The Atlantic Economy during the
Seventeenth and Eighteenth Centuries

The Carolina Lowcountry and the Atlantic World

Sponsored by the Lowcountry and Atlantic Studies Program of the College of Charleston

Money, Trade, and Power
Edited by Jack P. Greene, Rosemary Brana-Shute, and Randy J. Sparks

The Impact of the Haitian Revolution in the Atlantic World
Edited by David P. Geggus

London Booksellers and American Customers
James Raven

Memory and Identity
Edited by Bertrand Van Ruymbeke and Randy J. Sparks

This Remote Part of the World
Bradford J. Wood

The Final Victims
James A. McMillin

The Atlantic Economy during the Seventeenth and Eighteenth Centuries
Edited by Peter A. Coclanis

The Atlantic Economy
during the Seventeenth
and Eighteenth Centuries

Organization, Operation, Practice, and Personnel

Edited by Peter A. Coclanis

University of South Carolina Press

© 2005 University of South Carolina

Cloth edition published by the University of South Carolina Press, 2005
Paperback and ebook editions published in Columbia, South Carolina,
by the University of South Carolina Press, 2020

Manufactured in the United States of America

29 28 27 26 25 24 23 22 21 20
10 9 8 7 6 5 4 3 2 1

The Library of Congress has cataloged the cloth edition as follows:

Conference "The Emergence of the Atlantic Economy" (4th : 1999 : Charleston, S.C.)
   The Atlantic economy during the seventeenth and eighteenth centuries : organization, operation, practice, and personnel / edited by Peter A. Coclanis.
     p. cm. — (The Carolina lowcountry and the Atlantic world)
   Essays originally presented at the Carolina Lowountry and Atlantic World Program's fourth conference, "The Emergence of the Atlantic Economy," held at the College of Charleston, 14–16 October 1999.
   Includes bibliographical references and index.
   ISBN 1-57003-554-7 (cloth : alk. paper)
   1. North Atlantic Region—Commerce—History—17th century—Congresses.
   2. North Atlantic Region—Commerce—History—18th century—Congresses.
   3. North Atlantic Region—Economic conditions—17th century—Congresses.
   4. North Atlantic Region—Economic conditions—18th century—Congresses.
   5. North Atlantic Region—Economic integration. I. Coclanis, Peter A., 1952–
II. Title. III. Series.
   HF4045.C66 1999
   330.9182'1'09032—dc22

2004017358

ISBN 978-1-64336-104-8 (paperback)
ISBN 978-1-64336-105-5 (ebook)

Contents

List of Illustrations   vii
Acknowledgments   ix
Introduction   xi
    Peter A. Coclanis

The Dutch Atlantic Economies   1
    Jan de Vries

Self-Organized Complexity and the Emergence of an
   Atlantic Market Economy, 1651–1815   30
   The Case of Madeira
      David Hancock

Cloth and the Emergence of the Atlantic Economy   72
    Robert S. DuPlessis

The Organization of Trade and Finance in the British Atlantic
   Economy, 1600–1830   95
    R. C. Nash

Revisiting 1640; or, How the Party of Commercial Expansion
   Lost to the Party of Political Conservation in Spain's
   Atlantic Empire, 1620–1650   152
    Daviken Studnicki-Gizbert

Atlantic Trade and American Identities   186
   The Correlations of Supranational Commerce, Political Opposition,
     and Colonial Regionalism
    Claudia Schnurmann

Dutch and New Netherland Merchants in the Seventeenth-Century
   English Chesapeake   205
    April Lee Hatfield

Official Duplicity 229
    The Illicit Slave Trade of Martinique, 1713–1763
        Kenneth J. Banks

The Spanish Empire and Cuban Tobacco during the Seventeenth and
    Eighteenth Centuries 252
        Laura Náter

The Drudgery of the Slave Trade 277
    Labor at Cape Coast Castle, 1750–1790
        Ty M. Reese

Indians and the Economy of Eighteenth-Century Carolina 297
        Peter C. Mancall, Joshua L. Rosenbloom, and Thomas Weiss

Planters' Exchange Patterns in the Colonial Chesapeake 323
    Toward Defining a Regional Domestic Economy
        Laura Croghan Kamoie

The Characters of Commodities 344
    The Reputations of South Carolina Rice and Indigo
        in the Atlantic World
        S. Max Edelson

Contributors 361
Index 363

Illustrations

Figures

1. Wine imports into New York, 1700–1775   48–49
2. Expenditures on Indians by the colony of South Carolina   305

Tables

1. Capital invested in the West India Company by chamber and capitalization of Second West India Company   5
2. Wild Coast plantations: population and commodity exports   11
3. Value of Dutch commodity imports from Asia and the Western Hemisphere, 1640–1779   19
4. Wine imports into New York from all points, 1700–1775   44
5. Varieties of wines and other alcoholic beverages in probate inventories   50
6. Percentage of inventories with varying amounts of wine   51
7. Average wealth at death   52–53
8. Textile values in early Montreal, Philadelphia, Charleston, and New Orleans areas by type of cloth   74
9. Cloth values in 1730s South Carolina by type of business   76
10. Three views of cloth consumption in 1730s Louisiana   76
11. Cloth values in late Montreal, Philadelphia, Charleston, and New Orleans areas by type of cloth   78
12. The Royal African Company's trade with Barbados, 1680–1711   99
13. Contraband cargoes/ships seized 1729–1741, French Windward Islands   243
14. The population of the Lower South at selected dates, 1680 to 1800 (narrow definition of Indian population)   300
15. The population of the Lower South at selected dates, 1680 to 1800 (intermediate definition of Indian population)   302
16. The population of the Lower South at selected dates, 1680 to 1800 (broad definition of Indian population)   303
17. Tithables of the Northern Neck of Virginia, 1722–1783   325
18. The One Hundred   332
19. John Tayloe II tobacco and iron production, 1751–1774   338

Acknowledgments

The editor would like to thank Randy J. Sparks, Rosemary Brana-Shute, and S. Max Edelson for their early help with this project. He would also like to thank Matthew Brown for research assistance and for the index. The staff at the University of South Carolina Press—particularly Alex Moore, Bill Adams, and Linda Haines Fogle—proved creative, encouraging, and patient through the whole publication process.

Jack P. Greene inspired us all.

Introduction

Peter A. Coclanis

In recent years the idea that the histories of Europe, West Africa, and the Americas were sufficiently united during the "early modern" period as to invite unified treatment has gained a great deal of momentum. Whether the concern is ideas, institutions, commodities, or pathogens, scholars of this period increasingly frame their studies in a transatlantic way. In so doing, they typically emphasize the links and interrelationships between and among historical actors and actions in the various geographical areas comprising the Atlantic basin.[1] In light of this, it is not surprising that many younger scholars in particular now refer to themselves as "Atlantic historians" in preference to more-prosaic appellations such as "imperial historians" or "early American historians," much less the now déclassé label "colonial historians." We are (almost) all Atlanticists now, to misquote Richard Milhous Nixon.

Not that the general idea behind an integrated approach to the history of the Atlantic world is new. One can trace back the roots of the approach at least to the nineteenth century, and some would extend the genealogy all the way back to volume 1, part 8 ("The So-Called Primitive Accumulation") of Marx and Engels's *Capital*.[2] This invocation of Marx and Engels leads to another important point regarding "Atlantic history": the ideological pluralism, even eclecticism, associated with the approach. Indeed scholars over time have linked the approach to progenitors ranging from the imperial school of historians to Catholic universalists, and from Braudellians to Wallersteinians. As a result, people as diverse as Charles M. Andrews and Peter Linebaugh, Carlton J. H. Hayes and Paul Gilroy, Bernard Bailyn and Wilma Dunaway are in some ways all part of the same team.[3]

To say that Atlantic history is both highly popular and highly influential right now is not to suggest that it is without problems. As with other organizing conceits there are, of course, certain inadequacies associated with (if not inherent in) the Atlanticist perspective, at least in its current garb. Purported transatlantic connections are often opaque or oblique, for example. Just what *were* the connections between Iroquois and British constitutional thought? Did the so-called task system of slave-labor organization *really* owe all that much to West African antecedents and analogues? Just *how* important, relatively speaking, were New World silver and profits from the slave trade to economic developments in Europe?

Another possible problem relates to the scale and scope of the approach. Ironically, it is possible to argue in this regard that the Atlantic basin as a unit or frame of analysis is too *narrow*. Why? According to an increasing number of global historians the entire "Old World"—sometimes referred to by such historians as Afro-Eurasia—had been conjoined biologically, economically, and to a lesser extent culturally for millennia prior to 1492. To lock in on the Atlantic basin is thus severely to truncate the proper analytical frame for studying problems occurring in what Westerners refer to as the "early modern period." Would it not be more efficacious, then, to pursue a global rather than an Atlantic approach?[4] For some purposes, at least, the answer seems to be yes.

Such problems notwithstanding, there is no gainsaying the fact that the latest wave of Atlanticist scholarship—linked to a variety of antecedents that stretch back as far as a century or more—has encompassed numerous contributions. Because of the efforts of many fine scholars adopting the approach (or even sensibility), we now know a great deal more than we formerly did about what might be called the "systemics" of life around the Atlantic basin in the period roughly between 1500 and 1800 C.E. Nowhere is this truer than in the material realm, most notably regarding biotic, demographic, and economic phenomena.

In this volume the focus is on the last of these: economic phenomena. That factor and product markets around the Atlantic basin were becoming linked in the early modern period is now beyond doubt. Such links were quite loose in the sixteenth century, but during the seventeenth century and especially the eighteenth century a unified, coherent, and increasingly cohesive Atlantic economy truly began to take shape. Underpinning and reflecting this process we see an emerging economic "system" characterized by European and Euro-American domination and by increasingly sophisticated production complexes, commercial institutions and practices, and transportation and communications facilities. We see as well shifting value orientations among certain groups in the basin, shifts that manifested themselves in numerous ways, including increased industry (both in those whose orientations had changed and, indirectly, in those subject to their control), more aggressive entrepreneurship, and a greater or at least more sustained interest in capital accumulation.[5] Withal we see in some cases the rationalization of state power and, concomitantly, of governmental "capacities," especially in the fiscal realm. One important result and "marker" of the changes outlined above was the institutionalization of extensive and intensive economic growth in at least some constituent parts of the Atlantic economy. If the formal imperatives of empire still impeded integration even at the end of the period in question, enterprisers around the basin were frequently able to work the margins and interstices of empire, as it were, if not to "breach" imperial bounds altogether. Thus we find supranational traders and trade networks emerging and the insinuation and penetration of "foreign" personnel and capital illegally or only quasi-legally across imperial lines. By the end of the period such breaches were arguably becoming as necessary as they were commonplace.

The thirteen essays included in *The Atlantic Economy during the Seventeenth and Eighteenth Centuries* grew out of papers originally prepared for a conference titled "The Emergence of the Atlantic Economy," which was held in Charleston, South Carolina, in October 1999.[6] The purview of the conference was broad, but the organizers fully expected that most presenters would focus on the tried and true: that is to say, one or another empire, one or another key staple, one or another occupation, trade route, governmental policy, or legal statute. Over the course of the three-day conference, however, the organizers were surprised to find that most had chosen instead to focus on areas, groups, and problems that had hitherto been unexplored, underappreciated, or misunderstood. Again and again in Charleston conferees heard about the fluidity of the Atlantic economy, its casual borders, and its blurred lines. They learned about decentering and multifocality and about contraband, illegal activities, and outsider individuals and behaviors. Consumption often trumped production, and the domestic economies of several colonies were brought to light. Trade webs, networks, and matrices were in, and linear trade patterns, conveyor-belt metaphors, hub-and-spoke models, and triangular trades were out. Out, too, for the most part was early modern European economic thought: little was said, for example, about mercantilism, bullion, or the balance of trade. Indeed, most presenters shied away from the centers of things altogether, preferring margins, interstices, and peripheries to the metropolitan core. And after the shock of recognition, conferees were by and large thrilled by these results.

Herein readers will find a selection of the papers presented in Charleston. The volume is comprised of two principal parts: one relating to the shape, form, and organization of the Atlantic economy; the other to questions dealing with little-known trades, controversies, and activities in the same. The volume opens with a much-needed analytical assessment of the economic role of the Dutch in the Atlantic by the eminent economic historian Jan de Vries. Over the years scholars of the Dutch seaborne empire have quite correctly focused most of their attention on Dutch activities in Asia. De Vries does not challenge this overall orientation but points out that Dutch economic activities in the Atlantic world were more important than many realize. In support of this contention de Vries notes that by the 1770s the value of Dutch imports from the Americas was roughly equal in value to Dutch imports emanating from Asia, which point will surprise even specialists in the economic history of the early modern period.

Although de Vries offers up other surprises in his essay—he cannot resist the opportunity to set the record straight once and for all on the nature of Dutch patroonships in New York—his primary concerns are not to debunk or revise.

Rather, the overriding purpose of his essay is to provide a broad interpretive scheme for understanding the manner in which the Dutch presence in the Atlantic evolved over time. In this, de Vries has succeeded brilliantly, and virtually everyone present in Charleston agreed that his division of Dutch economic activities in the Atlantic into four discrete phases between the late sixteenth century and the end of the eighteenth century will soon become standard among specialists in the field.

David Hancock's comprehensive look at the organization of the Madeira wine trade is similarly revelatory. In his essay Hancock not only offers a systematic look at the evolution of the market for Madeira—production, marketing, finance, and consumption—but also attempts to extrapolate from this case to make some generalizations about the character of the Atlantic economy as a whole. According to Hancock, scholars in the past have often drawn too heavily on patterns prevailing in the sugar and tobacco trades when conceptualizing about the workings of the early modern Atlantic economy as a whole. Hancock concedes that simple linear models capture the sugar and tobacco trades fairly well as producers (or rather those who controlled production) in the so-called periphery shipped most of their surpluses directly to the core. He might have mentioned rice in this regard as well, for here too we see the quintessential mercantilist scenario holding true. But Hancock argues that the Atlantic trade during the early modern period did not begin and end with the staples mentioned above. Drawing on his research on Madeira and on recent theoretical literature on "complex systems," Hancock argues that patterns in many trades were much more open, adaptive, nonlinear, unpredictable, and contingent than scholars believe. In these trades multifocality, porosity, and cross-imperial economic assignations were the rule rather than the exception. In such trades, then, the proper metaphor, in Hancock's view, is not the hub and spoke but rather the spiderweb.

In his essay Robert S. DuPlessis too is concerned with cross-imperial questions, albeit of another sort. Employing textiles as a case, DuPlessis is concerned with ascertaining the degree to which an integrated Atlantic economy can be said to have existed in the eighteenth century. Timothy Breen, among other scholars, has argued that consumer societies were emerging in parts of the Atlantic world in the eighteenth century—British North America, for example—and that "material standardization" of many consumer products was at once a reflection and an outgrowth of both the emergence of such societies and market integration.[7] Breen focused on Britain and British America, but DuPlessis is interested in extending this line of analysis by exploring whether consumption patterns associated with material standardization crossed imperial lines. If so, according to DuPlessis, one could make the case that such standardization can be construed as ipso facto evidence that a unified Atlantic economy had emerged or at least was emerging. DuPlessis tests this hypothesis by studying the cloth markets in four North American urban centers in the late seventeenth century/early eighteenth century and again in the 1760s/70s. Two cities in British North America (Philadelphia and Charleston, South Carolina) and two cities in French North America (Montreal and New Orleans) were chosen. DuPlessis analyzes merchandise lists included in (postmortem) probate inventories of merchants' estates in the four cities to establish patterns relating to the mercantile stock of and presumably consumer demand for textiles in each. Although he unearths interesting local patterns and intriguing subpatterns for discrete demographic groups, his principal finding is that merchants' stocks and presumably consumer preferences regarding cloth converged over the course of the eighteenth century, with a growing partiality toward cottons and calicoes and a movement away from woolens becoming characteristic of all four cities. To DuPlessis (and indeed to this writer) the pattern found is consistent with the proposition that an Atlantic economy rather than an *assemblage* of empire-specific Atlantic economies was emerging.

Ironically, just as an *integrated* Atlantic economy was emerging in the eighteenth century, we witness the continued expansion and development of several imperial economies in the Atlantic, none more so than that of Great Britain. In his essay R. C. Nash offers readers a comprehensive survey of British Atlantic trade and finance during the entire period between 1600 and 1830, though his focus is clearly on the spectacular rise in importance of Britain's Atlantic trade in the eighteenth century. Not only does Nash creatively synthesize and reinterpret a vast literature, but by extending his temporal reach to 1830 he is also able to bridge the early modern/modern divide, as it were. In so doing he is able to assess the impacts of the American Revolution, the French Revolution, the Napoleonic Wars, and the Industrial Revolution on transatlantic trade organization. Suffice it to say that few scholars have attempted this before. Then again, few have been so well equipped to do so as Nash is.

Having invoked irony in the paragraph above, let me do so again, for the integration process and the benefits ultimately arising therefrom displayed other ironic incongruities too. How else would one characterize a process that by and large did not proceed smoothly through enlightened statesmanship but haltingly through illegal, extralegal, and quasi-legal means? The next four articles in the volume, each by a young scholar, focus on breaches of one sort or another in imperial economies, breaches that directly or indirectly are suggestive of the forces and counterforces associated with the process of integration. In his essay Daviken Studnicki-Gizbert lays out in rich detail a fascinating struggle over commercial policy in Spain during the "reign" of Olivares (1621–43). On one side of the battle were liberal Portuguese merchants and bankers who, using their own experience to guide them, favored opening up the empire via policies that would puncture "the seal of mercantilist boundaries." This group was countered, on the other side, by conventional mercantilists and Catholic conservatives who desired instead that the empire be hermetically sealed. Although, or perhaps more accurately because, the former group—made up largely of descendents of Jews who had been expelled from Spain in 1492—was allied with the reformer Olivares, it eventually lost this battle, which loss set back the cause of freer trade in the Spanish Empire for many years to come.

Although we have long known that the Dutch breached the English Atlantic during the seventeenth century, two rich and dense essays on the commercial relationships binding the English and the Dutch over the course of that century —written by Claudia Schnurmann and April Lee Hatfield, respectively—provide much new information and detail on where, when, and just how much. In her essay Schnurmann offers a broad perspective on these concerns, detailing the many ways in which "supranational networks" involving Dutch and English commercial personnel interacted in the seventeenth century not only in English and Dutch possessions in the New World but in the Old World as well. Hatfield, on the other hand, zeros in on the deep and tangled economic roots Dutch merchants and planters put down in the Chesapeake. Taken together, these two essays give us a much better sense of the transgressive tendencies inherent in commerce, tendencies made manifest in seventeenth-century economic practice.

Kenneth J. Banks is concerned with imperial breaches as well, but breaches in the eighteenth century (rather than the seventeenth century) that involved French possessions rather than those of the Spanish, English/British, or Dutch. More specifically, Banks is concerned with the illegal slave trade to the French plantation colony of Martinique. The colony, part of the Windward Island group in the West Indies, was a major site of sugar and tobacco production in the eighteenth century. According to Banks, the demand for slaves there was considerable, but the inability of French slavers to supply adequate numbers left an opening that illegal slavers stepped in to fill. Here again, then, an integrating breach—one that paid short-term, if not necessarily long-term, dividends to slavers and planters alike regardless of nationality, and one that in time helped to spur the creation by the French government of several authorized free ports in the Caribbean.

In the 1760s—just as the French Caribbean was beginning to open up—the Spanish, after generations of trying, had finally succeeded in rendering the colony of Cuba into a form that would in good mercantilist fashion complement Spain economically and contribute significantly to the fiscal well-being of the Crown. The principal mechanism through which this scenario was brought about was the Spanish tobacco monopoly, which Laura Náter examines in close detail in an essay entitled "The Spanish Empire and Cuban Tobacco during the Seventeenth and Eighteenth Centuries." Náter's piece marks a slight shift—at the margin, as economists like to say—in the purview of *The Atlantic Economy*. Her essay and the four that follow all deal with lesser known trades, controversies, and economic activities. To be sure, some of the earlier essays in the volume treat such matters as well, but the last five in the volume do so more explicitly and more systemically.

Introduction xvii

Náter, for example, traces the Spanish Crown's efforts from the 1680s on to create profitable complementarities among Cuban commodities, Seville's factories and manufactories, and the royal purse. The Crown placed its primary hopes in Cuba on tobacco—the island's rise to great prominence in sugar was a nineteenth-century phenomenon—and over the course of the eighteenth century it attempted at once to establish Cuba as a tobacco-producing export platform, to monopolize Cuban tobacco exports, and to develop Seville as the primary site of tobacco manufacturing, marketing, and reexportation. All this, one might add, was in the hope of benefiting the royal treasury. After decades of trying, the Crown got what it wished for, according to Náter, but economic dislocations associated with the American Revolution and the Haitian Revolution soon brought an end to the commercial strategy it had worked so long and hard to implement.

If the story told by Náter is largely unknown, that told by Ty M. Reese in the essay following hers is almost utterly so: the complex labor system employed at a British slaving station on the West African coast between 1750 and 1790. Despite increased interest in many aspects of the African slave trade in recent years, relatively little work has been done on what might be called the infrastructure of the trade. For this reason alone Reese's close examination of the labor force at the Cape Coast Castle slaving station on the Gold Coast in the second half of the eighteenth century is well worth reading. Certainly the elaborate labor system he finds there—the Cape Coast Castle labor force was comprised of an ever-shifting mix of unskilled European free laborers, unskilled African free laborers, slaves, convicts, so-called pawns, and skilled African canoemen—complicates our notions about the organization of the slave trade and begs for additional studies and follow-ups.

We move back across the Atlantic in the last three essays in the volume. In the first of these, historian Peter C. Mancall and economists Joshua L. Rosenbloom and Thomas Weiss collaborate to assess the economic role of Native Americans in the economy of eighteenth-century South Carolina. This piece is noteworthy for several reasons. First, the authors grant Indians agency and proceed under the assumption that Native Americans were economic actors operating to optimize their material well-being subject to their social and environmental constraints. Second, the authors lay out the principal issues, problems, and questions involved in assessing the Indians' role in early South Carolina. Third, through inspired, even ingenious methods Mancall, Rosenbloom, and Weiss provide some quantitative estimates of this role, giving us some rough orders of magnitude with which to work.

In the next essay Laura Croghan Kamoie examines another understudied aspect of economic life in the southern part of British North America: the domestic economy of the Chesapeake. For generations students of the Chesapeake economy and, indeed, the economies of South Carolina and Georgia have focused most of their attention on the export sector. Given the export/output ratios of these areas in the early modern period and the role of exports in promoting the expansion and growth of these regions, such attention has not necessarily been misplaced.[8] Nonetheless, it is becoming increasingly clear that the domestic economy, though more difficult to measure, was not unimportant, much less insignificant in the Chesapeake and Lower South, particularly by the second half of the eighteenth century.[9] After taking readers through the issues involved in studying the domestic economy of the Chesapeake, Kamoie offers a close examination of the involvement of one famous Virginia planter—John Tayloe II (1721–79) of Richmond County—in the domestic economy of the Northern Neck. If Tayloe's case is at all representative—or at least illustrative—students of the eighteenth-century Chesapeake would do well in the future to allocate more time to local and regional economic orbits.

S. Max Edelson changes tack in his essay, the final one in *The Atlantic Economy*. Drawing from his ongoing work on planters in the Lower South during the eighteenth century, Edelson takes up an important but extremely difficult subject: the relationship between agriculture and culture, as it were. More specifically, he is interested in the way in which the reputations and, indeed, the identities of South Carolina planters and merchants in the eighteenth century were related to the reputations of rice and indigo, the principal commodities exported from the colony. That Carolina rice had a good reputation in the Atlantic world while Carolina indigo did not mattered deeply to anxious elites in South Carolina, people who, according to Edelson, desired transatlantic recognition and ratification along with (and perhaps as much as) profits from abroad. It seems propitious to end the volume with this piece, which, in pushing us to connect the material realm to the cultural realm, highlights still another understudied dimension of the early modern Atlantic economy, broadly conceived: identity formation among Atlantic elites. To push any farther in the cultural direction, however, would seem to require another conference and perhaps another book.

Notes

1. The literature in the field of Atlantic history is quickly becoming quite imposing. On the genealogy of the concept "Atlantic history" and an introduction to the issues involved, see Bernard Bailyn, "The Idea of Atlantic History," *Itinerario* 20 (1996): 19–44. Also see Alan L. Karras and J. R. McNeill, eds., *Atlantic American Societies: From Columbus through Abolition, 1492–1888* (London and New York: Routledge, 1992). Alison Grames, "Introduction, Definitions, and Historiography: What Is Atlantic History?" *OAH Magazine of History* 18 (April 2004): 3–7.

2. Karl Marx, *Capital*, ed. Frederick Engels, trans. Samuel Moore and Edward Aveling, 3 vols. (1867–94; repr., New York: International Publishers, 1967), 1:713–74.

3. See, for example, Bailyn, "Idea of Atlantic History"; David Armitage, "Greater Britain: A Useful Category of Historical Analysis?" *American Historical Review* 104 (April 1999): 427–45; Nicholas Canny, "Writing Atlantic History; or, Reconfiguring the History of Colonial British America," *Journal of American History* 86 (December 1999): 1093–114;

Felipe Fernández-Armesto, "The Origins of the European Atlantic," *Itinerario* 24 (2000): 111–28. Also see Jerry H. Bentley, "Sea and Ocean Basins as Frameworks of Historical Analysis," *Geographical Review* 89 (April 1999): 215–24.

4. For a recent assessment of the strengths and weaknesses of "Atlantic history" as an organizing concept, see Peter A. Coclanis, *"Drang Nach Osten:* Bernard Bailyn, the World-Island, and the Idea of Atlantic History," *Journal of World History* 13 (Spring 2002): 169–82.

5. Jan de Vries, "The Industrial Revolution and the Industrious Revolution," *Journal of Economic History* 54 (June 1994): 249–70.

6. This international conference was sponsored by the College of Charleston's Program in the Carolina Lowcountry and the Atlantic World and was held at the college October 14–16, 1999. In 1998 Jack P. Greene, the director of the program, enlisted Peter A. Coclanis to organize the conference, which Coclanis did with the help of Greene and the other principals in the program at the time, Randy J. Sparks, Rosemary Brana-Shute, and S. Max Edelson.

7. Timothy H. Breen, "An Empire of Goods: The Anglicization of Colonial America, 1690–1776," *Journal of British Studies* 25 (October 1986): 467–99; Timothy H. Breen, "'Baubles of Britain': The American and Consumer Revolutions of the Eighteenth Century," *Past and Present,* no. 119 (May 1988): 73–104. Timothy H. Breen, *The Marketplace of Revolution: How Consumer Politics Shaped American Independence* (New York: Oxford University Press, 2004).

8. See John J. McCusker and Russell R. Menard, *The Economy of British America, 1607–1789* (Chapel Hill and London: University of North Carolina Press, 1991), 5–88.

9. John J. McCusker, "Measuring Colonial Gross Domestic Product: An Introduction," *William and Mary Quarterly,* 3rd ser., 56 (January 1999): 3–8, esp. 4; Lorena S. Walsh, "Summing the Parts: Implications for Estimating Chesapeake Output and Income Subregionally," *William and Mary Quarterly,* 3rd ser., 56 (January 1999): 53–94. Kamoie's forthcoming monograph elaborates on many of the themes treated in her essay in this volume. Also see A. Glenn Crothers, "'The Projecting Spirit': Social, Economic and Cultural Change in Post-Revolutionary Northern Virginia, 1780–1805" (Ph.D. diss., University of Florida, 1997); A. Glenn Crothers, "Banks and Economic Development in Post-Revolutionary Northern Virginia, 1790–1812," *Business History Review* 73 (Spring 1999): 1–39.

The Atlantic Economy during the
Seventeenth and Eighteenth Centuries

The Dutch Atlantic Economies

Jan de Vries

Within twenty years of the establishment of the United Provinces, Dutch seafarers and merchants had ventured from their familiar northern European trade routes into nearly every corner of the world. Their exertions exposed them to the frosty rigors of Nova Zembla and the unexpected and unwelcomed sun of the Australian coast; they rounded (and named) Cape Horn and made their way to distant Japan. The seaborne empire they constructed was primarily an empire of trade, and it left its deepest marks in Asia, where the Dutch East India Company ruled over far-flung possessions and trading posts for 200 years, before the Dutch state succeeded it to rule over the Netherlands East Indies for 150 more.

By comparison, the Dutch presence in the Atlantic world has long appeared both unimpressive and unimportant. When compared to the other European powers the Dutch institutional and cultural legacy has seemed negligible, and in comparison to Asia the New World ventures appear to have possessed a distinctly subordinate historical importance. But if the Dutch Atlantic has, until recently, suffered the neglect and condescension of historians, it was not ignored by the Dutch of the seventeenth and eighteenth centuries. And if their enterprise in the West never assumed the institutional form of their ventures in the East, this was not the product of their indifference.

In fact, from the early days of the Dutch Republic an "Atlantic dream"—a New World redeemed from its Spanish/Catholic yoke, populated by Dutch settlers and Calvinist Indians, forming a productive and profitable part of a global trading economy—captured the imaginations of merchants, the House of Orange, and many Reformed clergymen and their followers.[1] In 1630 the new Dutch West India Company published a pamphlet with this bit of promotional verse[2]:

> Westindjen kan syn Nederlands groot gewin
> Verkleynt 's vyands Macht brengt silver platen in.
> [West India can become the Netherlands' great source of gain,
> Diminishing the enemy's power as it garners silver plate.]

The "Atlantic reality" never came near to fulfilling the high hopes of the early promoters, but this was not for want of trying. The Netherlands launched repeated efforts to achieve something in the New World.[3] It fought and worked to build an empire—indeed, to construct a *groot desseyn*—grand design—in the Western Hemisphere comparable to the intra-Asian trading network operated out of Batavia. When this failed, it sought to organize and dominate an international trading system that penetrated the plantation colonies of all the Atlantic powers. When this strategy was checked by the increasingly effective mercantilist policies of its rivals, the Dutch Republic set its sights on the construction of plantation economies of its own. And as these showed signs of failing, the Netherlands refocused its New World hopes on investment possibilities in the new American republics, especially the United States. These successive rounds of enterprise engaged the Netherlands and its advanced commercial institutions with the political and economic challenges of the Western Hemisphere. This engagement was filled with frustration and disappointment, never resulting in a territorial, political or cultural presence that answered to the grand visions of succesive generations of advocates. Economically, Dutch engagement with the Atlantic world resulted in both success and failure, and it is an engagement not yet finished.

Dutch Institutions in the New World

The first Dutch trading ventures beyond European waters—to the west coast of Africa, Asia, and the Caribbean—were all private initiatives by small partnerships of risk-taking merchants. Whether sailing to West Africa for gold, Southeast Asia for spices, or Punta de Araya (on the coast of Venezuela) for salt, the merchants made use of the commercial institutions already familiar to them from trade within European waters. They pooled their capital in *partenrederijen*, partnerships in which investors held shares such as one-eighth or one-sixteenth and entrusted their capital in the hands of the active partner(s), usually for the duration of a voyage. The partnerships were contracted before notaries, who filed the documents and provided legal recourse in the event of problems. This flexible form of organization allowed merchants to distribute their capital among multiple ventures, thereby reducing their exposure to risk, and they could finance their voyages by contracting with private lenders, again via notaries, for bottomry loans (*bodemerijbrieven*) secured by the hull of a ship serving as collateral.

These early ventures of the 1590s were risky and even audacious in view of the monopoly claims of the Iberian colonial powers, but they were essentially trading ventures rather than colonizing projects. By 1600 discussions surfaced in both mercantile and governmental circles concerning the desirability of bundling the activities of private merchants into monopoly trading companies. The benefits of such a move were partially economic: a reduction of competition among the rival partnerships of the numerous Dutch trading cities, a larger capitalization for these long-distance trades, and a reduction of risk through the internalization of protection costs. But the establishment of such consolidated enterprises was also seen as a more effective way to do battle against the Spanish enemy in distant lands and, ultimately, to secure colonial outposts necessary to conduct trade more securely.

In 1602 the States General of the Republic chartered a United East India Company (Verenigde Oostindische Compagnie, or VOC)—united because it brought together the six merchant partnerships in as many cities already active in the trade with Asia. These merchants and many others, some eighteen hundred people in all, invested 6.4 million guilders to launch what would become for nearly two centuries the largest joint-stock firm in the world. The VOC quickly established itself as the dominant European trader in Asia. It augmented its large initial capitalization with short-term loans (5.6 million between 1613 and 1620) and with plowed-back profits (it paid few cash dividends for its first thirty years of operation) to amass a working capital stock of many tens of millions of guilders by the 1640s. The company moved quickly to supplement its Europe—Asia trade in spices with an intra-Asian trade, coordinated from its territorial base at Batavia on Java. From there it gradually secured strategic locations to enforce its control of Asian waters and territorial possessions to protect its access to Asian commodities. The Dutch empire in Asia was the possession of a company, not of the Dutch state.[4] The VOC was responsible for the defense and administration of its far-flung possessions and was expected to pay for this overhead cost from its trading profits (and the tax revenue it could secure from its colonial subjects), and so it would remain until the 1795 dissolution of the VOC in bankruptcy.[5]

The VOC had no dealings with the New World; its trading monopoly extended from the Cape of Good Hope eastward. But its dazzling success stood as a model for those urging the States General to charter a comparable monopoly company for the Atlantic zone. The government, which had pressed for the creation of the VOC in 1602, resisted such urgings in 1606 in anticipation of a hoped-for truce in the war with Spain—a truce secured in 1609. But when that truce expired in 1621 one of its first acts was to charter (fifteen precious years too late in the minds of the republic's most ardent advocates of colonialism) the West India Company (WIC), with monopoly rights over all trade in West Africa and the New World.[6]

Although the new company's organizational structure closely resembled the VOC (five chambers and a governing board of nineteen directors, compared to the VOC's six chambers and seventeen directors), the similar outer forms masked significant internal differences. Just as the VOC bundled the energies of predecessor trading ventures, so did the WIC, but while the Asian ventures had all competed in the same basic trade, the WIC predecessors were all different. Amsterdam's New Netherland Company was active in the Mohawk region fur and pelt trade;[7] various merchant consortia were active in the "Guinea" trade in West African gold and ivory; the merchants of Hoorn and Enkhuizen were committed to the Punta de Araya salt trade;[8] Zeeland merchants had their eye on the "Wild Coast" (the South American coast between the mouths of the Orinoco and Amazon rivers);[9] and yet others, in alliance with Portuguese "New Christians" who had settled in the Netherlands, sought their fortunes in the Brazilian sugar trade. It would be the WIC's task to knit these disparate interests into a single, coherent commercial company.

For aid in this task the newly floated WIC could hope to draw on the flourishing republic's abundance of capital, efficient commercial institutions, and enormous seafaring sector. But the new company initially found it difficult to gain access to these resources. It faced a reluctant investor community, which was suspicious that the new company, whose most enthusiastic backers were conspicuously motivated by religious and patriotic sentiments, would undertake costly military ventures that would undermine commercial profitability. It took two years and a great deal of government "jaw-boning" to assemble the initial capitalization of 7.1 million guilders.[10]

The First Dutch Atlantic Economy

In its first years the new company found it difficult to set a clear course. Its first military ventures, attacks on Bahia, Brazil, and Sa Jorge da Mina on the Gold Coast of Africa, both failed. In these years the WIC sustained itself on the existing trades of the predecessor firms and on privateering. Then in 1628 the company hit the jackpot, achieving suddenly the greatest financial success of its history. Adm. Piet Heyn captured the entire Spanish silver fleet, carrying a cargo of at least 11.5 million guilders worth of silver. That great prize filled the company's coffers while also making possible the payment of a 50 percent dividend (the only substantial return its investors would ever receive). This event in turn drove WIC share prices up on the Amsterdam *Beurs,* allowing the company to issue new shares, borrow even more funds, and thereby finance a large fleet to set out on the conquest of Brazil (see table 1 for the new sums invested).

From 1630, with the conquest of Pernambuco (Recife), until the company was finally forced out of New Holland, as the Dutch preferred to call it, the New World enterprise was focused on Brazil and its sugar. The existing population of Portuguese *moradores* (planters), settlers, mestizos, and mulattos was quickly joined by WIC employees (some 10,000 at the peak in 1639), and by *vrijlieden* ("civilian"; former employees and immigrants), numbering 3,000 adult males by 1645. One-third of these settlers were Portuguese Jews, who had played a leading role in the Brazilian enterprise from the outset.[11] The WIC acted quickly to supplement its African trade in gold and ivory with a new trade in slaves in order to expand Brazilian plantation agriculture.[12] In the twenty years after 1630 the company sent 31,533 slaves to Brazil. Meanwhile the Dutch ports became

Table 1A: Capital invested in the West India Company by chamber

Chamber	Initial capital	%	1629–39 shares	1641–71 bonds	Total	%
Amsterdam	f.2,846,585	40	6,984,885	3,104,754	12,936,224	54
Zeeland	1,379,775	19	1,069,203	2,096,330	4,545,308	19
Maas	1,039,702	15	277,677	432,295	1,749,674	7
Noorderkwartier	505,627	7	782,683	618,370	1,906,680	8
Groningen	836,975	12	482,909	222,479	1,542,363	6
States General	500,000	7	500,000			2
Other cities			891,637		891,637	4
Total	7,108,664		9,981,994	6,474,228	23,564,886	

Table 1B: Capitalization of the Second West India Company in 1674, by chamber

Chamber	Shares	Bonds	Total	%
Amsterdam	1,608,466	931,426	2,539,892	56
Zeeland	367,346	628,899	996,245	22
Maas	197,666	129,688	327,294	7
Noorderkwartie	196,932	66,743	263,675	6
Groningen	193,246	185,511	318,757	8
Total	2,563,596	1,942,267	4,505,863	

Source: Norbert H. Schneelock, *Actionäre der Westindischen Compagnie von 1674*, Beitrage zur Wirtschaftsgeschichte, Band 12 (Stuttgart: Klett-Cotta, 1982), 28–37; H. den Heijer, *Goud, ivoor en slaven: Scheenvaart en handel van de Tweede Westindische Compagnie op Africa 1674–1740* (Zutphen: Walburg, 1997), 47. Note: The subtotals do not always equate perfectly with the aggregate totals.

Europe's leading centers of sugar refining. As all this took shape the hope arose that the settlements on the Hudson River could supplement their fur trade with an expanded production of foodstuffs for the developing plantation economies.

This, then, was the grand design, but it was too large for the WIC to control and to internalize. Unlike the VOC in Asia, the WIC in the Atlantic could enforce its monopoly privileges against neither foreign competitors nor Dutch private traders. The "leakage" of commercial benefits to private interests prevented the company from earning a satisfactory return on its capital, which meant that it continued to depend on the issue of shares and the sale of bonds to finance its activities. In contrast, the VOC could almost immediately begin to finance its expansion internally, through retained profits.

In this setting the WIC retreated from its comprehensive but unenforceable claims to monopoly rights. In 1638 it allowed its shareholders to trade privately in its Atlantic realm, hoping that this concession would at least help maintain the company's share prices on the *Beurs*. Likewise, to encourage settlement in New Netherland, in 1640 it threw open the trade in beaver pelts to private traders in return for a recognition fee of one guilder per pelt. Even these measures did not satisfy the merchant community, 159 of whom petitioned the States General to allow free trade in the New World; by 1648 the WIC retreated further, allowing any Dutchman to trade in its New World territory on payment of a recognition fee to the company. Thus was the WIC in the New World transformed from a trading company to an administrative entity.

The Portuguese *moradores'* revolt against Dutch rule in Brazil, begun in 1645, exposed the economic and political weakness of the company. It was unable to finance the defense of New Holland by itself (indeed, a cost-cutting withdrawal of WIC troops had occasioned the initial Portuguese attack), but the merchant community at home was dubious of any intervention that would jeopardize trade within Europe (that is, Portuguese salt and wine).[13] At one point the Portuguese offered to return Brazil to the WIC in exchange for the restoration of Portuguese possessions in Asia. But in this the VOC showed even less interest than in a proposal to merge the two companies into a single Dutch colonial venture. To stop further talk of merger the VOC paid the WIC a onetime subsidy of 1.5 million guilders in 1649. It could be generous in this way for, in fact, the struggle over Brazil was a godsend to the VOC: so long as the Portuguese remained fully occupied in the Americas they were unable to defend their remaining Asian empire, which the VOC proceeded to pick apart. Meanwhile the WIC, without sufficient financial resources (its debt in 1649 stood at nearly 20 million guilders)[14] or sustained political support at home, had no choice but to abandon its last Brazilian foothold in 1654.

The Second Dutch Atlantic Economy

In the aftermath of the Brazilian adventure Dutch merchants stitched together a new Atlantic trading system. They made a virtue of necessity, exploiting the flexibility offered by the absence of a large territorial domain. This new Dutch Atlantic system integrated four key elements: (1) the WIC's monopoly trading functions were now restricted to Africa's gold, ivory, and slave trades; (2) private Dutch merchants and planters encouraged sugar production by extending credit to, establishing plantations in (many run by Sephardic Jewish planters who had left Brazil), and supplying manufactures to the Caribbean islands controlled by the British, French, and Spanish; (3) the expansion of food production was encouraged in New Netherland to sustain Curaçao (the slave entrepôt); and (4) Dutch shipping handled the transport of Caribbean produce to the Netherlands, specifically to the sugar refineries of Amsterdam. In this way the ships, African slave depots, and Amsterdam sugar refineries were kept operating despite the absence of a substantial base of production on Dutch-controlled territory.

This more modest version of a Dutch Atlantic economy, one focused on the trading center at Curaçao, proved to be more robust than the colorful but short-lived Brazilian escapade. In one respect this "interloper trade" was a more peaceful form of the privateering that had characterized the WIC—and especially its Zeeland chamber—from its beginning. So long as the Dutch were at war with the Spanish, the Dutch admiralties—again, with special gusto, the Zeeland admiralty—issued letters of marque (*kaperbrieven*). But after 1654 the Dutch were at peace with both Spain and Portugal, and the focus shifted toward the provision of commercial services to the entire Atlantic world.

As Dutch planters and merchants drifted away from Brazil they directed their attention to Barbados, speeding the transformation of that British possession from a tobacco-farming to a sugar-plantation economy.[15] Soon thereafter the French island of Martinique was similarly transformed. A third object of interest —renewed interest—was New Netherland. A publicist sought to console his countrymen over the loss of Brazil and attract settlers to the Hudson, Delaware, and Connecticut river valleys (the Noord [North], Zuid [South], and Verse [Freshwater] rivers, respectively, to the Dutch) with the following verse preface to Adriaen van der Donk's 1656 edition of *A Description of New Netherlands*:

> Why mourn about Brazil, full of base Portuguese?
> When Van der Donck shows us far much better fare;
> Where wheat fills golden ears, and grapes abound in trees;
> Where fruit and kine are good with little care;
> Men may mourn a loss, when vain would be their voice;
> But when their loss brings gain, they also may rejoice.[16]

A quickened pace of in-migration ushered in a prosperous period for the colony and helped raised the settler population of New Netherland to some eight to ten thousand by 1664.[17]

Everywhere in the Caribbean local planters tended to prefer Dutch commercial services to those of national monopolists, a preference reinforced by the Dutch hold over the slave trade. With Elmina (acquired in 1637), Luanda (1641), and some twenty other African forts under WIC control, the size of the Dutch slave trade was second only to the Portuguese until 1675. In the period 1650–74 the WIC shipped some fifty-seven thousand slaves, most destined for Curaçao to await sale to Spanish, French, and British planters. In the 1660s it looked for a time as though the buoyant French and British demand for slaves would revive the fortunes of the WIC while Dutch private traders would prosper as (illicit) suppliers of commercial services to the growing plantation economies. WIC shares, practically worthless in 1654, revived to 40 percent of par value by the end of 1664, and sugar shipments to the republic stood at least at the level achieved during the Brazilian adventure. In 1660 the republic's sixty-six sugar refineries, fifty of them in Amsterdam, supplied more than half of the refined sugar consumed in all of Europe.

This hardy commercialism functioned in an essentially hostile environment of mercantilism and could survive only by adapting to constraints that became steadily more restrictive. In the course of the 1660s rival colonial powers gradually developed the economic and military instruments sufficient to enforce their monopoly claims, thereby shrinking inexorably the Dutch interlopers' room for maneuver. The English Navigation Acts of 1651 were intended, among other things, to exclude the Dutch as suppliers of slaves and manufactures to and buyers of sugar from Barbados and other English islands. But these islands and the southern mainland colonies were Royalist nests eager to undermine the Commonwealth government of England. Consequently, St. Eustatius flourished as a center of sugar smuggling while New Amsterdam swept up the tobacco of the Chesapeake.[18]

By the mid-1660s, however, a restored monarchical England had conquered New Amsterdam while the Navigation Acts were enforced on Barbados with sufficient vigor to cause the Dutch to turn their attention to the French island of Martinique. But French trade ordinances of 1664 and 1673 had much the same intention as the Navigation Acts. Moreover, by 1665 English slave traders could begin to supply their own islands' labor needs at competitive prices, while the French Compagnie des Indes Occidentales, established in 1664, and the English Royal African Company of 1673 gradually marginalized the WIC's position as a supplier of slaves.[19] Dutch traders responded by cultivating their long-standing interloper trade with Spanish possessions, especially Cuba and Puerto Rico, and the coasts of Venezuela. Spain's colonial trading system lacked the capacity to exclude the Dutch—indeed, the colonists long continued to depend on them.[20]

Historians can identify another moment in the 1660s when a major Dutch role in the Atlantic might have been salvaged. The Second Anglo Dutch War (1664–67) began badly for the Dutch as the English swept through the Atlantic zone taking over Dutch possessions from New Netherland to Tobago and Guyana. But the tide turned, and by 1666 the English were being forced out of most of their recent acquisitions by Dutch and French naval expeditions. Moreover, by then the Dutch had defeated English fleets closer to home as well and even sailed up the Thames to plunder the Medway naval base and tow away the English flagship as war booty. At this point, with London on fire and disorganized by plague, the continuation of French-Dutch cooperation in the New World could have accomplished much. Indeed, the restoration of New Netherland was not beyond reach; after all, Adm. Cornelis Evertsen did just this with little effort in 1673, while Adm. Michael de Ruyter struck heavy blows against English positions in West Africa as he showed the Dutch flag throughout the Atlantic theater in 1674. "Nor," in the opinion of Jonathan Israel, "would there have been any difficulty in laying down reciprocal Franco-Dutch guarantees for the defence of New France, New Netherland, and the French and Dutch Antilles and Guianas."[21] What stood in the way—here and at several other junctures in the seventeenth century—was the chronic disjuncture between mutually advantageous alliances of European powers in the New World and those that made sense to rulers within Europe. The latter always trumped the former, and in the summer of 1667 Louis XIV turned his sights once again on the Spanish Netherlands, capturing Lille. Immediately the republic was in need of English support to defend its interests close to home, and in order to secure this aid it subordinated its colonial interests. Thus was a North American empire lost.[22]

The republic's inability to deploy either diplomacy or sufficient naval power to break out of the mercantilist box being constructed by its neighbors had economic consequences that can be read directly from the fate of Amsterdam's sugar refiners. In 1668 only thirty-four of the fifty were in operation; by 1680 only twenty remained. In addition the combination of commercial losses and military expenditures overwhelmed the always fragile finances of the WIC, which was forced to reorganize in 1674.

The product of this reorganization, the second WIC, was a slimmed-down affair shorn of the headstrong ambition that had marked its predecessor. It exercised monopoly rights to the Dutch slave trade until 1734, but from then until its dissolution in 1791 its only trading function was the Africa commodity trade. Otherwise its remaining task was administration of its colonial possessions (the African trading outposts with Elmina as headquarters, the six Caribbean islands, and the Wild Coast possessions, most notably Surinam), and its only revenues came from user fees and local taxes.[23] Until the fall of the republic the Dutch colonial empire was privately held (albeit subject to public pressure because of the periodic need to renew company charters).[24] With few exceptions public funds did not directly support either the East or West Indian ventures, a fact that placed Dutch empire builders at a distinct disadvantage vis-à-vis their competitors.[25]

In view of the WIC's early financial debility, its unpopularity with the merchant community, and the early abandonment of Atlantic monopoly companies by England and France, it is a wonder that the Dutch persisted so long with an institutional form manifestly unsuited to the New World environment. The WIC's bankruptcy in 1674 was a good opportunity to be rid of this chartered monopoly company; instead the States General pressured the holders of the company's worthless shares and bonds into injecting an additional 1.2 million guilders in order to float the second WIC.[26] It would appear that the Dutch Republic, a state with few central government powers over its constituent provinces, was not yet prepared to contemplate direct rule of its colonies.[27]

Ironically, the inability of the Dutch to project military power in the Atlantic zone after 1674 offered them some advantages. Spain turned to the Dutch as suppliers of slaves and commercial services to her colonial empire. The WIC and its

Curaçao trade center, its teeth having been drawn by British and French protectionism, prospered in the 1680s and 1690s as holder of the Spanish *asiento,* or slave supply contract, and as tolerated supplier of manufactured goods and shipping services to Spain's empire.

This Spanish connection provided a relatively stable setting in which the second WIC could actually pay some modest dividends (ranging between 2 and 8 percent; in 1687, 10 percent). But it usually paid nothing, and in 1713 even the possibility of participating in the Spanish *asiento* was lost as the Peace of Utrecht ending the War of Spanish Succession awarded this lucrative concession to England's new South Sea Company. The Curaçao slave entrepôt collapsed and with it the price of the second WIC's shares. The general expansiveness of the eighteenth-century Atlantic economy was such as to provide Dutch Caribbean trading centers (Curaçao and, increasingly, St. Eustatius) with occasional windfalls, usually the product of warfare among the major powers, but the idea that a second Dutch Atlantic economy based essentially on interloping could be a viable alternative to a colonial economy had been revealed much earlier to be wishful thinking.

The Third Dutch Atlantic Economy

By the 1680s it had become apparent that the only course of action still open was to develop plantation economies in the Dutch territories of modern Surinam and Guyana, and this can be said to inaugurate the third attempt to construct a Dutch Atlantic economy. The development of a Dutch plantation economy shared many similarities with the plantation economies of the other European powers active in the Caribbean. But it faced three important constraints unique to Dutch colonial policy. First, as noted above, the colonies remained the responsibility of the company, which is to say that the colonies had to pay their own way; the republic did not subsidize them in any significant way. Second, the colonies were subject to the typical mercantilist restrictions concerning where they could secure imports and services, but they did not enjoy any corresponding privileged access to the Dutch market. Their sugar, coffee, indigo, and other products fetched European market prices in Amsterdam, in contrast to the protected home markets enjoyed by the English, French, and Spanish colonies. Third, the planters could acquire slaves only from the WIC, which retained this monopoly until 1734. However, the WIC preferred to supply the Spanish market so long as it could since slave prices there were significantly higher. Consequently, 55 percent of the slaves shipped by the Dutch in the period 1674–1716 were destined for Curaçao (and Spanish America) while only 28 percent went to Surinam. The award of the Spanish *asiento* to England in 1713 was a bitter pill for the company but was greeted with enthusiasm by Dutch planters, who now expected a more elastic supply of slaves. Indeed, 78 percent of WIC-supplied slaves were directed toward the Surinam and Guyana plantations in 1716–38.

Table 2: Wild Coast plantations: population and commodity exports

SURINAM:

	Plantation	Slaves	Europeans	Total population*	Value of commodity exports (guilders)
1668	23			3,000	
1684	80	4,300	811	5,100	
1704	128	9,000		10,000	1.8 million
1737	370				
1750		51,100	2,133	53,800	5.8 million
1770	465	59,900	2,700	65,000	12.0 million
1795	533	48,200	3,350	53,110	15.9 million
1830	576	48,800	2,023	55,900	
1862		36,500		52,900	

GUYANA (Berbice, Essequebo and Demerary):

	Plantation	Slaves	Europeans	Total population*	
1750		8,000	726	8,780	
1770	250	25,000		c.27,000	

*Totals are approximate and include free blacks. They do not include Indians and the "morannen," escaped Africans.

Sources: Stanley Engerman and B. W. Higman, "The Demographic Structure of the Caribbean Slave Societies in the Eighteenth and Nineteenth Centuries," in *The Slave Societies of the Caribbean*, ed. Franklin W. Knight, vol. 3, *UNESCO General History of the Caribbean* (London: Macmillan Education Ltd., 1997); Alex van Stipriaan, *Surinaams contrast: Roofbouw en overleven in een Caraibische plantage economie, 1750–1863* (Amsterdam: Centrale Huisdrukkerij Vrije Universiteit, 1991), 327–29; Jan de Vries and Ad van der Woude, *The First Modern Economy: Success, Failure, and Perseverance of the Dutch Economy, 1500–1815* (Cambridge: Cambridge University Press, 1997), 478.

The WIC shifted the destination of its slave ships but did little to increase their number. This focused planter discontent on the WIC monopoly, and when this privilege was stripped from the company in 1734 the entry of private Dutch—overwhelmingly Zeeland—slave traders considerably increased the size of annual shipments. Free Dutch ships transported more slaves to the plantations in the sixty years after 1734 than the WIC had shipped to all American markets in its entire history.

Table 2 brings together the available data on the growth of the Dutch plantation economies. These data, sketchy though they are, show clearly that the plantation economy is largely a product of the century after 1680. Its eighteenth-century growth of 2.5 percent per annum was impressive by every standard except that of the Caribbean plantation economies of its French and English rivals, which grew even faster.

A century of rapid plantation growth required substantial capital investment. Until the 1750s the Dutch plantation economy was financed by a combination of private investment and commercial credit. Credit was essential to the operation of this economy, and most was extended and managed by merchant bankers in the republic.[28]

Each planter maintained a long-term relationship with such a banker, who extended credit to the planter, accepted the planter's bills of exchange, and received the planter's commodities, which the merchant banker transported, insured, and sold for a commission. A 1755 sample of planters' accounts with Amsterdam bankers reveals that the average plantation debt stood at thirty-two thousand guilders, between one-third and one-fourth of the assessed value of the plantations.[29]

This pattern of commercial relations, which differed little from plantation financing in British and French colonies, was disrupted by a major innovation in the 1750s. Willem Gideon Deutz, head of the merchant banking firm of W. G. en J. Deutz, introduced in 1753 the first *plantagelening,* or plantation loan. Also known as *negotiaties,* these were no longer short-term credits extended by the merchant banker but long-term loans secured by the value of the plantations with the funds provided by private investors. Deutz and later imitators pooled the mortgages of several plantations in a single unit trust, in which the investor bought shares. The value of the loan could be as much as five-eighths of the assessed valuation of the plantations (the bankers being rather more generous with other peoples' money than with their own). The investor received an interest rate usually of 6 percent (1 percent more than most foreign government bonds paid and nearly double the postfisc return on domestic public debt issues). Most of these bundled mortgages were structured to initiate a gradual return of principal after ten years. Presumably by that time the new productive facilities and the augmented slave labor forces financed by the loans would be fully operational.

This financial innovation stimulated a boom in the Dutch Caribbean. Amsterdam houses floated 241 unit trusts between 1753 and 1794 (when the practice came to a definitive end) with a total capitalization of about 80 million guilders. Half of this sum went to Surinam, a quarter to the Guyana settlements, and another quarter to foreign colonies, chiefly the Danish West Indies, where the Dutch were commercially dominant.[30]

The boom peaked in 1765–72, when nearly 6 million guilders per year was invested in plantation loans. The financial crisis of 1772–73 in Amsterdam was matched by trouble in the plantation colonies, as bad weather, falling coffee prices, and a revolt of the *Morranen* (runaway slaves) conspired to plunge the planters into a liquidity crisis. As major banking houses suspended payments, the flow of credit on which the plantations depended began to dry up, precipitating the bankruptcy of many plantations, the collapse of the Dutch slave trade, and the loss to Dutch investors of at least three-quarters of the capital that had been sunk over the years into the plantation loans.[31] In general, it appears that the plantation loan was a financial innovation that suited the immediate needs of cash-rich Dutch investors far more than it served the interests of the plantation economies. It took Surinam and Guyana a quarter-century to overcome the structural financial crisis into which the easy money of the plantation loans had plunged them. Only after 1800 would they grow again as productive sugar exporters.[32]

A Fourth Atlantic Economy? 1780–Present

The plantation loans display the curious combination of sophistication and naïveté that so often marks financial innovations. These loans were only one of several initiatives that marked the emergence of Amsterdam as the premier capital market of Europe. One might argue that a fourth Dutch Atlantic economy began to take shape with the 1781 search for loans for the newly proclaimed American Republic by John Adams's embassy to the Netherlands. The Dutch, as eager to support their enemy's enemy as to encourage a fellow republic, offered the American rebels their first foreign loan.[33] It was followed by many others and then by direct and portfolio investments in American land, railroads, and much more.[34] The United States was the recipient of 30 percent of all Dutch capital invested abroad in the period 1875–1900.[35] By 1914 this figure had risen to 40 percent, and in this era the Dutch invested an even larger share of its savings abroad than did even the British.[36] Today the volume of Dutch capital invested in the United States ranks directly after Britain and about even with Japan. But this is a story that cannot be entered into in any detail here.

Dutch Rule

Besides the financial presence of the Dutch in the Atlantic, there is its political and institutional legacy to consider. Brazil was not long governed by the WIC, but while it was it shared with New Netherland, Surinam, Curaçao, and Elmina (and the VOC's Cape Colony) the general pattern of company rule. The company directors (Heren XIX) appointed a governor-general or director-general with broad authority to govern the possession. These administrators represented the trading interests of the company and of the republic more generally; they frequently found themselves at odds with the interests of settlers. The several colonies varied in how these conflicts were handled. In Brazil a person of great independent stature, Count Johan Maurits of the House of Orange (the stadtholder's cousin), became governor-general. He established a parliament with representatives of both the Dutch and Portuguese planter communities. These settler interests were also represented in the lower courts and in the administration of the orphan chambers (important institutions for the transmission of property). In New Netherland the successive governors instituted an advisory council in which leading settlers were invited to participate, especially in times of military danger. They also conferred rights of local government in the form of local courts (chosen by the directors from "double lists" supplied by the inhabitants).[37] Finally, in 1653 New Amsterdam received a town charter, conferred burger rights, and formed a regular town council. According to Donna Merwick, "It was the only seventeenth-century North American city that consciously strove to imitate a European city."[38]

In the Caribbean possessions colonists were gradually admitted to the advisory councils (otherwise composed of high WIC officials) that supported the governors- or directors-general. The 1682 charter conferred by the States General for the WIC's governance of Surinam provided for a governor supported by a Policy Council and Council of Justice. The WIC-appointed governor selected the ten members of the Policy Council from double lists of candidates nominated by all free inhabitants (including the colony's numerous Jews, who formed 30–40 percent of the white population). This council advised the governor but on weighty matters could decide by majority vote. It also functioned as the criminal court. The Council of Justice—six members nominated by the Policy Council and elected by free men—heard civil cases.[39]

Dutch rule in colonies large enough to allow the development of more complex governing structures was too brief to move far beyond rule by company officials, although New Netherland on the eve of conquest enjoyed far more popular participation than the textbook accounts of "autocratic rule" allow—and far more than the English were prepared to allow for many decades.[40] However, throughout the Dutch colonial realm two traditions firmly rooted in the mother country were honored: freedom of conscience and free labor (for white settlers).

All of the Dutch colonial settlements (including the VOC's outpost at the Cape of Good Hope) were characterized by polyglot populations of Dutch, German, Huguenot, Jewish, and other European residents. Just as in the republic, religious pluriformity was the norm in most settlements. This norm was not the WIC's goal; after all, the company had been established in part to demonstrate the superiority of Calvinist colonization over Catholic subjugation of New World peoples. But this goal was subject to a set of Dutch Republican ideals that was enforced in the colonies as well. It is clearly expressed in the initial regulations—the *Provisionele Ordere* of 1624—that governed New Netherland: "No religious services will be held except those of the reformed religion, in the manner currently observed here [in the Netherlands] . . . without, however, persecuting anyone on account of their religion, but leaving for every [person] the freedom of conscience."[41] The two statements appear contradictory to the modern reader, simultaneously asserting a religious monopoly and freedom of religion. To the Dutch they identified the Reformed Church as the "Public Church," while forbidding any measures that forced individuals to attend, join, or conform one's beliefs to that church. That is, the state sanctioned the Reformed Church for the benefit of all inhabitants; its religious services were public and open to all, whether members or not. Other religions could be practiced but not publicly. Officially, this meant that individuals were free to worship as they pleased in their homes, in a family context. In many cases—especially for Lutherans and Jews but rarely for Catholics—local officials tolerated organized religious bodies on the condition that they did not create public scandal (openly challenge the Public Church).[42] Thus, while the English toyed for a time with theocracy and the Spaniards prosecuted with zeal all deviations from the Roman church, the Dutch colonies had a distinctly "multicultural" character.

Dutch law, unlike English law in this period, did not recognize the legality of indentures.[43] People were not free to sell away their freedom for extended periods of time; indeed, labor contracts in the republic generally extended for no more than six months.[44] Nor was impressment legal in the republic; the admiralties had to secure their sailors on the open market. Also it was not the republic's habit to forcibly transport prisoners and charity cases to its colonies or to establish penal colonies abroad.[45] Dutch penal institutions were then admired for their rehabilitative efforts. In sum, civil society for whites in Dutch colonies was uniquely free, even while public administration was in the hands of the companies. It is in this context that the single most famous Dutch colonial institution should be discussed: the patroonship.

The patroonship was a device intended to enlist private capital in the settlement and administration of the WIC's territories. In the absence of indentures the financing of settlers in the New World was difficult to arrange and almost always involved subventions by the WIC in the form of passage money, free land, and/or tax exemptions. To reduce its costs in a difficult period the company, after much debate, agreed to offer grants of land to private investors, patroons, in return for their commitment to send a minimum number of adult settlers (fifty in the case of the New Netherland patroonships) to the colony and provide the necessary farm capital and infrastructure. These settlers were free and could come and go from the patroon's lands as they pleased. But to reduce the WIC's administrative costs the patroons were granted the rights to administer "high, middle, and low justice" on their lands and to tax colonists up to a fixed amount to defray the costs of defense and governance. At the same time these colonists enjoyed a ten-year period of exemption from WIC taxation.

The first patroonships were established in the Caribbean (Berbice and Curaçao, 1627), followed by New Netherland (1629). Others followed on Tobago (in Dutch hands until 1678), Surinam, and the Leeward Islands, but the practice was soon judged unsuccessful and ended. In New Netherland five investors stepped forward to take advantage of the WIC's offer. Four of them formed a *partenrederijen*, whereby each patroonship was divided into five shares.[46] Each patroon held two shares of the estate he would direct and one in each of the others. They thereby sought to pool the risks of the venture in accordance with maritime commercial practice. In the event only one of the patroonships, that of Kiliaen van Rensselaer, became fully operational,[47] but these colonizing efforts, so thoroughly capitalist in their inspiration and organization (their purpose was analogous to U.S. railroad land grants of the late nineteenth century), have gone down in American historiography as attempts to transplant "feudalism" to the New World.

In 1846 E. B. O'Callaghan wrote that the patroonship provisions of the WIC "transplanted to the free soil of America the feudal tenure and feudal burdens of continental Europe."[48] He supposed that the patroonships were akin to the manors and seigneuries of the Old World, most likely because of the political functions given to the patroons—the administration of "high, middle and low justice." This, indeed, was a typical prerogative of European seigneurs. In this case, however, rulings of the patroon's court in excess of fifty guilders in value (about five pounds sterling) could be appealed to the colony's director and his council.[49] In other respects the settlers were tenants, not serfs or subjects or, for that matter, indentured servants or slaves. Thus, O'Callaghan and the unending stream of American historians who have unthinkingly repeated this calumny (to this day textbooks in U.S. history persist in referring to the patroonships as feudal or semifeudal[50]) perpetuate a misconception that has its origins in transparently Anglophilic attempts to put a progressive face on the English conquest of New Netherland. In reality, the patroonship was a commercial proposition for all parties involved, designed to save the capital and reduce the expenses of the WIC, encourage private investment and settlement, and expand trade. The patroons (who, far from being feudal lords, included in their number Jews[51] and Amsterdam merchants) entered into risk-reducing partnerships as they would have in any other commercial venture of the time. More to the point, the Hudson River Valley would have to wait for the arrival of the English to experience a regime in which land was distributed by privilege and by proximity to the throne. It would take English rule to cover the region with great estates, to teach the conquered Dutch settlers "that land was the reward given for loyalty or service," and to encourage the cultivation of gentry life in the Hudson River Valley.[52] Indeed, the English conquest of New Netherland, imposing the legal traditions of a more patriarchal and authoritarian society, gave rise to decades of legal friction between the new masters and the Dutch settlers.[53]

The patroonship's role as a settlement tool in New Netherland was brief and limited. By the 1650s the company bought back the rights to all but van Rensselaer's enterprise.[54] The experiment with the patroonship in New Netherland was the compromise result of a struggle within the WIC between directors who saw it as a trading post versus those who wished it to become a colony of settlements. In the course of the 1640s the WIC ceased to be primarily a trading company and became less reluctant to encourage settlement directly. By the 1650s—infused with refugees from Brazil—New Netherland was in a flourishing state as thousands of new settlers arrived with private financing.[55] Its exports of pelts and locally grown tobacco exceeded five hundred thousand guilders annually, and a large transit trade in Chesapeake tobacco and European consumer goods destined for the English colonies endowed New Amsterdam with a substantial autonomous merchant community. It was then in no sense a doomed or fatally misruled colony. Indeed, on the eve of the English attack a Dutchman, embroidering on a rich poetic tradition, took pen in hand to praise the colony:

> Nieuw Nederland is 't puijck,
> en 't eedelste van de Landen,
> een Seegenrijck,
> daar Melck en Honigh vloeijd
>
> [New Netherland is the epitome,
> and the noblest of all countries,
> a land of blessings,
> where milk and honey flow][56]

The colony was evidently a potent inspiration for poets; even Joost van Vondel, the greatest of Dutch seventeenth-century writers, was moved to declaim:

> Nieu Nederlant, bezaeit, belooft ons maght van koren.
> Een ander Polen schijnt voor Hollant daer geboren.
>
> [New Netherland, sown to crops, promises us an abundance of grain,
> another Poland appears to be born there for Holland.][57]

In the Caribbean the patroonship was succeeded by the colonizing society—a chartered corporation to encourage settlement and, typically, plantation agriculture. These became active on the Wild Coast settlements after the 1680s. Here again the WIC was prepared to encourage subsidiary ventures, each with its own capital and balance sheet, to spread the costs associated with colonial settlement and administration. The largest was the Sociëteit van Suriname, founded in 1682 with shares equally divided between a Zeeland investor, the city of Amsterdam (which wanted to encourage sugar production to bolster its large refining industry), and the WIC.

Standing against this record of free white labor, freedom of conscience, and relatively open, market-based governing institutions is the Dutch reputation for having been particularly severe slave masters. The reputation is based largely on John Gabriel Stedman's salacious exposé of Surinam plantation life of 1796. Stedman's book recounted his experiences twenty years earlier as a member of expeditions to capture runaway slaves. Its many illustrations of slave punishments attracted a large reading public prepared by the anti-slave-trade movement to think the worst of plantation owners, especially if they were not British. If the Dutch plantation system differed from the others, this may have derived from the strikingly high ratio of slaves to whites in eighteenth-century Surinam and Guyana (approximately 20:1). Such a ratio suggests the probable maintenance of a strict discipline, but direct evidence to support this surmise is not abundant. Unhappily, what Stedman reported may have been closer to a Caribbean norm than an exception.[58]

Whether unusually severe or not, slavery in the Dutch colonies was long lasting, being abolished only in 1863. The absence of an active Dutch antislavery discourse stands as a puzzle and challenge to prevailing interpretations of the origins of the British antislavery movement.[59] Perhaps the answer is to be found in the weak integration of the plantation owners, themselves forming a polyglot community, to the Netherlands. Indeed, a recent interpretation of Dutch colonialism in the Caribbean emphasized its "negligent" character; Gert Oostindie argues that after the seventeenth-century dreams of empire and wealth had faded, Dutch policy was icily instrumental.[60] Language, culture, and religion were not imposed on the inhabitants in ways comparable to the other colonial empires. Consequently, today Dutch is not the common language of the Netherlands Antilles, the Christian population is not primarily Calvinist, and neither high culture nor popular culture has a specifically Dutch stamp. While colonizers are usually faulted for cultural imperialism, Oostindie makes a good case for the long-term disadvantages (to the subject peoples) of colonial indifference. It certainly has not made these societies any less reliant on the "mother country."

Assessment and Speculation

From the perspective of a colonizer, Dutch participation in the Atlantic world of the seventeenth and eighteenth centuries presents a spectacle of frustration and failure. The Netherlands remain, to be sure, in possession of colonial territories even in the twenty-first century, but few besides cruise-ship passengers and tax evaders are touched by this institutional and cultural legacy. The great prizes, New Holland and New Netherland, slipped from Dutch control after only a brief period of colonization. Perhaps the Dutch had arrived too late in the Atlantic theater to establish firmly their grand design, and when they arrived, it was in the form of a trading company that could not possibly succeed as a colonizing power in the competitive environment of the Atlantic world without sustained state support.

When the early failure of the WIC and its grand design for the Western Hemisphere is placed beside the success of the VOC and its long reign as the dominant European power in Asia, historians have long been inclined to depreciate too much the importance of the New World to the Dutch Republic. But these instincts of modern nationalist historians were not those of most early modern

Table 3: Value of Dutch commodity imports from Asia and the Western Hemisphere, 1640–1779

Annual average revenue, in thousands of guilders

Period	Asia	West Indies	Approx. Total
1640–49	7,922	[4–5,000]*	12–13,000
1670–79	9,127	—	
1680–89	10,446	[2–3,000]**	12–13,000
1690–99	12,736	—	
1700–09	13,950	4,300	18,000
1710–19	16,370	4,900	21,000
1720–29	18,555	5,600	24,000
1730–39	16,705	5,600	22,000
1740–49	15,973	10,300	26,000
1750–59	18,796	11,900	31,000
1760–69	21,360	17,900	39,000
1770–79	19,951	22,400	42,400

*Commodities from Brazil and New Netherlands
** Commodities from Surinam and Curaçao

Sources: Asia (VOC revenues in Patria): De Vries and Van der Woude, *First Modern Economy*, 390, 444; West Indies (Surinam and Guyana): ibid., 478; Curaçao and Sint Eustatius: Wim Klooster, *Illicit Riches: Dutch Trade in the Caribbean, 1648–1795* (Leiden: KITLV Press, 1998), 176; 1640s estimate: De Vries and Van der Woude, *First Modern Economy*, 403; Jacobs, *Een zegenrijk gewest*, 219–28.

Dutch observers. In truth mournful, frustrated colonizers were few in the Dutch Republic. For most merchants and investors the Atlantic world was understood as a zone of commercial activity first and of colonization and political power second.

The Dutch political failures of the mid-seventeenth century did, indeed, produce a severe contraction in what had earlier been a large trade in New World commodities. But thereafter, especially after about 1680, the Dutch New World trade grew rapidly (see table 3). One must keep in mind the fact that total trade between Europe and the New World grew much faster than did the total Asian-European trade. In the very long run (1510–1780) total European trade with Asia grew in volume by about 1 percent per annum, while European trade with the New World grew by over 2 percent per annum.[61] Even a gradually declining share of this dynamic trade could loom large in comparison to a large but stationary share of the more slowly growing Asian trade. The small Dutch plantation sector of the 1680s was good for about 8 percent of total Caribbean commodity production. By the 1750s, the substantial growth of the Dutch plantations not withstanding, its share had fallen to 6 percent of total output, and after the plantation loan boom, in 1775, the share had fallen further to under 5 percent of a vastly larger total output (30–32 million kg. of sugar in the 1680s; 200 million kg. in the 1770s).[62] Despite this steadily declining share, the total value of Dutch imports from the New World rose to approximately equal those from Asia by the 1770s.[63]

Dutch participation in the Atlantic world was not negligible, but it was vulnerable because of the marginal character of its presence in the Caribbean. Under favorable circumstances (war between France and England, most obviously), the Dutch islands could become beehives of illicit trade. But this trade could disappear at the stroke of a pen, and when the Dutch Republic was involved in war (a prospect invited by its increasingly conspicuous military weakness) the consequences for her economic activity were serious indeed.

The marginalized political position of the Dutch combined with the inherently volatile character of long-distance trade exposed the republic fully to a highly risky economic environment. The republic had well-developed institutions to manage risk at the micro level, but its decentralized state structure was not well suited to create a protected environment in which its institutions might take root and protect investments abroad. At the macro level, the steadfast reliance on joint-stock trading companies to shoulder the financial burdens of empire building and the maintenance of free labor conditions (always excepting African slaves) placed the Netherlands at a severe political disadvantage in its competition with the other European colonial powers in the New World.

Both of these features—the joint stock company and free labor markets—meant that market forces would dominate colonial decision making. Attracting settlers required competition with the VOC's voracious appetite for men to sail to Asia. The superior returns available there insured that the flow of labor to the New World would never be more than a trickle. The prospective settler in New Netherland had to secure his passage and start-up financing; an ever-present alternative was to sign up with the VOC, which paid a signing bonus and monthly wages, and provided maintenance while in company service and the right to engage in a limited amount of private trading. The survivor could hope to return home with a significant nest egg. These hopes were not often realized, to be sure, but the *ex ante* calculation of costs and benefits seems to have made settlement in the New World uncompetitive.[64] The choices facing the potential migrant in the British Isles differed significantly so that in the seventeenth century, when Britain sent approximately 370,000 persons to the New World (the majority indentured servants and prisoners) and perhaps 100,000 to Asia (a significant minority of which died while in the English East Inda Company [EIC] service), the Netherlands sent 15,000 settlers to the New World and 375,000 to Asia (of whom 215,000 died either in Asia or at sea).[65]

Similarly, financing the military power needed to secure and hold a New World empire required attracting funds on the private capital market. The same was true in Asia, but the sustained profitability of the VOC allowed it to draw on retained profits to finance its expansion plans. In the New World the more competitive commercial setting denied the WIC this option, and after the 1630s private capital markets rarely judged the prospects for gain superior to alternative opportunities in Europe.

Perhaps the Dutch experience of the seventeenth and eighteenth centuries offers a test of the viability of the concept of an "Atlantic world." More than other European states, the Dutch Republic was prepared to participate in an international economy with colonies populated by a polyglot population of settlers. "Prematurely" modern, the Dutch launched multinational enterprises before the age of mercantilism had ended. The Atlantic world may have had a cosmopolitan aspect, but it was not, certainly not in the eighteenth century, a zone hospitable to such an approach. Despite this, the Dutch persevered and found and exploited weak spots in the armor of mercantilism whereby their economy might prosper even as their state's weakness became ever more manifest. It is a theme whose relevance has returned in recent decades.

Notes

1. Oliver A. Rink, *Holland on the Hudson: An Economic and Social History of Dutch New York* (Ithaca and New York: Cornell University Press, 1986), 50–64; Cornelius Ch. Goslinga, *The Dutch in the Caribbean and on the Wild Coast, 1580–1680* (Assen: Van Gorcum/Gainesville: University of Florida Press, 1971), 34–42, 87; Catharina Ligtenberg, *Willem Usselinx* (Utrecht: A. Oosthoek, 1914); W. J. van Hoboken, "The Dutch West India Company: The Political Background of Its Rise and Decline," in *Britain and the Netherlands*, vol. 1, ed. J. S. Bromley and E. H. Kossmann (London: Chatto and Windus, 1960), 41–61.

2. *Vrijheden by de Vergaderinghe van de Negenthiene vande Geoctoryeerde West-Indische Compagnie vergunt aen allen den ghenen die eenighe Colonien in Nieuw-Nederlandt sullen planten* (Amsterdam, 1630).

3. A detailed account of the successive phases of Dutch economic involvement in the New World is provided in Jan de Vries and Ad van der Woude, *The First Modern Economy: Success, Failure, and Perseverance of the Dutch Economy, 1500–1815* (Cambridge: Cambridge University Press, 1997), 396–402, 464–81.

4. When the VOC was disbanded, control of its possessions passed in 1798 to a government department of Buitenlandse Bezittingen en Coloniën (Foreign Possessions and Colonies). The appeal of a monopoly trading company did not fade, however, and in 1824 the Kingdom of the Netherlands established a firm with monopoly privileges in the Dutch East Indies, the Nederlandsche Handelsmaatschappij. Free access to the Asian colonies was not achieved until the 1870s.

5. The best general survey history of the VOC is Femme Gaastra, *Geschiedenis van de VOC*, 2nd ed. (Zutphen: Walberg Pers, 1991). In English one must still consult Charles R. Boxer, *The Dutch Seaborne Empire, 1600–1800* (London: Hutchinson, 1965).

6. Jonathan Israel, *Dutch Primacy in World Trade, 1585–1740* (Oxford: Clarendon Press, 1989), 84–85.

7. The New Netherland Company had been formed in 1615 (with a charter granting monopoly rights for only three years) as a fusion of four partnerships that traded for beaver pelts in the Hudson River area beginning in 1610, immediately after Henry Hudson's reconnaissance of the river in 1609. See Simon Hart, *The Prehistory of the New Netherland Company: Amsterdam Notarial Records of the First Dutch Voyages to the Hudson* (Amsterdam: City of Amsterdam Press, 1959).

8. Salt, a commodity in which the Dutch have long held an important trading position, is discussed in detail in Engel Sluiter, "Dutch-Spanish Rivalry in the Caribbean Area, 1594–1609," *Hispanic American Historical Review* 28 (1948): 165–96. The Punta de Araya salt pans were originally excluded from the WIC monopoly zone. When, in 1622, it became apparent that this profitable trade would be essential to the viability of the new company, the salt trade was included in the WIC's prerogatives, to the distress of the Hoorn and Enkhuizen merchants, who reacted by refusing to recognize the WIC's charter. It took several years to overcome this resistance. See Jaap Jacobs, *Een zegenrijk gewest: Nieuw-Nederland in de zeventiende eeuw* (Amsterdam: Prometheus–B. Bakker, 1999), 62–63.

9. Doeke Roos, *Zeeuwen en de Westindische Compagnie, 1621–1674* (Hulst: Van Geyt Productions, 1992), 9–11.

10. On the difficulty of raising capital, see P. J. van Winter, *De Westindische Compagnie ter kamer Stad en lande* (The Hague: Martinus Nijhoff, 1978), 12–18; Israel, *Dutch Primacy,* 158–59. The reluctance of Amsterdam investors was compensated for by stimulating the interest of investors in nonseaport cities. These presumably less knowledgeable but fervently anti-Spanish investors committed as much capital as did the Amsterdam commercial community.

11. Jan Lucassen, "Emigration to the Dutch Colonies and the USA," in *The Cambridge Survey of World Migration,* ed. Robin Cohen (Cambridge: Cambridge University Press, 1995), 22–23. Only about one-quarter of the *vrijlieden* resided in Brazil with families.

12. Until this time Dutch commentary on the Atlantic slave trade had been overwhelmingly negative. Such slaves as had been delivered to Dutch ports—by storm or the capture of enemy ships—had been freed; the playwright Bredero denounced the trade in slaves in a popular play, *Moortje,* of 1615; the great proponent of establishing the WIC, Willem Usselinx, insisted that Protestant colonization, in contrast to Catholic imperialism, could have no place for slavery. After 1630 these voices quickly fell silent. Usselinx continued to declaim against slavery, and Grotius, the jurist, made fine distinctions between slaves taken in just wars and those taken in unjust wars, but by 1640 the first of many theological pamphlets offering justifications for slavery had appeared. See Pieter Emmer, *De Nederlandse slavenhandel, 1500–1850* (Amsterdam: Arbeiderspers, 2000), 34–39.

13. Opinions about the value of Brazil varied: Zeeland, heavily committed to the New World enterprise, was eager to commit public funds; Holland was more reluctant. Amsterdam merchants tended to regard the preservation of Dutch access to the Portuguese market as far more valuable than the preservation of control over Brazil. Jonathan Israel notes that the Amsterdam merchants most committed to Brazil were Portuguese Jews.

Indeed, many of the *moradores* who had risen in revolt were indebted to these Jews for purchases of slaves and commercial services. Under the circumstances, Israel reasons, many of Holland's Christian merchants doubted whether the benefits of retaining Brazil could equal the costs (Israel, *Dutch Primacy,* 168–70). E. van den Boogaart acknowledges the role of the Jews but emphasizes the large debts of these planters to the company—the eleven largest *senhores de engenho* owed nearly 2 million guilders at the eve of the revolt; see E. van den Boogaart, "De Nederlandse expansie in het Atlantisch gebied, 1590–1674," in *Algemene geschiedenis der Nederland,* vol. 7, ed. Dirk Peter Blok, W. Prevenier, and D. J. Roorda (Haarlem: Fibula-Van Dishoeck, 1980), 237–38; Roos, *Zeeuwen,* 55–56.

14. Henk den Heijer, *Goud, ivoor en slaven: Scheepvaart en handel van de Tweede Westindische Compagnie op Afrika, 1674–1740* (Zutphen: Walburg, 1997), 38. In 1649 the WIC had issued shares with a total face value of 17 million guilders and bonds and short-term obligations totaling nearly 20 million guilders.

15. The role of Dutch commerce as a catalyst in the transformation of Barbados—and in the creation of the "second Atlantic system"—remains a topic of debate. The strong version of the story points to the reduction by the Dutch of prices of slaves, victuals, equipment, and sugar transport sufficient to make large-scale plantation-based sugar production possible. See Richard N. Bean and Robert P. Thomas, "The Adoption of Slave Labor in British America," in *Uncommon Market: Essays in the Economic History of the Atlantic Slave Trade,* ed. Henry A. Gemery and Jan S. Hogendorn (New York: Academic Press, 1979), 390–98; V. T. Harlow, *A History of Barbados, 1625–1685* (Oxford: Clarendon Press, 1926).

16. Evert Nieuwenhof, preface to Adriaen van der Donck, *Beschryvinge van Nieuw-Nederlant [A Description of New Netherlands],* 2nd ed. (Amsterdam: t'Aemsteldam by Evert Nieuwenhof, boeck-verkooper woonende op't Ruslandt in't Schrijf-boeck, 1656).

17. The process of Dutch settlement of New Netherland was not altogether stopped by the English conquest of 1664. In the three decades following 1664 the number of Dutch Reformed congregations nearly tripled, from eleven to twenty-nine. See S. B. Kim, *Landlord and Tenant in Colonial New York: Manorial Society, 1664–1775* (Chapel Hill: University of North Carolina Press, 1978). Then, in 1692, New York's mayor Charles Lodwick complained: "Our chiefest unhappiness here is too great a mixture of nations, and English the least part. . . . The Dutch are generally the most frugal and laborious, and consequently the richest, whereas the English are the contrary" (letter from Lodwick to two members of the Royal Society in London, in *Collections of the New-York Historical Society,* 2nd ser., 2 [New York, 1849], 243–50).

18. Jon Kepler, "Estimates of the Volume of Direct Shipments of Tobacco and Sugar from the Chief English Plantations to European Markets, 1620–1669," *Journal of European Economic History* 28 (1999): 116–18. By the 1650s tobacco replaced pelts as New Amsterdam's chief export. In the course of that decade imports to New Amsterdam nearly doubled, approaching 1 million guilders in annual value. Much of the imported merchandise was destined for the Chesapeake. See Jacobs, *Een zagenrijk gewest,* 222, 227.

19. Charles Wilson, *Profit and Power: A Study of England and the Dutch Wars* (London and New York: Longmans, Green, 1957), 115.

20. The hitherto unsuspected scope of Dutch trade with the Spanish Caribbean is revealed in Wim Klooster, *Illicit Riches: Dutch Trade in the Caribbean, 1648–1795* (Leiden: KITLV Press, 1998).

21. Jonathan Israel, "The Emerging Empire: The Continental Perspective, 1650–1713," in *The Origins of Empire,* ed. Nicholas Canny, vol. 1 of *The Oxford History of the British Empire,* ed. William Roger Louis (Oxford: Oxford University Press, 1998), 433.

22. The republic's most prominent theorist of political economy, Pieter de la Court, felt acutely the historic importance of the losses of New Holland and New Netherland. In the 1669 revision to his *Interest van Holland* he argued as follows for the necessity of settler colonies: "for when we consider, that all the trade of our common inhabitants is circumscribed or bounded well nigh within Europe, and that in very many parts of the same, as France, England, Sweden &c. our greatest trade and navigation thither is crampt by the high duties, or by patent companies . . . ; as also how small a part of the world Europe is, and how many merchants dwell in Holland, and must dwell there to support it; we shall have no reason to wonder, if all the beneficial traffick in these small adjacent countries be either worn out, or in a short time be glutted with an over-trade." The traditional European markets, he argued, were both overstocked with merchants and subject to protectionist measures of increasing effectiveness. De la Court was convinced that the future lay in the development of settler colonies and in the trade that would emerge on that solid foundation. From this perspective the unfolding crisis was doubly troubling, for the prospects of a New World territorial empire of any size had just been dashed with the losses of Brazil and New Netherland. "Nu zijn wij dit alles quijt" (Now all this has been lost to us), sighed de la Court, with palpable regret. See Pieter de la Court, *Aanwysing der heilsame politieke gronden en maximen van de Republieke van Holland en West-Vriesland* (Leiden, 1669); translated as *The True Interest and Political Maxims of the Republic of Holland* (London: J. Nourse, 1746; repr., New York: Arno Press, 1972).

23. The fiscal regimes established by the WIC (and the colonization societies) were transparent in their operation and light in their burden. Colonists paid an *akkergeld* (land tax), a *hoofdgeld* (head tax per colonist and per slave), and *handelsrecognitiën* (trade fees) of 2.5 percent on the value of imports and exports. Until the mid-eighteenth century taxes were usually paid in "commodity money," that is, sugar and beaver pelts. See Henk den Heijer, *De geschiedenis van de WIC* (Zutphen: Walburg, 1994), 181.

24. This exceedingly brief account cannot do justice to the history of the WIC. For more extended treatments, see den Heijer, *De geschiedenis van de WIC*; Charles R. Boxer, *The Dutch in Brazil* (Oxford: Clarendon Press, 1957); Goslinga, *Dutch in the Caribbean;* Pieter C. Emmer, "The West India Company, 1621–1791: Dutch or Atlantic?" in *Companies and Trade: Essays on Overseas Trading Companies during the Ancien Régime,* ed. L. Blussé and F. Gaastra (Leiden: Leiden University Press, 1981), 71–95. Emmer's article plus several of his important articles on the Atlantic economy and the Dutch slave trade are available in Pieter Emmer, *The Dutch in the Atlantic Economy, 1580–1880: Trade, Slavery, and Emancipation* (Aldershot: Ashgate, 1998).

25. In the case of the second WIC, the States General agreed in 1674 to provide a modest subsidy for military defense: the pay for two hundred soldiers and the maintenance costs for fortifications. All together this came to between twenty-five thousand and thirty-five thousand guilders annually.

26. For an account of the debates leading to the decision to end the old company and establish a new WIC, see den Heijer, *Goud, ivoor en slaven,* 39–49. Holders of WIC shares received shares in the new company at the rate of fifteen cents on the guilder on the condition that they injected new capital at the rate of 4 percent of the nominal value of the

old shares. Bondholders were issued new bonds with a face value of 30 percent of the old bonds on condition that they paid in 8 percent of the nominal value of the old bonds.

27. The Dutch colonial empire became "state property" only with the dissolution in bankruptcy of the WIC (in 1791) and the VOC (in 1795), but even then it took until 1806 for the then Batavian Republic to establish a colonial ministry. Only in 1816, with the return to Dutch control of colonial territories held by the British during the French occupation of the Netherlands, did modern Dutch colonialism properly begin. See J. van Goor, *De Nederlandse Koloniën: Geschiedenis van de Nederlandse expansie, 1600–1975* (The Hague: SDU, 1994).

28. The financing of slave purchases was to a large extent arranged by the WIC, so long as it lasted.

29. Alex van Stipriaan, *Surinaams Contrast: Roofbouw en overleven in een Caraïbische plantage economie, 1750–1863* (Amsterdam: Centrale Huisdrukkerij Vrije Universiteit, 1991), 220.

30. Details on the plantation loans are drawn chiefly from J. P. van de Voort, *De Westindische plantages van 1720 tot 1795: Financiën en handel* (Eindhoven: Drukkerg de Witte, 1973). See also van Stipriaan, *Surinaams Contrast*, chap. 7.

31. The issuance of new loans did not end immediately. Investors remained prepared to supply capital to British planters on Tobago and Barbados (where hurricane damage sent them to the capital markets), and the Danish islands also remained in favor. But by 1777–80 new loans amounted to no more than a half-million guilders per annum. See Charles Wilson, *Anglo-Dutch Commerce and Finance in the Eighteenth Century* (Cambridge: The University Press, 1941), 182–86; van Stipriaan, *Surinaams Contrast*, 223; van de Voort, *De Westindische plantages*, 268–323.

32. P. C. Emmer, "Capitalism Mistaken? The Economic Decline of Surinam and the Plantation Loans, 1773–1850: A Rehabilitation," *Itinerario* 20 (1996): 11–18.

33. James Riley, *International Government Finance and the Amsterdam Capital Market* (Cambridge: Cambridge University Press, 1980), 193. See also James Riley, "Foreign Credit and Fiscal Stability: Dutch Investment in the U.S., 1781–1794," *Journal of American History* 65 (1978): 654–78; Pieter J. van Winter, *American Finance and Dutch Investment, 1780–1805, with an Epilogue to 1840,* 2 vols. (New York: Arno Press, 1977).

34. James Riley, "Financial and Economic Ties: The First Century," in *A Bilateral Bicentennial: A History of Dutch-American Relations, 1782–1982,* ed. J.W. Schulte Nordholt and R. P. Swieringa (New York: Octagon Books/Amsterdam: Meulenhoff International, 1982); Augustus J. Veenendaal Jr., *Slow Train to Paradise: How Dutch Investment Helped Build American Railroads* (Stanford, Calif.: Stanford University Press, 1996), 8–13.

35. Wybren Verstegen, "National Wealth and Income from Capital in the Netherlands, c. 1805–1910," *Economic and Social History of the Netherlands* 7 (1996): 100; K. D. Bosch, *De Nederlandse beleggingen in de Verenigde Staten* (Amsterdam: Elsevier, 1948).

36. These are the best estimates of Veenendaal, *Slow Train to Paradise,* 174–75.

37. This process is described in detail in Jacobs, *Een zegenrijk gewest,* 147–57. The first three villages to establish *rechtbanken* were English settlements on Long Island; by 1664 a total of sixteen local governments had been established, besides the more elaborate urban government of New Amsterdam.

38. Donna Merwick, *Possessing Albany, 1630–1710: The Dutch and English Experiences* (Cambridge: Cambridge University Press, 1990), 143. By the 1650s direct company rule

was making way for the introduction of Dutch civic governance in New Netherland. The new settlement of Nieuwer-Amstel (modern New Castle, Delaware) was furnished with a charter that foresaw a government of three *burgemeesters* and five to seven *schepenen* (legal officers) to be drawn from a *vroedschap* of over twenty leading citizens elected by the inhabitants. See Jacobs, *Een zegenrijk gewest,* 129–30.

39. G. W. van der Meiden, "Governor Mauricius and the Political Rights of the Surinam Jews," in *The Jewish Nation in Surinam: Historical Essays,* ed. R. Cohen (Amsterdam: S. Emmering, 1982), 49–50. The colony's governing documents are available in J. J. Hartsinck, *Beschrijving van Guiana* (Amsterdam: G. Tielenburg, 1770).

40. According to Jacobs, "the development process of the governmental and legal administration [of New Netherland] was more a question of the growth of scale, following the existing forms prevailing in the Republic, than it was influenced by circumstances specific to North America" (Jacobs, *Een zegenrijk gewest,* 172).

41. F. C. Wieder, *De Stichting van New York in Juli 1625,* Werken Linschoten-Vereeniging, vol. 26 (The Hague: Martinus Nijhof, 1925), 112.

42. In Brazil, Surinam, and Curaçao, Jews (who made up large minorities of the white populations) readily secured the right to public worship. When the first Jews arrived in New Amsterdam in 1654 (directly from Recife, which had just fallen to the Portuguese), Director-General Stuyvesant was far from welcoming. His eagerness to see the Jews continue onward was countermanded by WIC directors. The city council of New Amsterdam then passed ordinances that greatly restricted the freedom of action of Jews. This, too, was ordered undone by company directors, who insisted that Jews receive the same (limited) rights in New Amsterdam as they enjoyed in Amsterdam. The solicitude of the directors was no doubt related to the importance of Jewish planters and sugar traders to the larger WIC enterprise in the Caribbean. In 1659 the WIC issued a charter to Jews settling in Cayenne, on the Wild Coast. The charter guaranteed freedom of worship, tax privileges, and partial autonomy. See Jacobs, *Een zegenrijk gewest,* 315–19; R. A. J. van Lier, "The Jewish Community in Surinam: A Historical Survey," in *The Jewish Nation in Surinam: Historical Essays,* ed. R. Cohen (Amsterdam: S. Emmering, 1982), 19–20.

43. For a nuanced discussion of this blanket assertion, see Ernst van den Boogaart, "The Servant Migration to New Netherlands, 1624–1664," in *Colonialism and Migration; Indentured Labour Before and After Slavery,* ed. P. C. Emmer (Dordrecht: M. Nijhoff/Higham, Mass.: Kluwer Boston, 1986), 55–81. Servants who contracted to work in New Netherland on multiyear contracts were not unknown, but their legal and economic positions are readily distinguishable from those of English and French indentured servants. For instance, their contracts could not be bought and sold. Over 60 percent of the 746,000 Europeans setting sail for British New World colonies before 1800 were bound to masters by extended indentures (calculated from David Eltis, "Slavery and Freedom in the Early Modern World," in *Terms of Labor: Slavery, Serfdom, and Free Labor,* ed. Stanley Engerman [Stanford, Calif.: Stanford University Press, 1999], 28–31).

44. The length of service contracts and the penalties for breaking them are good indicators of the practical freedom of "free labor." See David W. Galenson, "The Rise of Free Labor: Economic Change and the Enforcement of Service Contracts in England, 1351–1875," in *Capitalism in Context: Essays on Economic Development and Cultural Change in Honor of R. M. Hartwell,* ed. John A. James and Mark Thomas (Chicago: University of

Chicago Press, 1994), 114–37. Dutch practice seems to stand between the substantial contractual rigidity of England and the "anarchy" of the United States.

45. The republic did not populate its colonies with prisoners and paupers, but it did encourage orphans to settle in New Netherland. While plans to send orphans in large numbers were often discussed, little came of them. Altogether no more than one hundred orphans became apprentices in New Netherland. The number remained small, perhaps, because the plans were strictly voluntary; set skill, age, and health standards for the orphans; and included promises to settle assets (land and tax exemptions) on the orphans at the end of their apprenticeships. See Jacobs, *Een zegenrijk gewest,* 96–100.

46. The first five aspirant patrons were Michiel Pauw (estates on the Connecticut and Hudson rivers), Samuel Godijn (on the Delaware River), Albert Conraetsz Burg (also on the Delaware), Samuel Blommaert (on the Connecticut), and Kiliaen van Rensselaer (on the Hudson). All but Pauw participated in the *partenrederij.*

47. Godijn's colony of Swanendael, on the Delaware, was established in 1630, but the thirty-two inhabitants suffered extermination at the hands of Native Americans in 1632. See David Pietersz de Vries, *Korte Historiael ende Journaels Aenteykeninge van verscheyden voyagiens in de vier delen des werelts-ronde, als Europa, Africa, Asia ende America gedaen,* ed. H. T. Colenbrander, Werken Linschoten-Vereeniging, vol. 3 (The Hague, 1911), 147–48.

48. E. B. O'Callaghan, *History of New Netherlands; or, New York under the Dutch* (New York: G. S. Appleton, 1846), 120. Also influential in establishing this durable academic folk myth is John Romeyn Brodhead, *History of the State of New York* (New York: Harper & Brothers, 1872). He called the patroonship "that obnoxious instrument of 1629," with which the WIC "matured its selfish commercial scheme for the introduction of the feudal system into its American province" (187). Even the otherwise alert and well-informed work of Oliver Rink could not resist draping the Dutch peculiar institution with this term of opprobrium, describing the patroons' "vainglorious attempt to establish feudal estates on the Hudson River" (Rink, *Holland on the Hudson,* 65, 115).

49. Moreover, the law court (at Rensselaerswijk, the only patroonship that ever functioned in New Netherland) was not literally the possession of the patroon. It consisted of five persons: two representing the patron and three appointed by the colony's director as representatives of the colonists. See Jacobs, *Een zegenrijk gewest,* 123.

50. For a current example, see George Brown Tindall and David E. Shi, *America: A Narrative History,* 5th ed. (New York: W. W. Norton, 2000), 90.

51. For example, in 1659 a patroonship was granted to David Nassy and coinvestors to establish a Jewish colony at Cayenne. The French took control of the area in 1664, at which time Nassy and associates moved to neighboring Surinam, which came under Dutch control (from the British) in 1667. By 1694 Surinam had "92 Portuguese Jewish and 10 to 12 German Jewish families.... They were the owners of 40 sugar estates with a total of 9,000 slaves in that year" (van Lier, "Jewish Community in Surinam," 19). Nassy's famous descendent David de Isaac Cohen Nassy wrote *Essai Historique sur la colonie de Surinam* (Paramaribo, 1788), a celebrated Enlightenment work advocating Jewish civil emancipation. See G. J. van Grol, *De Grondpolitiek in het West-Indische Domein der Generalitieit* (Amsterdam, 1980), part 2:91–98.

52. Donna Merwick, "Dutch Townsmen and Land Use: A Spatial Perspective on Seventeenth-Century Albany, New York," *William and Mary Quarterly* 37 (1980): 77–78. The

American historiographical tradition of idealizing the yeoman farmer has long placed the large New York State landowners of the eighteenth century in bad odor. Frederick Jackson Turner managed to fit all of the stereotypical charges into a few pages of his *The Frontier in American History* (New York: H. Holt and Company, 1920): "From the time of the patroon grants along the lower Hudson, great estates had been the common form of land tenure [in New York].... These great patroon estates were confirmed by the English governors." After recounting how German settlers later left the region, Turner concluded with a moral lesson: "those [colonies] which imposed feudal tenures and undemocratic restraints, and which exploited settlers, were certain to lose" (80–82). Not only are the Dutch roots of this regime grossly overstated (the sixteen great manorial estates that came to dominate the province were the creation of English rule, not Dutch), so are the purported negative effects of tenancy. See Sung Bok Kim, "A New Look at the Great Landlords of Eighteenth-Century New York," *William and Mary Quarterly* 27 (1970): 581–614.

53. David E. Narrett, *Inheritance and Family Life in Colonial New York City* (Ithaca: Cornell University Press, 1992), 45–51.

54. The company issued a revised form of the ordinance governing patroonships (the *Vrijheden ende Exemptiën*) in 1650. This attracted at least three new investors who sought to establish estates on Staten Island, on the Hackensack River, and at Nieuw-Utrecht, in modern Brooklyn. None became a functioning patroonship, and the WIC closed the books on this settlement device in 1659. See Jacobs, *Een zegenrijk gewest,* 126–27.

55. Rink, *Holland on the Hudson,* 171.

56. Quoted in Albert Eekhof, *De Hervormde Kerk in Noord Amerika, 1624–1664,* vol. 2 (The Hague: M. Nijhoff, 1913), 68.

57. Quoted in Jacobs, *Een zegenrijk gewest,* 193.

58. Emmer, *De Nederlandse slavenhandel,* 178–81.

59. Seymour Dresher, "The Long Goodbye: Dutch Capitalism and Antislavery in Comparative Perspective," *American Historical Review* 99 (1994): 44–69. See also Emmer, *De Nederlandse slavenhandel,* 34–39, 185–206.

60. Gert Oostindie, *Het paradijs oversee: De 'Nederlandse' Caraïben en Nederland* (Amsterdam: B. Bakker, 1998).

61. Jan de Vries, "Connecting Europe and Asia: A Quantitative Analysis of the Cape Route Trade, 1497–1795," in *Global Connections and Monetary History, 1470–1800,* ed. Dennis Flynn, Arturo Giraldo, and Richard von Glahn (Aldershot: Ashegate, 2003), 35–106.

62. De Vries and van der Woude, *First Modern Economy,* 477.

63. The VOC earned revenues from the sale of Asian goods averaging 20 million guilders per year in the 1770s. Contemporary assessments put the annual value of commodities sent to Dutch ports from the Western Hemisphere at 18 million guilders, which is reported in de Vries and van der Woude, *First Modern Economy,* 497. The recent study by Klooster, *Illicit Riches,* offers evidence to indicate that Dutch New World trades were more valuable than this. In the 1770s the plantation economies of Surinam and Guyana delivered commodities valued at 12.6 million guilders (see de Vries and van der Woude, *First Modern Economy,* 478); meanwhile the legal and illegal trades of Curaçao and St. Eustatius were shipping goods, primarily from the Spanish and French colonies, valued at 9.8 million guilders (Klooster, *Illicit Riches,* 176), for a total value of 22.4 million guilders. Table 3 presents a revised assessment of Dutch commodity imports from the

New World. The trade volume of the 1770s was not to last. By the 1790s the trade of the commercial islands collapsed. English forces did their best to level the mountainous island of St. Eustatius, and they occupied Curaçao, prompting the flight of its commercial elite before the English confiscation of what remained.

64. One of the few eighteenth-century Dutch critiques of plantation slavery was written in response to news of a slave revolt in Berbice. Writing in *De Koopman* 4, no. 32 (1773), "Colonius Agricola" argued that gentler treatment would bring such revolts to an end since black slaves are no different than "we free Christians." He went on to ask why slavery was necessary in the first place: "Why not use free white workers? Are there not, after all, plenty of poor Germans?" Indeed, the flow of German migrants to the Netherlands was large and continuous; the Netherlands came to be known as the "graveyard of Germany." But this labor supply moved east, not west. See Roelof van Gelder, *Het Oost-Indisch avontuur: Duitsers in dienst van de VOC* (Nijmegen: SUN, 1997).

65. P. C. Emmer, ed., *Colonialism and Migration: Indentured Labour before and after Slavery* (Dordrecht: M. Nijhoff, 1986). Migration estimates are drawn from David Eltis, "Seventeenth Century Migration and the Slave Trade," in *Migration, Migration History, and History: Old Paradigms and New Perspectives,* ed. Jan Lucassen and Leo Lucassen (Bern and New York: Peter Lang, 1997); de Vries, "Connecting Europe and Asia."

Self-Organized Complexity and the Emergence of an Atlantic Market Economy, 1651–1815

The Case of Madeira

David Hancock

Each year ever more scholarly writing casts itself as "Atlantic history." In the past two decades published studies of migration flows, labor systems, intellectual influences and adaptations, and commercial exchanges have uncovered a hitherto neglected early modern Atlantic world. What was earlier dubbed Anglo or British, French, Spanish, or Portuguese America is now as often described as part of Atlantic America—a community that exchanged commodities, services, settlers, and laborers; waged war on itself; and shared political ideas and institutions, even while its constituent states also exhibited distinctive cultures. That community was "the scene of a vast interaction" among these old worlds, and in various ways the studies of this "single functional unit," both integrated and cohesive, strive to "encompass the entire Atlantic basin, not simply descriptively but conceptually" as well.[1]

My recent research into the Madeira wine complex develops these insights, extends them to particular projects of late seventeenth- and eighteenth-century men and women, and begins to raise the question of how this composite Atlantic system, its institutions, actors, and ideas, evolved over the century. My approach is to consider the Madeira wine complex of producers, distributors, and consumers, with its associated institutions and ideas, as a complex economic and social system.

In complex social and economic systems the actors have many specific links among themselves, and larger-scale phenomena are the outcomes of the multitudinous chaotic and decentralized interactions along these links.[2] The contrasts are with systems having only a few important links among actors, on the one hand, and with systems in which the abundance of interactions among individuals can be summarized as net, anonymous forces, on the other hand. These contrasting approaches are easier to analyze because fundamentally they posit simpler worlds, and no doubt in many instances they are adequate. But they do not do justice to the development of a composite Atlantic economy. Indeed, the many, specific links among people highlighted in a complex economic and social system are consistent with historians' well-developed, historically grounded intuition about how most of life was (and is) lived: as people today do, men and women in the past had lots of particular pressures and influences on them; and they responded to specific, named individuals.

Looking at the seventeenth- and eighteenth-century Atlantic economy as a complex economic and social system directs our attention to certain features rich in interpretative significance. First, it allows us to appreciate both the details and the self-organizing characteristics of this world. The idea of self-organizing systems comes from physics, chemistry, biology, geology, computer science, and artificial intelligence—all of which have investigated the ordered behavior of large-scale aggregates as the result of complex interactions among many smaller-scale elements that operate according to much simpler behavioral rules. With an understanding of this self-organization, larger-scale phenomena need not, indeed often do not, look like their constituent parts: the human body is not an organic molecule writ large; nor is it appropriate to describe a market as goal-seeking in the way that its members may be.

Considering structures and institutions from the vantage of their complexity also allows us to make sense of the decentralization of economic and social authority in much of the Atlantic world over much of the period. Metropolitan control was always contested, and for any one economic or social act, there were a variety of centers that actors had to consider and address. Regarding the emerging Atlantic economy as a complex economic and social system turns the searchlight away from the traditionally privileged center, the large European metropolis. That is not to say that central directives or influences were unimportant—only that they were not dispositive in the dominions. Much of what we have learned about material life suggests that the emerging Atlantic economy was decidedly multilocal and, even at larger-scale levels, ambivalently nonmetropolitan. These findings are at odds with the thrust of traditional scholarship, which examined in loving detail the tobacco and sugar trades and conceived the British Empire as a "hub-and-spoke" affair that ran from the "metropolis" to the "peripheries." But this model does not fit all the facts, or all the trades; many trades bore more resemblance to a "spider's web."[3] Furthermore, the continuity of any trading system was complicated by the porosity of Atlantic empires. To the annoyance of metropolitan mandarins but the profit of enterprising Europeans and Americans, transatlantic trade, both legal and illegal, among the British, Portuguese, Spanish, French, and Dutch across imperial boundaries was commonplace. Attempts to make the hub-and-spoke model fit are further complicated by the fact that most trade in the Americas or in Europe was not between the Americans and the Europeans but among Americans or among Europeans, even though both trades were linked to a vast commercial web covering the Atlantic and its rim.

Last, the complex systems lens shifts our understanding of how political, economic, and social conditions affected individuals' behavior: it is more insightful to view large-scale forces as *creating the conditions* for individuals' actions and reactions rather than as causing them. In their choices of explanatory devices, historians frequently favor the isolation of deterministic forces. But in a complex system such as the Atlantic market economy, for instance, Great Britain's Navigation Acts, the agricultural productivity of the Americas, and the changing nature of the labor force are more appropriately regarded as conditions, not causes, of the patterns of trade. The search for causation is much more appropriately focused on the decentralized activities of individuals. Large-scale conditions, of course, shaped the contours of the outcomes, but the outline of specific outcomes was drawn by the individuals directly involved.

An appreciation of social and economic complexity, and all that the concept connotes, provides a helpful intellectual apparatus for understanding the problem under study—the development of the eighteenth-century Atlantic economy, as glimpsed through the linked processes of Madeira wine's production, distribution, and consumption. We can see this at work in the transformation of the product, the ordering of the market, and the internationalization of consumer taste.

Production

Particular and reciprocal personal transatlantic linkages and exchanges among producers, distributors, and consumers transformed Madeira wine from a cheap, simple table wine into an expensive, complex, highly processed luxury wine over the course of the eighteenth century. Innovations in Madeira wine growing and wine making were the direct results of highly verbal, often contentious epistolary conversations among growers, the distributors' agents, wholesalers and retailers around the Atlantic, and consumers in America, Britain, and the East. As a result, producers increased the number of grape varieties from four to twenty-three, prepared unblended wines that ran the gamut from sweet to dry, fortified their wines with brandy, agitated the beverage to distribute the alcohol more evenly, aged the wine, and intentionally heated it.[4]

Fortification is often singled out as one of the hallmarks of Madeira's wine, but it was introduced into production and distribution only during the second quarter of the eighteenth century, and it took decades to become widespread. Although the practice was first prescribed by an English physician in 1633, the first descriptive mention of adding brandy to Madeira occurred in the 1743 edition of *Poor Richard's Almanack*, in which Benjamin Franklin urged his readers who were either shipping or selling Madeira to mix it with brandy. The first reference to island distributors adding brandy as a supplement appeared ten years later and suggests that the practice was gaining acceptance on the island by mid-century. Only after distributors and consumers blazed the trail did growers and producers adopt the technique.[5]

The practice of adding spirits to the wine "helped," it was firmly believed, "very indifferent and clear" grades. It imparted a smooth taste to rough, acidic, or full-bodied wines. As one firm explained to London purchasers, since Madeira's wine was "sweetish" in the must (the juice of the grapes), it needed more brandy "than was common" to other wines; brandy would "eat off the sweetness" and thereby "prevent fretting." In addition, fortifying wine added alcoholic strength and thereby pleased consumers in certain markets, in which "they like everything that is powerful and heady." However contemporaries described or justified it, by 1760 fortification appears to have been adopted by enough export firms to warrant the island government's banning the importation of expensive French brandy on the grounds that too much of it was being watered down and that diluted brandies sullied the reputation of export wines. Some export firms, especially those specializing in higher-quality wines, initially refused to add brandy; as late as 1807 they were still decrying such "spoilage" and arguing for its use only as a last resort. But despite the remonstrations of a few, the "brandy doctrine" was more or less universally accepted by 1790, even by growers and producers. Brandy became the "indispensable" component of all grades.[6]

Widespread fortification with brandy was largely consumer- and distributor-interactive; that is, it was the result of negotiated discussion. Such discourse "on the ground," among a lot of "small players," is most clearly seen in the decision of producers and distributors involved in production to add brandy to Madeira—a response to a multitude of local influences and incentives. There were many palates in the wine's principal market, British America, and island growers and merchants altered wine formulas to suit their clients, negotiating them with American distributors and buyers in each region in response to the preferences of purchasers there. Foremost in customers' minds were questions of color and taste. With no adulteration, new wine bore a reddish color and sweetish taste; old wine, having experienced additional fermentation and climatic heating, gained a lighter hue and a drier flavor. The addition of brandy accelerated both changes.

In the British West Indies and the southern colonies of British North America, where there was no concern for the wine spoiling for lack of heat, a love of wines of a darker hue and sweeter taste flourished. To satisfy these customers, who wanted to avoid the lightening and intoxicating effects of additional alcohol in hot climates, Madeira distributors put less brandy in their export; sometimes, in response to requests from Caribbean planters, they left it out altogether and sent a quarter-cask of red must and another of brandy along with a pipe (cask) of wine so that it could be colored and strengthened to taste. In contrast, consumers to the north asked for a paler, drier wine, and so producers and shippers added one or two gallons more brandy than they put in Caribbean wine. South Carolinians and Virginians ordered extremely pale, dry white wine ("white as water," they often requested) that had been heavily fortified, while Philadelphians requested golden wines with slightly less brandy and slightly more sweetness. New Yorkers wanted an amber, somewhat reddish drink that was even less brandied and more sugared. But here the Madeirans balked. If the islanders had had their way, they would have sent the wines to New York completely untouched: "our best wine," Thomas Murdoch informed John Campbell of New York, was "excellent only in proportion as it is simple." For decades they battled with importers over the amount of brandy, and in the end they succeeded with a formula for New Yorkers that was more fortified than they had wished yet less than New Yorkers had wanted at the outset. Each market demanded and, after rounds of negotiation, received its own distinctive formula.[7]

Distribution

Through the eighteenth century the Madeira wine trade spread to nearly every colony or possession in British or formerly British America, as it had to Portuguese America the preceding century, and over time the outlets for distribution in each place became more numerous and specialized. In 1700 Madeira merchants dispatched Portuguese, British, American, and Dutch ships from Funchal to South Carolina, Virginia, Pennsylvania, New York, and Massachusetts as well as Barbados, Antigua, St. Kitts, and Jamaica; one or two ships from Madeira dropped anchor in Connecticut, Rhode Island, or Bermuda, but these were rare. By 1800 ships regularly left the island for all the principal North American ports, plus lesser ones in Maryland (Baltimore), Massachusetts (Salem), Nova Scotia (Halifax), Newfoundland, Quebec, nearly all the Caribbean sugar islands, and India.

At the beginning this trade was haphazard and personal. Wine drinkers could not depend on its shipment and arrival. Madeira firms developed business with customers they already knew through blood tie or prior acquaintance in a large port town; gradually they increased the number of people to whom they shipped in that town until finally they expanded from that base, first to other centers in the colony and then to hitherto untapped adjacent colonies. On the North American mainland firms typically began in one of four cities with reliable shipping facilities—Boston, New York, Philadelphia, and Charleston—or in one of two plantation regions blessed with passable rivers—the Chesapeake and the South Carolina low country. Successful firms in time moved on to integrate into other, sometimes new distribution channels. At the beginning of the century Madeira merchants on the island and wholesalers/distributors in America were linked principally by arm's-length trade; but by the end of the eighteenth century many islanders also provided importation and distribution services, sending their own representatives to the colony to manage the entrance and first sale. From the cumulative actions of such men a transatlantic commodity distribution system emerged from a relatively semiorganized group unpredictably supplying its kin and friends and expanded to a set of substantial, reliable trading firms and outlets that managed to get the produce from the vineyards to the tables of complete strangers.

Given the extent to which Madeira's trading houses were initially built along family and kinship lines, it is not surprising that deploying familial, kin, and ethnic connections was the first important means of building correspondent bases. Newton & Gordon's first correspondent in Jamaica was the brother of Alexander Johnston, the Scot who first provided work in London for the Jacobite Francis Newton and later provided the capital to set up Thomas Gordon in business; of the fifty-two correspondents Newton & Gordon attracted over the next ten years, over three-quarters were either friends of their families, friends of Alexander Johnston, or other Scots.

But to succeed, a firm had to move well beyond the base of family, kin, and ethnic relations to more extended personal and business relations. Early friendships helped at the outset: "Early attachments are always the most lasting," noted one schoolfellow of Thomas Gordon; they "often reap much a happiness in point of society, business or advancement in life." There was "vast advantage," for instance, to boys "being sent to publick school"; certainly, Thomas Gordon's Mercer's School provided him an introduction to John Cone, James Plunderleath, Andrew Robertson, and Basil Cooper—all subsequent correspondents—in much the same way that John Leacock's Christ's Hospital alumni "network" subsequently funneled consignments to him.[8]

Later attachments were also grist for the mill. After he moved to Madeira from New York in 1756, Thomas Newton wrote a volume of letters with the intent of enlarging the orders to his firm from New York. He had no more tie to many of his correspondents than having lived eight years among them. Often he wrote twenty letters a day with the same message. Friendship and acquaintance were primary reasons for his approaching a New Yorker and expecting an order. "I rely on your *friendship* in giving me the preference of what you do this way," he wrote Anthony Sarly in 1756. From his "intimate friendship" with Malcolm Campbell, he flattered himself that Campbell would expend his "utmost endeavours to procure me soon the consignment of a vessel & to speak to all your friends & acquaintances to give me the preference." "Old acquaintance" with Dr. Robert Knox and "intimate friendship" with his brother were enough to win an order. Not just any acquaintance would do, of course; some were better than others. Most firms were "ever ambitious of extending ... connexions with gentlemen of character," and to them, "character" often meant having numerous friends and being willing to share them.[9]

As island competition mounted after 1750, Madeira merchants did not leave it up to their customers—a group with whom they had fewer and fewer direct ties—to come or write to them. The partners of firms visited primary markets on a regular basis "in order to acquire some more friends in those quarters." Most mid-sized and large firms sent partners to America and Britain every two or three years. In 1756 Dr. Richard Hill went to Maryland and Pennsylvania to "drive all before him," that is, to procure orders from old and new customers and arrange for return consignments, and he stayed for two years. Gedley Clare Burges of Madeira left his sometime partner Robert Jones in London and, with Jones's letters of recommendation, set out on an elaborate "visitation of the counties," taking in Liverpool, Dublin, Cork, Waterford, and Bristol. Early the next year his competitor George Spence of Newton & Spence made a similar journey to Scotland to drum up orders. In 1758, after Francis Newton parted with Spence and aligned himself with Thomas Gordon, Gordon and the London general merchant Alexander Johnston went to Bristol and Liverpool "to procure a good deal of business" for the new firm. Given the absence of other Madeirans, they met with success. In America, Newton's brother Thomas, the third partner in Newton & Gordon, and the New York merchant John Provoost traveled to various towns in New York and New England to do the same, but with less positive results, for there they encountered the likes of John Searle and James Anderson (an agent of the Madeiran Andrew Donaldson), who were also personally scouring the region with the intent of "procuring an opening to a larger correspondence." Even more purely personal trips, occasioned by, for example, the death of a parent or one's marriage, were turned into vigorous attempts to expand one's portfolio of customers.[10]

After 1750, as the necessity for expanding customer lists grew greater, not only because of the presence of more merchants on the island but also because of economic dislocations within Madeira's fragile economy, the firms appointed part-time and later full-time agents in London, Philadelphia, and New York. Eventually they settled their own partners there to monitor commercial developments and scout out and secure new correspondents.[11] After Francis Newton's arrival in Madeira in 1748, for instance, he relied on his former employer Alexander Johnston to handle London concerns. But by 1761 there were "so many partners" of competitors "residing in London" that Newton & Gordon began to worry. London-based partners could devote more time and procure more orders than a part-time agent with other interests and commitments could. Like nearly every firm of any size and ambition, they soon sent a partner there.[12] But it was not enough to cover only London; American ports needed to be managed personally as well. So in 1758 Newton & Gordon sent Thomas Newton to New York. After he died they made John Provoost and later Waddell Cunningham their agents, and at the end of the century their "transactions in America" went "more or less through the hands" of their agent Robert Lenox. "Having partners on the spot" came to be regarded as a sine qua non of working "in the Madeira Way."[13]

As competition among distributors continued to accelerate in the last quarter of the century, the exporters began to send their wine to purchasers in the countryside at the exporters' own expense. Some firms sent personal representatives to "go a drumming" up business and, when payment was received, shipped the wine via wagon trains or riverboats. Other, more aggressive retailers shipped the wine to backcountry retailers at the outset. Instead of requiring payment in advance, they struggled to procure repayment in the months ahead. The Quaker firm Lamar, Hill, Bisset & Co. combined both approaches.

Dr. Richard Hill naturally turned first to the colony and city he had left behind, and the first orders he filled were those submitted by family members or relatives still resident in Maryland and Philadelphia, such as his son Richard Jr., his son-in-law Samuel Preston Moore, and his cousins. Before five years had passed, however, he was also supplying many of the city's most successful import houses, firms that were more often than not headed by prominent Friends (members of the Society of Friends, or Quakers)—Israel Pemberton, John Smith, Burd & Swift, Baynton & Wharton. With each passing year Hill's firm added smaller and newer Philadelphia merchants and firms to its lists of correspondents. By the beginning of the Seven Years' War it had "engrossed most of the American business" in the city, by pushing on old friends and, in a move that probably swayed more than anything else, by "holding part of [their] vessels and being concerned in their cargoes." At the end of the war, customers included old acquaintances and mercantile connections—William Redwood, Reese Meredith, James Clunow, John Armit, George Smith, James Pemberton, Samuel McCall Sr., John Gibson, Shoemaker & Pennington, William Logan, Meredith Neave, Charles and Alexander Stedman, Robert Bulley, Joshua Maddox, John Sibbald, Samuel Parratt, James Wallace, and Samuel Miles, to name only a few—who took the wine for their own consumption or for resale to their own customers. In nearly all these cases the choice of correspondent was influenced mainly by specific family, religious, or social connections.[14]

After Dr. Richard Hill died in 1762 and his son and heir Henry took up residence in Philadelphia, the firm began to move farther afield in its search for customers. It cultivated the custom of general-store-keepers and tavern-keepers in the city. Years later the firm supplied wines to the new City Tavern, "a genteel tavern" with club rooms, a room for public entertainment, lodgings rooms "for the accommodation of strangers," and "every other conveniency," which Henry Hill and fifty-two other Philadelphia gentlemen-subscribers opened in 1773 "for the convenience and credit of the city."[15] Moreover, the firm took advantage of Philadelphia's role as commercial entrepôt and started directly supplying consumers, storekeepers, and tavern proprietors in surrounding counties and the backcountry.[16] According to Hill's books, accounts were opened with residents in Shippensburg and Carlisle, as well as with Hance Hamilton in York, Edward Shippen in Lancaster Town, John Harris Jr. at Harris's Ferry, and the frontier soldiers stationed at Fort Augusta, north of Harris's Ferry, in addition to a host of retailers and householders closer to home in Chester and Bucks counties. On occasion, Hill's backcountry customers (usually merchants, storekeepers, and tavern-keepers) came to his business office in his new house on South Fourth Street, where he kept an extensive cellar. But over time he more willingly seized the initiative and went to them. Most years from 1767 through 1785, when fighting during the American Revolution did not prevent him, he embarked on trade "missions" that took him to Christiana Bridge, York, Shippensburg, Harris's Ferry, Lancaster, and Reading, and then back again to Philadelphia. On these circuits he met with both established and potential customers, including several wagon-train leaders and pack-horse traders, whom he lured with a variety of samples and offers of easy credit. Each year Hill's expressed excuse for the trip was to visit a friend or relation; but the actual reason for his journey was to enlarge the firm's correspondence.[17]

Madeira wine's distribution system developed over the century in what seem predictable ways. In Madeira some firms that started better positioned with their customers, or more adept at responding to their evolving needs, or better skilled at deploying the rhetoric of cultural refinement became larger and more successful than their competitors and managed the trade more extensively. Yet the reasons for their success were always local or particular, the result of individual ambition, genius, skill, or luck. Moreover, no central governmental authority or culture emanating from Lisbon or London directed their work. Distribution channels in the Americas developed along similar lines. From the start they were individual, informal, and irregular. In some cases wine-trading houses in Madeira, ever attentive to the possibilities of family ties, kinship, ethnicity, and acquaintance, struck up commercial relationships with individual consumers, often the wealthiest in colonial communities.[18] Elite urban merchant families such as the Hancocks, Browns, Van Cortlandts, and Willings annually requested two and sometimes four pipes from Madeira, regardless of price, which they used in their homes. They also ordered a pipe or two of "the very best Madeira wine" for their friends and peers. In 1759 Thomas Hancock did this for the Massachusetts governor; eight years later his nephew John did the same with a pipe for its treasurer and two pipes for his friends John and Jonathan Amory, two wealthy Boston traders who were strangers to Madeira's distributors. Elite consumers also purchased in bulk for resale. Also in 1759 John Hancock placed the Amorys' order and requested six pipes that he then resold to several Boston public houses "where the Best Company resorts."[19]

Apart from individual exporters' occasional shipments to elite drinkers and subsequent distribution and resale by them, wine distribution was in the hands of American middlemen, such as John Harris of Harris' Ferry or the proprietor of the King George Hotel in Schaefferstown, Pennsylvania. At the high end of the entrepreneurial ladder, wine exporters shipped to wine importers, who in turn dealt with coastal- or port-town drink retailers (inn- and tavern-keepers), general-store-keepers, urban householders, and gradually similar men and women in the backcountry.[20] At the low end, there were wagon-train operators, pack-horse traders, and itinerant peddlers—workers who would take almost anything for a price and whose employment depended heavily on the presence and passability of roads, bridges, canals, and ferries and the general westward extension of American society. The means of the latter were often insufficient to purchase and transport whole barrels of wine; but on at least a few occasions a peddler was seen to be carrying bottles or barrels of wine and rum, as well as coffee and sugar, on his back or in his cart. In the backcountry peddlers, pack-horsemen, and wagoneers sold to consumers outright or to enterprising farmers, who in turn set up ad hoc retail establishments and dispensaries in their own houses and barns. Itinerants thus enabled rural enterprisers to supply their patrons with glasses of wine, alongside drams of whiskey and cider.[21] Yet, slowly the necessity for their work was eliminated. As the population of the backcountry grew and its economy prospered, such operations often took on the look of or were replaced by well-fixed stores, warehouses, inns, taverns, and dramshops, similar to those of the coastal port towns, and ad hoc establishments. Roaming interests pushed farther west.[22]

All these changes were uncoordinated. The provision of drink in each community was highly dependent on county officials, on local suppliers, and on neighborhood drinkers who frequented the stores and taverns; often little notice was given to what was going on in Philadelphia, much less in Funchal, London, or Lisbon, although even the humblest drinker was aware of his connection to the wider world. War among Europeans or famine in England, the Azores, or Italy—well covered in even the most provincial papers and often the subjects of discussion among strangers encountering one another along the frontier—forced shifts in everyday purchasing and consuming, and local buyers and consumers generally knew their causes. Backcountry concerns might be highly local, unique to each market, but these were related back to the retailers in Lancaster, Philadelphia, and eventually Funchal.

More than by personal distribution or small-scale retailing, the eighteenth century was characterized by a similarly uncoordinated proliferation of specialized services during the last four decades, and this had an immense effect on wine distribution in America, as it did on the distribution of almost all consumer goods.[23] At the beginning of the century everyday folk purchased wines and spirits in a tavern, ordinary, or dramshop, or in a general grocery or dry-goods store; by the end of the century they were just as likely to buy them in a storekeeper's shop or house that specialized as a wine and spirit store. That is because, over the course of the period 1663–1763, wine marketing and retailing emerged as a principal business.

Through the first 150 years of American settlement, wine selling had been an adjunct to other trades. Merchants who imported wine on their own account or as agents of European entrepreneurs always imported other things as well. They were in the truest sense of the term "general merchants." Wine to them was a product, not a business. For obvious reasons proprietors of inns, taverns, and ordinaries distributed wine, although the dispensing was only one of the many services they offered. But wine selling was not restricted to taverns. The *Pennsylvania Gazette,* which commenced publication in December 1728, contained only three wine advertisements in 1729 and 1730, and these hawked only "fine wines" or "good wine." By 1737 five different retailers advertised Madeira, red port, Canary, and claret; in 1738 one retailer floated Frontignan; in 1739 one retailer hawked Florence. All of these goods were put up for sale alongside dry goods. In fact, the most common distributors of imported wines in the colonies during the first half of the century were dry-goods wholesalers. As heavy importers of southern European and Wine Island fruit and salt, wholesale grocers also sometimes loaded and later dispensed the wines for many of the same reasons, but less frequently.[24]

Specialized wine traders first appeared in the newspaper advertisements, tax lists, and trade directories of Boston, New York, Philadelphia, and Charleston in the 1750s and 1760s, but they did not flourish until the fourth quarter of the eighteenth century. In Philadelphia, for example, no mention of a wineshop or wine store as a distinct establishment occurred until 1753 when Samuel Grisley began advertising "old choice Madeira wine, by the quarter cask, gallon and quart" and old Malmsey, Lisbon, and white wines by the bottle "at his wine store, below the Jersey market, where there is a green lamp before the door." No mention of a wine merchant occurred before the early1770s, although that is surely what Grisley was in 1753 and what William Braventon (who had resided in both London and Portugal and "acquired much experience in the art and mystery of the wine trade") was in the same year when he announced setting up shop as a "vintner" (blender) and "wine cooper" (blender and packager); both were professionals who for centuries had combined the work of selling wine with blending and packaging it. The lag in terminology notwithstanding, the niche was developed by the 1770s when John Mitchell opened a "Wine, Spirit, Rum and Sugar Store" on Front Street. His offerings testify to a focus and to a greatly expanded range: Madeira, claret, port, Lisbon, sherry, mountain, Tenerife, Fayal, Frontignan, French white, hock, and red Lisbon wine; Spanish brandy, Shone's, Kenton's, and Parker's London porter; Burton and Taunton bottled ale; West India and New England rum; Holland Geneva; plus a wide range of oils, teas, sugars, and spices, for example. Mitchell sold his wines "new or old," "dry or sweet," "genuine," "excellent," or "of the best quality" by the pipe, hogshead, quarter-cask, anchor, gallon, or dozen.[25]

During and after the American Revolution cellars, merchants, coopers, and vintners appeared in growing numbers. Some eighty-nine separate individuals and firms placed ads relating to wine in the newspapers between 1775 and 1783. Later on, Clement Biddle's *Philadelphia Directory* of 1791 notes the presence of eight wine specialists: not only four described as "wine merchant," including one who had previously worked in Madeira, and one described as "wine merchant and grocer," but also another as "wine cooper" and two more as "bottler[s] of liquors" (an occupation with tasks similar to those of a vintner). By 1811, when a *Census Directory* was published, the number had doubled: the city had at least six specialized wine merchants, five wine coopers, five liquor stores where wine was sold, and one proprietor of a bottling cellar.[26]

Thus, as the rise of specialization and the ramification of distribution outlets suggest, the extensive, multidirectional communication in the world of Atlantic commerce built the important ties that bound people together across imperial boundaries and transformed a collection of independent operatives and operations into a resilient commercial infrastructure. Because of this communication, a market emerged from a congeries of independent, disconnected individual behaviors. Particular conversations with their customers, suppliers, agents, and friends provided Madeira's traders with information, created understanding among parties, and helped build global organizations. Personal, conversation-based, negotiative relationships provided valuable sources of information about, for example, the opening of new markets, the successes and failures of other merchants on the other side of the ocean, local prosecution of infractions of the Navigation Acts, and the tastes of specific communities—all matters that were local to the arena of consumption and foreign to the distributor.

At the level of individual agents, the historical record shows them at work, responding to the opportunities that arose during their rather mundane lives and responding in ways heavily influenced by the specifics of their environments, their relations with their communities, and their own particular needs. Out of thousands of similar responses, a more highly elaborated and differentiated economy emerged: ships going to Madeira to off-load American staples became ships also going to Madeira to load island wine; one-off trades became multistep, multiplace exchanges managed by an army of employees; taverns became stores, and in turn general stores became wine stores. One sees a regularity and direction emerging out of the activities of all these disconnected people just doing what locally made sense to each one.

Consumption

Social and cultural institutions evolved in the eighteenth century alongside significant innovation in production and the elaboration of oceanic and inland distribution. Wine and wine drinking were part of these institutions and their evolution. A close examination of the linked markets for the production, distribution, and consumption of Madeira wine casts some light on these institutions and helps us understand how individual growers, traders, and drinkers deployed local tools at hand to promote specific commercial and social projects. It also shows how social norms and standards emerged and changed in a complicated and decentralized fashion, and here, too, an interactive transatlantic conversation was critical in forming and transmitting these standards.

As a result of a century of changes in the production and distribution of wine, late eighteenth-century imbibers could choose among more alcoholic drinks, more wines, and more types and grades of Madeira, as well as more places to procure them. On the consumption side, the story of Madeira is embedded in the story of other wines, spirits, and even some nonalcoholic drinks. Often the records do not distinguish among them and refer only to "wine," "liquor," or "drink" when complementary evidence suggests that what was drunk was Madeira wine. Over the century Madeira's share of the Americas' imported drinks market fell. Early in the early period, 1714–23, Madeira made up some 82 percent of British colonial wine imports; by 1805–6 that share had fallen to 8 percent of U.S. wine imports, although, given the tendency to label Madeira rather vaguely, that may be a conservative estimate. Nevertheless, the preference for Madeira was progressively reduced, and after the American Revolution the market was opened to other wines, particularly those of Spain and France. But the changes would have happened anyway. The white population of what became the United States grew twenty-fold over the century, while the productive capacity of Madeira remained flat. Some Madeira that had been wasted or drunk on the island early in the century was made available for export by 1775, but Madeira's markets grew too, in both Europe and India, and drew off not only the newly released product but also customary lots formerly sent to the Americas.

There are two principal sets of records that document the change in what Americans drank in the eighteenth century: shipping lists that show what traders were importing into British America; and probate inventories that show what people were storing at home at the time of their deaths. In the absence of other compilations, Naval Office Shipping Lists (NOSL)—quarterly lists of all ships entering and exiting colonial ports that were kept by naval officers appointed by the Treasury who lived in the port towns—and colonial port manifest books of entry provide the only available extensive quantitative source for figuring out the imports of wines and spirits to the colonies.[27] For some colonies and some periods it is possible to reconstruct an "imported beverage portfolio" with these records and track the changes in the composition of that portfolio.

Philadelphia and New York were the two principal ports for wine's importation. Of the two, New York is the better documented.[28] Wine imports into New York are detailed in table 4 and graph 1.[29] Before the French and Indian War total wine imports show a slow increase. In the earliest period for which the records survive, 1703 to 1707, 323 pipes of wine came in through the port of New York each year, on average. This increased to 494 pipes per year in 1749–55. The statistics for the French and Indian War period are much thinner; wars generally disrupted trade and its recording, and the results are not to be trusted. Yet, some want was felt, for in both 1763 and 1764 New Yorkers greedily imported over 1,700 pipes of wine. These extraordinarily high levels probably reflect the pent-up demand that accumulated during the war because the level of wine importation dropped thereafter. It averaged 571 pipes in 1768 to 1772.[30] Overall Madeira's share of total wine imports was high (68 percent), but over time it fell—from 74 percent in 1703–9 to 67 percent in 1753–55, 45 percent in 1763–64, and 47 percent in 1768.[31] Throughout the colonial years Madeira imports always exceeded those of the Azores, Canaries, Portugal, or Spain, but slowly the others gained ground.

As went New York's wine imports, so went the other colonies' wine imports. Grouping together all surviving British North American colonial port entries for 1700 to 1775 reveals that some 58 percent of all imported wine was Madeira, another 7 percent was Azorean, and 9 percent was Canary. Thus, wines from the Wine Islands dominated British North American markets. In contrast, wines from the Spanish mainland (Alicante, Malaga, mountain, Passado, and sherry) provided only 1 percent, and wines from the Portuguese mainland (Lisbon, Porto, and Viana) comprised only 0.3 percent,[32] even though Iberian wines such as port dominated the market in England and Wales.[33]

The removal of Great Britain's mercantile restrictions during the American Revolution accelerated some prewar trends. Madeira wine's hold on the market—already loosened—weakened further. Madeira's share of the wine imported into the United States fell from 31 percent in 1789–90 to 8 percent in 1805–6; it had averaged 36 percent in the immediate pre-1776 period. Wines from other wine-producing countries, such as Spain and France, were now regularly imported. Sherry and St. Lucar wines in particular had come into vogue and were introduced in greater volumes; in half of the years between 1794 and 1806 the total quantity of sherry imported actually exceeded that of Madeira. Nevertheless, Madeira remained the single most valuable of America's wine imports: given the high market price of Madeira, its share of the value of all wines totaled together was still unmatched.

Probate inventories, recording the possessions of an individual at the time of his or her death, paint a similar, if more complicated, picture of increasing choice among drinks and shed some light on the increasing distinctions among drinkers that that allowed. Few of these choices and distinctions had anything to do with Portugal or England directly, indeed with anything beyond the social and cultural world of the consumers. I have constructed consumer databases from probates of Suffolk County (Boston) and Hampshire County, Massachusetts; New York City and County, New York; and the colonies of South Carolina and Jamaica. For each region I surveyed all probates for a decade toward the beginning of the eighteenth century and another decade toward the end.[34]

Some results from the analysis of these inventories are arrayed in the tables that follow. First, table 5 confirms the increase in the variety of wines that were consumed. In the two northern metropolitan counties, the number of varieties of wine recorded in probate records at the end of the century was three to six times the number early on. (The numbers in this table suggest that the varieties of wine

Table 4: Wine imports into New York from all points (in 110-gallon pipes), 1700–1775

Year	Quarters of Extant NOSL	Wine-bearing Ships	Total	IMPORTS Madeira	Azoren	Portuguese	Canary	Spanish	Other
1700									
1701									
1702									
1703			417.49	354.75	40.99				15.25
1704			593.10	455.32	123.80				13.98
1705			299.71	177.44	74.00				51.78
1706									
1707			335.10	321.85					13.25
1708			179.50	20.00					159.50
1709			110.50	99.50					11.00
1710									
1711									
1712									
1713	cd	52	436.75	388.75					48.00
1714	abcd	27	355.75	245.50					110.25
1715	abcd	24	578.50	527.00					51.50
1716	bcd	7	647.50	646.50					1.00
1717	abcd	12	554.25	508.25	13.00		20.00		13.00
1718	abcd	8	285.25	240.25	44.00		1.00		
1719	ab d	12	341.50	337.50					4.00

Table 4 (continued)

Year	Quarters of Extant NOSL	Wine-bearing Ships	IMPORTS							
			Total	Madeira	Azoren	Portuguese	Canary	Spanish	Other
1720	abcd	9	516.50	515.50					1.00
1721	abcd	10	368.13	352.50			15.63		
1722	abcd	11	498.00	422.50			75.50		
1723	abcd	6	70.50	68.50	2.00				
1724	abcd	13	537.13	515.00	0.13		22.00		
1725	abcd	17	339.40	319.75			10.00	1.00	8.65
1726	abcd	11	470.00	406.75			51.00		12.25
1727	abcd	13	327.25	319.25	1.00		2.00		5.00
1728	abcd	17	977.25	964.25			1.00	12.00	
1729	abcd	16	292.25	267.25			11.00		14.00
1730	abc	19	293.00	270.50			20.25		2.25
1731	bcd	19	833.00	818.50			14.50		
1732	abcd	10	186.00	185.50					0.50
1733	abcd	15	581.25	577.25			2.00		2.00
1734	abcd	11	188.75	177.50			5.00		6.25
1735	abcd	14	555.75	535.25			15.00	2.00	3.50
1736	abcd	6	21.25	15.75					5.50
1737	bcd	12	213.50	111.25	8.00		75.00	19.25	
1738	abcd	18	559.58	368.78			181.25	9.00	0.55
1739	abcd	19	1,326.41	571.91			659.25	94.00	1.25

Table 4 (continued)

Year	Quarters of Extant NOSL	Wine-bearing Ships	Total	IMPORTS					
				Madeira	Azoren	Portuguese	Canary	Spanish	Other
1740	abcd	15	670.25	661.25	1.00	5.00	2.00		1.00
1741	abcd	8	310.00	285.00		8.00	1.00		16.00
1742	abcd	9	310.26	305.50					4.76
1743	ab	6	385.58	382.50					3.08
1744			442.75						
1745			440.50						
1746			331.75						
1747			476.50						
1748	bc	9	782.25	782.25					
1749			987.99						
1750			75.00						
1751	d	8	987.25	192.50	64.00				
1752									
1753	d	4	139.75	139.75					
1754	abcd	17	663.75	386.75	256.00		15.00		6.00
1755	abc	7	110.00	84.75	25.25				
1756		8							
1757		12							
1758		28							
1759		50							

Table 4 (continued)

Year	Quarters of Extant NOSL	Wine-bearing Ships	IMPORTS						
			Total	Madeira	Azoren	Portuguese	Canary	Spanish	Other
1760		51							
1761		14							
1762		23							
1763	abcd	24	1,742.38	775.88			624.75	216.50	125.25
1764	abcd	27	1,703.76	1,572.51	100.00		2.50		28.75
1765									
1766									
1767									
1768	abcd		1,238.70	586.10					
1769	abcd		543.60						
1770	abcd		255.90						
1771	abcd		433.50	420.00					
1772	abcd		384.80						
1773									
1774									
1775									
Total			22,367.34	18,680.79	753.17	13.00	1,826.63	353.75	740.05
Percentage of Total				68.3%	2.8%	0.05%	6.7%	1.3%	2.7%

Figure 1: Wine imports into New York, 1700–1775

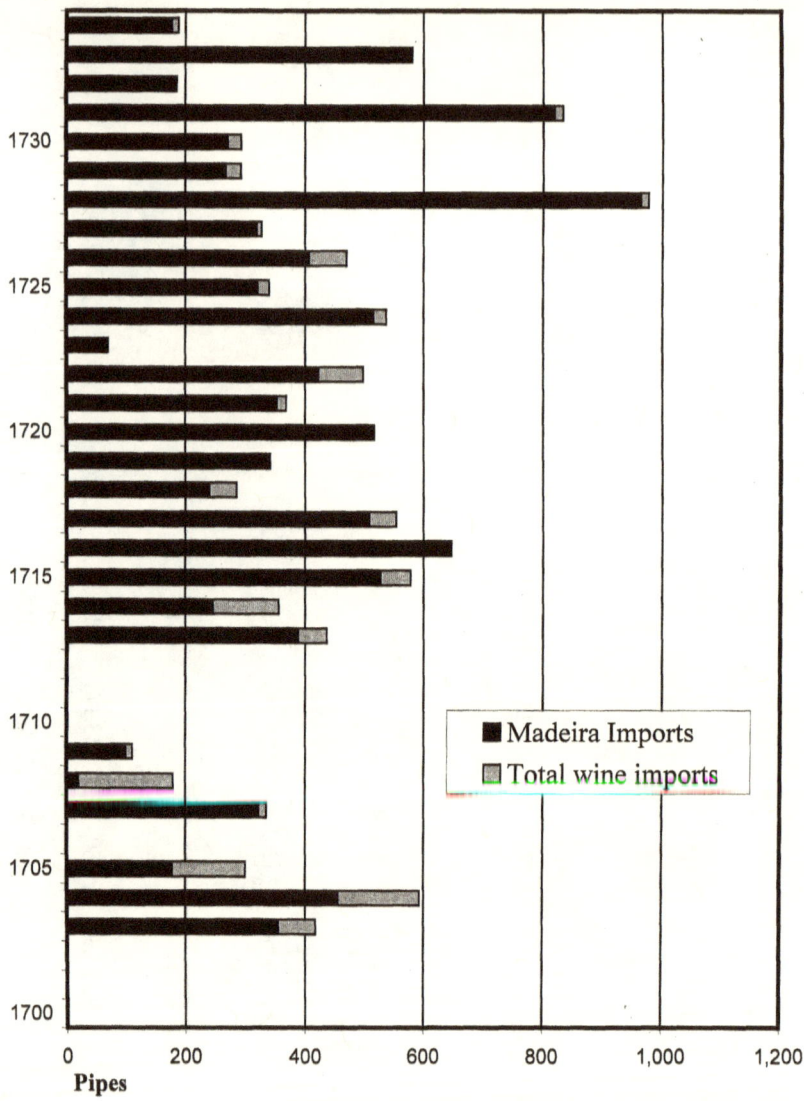

in New York inventories rose from one to thirteen, but that is because I have included "Made Here A"—what today we might consider a "Madeira-flavored beverage"—with true Madeira.) There is an only slightly smaller increase in the varieties of other alcoholic drinks. In backcountry Hampshire County the pattern is similar, but the variety is smaller, both early and late. This is to be expected because of the port cities' economic role and population density. There was actually no wine recorded in Hampshire County probate inventories in

Figure 1 (continued)

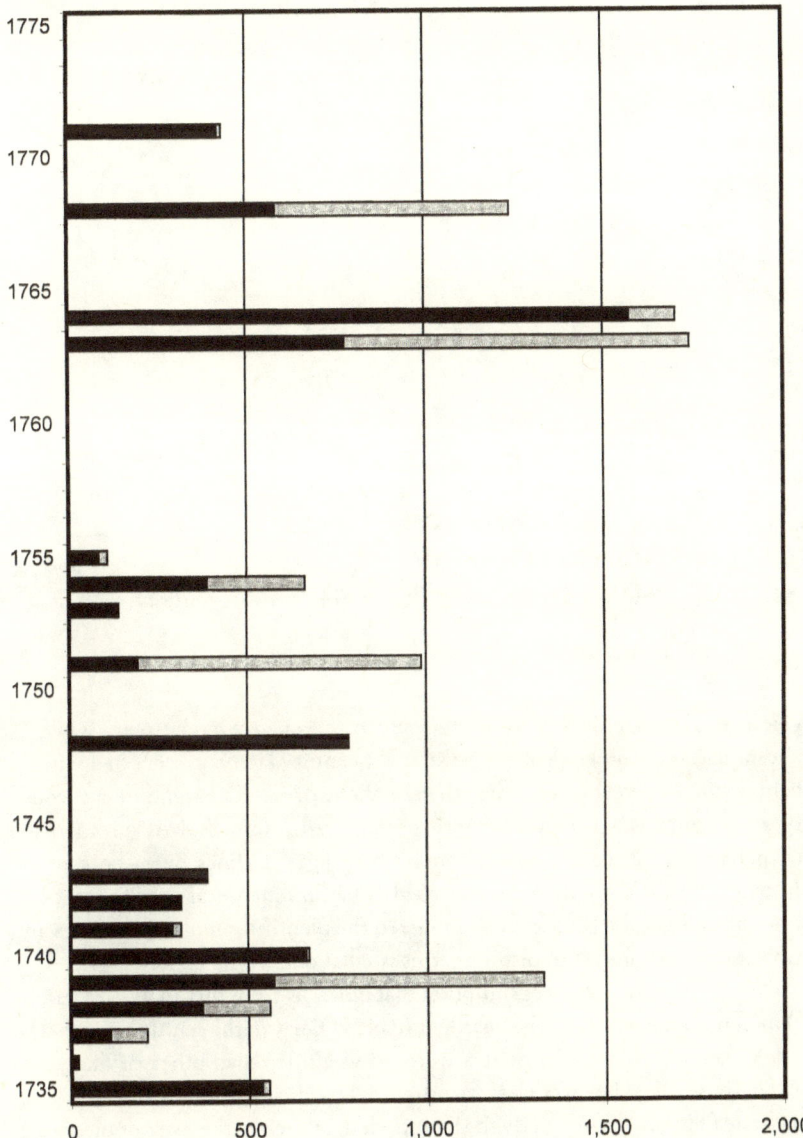

1703–7. Similar increases in variety took place to the south. The data suggest that this may have occurred earlier in Carolina and Jamaica than in the North, but we cannot be sure of this until New York City and County inventories are examined for midcentury.

As noted in table 6, in both urban and rural county estates alcoholic beverages such as rum or cider appeared more commonly than wine. Suffolk County was

Table 5: Varieties of wine and other alcoholic beverages in probate inventories

		Wines	Other Alcoholic Beverages
1700–1705	Jamaica	6	6
1703–1707	Hampshire County, MA	0	2
1703–1707	Suffolk County, MA	4	6
1703–1712	New York County, NY	1	7
1713–1716	Jamaica	3	9
1732–1736	Jamaica	13	16
1732–1741	South Carolina	6	6
1765–1774	South Carolina	23	31
1790–1799	New York County, NY	13	15
1803–1807	Hampshire County, MA	6	9
1803–1807	Suffolk County, MA	14	28

typical: in 1703–7 only 4 percent of all inventories had wine in them, while 11 percent had some other alcoholic beverage; a century later 6 percent had wine in them, while 12 percent had some other alcoholic drink. The trend in backcountry Hampshire was somewhat more pronounced. New York is an anomaly: the percentage of estates with alcoholic beverages declines over the century, although the varieties of drink increased. The dominance of spirits, especially rum, throughout the century is clear. Given the plentiful supply of molasses and Americans' push into rum distilling, this is what one would expect.

One more point about consumption that emerges from this analysis is its correlation with the wealth of the decedent (table 7) Early in the century people who had Madeira wine in their estates were no wealthier than other drinkers—in fact, in some cases they were less wealthy. Yet at some point in the 1720s or 1730s that state of affairs changed. By the later period, in each of the five samples, decedents who held Madeira wine were in almost all cases (barring Carolina) wealthier than decedents who held any wine, who in turn were wealthier than all decedents. Certainly the lots that were inventoried recorded fairly large and therefore expensive containers: tuns, pipes, hogsheads, and quarter-casks— requiring an outlay too steep for most middling urban or rural families, who more commonly got their wines from taverns or shops in rented bottles. At the

Table 6: Percentage of inventories with varying amounts of wine

		Just Wine	Just Other Alcoholic Beverages	Wine & Other Alcoholic Beverages	Wine or Other Alcoholic Beverages
1700–1705	Jamaica	1.0%	6.4%	3.4%	10.8%
1703–1707	Hampshire County, MA	0.0%	10.3%	0.0%	10.3%
1703–1707	Suffolk County, MA	0.6%	8.1%	2.9%	11.6%
1703–1712	New York County, NY	2.1%	12.5%	4.2%	18.8%
1713–1716	Jamaica	0.7%	4.7%	1.0%	6.4%
1732–1736	Jamaica	2.4%	4.9%	2.6%	9.9%
1732–1741	South Carolina	0.5%	5.1%	1.0%	6.6%
1765–1774	South Carolina	2.1%	6.3%	5.0%	13.4%
1790–1799	New York County, NY	1.1%	5.5%	3.8%	10.4%
1803–1807	Hampshire County, MA	0.0%	21.1%	0.9%	22.0%
1803–1807	Suffolk County, MA	2.2%	7.9%	3.6%	13.7%

same time, wine and, in particular, Madeira wine became more expensive compared to both overall price indices and the specific prices of other alcoholic drinks. The origins of this were dispersed around the globe: Asian and American demand increased, while the island's natural production increased slowly and then stagnated; the factory on the island raised export prices; and rituals appropriate to an expensive commodity accreted to the wine.

More than anything else, for the purposes here, probate inventories confirm what shipping lists suggest: Madeira wine became an international luxury good in the eighteenth century, and as we shall see, that status was closely associated with wealth, cultural refinement, and cosmopolitanism. In the 1670s and 1680s consuming wine in America as an accompaniment to a meal or an act all its own connoted few things. Wine was a nutritional supplement and a staple of the diet, and it generally provided individual physical satisfaction and stimulation—the quenching of thirst or easy intoxication. Moreover, it was a sign of social

Table 7: Average wealth at death (in pounds sterling)

Massachusetts

	Wealth at Death (in British Pounds Sterling)			
	1703–1707		1803–1807	
	Hampshire	Suffolk	Hampshire	Suffolk
Average Value of Total Estate of All Wealth-holders	129.0	336.0	408.14	1502.4
Average Value of Total Estate of All Wine-holders	0.0	209.1	1,443.73	4805.8
Average Value of Total Estate of All Madeira-holders	0.0	199.1	0.00	5107.0
Average Value of All Wine in All Estates with Wine	0.0	9.9	5.43	53.6
Average Value of All Madeira in All Estates with Madeira	0.0	8.5	0.00	81.5

New York

	Wealth at Death (in British Pounds Sterling)	
	1703–1712 New York	1790–1799 New York
Average Value of Total Estate of All Wealth-holders	971.6	1116.3
Average Value of Total Estate of All Wine-holders	229.9	1752.0
Average Value of Total Estate of All Madeira-holders	229.9	3831.2
Average Value of All Wine in All Estates with Wine	64.0	1840.9
Average Value of All Madeira in All Estates with Madeira	64.0	585.2

Table 7 (continued)

South Carolina	Wealth at Death (in British Pounds Sterling)	
	1732–1741	1765–1774
	All Counties	All Counties
Average Value of Total Estate of All Wealth-holders	721.2	1131.1
Average Value of Total Estate of All Wine-holders	1041.1	5181.5
Average Value of Total Estate of All Madeira-holders	616.0	5220.4
Average Value of All Wine in All Estates with Wine	12.9	19.1
Average Value of All Madeira in All Estates with Madeira	6.3	32.4

Jamaica	Wealth at Death (in British Pounds Sterling)		
	1700–1705	1713–1716	1732–1736
	All Counties	All Counties	All Counties
Average Value of Total Estate of All Wealth-holders	759.6	777.0	1636.2
Average Value of Total Estate of All Wine-holders	710.5	672.8	3215.2
Average Value of Total Estate of All Madeira-holders	1072.5	292.5	4214.8
Average Value of All Wine in All Estates with Wine	98.2	5.3	63.7
Average Value of All Madeira in All Estates with Madeira	186.9	2.3	130.9

communion and hospitality. However, in the century that followed—a century marked by the proliferation of choice—imported wine began satisfying new motivations and conveying new meanings.

Few wines had given rise to many wines. This increased product differentiation provided the conditions for individuals to use wine to make social distinctions: some wine could be distinguished as fine wine and connected to specific classes, persons, venues, or events. In America the finest was Madeira wine, and its case is exemplary. Few of its connotations had much to do with metropolitan London culture, greater British culture, or provincial Portuguese customs. They were the product of North American people and circumstances, although at each step along the way they were influenced by their conversations with Madeira producers and distributors. The change in Madeira's status was accompanied by a rise in wine ceremony and celebration and an increase in the use of drinking artifacts and rituals. The composite wine culture that George Washington partook of at the end of the century was not something William Byrd would have known or understood at the beginning; nor would Washington's contemporaries in England or Portugal necessarily have appreciated it.

Contemporaries' stray and often terse remarks in, for example, diaries, letters, and newspaper accounts reveal both the persistence of older meanings for Madeira and the emergence of new ones. Consider these meanings under three headings: wealth, refinement, and cosmopolitanism.

Wealth

Wine consumption came to signify the possession of wealth. As the probate analysis tells us, after the 1730s the "quality" in America preferred a wider range of drinks, and some drinks over others. Certain wines such as Madeira after midcentury became markedly more expensive when compared to other imported wines such as Canary or Lisbon, or locally manufactured spirits such as whiskey or rum. Over time Madeira gained a reputation as a luxury, while others gained notice as ordinary, cheaper alternatives.

That reputation was not lost on contemporaries; it was noticed and remarked on extensively. "People of Fortune" in New Hampshire drank "very good" Madeira and old rum, observed the traveler James Birket in 1751, whereas "the lower sort" drank cider, new rum locally distilled, and common Wine Island Vidonia. After 1755, according to the century's leading expert on the history of wine, John Wright, "the tables of the opulent in our East and West Indies seldom exhibited any other wine" but Madeira wine. The "extravagance of the planters in Virginia," "many of whom had great estates," was evidenced by their preference for rich, rare wines such as Madeira. One of the reasons the earl of Bute's administration strove to lay a high import duty on Madeira in the 1764 Sugar Act was to tap the wealth of wine drinkers and use it to extricate the Crown from its large postwar debt.[35]

Especially after the American Revolutionary War, the price of Madeira kept it off many tables, and it was frequently mentioned as a luxury fit only for "the quality." In trying to revive his flagging business, William Lee, a planter and wine merchant who worked from his James River plantation Green Springs, near Williamsburg, noted somewhat sadly that the "gentry here ... are the only people that drink wine in this country." This was not true just in Tidewater Virginia but everywhere in North America. Wherever the Scots arriviste Patrick Campbell looked between Albany and Montreal in 1791, he could find neither wine nor punch: the product "of these new settlements cannot as yet afford this luxury," he surmised, and he had no choice but to drink grog and rasp rum, poured from glass decanters into glass tumblers. Even George Washington in 1794 noted that the duty on Madeira wine made it "one of the most expensive liquors that is now used," and accordingly he advised his niece to use claret rather than Madeira, "*unless* it be on extraordinary occasions." Yet, if he succeeded in convincing her, or if in fact he abstained, he was unique, for few rich Americans could "do without either a horse or a pipe of Madeira."[36]

Cultural Refinement

In September 1736 William Allen, Philadelphia's mayor, gave a feast. It was deemed "the most elegant Entertainment" in Philadelphia's history because it possessed four ingredients: good food, fine wines, acceptable guests, and "easiness & order."[37] Fine wine had become a declaration of gentility, sophistication, and allegiance to the goal of living well. But merely owning and serving fine wines was fast becoming insufficient to engender politesse; in addition the consumer had to know how to use them and how to talk about them. The wines had to be served with appropriate fanfare and ritual, requiring appropriate paraphernalia, and they had to be worthy of detailed discussion, in order to impart an elegance to the event and host.

Steps in serving wine were elaborated over the course of the eighteenth century and then scrutinized by drinkers: matching wine to food, choosing wine, opening the bottle, allowing the wine to breathe, decanting the wine (choosing the decanter, presenting it, and using it to pour), and serving the wine (choosing the glassware and pouring the wine). Key to the acceptance of their distinctions was their transmission by local friends one respected and their application in local circumstances.

The shrewish Princetonian Philip Vickers Fithian, who was serving as tutor to the children of Robert Carter III at Carter's seventy-thousand-acre estate, Nomini Hall in northern Virginia, in the early 1770s, had perhaps the most refined sense of the service of wine in the last three decades of the century and the tongue to go with his palate. When he attended a ball in January 1774, for instance, he pronounced the dinner "as elegant as could be well expected" for there were "several sorts of Wine, good Lemon Punch, Toddy, Cyder, Porter

& c." Several months later, "an elegant Supper" was noted only for its "good Porter & Madeira." But Fithian was not alone in his judgments. John Pope, on a tour through the western and southern territories of the new United States, visited Charleston and witnessed the ritual of drinking Madeira wine in full form. On arriving, he visited Col. William Washington, "in Company with" his old preceptor the Reverend Wilson. "They were seated opposite to each other, about 5 feet asunder, separated by two Glasses and a Decanter of generous old *Madeira*." On entering the room, after proffering congratulations and "mutual Professions of Friendship," "a third Glass and another Decanter (as if by Enchantment) made their Appearance on the Table, and the Duumvirate was soon converted into a Triumvirate."[38]

The possibilities for social failure in drinking wine were increasingly great. When wine was used by men or women of a false gentility and a thin sense of discernment, those who set themselves up as social arbiters noted it immediately. In July 1774 a tobacco inspector paid a visit to Nomini Hall and dined with the Carters. The inspector, Fithian quipped, was "rather Dull" and "unacquainted with company," "for when he would . . . drink our Health" in a toast, he "held the glass of Porter fast with both his Hands, and then gave an insignificant nod to each one at the Table, in Hast, & with fear, & then drank like an Ox." A tragedy of errors, it seems. Even one so young as the censorious Presbyterian tutor knew not only that porter was the wrong drink to choose for such a toast, but also that the way he held the glass was uncouth and his phrasing of the toast lacking in all "manner."[39]

With such perils in mind, American men and women devised a cultural and social assemblage to make their refinement even more manifest, much as they did across the sea. Sometimes they copied their betters or peers in Europe and sometimes local worthies. Sometimes they struck out on their own and improved. They elaborated the art of toasting—devising appropriate surroundings, proper sequencing, witty phrasing, and correct handling—and they adopted and extended an art of presentation that made use of not only new rules of etiquette but also new glass or metal wine-drinking paraphernalia—glasses, decanters, labels, coasters, and cisterns or coolers. Perhaps most telling, they incorporated and modified when appropriate the distinctions in cultural language that the distributors and others were peddling; for theirs was a world where the discussion, and detail, of the wines was fast becoming "an important part of social conversation."[40]

This particular social conversation between Madeirans and Americans amplified the number of traits used to describe each variety: body, smoothness, color, and taste. Each trait had its own lexicon, which had to be mastered if one were to be regarded as a connoisseur of wine.[41] Madeira's consumers read the letters of their suppliers for detailed descriptions of discriminating customs. Madeira distributors such as Newton & Gordon or Leacock & Sons loved to expatiate on how best to package the cask, fine the wine, and furnish a table with imported glassware.[42]

The subject of fining was of "greatest consequence" since their wine would be deprived "of the only valuable essential, full body & high flavour" if it should be "treated in a wrong & in an injurious manner by a Quack." Through "many experiments on the subject" in 1791 and 1792, Newton & Gordon and competing firms formed distinct ideas about how their customers should fine their wine, and many precepts contravened reigning fashion in London: blood would, they admitted, produce "different shades of colour," but (playing to their audience of would-be cognoscenti) "surely to a man who knows what genuine Madeira was, it would be as ridiculous [to speak] of a particular shade of paleness . . . as it would be to talk to a Jockey of the particular colour of a horse, provided the animal was possesst of every part of excellence." Milk, too, was "infinitely too strong for the man who setts a value on the body & fine fruity flavour of his liquor"; besides, it left "a ropy kind of film on the liquor" that impeded viewing. Likewise, isinglass had "a bad smell." Instead one island wine firm urged buyers in America to adopt "the method practiced long in the house & still practiced by most of our neighbours of putting 24 to 30 whites of eggs together with the shells (comminuted & mixed together) to each pipe." The wine was to be fined "the day" the American got it "from on board ship," and "in six weeks it will have recovered sufficiently" to be drinkable. Nevertheless, it still needed to be immediately racked, allowing it to sit for ten or fifteen more days before tasting.[43]

Fining, as Newton & Gordon assured their clients, was only the first among many steps to be taken by a connoisseur. In the case of a "very old and very fine" Sercial—"a great rarity"—Newton & Gordon advised John Gibbes of Charleston to bottle it once he had fined it and allowed it "to become perfectly clear," "for it is a capricious liquor." The bottles were "to lie on their side"; by no means were they "to stand on their bottom," as was the practice in some parts of Britain. Newton & Gordon wrote from their experience, not from their reading, and suggested that Gibbes apply their method "not with Sercial only but all other liquors." Because of Sercial's scarcity, American connoisseurs were urged to take "only a glass or two during dinner." Competing firms had just as many ideas about connoisseurship, a word they all began to bandy about with greater frequency.[44]

Pronouncements by distributors were more often than not responses to consumers' queries about how to care for, display, or drink the wine. Sometimes distributors' communications concerned consumers inasmuch as the directives could be at odds with the practices promulgated by local grandees or dispensers. This provoked extended correspondence until the matter, for instance fining, was reengineered to the satisfaction of producers, distributors, and consumers— an arduous task. Somewhat more independent commentary was penned by medical men or men of means who enjoyed their bottles and reveled in travel.

These accounts and manuals by doctors and aesthetes of all nations—mainly British but some French, Spanish, and Italian—began appearing in the last quarter of the eighteenth century to educate and improve wine-drinking audiences. John Croft's 1788 *Treatise* is typical for the multiplicity of distinctions he dispenses:

> Perhaps sound, old mellow Madeira may be preferred to any other sort of Wine as a good stomachic. There are two sorts which grow in the island from whence it takes its name, though properly of the same grape. The genuine, natural, and best sort, is of the colour of oil, and tinges in the glass, affording a hue or shade of a light blue, and has a kernelly taste like a walnut. The commoner sort is made of the ordinary grape, and they tinge it in the Wine-press with the *uva roxa,* or red grape, which they cultivate on the island for that purpose, and it makes the wine of a foxy or deep colour. As the caprice of fashion has reigned in England of later years in respect to Wines, as well as other articles of luxury, sometimes they required them of one colour, and at other time of another, as said before.

In addition, Croft advised his readers on "the proper time to begin to drink" and "the best time to bottle" wine. Duncan McBride was no less reluctant, and his 1793 *General Instructions for the Choice of Wines and Spirituous Liquors* he included an accounting of "those Wines which are best to be used at the Tables of the Opulent." Thus, when the doctor John Wright educated his readers in 1795 on "the component parts of wine," his readers were ready. Specialized books for wine-thirsty audiences were published with increasing frequency and in increasing volume in the two decades that succeeded the close of the American Revolution.[45]

Cosmopolitanism

As Madeira wine became more expensive, and so indicative of wealth, refinement, and gentility, its European-ness and worldliness were also highlighted. For eighteenth-century Americans, consumption of wine came to signify for some drinkers a cosmopolitanism—the attitude that the drinker was worldly and had transcended local, regional, or national limitations. In the last quarter of the century, American cosmopolites often chose their wines for this reason.

Often Americans used gifts of wine to honor or thank their countrymen as well as Europeans in a way that demonstrated the giver's familiarity with transatlantic conventions and tastes. In 1735 Governor Gooch of Virginia sent the bishop of London some Madeira wine. To placate their friend Thomas Hancock for some slight, Messrs. Harris & Crisp sent the merchant a "present of wine." Benjamin Franklin both sent and received European and American wines in great quantity; he regarded such beverages as ideal transatlantic gifts. The London overseas trader John Sargent II returned the favor and sent Franklin's son "a little Present of Wine" in July 1773. Thomas Everard of Virginia ordered ninety-six bottles of "fine old Madeira" to be sent from Madeira to London, where one Mrs. Horrocks, a Virginia planter, was visiting the metropolis and intending "to distribute [them] among her friends." During the American Revolutionary War such "civilities" and their associations were not wholly banished. In a rather curious twist, the Marquis de Chastellux sent to General Washington, the commander in chief, a cask of claret as a token of his esteem—claret because it was *not* Madeira and a reminder of Portugal's support of Britain in the war. John Marsden Pintard, the New Yorker recently appointed by Congress to be the U.S. commercial agent on Madeira, sent the president of Congress some Madeira as "a mark of remembrance" in 1783. The giving of wine gifts went on and on and on.[46]

Giving wine as a gift whose status was seen as a luxury had a triple effect: it showed the recipient that he or she was an object of great respect; it displayed the giver as a person of some means and discernment; and it projected European connections. Many regarded the European-ness of a wine as a distinct virtue. Early on, in one Boston newspaper, a writer asked the reader: "And who can keep a genteel House without a cask of wine in his cellar? How very *impolite* to invite a friend to Dine, and be wanting in wine or punch. So very *sickish*" it was to serve "any thing of our own Country make." With such constraints in mind, Madeira—the expensive Portuguese wine grown on an island in the middle of the Atlantic that was by most geographers' reckoning more part of Africa—was best suited for the purpose of reconnecting ties to the Old World. Wines, in this sense, were not unlike languages spoken in coffeehouses or dresses worn in public: after the war for America, "every language of Europe is now spoken" in American taverns and "every dress of Europe is now seen" in American streets. As with clothing and languages, Madeira wine could signify to others that America was tied to Europe.[47]

Conclusion

The eighteenth-century Atlantic world was a remarkable place. The conditions under which individuals lived and acted are well known: the economic success of the New World, for instance; the contests among the European powers to dominate that world; the mercantilist ideology that translated the contests into trade relations and government policies. Into this world stepped a group of particularly situated individuals who sought economic and social success in the local environments in which they found themselves. Few if any of these local actors in the story of Madeira wine regarded themselves as moving about an Atlantic stage, whether by setting standards of connoisseurship and determining social hierarchies, solving short-run distribution problems, or inventing new products. Most of them—to the extent that they articulated it—thought of themselves as making do in their particular social milieus and with the particular economic opportunities they found for themselves. Achieving success was generally enough.

And yet collectively they changed the world. Madeira wine metamorphosed from common plonk into the highest status, most expensive wine in America. It was suitable for occasions of state and the tables of the rich and refined, and its taste and the taste of Americans were internationalized. The distribution infrastructure of the Atlantic and inland North America was developed, elaborated, differentiated, and regularized. A sterling example of preindustrial product and process innovation took place. The market for Madeira wine organized a congeries of local decisions with little or no central direction. In tandem the social and ideational concomitants also organized, each influencing the other through the continuous, conversational feedback participants provided each other.

In 1700 an individual could have predicted that if the number of Americans and their wealth grew apace, a relatively undifferentiated wine drink would become differentiated. Producers would respond to the growing market by going after different parts of the market, and consumers would respond to increased variety offered by making differing symbolic uses of different drinks thus proffered. This is the regularity favored by economists: "the differentiation of product is governed by the extent of the market" (a variation of the title Adam Smith attached to chapter 3 of book 1 of *The Wealth of Nations*). The particularity beloved of historians is that in 1700 it was impossible to predict that Madeira wine would be the premier luxury drink, with cider the common beverage and port hardly known. With hindsight one can only understand that outcome by looking at the particular unfolding of the market.

The outcome of this rather exciting picture is that it shatters much of the reigning mental picture of the eighteenth-century British American world, one part of which concerned wine. That picture is Anglo-centric: primarily peopled with Great Britons and managed from its metropolis; more or less rigid in the operation of imperial institutions and initiatives; static from an entrepreneurial standpoint; and focused on the mother country and metropolis in social and cultural norms and affairs.[48]

The world of Madeira wine, and wine drinking in America, though, was anything but that.[49] It was not Anglo-centric; if anything it was centered on an island in the middle of the Atlantic, a province over which the Kingdom of Portugal always had difficulty exerting control. In practice, the wine's world had no core. The trade was not managed from any center—London, Lisbon, or Funchal; actual strategies, choices, and decisions were made in an ongoing set of decentralized negotiations between men and women on both sides of the Atlantic, in at least four or five places. Rather than rigid, the trade and its practitioners were flexible—protean men, working in an uncertain and porous environment, with an opportunistic approach to everyday business. Innovation was more the order of the day than was any passive imprisonment to inherited traditions and resources; these preindustrial people were enormously dynamic—witness the turnover of businesses, the development of new commodities, and the derivation of new socially significant uses. And finally, the styles of consuming did not take their cues from the centers of the empires: drinkers around the Atlantic Ocean rim were focused more on their own opportunities and needs than on the fashions and dictates of the mother countries' gentility. Such deviations from the norm should cause us to reconsider characteristic traits before we apply them to the larger functioning unit we now call the "Atlantic world."

Notes

1. D. W. Meinig, *The Shaping of America: A Geographical Perspective on 500 Years of History*, vol. 1 (New Haven: Yale University Press, 1986), 65; Bernard Bailyn, "The Idea of Atlantic History," *Itinerario* 20 (1996):12–14. For examples of this scholarship, see Ralph Davis, *The Rise of the Atlantic Economies* (Ithaca and London: Cornell University Press, 1973); Jacob M. Price, *Capital and Credit in British Overseas Trade: The View from the Chesapeake, 1700–1776* (Cambridge: Harvard University Press, 1980); Ian Steele, *The English Atlantic, 1675–1740: An Exploration of Communication and Community* (New York: Oxford University Press, 1986); Kenneth Morgan, *Bristol & the Atlantic Trade in the Eighteenth Century* (Cambridge: Cambridge University Press, 1993); David Hancock, *Citizens of the World: London Merchants and the Integration of the British Atlantic Community, 1735–1785* (Cambridge: Cambridge University Press, 1995).

2. Complex, nonlinear, dynamical, adaptive systems have been increasingly studied by specialists in a variety of fields, such as chemistry, geology, physics, and artificial intelligence. The most succinct introductions to the many ideas appear in R. Lewin, *Complexity: Life at the Edge of Chaos* (New York: Macmillan, 1992); G. Nicolis and I. Prigogine, *Exploring Complexity* (New York: W. H. Freeman, 1989). In economics, see W. Brian Arthur, "Inductive Reasoning and Bonded Rationality," and Paul Krugman, "Complex Landscapes in Economic Geography," both in *American Economic Review: Papers and Proceedings* 84 (May 1995): 406–16. It is, perhaps, a little overblown to describe this way of thinking as a *theory*, whether "complexity theory" or something else. This is because it does not now rise to the level of a set of propositions from which the investigator can make deductions about how events will unfold. It may develop into a theory or it may not. Given the state of today's knowledge, it would be more accurate to call it a *point of view*, a perspective on how human life unfolds in time. The perspective is explored at greater length in David Hancock, "Complex Adaptive Systems in Early-Modern Atlantic History" (unpublished paper presented at the Workshop on Early-Modern History, the University of Chicago, February 2001), and David Hancock, "Introduction," in *Oceans of Wine, Empires of Commerce: Madeira and the Self-Organization of the Early-Modern Atlantic Economy* (forthcoming).

3. On tobacco, see Jacob M. Price, "The Rise of Glasgow in the Chesapeake Tobacco Trade, 1707–1775," *William and Mary Quarterly,* 3rd ser., 11 (1954): 179–99; Jacob M. Price, "The Economic Growth of the Chesapeake and the European Market, 1697–1775," *Journal of Economic History* 24 (1964): 496–511; Jacob M. Price, *France and the Chesapeake:*

A History of the French Tobacco Monopoly, 1674–1791, and of Its Relationship to the British and American Tobacco Trades, 2 vols. (Ann Arbor: University of Michigan Press, 1973). On sugar, see Richard Pares, "The London Sugar Market, 1740–1769," *Economic History Review,* 2nd ser., 9 (1956): 254–70; Richard Pares, "A London West India Merchant House," in *Essays Presented to Sir Lewis Namier,* ed. Richard Pares and A. J. Taylor (London: Macmillan, 1956), 75–107.

4. David Hancock, "Commerce and Conversation in the Eighteenth-Century Atlantic: The Invention of Madeira Wine," *Journal of Interdisciplinary History* 39 (Autumn 1998): 197–219.

5. Among Iberian wines, Madeira was the first to be fortified. On its fortification, see William Vaughan, *Directions for Health, Natural and Artificiall,* 7th ed. (London: Thomas Harper, for John Harison, 1633), a reworking of his *Natural and Artificiall Directions for Health* (London, 1600); Richard Saunders, *Poor Richard, 1743* (Philadelphia, 1743), in *The Papers of Benjamin Franklin,* ed. Leonard W. Labaree, 36 vols. to date (New Haven: Yale University Press, 1959–), 2:367; Francis Newton to Thomas Newton, August 4, 1753, and Francis Newton to George Spence, October 27, 1753, Newton & Gordon Letterbooks, private collection, Suffolk, England, vol. 1, fols. 62, 77. However, by the seventeenth century the Dutch were already rectifying brandy and adding it to common beverage wines to make *brandewijn,* a drink more suitable for long-distance travel. On the fortification of port and other wines, see Alan D. Francis, *The Wine Trade* (London: A. and C. Black, 1972); Warner Allen, *Sherry and Port* (London: Constable, 1952); George Robertson, *Port,* 4th ed. (London and Boston: Faber and Faber, 1978), 12, 15, 16; Julian Jeffs, *Sherry,* 4th ed. (London: Faber and Faber, 1992).

6. Newton & Gordon to Kearny & Gilbert, January 25, 1768, vol. 4, fol. 171, and Thomas Murdoch to Thomas Gordon, January 28, 1789, both in Newton & Gordon Letterbooks; John Leacock to Michael Nowlan, June 2, 1779, Leacock Papers; Johann Wilhelm Von Archenholz, *A Picture of England* (Dublin: P. Byrne, 1791), 203; James Gordon to Alexander Gordon, March 14, 1768, Gordon of Letterfourie Papers, Buckie, Banffshire, Scotland; Provedoria da Fazenda, no. 942, fols. 19–20, Arquivo Regional Madeira, Funchal, Portugal. See also Newton & Gordon to Kearny & Gilbert, January 25, 1768, vol. 4, fol. 171; Thomas Murdoch to Thomas Gordon, January 28, 1789, vol. 11, fol. 218; Thomas Murdoch to Thomas Gordon, January 28, 1789, vol. 11, fol. 218, and June 15, 1789, vol. 12, fol. 86; Newton & Gordon to Thomas Gordon, August 19, 1789; James Gordon to Thomas Gordon, September 3, 1803; and Thomas Murdoch to Robert Lenox, September 30, 1803, vol. 25, fol. 173—all in Newton & Gordon Letterbooks. Also see James Gordon to Alexander Gordon, May 22, 1769, Letterfourie Papers; Newton & Gordon to Thomas Gordon, January 28, 1789, vol. 11, fol. 177, Newton & Gordon Letterbooks; John Leacock Sr. to William Leacock, May 29 and June 27, 1799, Leacock & Sons Letterbook 1799–1802, fols. 35, 52–58, Leacock Papers; Michael Nowlan to Gedley Clare Burges, February 25, 1762, Nowlan & Burges Letterbook, Leacock Papers. Today we know that brandy ensures microbiological stability, rendering impotent most bacteria and strains of yeast and thereby precluding further fermentation.

7. Thomas Murdoch to Pierce Butler, October 18, 1800, Newton & Gordon Letterbooks; Spence, Leacock & Spence to John Erskine, June 26, 1762, and John Leacock to William Leacock, May 10, 1796, Leacock Papers; Henry Laurens to Corsley Rogers &

Son, May 16, 1755, in *Papers of Henry Laurens,* ed. David R. Chesnutt, 16 vols. (Columbia: University of South Carolina Press, 1968–2002), 1:248; Newton & Gordon to Capt. John Diffell, January 17, 1776, vol. 6, fol. 38, Newton & Gordon Letterbooks; Thomas Newton to Newton & Gordon, November 26, 1759, Thomas Newton Letterbook, Madeira Wine Company Archives; Baynton & Wharton to Thomas Newton, October 2, 1763, box 2, Cossart & Gordon Papers, Liverpool University Archives; Newton & Gordon to John Campbell, April 14, 1798, vol. 18, fol. 316, and William Johnston to Francis Newton, January 22, 1786, both in Newton & Gordon Letterbooks.

8. John Corrie to Thomas Gordon, January 7, 1771, box 5, bundle 1770–71, Cossart & Gordon Papers, Liverpool University Archives.

9. Thomas Newton to Anthony Sarly, January 22, 1756; Thomas Newton to Malcolm Campbell, January 22, 1756; Thomas Newton to Dr. Robert Knox, March 23, 1756; Thomas Newton to Evan Cameron, June 3, 1756—all in Thomas Newton Letterbook, fols. 1, 3, 7, Madeira Wine Company Archives.

10. Daniel Henry Smith to James Gordon, July 25, 1774, Letterfourie Papers; Francis Newton to George Spence, June 9, 1756, December 6, 1756, February 17, 1757, Newton & Gordon Letterbooks, vol. 1, fols. 208, 235, 248; Gedley Clare Burgess to Michael Nowlan, July 29, 1756, Burgess & Nowlan Letterbook, fol. 23; Thomas Newton to Francis Newton, October 31, November 29, 1758, September 4, 1759, Thomas Newton Letterbook, fols. 44, 46, Madeira Wine Company Archives; Thomas Newton to Newton & Gordon, July 10, 1762, box 8, bundle 1774–75, Cossart Gordon Papers, Liverpool University Archives; Newton & Gordon to Thomas Newton, June 9, September 3, 1763, May 15, 1765, Newton & Gordon Letterbooks, vol. 3, fols. 154, 193, 407.

11. The Madeirans appear to be effecting what economists have noted for later periods. For a discussion of how economies first worked across markets and later worked across hierarchical firms, see the studies by Ronald H. Coase, "The Nature of the Firm," *Economica* 4 (1937): 386–405; Oliver E. Williamson, *Markets and Hierarchies: Analysis and Antitrust Implications* (New York: Free Press, 1975); and Douglass C. North, *Institutions, Institutional Change and Economic Performance* (Cambridge: Cambridge University Press, 1990). The most recent contribution to this literature—Bengst Holmaström and John Roberts, "The Boundaries of the Firm Revisited," *Journal of Economic Perspectives* 12 (Fall 1998): 73–94—in looking at Japanese subcontracting, American steelworking, airline alliances, and broadcasting systems, observes for the late twentieth century what the Madeirans learned in the eighteenth century: ownership patterns and behaviors are responsive not only to "the provision of investment incentives and the resolution of holdups" but also to "agency problems, concerns for common assets, difficulties in transferring knowledge, and the benefits of market monitoring" (75).

12. Newton & Gordon to Alexander Johnston & Co., June 19, 1761, Newton & Gordon Letterbooks, vol. 2., fol. 308. Nearly every other firm of Newton & Gordon's size, scale, and ambition also sent partners to London to reside. Robert Scott Sr. had moved there in the late 1730s, and John Pringle joined him in the late 1750s. In 1760 James Gordon followed them, as did Thomas Lamar in 1762 and Charles Fergusson in 1763.

13. Francis Newton to Waddell Cunningham, July 4, 1755; Francis Newton to John Provoost, August 2, 1758; Newton & Gordon to David Barclay, December 6, 1764; Francis Newton to John Provoost, July 23, 1766; Francis Newton to Mackintosh & Hannay,

July 8, 1767; Francis Newton to Colt, Baker & Day, October 11, 1798; Francis Newton to William Cole, August 16, 1802—all in Newton & Gordon Letterbooks, vol. 1, fols. 165, after 281, vol. 3, fol. 353, vol. 4, fols. 33, 105, vol. 19, fol. 105, vol. 23, fol. 392.

14. Francis Newton to George Spence, March 7, 1757, Newton & Gordon Letterbooks, vol. 1, fol. 248. Likewise, the Searle firm tried to engross all the New York business to itself. They had "great friends there" and during the war were "very industrious in procuring them consignments." One "friend," their cousin Lewis Pintard, procured "a vast deal of business to their friends . . . by getting intelligence of every vessel" that left New York, Connecticut, and the Jerseys for the island and by "getting intimately acquainted with the captains & owners." Like the Hills, the Searles also took "a concern in several [ships] to promote the interest of the house." Often the house took a one-third share and Pintard and the owner the remainder. By midcentury it seemed clear to most in the American trade that "there is no doing anything considerable here without being concerned in a vessel & even some part of the cargo." See Francis Newton to Thomas Newton, August 31, 1753, Newton & Gordon Letterbooks, vol. 1, fol. 70; Thomas Newton to Malcolm Campbell, October 20, 1756, Thomas Newton to Francis Newton, December 26, 1758, and Thomas Newton to Francis Newton, February 19, 1759—all three in Thomas Newton Letterbook, fols. 22r, 77r, 52v.

15. John D. R. Platt, *The City Tavern: Historic Resource Study* (Denver: National Park Service, 1973), 8–20, 243–45. For the use of Hill's Madeira at the tavern, see Penelope H. Batcheler, *The City Tavern: Historic Structure Report—Architectural Data Section* (Denver: National Park Service, 1973), 113–21; Constance V. Hershey, *The City Tavern: Historic Furnishings Plan* (Denver, 1974), 61–72.

16. Before the mid-1770s many of the firm's wine customers in the city of Philadelphia had managed the trade to the hinterland. In the early 1770s, for instance, William Pollard regularly supplied Madeira wine to Black Log Valley settlers. See William Pollard Letterbook "1772–1774," Historical Society of Pennsylvania (HSP), Philadelphia.

17. The redistributive work performed by Henry Hill's customers can also be fruitfully studied. Lancaster County distribution sources include the John Harris Ledgers, 1748–75 and 1770–91, HSP; James Burd Account Book, 1747–48, American Philosophical Society (APS), Philadelphia; Burd-Shippen Family Papers and Edward Shippen Thompson Papers, Pennsylvania State Archives, Harrisburg; Edward Shippen Papers, HSP; William McCord Ledger, 1761–66, Day Book, 1763–67, Invoice Book, 1764–67, Pennsylvania State Archives; F. S. Weiser and L. M. Neff, eds., *Records of Purchases at the King George Hotel . . . 1762–1773* (Birdsboro: Pennsylvania German Society, 1987). Apart from Jerome Wood's study *Conestoga Crossroads* (Harrisburg, 1979), little work has been done on Lancaster County. Even less has been done on other counties supplied by Hill. There is nothing on Berks, apart from the biography by Paul A. W. Wallace, *Conrad Weiser, 1696–1760: Friend of Colonist and Mohawk* (Philadelphia: University of Pennsylvania Press, 1945), and an edition of his account book published by the Pennsylvania German Society. Nor has work been done on the developing economies of York and Cumberland counties, despite useful materials in the Hance Hamilton Papers, box 1, HSP.

18. See, for example, Robert Carter to John Hyde, May 26, 1729, and Robert Carter to Micajah Perry, July 2, 1729, Robert Carter Letterbook, fols. 62, 77, Virginia Historical Society, Richmond.

19. John Hancock to Lamar, Hill, Bisset & Co., January 20, November 12, 1767, Hancock Papers, Special Collections, Harvard Business School, Boston. After the American Revolution, Lamar, Hill, Bisset & Co. resumed their shipment of two pipes per year.

20. Inns, taverns, ordinaries, and general stores spread with remarkable speed as metropolitans, colonials, and Indians clashed with the French during the 1750s and 1760s. War-time food and drink demands were greater than those that could be supplied by ordinary farmers; as a result more well-equipped, institutionalized dispensaries arose to meet them in western Virginia, Pennsylvania, and New York. The dispensaries remained to serve incoming settlers after the French and Indian War was concluded. See Robert D. Mitchell, *Commercialism and Frontier: Perspectives on the Early Shenandoah Valley* (Charlottesville: University Press of Virginia, 1977), 144–45. See also, more generally, Charles J. Farmer, "Country Stores and Frontier Exchange Systems in Southside Virginia during the Eighteenth Century," 2 vols. (Ph.D. diss., University of Maryland, 1984).

21. The farmer-retailers bought as readily from local county merchants and wagon-train traders as from pack-horse traders and itinerant peddlers. On the wagons, see Wood, *Conestoga Crossroads,* 108–9. The literature on itinerant peddlers is not extensive. See Richard R. Beeman, ed., "Trade and Travel in Post-Revolutionary Virginia: A Diary of an Itinerant Peddler, 1807–1808," *Virginia Magazine of History and Biography* 84 (1976): 174–88; Daniel H. Usner Jr., "The Frontier Exchange Economy of the Lower Mississippi Valley in the Eighteenth Century," *William and Mary Quarterly,* 3rd ser., 44 (1987): 165–92; Daniel B. Thorp, "Doing Business in the Backcountry: Retail Trade in Colonial Rowan County, North Carolina," *William and Mary Quarterly,* 3rd. ser., 48 (1991): 400. Much work remains to be done on the pack-horse trade.

22. On the quite remarkable growth of taverns and dramshops in the towns and counties of Massachusetts, see David Conroy, "The Culture and Politics of Drink in Colonial and Revolutionary Massachusetts, 1681–1790" (Ph.D. diss., University of Connecticut, 1987), 179. On taverns and tavern-keepers generally, see Kym Rice, *Early American Taverns: For the Entertainment of Friends and Strangers* (Chicago: Regnery Gateway, 1983); Robert Graham, "The Taverns of Colonial Philadelphia," *Transactions of the American Philosophical Society* 43 (1953): 318–25; Peter Thompson, "A Social History of Philadelphia's Taverns, 1663–1800" (Ph.D. diss., University of Pennsylvania, 1989); Patricia Gibbs, "Taverns in Tidewater Virginia, 1700–1774" (A.M. thesis, College of William and Mary, 1968); Anne Hedges, "Richmond's Taverns in the Years 1775–1810" (A.M. thesis, University of Richmond, 1993); James W. Hosier, "Travelers' Comments on Virginia Taverns, Ordinaries and Other Accommodations from 1750 to 1812" (A.M. thesis, University of Richmond, 1964); Paton Yoder, "Tavern Regulation in Virginia," *Virginia Magazine of History and Biography* 87 (1979): 259–78; Gretchen Sorin, "Tavern Fare Comestibles in Alexandria, 1770–1810," *Northern Virginia Heritage* 3 (1981): 3–20.

23. Two other sales outlets also grew in importance in the 1700s: urban vendue masters and the assignees of bankrupts. In 1766, for instance, New York had two vendue masters—Nicholas William Stuyvesant, and Moore & Lynsen—whose public auctions were held at their offices, the site of the property being sold, a coffeehouse or tavern, or a dock. See *New-York Mercury,* June 9, 1766, 4.

24. *Pennsylvania Gazette,* May 12, 1737 (John Valentine), November 16, 1738 (Evan Morgan). In the first twenty years of its publication (1731–49), some twenty-one wholesalers and retailers advertised Madeira wine in the *Pennsylvania Gazette* on forty-eight

separate occasions. The first mention of Madeira appeared on August 22, 1734, when seven pipes were put up at public vendue.

25. *Pennsylvania Gazette,* September 13, 1753, and June 26, 1755. See also May 17 and August 21, 1773, and May 11 and 12 (Bache's Wine Store), November 23 (Mitchell's Wine, Spirit, Rum & Sugar Store), 1774. Benjamin Morgan had advertised his services as a wine cooper as early as 1729 (ibid., March 4, 1729). In March 1772 the German Ludwig Kuhn described himself as a clerk who "would suit a wine merchant best, as in Europe he has been a considerable time in that trade, as well for himself as others, and consequently is a good judge of wines" (*Pennsylvania Gazette,* March 26, 1772). Similar specialization occurred outside Philadelphia at roughly the same time. To the west in Lancaster, for instance, the Scot James Burd, who had previously worked as a merchant in Philadelphia, was the first to open a "Win Store" in 1759, in concert with his father-in-law Edward Shippen Sr. There Burd sold several qualities of Madeira, which he obtained either directly from the Hill firm or indirectly from his brother-in-law Edward Shippen Jr. and Thomas Willing in Philadelphia, as well as Tenerife, Malaga, rum, spirits, brandy, and sugar. See Lily L. Nixon, *James Burd: Frontier Defender, 1726–1793* (Philadelphia: University of Pennsylvania Press, 1941), 127; Wood, *Conestoga Crossroads,* 98. Despite the onset of specialization, the combination of retail services persisted, especially in nonurban or undeveloped regions. As late as 1797 the proprietor of the Spring House Store, eight miles from Chestnut Hill on the road to Bethlehem, announced the sale of "dry and wet goods." Tavern-keepers, he advertised, would be "supplied with wines and liquors warranted free of adulteration on very moderate terms," as well as "every article suitable for a store" (*Pennsylvania Gazette,* May 31, 1797).

26. Clement Biddle, *The Philadelphia Directory* (Philadelphia: Johnson, 1791); Anon., *Census Directory for 1811* (Philadelphia, 1811). Thomas M. Doerflinger, *A Vigorous Spirit of Enterprise* (Chapel Hill: University of North Carolina Press, 1985), 77, sketches the ancillary specialization by region and by commodity in Philadelphia's import trading community, a process fixed by the 1780s. For similar growth in wine specialists in other American towns and cities, see Anon., *The Boston Directory* (Boston, 1789); Edward Cotton, *The Boston Directory* (Boston, 1807); William Duncan, *The New York Directory and Register, for the Year 1792* (New York: T. and J. Swords, 1792); *Longworth's American Almanac, New-York Register, and City Directory for the Thirty-Second Year of American Independence* (New York: David Longworth, 1807); Eleazer Elizer, *A Directory for 1803* (Charleston, S.C.: W. P. Young, 1803). David Hancock, "Markets, Merchants, and the Wider World of Boston's Wine, 1700–1775," in *Entrepreneurs: The Boston Business Community, 1700–1850,* ed. Conrad Wright and Katheryn Viens (Boston: Massachusetts Historical Society, dist. by Northeastern University Press, 1997), 21–22, 28–33, documents the increase in captains and merchants shipping and trading wine in Boston and Massachusetts. The New York City case was the most pronounced. Some 175 enterprisers (vendue masters, merchants, wholesalers, retailers, store owners, specialists such as cork cutters, and brokers) advertised the sale of wine between 1768 and 1775; during the war 387 individuals advertised. The average number of advertisements more than doubled from 42 in the prewar period to 98 in the war period, and the level was maintained after the war. See Robert Dructor, "The New York Commercial Community: The Revolutionary Experience" (Ph.D. diss., University of Pittsburgh, 1975).

27. On the sources for reconstituting wine imports and their use, see David Hancock, "A 'Revolution in the Trade': Madeira Wine and the Development of the Infrastructure of the Atlantic Market Economy, 1703–1807," in *The Early Modern Atlantic Economy,* ed. John McCusker and Kenneth Morgan (Cambridge: Cambridge University Press, 2000), 105–53.

28. On imports into New York, see William I. Davisson and Lawrence J. Bradley, "New York Maritime Trade: Ship Voyage Patterns, 1715–1765," *New York Historical Society Quarterly* 55 (1971): 308–17; Cathy Matson, "Commerce after the Conquest: I: Dutch Traders and Goods in New York City, 1664–1764," *De Halve Maen* 59 (March 1987): 8–12; Philip L. White, *The Beekmans of New York in Politics and Commerce, 1647–1877* (New York: New York Historical Society, 1956); David A. Armour, *The Merchants of Albany, New York, 1686–1760* (New York: Garland, 1986), 178. Data for wine imported into New York are contained in the following record series: Julius M. Bloch, Leo Hershkowitz et al., eds., *An Account of Her Majesty's Revenue in the Province of New York, 1701–1709* (Ridgewood, N.J., 1967), for 1703–5 and 1701–10; Naval Office Shipping Lists (NOSL), CO 5/1222–1228, Public Record Office, London, for 1713–43, 1751, 1753–55, and 1763–64; Manifest Books, vols. 13–39, New York State Archives, Albany, for April 1743–October 1762; American Inspector-General Abstracts, based on NOSL, no longer extant, Customs 16/1, Public Records Office, London. The New York manifest books from 1757 to 1761 are heavily damaged by smoke and fire; one can extract the number of ships entering with wine but the portion of the page in the volumes containing the number of pipes is destroyed or unreadable. See also E. D. Beechert Jr., "The Wine Trade of the Thirteen Colonies" (M.A. thesis, University of California, Berkeley, 1949); Robert M. Dructor, "The New York Commercial Community."

29. The data series of wine imports is quite noisy due to weather conditions that affected the crop and shipping. The five-year moving averages reduce the effect of the noise.

30. Comparing the imports to the size of the colony's white population (as estimated by John McCusker in "Rum and the American Revolution: The Rum Trade and the Balance of Payments of the Thirteen Continental Colonies, 1650–1775" [Ph.D. diss., University of Pittsburgh, 1970]), it appears that average per capita importation was 2.1 gallons of wine in 1714–18, 1.6 gallons in 1749, 0.9 gallons in 1754, 1.5 gallons in 1763–64, 0.4 gallons in 1768–72, and 0.6 gallons in 1789/90.

31. In 1703–7 only 13.8 percent of the wine imports were denoted "Madeira." Another 82.7 percent were labeled "Wine." Since 75.9 percent of all wines entered into the port came on ships coming directly from Madeira, it is safe to assume that at least two-thirds of the wine was Madeira wine. The rise to 97 percent in 1771 is almost certainly an aberration, having to do with the end of colonial nonimportation, a run of low vintages in the Azores and Canaries, and most important, the fact that inexplicably the source for the years 1768–72, Customs 16/1, 1768–72 Public Record Office, London, Newfoundland, does not include Azorean wines.

32. A final category of "other" wines, including French, Italian, and those listed simply as "wines," constituted 16.9 percent.

33. Port wine at the end of the century was "the most universal in Britain" and had been so throughout the century. See Arthur W. Secord, ed., *Defoe's Review,* vol. 1, bk. 2 (New York: Columbia University Press, 1938), 362 (January 2, 1705), 358 (December 30,

1704). By 1755 Madeira wine was not uncommon in Britain, but that was not saying much. Within forty years it was "scarcely reckoned one of" their wines. Similarly, sherry, which was around 1780 "in vast vogue," was by 1795 "retiring from our acquaintance." See John Wright, *An Essay on Wines, Especially on Port Wine* (London, 1795), 19, 42–43.

34. The database was compiled on three principles. First, four colonies were selected, largely on the basis of geographical distribution: Massachusetts, New York, South Carolina, and Jamaica. Second, within two of those colonies, a metropolitan county (that housed the seat of government) and a less-developed interior county were selected: for Massachusetts, Suffolk and Hampshire; for New York, New York and Albany. *County* officials in these two colonies were responsible for the recording of testamentary dispositions, probate inventories, and related deeds. In Carolina and Jamaica, however, *colony* officials were responsible for collecting and collating such records; sometimes they noted the residence of the decedent, but sometimes not. As a result, it is not always possible to distinguish metropolitan from backcountry decedents. Accordingly, the samples for Carolina and Jamaica were constructed to include inventoried decedents from all counties and parishes. For each jurisdiction, whether colony or county, a database of all decedents whose estates were inventoried for two periods was compiled—a decade or half-decade near the beginning of the century and a decade or half-decade near the end. Since the survival of probate records has not been uniform across colonies, exact overlap of all four studied regions was impossible to effect. For instance, the Massachusetts county records were culled for the years 1703–7 and 1803–7; New York probate inventories were culled for 1703–12 and 1790–99. Jamaica records are spottier, however, and as a result in the earliest decade could yield data only for the years 1700–1705 and 1713–16; the records for intervening years are inaccessible. Similarly, Carolina probates were not recorded until the 1730s; the first decade surveyed is therefore 1732–41. The data, then, in some cases are scattered across time, although enough overlaps have been constructed to permit comparison among regions.

35. James Birket, *Some Cursory Remarks Made by James Birket in His Voyage to North America, 1750–1751* (New Haven: Yale University Press, 1916), 9–10; Wright, *Essay on Wines,* 42; Oliver M. Dickerson, *The Navigation Acts and the American Revolution* (Philadelphia: University of Pennsylvania Press, 1951), 172, 188; Edmund Morgan and Helen Morgan, *The Stamp Act Crisis: Prologue to Revolution,* new rev. ed. (New York: Collier Books, 1962), 39, 41, 45; R. C. Simmons and P. D. G. Thomas, eds., *Proceedings and Debates of the British Parliaments Respecting North America, 1754–1783,* 6 vols. (Milwood, N.Y.: Kraus International Publications, 1982), 1:487–93, 508–11; Newton & Gordon to George & John Riddell, June 3, 1765, Newton & Gordon Letterbooks, vol. 3, fol. 413.

36. William Lee to Lamar, Hill, Bisset & Co., January 5, 1784, William Lee Letterbooks, Virginia Historical Society, Richmond; Matthew Miller (Gosport) to Newton & Gordon, February 2, 1780, unnumbered bundle, box 1780/81, Cossart Gordon Papers, Liverpool University Archives; George Washington to William Pearce, November 23, 1794, in *The Writings of George Washington,* ed. John C. Fitzpatrick, 39 vols. (Washington, D.C.: U.S. Government Printing Office, 1931–44), 34:41–42, 53; Robert Beverley to William Beverley, August 22, 1794, *Virginia Historical Magazine* 21 (1913): 102; Patrick Campbell, "Travels in North America," in his *The Publications of the Champlain Society* (Toronto, 1937), 46; William Bentley, *The Diary of William Bentley D.D.,* 4 vols. (Gloucester, Mass.: P. Smith, 1962), 1:299 (September 8, 1791).

37. *Pennsylvania Gazette,* September 30, 1736; William Smith Jr., *The History of the Province of New York,* ed. Michael Kammen, 2 vols. (Cambridge: Belknap Press of Harvard University Press, 1972), 1:227.

38. Philip V. Fithian, *Journal & Letters* (Williamsburg, 1943), 57 (January 18, 1774), 77 (March 12, 1774); John Pope, *A Tour through the Southern and Western Territories of the United States of North-America; the Spanish Dominions on the River Mississippi, and the Floridas; the Countries of the Creek Nations; and Many Uninhabited Parts* (Richmond, Va.: J. Dixon, 1792), 84.

39. Landon Carter, *The Diary of Colonel Landon of Sabine Hall, 1752–1798,* vol. 2, ed. Jack P. Greene (Richmond, 1987), 1001. On March 15, 1776, Carter prided himself on serving only one bottle of wine after dinner. On his second attempt, even having "seen a little our Manner," he made the toast to "Ladies, when only Mrs. Carter was in attendance" (Fithian, *Journal,* 138 [September 12, 1774]).

40. Edward Warren, *The Life of John Collins Warren, Md.,* 2 vols. (Boston: Ticknor and Fields, 1860), 1:14.

41. Thomas Murdoch to Pierce Butler, October 18, 1800, Newton & Gordon Letterbooks; Spence, Leacock, & Spence to John Erskine, June 26, 1762, and John Leacock to William Leacock, May 10, 1796, Leacock Papers. On colors appropriate for the London market, where "high coloured wines will never please," see March 12, 1774, Liverpool University Archives; for the Glasgow market, where "high coloured wines ... were [also] not so salable," see Andrew Ramsay to Newton & Gordon, September 24, 1759, Cossart & Gordon Papers—Loose Papers, Madeira Wine Company; and for the New York and New England market, see John and William Gordon to Robert Lenox, October 11, 1805, Newton & Gordon Letterbooks, Cossart Collection. Also see Henry Laurens to Corsley Rogers & Son, May 16, 1755, in *Papers of Henry Laurens,* 1:248; Thomas Newton to Newton & Gordon, November 26, 1759, Thomas Newton Letterbook, Madeira Wine Company Archives; and Baynton & Wharton to Thomas Newton, October 2, 1763, box 2, Cossart Gordon Papers, Liverpool University Archives.

42. On packaging the casks, see Newton & Gordon to Evans, Offley & Sealy, September 23, 1797, Newton & Gordon Letterbooks, vol. 18, fol. 80. On choosing correct glassware, see Leacock & Sons Letterbook 1797–97, fol. 6, where Leacock suggests "small glass tumblers which hold half a pint & a quarter pint" that were "fit for seeing wine." Wine glasses had become as much instruments for viewing wine and all its characteristics as receptacles for holding alcohol. "Drinking glasses for Madeira wine" by the end of the century had to be "decent." Such was the kind that Thomas Murdoch probably ordered from England for his own house on the island where he lectured houseguests on the art of holding, viewing, tasting, and describing Madeira wine. Until glass manufacturers began producing specially made Madeira glasses in the third quarter of the nineteenth century, Madeira drinkers probably used small glasses or cordial glasses—ideally, "low, heavy glasses" designed "to hold as little as possible"—one-third or two-thirds the volume of a common wine glass. See Newton & Gordon to Johnston & Jolly, December 18, 1767, Newton & Gordon Letterbooks, vol. 4, fol. 67.

43. Newton & Gordon to William Mitchell, May 4 and June 4, 1792, Newton & Gordon Letterbooks, vol. 14, fols. 180, 224. A similar fining recipe (according to "the Lisbon way") calling for more egg white was previously propounded by James Jenks in *The Complete Cook* (London: E. and C. Dilly, 1768), 322. On various methods of fining employed,

see Paul V. Thompson and Dorothy J. Thompson, eds., *The Account Books of Jonathan Swift* (Newark: University of Delaware Press, 1984), 191 (1718: eggs); Aaron Hill, *The Works of the Late Aaron Hill, Esq.,* 2nd ed., 4 vols. (London, 1754), 2:103 (1740: gesso or lime); *The Annual Register,* vol. 2 (1759), 383; Temple Henry Crocker, *The Complete Dictionary of Arts and Sciences,* vol. 2 (London, 1764–66) (sub. "wine"; 1765: isinglass); Francis Norton Mason, ed., *John Norton & Sons, Merchants of London and Virginia* (Richmond, Va.: Dietz Press, 1937), 191. In ancient times, noted Dr. James Hardy, lead, gypsum, and arsenic were used as fining agents; see Hardy, *A Candid Examination of What Has Been Advanced on the Colic of Poitou and Devonshire* (London: W. Mackintosh, 1778), 83. As early as 1669 Dr. Walter Charleton held up the Spanish practice of adding gesso as admirable; see Charleton, *Of the Mysterie of Vintners* (London, 1669), 203. By 1800 more writers on wine were detailing the art of fining; see C. H. Kauffman, *The Dictionary of Merchandise & Nomenclature* (Philadelphia: James Humphreys, 1805), 363–64; William Gourlay, *Observations on the Natural History, Climate, and Diseases of Madeira, during a Period of Eighteen Years* (London: J. Callow, 1811), 18.

44. Newton & Gordon to John Gibbes, May 29, 1802, Newton & Gordon Letterbooks, vol. 23, fol. 312; Newton & Gordon to Joseph S. Lewis, April 18, 1804, vol. 25, fol. 387, Newton & Gordon Letterbooks.

45. John Croft, *A Treatise on the Wines of Portugal,* 2nd ed. (York, 1780), 24, 283; Wright, *Essay on Wines,* 34; McBride, *General Instructions for the Choice of Wines and Spirituous Liquors* (London, 1793), 22–46.

46. Charles Wolley, *A Two Years' Journal in New York and Part of Its Territories in America* (Cleveland, 1902), 65–66, 68; *Virginia Magazine of History and Biography* 32 (1735): 328; Thomas Hancock to Harris & Crisp, August 23, 1750, Thomas Hancock Letterbook 1750–62, Hancock Papers, Harvard Business School; Leonard W. Labaree, ed., *The Papers of Benjamin Franklin,* 36 vols. (New Haven, 1959–), 8:120 (Mary Fisher to Benjamin Franklin, August 14, 1758), 14:309–10 (Thomas Livezey to Benjamin Franklin, November 18, 1767), 20:328 (Benjamin Franklin to William Franklin, July 25, 1773); Frederick Smyth to Aaron Lopez and Jacob Rivera, January 8, 1773, Aaron Lopez Papers, box 14, fol. 10, Collections of the American Jewish Historical Society, Waltham, Mass.; Thomas Everard to John Norton, September 25, 1772, in Mason, *John Norton & Sons,* 276; Thomas Jefferson to William Small, May 7, 1775, in Julian P. Boyd, ed., *The Papers of Thomas Jefferson,* 39 volumes to date (Princeton, N.J.: Princeton University Press, 1950–), 1:165; Marquis de Chastellux, *Travels in North America in the Years 1780, 1781 and 1782,* vol. 1 (Chapel Hill: University of North Carolina Press, 1963), 153 (December 7, 1780); John Marsden Pintard to Elias Boudinot, April 3, 1783, Boudinot Correspondence, fol. 41, American Bible Society, New York City; Anne Grant, *Memoirs of an American Lady,* vol. 1 (New York: Dodd, Mead, 1901), 272.

47. *Boston Weekly News-Letter,* October 11, 1750; *Pennsylvania Gazette,* June 12, 1781.

48. Russell R. Menard, "British Migration to the Chesapeake Colonies in the Seventeenth Century," in *Colonial Chesapeake Society,* ed. Lois G. Carr et al. (Chapel Hill: University of North Carolina Press, 1988), 99–132; David Galenson, *White Servitude in Colonial America* (Cambridge: Cambridge University Press, 1981); James Horn, *Adapting to a New World: English Society in the Seventeenth Century Chesapeake* (Chapel Hill: University of North Carolina Press, 1994); David H. Fischer, *Albion's Seed: Four British Folkways in America* (New York: Oxford University Press, 1989); Stephen S. Webb, *The*

Governors-General: The English Army and the Definition of the Empire, 1569–1681 (Chapel Hill: University of North Carolina Press, 1979); Alison Olson, *Making the Empire Work: London and American Interest Groups, 1690–1790* (Cambridge: Harvard University Press, 1991); James A. Henretta, *"Salutary Neglect": Colonial Administration under the Duke of Newcastle* (Princeton, N.J.: Princeton University Press, 1972); Thomas C. Barrow, *Trade and Empire: The British Customs Service in Colonial America, 1660–1775* (Cambridge: Harvard University Press, 1967). In the area of culture and consumption, see Timothy H. Breen, "An Empire of Goods: The Anglicization of Colonial America, 1690–1776," *Journal of British Studies* 25 (October 1986): 467–99; Timothy H. Breen, "'Baubles of Britain': The American and Consumer Revolutions of the Eighteenth Century," *Past and Present*, no. 119 (May 1988): 73–104; and the summary by Cary Carson titled "The Consumer Revolution in Colonial British America: Why Demand?" in *Of Consuming Interests: The Style of Life in the Eighteenth Century,* ed. Cary Carson et al. (Charlottesville: University Press of Virginia, 1994), 483–697. On connections between Britain and America, see Richard L. Bushman, "American High-Style and Vernacular Cultures," in *Colonial British America*, ed. J. P. Greene and J. R. Pole (Baltimore: Johns Hopkins University Press, 1984), 366, who argues that "cultural evolution in England and America" was "a single integrated process."

49. Recent works similarly question the Anglicized orientation of British America. See George F. Jones, *The Salzburger Saga: Religious Exiles and Other Germans along the Savannah* (Athens: University of Georgia Press, 1984); Mack Walker, *The Salzburg Transaction: Expulsion and Redemption in Eighteenth-Century Germany* (Ithaca: Cornell University Press, 1992); A. G. Roeber, *Palatines, Liberty and Property: German Lutherans* (Baltimore: Johns Hopkins University Press, 1993); Rosalind Beiler, "The Transatlantic World of Caspar Wistar: From Germany to America in the Eighteenth Century" (Ph.D. diss., University of Pennsylvania, 1994).

Cloth and the Emergence of the Atlantic Economy

Robert S. DuPlessis

The growth of the Atlantic economy should be one of the great themes of early modern history. But the actual emergence and precise contours of that economy are difficult to discern. The data that reveal the increasing dynamism and commercial importance of the Atlantic basin were generated within empires constituted by and centered on European metropoles,[1] and up to the present, scholarship has largely remained within and mirrored those imperial boundaries. As a result, it is difficult to discern when (if at all) and the extent to which *an* economy rather than an aggregate of economies formed in the Atlantic basin. Is it, in fact, correct to speak of an Atlantic economy, or should we refer to the English imperial Atlantic economy, the French Atlantic economy, the Dutch, and so forth?

One way to try to answer this question is to look at goods consumed within the Atlantic world. If an Atlantic economy was coming into existence, we would expect that the process of material standardization that Timothy Breen has proposed for eighteenth-century British North America would obtain more widely.[2] Is that what happened? Did European expansion issue in common Atlantic consumption patterns? Or was the fact that New World colonies were established by distinct European nations reflected in diverse colonial or imperial material cultures?

The Atlantic—even just the North Atlantic—covers a large space, and even in the early modern period the commodity flows were substantial. So in order to get a handle on them, and on the larger issue, this chapter concentrates on imported cloth in four cities in continental British and French North America and their more and less distant market areas, together with brief comparisons with England and France. It employs primary data bearing on (and for the most part still housed in) Montreal, Philadelphia, Charleston, and New Orleans and their commercial hinterlands. Each of these cities was a leading center in its empire and its region, trading with Native Americans, African Americans, and European Americans alike to export staples and supply necessary imports.

This essay encompasses the period from the late seventeenth century to the 1760s/70s, a time when, scholars hold, the most rapid and major changes in consumption occurred, adding up, in some accounts, to a consumer revolution.[3] The analysis focuses on two periods: as early as adequate documentation first becomes available and as close as possible to the end of the original colonial regimes. For Montreal and Philadelphia, the initial data come from the 1680s and 1690s, and the later information from the early 1770s; for Charleston and New Orleans, from the early 1730s and the 1760s. Hence the inquiry brackets the 1740s and 1750s, the time when colonial habits of consumption are said to have most significantly changed.[4]

For several reasons the study focuses on textiles imported into the New World. For one thing, they were the largest single category of consumer items—and usually the most valuable—sent to the colonies, and their share of trade was growing.[5] For another, as major items of consumption among all segments of the populace, irrespective of age, gender, ethnic group, locality, or occupation, cloth and the clothing and furnishings fashioned from it constituted the second biggest item, after food, in household budgets.[6] Textiles, including cloth garments, were likewise major components of colonists' trade with Native Americans.[7] As a result, consumption of imported cloth should reveal important information about the constitution and composition of whatever Atlantic consumer economy came into being.[8]

This chapter is based on a variety of sources, among the most important of which are the detailed lists of merchandise included in probate (postmortem) inventories of merchants.[9] These documents are particularly valuable because few merchant accounts or similar records survive from this period. Inventories, of course, record possessions at death; they do not register sales over the decedents' mercantile careers. Still, merchants who stayed in business during their lifetimes, as those presented here did (I have avoided bankruptcy inventories), must have been reasonably well attuned to their markets and therefore possessed inventories representing actual consumption fairly well.[10] Although it would be preferable to study both the quantities (yardage or ellage) and the values of the cloth, the sources only permit calculations based on value. Admittedly, this focus tends to minimize the significance of less expensive textiles, many of them linens, while overstating that of more costly fabrics such as woolens and silks. But if we thereby gain a somewhat distorted sense of the volume of the various textiles that were in circulation, focusing on values does indicate the manner in which consumers allocated their expenditures among the various types of textiles.

Patterns of Textile Consumption

What kinds of cloth, then, did North Americans acquire? How similar were their purchases within and between empires? To what extent did social characteristics (for example, ethnicity, gender) affect their textile possessions? Did their consumption patterns shift over time? Table 8 presents a first approximation of the situation obtaining during the late seventeenth and early eighteenth centuries.

Table 8: Textile values in early Montreal, Philadelphia, Charleston, and New Orleans areas* by type of cloth

(values as percentage of total merchant textile stocks)**
n=number of merchant inventories

Type of cloth	Montreal (n=12)	Philadelphia (n=9)	Charleston (n=19)	New Orleans (n=6)
Linens	19	44	27	57
Woolens	67	38	57	15
Cottons	3	4	8	23
Mixed	5	5	2	0
Silks	5	3	5	2

*Montreal and Philadelphia = 1680s–90s; Charleston and New Orleans = 1730s
**Textiles insufficiently described to classify constituted the remainder.

Sources: Archives nationales du Québec à Montréal (henceforth ANQM), all notaries operating in 1680s–90s; the collections of Philadelphia-area inventories, 1680–99, at the Historical Society of Pennsylvania, Philadelphia, and the Chester County Archives and Record Services (henceforth CCA), West Chester, Pennsylvania; Charleston County, South Carolina, Wills and Miscellaneous Records, vols. 62–65 (1730s); Louisiana Historical Center (henceforth LHC), French Superior Council Records (henceforth FSC), Inventories, 1730–39; New Orleans Notarial Archives Research Center, New Orleans (henceforth NONA), Inventories.

Table 8 suggests that each region had a fairly distinctive textile consumption profile in its early years.[11] Individual inventories and contemporary comments alike imply that climate had something to do with the differences. For example, New France's harsh weather encouraged purchases of woolens, notably among groups that were most exposed to the rigors of long, bitterly cold winters,[12] whereas hot summers made thinner fabrics attractive in Pennsylvania.[13] Yet this explanation seems less convincing when we look at Charleston and New Orleans. Merchant inventories from South Carolina are heavily weighted toward woolen fabrics, whereas those from Louisiana were just as heavily tilted toward linens. Equally striking is the stark opposition between the two cities with respect to cotton textiles. These contrasts existed, moreover, despite climates that had much more in common than either had with Philadelphia, much less Montreal. What, then, better explains the diversity among the selections available in merchant shops?

A closer look at the inventories from 1730s Charleston together with additional documentation from 1730s New Orleans allows us to begin to answer this question. Table 9 indicates that people living in and around Charleston had strongly different demand preferences than those buying cloth on the frontier. In fact, the overall proportions derived from the inventories of urban Charleston merchants in the 1730s (table 9, column 3) look a lot like those derived from contemporary inventories of Louisiana merchants (reported in table 8, column 5), all of whom lived in New Orleans. Further clarification results when we consult fresh sources for Louisiana to supplement the urban merchant inventories. Table 10 reveals considerable divergence in the textile market in and around New Orleans (column 2, reproduced from table 8, column 5) as compared to those obtaining more widely over backwoods Louisiana and on into Illinois and other inland areas, which can be discerned from columns 3 and 4. Probably the best indicator of frontier demand is column 4, and it resembles nothing so much as table 9, column 4, the South Carolina frontier traders.

Taken together, tables 9 and 10 indicate that textile demand already displayed some similarities across imperial frontiers in the early eighteenth century. On the one hand, consumption in the southern borderlands of both British and French colonial North America was strongly oriented toward woolens.[14] Who were the consumers in these areas? Many, if not most, were Native Americans,[15] who swapped furs for heavy and durable woolens such as stroud (French *écarlatine*), limbourg, melton (French *molton*), broadcloth, halfthicks, or duffel (duffil).[16] On the other hand, both the Charleston and the New Orleans urban zones show a more varied textile consumption, with a marked taste for lighter linens and cottons and rather less for woolens.

These patterns appear, moreover, to have prevailed more widely over British and French North America. Although the Montreal data cannot adequately be disaggregated, the fact that nearly all the late-seventeenth-century merchants inventoried in that city participated substantially in trade with Amerindians—usually by outfitting coureurs de bois and voyageurs who traveled to the West—is likely to have contributed significantly to the pronounced bias for woolens displayed in table 8, column 2.[17] Individual inventories indicate, furthermore, that colonists who lived in Montreal opted for linen garments much more often than farmers and rural artisans did.[18] Again, the fact that Philadelphia's late-seventeenth-century merchants played only a minor role in frontier commerce, focusing instead on the settler population, probably helps explain why woolens bulked less large in that area's textile profile (table 8, column 3), which looks more like that reported for the more urban-oriented merchants in South Carolina and Louisiana (table 9, column 3, and table 10, column 2).

Unfree colonists—slaves—also significantly and similarly affected merchant stocks and inventories in both the Charleston and New Orleans regions.[19] Slaves' consumption is difficult to discern from the merchant data because no shopkeepers or traders specialized in trade with slaves, most of whose textiles were purchased by their owners. However, two-fifths of all the woolens sold by Rasteau in New Orleans in 1736–37 (table 10, column 3) consisted of *étoffe à Nègre*, a cheap fabric specifically designed for slave clothing; it is entirely absent from both the fur traders' invoices and merchant inventories.[20] Again, nearly a third of the linens he sold comprised cheap Halle and brin (a plain-wevae strong linen, made of hemp), varieties also largely intended for slaves. No documents of this

Table 9: Cloth values in 1730s South Carolina by type of business
(values as percentage of total merchant cloth stocks)*
n = number of merchant inventories

(1) Type of cloth	(2) All merchants (n=19)	(3) Charleston (urban) merchants (n=12)	(4) Frontier traders (n=7)
Linens	27	52	5
Woolens	57	20	92
Cottons	8	14	3
Mixed	2	3	0
Silks	5	11	0

* Textiles insufficiently described to classify constituted the remainder.
 Sources: Charleston County, S.C., Wills and Miscellaneous Records, vols. 62–65, merchant inventories from 1730 to 1739.

Table 10: Three views of cloth consumption in 1730s Louisiana
(values as percentage of total cloth stocks or sales)*
n = number of merchant inventories, accounts, or invoices

(1) Type of cloth	(2) All merchants (n=6)	(3) Store Accounts (n=1)	(4) Frontier traders (n=5)
Linens	57	39	12
Woolens	15	31	80
Cottons	23	25	6
Mixed	0	0	2
Silks	2	3	0

*Textiles insufficiently described to classify constituted the remainder.
 Sources: LHC, FSC, docs. 1730011601, 1730033002, 1737041801, 1738012101, 1739092503; NONA, September 14, 1735; accounts from Paul Rasteau's store, October 2, 1736–October 2, 1737; LHC, FSC, doc. 1737100201 (this business sold both retail and wholesale, outfitting residents of New Orleans, planters in the vicinity, and traders to the Illinois Indians); LHC, FSC, docs. 1737081405, 1737081501, 1739031002 (two invoices), 1739070701.

type have survived for early South Carolina, but about one-fifth of the woolens in merchant inventories were "plains," an inexpensive flannel-like woolen that many owners bought for slaves; duffel, used for slave as well as Amerindian blankets, comprised another two-fifths. Nearly 30 percent of linens enumerated were osnaburgs (or osnabrig, a cheap, coarse, unbleached linen, used especially for shirts and shifts), likewise destined largely for slave clothing.[21] Indeed, with their heavy orientation to woolens together with a notable minority of linens, textile expenditure patterns for African American slaves in the 1730s resemble nothing so much as the Native American markets in both French and British North American colonies, although the particular types of woolens and linens consumed by each group only partially overlapped.

No later than the 1730s, then, colonial British and French textile cultures displayed a good degree of similarity across imperial boundaries. This was true even though the garments specific to each group, and some of the varieties of cloth each used, differed as a function of their dissimilar social ecologies. The free settler population enjoyed access to the greatest variety of fabrics, and Native Americans and African Americans had rather less.[22] Already before the postulated mid-century "consumer revolution," in other words, a process of consumption standardization by broad social groups was well under way in continental North America. The variety depicted in early merchant inventories thus mainly reflected the disparate weight of different groups in each area's trade, which in turn expressed to some degree the distinct social composition of each colony, rather than any broad differences among empires as such.

Over time, standardization both extended its reach and fragmented. Even without distinguishing among submarkets or distinctive categories of consumers, table 11 shows an increasing resemblance, by the end of the colonial regimes, among *all* the areas' cloth cultures in terms of the three major kinds of fabrics. (As before, Charleston and New Orleans and their respective commercial zones exhibit the strongest deviation from the norm, but now with respect to only one textile category.) The conspicuous popularity of cottons (including calicoes) and the waning of demand for woolens were equally striking manifestations of this consumption convergence. In merchant stocks, at least, a continental North American model that largely ignored political and social boundaries both between the British and French empires and between colonies within the same empire had become evident by the 1760s and 1770s. Following Louisiana's precocious lead, the consumption of cotton fabrics had increased so impressively in every colony (even Charleston showed nearly a doubling in just three decades) that it does not seem fanciful to speak of a "cotton revolution" of the mid-eighteenth century. What explains this growing congruence?

Part of the reason may lie with changing Native American tastes. Already in the 1730s and 1740s cottons (including calicoes) accounted for perhaps 15 percent of the value of the cargoes that Montreal merchants sent to the Illinois Indians

Table 11: Cloth values in late Montreal, Philadelphia, Charleston, and New Orleans areas* by type of cloth
(values as percentage of total merchant cloth stocks)**
n=number of merchant inventories

(1) Type of cloth	(2) Montreal (n=8)	(3) Philadelphia (n=8)	(4) Charleston (n=18)	(5) New Orleans (n=7)
Linens	24	31	39	44
Woolens	33	25	33	11
Cottons	30	31	14	33
Mixed	4	5	8	9
Silks	4	7	3	3

*Montreal and Philadelphia = 1770–74; Charleston and New Orleans = 1760s
**Textiles insufficiently described to classify constituted the remainder.

Sources: ANQM, all notaries operating in 1770–74; the 1770–74 merchant inventories in the collections of Philadelphia-area inventories at the CCA and (on microfilm) the Winterthur Library, Wilmington, Delaware; the 1774 wills printed in Alice Hanson Jones, *American Colonial Wealth: Documents and Methods,* vol. 3 (New York, 1977); Charleston County, S.C., Wills and Miscellaneous Records, vols. 68, 71; LHC, FSC, Inventories, 1760–69; NONA, Inventories; Natchitoches Parish Court House, Louisiana, Conveyance Record Book 1 (microfilm copy).

(who lived southwest of the Great Lakes) and to the Green Bay, Rainy Lake, and Michilimackinac fur-trade posts around the northern Great Lakes; woolens were some 55 percent and linens about 30 percent.[23] In 1758, when the last cargoes of the French era went out to the Detroit post, linens made up 47 percent of the consignments, woolens 27 percent, and cottons and calicoes just under 25 percent.[24]

Evidence from Philadelphia's increasingly vigorous commerce with Native Americans indicates less change, however.[25] In the mid-1750s the value of cloth and clothing held by western Pennsylvania Indian traders included 73 percent woolens, 25 percent linens, and just 1 percent cottons.[26] Again, gifts of fabrics and garments presented by "The Friendly Association for Regaining & Preserving Peace with the Indians by Pacific Means" in 1761 comprised (by value) 84 percent woolens and 15 percent linens, while the nearly contemporaneous "List of a Large Assortment of Indian Goods suitable at this time at Pittsburg Nov 24th 1761" showed the clear dominance of woolens (forty-eight bales of stroud, halfthicks, and blankets), as against ninety-five pieces of linen, thirty pieces of the "brightest" calico, and six dozen silk handkerchiefs.[27] Two years later Indian trade goods at the Susquehanna Valley frontier post of Fort Augusta included (by value) 78 percent woolens, 10 percent linens, and 12 percent cottons and calicoes, the latter representing the high point of cottons' market penetration among Amerindians in the colonial Pennsylvania borderlands.[28] South Carolina sources suggest much the same pattern, for among the gifts presented to Indians by the South Carolina provincial government in the spring of 1758 were (by value) about 70 percent woolen fabrics, blankets, and garments; some 20 percent linens (many in the form of shirts); and about 10 percent cottons and calicoes.[29]

While open to new varieties of fabrics, then, Amerindians continued to opt for woolens at a rate above that of the North American population as a whole.[30] No matter what their preferences, however, by the 1760s and early 1770s Native American consumers were much less important to the textile market than earlier. Both absolutely and relatively, Amerindians formed a decreasing part of the North American population across most of the eighteenth century.[31] Given Indians' preference for woolens, there can be little doubt that their declining weight in the market, even more than the partial diversification of their tastes, explains some of the waning of demand for woolens registered in table 11. Little wonder that even at Camden, in the South Carolina backcountry, stroud and duffel accounted for less than 15 percent of Ely Kershaw's woolen fabric sales in the years around 1770.[32]

Not all of woolens' decline can be attributed to alterations in the Amerindian market, however. Important changes occurred among settlers, and given the dramatic growth in their numbers,[33] their tastes had the largest impact on the relative fortunes of specific types of fabric.[34] Among free colonists, to begin with, the personal and domestic uses of linens and particularly cottons had expanded dramatically by the 1760s–70s. Little mentioned in the late seventeenth century, save for kerchiefs and cravats as well as an occasional shirt, blouse, or curtain, by the early 1770s cottons had been transformed from novelties to widely and regularly employed everyday products. Skirts, vests, jackets, breeches, gowns, shirts, and blouses were all tailored from cottons and calicoes (as well as from linens). Strikingly, in light of the continuing rigors of winter in New France, in Montreal cloaks and capes (especially those worn by women) and even the occasional greatcoat, all previously the exclusive preserve of woolens, were now more likely to be fashioned from cottons.[35] Concomitantly, as the inventories of individuals in Montreal and New Orleans disclose, woolens lost ground among nearly all groups of settlers.

Of great consequence, too, were transformations taking place in the dwellings of European Americans, who during the eighteenth century came to enjoy a higher level of domestic comfort than their pioneer ancestors had. Because they set fancier tables, put hangings over their larger and more abundant windows, cleaned themselves and their quarters more adequately, and slept in less vermin-infested beds, they used greater amounts of linens and cottons for napkins, tablecloths, curtains, towels, sheets, and pillow covers. Conversely, woolens were rarely employed for such purposes; bed curtains and blankets formed the main exceptions, but even for those purposes woolens could claim no monopoly. Thus woolens benefited little from the growing consumption of cloth to enhance both the body and the household environment of European Americans.[36]

Clothing slaves also affected textile consumption patterns in the southern colonies, but in quite discrepant ways. In South Carolina, where the slave population increased dramatically in both absolute and relative terms,[37] owners' preferences slowed the shift away from woolens and linens. In 1760–65 woolens accounted for 43 percent of the textiles sold by the Charleston merchant James Poyas, who counted planters among his leading customers, and 60 percent of the woolens were plains.[38] Other woolens—mainly flannel, Russian "drab," and occasionally stroud—were also used for slave garments, and duffel continued to be favored for slave blankets, but all evidence shows the overwhelming predominance of plains for caps, jackets, and breeches.[39] The annual summertime destruction of woolens by moths, frequently alluded to in merchant letters,[40] assured that demand would remain vigorous year in and year out. The increase in Charleston merchant holdings of linens can likewise probably be traced to the rising South Carolina slave population since plantation owners maintained their partiality for osnaburg and similar varieties of cheap linen.[41]

Although I have found no contemporaneous account books there, Louisiana inventories indicate that, contrary to South Carolina, slaves in the French colony wore few woolens by the 1760s.[42] Instead, Louisiana slaves dressed largely in cheap kinds of linen as well as in "couty" and "siamoise" (cotton or cotton-linen mixtures).[43] Why the two colonies clothed their slaves so differently is not clear. Price does not seem to have been crucial, for in South Carolina as in Louisiana planters chose inexpensive fabrics. Perhaps the secret lay in supply rather than demand. Were French woolens manufacturers unable not only to satisfy Native American consumers but also to develop a cheap light woolen adequate for clothing slave populations? Or, to look at the issue from another perspective, were British cotton manufacturers unable to come up with viable substitutes for the woolens that were destined to be eaten ragged each summer in the low country?

An Atlantic World of Goods

The rising North American partiality for cottons and calicoes, and the withdrawal of custom from woolens, was part of a wave breaking on both sides of the Atlantic. Studies of England by Lemire and of France by Roche have established that cottons captured comparably large shares of the market in those countries as well, as "ordinary, everyday people" (in Lemire's words) began to use them.[44] Based on detailed analysis of Parisians' clothing, in fact, it appears plausible to speak of an eighteenth-century "cotton revolution." Whereas in 1700 cotton was the least important garment fabric for all social groups from servant to noble, by

1789 it had become the leading one for all save aristocrats, *officiers,* and professionals.[45] In light of this consumption convergence, not only might we extend across imperial borders Breen's thesis about the growing standardization of colonial consumer goods,[46] but we might also speak of an Atlantic world of goods that extended from London to Louisiana, Paris to Pennsylvania.

The process of textile standardization did not occur uniformly, however. First, some regional variation continued. Besides the prominent Charleston–New Orleans contrast, table 11 indicates a positive north-south gradient with respect to linens and the absence of a similar slope among cottons. Taken together, these figures reveal the interweaving of price and bondage since linens were considerably cheaper light fabrics than cottons, which free colonists increasingly favored. Second, what looks like a notable transatlantic difference developed—although, after other parts of Europe are studied, it may turn out to be a distinction between metropolitan capitals and hinterlands on both sides of the Atlantic. For not only was the most popular garment fabric of the late eighteenth-century Parisian elite silk (it made up a third or more of their clothing), but even the armoires of wage earners and domestic servants, at the bottom of the Paris hierarchy, boasted 12–15 percent silk items.[47]

The data presented in this essay indicate that no North American merchant stocked or sold anywhere near as many silk textiles. Individual inventories tell a similar, yet slightly nuanced story. In and around Montreal (where the documentation is most complete), the overall proportion of silk garments did not increase from the late seventeenth century to the early 1770s (it rose from 4 to 5 percent of the total, a change that is not statistically significant). But silk expanded its clientele socially. People of middling wealth began to display more silk kerchiefs, cravats, and other accessories—the kinds of silk items of which their homologues would have had just one, if that, in the late seventeenth century—and by the 1770s most of them had also acquired a few basic silk garments such as jackets or skirts for their wardrobes. Indeed, even some of the poorer Canadian colonists, including one of every two artisans and farmers, could sport an item made from a cheaper grade of silken fabric.[48] Thus in New France, as in France, silk garments remained disproportionately represented in the dress of the well-to-do, while losing their status as markers of social exclusivity. Yet in the colonies they were unable to lay claim to anything resembling the high proportion of total clothing expenditures found in the metropole.

In short, cloth served not only to integrate but also to separate the North Atlantic. And silk was not the only fabric that defined social and spatial divisions. Even the cotton revolution had its active and passive citizens. Thus whereas Louisiana planters clothed themselves and their families in the more expensive grades of linens, cottons, and calicoes, they dressed their slaves largely in cheap types. In South Carolina slaves do not appear to have received much of even low-cost varieties of cottons or cotton-linens, although checked cottons and calicoes were included in the list of fabrics to which slave clothing was restricted after 1735.[49] Nevertheless, there too slaves came to wear garments fashioned of a distinctive textile, plains or Negro cloth. In the early eighteenth century these were commonly conferred on Amerindians and bought by poorer farmers, but by the 1760s, although still listed in one frontier price list, they seem no longer to have been given as presents to Native Americans nor purchased by free colonists.[50] By that point advertisements for runaway slaves in the *South Carolina Gazette* suggest that many slaves wore virtually a uniform consisting of plains trousers and jackets together with osnaburg shirts.[51] And—again parallel to Louisiana—their masters fancied expensive woolens.[52]

Specific types of textiles played a more complicated role in distinguishing Amerindians from colonists than in setting off slave from free.[53] Admittedly, both stroud and what the French called "trade" linen and the English "garlix" were expressly intended for Indians. Yet South Carolina slaves, at least, also wore stroud and could, under the terms of the 1735 law, have had garlix garments, and settlers bought tidy amounts of garlix for themselves. Similarly, Native Americans purchased linens not specifically aimed at their custom, and they were given or otherwise acquired many if not most of the same fabrics as their European American neighbors in both the French and the British colonial backcountry. Even expensive "holland" linen, destined mainly for colonists, was regularly distributed in presents to Native American leaders. Still, it seems clear that woolens and linens remained more prominent on the bodies of Native Americans than on those of European Americans; in that important way African and African American slaves resembled Native Americans more than they did European Americans. And although not unchanging, the textile markets oriented to Amerindians and slaves did prove the most stable across the eighteenth century.

Finally, certain categories of textiles acquired something of a gender identification. Evidence from individual inventories shows that by the 1760s and 1770s women in Montreal and Louisiana owned three to four times as many cotton garments as men did; in contrast, woolen clothing was male by a ratio of two or three to one on the banks of the Mississippi and the St. Lawrence. These ratios have much to do with garments specific to each gender as well as with their distinctive occupations. But the gendered nature of cotton cloth does not seem to have been limited to French colonies nor only to European Americans. The detailed barter and gift lists that South Carolina officials drew up when dealing with Native Americans mention calico only in relation to Amerindian women.[54] In short, while many groups had some form of access to an increasingly homogeneous Atlantic world of goods, levels of actual participation varied considerably, particularly along lines of ethnicity, status, and gender.

These distinctions are not just a matter of historical typology; they actively shaped aspiration and action, as the story of a Louisiana slave girl exemplifies. In early October 1765 the eleven-year-old Babete, who declared herself "catholic and apostolic and roman, a creole of this town" of New Orleans, found herself working for the city's jailer and his wife, to whom she had been leased by her owner. Yielding to temptation one day, Babete took "some piastres" from "a chest that she found open, that is, not locked," then set off with another slave woman to make the rounds of shops and hawkers. Although she bought some candies and a cheap gold ring, most of Babete's funds (including the paper piastre she received in change after one of her purchases) went toward two ells of expensive cotton that she turned into a skirt, four ells of *indienne* or printed calico (out of which she fashioned another skirt), a *casaquin* (a short overjacket of unspecified fabric), a silk kerchief, and a blue kerchief (probably of linen). She also tried to buy some red linen (again for a skirt), but the merchant she asked had none in stock.[55]

The documents that contain the interrogations of Babete and the men and women who sold goods to her in flagrant violation of the *Code Noir* are as rich as they are rare. They provide fascinating glimpses into the actual workings of the slave system: some of the sellers admitted to knowing about the *Code Noir's* prohibition, but all, for one reason or another, felt justified in contravening it; and apparently no one doubted that even a young slave could have been given money, as she claimed, to make purchases for her mistress (in fact, most sellers did not even bother to ask Babete where she had gotten her cash). The court records also instruct about the formal and informal sites of consumption and the broad range of participants in trade: Babete's sources included a shoemaker's wife, a drummer in the New Orleans garrison, a soldier in M. Duplessy's company, another woman, and just two individuals who identified themselves as merchants, one of whom was better known as a ship's captain. What needs most to be underlined in this context, however, is that the fabrics Babete bought were commonly found in New Orleans but were more expensive than those that masters typically distributed to slaves. Her purchases thus represented a bold attempt to surmount the boundaries imposed on her by the normal cloth culture, a bid to participate more fully in a common North Atlantic world of cloth and clothing. But because Babete could hope to buy them only thanks to stolen funds, her acquisitions also demonstrate just how effectively—and how frustratingly—those boundaries ordinarily operated.

Babete's story likewise points once again to limits on the process of Atlantic standardization. The "shared language of consumption" that Breen postulates was not the only tongue being spoken in the early modern North Atlantic world, and there seems to be some justice in Richard Bushman's argument that eighteenth-century clothing patterns reinforced the traditional hierarchy.[56] As a result of simultaneously convergent and contrary developments a normalizing Atlantic consumer economy and distinctive consumer subeconomies founded on region, status, wealth, and gender emerged hand in hand during the eighteenth century.[57]

Appendix: The significance of textiles to English and French Atlantic trade during the eighteenth century

A. English textile exports and re-exports*
(amounts in £ sterling)

	1699–1701	1722–1724	1752–1754	1772–1774
Cloth exports only to Americas and West Africa	237,000	378,000	701,000	2,138,000
As percent of all cloth exports	7.54	12.17	15.99	40.07
Cloth re-exports only to Americas and West Africa**	216,000	384,000	409,000	580,000
As percent of all cloth re-exports	32.14	35.89	36.81	38.06
Cloth exports and re-exports to Americas and West Africa	453,000	762,000	1,110,000	2,718,000
As percent of all cloth exports and re-exports	11.87	18.24	20.20	39.62

*Calculated from Ralph Davis, "English Foreign Trade, 1700–74," *Economic History Review*, 2nd ser., 15 (1962–63): 302–3.
**Calicoes, silks and related textiles, linens.

B. The Place of Specific Textiles

About 1770, according to McCusker and Menard, "[a]round half of all English exports of . . . silk goods, printed cotton and linen goods, and flannels were shipped to colonial consumers. Between two-thirds and three-quarters of all exported English . . . linen and Spanish woolen goods went to British America."[1] According to their calculations, 79.2 percent of all linen exported from England went to British America. This was the highest proportion of twenty-seven items; calicoes (enumerated as printed cotton and linen), 58.9 percent of which ended up in the same destination, ranked sixth from the top.[2]

Although detailed figures are lacking, cloths also loomed large in France's Atlantic exports. John Clark's study of La Rochelle's commerce found that "[t]extile products composed the single most important category of trade goods to the West Indian and mainland colonies. . . . During the first half of the eighteenth century, textiles often exceeded one-half of total exports to Africa and the colonies."[3] Contemporaries were fully aware of the situation. In 1761 the Chamber of Commerce of Marseilles reported that Canada "consumes a great quantity . . . of woolens of every type [and] of linens." Thus the anticipated loss of the colony as a result of the Seven Years' War would be a harsh blow to the French textile industry, which furnished a large (but unknown) proportion of cloth exports.[4]

1. McCusker and Menard, *Economy of British America,* 286. See also Carole Shammas, *The Pre-Industrial Consumer in England and America* (Oxford: Clarendon Press, 1990), 67 (tab. 3.4).

2. McCusker and Menard, *Economy of British America,* 284 (tab. 13.2).

3. John Garretson Clark, *La Rochelle and the Atlantic Economy during the Eighteenth Century* (Baltimore: Johns Hopkins University Press, 1981), 112.

4. See "Réponse de la Chambre de Commerce de Marseille à Messieurs de La Rochelle touchant la conservation du Canada," December 21, 1761, in "Les Chambres de Commerce de France et la cession du Canada," *Rapport de l'archiviste de la province de Québec* 5 (1924–25): 205.

Notes

1. By the eighteenth century, the first era for which aggregate data exist, growth in Atlantic exports and imports far outstripped that of any other sector, at least for England and France. According to calculations based on the data in Ralph Davis, "English Foreign Trade, 1700–74," *Economic History Review,* 2nd ser., 15 (1962–63): 300–303, imports to England from the Americas and Africa increased 331 percent between 1699–1701 and 1772–74, and exports (including reexports) 505 percent (compared with overall growth of 118 and 144 percent, respectively). Imports from these areas were 19 percent of England's total in 1699–1701 and 39 percent in 1772–74; they took respectively 13 and 38 percent of exports and reexports (13 and 47 percent of manufactures). Calculations based on Paul Butel, *L'economie française au XVIIIe siècle* (Paris: Sedes, 1993), 88, show French imports from America and Africa (which started from a smaller base) rising 2741 percent between 1716 and 1772 and exports rising 1567 percent, as compared to overall increases of 680 and 624 percent, respectively. These areas' share of total French imports rose from 12 to 42 percent over the period; their share of total exports rose from 4 to 10 percent.

2. Timothy H. Breen, "An Empire of Goods: The Anglicization of Colonial America, 1690–1776," *Journal of British Studies* 25 (October 1986): 467–99; Timothy H. Breen, "'Baubles of Britain': The American and Consumer Revolutions of the Eighteenth Century," *Past and Present,* no. 119 (May 1988): 73–104.

3. The bibliography on this topic is large and rapidly growing. Only a few of the more important works can be cited: the classic statement by Neil McKendrick, "The Consumer Revolution of Eighteenth-Century England," in *The Birth of a Consumer Society: The Commercialization of Eighteenth-Century England,* ed. N. McKendrick, J. Brewer, and J. H. Plumb (Bloomington: Indiana University Press, 1982), 9–33, which links consumer and industrial revolutions; Breen, "Baubles of Britain," which connects consumer and political revolutions; and for a recent French overview more focused on changes in material culture and standards of living, Daniel Roche, *Histoire des choses banales* (Paris: Fayard, 1997), translated as *A History of Everyday Things: The Birth of Consumption in France, 1600–1800* (Cambridge: Cambridge University Press, 2000).

4. See Breen (n. 2) or Lois Carr and Lorena Walsh, "Changing Lifestyles and Consumer Behavior in the Colonial Chesapeake," in *Of Consuming Interests: The Style of Life in the Eighteenth Century,* ed. C. Carson, R. Hoffman, and P. Albert (Charlottesville: University Press of Virginia, 1994).

5. For the view from the perspective of exports, see the sources cited in the appendix and, more generally, Robert DuPlessis, *Transitions to Capitalism in Early Modern Europe* (Cambridge: Cambridge University Press, 1997). For the import perspective, see Louise Dechêne, *Habitants and Merchants in Seventeenth Century Montreal* (Montreal and Buffalo: McGill-Queen's University Press, 1992; trans. by Liana Vardi from *Habitants et merchands de Montréal au XVIIe siècle* [Paris: Plon, 1974]), on the basis of whose table 17 on p. 79 it can be calculated that cloth (and goods made of textiles) constituted 30 percent of merchant stocks in Montreal before 1664 and more than half between 1680 and 1720. As Dechêne summarizes (78), "[t]he principal import was finished fabrics."

6. Fabrics and garments formed "the second largest single expenditure on the people in the household" in late seventeenth- and eighteenth-century Britain, according to Lorna Weatherill, *Consumer Behavior and Material Culture in Britain 1660–1760* (London and

New York: Routledge, 1988), 119; see also 133 (table 6.4), where she quotes account books and contemporary estimates that place cloth and clothing expenses at 8–15 percent of annual budgets, with most figures at the upper end. Cf. Daniel Roche, *The Culture of Clothing: Dress and Fashion in the "Ancien Régime"* (Cambridge and New York: Cambridge University Press, 1994; trans. from *La culture des apparences* [Paris: Fayard, 1989]), chap. 5, although Roche discusses only garments as a proportion of total moveable wealth at death.

7. For two exemplary studies, see Kathryn E. Holland Braund, *Deerskins & Duffels: The Creek Indian Trade with Anglo-America, 1685–1815* (Lincoln: University of Nebraska Press, 1993), esp. 121–27; and Dean L. Anderson, "The Flow of European Trade Goods into the Western Great Lakes Region, 1715–1760," in *The Fur Trade Revisited: Selected Papers of the Sixth North American Fur Trade Conference* (East Lansing: Michigan State University Press, 1994), 93–115. Sales to Indian traders and Amerindians could loom large in the trade of individual merchants: for example, they represented three-quarters of the cloth and clothing transactions, and nearly half the total business, of the leading Montreal merchant Alexis Lemoine Monière in 1715–24, as calculated from Dechêne, *Habitants and Merchants,* 307 (graph 11).

8. Of course, textiles woven within the colonies, most often by professional weavers using thread spun by farm families, were also consumed, but they are only a peripheral concern of this chapter. On the one hand, they were rarely to be found in the merchant inventories on which this study is mainly based because for the most part buyers ordered them directly from weavers (the "bespoke" method). On the other hand, they formed a small part of overall consumption. In the British colonies this was partly because cloth making was hobbled by the Navigation Acts, which in good mercantilist fashion severely limited or outright forbade the manufacture of many items in the colonies in order to protect metropolitan producers. The effects of these laws should not be overestimated, however. They were flouted during periods when restive British colonists, decreeing nonimportation agreements to challenge taxes and other actions taken by the imperial government, turned to their own manufactures. More important, it would seem, colonists mainly chose to specialize in exportable foodstuffs and raw materials, for which prices generally rose across the eighteenth century, and to purchase mostly imported manufactures, for which prices were generally falling. As Carole Shammas and Adrienne Hood have shown, the myth of British American colonial self-sufficiency and reliance on domestically produced goods is just that—a myth; to the contrary, colonists were customers for external suppliers of consumer goods (Shammas, "How Self-Sufficient Was Early America?" *Journal of Interdisciplinary History* 13 [1982]: 247–72; Hood, "The Material World of Cloth: Production and Use in Eighteenth Century Rural Pennsylvania," *William and Mary Quarterly,* 3rd ser., 53 [1996]: 43–66). See also Mary Schweitzer, *Custom and Contract: Household, Government, and the Economy in Colonial Pennsylvania* (New York: Columbia University Press, 1987), 71–77, esp. 72 (table 2.7). French policy was, at least on its face, less opposed to colonial cloth production; in fact, various initiatives were sponsored or at least favored by colonial authorities (see Dechêne, *Habitants and Merchants,* 78–79). But no Canadian textile industry of any size ever got going during the French period. The extensive domestic production often thought characteristic of rural New France actually emerged in the late eighteenth and early nineteenth centuries; see

David-Thierry Ruddel, "Domestic Textile Production in Colonial Québec, 1608–1840," *Material History Bulletin* 31 (1990): 39–49. See also Robert DuPlessis, "Transatlantic Textiles: European Linens in the Cloth Culture of Colonial North America," in *The European Linen Industry in Historical Perspective,* ed. B. Collins and P. Ollerenshaw (Oxford: Oxford University Press, 2003), 123–37. The situation in the French colonies deserves more careful study, but I would suggest that a similar explanation to Shammas's and Hood's may account for the similar outcome. I cannot go into this issue here, but for relative agricultural and industrial prices that point in this direction, see Marc Egnal, *New World Economies: The Growth of the Thirteen Colonies and Early Canada* (New York: Oxford University Press, 1998), 154, 155 (figs. 9.11, 9.12).

9. Good introductions to probate inventories are provided by Lois Green Carr and Lorena S. Walsh, "Inventories and the Analysis of Wealth and Consumption Patterns in St. Mary's County, Maryland, 1658–1777," *Historical Methods* 13, no. 2 (Spring 1980): 81–104; A. van der Woude and A. Schuurman, eds., *Probate Inventories: A New Source for the Historical Study of Wealth, Material Culture and Agricultural Development* (Wageningen: Afdeling Agrarische Geschiednis, Landbouwhogeschool, 1980); and Peter Benes, ed., *Early American Probate Inventories* (Boston: Boston University Press, 1989). Below I also use information about clothing taken from the inventories of individuals in New France and Louisiana. As scholars have repeatedly noted, of course, probate inventories are a problematic source; for a discussion of why, for the study of garments, the advantages of individual inventories in the French (but not the British) colonies outweigh their (real and alleged) deficiencies, see Robert S. DuPlessis, "Was There a Consumer Revolution in Eighteenth-Century New France?" *French Colonial History* 1 (2002): 193–59.

10. The fact that the inventories used in this study come, in every area, from all times of the year minimizes the possibly distorting effects of seasonality.

11. For what it is worth, the two surviving merchant inventories from 1690s Charleston already show a distribution quite similar to that present a third of a century later, with the exception of cottons, where the much lower proportion is consistent with that found in contemporary Montreal and Philadelphia. The precise proportions are 31 percent linens, 54 percent woolens, 2 percent cottons, 4 percent mixed, 8 percent silks. See Charleston County, South Carolina, Wills and Miscellaneous Records, vol. 53 (Works Progress Administration transcription), inventories of Wilson Dunston, April 17, 1692 (117–32), and John Vansusteren, May 23, 1694 (199–204).

12. Woolen garments predominated in the armoires of all Montreal-area colonists in the late seventeenth century, but farm families held proportionately the largest share, followed by artisans. Conversely, urban dwellers, most notably merchants, clothed themselves more in linens and other fabrics. For more details, see DuPlessis, "Was There a Consumer Revolution?"

13. A mid-eighteenth-century German pastor visiting Pennsylvania noted that due to the intense summer heat, "light coats or jackets are worn which are neatly made of fine linen or dimity [a sturdy and serviceable cotton fabric]" (Gottlieb Mittelberger, *Journey to Pennsylvania in the Year 1750 and Return to Germany in the Year 1754,* trans. C. Eben [Philadelphia: J. J. McVey, 1898], 118).

14. It might be argued that because some linen was tailored into shirts and blouses in Europe or in the ports before being exchanged with Native Americans, the proportion of

linen in the Amerindian trade is underestimated by the figures quoted in tables 9 and 10. For instance, Rasteau (table 10, col. 3) sold linen shirts worth about one-fifth as much as his total sales of linen cloth; moreover, 95 percent of those shirts were tailored of so-called "trade linen" (*toile de traite*), designed specifically for—though not actually sold exclusively in—the Native American market. Even earlier the "Statement of expenses for Mississippi for 1703" listed outlays of 1,240 livres for cloth and clothing "to give to persons dispatched to friendly [Amerindian] nations," 250 livres (20 percent) of which paid for one hundred men's linen shirts (the rest was spent on woolens: 300 livres for thirty ells of "red cloth," 240 for red cloth overcoats, and 450 for three hundred ells of red stuff for breechclouts); see Jeffrey Brain, *Tunica Treasure* (Cambridge: Peabody Museum of Architecture and Ethnology, Harvard University/Salem, Mass.: Peabody Museum of Salem, 1979), 294. Still, as this example demonstrates, woolen fabrics were also made up into garments before being shipped to the frontier, and these, like linen shirts, were not enumerated in the textile lists; what is more, woolen garments were on the whole more expensive both individually and collectively. Overall, it seems safe to conclude, Native American demand for cloth and clothing in late seventeenth- and early eighteenth-century British and French North America embraced a respectable minority of linens (perhaps 15 to 20 percent by value) but was mainly focused on woolens.

15. Peter Mancall, Joshua Rosenbloom, and Thomas Weiss, "Indians and the Economy of Eighteenth-Century Carolina" (essay in this book), in table 16 calculate that Indians numbered about 40,000 of the 100,000 people in the Lower South (the Carolinas and Georgia) in 1730. It should be noted that the Amerindian population not only formed the largest single group (whites were some 34 percent, blacks 26 percent) but also would have been a much larger proportion of the population living on or near the frontier. Similar figures are not available for Louisiana; but the estimates of 150,000 Native Americans in 1699 and around 70,000 in 1763 by Thomas N. Ingersoll, *Mammon and Manon in Early New Orleans: The First Slave Society in the Deep South, 1718–1819* (Knoxville: University of Tennessee Press, 1999), 18, suggest a 1730s Native American population that was both absolutely and proportionally much larger than the settler population, both free and unfree, which numbered about 5,740 in 1731.

16. In a 1743 letter Robert Pringle called stroud and duffel blanketing the "most Material Articles for the Indian trade"; see Walter B. Edgar, ed., *The Letterbook of Robert Pringle*, 2 vols. (Columbia: University of South Carolina Press, 1972), 2:646. Cf. a 1762 letter by Henry Laurens, in *The Papers of Henry Laurens,* ed. Philip M. Hamer et al., 14 vols. (Columbia: University of South Carolina Press, 1968–88), 3:110. See also Philip Brown, "Early Indian Trade in the Development of South Carolina: Politics, Economics, and Social Mobility during the Proprietary Period, 1670–1719," *South Carolina Historical Magazine* 76 (1975): 123; and Verner Crane, *The Southern Frontier 1670–1732* (Durham, N.C.: Duke University Press, 1928), esp. 332–33, app. B.

17. Cf. Richard White, *The Middle Ground* (Cambridge and New York: Cambridge University Press, 1991), 136–38, who shows that the ellage of woolen cloth and the number of blankets taken west by Canadian fur traders at least doubled and may have tripled between the 1670s and 1690s, as Indians began to adopt woolen clothing in place of that made of skins.

18. See n. 13, above.

19. According to Mancall, Rosenbloom, and Weiss, "Indians and the Economy of Eighteenth-Century Carolina," table 16, the 26,000 slaves in the Lower South in 1730 formed 26 percent of the area's total population or 43 percent of the area's settler population; by 1740 their numbers had risen to 41,000 (respectively, 30 percent and 42 percent). In Louisiana the 4,112 slaves counted in 1731 formed 72 percent of the settler population; my calculations are from Ingersoll, *Mammon and Manon,* 18.

20. Cheap woolens for slaves are cited in the list of "Ammunitions and merchandise for the Colony of Louisiana for 1734," put up for bid at La Rochelle, which includes "1,000 ells of *tirtaine* from Amiens for the negroes [*sic*]"; see Brain, *Tunica Treasure,* 300. No linens are mentioned in this document. "Tir[e]taine" was a cheap, coarsely woven woolen or linsey-woolsey. I have not encountered it in any Louisiana inventories or invoices.

21. For the identification of these fabrics as particularly destined for slaves, see "Expense of purchasing [and operating] a plantation in South Carolina, within 40 miles of Charles Town," a 1755 document that lists five yards of white plains per slave per year, a blanket every third year, and unspecified amounts of "ozinbrig" [osnaburg] linen annually; see "C.W." [Charles Woodmason], "The Economics of a Plantation Venture, 1755," in *The Colonial South Carolina Scene: Contemporary Views, 1697–1774,* ed. H. Roy Merrens (Columbia: University of South Carolina Press, 1977), 162.

22. From 1735 the textiles that slaves in South Carolina could wear were restricted by a kind of sumptuary law. The list of permissible fabrics comprised "Negro cloth, duffils, coarse kerseys, oznabrigs, blue linnen, checked linnen, coarse garlix, callicoes, checked cottons or scotch plaids." It is cited in Audrie Hadow Michie, "Goods Proper for South Carolina: Textiles Imported 1738–1742" (M.A. thesis, University of North Carolina at Greensboro, 1978), 19.

23. ANQM, Fonds Chateau de Ramezay P 345, Monière, Journals 3 and 4; Montreal Merchants Records Project (henceforth MMR), microfilm ed., Historical Society of Minnesota, St. Paul, 1971–75, "Trade goods." The value of the numerous linen shirts and considerable amounts of woolen clothing (mainly greatcoats and other pieces of outerwear) and blankets (often used as draped garments) that were also in the cargoes has been included in these proportions.

24. MMR, "Trade goods."

25. That trade had received a major boost in the mid-1740s when naval actions consequent on Franco-British conflicts disrupted supplies of European goods to New France; see Neal Salisbury, "The History of Native Americans from Before the Arrival of the Europeans and Africans until the American Civil War," in *The Cambridge Economic History of the United States,* vol. 1, *The Colonial Era,* ed. Stanley Engerman and Robert Galiman (New York: Cambridge University Press, 1996), 33.

26. Ironically, we know about these shipments because they were regularly seized by the Indian allies of the French, who claimed the area; see Historical Society of Pennsylvania (HSP), Philadelphia, Etting Collection, vol. 40, dossiers 7, 17, 29, 30.

27. HSP, Cox-Parrish-Wharton Family Papers, box 18, folder 13; HSP, Etting Collection, vol. 40, dossier 36. Given relative prices, the dominance of woolens would have been higher than the amounts cited imply.

28. HSP, Gratz Collection, box 10, case 14, "Invoice . . . from the Trading House at Fort Augusta," August 22, 1763. Cf. the 1760 account book of the Philadelphia merchant

David Franks, HSP, Ms. Am. 0684. Franks outfitted numerous fur traders, so his sales—of which woolens comprised 61 percent by value, linens 30 percent, and cottons and calicoes 8 percent—likely reflect Native American preferences.

29. My calculations are based on W. L. McDowell, ed., *Documents Relating to Indian Affairs 1754–1765* (Columbia: South Carolina Archives Department, 1970), 457–58. Nine separate groups of presents were distributed in all in April and May. That these distributions were typical is suggested by gifts bestowed on the Chicksaw nation in September and October 1757 by Jerome Courtonne, agent of the South Carolina provincial government; on these occasions, too, the textiles included only woolens (duffel and stroud) and shirts (ibid., 445–46). Gifts awarded to headmen were even more heavily dominated by woolens. Thus "a Present for the Head Warriour" of the Chicksaws on March 30, 1756, once again given by Courtonne, included "1 Pr. Strouds, 1 Suit Scarlet Cloaths, 20 Yards of Embroidered Serge, 2 Shirts"—all of it woolens save the last (ibid., 114). In neither of these cases is it stated what material went into the shirts, but if the 1758 information is any guide, they would have been tailored of check linen.

30. Native American preference for woolens made them discerning and demanding consumers, as French officials repeatedly acknowledged; see MMR, "Ecarlatines." In the Southeast, for instance, both merchants and trading post garrisons sought British woolens for their trade with Creeks and Choctaws; see Gregory Waselkov, "French Colonial Trade in the Upper Creek Country," in *Calumet and Fleur-de-lys: Archaeology of Indian and French Contact in the Midcontinent,* ed. J. Walthall and T. Emerson (Washington, D.C.: Smithsonian Institution Press, 1992), esp. 42–43. Price played some role in this preference: in 1718, for example, some French traders operating in the South demanded twenty deerskins for a blanket, the English eight. See Patricia Dillon Woods, *French-Indian Relations on the Southern Frontier 1699–1762* (Ann Arbor, Mich.: UMI Research Press, 1980), 40, in which, in general, she claims (210–11 n. 48) that English traders in the South could sell their goods for half the price the French charged. Again, in 1741, a French official admitted that French limbourg cost twice as much as stroud, though he assured his Cherokee interlocutors that limbourg was much more durable; see "Journal of Antoine Bonnefoy, 1741–1742," in *Travels in the American Colonies,* ed. Newton D. Mereness (New York: Macmillan, 1916), 250.

Not all French officials agreed with Bonnefoy's quality claims. In the 1730s Governor Bienville of Louisiana, acknowledging that the Indians showed a marked preference for better English blankets, tried to have the English ones copied in France; see Woods, *French-Indian Relations,* 117. This policy of learning from (or at least imitating) the competition was still being urged in 1757 by Bougainville, though he believed that Indian objections rested less on the intrinsic excellence of the cloth than on taste (*goût*), Carcassonne manufacturers not understanding how to dye satisfactory black bands on their blankets; see Louis Antoine de Bougainville, "Mémoire sur l'état de la Nouvelle-France, 1757," *Rapport de l'archiviste de la province de Québec* 4 (1923–24): 63. In his (wistfully defensive but not necessarily incorrect) words, "Ce n'est pas que les draps [de Carcassonne] n'en fussent meilleurs et n'en fussent aussi beaux pour les couleurs, mais on n'a pu encore y faire les bandes d'un beau noir; en général nos marchandises valent mieux pour la qualité que celles des Anglais, mais les Sauvages préfèrent les leurs." Bougainville also admitted (ibid.) that in times of war, prices at the fur trade posts became "very excessive" (*trop excessif*). Although I cannot pursue this subject here, Bougainville's comments, like those of Bienville, demonstrate how widely across imperial boundaries knowledge of textiles was diffused.

Quality is a more controversial issue among modern historians. Braund, no admirer of French goods, nevertheless reports that limbourg was "reputed to be of better quality than [stroud]" (*Deerskin & Duffels,* 123). For a more generally favorable verdict, see Wilbur R. Jacobs, *Wilderness Politics and Indian Gifts: The Northern Colonial Frontier, 1748–1763* (1950; repr., Lincoln: University of Nebraska Press, 1966), 69: "During the 1750s, the Indians desired French fabrics because they were of a better quality than the British merchandise." In a later article, however, Jacobs's judgment is more reserved. While noting that one British colonial official "considered the French blankets to be superior to those made in England," he concedes that "French cloth used for gifts was often poorly dyed and of an inferior grade"; see Wilbur Jacobs, "White Gift-Giving: French Skills in Managing the Indians," chap. 4 of his *Dispossessing the American Indian: Indians and Whites on the Colonial Frontier* (New York: Scribner, 1972), 52.

31. The data in Mancall, Rosenbloom, and Weiss, "Indians and the Economy of Eighteenth-Century Carolina," table 16, suggest that Amerindians, although numbering around thirty-seven thousand individuals, constituted less than 15 percent of the Lower South's population in the 1760s. Although no other area has benefited from a similarly careful and detailed study, there is no doubt that Native American populations across North America declined relatively and absolutely during much of the eighteenth century. Problems such as those in the South Carolina deerskin trade must have depressed Indian demand even further, in particular making it difficult for native people to purchase expensive fabrics such as woolens or even cottons, both of which cost more than linens. For the deerskin trade, see Peter Coclanis, *The Shadow of a Dream* (New York: Oxford University Press, 1988), 62–63, 80–81.

32. Ely Kershaw Account Book 1769–74, South Carolina Historical Society (SCHS), Charleston, MS 34/613.

33. If references are needed, see John J. McCusker and Russell R. Menard, *The Economy of British America, 1607–1789,* 2nd ed. (Chapel Hill: University of North Carolina Press, 1991), 112 (table 5.3), 220, 221 (figs. 10.2, 10.3); Egnal, *New World Economies,* 138 (fig. 8.7).

34. It is likely, for example, that some of the change noted in the shipments to Detroit resulted from the rise of the settler population there rather than shifts in Amerindian demand, for already by the 1740s Detroit had become the largest of the western colonial settlements; see Norman Caldwell, *The French in the Mississippi Valley 1740–1750* (Urbana-Champaign: University of Illinois Press, 1941), 37.

35. Whereas in 1651–1700 woolens had constituted (by value) 78 percent of Montreal decedents' outerwear and cottons none, in 1770–74 the proportions were 26 and 38 percent, respectively. For more details on clothing, based on Montreal-area inventories, which are by far the most complete, see DuPlessis, "Was There a Consumer Revolution?"

36. This statement should not be taken to suggest that imports of woolens, much less any other type of fabric, declined in absolute terms. Calculating from the figures in Davis, "English Foreign Trade, 1700–74," 302–3, between 1722–24 and 1772–74 English exports of woolens to the Americas and West Africa grew 3.8 times, linens 31 times, silks 3.5 times, and cottons 11.7 times; reexports from England to "America" expanded 1.3 times for linens, 1.8 times for silks, and 1.9 times for calicoes (woolen reexports are not listed). Total exports of manufactures grew 5.9 times between those dates; total reexports of manufactures grew

1.4-fold. These figures make it obvious, however, that British linens and cottons, not woolens, were the growth sectors.

37. On slave populations, see Coclanis, *Shadow of a Dream*, 64–65 (tables 3–1, 3–2); and Mancall, Rosenbloom, and Weiss, "Indians and the Economy of Eighteenth-Century Carolina," table 16, who suggest that the number of slaves rose from 26,000 in 1730 (26 percent of the total population of the Lower South) to 94,000 in 1760 (38 percent) and 155,000 in 1770 (41 percent). White population was also growing absolutely and relatively, whereas Native American numbers, as we have seen, were falling sharply, especially in relation to total population.

38. Calculated from James Poyas Account Book, Charleston Museum, Charleston, S.C. Another 40 percent of his cloth sales consisted of linens, while cottons added up to just 10 percent.

39. Based on the five yards of white plains per slave per year specified in "C.W.," "The Economics of a Plantation Venture, 1755," 162, the 1770 slave population in the Lower South translates into annual plantation consumption of 775,000 yards just of that one cloth. The letters of Charleston merchants are filled with references to the purchase and sale of large quantities of plains. On May 9, 1768, for example, Henry Laurens, a prominent merchant who also had several large plantations, ordered 1,200 yards of white plains from William Cowles & Co. at Bristol, specifying that he needed them "for my own use, so that [a]ny disappointment in these will prove injurious to my planting affairs"; see *Papers of Henry Laurens*, 5:678. The quantity cited would have clothed 240 slaves. When plains were unavailable, Laurens substituted stroud; see his letter to Abraham Schad, at Wambaw (plantation), October 7, 1765, ibid., 5:19. In another letter to Schad (ibid., 4:665–66), Laurens sends both white plains and stroud, with instructions to use the plains first.

40. For just two references among many devoted to "the moth," see Edgar, *Letterbook of Robert Pringle*, 1:33; *Papers of Henry Laurens*, 3:253.

41. In a 1764 letter to the manager of his Mepkin plantation (*Papers of Henry Laurens*, 4:319), Laurens cites a figure of three yards of osnaburg and five yards of plains per slave, together with a kerchief (probably linen), blanket (almost always duffel), and hat (most likely woolen).

42. Together with the apparent disappearance of woolens from slave wardrobes, the fact that slaves formed a diminishing proportion of the Louisiana population across our period probably helps explain the decline of woolens in merchant stocks despite demand generated by the Indian trade and consumption of fancy woolens by planters. For the falling slave proportion, see Ingersoll, *Mammon and Manon*, 95.

43. The predominance of these fabrics, and the virtual absence of woolens of any sort, is clear in the sale of the effects of the planter and merchant Sieur Lalande in LHC, FSC, doc. 80 (undated, circa 1758). Our understanding of clothing in early Louisiana will be immeasurably advanced by the publication of the University of London doctoral dissertation recently completed by Sophie White, "Trading Identitites: Cultures of Consumption in French Colonial Louisiana (1699–1769)"; for a foretaste, see White, "Dress in French Colonial Louisiana, 1699–1769: The Evidence from Notarial Sources," *Dress* 24 (1997): 69–75.

44. Beverly Lemire, "'A Good Stock of Cloaths': The Changing Market for Cotton Clothing in Britain, 1750–1800," *Textile History* 22 (1991): 311–28; Beverly Lemire, *Fashion's Favourite: The Cotton Trade and the Consumer in Britain, 1660–1800* (Oxford: Oxford University Press, 1991); Roche, *Culture of Clothing*.

45. Roche, *Culture of Clothing,* 127, 138 (tables 10, 14).

46. See esp. Breen, "Empire of Goods."

47. Roche, *Culture of Clothing,* 127, 138 (tables 10, 14).

48. In the late seventeenth century high-wealth Montreal decedents (15 percent of the total inventoried) possessed 57 percent of the silk clothing; by 1770–74 this group (still 15 percent of the total inventoried) owned 29 percent of all silk garments. In 1770–74 those in the lowest wealth category (57 percent of all inventoried decedents) also had 29 percent of all silk garments, while the middling (28 percent of inventories) had acquired the remaining 42 percent. *Habitants* (farmers) and artisans had just over half of all silk items, lower than their proportion in the decedent group (84 percent), and the lowest proportion of all types of cloth composing the garments they owned.

49. See n. 27, above.

50. Compare *Journals of the Commissioners of the Indian Trade, September 20, 1710–August 29, 1718* (Columbia: South Carolina Archives Department, 1992), 124, 204, 269, 281; with W. L. McDowell, ed., *Documents Relating to Indian Affairs May 21, 1750–August 7, 1754* (Columbia: South Carolina Archives Department, 1958) (no entries); and McDowell, *Documents Relating to Indian Affairs 1754–1765,* 568 (only citation).

51. See Lathan A. Windley, *Runaway Slave Advertisements: A Documentary History from the 1730s to 1790,* vol. 3 (Westport, Conn.: Greenwood, 1983).

52. In South Carolina planters and merchants (often the same individuals practiced both occupations) particularly fancied woolen garments, although if the examples of Robert Pringle or Henry Laurens are any guide, they were likely to order them ready-made from London tailors. See, for instance, Pringle to the London tailor David Glen, January 22, 1739, in Edgar, *Letterbook of Robert Pringle,* 1:63–64, in which Pringle ordered several garments made up from very expensive varieties of woolen fabric: a riding coat and vest "of the Best superfine Drabb," "a Best superfine Scarlett Broad Cloath Jackett or Waist Coat," a banyan (loose gown) "of a very fashionable worsted Damask of the finest & best sort," and a "superfine fashionable broad Cloth Fly Coat & Breeches." See also ibid., June 11, 1744, 2:706–7; or *Papers of Henry Laurens,* 1:195, December 26, 1748. These intercolonial similarities lend some credence to the claim by Ingersoll, *Mammon and Manon,* 122 (which is based on other considerations altogether), that early Louisiana was much more like "coastal South Carolina" than St. Domingue, to which it is usually compared.

53. Besides the fabrics already cited, it is worth noting that if tiretaine was used for slave clothing in Louisiana, it never showed up in free decedents' inventories.

54. See McDowell, *Documents Relating to Indian Affairs 1750–1754,* 376, 545; McDowell, *Documents Relating to Indian Affairs 1754–1765,* 282, 319, 475.

55. LHC, FSC, docs. 1765101001, 1765101102.

56. Richard L. Bushman, *The Refinement of America: Persons, Houses, Cities* (New York: Knopf, 1993), 69–74; Breen, "Baubles of Britain," 776.

57. The research for this chapter was supported by a Fellowship for College Teachers and Independent Scholars from the National Endowment for the Humanities, and by faculty research grants from Swarthmore College.

The Organization of Trade and Finance in the British Atlantic Economy, 1600–1830

R. C. Nash

British trade with America had its origins in the mid-sixteenth century, partly in the sporadic and clandestine commercial ventures mounted to Spanish and Portuguese America, which made a minor dent in the Iberian monopoly of transatlantic trade, but mainly in the less dramatic but more substantial fish trade from Newfoundland to southern Europe. The major growth of trade, however, occurred after 1600 with the foundation of permanent British colonies in America and did so in three stages. First, given the small scale of trade with the indigenous Native American population, commercial expansion had to wait for widespread agricultural settlement in the sugar and tobacco colonies in the Caribbean and southern mainland, which throughout the seventeenth century provided 80 percent or more of the colonies' exports to England. The creation of a plantation export economy depended, in turn, on a large-scale transatlantic traffic in coerced labor, first in white indentured servants and then, from circa 1650, in black African slaves. Nevertheless, the development of a staple-producing economy in British America, and of an appropriate commercial infrastructure, was a slow business; by 1700, after a century of colonization, imports from America comprised 20 percent of total British imports, while exports to America made up about 12 percent of total exports. In the second stage of Anglo-American commercial expansion, from 1700 to 1780, the rapid growth of the colonies' agriculture and population, including that of the northern mainland colonies, complemented by industrial diversification in Britain, shifted transatlantic trade from the margins to the core of Britain's international economy. To growing imports from the colonies of tobacco and sugar was added an array of new or much enlarged trades in rice, dyestuffs, rum, coffee, and grain. By 1772–74 the American colonies provided 40 percent of British imports, nearly all agricultural in origin, and took over 40 percent of British domestic exports, almost all of them manufactures. There were also three substantial, multilateral, or triangular export trades organized by English merchants to the colonies: in slaves from West Africa; in provisions from Ireland; and in wine from the Atlantic islands of Madeira and the Canaries. Taken together, these multilateral export trades were worth about 30 percent of direct exports. Third, from 1780 to

1830 British Atlantic trade in the post-Revolution era grew at unprecedented rates, on the complementary bases of the demand generated by the further massive expansion of American population and agriculture and, on the supply side, by the great cheapening of output in the revolutionized British-export industries. British transatlantic exports after 1780 were dominated by manufactures produced in the modernized industries, above all cotton textiles; imports consisted of sugar and the other nonessential foodstuffs, which had held the stage before 1780, and a greatly increased proportion of raw materials, especially cotton.[1]

The purpose of this chapter is to provide a broad review of research into the organization of the trading and financial systems that underpinned the expansion of the British Atlantic economy over the period 1600–1830. The first section presents three key questions concerning commercial organization: (1) What major changes took place in the methods by which British colonial trade was organized in the period from the settlement of the colonies to the Revolution? (2) What was the impact of the American and French Revolutionary Wars and of the British Industrial Revolution on transatlantic trade organization? (3) Did merchants become more specialized in their business activities and was trade increasingly concentrated in the hands of fewer merchants in the seventeenth and eighteenth centuries? The second section asks two fundamental questions about the role of merchant capital in the expansion of the British Atlantic economy: (1) How was transatlantic trade financed in the colonial period? (2) What impact did the British industrial and the British and American financial revolutions have on the financing of British-American trade from 1780 to1830?

The Organization of British Colonial Trade, 1600–1780

Until circa 1625 the major initiatives in transatlantic trade were taken by established London merchants in the Levant and East India trades, who made subsidiary investments in the trading companies and syndicates that undertook much of the colonization of English America and that controlled its early trade. However, these enterprises, besides being underfinanced, were usually founded on wholly unrealistic expectations about economic conditions in America: they emphasized the commercial prospects of the cloth trade with the native population, of manufacturing, of mineral wealth—almost anything but the agricultural staple production that was to provide the true basis of the colonies' material future. Most of these early corporate ventures had therefore failed by 1630, and the prominent merchants who invested in them saw little if any return on their capital, a chastening experience that discouraged London's established merchants from taking much further interest in colonial trade. Their place was taken by an influx of persons from outside the circle of London's conventional merchants—shopkeepers, tradesmen, ships' captains, and others—groups that hitherto had been excluded from participation in foreign trade. This mass of petty dealers remained of some significance throughout the century, but from within their ranks there slowly emerged inner groups of professional merchants, who traded in small partnerships rather than in corporate groups and who, by the 1680s, dominated London's trade to America. Colonial trade in the outports, on the other hand, remained widely dispersed among large and much less professionalized business communities.[2]

These London and outport merchants, acting as independent entrepreneurs, consigned cargoes of manufactures and other consumer goods, indentured servants, Irish provisions, and Madeira wine to their representatives in the colonial ports, from whom the proceeds of export sales were remitted in sugar, tobacco, and minor colonial staples. In the early years of colonization these representatives comprised a motley collection of colonial tradesmen and planters as well as a sprinkling of salaried factors employed by English merchants. In time, the growth in the scale of business in colonial ports bred groups of specialized native merchants, who worked as agents on an ad hoc commission basis for English principals.[3] In general, London dominated the British colonial trades, controlling 80 percent of imports and exports as late as 1700. London's only serious provincial rival was Bristol, which had a share in all the major colonial trades other than that in slaves, which was an official monopoly of the Royal African Company of London until 1698. Smaller southwestern ports exploited their locational advantages to participate in the tobacco reexport trade to the Low Countries or used their workaday Irish connections to break into the Irish provisions and indentured servant trades to the West Indies.[4]

From the late seventeenth century, the rapid expansion of British foreign trade was accompanied in some overseas trading sectors by decisive innovations in methods of commercial organization and finance, while other sectors were marked by a high degree of continuity in commercial practice. The extent to which trade was reorganized reflected the level of economic and commercial development achieved by Britain's trading partners. The organization of the trades with Asia, southern Europe, the Mediterranean, and the Levant was marked by continuity. Here, British merchants had to continue in their role as independent entrepreneurs, controlling trade and shipping and employing local agents as their representatives, because indigenous mercantile development in these regions was too backward or insufficiently integrated into Europe's financial system to carry the burden of organizing trade. In trade, on the other hand, with overseas regions that possessed strong indigenous mercantile groups and financial institutions, namely northwest Europe and the Baltic (excluding Russia), British merchants ceased, for the most part, to trade as independent entrepreneurs and instead became factors or agents who handled trade on commission for the account and risk of overseas traders and producers. In the Baltic countries foreign trade was nationalized by powerful indigenous groups of merchants, shipowners, and producers who received strong support from their national governments, which placed punitive restrictions on British merchants and shipping.

The foreign takeover of Britain's trade to northwest Europe, on the other hand, reflected the decline of the Company of Merchant Adventurers, the once all-powerful trading corporation that had formerly monopolized cloth exports to the region, and the movement to London of numerous Dutch, Jewish, German, and above all Huguenot merchants, who "cosmopolitanized" London's merchant community from the 1690s. These merchants naturally concentrated in London's cloth and colonial reexport trades to northwest Europe because there they could exploit their excellent continental connections by acting as London agents for foreign principals in Germany and the Netherlands.[5]

The organization of commerce to British America was marked by elements of both change and continuity, in a complex commercial milieu made up of a dense web of transatlantic trades coordinated by specialist mercantile groups on both sides of the Atlantic. To simplify matters, a description of and explanation for the major changes that took place in the organization of trade are needed.

Commercial innovation in the Atlantic economy was centered on the trades with the West Indies, with that part of the Chesapeake's trade controlled by the richer tobacco planters, and with the trade to the northern colonies (New England, New York, and Pennsylvania). In these trades there was a fundamental shift to the commission system, by which British merchants came to act not as independent entrepreneurs but as agents who sold consignments of goods received from American planters and merchants on commission; in return, they sent out manufactured goods to the order of their colonial clients and supplied them with a wide range of mercantile and quasi-banking services, including the provision of shipping, insurance, and eventually finance.

The first decisive shift to the commission system took place from the 1660s in British trade with the West Indies. Here the sugar planters turned entrepreneurs and chose to sell their sugar not in the colonies but in London through commission agents. In a classic study Davies located the origins of the system in the trade with Barbados and argued that it was hardly known in the other islands before the eighteenth century.[6] Hancock, however, has argued in a recent essay that commission trading by 1680 was "flourishing not only in Barbados but also in Jamaica and the Leeward Islands," and he shows that the leading London commission agency dealing with the Leewards received consignments of goods from at least fifty Leeward merchants and planters at this time.[7]

Nevertheless, it appears that the commission system did indeed achieve a much higher pitch of development in Barbados than in the other islands in the late seventeenth century. This is shown by Davies's basic source, the bills of exchange drawn by planters on their London commission agents for the payment of slaves bought from the Royal African Company. Bills of exchange, alongside the consignment of goods for sale in London, were the key link between the planter and his commission agent, and every sugar planter of any standing bought slaves from the company. Of the fifteen hundred West India

Table 12: The Royal African Company's trade with Barbados, 1680–1711
(annual averages: £s)

	Value of Slaves Delivered in Barbados	Bills of Exchange Remitted	Value of Sugar Remitted
1680–1688	24,982	17,451	1,484
1689–1697	16,039	7,498	5,204
1698–1701	12,726	1,079	10,051
1702–1711	16,610	66	4,473

bills received by the company in payment for slaves in the years 1672–94, 94 percent were drawn from Barbados, 4 percent from Jamaica, and 2 percent from the Leeward Islands. Furthermore, for every slave the company delivered to Barbados in the period 1680–88, it remitted 1.25 cwts. of sugar from the island; for every slave delivered to the Leewards in the same period the company brought home 10 cwts. of sugar. In other words, in the 1680s Barbados planters bought their slaves with bills and sold their sugar not in the islands but by consignment to London. The Leeward planters, on the other hand, paid for their slaves with funds raised by selling sugar locally, and they had no documented connection with the bill of exchange system.[8]

It is also unclear that the commission system was securely established in any part of the West Indies before the eighteenth century; certainly its operation was temporarily suspended in the war years 1689–1713, when the heavy losses of sugar ships from the West Indies shattered the bill mechanism between the islands and England. So the great majority of bills drawn by planters, nearly all of them of Barbados, on their commission agents in favor of the African Company in the 1690s and 1700s were "protested," that is, rejected for payment, because the planters' consignments to London designated to cover these bills were lost to enemy ships. The Barbados planters therefore reverted to the policy of selling their crops on the island, rather than in London, from where the company remitted its effects not in bills but in sugars purchased locally, a turnaround in commercial arrangements documented in table 12.[9]

The company's trading policy of the 1680s, and by implication that of the English West India merchants in general, was reversed after 1688. The Barbados sugar market, which had virtually disappeared in the 1680s, was restored to full working order in the war years, while the commission system stuttered to a near halt; even in the prosperous peace years 1698–1701, returns for slaves were made in sugar rather than in bills. The Leewards and Jamaica planters, of course, continued to pay for their slaves in sugar as they did before the war.[10] After the war the commission system was reinvigorated in the Barbados trade, as normal market conditions in the Anglo–West Indian trade were resumed, and it was also consolidated in Jamaica and the Leeward Islands. Henceforth, the great majority of West Indies planters consigned their sugar for sale in London, a practice they followed in times of war as well as in peace through the rest of the colonial period.[11]

The commission system also developed in the Chesapeake colonies, although the periodization of its development was quite different from that in the West Indies. In the tobacco trade the commission system did not emerge as an important mode of commerce until the war years 1689–1713, when it was in full decline in the West Indies. The system was used by the richer planters who generally produced the better grades of sweet-scented tobacco, which they consigned to London agents on commission, merchants who also imported tobacco on their own account. The consignment trade was of great significance to the wealthier producers, but it was not predominant in the trade as a whole, accounting for about 20 percent of all the tobacco exported to England in the war years. The tobacco consignment trade was feasible in wartime because it suffered much less from shipping losses than did sugar consignment trade, although the capture of many tobacco ships in 1706–7 prompted the London commission agents to reject numerous bills of exchange drawn on them by their clients in the Chesapeake. The history of the commission system in the two plantation regions continued to diverge in the later colonial period. While its postwar triumph in the West Indies was a permanent one, its heyday in the Chesapeake, even among the wealthier planters, lasted only until circa 1740. From then until the Revolution a growing proportion of even the better grades of tobacco produced on the larger plantations was marketed either through indigenous merchants, in the "cargo trade," or through the chains of stores operated in the Chesapeake by British merchants who traded independently.[12]

In the trade of the northern mainland colonies it was native colonial merchants rather than planters who took the initiative in revolutionizing British American commercial relations. Indigenous merchants trading as independent entrepreneurs first emerged in Boston in the mid-seventeenth century on the twin bases of the local fishing and shipbuilding industries. So Boston merchants, with London connections, began from circa 1640 to supply fish to London ships that called in at Massachusetts en route to southern Europe. Fishing stimulated a substantial shipbuilding industry, and merchants seized the chance of using locally built vessels to ship fish cargoes on their own account to southern Europe and then mixed cargoes of lumber and provisions to the West Indies and Newfoundland. By the late 1670s Boston merchants dominated the supply of foodstuffs to the West Indies and the region's inter-island trade. New England's direct exports to England were less significant than those to other destinations, but England was the only market where large numbers of ships, an important New England export at this time, could be sold and the only source of manufactured goods. Boston also acted as a major entrepôt for the distribution of imported West India and British goods, drawing the vast region from Newfoundland to

Pennsylvania into its commercial hinterland. Boston merchants in their overseas trading ventures invariably owned the ships as well as the cargoes, and this close association between shipping and trade meant that they generated freight earnings comparable in value to their merchandizing profits. All these trades were conducted on Boston account, save that in imports from England, which was handled in the middle decades of the seventeenth century on English account. However, by circa 1700 this trade too had largely been transferred from the control of British to Boston merchants, who employed London agents to provide mercantile services.[13]

The degree to which merchants in New York and Philadelphia had achieved commercial independence by circa 1700 is less clear than that for merchants in Boston, as recent studies by Matson (on New York) and Nash (on Philadelphia) do not discuss the extent to which trade in these ports was controlled on American account. However, these studies do show that first-generation merchants in both ports, circa 1700, were much less wealthy than subsequent generations, suggesting that they had insufficient resources to carry on independent trading. There were, of course, wealthy merchants in New York at this time, but nearly all of them were Dutch, who traded mainly to Amsterdam. In contrast, New York's first-generation merchants of English origin possessed modest resources. However, both cities enjoyed a rapid growth in trade and shipping after 1700 and by circa 1720 had escaped from Boston's dominance in intercolonial trade and were on the verge too of wresting control of transatlantic trade from British merchants.[14]

The trade of Boston, New York, and Philadelphia for the later colonial period is thoroughly documented in studies, and these make abundantly clear that the great bulk of the swelling volume of manufactures imported into the northern ports from Britain, and by far the greater part of the shipping used in their transatlantic trades, was controlled by indigenous merchants. For example, in Philadelphia in the 1760s and 1770s the large import trade from England was in the hands of 250–300 independent, local merchants who were supplied with manufactures by a core of 15–20 British agencies, of whom the most important were a dozen or so great London commission firms.[15]

The expansive potential of the commission system is further shown by the development after 1750 of the so-called "cargo trade." This became a major system of trade in all the *slave-plantation* colonies in the later colonial period, being described, for example, as "the most dynamic feature of the Chesapeake economy in the years 1763–1774." Cargo trade was intimately connected to the London commission system, although it was mobilized not by planters but by indigenous colonial merchants. It originated in the West Indies where, after 1730, local merchants began to import dry goods on credit from the same London commission houses that marketed the planters' crops, although these merchants made their returns in bills of exchange rather than in sugar. After 1750 the cargo trade spread to the mainland plantation colonies—first to Virginia and Maryland. There native merchants received cargoes of dry goods on their independent account mainly from enterprising London tobacco commission agents, who diversified into this business in response to the stiff competition they faced in the tobacco trade from the independent traders of Liverpool and Glasgow. The native merchants made some of their returns to London in bills, but they sent back a higher proportion of commodities, that is, tobacco, than was the case with the native merchants of the West Indies. At about the same time yet another version of the cargo trade sprang up in South Carolina. Indeed, from the 1750s the greater part of the rising tide of English exports to South Carolina was shipped by a coterie of leading London firms on commission to Charleston merchants who traded independently. The Charleston merchants made part of their returns in rice and indigo, although as the staple-export trades were largely in the hands of other groups of merchants, the major means of remittance, as in the West Indies, was in bills.[16]

The largest indigenous mercantile firms in the plantation colonies, however, dealt in slaves rather than in manufactured goods. Slaves were supplied by independent Bristol and Liverpool slave merchants, but in America they were consigned to local "slave factors," the most eminent merchants in their respective colonies. The biggest business was done in Jamaica and Barbados and, on the mainland, in Charleston, where an inner group of ten merchants in the period 1735–75 participated in a series of overlapping firms that imported 57 percent of all Charleston's slave imports in these years. The colonial slave factors, in exchange for the large commissions they received, had to shoulder an increasing burden of financial obligations heaped on them by the British slave merchants. From the 1740s, first in the West Indies and then in South Carolina, the slave factors who "insensibly became the real purchasers of the slaves" were required to pay for slave cargoes at the time of delivery, in sets of long-dated bills of exchange, months or years before they gathered in the proceeds of slave sales from the planters. These financial arrangements were inextricably connected with the commission system; an indispensable precondition imposed by the British slave merchants on the colonial slave factors, without which their business would have shuddered to a halt, was that their bills should be guaranteed by British financiers, the great majority of whom were London commission agents in the appropriate trade.[17]

The business of the independent merchants in the plantation colonies appears to have rivaled that of the northern colonial port merchants, but, in fact, their control of trade was a much less comprehensive one. They were importers of slaves and dry goods rather than staple exporters, making their returns to Britain in bills and specie rather than in commodities. As a result, they failed to gain more than a subsidiary share of either intercolonial trade or the growing export trades in rice, tobacco, and cereals to Europe. In contrast, the merchants of the northern ports took preponderant control of *all* their import and export trades, including those with Britain, the Caribbean, and southern Europe. The key difference between the two sets of merchants lay in their respective investment policies. The merchants of the northern ports invested in large shipping fleets and commodity stocks, while merchants in the plantation colonies did not. The latter shied away from the staple-export trades because their widespread participation in this business would have required a massive, local investment in shipping and in stocks of commodities, which they were unwilling to make.[18]

Instead, the merchants of the plantation colonies specialized in the importing of slaves and dry goods because the finance for these trades was supplied from the huge financial resources of the London commission merchants. Yet, given the considerable wealth accumulated by merchants in the plantation colonies in the eighteenth century, it seems unlikely that their refusal to make greater investments in trade was caused by any absolute shortage of capital. Rather, for these merchants, the lure of investing in slave-plantation agriculture proved a stronger attraction than did any impulse to concentrate resources in the foreign trade sector. In the West Indies and South Carolina virtually all successful merchants became large-scale owners of land and slaves and, moreover, lent money to aspiring planters in the local capital markets. In the Chesapeake the most prominent merchants until the late colonial period started out as owners of slave plantations or invested heavily in land and slaves during their careers.[19]

In the northern colonies, in sharp contrast, merchants did not disperse urban trading capital in investments in land and slaves, but rather kept it concentrated in urban property investments and in trade. In Philadelphia, for example, only first-generation merchants acquired a great deal of land, basically because it was virtually free for the taking. But few Philadelphia merchants of the later generations owned nonurban property, and the overwhelming majority, even among the wealthiest, owned only one or two slaves. The most successful merchants, it is true, established themselves, or their sons, as leisured gentlemen, but they remained an urban class, one that drew a rentier income from city property and from loans to active and aspiring merchants.[20]

To sum up: the commission system, which was overwhelmingly centered on London, came to dominate the greater part of British Atlantic trade. On the import side, the commission trades included the trade from the West Indies in sugar and other commodities, which, circa 1770, provided about 60 percent of total English imports from America; a substantial proportion of tobacco imports, although these were relayed more and more to London commission agents by Chesapeake merchants in the cargo trade than by planters; and the great bulk of imports from the northern colonies into England. On the export side, by far the greater part of the massive volume of English exports to British America was shipped by commission agents on the account of a mixture of colonial clients: to the merchants of Philadelphia, New York, and Boston; to individual sugar and tobacco planters, in return for their consignments; and, at the end of the colonial period, to resurgent groups of native merchants throughout the plantation regions. In all, we can roughly estimate that about 80 percent of England's bilateral trades with America flowed through commission channels.

Nevertheless, important and flourishing colonial trades remained within, or passed into, the control of British merchants who traded independently, although the aggregate value of these trades was far less than that of the commission trades. The "independent" trades were focused on Britain's provincial ports, especially Bristol, Liverpool, and Glasgow. First, in the Chesapeake the cheaper tobacco produced by the middling and lesser planters, which made up the great bulk of output, was sold locally, as it always had been. London had a large share of this trade in the early eighteenth century and retained an important connection with it as late as circa 1770, but from the 1740s the pacemakers in the Chesapeake were the independent and aggressive merchants of Liverpool and, above all, Glasgow, who in America set up chains of stores staffed by salaried managers appointed locally or sent out from Britain and who reexported the bulk of imported tobacco to Holland and France.[21]

Second, in South Carolina the rice planters did not consign their rice to commission agents in London to any degree, but rather sold it in Charleston to the agents of British merchants. About 1700 the rice trade was mainly in London hands, but from the 1730s provincial merchants, especially of Bristol, came to control the bulk of the trade. Rice was shipped, mainly on British account, from Charleston to British ports on the south coast, from where it was reexported to its major markets in Holland and Germany, although much was shipped directly to southern Europe.[22]

Third, the African slave trade to the West Indies and to the southern plantation colonies was controlled, at least to the point when slaves were delivered to slave factors in America, by independent British merchants: first, by the Royal Africa Company (1672–98), then by London merchants (1698–1720), and subsequently by the merchants of Bristol (1720–40) and Liverpool (1740–1807).[23] Finally, the (declining) British share of the fish trade from Newfoundland to southern Europe was dominated by the provincial ports, while the substantial and expanding export trade in Irish provisions to America was shared roughly equally between Irish and English provincial ports and London in the later colonial period.[24]

The notable innovation in the organization of the transatlantic trades from the late seventeenth century, then, was the rise of the commission system, a commercial method or mode that dominated the trades with northwest Europe and the Baltic as well as trade to America, although it was largely absent in commerce to southern Europe, the Mediterranean, and Asia. This raises an obvious major question, although one that has almost never been posed, even by the most eminent authorities on the subject: why did the fundamental shift to the commission system in the colonial trades take place? Before answering this question it is necessary to consider Hancock's recent major study, which in part has challenged the received view that the commission system did indeed become of overwhelming predominance in transatlantic trade; an acceptance of Hancock's views would naturally render explanations of the commission system's triumph largely irrelevant.

Historians of trade, Hancock argues, have perpetuated a myth in accepting Joseph Massie's view, expressed in 1759, that British merchants had been reduced to "the diminutive Characters of Agents, Factors, &c. instead of appearing as PRINCIPALS [that is, independent merchants] in the TRADE of their OWN COUNTRY." Hancock has undertaken an exhaustive study of an important group of associated London colonial merchants and argues that Massie's stark description does little justice to their multifarious and imaginative business activities, which went far beyond commission trading. For Hancock's merchants, the commission business was a means to an end, not an end itself. It was the easiest way to enter the colonial trades because it required the least capital and the fewest connections; but it acted as a mere starting-point and complement to other, more profitable activities. London merchants operated intricate portfolios that combined commission merchandizing with independent trade, but it was the latter—"principal enterprising"—that provided the true basis of their fortunes. Hancock further argues that even when London merchants acted as commission agents their primary functions were shipping and trade, not, as many historians have contended, the provision of finance.[25]

Hancock has set a challenging agenda for the study of colonial trade organization, and it may well be that future studies, if they can emulate his remarkable standards of research, will indeed confirm his view that London colonial merchants, in general, managed much more complex commercial portfolios and conducted trade on a far more independent basis than scholars have hitherto appreciated. In the meantime, one can make three provisional responses to his revisionist thesis. First, while his conclusions are based on an exhaustive study of an important London merchant group, much of his detailed evidence on their trade bears on their activities as slave merchants and as shipowners and freighters in the Caribbean trades, especially in the late 1750s and 1760s.[26] These are two areas of trade and shipping, however, in which it is agreed that British merchants did act independently. The London slave trade, which enjoyed a notable revival from the 1750s, was conducted on independent London account, while much of the shipping in the British West Indies trade was similarly operated not by commission agents but by independent shipowners and merchants.[27]

Second, recent research does not substantiate Hancock's view that independent London merchants took the initiative in transatlantic trade in the late colonial period. With respect to the Chesapeake, while it is true that independent Liverpool and Glasgow merchants increased greatly their share of the region's trade from the 1740s, these were provincial, not London, traders. The more enterprising London merchants trading to the Chesapeake extended their trading portfolios not by trade on their own account, but by acting as *commission agents* to independent indigenous merchants in the cargo trade. Turning to the northern colonies, we can draw on Doerflinger's recent study of Philadelphia, which shows that local merchants who imported manufactured goods from London commission agents retained their "overwhelming predominance" in the trade. Doerflinger rejects the frequently expressed view that London merchants attempted to bypass this traditional Philadelphia merchant group in the 1760s and 1770s by exporting manufactures to the city on their own account or by consigning them for sale to local shopkeepers and auctions. It is true that certain London and provincial commission agents invaded the Philadelphia–West Indies trade from the 1760s, which had formerly been wholly dominated by Philadelphia interests; but even here the cargoes of provisions exported from Philadelphia to the West Indies, in ships outward bound from England, were carried on the account of the importing West India planters and merchants for whom the English agents and shipowners provided commission and transport services.[28]

Third, the view that many London colonial merchants shifted from a trading to a primarily financial role in the eighteenth century does have much to recommend it. After all, London took over Amsterdam's position as the world's leading financial center from circa 1750, an outcome based on a long prehistory of London merchants specializing in finance. London's financial role was further underwritten by the large influx of foreign merchants into the London merchant community, many of whom were as much or more financiers than traders.

Why, then, did commission trading become so significant in colonial commerce, and what determined if (and when) a particular trade would be drawn into its orbit or would remain under the control of independent merchants? The commission system, from the late seventeenth century, was adopted by the planters of the West Indies and the Chesapeake and by the merchants of the northern mainland ports. Three essential preconditions had to be fulfilled before the commission system emerged in the plantation colonies. First was the growth of a wealthy class of producers, as only rich planters could both absorb the entrepreneurial risks and marketing delays inherent in the system and provide a large enough scale of business to attract the services of London agents. Of course, planters in theory could have financed the wider costs of commission marketing by drawing on the resources of London commission agents, as was common in the later colonial period when financial matters tended to dominate the agent-client relationship. However, before circa 1730 commission agents did not advance finance to their planter-correspondents on any scale. Hence, the commission system was used by planters for *commercial* rather than purely financial advantages, and its adoption required an established planter class who possessed both the resources to wait a year or more for the proceeds of their crops and information about and contacts in transatlantic markets.[29]

The second precondition was the return to London by enough planters and merchants from the colonies to form the nucleus of a network of metropolitan commission agencies. It was absentee planters, above all, who pioneered the commission system in London. They began by marketing the produce of their own plantations and went on to sell the crops of resident planters, who were mostly friends and business associates encountered during their period of colonial residency and who, in turn, recommended the agents' services to fellow planters. The professional relationship was sustained by personal connections and mutual interests that bound planters and agents tightly together. Many agents continued to own plantations in the colonies, creating a strong identity of interest between themselves and their clients because agents, as absentee planters, experienced many of the same problems and anxieties faced by resident planters and, moreover, depended on the latter to provide advice and assistance in the running of their estates. The links were reinforced by the many services the agents supplied, other than arrangements for the sale of cargoes: in particular, the planters found that by far the best way to pay for their substantial purchases of slaves in the colonies was to draw bills of exchange on their London agents for that purpose. Of course, some commission agents had never been resident in the colonies, but many of these were allied by marriage or business partnerships to London agents who had resided there.[30]

The third precondition was that the commodities consigned in the commission trade should have two characteristics: they should be goods for which London was by far the major market; and they should be subject to large variations in quality, giving producers the incentive of gaining *premium* prices for higher grades by consigning them for sale in London, where the largest number of specialist buyers for the home and foreign markets were gathered. Sugar and the better-quality grades of tobacco consigned to commission agents shared these characteristics. All the planter had to do to turn entrepreneur was to establish a correspondence with one or two reputable commission agents; the agents did the rest, leaving the planter to concentrate on production with no requirement that he should exercise a considerable entrepreneurial expertise or energy in the marketing of his crops.[31]

In the West Indies trade these preconditions first came into place in the 1660s, when a class of major planters was established in Barbados, although the definitive appearance of such a class in Jamaica was delayed until the 1680s and 1690s and in the Leeward Islands until the years from circa 1690 to 1710. It was also in the post-Restoration period that planters perfected the production of higher-quality sugars and when London consolidated its position as the chief focus for England's West India trade, accounting for 85 percent and 95 percent, respectively, of England's sugar imports and reexports.[32] The planters' decision to actually adopt the commission system was triggered by falling sugar prices in the *colonial* sugar markets, which persuaded the bigger estate owners that they would be better off selling their sugar in London. Sugar prices were high in the 1640s but fell steeply from the late 1650s, and by the mid-1680s prices had plummeted to the lowest level seen in the West Indies in the entire colonial period. Planters therefore switched to the consignment system, as "when profits were being cut to the bone . . . the chance of an extra shilling or even a few pence on 100 lbs. sugar could not be ignored by those planters who could afford the delay in dispatching their goods to London."[33] In the period 1689–1713, however, the war-affected European market was starved of sugar, with the result that sugar prices in the British colonial markets were 50 percent higher on average in the war years than in the mid-1680s. This strong price recovery, combined with the high risks of capture faced by sugar ships in wartime, persuaded planters to sell their crops in the islands rather than consign them to London. Sugar prices remained steady in the postwar boom, but they fell in the renewed depression that engulfed the trade in the late 1720s and 1730s, as they had from the late 1650s—trends that persuaded the great majority of planters in all the islands to sell their sugar in London rather than locally.

The commission system did not become a significant method of trade in the Chesapeake until 1690–1720, a lagged development explained by two contrasting features in the economic and social development of the sugar and tobacco colonies. First, a substantial cadre of slave-owning planters wealthy enough to initiate commission trading did not appear in the Chesapeake until slaves began to be imported in larger numbers around 1680, when the depression in the sugar industry diverted slave cargoes from the Caribbean to the mainland. By the same token, it was not until then that tobacco planters found a need for an elaborated system of bills of exchange to pay for slaves. So in the 1690s in Virginia planters could buy indentured servants with tobacco but were required to buy slaves with bills of exchange.[34] Second, tobacco prices in the colonies fell to their lowest historical levels not in the 1670s and 1680s but in the war years 1689–97 and 1702–12, when the Chesapeake was afflicted by continuous shortages of shipping that caused a chronic, local oversupply of tobacco; conversely, Virginia tobacco prices in Europe were, on average, a third to a half *higher* in the war years than in the years 1674–88. It was this evident and widening gulf between colonial and European prices that persuaded the wealthier planters in the Chesapeake to consign far more tobacco to London from 1690 to 1720 than they had in the preceding period.[35]

The essential precondition for the commission system in the northern colonies was the growth not of a class of wealthy agriculturalists but of an indigenous merchant and ship-owning community with substantial resources and widespread trading interests. Such a group first emerged in Boston in the second half of the seventeenth century. These merchants conducted much more complex business operations than did the sugar and tobacco planters. Planters owned little shipping circa 1700, and their business consisted simply of the bilateral shuttling of goods to and from England, complemented by dealings in the local island markets. The Boston merchants, on the other hand, consigned their exports to markets all over the Atlantic world and were frequently required to remit the commodities and specie generated by their shipping and trade earnings to London rather than Boston. New England merchants therefore found it indispensable to have an agency in London, not as a source of finance but as a clearinghouse, where the many aspects of their complex businesses could be centralized and expedited. Such agencies first came into existence in the 1680s, and their numbers grew in the early eighteenth century as they came to deal with the independent merchant groups of New York and Philadelphia. For example, David Waterhouse, the leading London commission agent in the New England trade in the 1690s and 1700s, acted as the London correspondent for a great many of Boston's major merchants: he sold their consignments of goods from numerous ports in the British and Spanish colonies and southern Europe; he managed the refitting and freighting of their ships whenever they docked in British ports, issued instructions to their captains for subsequent voyages, and sold many of these vessels on their behalf; he negotiated their bills of exchange, organized groups of London underwriters to insure their ships and cargoes, and shipped out orders of manufactures on their account—to mention only the major services he provided. Occasionally he traded on joint account with Boston merchants, although the great bulk of his large and demanding business was on commission account.[36]

The causes of the rise of the commission system can also be investigated by considering a negative case, the important South Carolina rice trade. Here the system was not adopted despite the fact that important preconditions for its existence were fully in place by the 1720s: namely, a wealthy group of rice planters had emerged in South Carolina while the merchant community in London dealing with the colony was dominated by merchants formerly resident for long spells in Charleston. However, rice was a bulky, standardized commodity exported from South Carolina not only to London, although much was in the early eighteenth century, but also to a wide variety of markets in America and Europe. The rice planters were discouraged from consigning their crops on their own account because this fragmentation of the markets for rice, and the high costs of its shipment relative to its value, required from planters a greater knowledge of commodity and freight markets than they possessed or wished to acquire. Moreover, there were far fewer gradations in quality in rice than in tobacco and sugar, which meant that rice planters had few opportunities to earn premium prices for higher grades by consigning their rice for sale in British markets. The commission system played a far greater part in the South Carolina indigo trade, which came to prominence from the mid-1750s, because commercial conditions for indigo were similar to those found in the sugar and higher-quality tobacco trades. First, virtually all indigo exports were shipped to London, while freight costs for indigo were low because the staple had a high value to bulk ratio. Planters were therefore able to market their own crops without the need to possess any great commercial expertise in the international commodity and freight markets. Second, indigo was a staple marked by great variations in quality; premium prices for quality grades were much more likely to be earned in British than in colonial markets, and this further encouraged the richer indigo planters to market their own crops in Britain on their own account and risk.[37]

The commission trades, then, were dominated by London from the late seventeenth century, and London's supremacy was never seriously challenged during the colonial period. It is true that Bristol developed a substantial commission trade in sugar in the first half of the eighteenth century and that there appears to have been a tendency for the outports, in general, to have increased their participation in the commission trades both to the West Indies and to the northern colonies in the decade before the American Revolution, although this subject has never been systematically studied.[38] But as late as 1770 London still controlled 75 percent of England's sugar imports and retained the lion's share of the commission trade in tobacco, as the outports, including Bristol, went over more and more to the direct purchase system for tobacco. Moreover, in certain respects, London intensified its control over the commission trades. First, from circa 1730 London commission agents advanced large sums of capital and credit to their clients, whether they were sugar and tobacco planters or merchant firms in the northern ports. From circa 1750 London also financed the cargo trades and the sale and distribution of slaves in the plantation colonies. These financial advances bound the interested parties in the colonies to their London agents, and the interest charged on these loans, together with the agents' fees and commissions, provided the basis of mercantile fortunes in the London commission trades.[39]

London's prominence throughout the colonial period in the operation and financing of the commission trades was rooted in its comparative advantages over the provincial British ports, namely in its undisputed role as Britain's premier market and financial center. London was the major national market for the distribution of sugar, coffee, dyestuffs, and the higher grades of tobacco, which were consumed in the domestic market rather than reexported. London was even more dominant as a wholesale emporium for the manufactured goods that were the staples of the export and reexport trades to the colonies: namely, English woollen and cotton textiles and metal goods, Asian calicoes, and European and Irish linens. In addition London's financial resources were immensely greater than those of the English regions, and hence London was able to finance the expanding volume of credit associated with the commission trades from circa 1730 in a way that the provincial ports could not match.[40]

However, in the course of the eighteenth century London relinquished its grip on the noncommission colonial trades that gravitated to the outports, that is, the import and reexport trades in rice and the tobacco produced by the lesser planters, and the export trades in slaves, Irish provisions, and Newfoundland fish. The trades that came under provincial control formed a heterogeneous group, but they had one thing in common: they were all long-distance and multilateral *bulk* trades, in which port and shipping charges made up a high proportion of total costs. This was true even of tobacco as London tended to import the dense and expensive sweet-scented varieties for the domestic market, while Glasgow and the English provincial ports dealt in the cheaper grades for the reexport market with a rather lower value to bulk ratio. The provincial ports wrested the transatlantic bulk trades away from the metropolis in the eighteenth century by exploiting *their* comparative advantage, that is, their ability to supply shipping and port facilities much more cheaply than London did.[41] The continuing advantage of the provincial ports in these respects is shown by the fact that from 1680 to 1770 London's foreign-going shipping fleet remained static in size at 150,000 tons, while the tonnage of the outports' fleet more than doubled from 190,000 to 450,000 tons.[42] In the provincial ports costs were lower, including those of seamen's wages and dock labor; of port facilities, including administrative fees; and of the procurement, provisioning, and refitting of ships.[43] Costs were further reduced by shorter voyages, partly because the provincial ports were nearer to American markets but mainly because their ships achieved much shorter turn-around times in colonial ports. London ships freighting from the West Indies and the Chesapeake were filled with goods consigned by planters and merchants to their London agents, and these ships often spent months in the colonies as cargoes were laboriously assembled from numerous freighters.[44] The Glasgow tobacco ships, the Bristol rice ships, and the Liverpool slavers, on the other hand, were operated on different and far more efficient principles: they dealt not with an array of dilatory planters but with single agents or salaried factors, colonial representatives who were primed to dispatch ships as rapidly as possible partly because as men of business they possessed good information about local freight markets and partly because, under instructions from the ships' owners, they purchased cargoes or part-cargoes in advance of the ships' arrival.[45]

Of course, the division of the Atlantic trades between London and the provincial ports cannot solely be explained in terms of relative transport costs. First, Glasgow flourished in the tobacco trade partly because the giant tobacco firms that dominated the business mobilized a considerable part of western Scotland's surplus capital to finance an extension of credit to thousands of small and middling tobacco producers in the Chesapeake—as vital an element in Glasgow's trading success as was the efficiency of its shipping fleets. Second, it was Yorkshire merchants, rather than those of London, who controlled the rapidly growing woolen trade to America in the years 1750–75. The specialist Yorkshire merchants were much better informed about foreign markets and the intricacies of the local manufacturing of woolens than were the London merchants, for whom woolen exports were merely one aspect of a general export business, and hence were far quicker to grasp and implement the changes in products, fashions, and prices demanded by the American and other consumer markets. Third, Liverpool merchants from the 1740s were highly ingenious in solving the major entrepreneurial problem posed by the slave trade, which was how to remit the proceeds of slave cargoes in America.[46]

Merchant Specialization and Growth in the Scale of Business, 1600–1780

Did merchants become more specialized in their activities in the seventeenth and eighteenth centuries, and was trade increasingly concentrated in the hands of fewer merchants? By 1600 the activities of English merchants already demonstrated a clear degree of specialization. First, the most important trades were dominated by trading companies, such as the Merchant Adventurers, the members of which used their state-sponsored privileges to exclude competition from retailers and other domestic dealers. Second, merchants restricted their principal activities to one trading company and hence to one geographical area. Nevertheless, within these areas merchants carried on a general business. They did not specialize in one commodity, nor did they trade in a single direction; rather they were composite import-export merchants who traded in all the commodities appropriate to the area in which they possessed corporate trading privileges.[47] In the seventeenth and eighteenth centuries mercantile specialization became much more marked so that by the 1680s and 1690s the great majority of London merchants trading to Europe focused their business on one commodity or in trade to one region. Moreover, in any particular branch of London's trade, merchants were divided into exporters, or importers, or reexporters—that is, they specialized by the direction of trade. Of course, not all merchants specialized, and even the majority who did usually broadened their activities to include subsidiary interests in other trades, although these were normally related to their main specialism.[48] It is often said that, in contrast to the Londoners, provincial merchants were nonspecialists, but in fact the evidence points to the opposite conclusion, namely, that outport merchants specialized by region and that exports were handled by one group of merchants and imports by another.[49]

These conclusions about mercantile specialization in the European trades have also been applied to the colonial trades. Indeed, Price and Clemens have doubted "that there ever was an age of sustained nonspecialization in the Atlantic trades."[50] However, before the 1640s, it would appear that London merchants moved freely between the import trades from different colonial regions and had extensive interests in activities such as East Indies interloping, while in Bristol, nonprofessional merchants had a large share of trade throughout the century.[51] But by the 1680s the great majority of London's colonial merchants specialized in importing either sugar or tobacco but did not deal in both. Specialized trading continued in London in the eighteenth century and also came to characterize the provincial ports when sugar and tobacco commission agents formed quite distinct groups while the trade to the northern mainland colonies was handled by yet another set of merchants.[52] However, merchants trading to the colonies in the eighteenth century were less likely to specialize by direction than those trading to Europe were. This is best explained by the Navigation Acts, which dictated that transatlantic trade had to be routed through England in both directions and by the close economic ties that bound British commission agents to colonial planters. For instance, London and Bristol commission agents sold sugar for individual planters and in return shipped out their orders of manufactured goods.[53]

The growth of specialization was accompanied by an increasing concentration of English trade in the hands of fewer merchants, a trend which, for the eighteenth century, has been described as a "revolution of scale in overseas trade." In fact, the process by which trade became more concentrated was a far from continuous one. By circa 1600 trade was already highly concentrated. In the major English trades at this time, namely the London cloth-export trades to northwest Europe, the Levant, and Iberia, the pattern of concentration was remarkably similar: in each trade an inner core of some twenty to thirty merchants, out of a total of about two hundred participants, controlled about 50–60 percent of exports.[54] In the seventeenth century, indeed, trade became *less* concentrated both because of the major growth of cloth exporting from provincial ports and because of the inflow of nonprofessional London and provincial merchants into the unregulated trades to America and the Iberian Peninsula. In Bristol, for example, colonial trade was dispersed widely among members of the city's business community; in 1654–56 only one-fifth of the 461 importers from the colonies were bona fide "merchants."[55] From the later seventeenth century, however, the degree of concentration became once more very marked in *every* foreign trade for which we have evidence. In the London colonial trades in the 1680s there were hundreds of importers of sugar and tobacco, but a small number of merchants dominated trade: in 1686, for example, forty firms handled 86 percent of London tobacco imports; by 1775, when London tobacco imports had trebled in volume, 90 percent of the trade was handled by just twenty-eight firms.[56] In the outports the process of concentration was delayed until circa 1730: in the Bristol sugar trade there were over five hundred importers in 1728, few of whom traded on a large scale; by 1788, 98 percent of an enlarged trade was handled by twenty-six importers. In Liverpool in the early 1780s as few as a dozen firms handled two-thirds or more of the port's vast slave trade.[57]

Why was there a growth in specialization and concentration in foreign trade? There were factors that encouraged a high degree of specialization, but in the limited discussion possible here it is worth emphasizing two in particular. First, merchants naturally preferred to specialize in the trades in which they had their greatest expertise, usually acquired through overseas residence as factors or producers. In the Atlantic trades the connection between specialization and former residency in the colonies was strong. So most London sugar commission firms throughout the colonial period were founded by individuals who had been merchants or planters in the West Indies, while the majority of the major London merchants trading to South Carolina after 1720 had also spent lengthy periods in Charleston. Second, and linked to this, most merchants specialized in the trade of one or two regions to avoid the difficulty they experienced in their careers in establishing more than a handful of personal and professional relationships with creditworthy and reliable overseas agents. Merchants, in other words, tended to stick to those trades in which their local knowledge and experience were great enough to allow them to forge secure ties with a circle of dependable overseas representatives.[58]

A higher degree of specialization, it could be argued, was almost bound to lead to greater *concentration* simply because a merchant was more likely to build up a leading position in a trade that was his sole concern than he was in several trades. Certainly, in the seventeenth century increasing specialization in the colonial trades ran parallel with the growth in the scale of business handled by merchant firms. However, as Price and Clemens's recent comprehensive study has shown, the degree of merchant specialization in the colonial trades reached its high point circa 1680, while the process of concentrating trade in fewer firms continued unabated for another century, both in London and in the provincial ports. They suggest, therefore, that the process of concentration was a self-reinforcing one, that larger firms grew ever larger because of their competitive advantages over smaller ones: they had lower unit transaction costs, and they gained cheaper and more abundant credit, both from wholesale suppliers and in the capital markets, because they were deemed more creditworthy than smaller firms were.[59]

While Price and Clemens's thesis is a compelling one, it has not been empirically tested across trades. Indeed, the links between firm size and market competitiveness have been assessed in only one transatlantic trade, the late eighteenth-century slave trade. Here, Inikori has argued that the entry of merchants to the slave trade was restricted circa 1790; a few giant Liverpool firms dominated the commerce because the scale of their business gave them privileged access to credit and to supplies of export goods.[60] In a critique of Inikori's thesis, however, Anderson and Richardson riposte that "levels of concentration . . . in the British slave trade around 1790 were not [unusually high] and were insufficient to allow the larger firms to wield the market power" that Inikori's model assumes; they conclude that all firms, large and small, had excellent access to credit and to supplies of trade goods—in other words, the large slave firms were *not* able to exploit the kinds of market advantages over the smaller concerns emphasized by Price and Clemens.⁶¹ The notion, then, that a growing concentration in colonial trade in the eighteenth century was a self-reinforcing process is an attractive one, but as yet the hypothesis has not been definitively established for any branch of transatlantic trade. Indeed, commercial organization may have been based on a paradox: that trades became highly concentrated in fewer hands but, at the same time, presented few barriers to new merchants who wished to enter them.

Whatever the causes of increasing specialization and concentration, it is clear that these developments underpinned the position of the elites of wealthy professional merchants who dominated British foreign trade until 1780, leaving little room for the participation of retailers and manufacturers in foreign commerce. In the early seventeenth century nonprofessional merchants had been excluded from the most important trades by the hostility of the trading companies, yet neither were they favored by the system of freer trade that eventually replaced corporate control. It is true that the sheer scale of the growth of demand in eighteenth-century American markets encouraged manufacturers and domestic tradesmen to sidestep merchants and make direct sales to the colonies. But this development did not gain any impetus until about 1750, and in general, the importance of nonmerchant exporters in the colonial trades before the American Revolution is easily exaggerated, as several examples show. First, the New York merchant James Beekman imported less than 2 percent of his British dry goods directly from manufacturers in the period 1753–75, with the rest of his needs supplied by merchants. Second, Joshua Johnson, a Maryland tobacco merchant in London in the early 1770s, found it impossible to buy any quantity of goods directly from Midlands manufacturers for shipment to America because they could not match the long credits offered by the London wholesalers, who consequently remained his major suppliers. Tradesmen and manufacturers were relatively more important as exporters outside London, for example in Bristol, but even there they traded on a much smaller scale than the professional merchants.⁶² Manufacturers did not dislodge the merchants' traditional grip on the export trades in the colonial period. This had to await the early nineteenth century, when revolutionary changes in the British financial system enabled manufacturers to overcome what had hitherto been the insurmountable obstacle to their direct exporting: lack of export finance.

The Organization of British Atlantic Trade, 1780–1830

Until recently Buck's classic study provided the general framework for our understanding of the major innovations that occurred in the organization of Anglo-American trade in the late eighteenth and early nineteenth centuries. Buck argued that until circa 1815 the export trade to America was organized by British merchants who traded on their own account and risk but that from 1815 to 1830 there was a decisive change in commercial structure: the independent merchants were replaced by the manufacturers, who became the chief exporters of industrial goods. In recent years, however, Chapman has proposed a radically different interpretation of developments. The large-scale involvement of manufacturers in direct exporting, he argues, commenced in the boom in textile exports to America from the 1770s, exports that could not be marketed through the existing mercantile system, dislocated as it was by the volatile trading conditions of the American (1776–82) and French revolutions (1793–1815), which bankrupted or forced into retirement many traditional merchants. The differences between the two interpretations are greatest for the years before 1815, but even for the period 1815–30 there is little real agreement between them: Buck sees the years after 1815 as a period when manufacturers began to export directly to foreign markets, whereas Chapman argues that this system of marketing in fact declined in these years. In truth, both of these interpretations can be challenged. Buck's is flawed because he misunderstood the role of English export merchants before 1815, conferring on them a predominantly independent role in trade that they had not in fact occupied for over a century, while Chapman anticipates the true date of the demise of the old-style merchants by thirty to forty years.[63]

In fact, the notable feature of the period from 1780 to 1800, or even later, is the continuity in methods used to organize trade: there was a huge increase in the volume of commerce, but it was accommodated by a reconstruction of the modes that had existed before the American Revolutionary War rather than a revolution in trading methods. This reconstruction was accompanied, it is true, by the appearance of novel elements in British-American commercial organization, but it was not until after 1810 that these innovations matured to the point where they displaced the old system of trade. After the Revolution the British-American export trade was served by merchants whose business methods closely resembled those prevalent in the colonial period, and who in the long, post-1782 boom in trade flooded the U.S. market with manufactures. The major exports were Lancashire cotton textiles and Yorkshire woolens. Cotton exports were controlled by two sets of merchants. First, London merchants exported cottons partly to American orders but also increasingly on their own accounts, and they bought their cotton manufactures from London wholesalers, who acted in a traditional capacity as links between the northern manufacturers and the London export merchants. Second, Liverpool merchants, who had entered trade before the war, shipped out a rapidly growing volume of cottons, mainly on account of American importers. The Yorkshire cloth trade to the United States continued to be handled by many of the Leeds firms that had dominated exports in the late colonial period, although many new firms entered the trade, which was increasingly being channeled through Liverpool rather than London. The Yorkshire merchants, however, consigned a far higher proportion of woolen exports on their own account than had been customary before the war. Conventional merchants also continued to control the import trades. For example, imports of sugar and other goods from the West Indies, which trebled from 1782 to 1802, were mainly handled by long-established London commission agents that had been active in trade before the American War. These long-established commission agents were supplemented by new firms, mainly of London but some of them based in Liverpool, which were prominent in the financing of the massive slave trade to newly acquired islands such as Grenada.[64]

From the 1770s, as Chapman suggests, British manufacturers did increase direct exports on their own accounts to the United States, and in time they superseded the traditional London and provincial merchants who had controlled Anglo-American trade for two centuries or more. However, the winning of this initiative was a much slower and discontinuous business than Chapman allows. In cottons, some large-scale concerns did export directly to America in the 1780s and 1790s, but these industrial giants were exceptional and the mass of lesser manufacturers, who dominated output, simply did not have the capital resources to break into foreign trade. In woolens, the declining West Country and East Anglian industries made little progress in foreign markets in the late eighteenth century. The West Country manufacturers had marketed their cloth through London cloth dealers since the sixteenth century, and from 1770 only a few of the largest firms made perfunctory and unsuccessful attempts to engage in direct exporting. The East Anglian manufacturers did export directly to Europe on their own account after 1783, but these efforts petered out in the 1790s when the French wars made trading conditions hazardous. In Yorkshire, the main branch of the woolen industry, on the other hand, some broadcloth manufacturers, who built the first generation of woolen factories from 1785 to 1800, did use the handsome profits they made as pioneers of mechanization to finance direct export sales to the booming United States market. This strategy was not, however, emulated by the Yorkshire worsted manufacturers, who failed to centralize production before 1815 and hence lacked access to the sort of inflated industrial profits that the broadcloth producers used to finance direct exporting.[65]

From 1800 the wartime closure of Britain's main markets, first in Europe and then in the United States, created the first major reversals for the modernizing textile industries: in Lancashire manufacturers experienced waning profits and there was a clear deceleration in factory investment; in Yorkshire the first factory boom of 1785–1800 came to an end and from 1800–1812 the broadcloth industry experienced disinvestment, as "more mills ceased working . . . than entered the industry." The depth of the trading and industrial crisis persuaded many woolen and cotton producers to undertake further experiments in the organizing of trade. Manufacturers exported on their own account to commission agents who sprang up in outlying ports such as Heligoland and Trieste, and from there textiles were smuggled into the areas closed to British exports by Napoleon's Continental System; or they rushed into the Latin American market, which for a year or two took a greater value of woolen exports than did Europe or the United States.[66] However, despite the many initiatives taken by manufacturers, it appears that outside Latin America neither cotton nor woolen producers came near to dominating the overseas marketing of their respective products during the French wars. As Hudson comments on the Yorkshire woolen industry: "although there is some evidence of . . . manufacturers getting directly into the Atlantic trade from an early date . . . this accounted for only a small proportion of trade before the 1820s."[67]

However, from 1815, as Buck argued, the manufacturers shifted decisively into direct exporting to the United States market. This development reflected postwar production conditions in the textile industries: a constant rise in output, especially in cottons, and a continuous fall in prices caused by the acceleration of productivity gains in manufacturing, the cheapening of raw materials, and the strong deflationary pressures induced by Britain's "return to gold" in 1816. These trends created the most intense competition ever seen in Britain's domestic and foreign markets. Manufacturers, faced by excess capacity at home, were forced to export a growing proportion of output on low profit margins but found the existing mercantile structure inadequate to the task. The problem was that few London merchants vigorously promoted exports on the manufacturers' behalf. Instead, they either responded passively to orders from American merchants or, if they traded, as many did, on their own accounts, were unwilling to take the financial risks of pushing exports in an aggressive manner that would, of course, have entangled them in a massive and hazardous extension of credits to the American market. The provincial merchant groups were also found wanting. The Yorkshire merchants had long been specialists in broadcloths, and they refused to shift their interests to the cheaper worsted cloth that dominated the American market after 1815. Indeed, by 1830 virtually all the major Leeds merchant houses had gone into retirement. Liverpool merchants were more enterprising than most, but their trade was crippled by the mutually antagonistic commercial policies followed after 1805 by Britain and the United States, and by 1815 many Liverpool merchants were bankrupted or had retired.[68]

Textile manufacturers after 1815, therefore, bypassed or elbowed aside the traditional merchant cadres, whose centuries-old dominance of Anglo-American trade was abruptly terminated. The cotton and woolen manufacturers adopted one of three new marketing strategies, each of which included marketing exports on their accounts and risks. First, they directly exported to agents in the United States, often relatives who had been sent abroad to represent the home firms. So Yorkshire manufacturers of worsteds, who doubled the number of worsted mills between 1815 and 1822, were represented in the United States by a wave of post-1815 migrants. Second, they consigned their exports to commission agents in Great Britain, who reconsigned them to their agents overseas. These were *not* established firms of the pre-1815 period but new Liverpool and

Manchester firms that now handled the bulk of exports to the United States. A variation on this policy was to consign exports directly to British commission agents resident in foreign ports, the normal method of trade in, for example, the Latin American market. Third, from 1820 many British export manufacturers sold—in effect dumped—massive quantities of goods at American auctions for low prices and cash payment. Thus, in the mid-1820s over half of British manufactured exports to the United States were sold under the hammer at New York auctions, mainly on behalf of the manufacturers.[69] Of course, the crucial element in the new system of trade, as in the old, was the financial one. The manufacturers and new commission agencies took control of trade because they gained access to new and abundant sources of finance, without which the post-1800 revolution in the organization of trade could not have occurred.

So far this account of the reorganization of British-American commerce after 1780 has emphasized revolutionary innovations at the British end of the business, but there were equally profound changes in the structure and commercial activities of the merchant communities in the United States.[70] This is a large subject, and here these changes are merely sketched in, with an emphasis on three distinct phases: 1782–92, 1793–1808, and 1809–30. During the Revolutionary period the pattern of American trade changed: from 1768–72 to 1790–92 exports from the northern colonies, mainly of food and grain, more than doubled, while southern exports of tobacco and rice stagnated. There was also a major boom and then an equally severe crash in the import of manufactures from Britain, the fallout from which helped cause a deep recession in the wider economy.[71] Many American merchants had died or retired in the Revolution, although the loss of personnel was more than made good by the British and Irish merchants who flooded into the United States after the war, many of whom acted as agents of London and Liverpool merchants shipping manufactures on their own account. These migrants, and American merchant-importers, were supplied with, and themselves sold on, British manufactures on such liberal credit terms that by 1785–86 most American importers were massively in debt to Britain. The London debts of one American firm in the relatively minor port of Annapolis, for example, reached 240,000 pounds by 1785, a sum that would have staggered even the most reckless of prewar merchants and that took the firm nearly twenty years to liquidate. Many American merchants who suffered in "the critical period" gave up importing from Britain altogether and shifted their horizons to the trades in foodstuffs to the West Indies and southern Europe and to the new trades to Asia and Europe, from which they had hitherto been excluded by the Navigation Acts.[72]

From 1793 to 1808 American trade was revolutionized. The United States took advantage of its neutrality while Europe was at war, and its merchants built on the initiatives of the 1780s and captured a large part of Europe's carrying trades to the West Indies, to central and southern America, and to China, India, and the Dutch East Indies. In many years to 1808 U.S. reexports of Asian and American goods made up half or more of total exports, which at their peak were six to seven times as great by value as in 1768–72. The carrying trades, moreover, required an enormous freight capacity, and by 1810 America's shipping fleet, which now hauled 95 percent of the country's trade due to American advantages in operating shipping, totaled 1.25 million tons, rivaling that of Britain's in size. The boom in trade and shipping was punctuated, it is true, by a great volatility in prices and demand and by hazardous conditions for American shipping, which was often attacked or impeded by French and British privateers and warships.[73] Nevertheless, the commercial expansion underpinned the rapid growth of the four great seaports, Baltimore, New York, Philadelphia, and Boston, at least to 1808 (although it had more muted effects on the wider economy), and enabled American merchants, for the first time, to make large fortunes in businesses that were only tangentially connected to British-American trade.[74]

Many firms, however, mindful of the commercial debacle of the mid-1780s, steered clear of the trade in manufactures from Britain. Indeed, a large share of this trade was handled by British immigrants, who continued to settle in American ports in large numbers after 1790, as they had in the 1780s. Many of them represented British merchants, although some acted for woollen and cotton manufacturers. British business interests thus consolidated the more controlling position they had achieved in the organization of Anglo-American trade in the 1780s. Nevertheless, the high prices that scarce British goods commanded in the United States in wartime attracted the renewed interest of some indigenous merchant firms in importing from Britain, the more enterprising of which established permanent representatives in London or Liverpool.[75]

From 1808 everything changed: U.S. trade and shipping were hit by embargoes and by the war with Britain and then, from 1815, by the resurgence of European competition in the transoceanic carrying trades, in a context of a sharp and worldwide postwar deflation in commodity and industrial prices. The value of U.S. imports and of domestic exports, other than raw cotton, declined, while that of reexports and shipping earnings, which had driven the foreign trade boom in the war years, plummeted. The decline of trade and shipping, and the squeezing of commercial profits, brought about the retirement or bankruptcy of numerous American merchants in all the major seaports and a general reallocation of mercantile capital from the foreign trade sector to the domestic economy. Merchants switched their capital to manufacturing, especially cotton textiles, to federal and state securities and banking, and to land speculation and the financing of internal trade, in an economy where population and settlement were growing at an exponential rate.[76]

The American merchants' reversals, however, were greatest in a trade that was in fact growing rapidly, at least in volume if not in value, but in which competition was fiercest—namely the import trade in British manufactures. Britain inundated the United States with manufactures after 1814, exports accompanied by yet another wave of British merchant-migrants. The independent New York merchants, who had cornered the largest share of the trade in manufactures at the expense of Philadelphia and Boston, were hit hard by this renewed competition and devastated by the leap in New York auction sales from 1818, which bypassed them altogether. Henceforth, most leading New York merchant firms traded as shipping and commission agents rather than on their own account. From 1815 American merchants in the northern ports found that they could only act as independent entrepreneurs in the British-American trade if they specialized, either in the raw cotton export trade from New York or the South, or in the importing from Britain of specialist categories of metal goods or high-quality textiles. To sum up: the revolutionary changes in the organization and financing of trade in Britain in the early nineteenth century swept away the conventional British merchants who had ruled trade for two centuries; but they also forced major changes in the composition and business practices of the merchant communities in the United States.[77]

Capital and Credit in the British Atlantic Economy, 1600–1830

The Financing of British Colonial Trade, 1600–1780

Nearly all of the overseas regions with which Britain traded in the seventeenth and eighteenth centuries were rich in natural resources or in labor but poor in capital. The essential precondition for the expansion of Britain's overseas trade in the preindustrial period was therefore that British merchants advance substantial and increasing sums of capital to foreign traders and producers. Thus, a high proportion of British exports to Spain and Portugal was reexported to Spanish America and Brazil, and as British merchants were usually not paid until proceeds had been remitted from America, they found it necessary from circa 1700 to extend credit in Iberian markets for two to three years. The import-oriented trades also required a heavy financial commitment.[78] In fact, the only trading region that did not tap into English capital was the advanced economy of northwest Europe, from which, indeed, there was a large net inflow of funds.[79]

Of all Britain's foreign trades, that to colonial America grew fastest and thus made the greatest demands on British mercantile capital. The pattern of the distribution of capital and credit within this Atlantic system was determined by the modes of trade organization discussed in the first half of this chapter. In the early seventeenth century, when colonization was controlled by institutions such as the Virginia Company, English company merchants and other corporate investors directly invested in plantation and infrastructural development. Because from circa 1630 such collective investments ceased to be of much significance in the financing of colonial trade, this financing came to be dominated by independent British merchants who extended trade credit of about six months on average to colonial customers for manufactures and other exports. The slave business, on the other hand, was largely financed by the Royal Africa Company, which came to be saddled with trade debts in the West Indies that circa 1700 peaked at 160,000–170,000 pounds. The company's capital was not provided by merchants trading to the colonies, few of whom bought the company's stock, but by other merchants and businessmen and by large-scale borrowings on bond in the London money market.[80]

From the late seventeenth century the commission system became the principal mode of trade organization in the colonial trades, and in the long run it supplied more capital to the colonies than the independent traders ever did. However, from its introduction in the 1670s until the 1720s, by which time commission trading was in widespread use, the system failed to provide a major means by which British capital was transmitted to the colonies. In the West Indies trade Davies found no evidence that commission agents advanced loans to their planter-clients in the late seventeenth century, and he showed that the bill system collapsed in the war years 1689–1713, when the majority of bills drawn by Barbadian planters in favor of the Royal Africa Company were "protested"; when the planters were most in need of credit, their London commission agents deserted them.[81] More recent research on Jamaica in the late seventeenth and early eighteenth centuries corroborates the view that the commission system was not a major source of finance for West Indian planters. Zahedieh and Sheridan have shown that the majority of deceased sugar planters' estates owed no debts to London merchants and that circa 1720 many held sterling cash balances with their commission agents, as well as investments in the English funds, in company stocks, and in land.[82]

The London commission agents also failed to extend large credits to the Chesapeake tobacco in the period to 1730. In the 1680s and 1690s, indeed, many leading planters strove to maintain substantial cash balances with their commission agents in London. It is true that, after 1700, the commission firm of Micajah Perry advanced sums of 1,500–3,000 pounds to great planters, but this was by far the biggest firm in the trade, one that sought to cultivate a close relationship with the greater planters, and we can assume that the smaller commission firms advanced less capital. This is suggested by the fact that from 1704 to 1710 the great majority of bills drawn by planters on London tobacco commission agents were protested.[83]

Tight credit conditions were also imposed by London commission agents on their correspondents in the northern mainland colonies in the late seventeenth and early eighteenth centuries. David Waterhouse, for example, who acted for many leading Boston merchants in the 1690s and 1700s, never extended credit.[84] Samuel Storke, a London commission agent dealing with Boston and New York in the 1720s, "did not purchase goods for his [commission] correspondents until he had cash . . . or bills of exchange from them . . . , more often than not his customers' accounts showed a small credit balance in their favour."[85] Until 1730, then, commission agents did not advance substantial capital to colonial planters and merchants, and there is no evidence that merchants trading on an independent basis were any more liberal in providing credit. In the slave trade, for example, slaves were sold in the West Indies on an average credit of six to nine months in the 1680s and 1690s; in the war years 1689–1713 these credit terms were considerably tightened, after which they returned to their prewar levels.[86]

If, from 1680 to 1730, commission agents and independent merchants extended no more than short-term credits to colonial merchants and planters, and refrained from investing directly in plantation development, it follows that British-American economic development in these middle years of the colonial period was financed from internal, not external, sources. In the West Indies the tripling of sugar output from 1680 to 1730 was capitalized by three main means: by the investment of local mercantile profits in plantation development, of particular importance in Jamaica before 1700; by the ploughing back of plantation profits; and through loans extended by established resident planters to aspiring producers. For example, when Peter Beckford died in Jamaica in 1739, his estate was worth about 300,000 pounds, of which 135,000 pounds consisted of debts owing to him from other Jamaican planters. Thus, this *one* Jamaican magnate lent almost as much money to his fellow planters as the mighty Royal African Company had done at its peak, circa 1700.[87]

The view that colonial economic development from 1680 to 1730 was financed from domestic rather than British resources seems equally applicable to the Chesapeake region, where there was a big difference between the rates of growth in the internal and external economies. While the region's population grew nearly fourfold from 1680 to 1730, the volume of tobacco exports only doubled. By necessity Chesapeake resources were diverted into the production of cereals and other goods, but these products were not exported to any extent by 1730 and hence cannot have acted as a channel by which capital entered the region from overseas. One must conclude that regional growth was mainly financed internally, as in the West Indies, through reinvested agricultural profits and increased lending on the part of indigenous creditors. This accounts for the prominence of the merchant-planter elite in the tobacco colonies, to whom nearly all the lesser planters were indebted and whose central importance in the Chesapeake economy in the early eighteenth century has been highlighted by recent research.[88]

From the 1730s, however, there was a huge increase in the volume of capital advanced to the colonies by the specialist groups of commission agents who dealt with each region. First, commission agents lent capital sums to tobacco and, above all, sugar planters that dwarfed the loans made before circa 1730. Richard Pares argues that the sterling debts of virtually every sugar planter piled up from the mid-eighteenth century: the colonies "were ceasing to be communities of debtors and creditors, and becoming communities of debtors alone"; London commission agents regularly advanced individual West Indian planters unsecured loans of 10,000–20,000 pounds.[89] No precise estimates have ever been made of the total West Indian debt, although given that there were well over a thousand major sugar planters, a great many of whom were in debt, it is probable that the total sum owing to London merchants by circa 1770 had reached several million pounds.[90] This takes no account of the large sums owing from merchants and slave factors in the West Indies, who were backed by London sugar agents and whose appetite for credit was as hard to control as that of planters. Thus, in the 1760s one London commission agency was owed 140,000 pounds by a single firm in Jamaica, largely as a result of slave dealings.[91] Second, other groups of London commission agents financed exports both to the northern and, in the cargo trades, southern mainland colonies. Thus, many large firms in the northern ports were indebted to their London agents for sums of 10,000 pounds or more, while many Charleston importers of dry goods owed their London agents similar or larger sums in the early 1770s. Moreover, in the South Carolina slave trade some Charleston slave factors were indebted to London agents to the tune of 30,000–50,000 pounds in the late 1760s and 1770s.[92] The total mercantile debt owed by the mainland colonies to London, nearly all of which arose from the various commission trades, peaked at roughly 3.0 million pounds in 1774, although this sum was reduced to about 1.3 million pounds by 1776.[93]

British merchants also advanced a great deal of credit to the colonies in those trades in which they acted as independent entrepreneurs. In the 1740s the tobacco merchants of Liverpool and Glasgow set up chains of stores in the Chesapeake that extended their reach to virtually every tobacco planter, all of whom could obtain store credit over the crop cycle. On the eve of the Revolution, indeed, Glasgow was owed 1.3 million pounds by the tobacco colonies, a sum equal to the mainland colonies' total debts to London although far less than the debts that were suggested above for the West Indies.[94] In the slave trade from the 1740s, Liverpool merchants delivered slaves to colonial factors in exchange for postdated bills of exchange with an average duration of twelve to eighteen months, thus creating far longer credits than had been the case in the slave trade before circa 1730.[95] However, trade on independent British account did not always lead to British merchants granting more liberal credit. Again it was the mode of trade organization employed that shaped the flow of capital. In the South Carolina trade, British importers bought their rice not directly from planters but rather from agents in Charleston. The agents bought rice for cash and then drew bills of exchange on their English principals to recoup their outlays—bills, however, that were not paid in England until some months had elapsed. In the British import trade from South Carolina, then, British merchants obtained credit from colonial merchants rather than the other way around, and Charleston merchants were unable to tap into supplies of British finance.[96]

This survey of the financing of colonial trade from circa 1730 suggests that the key questions remain those first systematically investigated by Pares: why were British merchants more willing to advance capital to the colonies in the later colonial period; and where did they get this money?[97] Part of the answer lies in the inflow of capital from northwest Europe, mainly in the form of enormous eighteenth-century Dutch investment in the English public funds and augmented by the numerous foreign merchants who moved to London from the 1680s, whose own capital resources were supplemented by the credit made available to them by their continental correspondents. This inflow, Ormrod argues, freed English mercantile capital formerly tied up in the trades with northwest Europe, which was then reinvested in the Atlantic trades. The greater willingness to lend money to the colonies was further stimulated by a sharp drop in the rates of return in the British capital markets from the mid-1730s to the mid-1770s, when, for example, yields on most government-funded debts fell to a historical low of 3–3.5 percent, although rates were higher in the Seven Years' War. As Davis comments, Britain in the middle decades of the eighteenth century, partly as a consequence of Dutch and other foreign investments, "was constantly trembling on the edge of depression because savings were generated on a scale that could not readily find outlets." In contrast, a standard 5 percent interest was charged on colonial debts contracted in Britain and 6–8 percent on money advanced in the colonies, rates of return that favored a reallocation of capital from the British domestic to the colonial money markets. Risks on colonial loans were higher than those made to British debtors, but they were reduced from circa 1730, partly because long-term economic growth in America increased the colonists' assets and hence their collateral, and partly because the ability of British creditors to distrain the assets of defaulting colonial debtors was improved by legislation and by the perfecting of punitive means of securing loans such as bonds and mortgages.[98]

Where did British merchants acquire the capital to lend to the colonies? Of course, merchants entering trade disposed of equity capital, the bulk of which was raised by loans from relatives, augmented by marriage portions and such funds as tyro merchants had accumulated during their years as factors. However, in order to build large fortunes merchants had to supplement their start-up capitals from external sources. They could borrow from banks, but there were few banks before 1780, especially outside London, and these met "only a fraction of the merchants' credit needs."[99] Much more important were loans raised in the informal capital markets, from landowners, widows, and retired merchants who were willing to lend on bond to active merchants, often for indefinite periods. For example, in eighteenth-century Glasgow, loans made by banks to the city's leading merchants were dwarfed by those granted by private individuals; while in Lancashire and Yorkshire, a good deal of the community's surplus capital was lent through attorneys, much of which was borrowed by merchants.[100]

However, the most important source of merchants' expanded trading capital, as Price has shown, was the credit that export merchants obtained from the middlemen who supplied them with manufactured goods. Davis argues in a European context that, "on the whole, trade was financed by credit from industry," but in England industry played a limited direct role in the financing of commercial credit before circa 1800. In the early seventeenth century London merchants bought their cloth directly from the manufacturers, to whom they paid cash or advanced credit—that is, the merchants financed industry rather than the other way around. Subsequently, the direct links between the provincial clothiers and London exporters were broken and new categories of entrepreneurs came into existence to finance trade. From the mid-seventeenth century clothiers sold their cloth in London through the Blackwell Hall factors, who supplied credit both to the clothiers *and* to the export merchants who bought the cloths.

In the eighteenth century the factors found it impossible to sustain this double burden of credit and therefore concentrated on supplying finance to the manufacturers. They therefore ceased, for the most part, to sell cloth to merchants and sold instead to drapers, packers, and warehousemen who, despite their names, included some of the richest businessmen in England. In turn, these wealthy wholesalers supplied the export merchants, customarily on a year's credit. London wholesalers also provided key financial services in the other two major pre-1780 colonial export trades, those in metals and linens. Midlands ironmongers sent their products to wholesalers in London, who sold them to export merchants; in the linen trade London wholesale drapers, who imported on commission from Dutch, German, and Irish producers, also supplied the export sector.[101]

Price has made the most important contribution to our understanding of the financing and organization of colonial trade since Pares's pioneering researches; however, his singular emphasis on the role of London middlemen tends to neglect the contribution made by provincial sources of capital to the financing of the export trades. First, from the 1720s Yorkshire merchants steadily increased their woolen exports to the European and later the American markets, and by the early 1770s they were handling about 2.3 million pounds of woolen exports per year, over half the national total. These merchants bought cloth directly from small-scale clothiers for cash. From circa 1750 the bulk of this cloth was dispatched to the order of European and American merchants, on long credits financed by the Yorkshire merchants, although some cloth was sold to London export merchants who were required to make speedier payments.[102] Second, Liverpool and Bristol slave merchants and general export merchants received extensive credit from suppliers of manufactured goods in Lancashire and the Midlands. Provincial exporters, whose trade was increasing fast from midcentury, did not therefore depend on the capital of London middlemen but on their own resources or on credit drawn from the manufacturers.[103]

British merchants, then, assembled their capital portfolios from three main sources: start-up capitals; loans drawn from the informal capital market; and most important, from credit granted by London wholesalers and provincial manufacturers. To put these various sources of capital in perspective, we can refer to Price's estimate that the total investment of British mercantile firms in the Chesapeake trade in 1774 amounted to 4 million pounds: of this, the tobacco firms' equity capital, that is, their start-up capitals *plus* reinvested profits, accounted for about 1 million pounds; borrowings on bond 0.5 million pounds and from banks 0.1 million pounds; about 0.4 million pounds invested by outside firms in ships and other real assets; and the remaining 2 million pounds in the form of commercial credit advanced by London and provincial wholesalers to the tobacco merchants.[104] To build up large capitals, firms had therefore to do two things: first, extend their start-up capitals by borrowing on bond and through commercial credit; second, reinvest the profits they made on this extended trading capital, rather than distribute them to the firms' partners for their personal use. In years of good trade and high prices, firms could accumulate capital at a spectacular rate. So tobacco and sugar commission agents accumulated large capitals by reinvesting what appear, at first sight, to have been the trivial 2.5 percent commissions derived from the sale of colonial consignments and the 5 percent interest charged on loans. The London tobacco agency of James Buchanan and Co., for example, quadrupled its capital from 12,000 pounds to 48,000 pounds in the years 1758–68 by retaining 80 percent of its profits in the firm and extending its business through energetic innovation in the cargo trade.[105] Recent research on mercantile capital accumulation has, therefore, confirmed Pares's views, summarized in the last lines he published: "Adam Smith was wrong: the wealth of the British West Indies did not all proceed from the mother country; after some initial loans in the earliest period which merely primed the pump, the wealth of the West Indies was created out of the profits of the West Indies themselves."[106]

The Mobilization of Capital in the Atlantic Trades in Britain and the United States, 1780–1830

From 1780 Britain's Atlantic trades grew at a faster rate than in any previous period, while the period of credit granted to foreign customers for British textile exports, and to foreign suppliers of Britain's imports, was extended in virtually every branch of trade—at least until the late 1820s, when credit terms became less liberal. How was the tremendous growth in trade and credit financed? There was, of course, a high degree of continuity with the methods used before the American Revolution, although eventually there were important and indeed revolutionary changes in the financing of trade both in Britain and the United States.

In the 1780s and 1790s the most important source of British finance in the export sector remained the credit supplied by London wholesalers and provincial manufacturers. Thus, in London the wholesalers dealing in the enormous market in Lancashire cottons gave a year's credit to merchants exporting to America. In Liverpool and Bristol slave and export merchants expected and got fifteen to eighteen months' credit on goods supplied to them by northern textile manufacturers for the African and transatlantic trades. The most important innovation in trade financing resulted when London wholesalers universalized the practice by which the cotton manufacturers, at the time of delivery of goods, were permitted to draw long-dated bills on them for the whole or greater part of the value of textiles supplied. The manufacturers then discounted the bills with Lancashire banks, which specialized in discounting rather than in note issues, by which means they raised the funds needed to finance the next cycle of production. There was a similar mixture of old and new financial practices in the Yorkshire cloth-export trade to America, which also increased at a spectacular rate in the 1780s and 1790s. The Yorkshire merchants, as before the war, received little or no credit from the local clothiers but were required to grant far more extensive credit in American markets, where they now sold a much higher proportion of cloth on their own account. The solution to their pressing financial problems was twofold. First, they paid the clothiers not solely in cash, as they had formerly done, but mainly in innumerable small drafts drawn at one or two months' notice on country banks and in longer-dated bills drawn on themselves, which the clothiers could discount with local banks. Second, the merchants discounted the American bills, usually drawn on London, that they received in payment for woolens sold on their account in the United States.[107] So in woolens, as in cottons, a large part of the responsibility for financing trade was shifted to banks.

Indeed, the growing use in the 1780s, 1790s, and most notably after 1800 of bills of exchange and the discount market, as well as bank drafts and overdrafts, represented the central elements in the creation of a reordered financial system. This system was much more attuned to the needs of British foreign trade than that current in the colonial period had been, and it was the essential precondition for revolutionary changes in the organization of trade. The expansion of these financial instruments was mainly a function of the growth of banking. In London the number of private banks grew from eighteen in 1754 to seventy in 1800; the number of country banks trebled from 1784 to 1797 and then doubled again, to a peak of about six hundred banks by 1820. The impetus behind this latter multiplication of country banks was the suspension of cash payments from 1797 to 1816, which allowed an immense increase in bank note issues, thus creating "a more or less continuous credit expansion from 1797 to 1815 ... fertile ground for the breeding of swarms of new banks."[108]

From the point of view of financing foreign trade, however, the main contributions of banks lay not in their note issues but in the provision of loans and, most crucially, in the discounting of bills of exchange.[109] In London bankers such as Boyd and Benfield made loans to West Indies commission agents in the

French wars that ran into hundreds of thousands of pounds, unthinkable sums before 1780. In the provinces merchants borrowed on a smaller scale from country banks, but even here the size of loans shot up especially in the period of easier credit after 1797, and such borrowings were often critical to the expansion, or the survival, of provincial mercantile businesses.[110] The Bank of England, the private London banks, and their country cousins in the industrializing regions also discounted the mass of inland bills acquired by the manufacturers in sales to London, Yorkshire, and Liverpool export and slave merchants, as well as the flow of foreign bills of exchange received by the same merchants from the proceeds of their sales in America. The Bank of England, by the early 1780s, for example, discounted bills at the rate of 1.5–2.0 million pounds per month.[111] However, it became more difficult to negotiate bills with London banks during the French wars, partly because higher interest rates increased the discount rate but mainly because the Bank of England and London private banks diverted their capital from discounting to loans to the state. Thus, the Bank of England discounted fewer commercial bills in the mid-1790s than it had in the early 1780s, although there was a great resurgence in its discounting in some years after 1800. The vacuum in the discount market was filled by a huge interregional circulation of capital *between* country banks that, as noted, trebled in numbers during the suspension of cash payments period. Thus, inland bills of exchange received by, say, textile manufacturers and drawn on Yorkshire woolen merchants or London cotton wholesalers were taken up by country banks in the commercial areas and discounted, *via* London bill brokers, by banks in the agricultural areas, regions that generated massive surpluses of funds in a period of abnormally high agricultural prices and profits.[112]

It was the consolidation of further changes in the financial system that enabled manufacturers, from 1800 and with greater force after 1815, to circumvent the old-style merchants and wholesalers and to become major exporters in their own right. The manufacturers' initiative generated a huge requirement for export finance, as manufacturers who exported directly to the United States had to finance manufacturing operations *and* extend long credits to foreign customers, financial tasks that had formerly been divided among intermediaries. Some manufacturers financed exports by bank overdrafts or by subsidizing trade from their manufacturing profits; but in general these expedients proved inadequate, as manufacturers lacked access to the credit of the big London banks and found after 1805 that profits were highly variable.[113] Manufacturers therefore consigned their direct exports to America on their own accounts *via* new breeds of Liverpool and London or American-based commission agents. In dispatching goods, it became the universal rule for manufacturers to draw long-dated bills on these commission agents for two-thirds to three-fourths the value of the invoiced cargo at the time of delivery. The commission agents, who were not well capitalized, had connections with London or Liverpool financiers, who "accepted," in effect guaranteed, future payment of the bills that the agents signed or endorsed for the manufacturers. Likewise, merchants in the United States, who imported goods directly from the manufacturers on American account, paid for these goods with bills drawn on, and "accepted" by, London, Liverpool, and more rarely, U.S. merchant bankers.

These "acceptance houses" thus came to form the final key ingredient in the financing of Anglo-American trade in the early nineteenth century, and from circa 1800 the total bills guaranteed by merchant banks for British commission agents and U.S. merchants ran to many millions of pounds per year. The merchant bankers were usually of émigré or Anglo-American families, such as the London Barings or the Baltimore and New York Browns, and invariably graduated to careers in mercantile finance from the textile trades. The manufacturers discounted the bills accepted by the merchant banks with local and London banks and bill brokers, creating the liquid funds to finance the next round of production, bills that were then sold on, especially to country banks in the agricultural areas.[114] Finally, from circa 1820, as credit conditions in the economy tightened, the export manufacturers reduced their ever-increasing exposure, partly by shortening the credit terms they offered to foreign customers but mainly by dumping goods at American auctions for more or less immediate cash payment.[115] The auction system, requiring less credit, tended to reduce the role of the merchant bankers, although from 1830 further innovations in Anglo-American commercial methods gave them once again an absolutely central role in the financing of trade.

There were also major innovations from 1780 in the financing of foreign trade in the United States, at the heart of which was the creation of an efficient banking system geared to the needs of foreign and internal trade, something that the colonial economy had entirely lacked. In 1780 there were no banks in America; by 1799 there were twenty-two state-chartered institutions, eighteen of them located in coastal and four in inland ports.[116] The great majority of these banks were formed by established merchants, and their core business, which provided them with nearly all their profits, was the discounting of commercial paper, that is, promissory notes and bills of exchange, and accommodation paper. The banks accepted this paper from "insiders," that is, from stockholders, their relatives, and business associates, and from members of the wider trading community who stood in good repute. So in the early 1790s, of the active discounters at the Bank of North America in Philadelphia, 57 percent were merchants and 32 percent retailers.[117] The volume of discounting was a large and growing one. The First National Bank of Massachusetts discounted $3 million worth of paper per year in the late 1780s and early 1790s, and $20 million per year by 1810–15. The First Bank of the United States provided $6–8 million of discounts in 1795 in a business that had more than doubled by 1809.[118]

What overall impact did this banking revolution have on the financing of transatlantic trade at the American end? The best evidence on this question, as

Doerflinger notes, is found not in bank records but in merchants' papers. Doerflinger uses a small sample of such papers to argue that in the 1780s Philadelphia's merchants seized the opportunity of the formation of the Bank of North America (1781) to effect radical changes in the methods by which trade was financed. Before the Revolution there was little or no commercial paper in circulation in Philadelphia. In the 1780s, however, merchants converted some book debts, that is, the nonnegotiable sums owed to them by customers and entered into their ledgers, into formal paper instruments, namely promissory notes, which they promptly discounted at the bank. Commercial paper therefore made a sudden appearance in Philadelphia merchant portfolios, increasing in proportion both to book debts and more especially in relation to holdings of cash, for which the new forms of paper acted as a flexible substitute; cash was deposited in the bank, where it generated banknotes and credit. Unfortunately, such studies of the financial revolution from the merchants' point of view are rare, although Bruchey's work on the Olivers indicates that banks played a similar role in Baltimore after 1790 as in Philadelphia from 1780. Robert Oliver, indeed, soon came to equate a "scarcity of money" with the banks' incapacity to discount sufficient commercial paper.[119]

America's banking revolution from the early 1780s thus transformed the quotidian financial methods used by merchants in the major trading ports. Commercial capital circulated much more freely than in the colonial period, when the merchants' portfolios had been clogged with nonnegotiable book debts waiting to be collected. Moreover, banks oversaw the transfer of funds between merchants, by adjusting merchants' deposit accounts as the commercial paper held by the banks reached its maturity dates. Greater liquidity "mobilized and extended" mercantile capital, which quickened the pace of mercantile transactions in the ports and rippled out into their hinterlands, where merchants extended more credit to the country producers.[120] These factors stimulated the expansion of U.S. domestic exports and reexports, which increased at breakneck speed from the early 1790s to 1808, an expansion grounded both in the enlarged flow of agricultural commodities from the farms to the ports and in the multiplication of mercantile transactions in the entrepôt trades in sugar, coffee, and other commodities.[121] The banking system also stimulated exports in the southern plantation economy, although there were far fewer banks in this region. So American exporters of cotton to Britain after 1800 drew bills on the British importers, or much more commonly on their New York representatives, for two-thirds to three-fourths the value of their shipments at the time cargoes were dispatched; these bills could be sent north and sold to private buyers or "readily discounted at any commercial bank."[122]

However, the significance of American financial institutions for U.S. trade was limited by two factors. First, banks followed cautious policies. Their standard terms were to provide nonrenewable discounts on paper that had a maximum of thirty or sometimes sixty days to run to maturity, although after 1800 the periods of discount became longer and the likelihood of renewal greater. As Price has remarked, albeit in the context of London banking in the colonial tobacco trade, such short-term credit facilities were "obviously a convenience to a merchant firm but hardly a precondition for its operation."[123] Moreover, the supply of bank credit was erratic and frequently inadequate to the needs of trade. So only merchants of very good standing were granted discounts, and even these were curtailed in trading recessions when the banks' reserves were depleted of specie. In the depression of the mid-1780s, for example, the Bank of North America ceased discounting altogether; in other words, merchants tended to be denied credit when they were most in need of it. The Olivers of Baltimore, for instance, "repeatedly complained of the scarcity of money in 1796, 1797, and later as well."[124]

Second, while American banks lubricated the commercial transactions that underpinned the country's export trades, other branches of trade remained outside their financial orbit. British exports to America were sold on long credits granted to American importers, but this trade was underpinned by British finance: the importers, after 1800, paid British manufacturers, or their commission agents, with bills drawn on and endorsed by British, not American, banks. Furthermore, the sources of America's reexport trades, the cargoes bought by American ships in Europe, the West Indies, Latin America, and Asia, were bought with bills of exchange drawn on merchant bankers, bills that had to be guaranteed by letters of credit from the same. These bills and letters of credit, before 1830, were again invariably negotiated with London, not American, merchant bankers. Indeed, American banks until 1810 or even later appear to have mainly handled promissory notes and drafts arising from strictly local transactions; it was only subsequently that they accepted a high proportion of foreign bills, largely generated in the cotton export trade, and especially of accommodation paper, that is, paper arising not from commodity dealings but from arrangements of a purely financial nature.[125]

Every American foreign-trade merchant of any standing therefore required a London or Liverpool agency to act as a clearinghouse for his multifarious and multilateral trading and financial activities, even when, as was common, those activities hardly touched on British ports. Such agencies had existed since the late seventeenth century. But the main function of the early nineteenth-century agencies, which distinguished them from these remote antecedents, was financial: to provide American merchants with large, long-term credits that were simply unobtainable from American banks.[126] America had plenty of chartered banks by 1800 and many more by 1810, but its systems of merchant banking and of issuing internationally acceptable letters of credit were in "their infancy" in the early nineteenth century, and even the great and coming House of Brown did not finance international transactions on a large scale until the late 1820s.[127]

Conclusion

Professional merchants ruled transatlantic trade until 1780: they had traded on their own account until circa 1680, but thereafter the bulk of British-American trade was conducted on a commission basis. The commission trades were focused on London, reflecting its great advantages as a national market and as a center of mercantile and insurance services and, above all, of finance. London's merchants progressed in the classic sequence followed earlier by other premier business communities in Europe, such as those of Antwerp and Amsterdam— that is, from merchandizing and ship owning, to commission trading and insurance, and ultimately to finance and merchant banking. The shift toward the commission system was inspired by colonial planters and merchants in the late seventeenth century, but in the eighteenth century it was consolidated by London merchants who found that as merchant-agents and bankers they made as much in profits as they did in trade on their own account. The noncommission trades, on the other hand, gravitated to the provincial ports, partly because shipping and bulk merchandizing were handled there much more cheaply than in London and partly as a result of the entrepreneurial flair demonstrated by the Glasgow tobacco lords, the Leeds woolen merchants, and the Liverpool slavers.

As British merchants increased the share of trade conducted on their account and risk, the British-American trading system was modified in the 1780s and 1790s, but by no means out of all recognition. From 1800, however, and decisively from 1815 the old structure was swept away. The functions of marketing exports were transferred from old-style British merchants to manufacturers, who took the initiative in consigning exports on their own account, with the assistance of Liverpool and foreign-based commission agents. The essential instruments of trade financing, without which the reorganization of trade would have been impossible, were provided by London and Liverpool financial institutions and by the integration of London and regional capital markets through the expansion of bill discounting and of the country banking system. In America there was a boom in the export and reexport trades from the early 1790s, which was organized by American merchants and partially financed by the banking revolution in the leading seaports. However, the foundations of American trading success, a maritime war in Europe and free access to colonial markets for American shipping, crumbled after 1808, and American trade in the 1810s and 1820s never recovered its peak wartime levels. American merchants were further undermined by the British manufacturers' takeover of the export trade to the United States and by the rise of the New York auction system. Radical changes in the methods by which British trade was organized and financed in the early nineteenth century abruptly removed the conventional British merchants from the scene, but they also wreaked havoc among the merchant communities of the United States.

Notes

1. The classic studies of British trade in this period are Ralph Davis, "English Foreign Trade, 1660–1700" and "English Foreign Trade, 1700–1774," repr. in *The Growth of English Overseas Trade in the Seventeenth and Eighteenth Centuries,* ed. W. E. Minchinton (London: Methuen, 1969), 78–98 and 99–120; Ralph Davis, *The Rise of the English Shipping Industry in the Seventeenth and Eighteenth Centuries* (London: Macmillan/New York: St. Martin's Press, 1962); Ralph Davis, *The Industrial Revolution and British Overseas Trade* (Leicester: Leicester University Press/Atlantic Highlands, N.J.: Humanities Press, 1979). For sixteenth-century trade, see C. G. A. Clay, *Economic Expansion and Social Change: England 1500–1700,* 2 vols. (Cambridge and New York: Cambridge University Press, 1984), 2:130–36; and for the multilateral export trades, see R. C. Nash, "The Balance of Payments and Foreign Capital Flows in Eighteenth-Century England: A Comment," *Economic History Review* 50 (1997): 122–23.

2. Carole Shammas, "English Commercial Development and American Colonization, 1560–1620," in *The Westward Enterprise: English Activities in Ireland: The Atlantic and America, 1480–1650,* ed. K. R. Andrews et al. (Detroit: Wayne State University Press, 1979), 151–74; Richard Pares, *Merchants and Planters, Economic History Review,* supp. no. 4 (1960): 1–13, 26–33; Robert Brenner, *Merchants and Revolution: Commercial Crisis, Political Conflict, and London's Overseas Traders: 1550–1653* (Princeton, N.J.: Princeton University Press, 1993), 92–112; Theodore K. Rabb, *Enterprise and Empire: Merchant and Gentry Investment in the Expansion of England, 1575–1630* (Cambridge: Harvard University Press, 1967); K. G. Davies, *The North Atlantic World in the Seventeenth Century* (Minneapolis: University of Minnesota Press, 1974), 94–96; Jacob M. Price, "Sheffeild v. Starke: Institutional Experimentation in the London–Maryland Trade c. 1696–1706," *Business History* 28 (1986): 26–35; Jacob M. Price and Paul E. Clemens, "A Revolution of Scale in Overseas Trade: British Firms in the Chesapeake Trade, 1675–1775," *Journal of Economic History* 47 (1987): 2–8; David Harris Sacks, *The Widening Gate: Bristol and the Atlantic Economy, 1450–1700* (Berkeley: University of California Press, 1991), 258–59.

3. Jacob M. Price, "Transaction Costs: A Note on Merchant Credit and the Organization of Private Trade," in *The Political Economy of Merchant Empires,* ed. James D. Tracy (Cambridge and New York: Cambridge University Press, 1991), 279–82; Price and Clemens, "Revolution of Scale," 4–8; R. C. Nash, "The Organization of Trade and Finance in the Atlantic Economy: Britain and South Carolina, 1670–1775," in *Money, Trade, and Power: The Evolution of South Carolina's Plantation Society,* ed. Jack P. Greene, Rosemary Brana-Shute, and Randy J. Sparks (Columbia: University of South Carolina Press, 2001), 74–107; Nuala Zahedieh, "The Merchants of Port Royal, Jamaica, and the Spanish Contraband Trade, 1655–1692," *William and Mary Quarterly* 53 (1986): 570–93.

4. Stanley Gray and V. J. Wyckoff, "The International Tobacco Trade in the Seventeenth Century," *Southern Economic Journal* 7 (1940): 1–26; Paul E. Clemens, "The Rise of Liverpool, 1660–1750," *Economic History Review* 29 (1976): 211–17; Davis, *Rise of the English Shipping Industry,* 298–99; R. C. Nash, "Irish Atlantic Trade in the Seventeenth and Eighteenth Centuries," *William and Mary Quarterly* 52 (1985): 345–47; Sacks, *Widening Gate.*

5. H. S. K. Kent, *War and Trade in Northern Seas: Anglo-Scandinavian Economic Relations in the Mid-Eighteenth Century* (Cambridge: Cambridge University Press, 1973), 4–19,

31–36; Sven-Erik Astrom, *From Cloth to Iron: The Anglo-Baltic Trade in the Late Seventeenth Century*, part 1, *The Growth, Structure and Organisation of the Trade* (Helsingfors, 1963), 148–52; David Ormrod, "The Atlantic Economy and the 'Protestant Capitalist International,' 1651–1775," *Historical Research* 66 (1993): 201–5; David Ormrod, "The Demise of Regulated Trading in England: The Case of the Merchant Adventurers, 1650–1730," in *Entrepreneurs and Entrepreneurship in Early Modern Times: Merchants and Industrialists within the Orbit of the Dutch Staple Market*, ed. C. Lesger and L. Noordegraaf (Den Hagg, 1995), 253–68; D. W. Jones, *War and Economy in the Age of William III and Marlborough* (Oxford and New York: B. Blackwell, 1988), 249–60; Nash, "Balance of Payments," 120–21, and the literature cited therein. Britain controlled the trade with Russia where mercantile development was extremely backward in this period; see Douglas Kuglar Reading, *The Anglo-Russian Commercial Treaty of 1734* (New Haven: Yale University Press, 1938).

6. K. G. Davies, "The Origins of the Commission System in the West Indies Trade," *Royal Historical Society Transactions* 2 (1952): 89–107.

7. David Hancock, "'A World of Business to Do': William Freeman and the Foundations of England's Commercial Empire, 1645–1707," *William and Mary Quarterly* 57 (2000): 29–30. David Hancock, *The Letters of William Freeman, London Merchant, 1678–1685*, London Record Society Publications, 36 (London: London Record Society, 2002), esp. xxv–xxviii, xxxviii–xlvii. However, it appears from this letters that Freeman's trade on account of himself and his business partners was rather larger than the modest commission sales he undertook for Leeward Island planters who consigned him sugar.

8. Hancock, *Letters of William Freeman*, liii–lv; Davies, "Origins of the Commission System," 99–101; K. G. Davies, *The Royal African Company* (London and New York: Longmans, Green, 1957), 335–43, 358–60, 361–63. Revised estimates of the numbers of slaves delivered to the West Indies are given in David Eltis, "The British Transatlantic Slave Trade Before 1714: Annual Estimates of Volume and Direction," in *The Lesser Antilles in the Age of European Expansion*, ed. Robert L. Paquette and Stanley L. Engerman (Gainesville: University Press of Florida, 1996), 182–205.

9. Davies, "Origins of the Commission System," 89–107; Davies, *Royal African Company*, 358–60; Pares, *Merchants and Planters*, 33–35. For the losses of sugar ships in wartime, see R. C. Nash, "English Transatlantic Trade, 1660–1730: A Quantitative Survey" (Ph.D. diss., University of Cambridge, 1982), 109–18; and esp. Jones, *War and Economy*, 164.

10. See Nash, "English Transatlantic Trade," 137–66, for the relative importance of the commission and independent systems in the organization of West Indies trade, 1689–1730. For evidence of London merchants importing substantial quantities of sugar on their own accounts in the 1710s and 1720s, see Jones, *War and Economy*, 272.

11. Richard Pares, "A London West-India Merchant House, 1740–1769," in his *The Historian's Business and Other Essays* (Oxford: Clarendon Press, 1961), 198–226; Richard Pares, *War and Trade in the West Indies, 1739–1763* (Oxford: Clarendon Press, 1936), 514–16; Richard B. Sheridan, *Sugar and Slavery: An Economic History of the British West Indies, 1623–1775* (Baltimore: Johns Hopkins University Press, 1974), 298–305, 322–31, 335–37, 420; D. W. Thoms, "The Mills Family: London Sugar Merchants of the Eighteenth Century," *Business History* 11 (1969): 3–10.

12. R. Beale Davis, ed., *William Fitzhugh and His Chesapeake World, 1676–1701* (Chapel Hill: University of North Carolina Press, 1963), 138, 166, 180–81, 196, 220, 239, 322–23, 337–38, 353; Jacob M. Price, *Perry of London: A Family and a Firm on the Seaborne Frontier, 1615–1753* (Cambridge: Harvard University Press, 1992), 64–67; Jacob M. Price, "Merchants and Planters: The Market Structure of the Colonial Chesapeake Reconsidered," in his *Tobacco in Atlantic Trade: The Chesapeake, London and Glasgow, 1675–1775* (Brookfield, Ver.: Variorum, 1995), 25–31; Price, "Transaction Costs," 290; Jacob M. Price, "The Last Phase of the Virginia–London Consignment Trade: James Buchanan & Co., 1758–1768," *William and Mary Quarterly* 43 (1986): 82–96; Nash, "English Transatlantic Trade," 111–18, 125–57, 179–85; Jones, *War and Economy,* 164.

13. Bernard Bailyn, *The New England Merchants in the Seventeenth Century* (Cambridge: Harvard University Press, 1955), 76–86, 90–91; Curtis P. Nettels, *The Money Supply of the American Colonies Before 1720,* University of Wisconsin Studies, 20 (Madison: University of Wisconsin Press, 1934), 73–79, 99–114; John J. McCusker and Russell R. Menard, *The Economy of British America, 1607–1789* (Chapel Hill: University of North Carolina Press, 1985), 92–101; Ian K. Steele, *The English Atlantic, 1675–1740: An Explanation of Communication and Community* (New York: Oxford University Press, 1986), 62–66. See also n. 33, below.

14. Cathy Matson, *Merchants and Empire: Trading in Colonial New York* (Baltimore: Johns Hopkins University Press, 1998), 50–54, 73–74, 87–89, 135–36, 150, 153–54; Gary B. Nash, "The Early Merchants of Philadelphia: The Formation and Disintegration of a Founding Elite," in *The World of William Penn,* ed. Richard S. Dunn and Mary Maples Dunn (Philadelphia: University of Pennsylvania Press, 1986), 337–62. See also Jacob M. Price, "The Great Quaker Business Families of Eighteenth-Century London," in *The World of William Penn,* ed. Richard S. Dunn and Mary Maples Dunn, 366–67; Steele, *English Atlantic,* 66–76, 298–301; Marion Balderston, *James Claypoole's Letter Book: London and Philadelphia* (San Marino, Calif.: Huntington Library, 1967), 222–42; James G. Lydon, "Philadelphia's Commercial Expansion, 1720–1739," *Pennsylvania Magazine of History and Biography* 91 (1967): 401–18; William I. Roberts III, "Samuel Storke: An Eighteenth-Century London Merchant Trading to the American Colonies," *Business History Review* 39 (1965): 147–70; Thomas J. Archdeacon, *New York City, 1664–1710: Conquest and Change* (Ithaca: Cornell University Press, 1976), 66–77.

15. Thomas Doerflinger, *A Vigorous Spirit of Enterprise: Merchants and Economic Development in Revolutionary Philadelphia* (Chapel Hill: University of North Carolina Press, 1986), 82–97, 168–73; Virginia D. Harrington, *The New York Merchant on the Eve of the Revolution* (New York: Columbia University Press, 1935), 176–98; Philip L. White, *The Beekmans of New York in Politics and Commerce, 1647–1877* (New York: New York Historical Society, 1956), 318–19, 330–31, 362–81; Matson, *Merchants and Empire,* 153, 379–80 n. 74; W. T. Baxter, *The House of Hancock: Business in Boston, 1724–1775* (Cambridge: Harvard University Press, 1945), 59–61; John W. Tyler, *Smugglers and Patriots: Boston Merchants and the Advent of the American Revolution* (Boston: Northeastern University Press, 1986), 11–12, 123–38, 258–77; Edward Countryman, "The Uses of Capital in Revolutionary America: The Case of the New York Loyalist Merchants," *William and Mary Quarterly* 49 (1992): 20–22. For shipping data, see James F. Shepherd and Gary M. Walton, *Shipping, Maritime Trade and the Economic Development of Colonial North America* (Cambridge: Cambridge University Press, 1972), 122–23. Jacob M. Price, "Economic

Function and the Growth of American Port Towns in the Eighteenth Century," *Perspectives in American History* (1974): 159–60, emphasizes that British merchants continued to control part of the trade of the northern ports.

16. See Pares, who first referred to the "cargo business," "London West-India Merchant House," 221–25; Richard Pares, *A West-India Fortune* (New York: Longmans, Green, 1950), 240–41; Jacob M. Price, *Capital and Credit in British Overseas Trade: The View from the Chesapeake, 1700–1776* (Cambridge: Harvard University Press, 1980), 127–36, quotation from 128; Jacob M. Price, "Joshua Johnson in London, 1771–1775: Credit and Commercial Organisation in the British Tobacco Trade," in *Statesmen, Scholars and Merchants: Essays in Eighteenth-Century History Presented to Dame Luch Sutherland,* ed. Anne Whiteman, J. S. Bromley, and P. G. M. Dickson (Oxford: Clarendon Press, 1973), 157–58; Jacob M. Price, "One Family's Empire: The Russell-Lee-Clerk Connection in Maryland, Britain, and India, 1707–1857," *Maryland Historical Magazine* 72 (1977): 176–77, 186–87; Jacob M. Price, "Buchanan and Simson, 1759–1763: A Different Kind of Glasgow Firm Trading to the Chesapeake," *William and Mary Quarterly* 40 (1983): 3–4, 19–29; Price, "Last Phase of the Virginia–London Consignment Trade: James Buchanan & Co.," 82–95; Edward C. Papenfuse, *In Pursuit of Profit: The Annapolis Merchants in the Era of the American Revolution, 1763–1805* (Baltimore: Johns Hopkins University Press, 1975), 43–44, 52–53, 73–75; Charles G. Steffen, "The Independent Merchant in the Chesapeake: Baltimore County, 1660–1769," *Journal of American History* 76 (1989): 11, 28–32; Nash, "Organization of Trade."

17. Pares, "London West-India Merchant House," 222–25, quotation from 222; Richard B. Sheridan, "The Commercial and Financial Organization of the British Slave Trade, 1750–1807," *Economic History Review* 11 (1958): 249–63; Jacob M. Price, "Credit in the Slave Trade and Plantation Economies," in *Slavery and the Rise of the Atlantic System,* ed. Barbara L. Solow (Cambridge: Cambridge University Press, 1991), 310–23; Nash, "Organization of Trade"; Kenneth Morgan, ed., "Calendar of Correspondence from William Miles to John Tharp, 1770–1789," in *A Bristol Miscellany,* Bristol Record Society's Publications, 37, ed. P. V. McGrath (Bristol: Bristol Record Society, 1985), 102, 111–12, 116; Kenneth Morgan, "Slave Sales in Colonial Charleston," *English Historical Review* 113 (1998): 923–27; Trevor Burnard and Kenneth Morgan, "The Dynamics of the Slave Market and Slave Purchasing Patterns in Jamaica, 1655–1788," *William and Mary Quarterly* 58 (2001): esp. 212–215; Kenneth Morgan, "James Rogers and the Bristol Slave Trade," *Historical Research* 76 (2003): 207–09.

18. The Chesapeake merchants in the cargo trade, it is true, shipped a good deal of tobacco, but they did so in ships owned not by themselves but by the London commission agents.

19. Pares, "London West-India Merchant House," 222–25; Richard B. Sheridan, "The Rise of a Colonial Gentry: A Case Study of Antigua, 1730–1775," *Economic History Review* 13 (1961): 346–47, 356; see also refs. to West Indies in n. 77, below. See Nash, "Organization of Trade"; Russell R. Menard, "Financing the Lowcountry Export Boom: Capital and Growth in Early South Carolina," *William and Mary Quarterly* 51 (1994): 671–74. However, Steffen has shown for Baltimore County, Maryland, that only the merchants of the era before 1760 aspired to the patriarchal ideal of slave-plantation ownership. The more "bourgeois" merchants of the 1760s and 1770s, who made their money as much in the grain trade as in the tobacco trade, bought land for speculative purposes and

invested far less in slaves. See Charles G. Steffen, "Gentry and Bourgeois: Patterns of Merchant Investment in Baltimore County, Maryland, 1658 to 1776," *Journal of Social History* 20 (1986–87): 536–42.

20. Nash, "Early Merchants of Philadelphia"; Doerflinger, *Vigorous Spirit of Enterprise,* 129–33, 375–78. Countryman's study of a small and possibly unrepresentative sample of New York loyalist merchants shows that they invested a higher proportion of their wealth in land, especially those who had retired from trade. However, active merchants held most of their assets in book debts and in bonds and notes. See Countryman, "Uses of Capital," 15–20.

21. Jacob M. Price, "The Rise of Glasgow in the Chesapeake Tobacco Trade, 1707–1775," *William and Mary Quarterly,* 3rd ser., 11 (1954): 190–96; Jacob M. Price, "The Economic Growth of the Chesapeake and the European Market, 1697–1775," *Journal of Economic History* 24 (1964): 496–511; John W. Tyler, "Foster Cunliffe and Sons: Liverpool Merchants in the Maryland Tobacco Trade, 1738–1765," *Maryland Historical Magazine* 73 (1978): 246–79.

22. Nash, "Organization of Trade," 77–80.

23. Davis, *Rise of the English Shipping Industry,* 94–95, 292–97; David Richardson, "The Eighteenth-Century British Slave Trade," *Research in Economic History* 12 (1989): 185–95.

24. Davies, "Origins of the Commission System," 97–102. London commission agents shipped Irish provisions to the West Indies on their planter-clients' account while the provincial trade was organized by British and Irish merchants wholly on their own account. See Nash, "Irish Atlantic Trade," 344–49; Pares Transcripts, MS West Indies, ser. 5, Rhodes House Library, Oxford, U.K., box 4, H363, H365.

25. David Hancock, *Citizens of the World: London Merchants and the Integration of British Atlantic Community, 1735–1785* (Cambridge and New York: Cambridge University Press, 1995), esp. 115–42, 172–220, quotations from 130–31.

26. Hancock, *Citizens of the World,* 115–23, 131–42, 198–214. For example, Hancock's meticulously assembled database (118) of the nine hundred voyages in which his merchants invested is essentially concerned with shipping management, not with trading activities.

27. For London's slave trade, see Richardson, "Eighteenth-Century British Slave Trade"; James A. Rawley, "The Port of London and the Eighteenth Century Slave Trade: Historians, Sources and a Reappraisal," *African Economic History* 9 (1980): 86–98. For West India shipping, see Pares, *West-India Fortune,* 207–9; Davis, *Rise of the English Shipping Industry,* 271–73, 276–81. Hancock's merchants were exceptional for the size of their slave shipments and for their acquisition of a permanent trading factory on Bance Island. For information on an earlier "floating factory" established by a London-merchant syndicate in 1737–43, see Conrad Gill, *Merchants and Mariners of the 18th Century* (London: E. Arnold, 1961), 91–97.

28. Doerflinger, *Vigorous Spirit of Enterprise,* 168–73, quotation from 170; Marc Egnal, "The Changing Structure of Philadelphia's Trade with the British West Indies, 1750–1775," *Pennsylvania Magazine of History and Biography* 96 (1975): 171–79.

29. Davies, "Origins of the Commission System," 97–102; Nash, "English Transatlantic Trade," chaps. 3, 4.

30. Davies, "Origins of the Commission System," 104–7; Hancock, "'World of Business to Do,'" esp. 22–33. Pares originally noted that the commission system harmonized

relations between planters and merchants: "The merchant and the planter ceased to face each other as adversaries in buying and selling [and] in the long run, the interests of merchants and planters were the same" (Pares, *Merchants and Planters,* 36).

31. Pares, *Merchants and Planters,* 35–36; R. C. Nash, "Urbanization in the Colonial South: Charleston, South Carolina as a Case Study," *Journal of Urban History* 19 (1992): 13–14. As Price comments, planters who grew the best tobacco "continued to send [it] to consignment merchants in London because they expected a premium price for a premium product"; see Jacob M. Price, "Who Was John Norton? A Note on the Historical Character of Some Eighteenth-Century London Virginia Firms," *William and Mary Quarterly* 29 (1962): 407.

32. Richard S. Dunn, *Sugar and Slaves: The Rise of the Planter Class in the English West Indies, 1624–1713* (Chapel Hill: University of North Carolina Press, 1972), 76–82, 131–43, 170–76, 264–67; Richard S. Dunn, "The Barbados Census of 1680: Profile of the Richest Colony in British America," *William and Mary Quarterly* 36 (1969): 3–30; see also Nuala Zahedieh, "Trade, Plunder and Economic Development in Early English Jamaica, 1655–89," *Economic History Review* 39 (1986): 210–11.

33. Davies, "Origins of the Commission System," 100–104, quotation from 104. Pares, *Merchants and Planters,* 33–36, 79 nn. 61, 64, provides, among other things, evidence of commission trading from Barbados as early as 1660. This coincided with the imposition of the Navigation Acts in the 1650s and early 1660s, which, by excluding the Dutch, reduced competition for the planters' sugars in the islands and focused the sugar trade on London rather than the Netherlands.

34. In 1674–79 slaves made up about 20 percent of bound labor, white and black, in Maryland and 34 percent in York County, Virginia; by the early 1690s the proportions had reached 78 percent in Maryland and 93 percent in York County. There was, in general, a sizable increase in wealth inequality and in the proportion of upper-middle and wealthy households in the Chesapeake from the 1650s to the 1680s. See Russell R. Menard, "From Servants to Slaves: The Transformation of the Chesapeake Labour System," *Southern Studies* 16 (1977): 361–62; David W. Galenson, "Economic Aspects of the Growth of Slavery in the Seventeenth-Century Chesapeake," in *Slavery and the Rise of the Atlantic System,* ed. Barbara L. Solow (Cambridge: Cambridge University Press, 1991), 266–67, 281–83; Lois G. Carr and Russell Menard, "Wealth and Welfare in Early Maryland: Evidence from St. Mary's County," *William and Mary Quarterly* 56 (1999): 106–11; on the use of bills, see Price, *Perry of London,* 30–40.

35. Arthur Pierce Middleton, *Tobacco Coast: A Maritime History of the Chesapeake Bay in the Colonial Era* (Newport News, Va.: Mariner's Museum, 1953), 104–10; Price, *Perry of London,* 30–33, 37–40; Jacob M. Price, "The Tobacco Adventure to Russia," *American Philosophical Society Transactions* 51, part 1 (1961): 87–89; Jacob M. Price, *France and the Chesapeake: A History of the French Tobacco Monopoly, 1674–1791, and of Its Relationship to the British and American Tobacco Trades,* 2 vols. (Ann Arbor: University of Michigan Press, 1973), 2:852; Russell R. Menard, "The Tobacco Industry in the Chesapeake Colonies, 1617–1730: An Interpretation," *Research in Economic History* 5 (1980): 138–42, 159–60; Nash, "English Transatlantic Trade," 179–89 (for the effects of shipping shortages on local markets and prices).

36. Robert Hackshaw, another major London agent, conducted a similar business with New York and New England merchants until his death in 1723. See Chancery Masters'

Exhibits, C104/15–16, *Waterhouse v. Lillie,* 1690–1710, Public Record Office (hereafter PRO); Prob. 3/23/10, January 23, 1723, Robert Hackshaw, PRO. On Hackshaw, see Jones, *War and Economy,* 265.

37. Nash, "Organization of Trade"; Nash, "Urbanization in Colonial America," 12–14.

38. Kenneth Morgan, *Bristol & the Atlantic Trade in the Eighteenth Century* (Cambridge: Cambridge University Press, 1993), 193–98; Egnal, "Changing Structure of Philadelphia's Trade," 171–79; Harrington, *New York Merchant,* 353–55.

39. Pares, *Merchants and Planters,* 48–50; Samuel M. Rosenblatt, "The Significance of Credit in the Tobacco Consignment Trade: A Study of John Norton and Sons, 1768–1775," *William and Mary Quarterly* 29 (1962): 388–89, 398–99 (for the large revenues derived from the commission trades); see also n. 106 below.

40. See, among a large literature, Clay, *Economic Expansion,* 1:198–201; Gordon Jackson, *Hull in the Eighteenth Century: A Study in Economic and Social History* (London and New York: Oxford University Press, 1982), 53–76, 82–87; Price, *Capital and Credit,* 69–77, 101–21; Ormrod, "Atlantic Economy," 201–5.

41. The point was first made by Price, "Rise of Glasgow," 185–91; see also Jacob M. Price, "Who Cared about the Colonies? The Impact of the Thirteen Colonies on British Society and Politics, ca. 1714–1775," in *Strangers within the Realm: Cultural Margins of the First British Empire,* ed. Bernard Bailyn and Philip D. Morgan (Chapel Hill: University of North Carolina Press, 1991), 420–21.

42. Davis, *Rise of the English Shipping Industry,* 27.

43. Price, "Rise of Glasgow," 189–90.

44. Richard F. Dell, "The Operational Record of the Clyde Tobacco Fleet, 1747–1775," *Scottish Economic and Social History* 2 (1982): 1–17 (who also shows that tobacco ships were turned around rapidly in Glasgow).

45. Pares, *West-India Fortune,* 224–28; Nash, "Urbanization in the Colonial South," 16–18; Morgan, *Bristol & the Atlantic Trade,* 199–201.

46. T. M. Devine, *The Tobacco Lords: A Study of the Tobacco Merchants of Glasgow and Their Trading Activities* (Edinburgh: Donald, 1975), 89–98; R. G. Wilson, *Gentlemen Merchants: The Merchant Community in Leeds, 1700–1830* (Manchester: Manchester University Press/New York: A. M. Kelley, 1971), 50–53; John Smail, "The Sources of Innovation in the Woollen and Worsted Industry of Eighteenth-Century Yorkshire," *Business History* 41 (1999): 1–11; John Smail, *Merchants, Markets and Manufacture: The English Wool Textile Industry in the Eighteenth Century* (Basingstoke: Macmillan, 1999), 86–93. Woolen exports from England to the American colonies trebled from 1750 to 1775, the period when America first became an important market for the industry; virtually all of the additional exports came from Yorkshire. See Price, "Credit in the Slave Plantation Economies," 313–17; Price, *Capital and Credit,* 23–29.

47. Astrid Friss, *Alderman Cockayne's Project: The Commercial Policy of England, 1603–1625* (London: Oxford University Press, 1927), 100–102; Brenner, *Merchants and Revolution,* 22–23, 75–77; R. W. K. Hinton, *The Eastland Trade and the Common Weal in the Seventeenth Century* (Cambridge: Cambridge University Press, 1959), 57, 116–17; Wolf-Rüdiger Baumann, *The Merchants Adventurers and the Continental Cloth-Trade (1560s–1620s)* (Berlin and New York: W. de Gruyter, 1990), 156–61, 341, 349–50.

48. See Jones, *War and Economy*, 260–73; D. W. Jones, "London Merchants and the Crisis of the 1690s," in *Crisis and Order in English Towns, 1500–1800*, ed. Peter Clark and Paul Slack (London: Routledge and K. Paul, 1972), 311–55; Astrom, *From Cloth to Iron*, 143, 169–78; Kent, *War and Trade*, 34.

49. Jackson, *Hull in the Eighteenth Century*, 96; W. B. Stephens, *Seventeenth-Century Exeter: A Study of Industrial and Commercial Development, 1625–1688* (Exeter: University of Exeter, 1958), 46–47, 160; Morgan, *Bristol & the Atlantic Trade*, 93–97 (although in Bristol, large-scale West Indies traders were both importers and exporters).

50. Price and Clemens, "Revolution of Scale," 25–36, quotation from 36.

51. Brenner, *Merchants and Revolution*, 168–81; Sacks, *Widening Gate*, 258–59.

52. Price and Clemens, "Revolution of Scale," 35–37.

53. Morgan, *Bristol & the Atlantic Trade*, 95–96, 189–93, 222–23; Simon Smith, "The Significance of New World Demand for English Wool Textiles 1699–1783," University of York, Discussion Papers in Economics, no. 93/6, 21.

54. Friss, *Alderman Cockayne's Project*, 78–81, 94–101; Baumann, *Merchants Adventurers*, 155–65; Harland Taylor, "Price Revolution or Price Revision? The English and Spanish Trade after 1604," *Renaissance and Modern Studies* 12 (1968): 11–14; Richard Grassby, *The Business Community of Seventeenth-Century England* (Cambridge and New York: Cambridge University Press, 1995), 64–65.

55. Sacks, *Widening Gate*, 258.

56. Price and Clemens, "Revolution of Scale," 24–36; Nuala Zahedieh, "Credit, Risk and Reputation in Late Seventeenth-Century Colonial Trade," in *Research in Maritime History*, 15.

57. Morgan, *Bristol & the Atlantic Trade*, 191–93; J. E. Inikori, "Market Structure and the Profits of the British African Trade in the Late Eighteenth Century," *Journal of Economic History* 41 (1981): 750; Nuala Zehediah, "Credit, Risk and Reputation in Late Seventeenth-Century Colonial Trade," in *Merchant Organization and Trade in the North Atlantic, 1660–1815*, ed. Olaf Uwe Janzen, *Research in Maritime History* 15 (1998), tables 4, 5. The import trades in Levant silk, Scandinavian timber, and Portuguese wine also became highly concentrated from circa 1700.

58. Jones, *War and Economy*, 272; Astrom, *From Cloth to Iron*, 122–52, 160–65; Philip Riden, "An English Factor at Stockholm in the 1680s," *Scandinavian Economic History Review* 35 (1987): 191–207; Ralph Davis, *Aleppo and Devonshire Square: English Traders in the Levant in the Eighteenth Century* (London: Macmillan, 1967), 65–68; Brenner, *Merchants and Revolution*, 113–20; Sheridan, "Rise of a Colonial Gentry," 350–57; Sheridan, *Sugar and Slavery*, 285–88, 298–305; Richard B. Sheridan, "Planters and Merchants: The Oliver Family of Antigua and London, 1716–1784," *Business History* 13 (1971): 104–13; Kenneth Morgan, "Bristol West India Merchants in the Eighteenth Century," *Royal Historical Society Transactions* 3 (1993): 191–94; Katherine A. Kellock, "London Merchants and the Pre-1776 American Debts," *Guildhall Studies in London History* 1 (1974): 109–49 (for early careers of many of London's leading colonial merchants); Sacks, *Widening Gate*, 264–65; W. E. Minchinton, "The Merchants in England in the Eighteenth Century," *Explorations in Entrepreneurial History* 10 (1957): 64; Nash, "Organization of Trade"; Zahedieh, "Credit, Risk and Reputation," 66–68; Hancock, *Citizens of the World*, 46–69.

59. Price and Clemens, "Revolution of Scale," 36–37; Price, "Transaction Costs."

60. Inikori, "Market Structure," 745–76.

61. B. L. Anderson and David Richardson, "Market Structure and the Profits of the British African Trade in the Late Eighteenth Century: A Comment," *Journal of Economic History* 43 (1983): 713–21; 45 (1985): 705–7, quotation from 705.

62. White, *Beekmans,* 642; Price, "Joshua Johnson," 158–60. See also Herbert Heaton, "Yorkshire Cloth Traders in the United States 1770–1840," *Publications of the Thoresby Society* 37 (1941): 232; Kellock, "London Merchants," 109–49 (for examples of major wholesaler-merchants exporting to the colonies); B. A. Holderness, "A Sheffield Commercial House in the Mid-18th Century: Messrs Osborne and Gunning around 1760," *Business History* 15 (1973): 32–34, 39–41; Eric Hopkins, "The Trading and Service Sectors of the Birmingham Economy 1750–1800," *Business History* 15 (1973): 87–88; Stanley D. Chapman, "British Marketing Enterprise: The Changing Role of Merchants, Manufacturers, and Financiers, 1700–1860," *Business History Review* 53 (1979): 208–10; Kenneth Morgan, "Business Networks in the British Export Trade to North America, 1750–1800," in *The Early Modern Atlantic Economy,* ed. John J. McCusker and Kenneth Morgan (Cambridge: Cambridge University Press, 2000), 72–74; Morgan, *Bristol & the Atlantic Trade,* 95–97. For nonmerchant participants in the expanding Irish trade, see L. M. Cullen, *Anglo-Irish Trade, 1660–1800* (New York: A. M. Kelley, 1968), 113–14.

63. Norman Sidney Buck, *The Development of the Organisation of Anglo-American Trade, 1800–1850* (New Haven: Yale University Press, 1925), 99–117, 121–50; Chapman, "British Marketing Enterprise," 205–33; Stanley D. Chapman, *Merchant Enterprise in Britain from the Industrial Revolution to World War 1* (Cambridge and New York: Cambridge University Press, 1992), 59–74. See also Price, *Capital and Credit,* 143–45.

64. M. M. Schofield, "The Virginia Trade of the Firm of Sparling and Bolden, of Liverpool, 1788–1799," *Transactions of the Historic Society of Lancashire and Cheshire* 116 (1964): 117–62; S. R. Cope, "Bird, Savage and Bird of London: Merchants and Bankers, 1782–1803," *Guildhall Studies in London History* 5 (1981): 202–17; Robert Allen Davison, *Isaac Hicks: New York Merchant and Quaker, 1767–1820* (Cambridge: Harvard University Press, 1964), 24–52; Elva Tooker, *Nathan Trotter, Philadelphia Merchant, 1787–1853* (Cambridge: Harvard University Press, 1955), 40–43, 75; Doerflinger, *Vigorous Spirit of Enterprise,* 242–49, 261–67; Wilson, *Gentlemen Merchants,* 77–81, 112–13; Pat Hudson, *The Genesis of Industrial Capital: A Study of the West Riding Wool Textile Industry c. 1750–1850* (Cambridge and New York: Cambridge University Press, 1986), 158–60, 163–67; R. G. Albion, *The Rise of Port of New York, 1815–60* (New York: Charles Scribner's Sons, 1939), 275–78; M. M. Edwards, *The Growth of the British Cotton Trade, 1780–1815* (Manchester: Manchester University Press, 1967), 161–63, 176–81; B. H. Tolley, "The American Trade of Liverpool in the Early Nineteenth Century and the War of 1812" (M.A. thesis, University of Liverpool, 1967), 67–85; C. H. Lee, *A Cotton Enterprise, 1795–1840: A History of McConnel and Kennedy, Fine Cotton Spinners* (Manchester: Manchester University Press, 1972), 48–57, 50–57; Buck, *Development,* 102–3; S. G. Checkland, "Finance for the West Indies, 1780–1815," *Economic History Review,* 2nd ser., 10 (1957–58): 461–69; Chapman, *Merchant Enterprise,* 59–74.

65. Edwards, *Growth of British Cotton Trade,* 161–63, 176–81; J. de L. Mann, *The Cloth Industry in the West of England from 1640–1880* (Oxford: Clarendon Press, 1987), 81–86, 223–24; Trevor Fawcett, "'Argonauts and Commercial Travellers': The Foreign Marketing

of Norwich Stuffs in the Later Eighteenth Century," *Textile History* 16 (1985): 151–82; Wilson, *Gentlemen Merchants,* 94–96, 111; Hudson, *Genesis of Industrial Capital,* 163.

66. Edwards, *Growth of British Cotton Trade,* 15–24, 57–62, 68–72, 212; D. T. Jenkins, *The West Riding Wool Textile Industry, 1770–1835: A Study of Fixed Capital Formation* (Edington: Pasold Research Fund, 1975), 171–80, quotation from 179; Lee, *Cotton Enterprise,* 48–57; Wilson, *Gentlemen Merchants,* 111–21; B. W. Clapp, *John Owens, Manchester Merchant* (New York: A. M. Kelley, 1965), 28–23, 71–72; Patrick K. O'Brien, "Merchants and Bankers as Patriots or Speculators? Foreign Commerce and Monetary Policy in Wartime," in *The Early Modern Atlantic Economy,* ed. John J. McCusker and Kenneth Morgan (Cambridge: Cambridge University Press, 2000), esp. 264–71; D. C. M. Platt, *Latin America and British Trade, 1806–1914* (London: A. and C. Black, 1972), 148–51; Herbert Heaton, "A Merchant Adventurer in Brazil 1808–1818," *Journal of Economic History* 6 (1946): 1–5.

67. Hudson, *Genesis of Industrial Capital,* 153.

68. Arthur D. Gayer et al., *The Growth and Fluctuation of the British Economy,* 2 vols. (Oxford: Clarendon Press, 1953), 1:154–57; Tolley, "American Trade of Liverpool," 344–45, 367–68, 374–75; Tooker, *Nathan Trotter,* 79–82; Buck, *Development,* 121–24; Wilson, *Gentlemen Merchants,* 111–16.

69. Ray B. Westerfield, "Early History of American Auctions: A Chapter in Commercial History," *Transactions of the Connecticut Academy of Arts and Sciences* 23 (1920): 159–210; Ira Cohen, "The Auction System in the Port of New York, 1817–1837," *Business History Review* 46 (1971): 488–510; Buck, *Development,* 121–35; Albion, *Rise of Port of New York,* 57–61, 276–82, 410; Price, *Capital and Credit,* 143–44; Heaton, "Yorkshire Cloth Traders"; Heaton, "Merchant Adventurer," 1–5, 23; Platt, *Latin America,* 48–51; Chapman, *Merchant Enterprise,* 62–78; Hudson, *Genesis of Industrial Capital,* 155–74; Buck, *Development,* 135–48; Edwin J. Perkins, *Financing Anglo-American Trade: The House of Brown, 1800–1880* (Cambridge: Harvard University Press, 1975).

70. The rise of Liverpool after 1780, from being merely the leading provincial port to the position, circa 1800, where its trade and shipping surpassed that of London, represents the other major innovation in the organization of British-American trade; see R. C. Nash, "On the Waterfront: Liverpool's Trade and Shipping, 1660–1830," University of Manchester, *Working Papers in Economic and Social History,* no. 27 (1998).

71. James B. Shepard and Gary M. Walton, "Economic Change after the American Revolution: Pre- and Post-War Comparisons of Maritime Shipping and Trade," *Explorations in Economic History* 13 (1976): 397–422; Jacob M. Price, "New Time Series for Scotland's and Britain's Trade with the Thirteen Colonies and States, 1740 to 1791," *William and Mary Quarterly* 22 (1975): 325; Curtis P. Nettels, *The Emergence of a National Economy: 1775–1815* (New York: Holt, Rinehart, and Winston, 1962), 45–64.

72. Among a large literature, Nettels, *Emergence of a National Economy,* 65–75; McCusker and Menard, *Economy of British America,* 370–72; Papenfuse, *In Pursuit of Profit,* 189–215, 231–32; Doerflinger, *Vigorous Spirit of Enterprise,* 215–18, 242–50, 261–67; Stuart Weems Bruchey, *Robert Oliver, Merchant of Baltimore, 1783–1819* (Baltimore: Johns Hopkins University Press, 1956), 52–54; James Blaine Hedges, *The Browns of Providence Plantations: Colonial Years* (Cambridge: Harvard University Press, 1952), 291–305; White, *Beekmans,* 540–41; Davison, *Isaac Hicks,* 24–52; Gedalia Yogev, *Diamonds and Coral:*

Anglo-Dutch Jews and Eighteenth-Century Trade (New York: Holmes and Meier, 1978), 188–89.

73. See Nettels, *Emergence of a National Economy,* 232–38; Douglas C. North, *The Economic Growth of the United States 1790–1860* (Englewood Cliffs, N.J.: Prentice-Hall, 1961); Doerflinger, *Vigorous Spirit of Enterprise,* 335–44; U.S. Bureau of the Census, *Historical Statistics of the United States: Colonial Times to 1970,* vol. 2 (Washington, D.C.: Department of Commerce, Bureau of the Census, U.S. Government Printing Office, 1975), 2, 744, 750, 904–5; and esp. François Crouzet, "Variations on the North American Triangle from Yorktown to Waterloo: Substitution, Complementarity, Parallelism," in *Economics in the Long View; Essays in Honor of W. W. Rostow,* ed. C. P. Kindleberger and Guido di Tella, vol. 2, *Applications and Cases, Part I* (New York: New York University Press, 1982), 44–63. François Crouzet, "America and the Crisis of the British Imperial Economy, 1803–1807," in *The Early Modern Atlantic Economy,* ed. McCusker and Morgan, 278–315. Space does not permit a discussion of the problems of measuring and comparing shipping tonnages.

74. Gordon C. Bjork, "Foreign Trade," in *The Growth of the Seaport Cities, 1790–1825,* ed. David T. Gilchrist (Charlottesville: University Press of Virginia, 1967), 54–61. Robert Oliver of Baltimore, for example, made his million in the West Indies trade and above all by reexporting European manufactures to Vera Cruz, and the Browns of Providence specialized in the trades to Canton and Batavia and in reexporting Asian and West Indian goods to Europe; see Bruchey, *Robert Oliver,* 232–33, 314–18, 329; James Blaine Hedges, *The Browns of Providence Plantations: The Nineteenth Century* (Providence, R.I.: Brown University Press, 1968). See also François Crouzet, "Opportunity and Risk in Atlantic Trade during the French Revolution," in *Interactions in the World Economy: Perspectives from International Economic History,* ed. Carl-Ludwig Holtfrerich (Hemel Hempstead: Harvester Wheatsheaf, 1989), 90–150. For the trade boom's effects on the wider U.S. economy, see Claudia D. Goldin and Frank D. Lewis, "The Role of Exports in American Economic Growth during the Napoleonic War, 1793–1807," *Explorations in Economic History* 17 (1980): 6–7, 22–23; Crouzet, "Variations on the North American Triangle," esp. 51–52.

75. Buck, *Development,* 104–8; Herbert Heaton, "The American Trade," in *Trade Winds: A Study of British Overseas Trade during the French Wars, 1793–1815,* ed. C. Northcote Parkinson (London: G. Allen and Unwin, 1948), 213; Kenneth Wiggins Porter, *The Jacksons and the Lees: Two Generations of Massachusetts Merchants, 1765–1844,* vol. 1 (Cambridge: Harvard University Press, 1937), 629–30; Bjork, "Foreign Trade," 64–65; Perkins, *Financing Anglo-American Trade,* 88–89; Frances W. Gregory, *Nathan Appleton: Merchant and Entrepreneur, 1779–1861* (Charlottesville: University Press of Virginia, 1975), 14–56, 92–93, 116–17; Tooker, *Nathan Trotter,* 43–44, 75–80; John R. Killick, "Bolton Ogden and Co.: A Case Study in Anglo-American Trade, 1790–1850," *Business History Review* 48 (1974): 503–8. The Olivers and the Browns are examples of two major firms that avoided the import trade in manufactures from Great Britain.

76. See Bjork, "Foreign Trade," 66–67; Doerflinger, *Vigorous Spirit of Enterprise,* 342–44; Ralph W. Hidy, *House of Baring in American Trade and Finance: English Merchant Bankers at Work, 1763–1861* (Cambridge: Harvard University Press, 1949), 56–57, 78–79, and refs. in nn. 63, 66 to studies of individual American merchant firms.

77. Buck, *Development*, 149; Albion, *Rise of Port of New York*, 68, 274–79; John B. Hutchins, "Trade and Manufactures," in *The Growth of the Seaport Cities, 1790–1825*, ed. David T. Gilchrist (Charlottesville: University Press of Virginia, 1967), 86–87; Diane Lindstrom, *Economic Development in the Philadelphia Region, 1810–1850* (New York: Columbia University Press, 1978); Killick, "Bolton Ogden and Co.," 508–15; Perkins, *Financing Anglo-American Trade*, 85–86, 93–94.

78. For example, the East India Company maintained its major flow of calico imports by advancing cash to Indian merchants, who then put out raw materials on credit to rural calico weavers; see K. N. Chaudhuri, *The Trading World of Asia and the East India Company* (Cambridge: Cambridge University Press, 1978), 253–62, 305–12. English merchants after 1700 also advanced substantial capital, through local merchants, to producers in Portugal, the Levant, Scandinavia, and Russia; see L. Sutherland, *A London Merchant, 1695–1774* (London: Oxford University Press, H. Milford, 1933), 29; H. E. S. Fisher, *The Portugal Trade: A Study of Anglo-Portuguese Commerce, 1700–1770* (London: Methuen, 1971); Astrom, *From Cloth to Iron*, 150–52; Henry Roseveare, ed., *Markets and Merchants of the Late Seventeenth Century: The Marescoe-David Letters, 1668–1680* (Oxford and New York: Oxford University Press, 1987), 37–40, 48–50, 130; Kent, *War and Trade*, 50–53, 71–76; Reading, *Anglo-Russian Commercial Treaty*, 47–53, 190–91; Davis, *Aleppo and Devonshire Square*, 208–12.

79. Ormrod, "Atlantic Economy," 197–208; Jones, *War and Economy*, 254–60; L. Neal, *The Rise of Financial Capitalism: International Capital Markets in the Age of Reason* (Cambridge and New York: Cambridge University Press, 1990), 10–13; Wilson, *Anglo-Dutch Commerce*, 70–79. Elise S. Brezis, "Foreign Capital Flows in the Century of England's Industrial Revolution: New Estimates, Controlled Conjectures," *Economic History Review* 48 (1995): 46–67, argues, indeed, that England had a massive and structural balance of payments deficit until late in the eighteenth century; for a critique, see Nash, "Balance of Payments."

80. Pares, *Merchants and Planters*, 1–13, 26–32; Brenner, *Merchants and Revolution*; Davies, *Royal African Company*, 63–69; Nash, "English Transatlantic Trade," 35–37.

81. Davies, "Origins of the Commission System," 97–99; Davies, *Royal African Company*, 358–60; Nash, "English Transatlantic Trade," 155–59; Royal African Company, T. 70, 277–83, 289–93, Accounts, Bills of Exchange, PRO.

82. Zahedieh, "Trade, Plunder and Economic Development," 212–13; Sheridan, *Sugar and Slavery*, 224–25, 285–86, 295–98, although see n. 81, below.

83. Price, *Perry of London*, 66–71. Some Virginia planters, circa 1720, kept balances of several thousand pounds in Perry's hands, as they had in the 1680s—surpluses, however, that soon disappeared from the trade; see Royal African Company, T. 70, 277–83, 289–93, Accounts, Bills of Exchange, PRO.

84. This policy was applied even to Samuel Lillie, Waterhouse's chief correspondent and probably the greatest Boston merchant and shipowner of his day. Waterhouse commenced a Chancery suit in 1705 against him over protested bills worth a few hundred pounds. Lillie then shifted his business to another major London agent trading to Boston, Robert Hackshaw. Within a few years it was Hackshaw's turn to sue Lillie over unpaid debts that amounted to a similar sum, although some years later, at his death in 1722, Hackshaw was owed significant sums by some New England merchants. See Chancery

Masters' Exhibits, C104/15–16, *Waterhouse v. Lillie,* 1690–1710, PRO; C107/207, *Lillie v. Hackshaw,* 1713–15; Prob. 3/23/10, January 23, 1723, Robert Hackshaw, PRO. On Lillie, see Bernard Bailyn and Lotte Bailyn, *Massachusetts Shipping, 1697–1714: A Statistical Study* (Cambridge: Belknap Press of Harvard University Press, 1959), esp. 91–95.

85. Roberts, "Samuel Storke," quotation from 158.

86. Hancock, *Letters of William Freeman,* xix; Price, "Credit in the Slave Trade," 302–5. For credit terms in the South Carolina trade, see Nash, "Organization of Trade."

87. J. R. Ward, "The Profitability of Sugar Planting in the British West Indies, 1650–1834," *Economic History Review* 31 (1978): 204, 208; Sheridan, *Sugar and Slavery,* 216, 224–25, 228–29, 375; Michael Craton and James Walvin, *A Jamaican Plantation: The History of Worthy Park, 1670–1970* (Toronto: University of Toronto Press, 1970), 49, 53, 57; Zahedieh, "Trade, Plunder and Economic Development," 218–22. For the flourishing intra–West Indies capital market, see Pares, *West-India Fortune,* 36–42; Pares, *Merchants and Planters,* 25; and the rich documentation in Pares Transcripts, MS West Indies, s. 5, Rhodes House Library, Oxford, U.K. See also n. 80, below, Chancery records.

88. McCusker and Menard, *Economy of British America,* 136; Aubrey C. Land, "Economic Base and Social Structure: The Northern Chesapeake in the Eighteenth Century," *Journal of Economic History* 25 (1965): 649–51; Aubrey C. Land, "Economic Behavior in a Planting Society: The Eighteenth-Century Chesapeake," *Journal of Southern History* 33 (1967): 477–80; Price, *Perry of London,* 31–36, 67–71; Steffen, "Independent Merchant," 18–22; Menard, "Tobacco Industry," 150–61; Lorena S. Walsh, "Summing the Parts: Implications for Estimating Chesapeake Output and Income Subregionally," *William and Mary Quarterly,* 3rd ser., 56 (January 1999): 55–72; Carr and Menard, "Wealth and Welfare in Early Maryland," 96–101.

89. Pares, *Merchants and Planters,* quotation from 47; Pares, "London West-India Merchant House," 219–26; Morgan, "Calendar of Correspondence," esp. 83, 99, 114–15, 117–21. There is a mass of evidence bearing on the large increase in West Indian, especially Jamaican, planters' debts from the 1720s to the Revolution and beyond in the Chancery papers in the PRO. See, for examples, Chancery Masters' Exhibits: C104/108, *Walter v. Evans,* 1744–82; C107/148, *Clark v. Knight,* 1720–87; C108/85, Roberts, circa 1740; C109/338, *Richardson v. Baxter,* 1753–74; and Chancery, Petty Bag, Misc., C217/86/1–2 Tarbutt Papers. For tobacco planters, see Francis N. Mason, *John Norton & Sons, Merchants of London and Virginia* (New York: A. M. Kelley, 1968), xxvi–xxvii, 129–31; Rosenblatt, "Significance of Credit," 396; Price, "Last Phase of the Virginia–London Consignment Trade: James Buchanan & Co.," 86–93.

90. For the (qualified) view that the debts of sugar planters have been exaggerated, see Sheridan, *Sugar and Slavery,* 292, 296–98; Sheridan, "Planters and Merchants," 111–13. His argument is based on the reasonably healthy financial position of Jamaican planters as depicted in their Jamaican probate inventories for the period 1741–75, although one notes that it is a characteristic of inventories made in the colonies to give full lists of assets and incomplete ones of liabilities. For the number of sugar estates, see Sheridan, *Sugar and Slavery,* 145, 173, 223, 231. A recent study of Jamaica, based on the views of contemporaries rather than on merchants' accounts, estimates that Jamaica's total debt to Britain at the end of the colonial period stood at only £2,000,000; see Trevor Burnard, "'Prodigious Riches': The Wealth of Jamaica before the American Revolution," *Economic History Review* 54 (2001): 512–13.

91. Pares, "London West-India Merchant House," 222–25. Henry Lascelles made a *direct* investment of £40,000 in the African slave trade in 1740, although he soon regretted this decision; see Gill, *Merchants and Mariners,* 92–97.

92. Richard Pares, *Yankees and Creoles: The Trade between North America and the West Indies before the American Revolution* (Cambridge: Harvard University Press, 1956), 161–63; Doerflinger, *Vigorous Spirit of Enterprise,* 96–97; Baxter, *House of Hancock,* 59–61, 280–85; Harrington, *New York Merchant,* 185–86; Hedges, *Browns of Providence Plantations: Colonial Years,* 182–83; Nash, "Organization of Trade"; Gifts and Deposits, 30/8/343, PRO, fols. 167–69, lists the debts claimed by British merchant houses from the colonies in 1776. Some merchants remained free of debt, usually if they started with some capital and followed steady, rather than aggressive, trading policies; see, for examples, the New York merchant James Beekman and Henry Laurens and John Guerard, Charleston slave factors. See White, *Beekmans,* 380–81; R. C. Nash, "Trade and Business in Eighteenth-Century South Carolina: The Career of John Guerard, Merchant and Planter," *South Carolina Historical Magazine* 96 (1995): 28. On the other hand, British merchants who refused to extend long credits to their colonial correspondents made little progress in the export trade to the northern colonies; see William I. Roberts III, "Ralph Carr: A Newcastle Merchant and the American Colonial Trade," *Business History Review* 42 (1968): 271–87.

93. Price, *Capital and Credit,* 8–11. As stated, these debts were owed to commission agents, other than certain debts owed by Chesapeake planters to the independent tobacco importers of London, for example, William Molleson. The origins of the debts and the nature of the trading relationships between colonial debtors and London creditors can be traced in the voluminous files in T. 79, Claims of British subjects for unrecoverable pre-1776 American debts, PRO. For detailed references to the South Carolina evidence from this source, see Nash, "Organization of Trade."

94. Devine, *Tobacco Lords,* 55–64; Price, *Capital and Credit,* 8–11. The Chesapeake debt owing to Glasgow increased rapidly from the mid-1760s to 1774 and was then sharply reduced in 1775.

95. Richard B. Sheridan, "The British Credit Crisis of 1772 and the American Colonies," *Journal of Economic History* 77 (1960): 161–86; Price, "Credit in the Slave Trade," 310–16.

96. Nash, "Organization of Trade," 93–97, and "Trade and Business," 25–28. In the British export trades to South Carolina, as explained above, much British capital was advanced to Carolina importers.

97. Pares, *Merchants and Planters,* 44–49.

98. Ormrod, "Atlantic Economy"; David Ormrod, *The Rise of Commercial Empires: England and the Netherlands in the Age of Mercantilism, 1650–1770* (Cambridge & New York: Cambridge University Press, 2003), esp. 63–66, 134–37; Davis, *Industrial Revolution,* 74; L. S. Pressnell, "The Rate of Interest in the Eighteenth Century," in T. S. Ashton, *Studies in the Industrial Revolution: Presented to T. S. Ashton* (London: University of London, Athlone Press, 1960), 178–214; A. H. John, "Insurance Investment and the London Money Market of the Eighteenth Century," *Economica* 20 (1953): 137–58; Pares, *Merchants and Planters,* 44; Pares, "London West-India Merchant House," 219–20; Sheridan, *Sugar and Slavery,* 288–92, 296–98; Thoms, "Mills Family," 8, 10; Price, "Credit in the Slave Trade," 306–10.

99. Price, *Capital and Credit*, 30.

100. Ibid., 66–69, 75–76, 92–93. Grassby, *Business Community*, 82–91; Peter Earle, *The Making of the English Middle Class: Business, Society, and Family Life in London, 1660–1730* (Berkeley: University of California Press, 1989), 35, 108–12, 141–42; Hancock, *Citizens of the World*, 241–47; Wilson, *Gentlemen Merchants*, 68; T. M. Devine, "Sources of Capital for the Glasgow Tobacco Trade, c. 1740–1780," *Business History* 16 (1974) 123–25; D. M. Joslin, "London Bankers in Wartime," in Ashton, *Studies*, 171–75; A. P. Wadsworth and J. de L. Mann, *The Cotton Trade and Industrial Lancashire, 1600–1780* (Manchester: Manchester University Press, 1931), 249–50; B. L. Anderson, "The Attorney and the Early Capital Market in Lancashire," repr. in *Capital Formation in the Industrial Revolution*, ed. François Crouzet (London: Methuen, 1972), 233–35; Hudson, *Genesis of Industrial Capital*, 211–14; quotation from 30.

101. Davis, *Rise of the Atlantic Economies*, 238; Conrad Gill, "Blackwell Hall Factors, 1795–1799," *Economic History Review* 6 (1953–54): 268–81; Mann, *Cloth Industry*, 65–84; Price, "Joshua Johnson," 157–61; and esp. Price, *Capital and Credit*, 101–23, 140–43.

102. Herbert Heaton, *The Yorkshire Woollen and Worsted Industries: From the Earliest Times up to the Industrial Revolution*, 2nd ed. (Oxford: Clarendon Press, 1965), 385–86; Wilson, *Gentlemen Merchants*, 52–53, 74–81; Hudson, *Genesis of Industrial Capital*, 156–60; Smail, *Merchants, Markets and Manufacture*, 34–40, 69–70. However, London *import* merchants helped to finance the woolen export trade by purchasing bills from the Yorkshire merchants drawn on the latter's foreign customers; see Jones, *War and Economy*, 262.

103. Wadsworth and Mann, *Cotton Trade*, 224–31; J. E. Inikori, "The Credit Needs of the African Trade and the Development of the Credit Economy in England," *Explorations in Economic History* 27 (1990): 210–14; Morgan, *Bristol & the Atlantic Trade*, 97–114; Price, "Credit in the Slave Trade," 338.

104. These figures, which are necessarily approximate ones, are summarized in Price, *Capital and Credit*, 122–23.

105. Another tobacco agency, Norton and Sons, followed more conservative trading policies and retained only 25 percent of profits; yet, from commencing trade in 1764, with an equity capital of £6,000, the firm succeeded in making loans to Virginia planters and merchants worth £41,000 by 1773. The Pinneys of Bristol, minor commission agents by London standards, who began business in 1783 with a capital of £12,000 came, through careful lending and a high retention of earnings, to hold debts in the West Indies worth by the 1830s £340,000. In an earlier period the Perrys, the most important tobacco firm in London, expanded rapidly in the 1690s by reinvesting the great bulk of their profits, which averaged £5,000 per annum. The London Huguenot merchant David Marescoe doubled his capital from £20,000 to £40,000 between 1664 and 1670, on the basis of reinvesting the commissions he earned in Baltic importing during the second Anglo-Dutch War. His successors, his widow and her new husband, did not add to this fortune because they spent their trading profits on an extravagant lifestyle. See Pares, *Merchants and Planters*, 49; Pares, *West-India Fortune*, 174–80, 322–28; Mason, *John Norton*, xxvi–xxvii, 129–31; Rosenblatt, "Significance of Credit," 396; Price, "Last Phase of the Virginia–London Consignment Trade: James Buchanan & Co.," 86–87; Price, *Perry of London*, 48–51; Roseveare, *Markets and Merchants*, 112–20, 203–6. For other examples of rapid merchant-capital accumulation, see Price, *Capital and Credit*, 20–39.

106. Pares, *Merchants and Planters,* 50. However, a recent important study of a London West-India merchant house lending money in the West Indies in the 1730s and 1740s sides with Adam Smith rather than Pares, arguing that much new capital was invested in the West Indies in addition to recycled mercantile trading profits; see S. D. Smith, "Merchants and Planters *Revisited,*" *Economic History Review* 55 (2002): 434–65.

107. See n. 64, above, and Wadsworth and Mann, *Cotton Trade,* 262–63; Schofield, "Virginia Trade," 132–41; Edwards, *Growth of British Cotton Trade,* 178–79, 227–28; Hudson, *Genesis of Industrial Capital,* 161–66; Inikori, "Market Structure," 718–19, 756–58; Inikori, "Credit Needs," 212–14.

108. L. S. Pressnell, *Country Banking in the Industrial Revolution* (Oxford: Clarendon Press, 1956), 4–11, quotation from 8; Price, *Capital and Credit,* 67–89; O'Brien, "Merchants and Bankers," 255–67, 275–77.

109. Contemporaries estimated that £200 million of foreign bills were drawn annually in circa 1812; see Pressnell, *Country Banking,* 171–73.

110. In Liverpool, for example, dozens of the port's merchants borrowed sums of up to £40,000 from Leyland, Bullins & Co. from 1812 to 1823. The Leeds woolen-manufacturing firm of Rhodes and Glover became indebted to their Leeds bankers for £22,000 by 1814, because of delayed returns from direct cloth sales in the Brazilian market; see Pressnell, *Country Banking,* 361–65, 532–34; R. G. Wilson, "The Fortunes of a Leeds Merchant House, 1780–1820," *Business History* 9 (1967): 80–83. See also Wilson, *Gentlemen Merchants,* 154–58; Hudson, *Genesis of Industrial Capital,* 167; S. R. Cope, *Walter Boyd: A Merchant Banker in the Age of Napoleon* (Gloucester: A. Sutton, 1983), 36, 41–42, 162, 172. For Leeds and Hull trading banks, see Jackson, *Hull in the Eighteenth Century,* 209–33.

111. The Bank of England until the early 1780s largely discounted bills presented by merchants in the inland and foreign trades rather than by banks. See Jacob M. Price, "The Bank of England's Discount Activity and the Merchants of London, 1694–1773," in his *Overseas Trade and Traders: Essays on Some Commercial, Financial, and Political Challenges Facing British Atlantic Merchants, 1660–1775* (Aldershot, U.K. and Brookfield, Vt.: Variorum, 1996), 107–14.

112. John Clapham, *The Bank of England: A History,* 2 vols. (Cambridge: The University Press/New York: Macmillan, 1945), 1:205–8, 269, 301–2; 2:1–30, 433; Ian Duffy, "The Discount Role of the Bank of England during the Suspension of Cash Payments, 1797–1821," *Economic History Review* 35 (1982): 67–82; Seymour Shapiro, *Capital and the Cotton Industry in the Industrial Revolution* (Ithaca: Cornell University Press, 1967), 79–87; Pressnell, *Country Banking,* 89–104, 142–60, 171–73, 434–40, 460–61; Edwards, *Growth of British Cotton Trade,* 223–24; Peter Mathias, *The First Industrial Nation: An Economic History of Britain, 1700–1914* (London: Methuen, 1969), 173–75; Price, "Transaction Costs," 286; Inikori, "Credit Needs," 215–18, 434–39; Gayer, *Growth and Fluctuation,* 1:11, 45, 105, 132–33, 205; Buck, *Development,* 133–35.

113. For example, Clapp, *John Owens,* 28–30, 40–45; also see n. 99, above.

114. For example, the firm of Burys, Lancashire calico printers and exporters, discounted hundreds of thousands of pounds of bills of exchange in the period 1811–15 with Manchester and London bankers and bill brokers, bills drawn on London and Liverpool commission agents and "accepted" by merchant banks; see Edwards, *Growth of British Cotton Trade,* 176–77, 218–25. See also Ralph W. Hidy, *House of Baring,* 37, 73–74, 102–3,

129–30; Ralph W. Hidy, "The Origins and Functions of Anglo-American Merchant Bankers, 1815–1860," *Journal of Economic History* 1 (1941): supp., 53–66; Stanley D. Chapman, *The Rise of Merchant Banking* (London and Boston: Allen and Unwin, 1984), 9–15, 105–6, 115–20; Stanley D. Chapman, "The Foundation of the English Rothschilds," *Textile History* 8 (1977): 106–9; Chapman, *Merchant Enterprise*, 68–74; Hudson, *Genesis of Industrial Capital*, 165–70; Buck, *Development*, 117–20, 131–35; Gregory, *Nathan Appleton*, 18, 65–66; Perkins, *Financing Anglo-American Trade*, 88–90, 93–94; Edwin J. Perkins, *American Public Finance and Financial Services, 1700–1815* (Columbus: Ohio State University Press, 1994), 318–19. The Browns of Liverpool, for example, were quite happy to advance funds to English manufacturers, in order to get consignments of goods to their U.S. branches.

115. Westerfield, "Early History of American Auctions," 159–210; Buck, *Development*, 121–35; Cohen, "Auction System," 488–510; Buck, *Development*, 135–48; Albion, *Rise of Port of New York*, 57–61, 276–82, 410; Price, *Capital and Credit*, 143–45; Hudson, *Genesis of Industrial Capital*, 170–74; Tooker, *Nathan Trotter*, 80–83.

116. Nettels, *Emergence of a National Economy*, 295–98; see also Richard Sylla, "U.S. Securities Markets and the Banking System, 1790–1840," *Federal Reserve Bank of St. Louis Review* 80 (1998): 83–98; Perkins, *American Public Finance*. In addition there was the First Bank of the United States. The number of banks increased rapidly after 1800, although many of these had little to do with foreign trade.

117. Doerflinger, *Vigorous Spirit of Enterprise*, 304–5; Herman E. Krooss, "Financial Institutions," in *The Growth of the Seaport Cities, 1790–1825*, ed. David T. Gilchrist (Charlottesville: University Press of Virginia, 1967), 110–11; N. S Gras, *The Massachusetts First National Bank of Boston, 1784–1934* (Cambridge: Harvard University Press, 1937), 46–49, 600–612; Robert E. Wright, "Bank Ownership and Lending Patterns in New York and Pennsylvania, 1781–1831," *Business History Review* 73 (1999): 41–43, 54–55; Naomi R. Lamoreaux, *Insider Lending: Banks, Personal Connections and Economic Development in Industrial New England* (Cambridge and New York: Cambridge University Press, 1994); Perkins, *American Public Finance*, 123–44, 253.

118. Gras, *Massachusetts First National Bank*, graph opposite p. 38, 600–612; Perkins, *American Public Finance*, 253–56. As a point of comparison, contemporaries estimated that British banks and other financial institutions discounted foreign and inland bills worth £1.2 billion ($3.5–4 billion) circa 1812 and £300–400 million ($1–1.3 billion) in the 1820s and 1830s; see Pressnell, *Country Banking*, 171–73.

119. Doerflinger, *Vigorous Spirit of Enterprise*, 296–310; A. Glenn Crothers, "Banks and Economic Development in Post-Revolutionary Northern Virginia, 1790–1812," *Business History Review* 73 (Spring 1999): 10–11. Doerflinger seems to overdraw the contrast between pre- and postwar financial practice in stating that "in colonial Philadelphia there was almost no commercial paper . . . prewar ledgers and journals make no mention of [promissory] notes and bills [of exchange]" (306). It seems improbable that *no* commercial paper circulated in colonial Philadelphia, given its widespread existence in other regions. Indeed, promissory notes circulated as negotiable instruments, to a limited degree, even among Massachusetts farmers in the colonial period; see Winifred B. Rothenberg, "The Emergence of a Capital Market in Rural Massachusetts, 1730–1838," in *The Economy of Early America: The Revolutionary Period, 1763–1790*, ed. Ronald Hoffman et al. (Charlottesville: University Press of Virginia, 1988), 140–42. See also Countryman, "Uses of

Capital," 16–21; Alice H. Jones, *American Colonial Wealth: Documents and Methods,* vol. 3 (New York: Arno Press, 1988), Charles Town District, S.C., 1473–1618. The Charles Town inventories include numerous examples of debtors' "notes" and other forms of paper. It may be that evidence of commercial paper is more common in probate inventories than in business ledgers, a source that by and large Doerflinger did not use. The Olivers' local financial dealings were focused on Baltimore banks; these discounted the bills and notes that the firm obtained from its customers in lieu of book debts, which in turn created the deposit funds on which numerous checks were drawn to pay the firm's own creditors. See Bruchey, *Robert Oliver,* 109–22.

120. Crothers, "Banks and Economic Development," 21–22; Perkins, *American Public Finance,* 134, 317; Bruchey, *Robert Oliver,* 115–21; B. Hammond, "Long and Short Term Credit in Early American Banking," *Quarterly Journal of Economics* 49 (1935): 80–81; Paul A. Gilje, "The Rise of Capitalism in the Early Republic," *Journal of the Early Republic* 16 (1996): 162–65.

121. Doerflinger, *Vigorous Spirit of Enterprise,* 305–10, quotation from 305.

122. Buck, *Development,* 73, 81–86; Perkins, *Anglo-American Trade,* 109, from which the quotation is taken.

123. Price, *Capital and Credit,* 90; Hammond, "Long and Short Term Credit," 88–90.

124. Krooss, "Financial Institutions," 119, 122–25; Bruchey, *Robert Oliver,* 117–18, quotation from 118.

125. Hidy, *House of Baring,* 30, 37, 66, 102–3, 130–33; and the literature on American merchants referred to in nn. 63, 66. The nature of the commercial and other paper discounted by banks has not been systematically studied, but see Gras, *Massachusetts First National Bank,* 46–49; Krooss, "Financial Institutions," 119; Lamoreaux, *Insider Lending,* 1–3; and esp. Bray Hammond, *Banks and Politics in America from the Revolution to the Civil War* (Princeton, N.J.: Princeton University Press, 1957), 71–80, 315–19.

126. The Codmans, a medium-sized Boston firm, for example, increased its debts to Baring and Co. from £12,000 to £50,000 from 1794 to 1798; see Crouzet, "Opportunity and Risk," 126–30. For the role of London agencies, see the literature on American merchants cited in notes 63, 67.

127. For American private and merchant banks, some of which sought chartered status after circa 1810, when the states legislated to restrict their activities, see Richard Sylla, "Forgotten Men of Money: Private Bankers in Early U.S. History," *Journal of Economic History* 36 (1976): 173–88; see also Krooss, "Financial Institutions," 106–7; Perkins, *Financing Anglo-American Trade,* esp. 32, 118; Perkins, *American Public Finance,* 280, 398, quotation from 323. Letters of credit circulated inside the United States—for example, northern merchants sent them to the southern ports when buying cotton.

Revisiting 1640; or, How the Party of Commercial Expansion Lost to the Party of Political Conservation in Spain's Atlantic Empire, 1620–1650

Daviken Studnicki-Gizbert

The twenty-two years of the Count-Duke of Olivares's informal rule of the Spanish Empire (1621–1643) can be read as the story of a reform movement's inability to recover a society from deepening crisis. In stark comparison to his predecessors, Olivares was an activist minister. In his view the state could and should intervene in a variety of social spheres for the sake of the *bien comun,* or commonwealth.[1] Moreover, the scale of intervention had to be equal to the extent of the crisis at hand. Thus, from the first days of his regime Olivares instituted policies aimed at the reform of the full swath of Spanish society: education, taxation, administrative structures, manners and morals, noble privileges, the military, the church, trade, and the economy.[2]

The revival of commerce in the Spanish Empire, the main problem examined in this essay, was arguably one of the central pillars supporting the overall project of reform.[3] The ultimate aim of reform was to restore the Spanish Empire to its past glory during the reign of Philip II, a golden age when its dominion stretched around the globe and fettered the enemies of nation and religion. Imperial power, however, rested on the financial capacities of the state. This was especially true during Olivares's tenure of government when his ambitious military and foreign policies drove state expenditures ever upward.[4] In one ten-year stretch (1621–31) Crown spending more than doubled, jumping from 8 million to 18 million ducados per year.[5] The fiscal health of the Spanish Empire rested, in turn, on the affluence of its commercial sector, whose activities—the transatlantic trades in particular—provided the Crown with the silver needed to fund its European and overseas campaigns. In the view of the writers of the period, "the expansion of commerce guarantees the common wealth of your [Philip IV] vassals,"[6] who "are truly the Kingdom's best walls and fortresses."[7] By the 1620s, however, it was abundantly clear that the commercial foundations were beginning to crumble. As Mendo da Mota—a Portuguese adviser to the count-duke—

pointed out, the empire had conquered the entire world by force of its arms, but having neglected matters of trade, its dominion lacked the means of its sustenance, "[because] it no longer enjoyed the fruits of any of the World's trades."[8] If Olivares wanted to recover the imperial grandeur of the past, he had to transform the Spanish Empire into a commercial power as well as a military one.

Though he may have been the chief protagonist of reform, the count-duke was not alone in his efforts. He constantly recruited individuals to counsel him over the formulation and implementation of reformist policy. With regard to the Crown's commercial policy, Olivares relied heavily on the expertise of men of experience: individuals drawn from the banking and trading communities of the period. Given the ambit of the Spanish Empire's economic concerns and the predominance of non-Castillians in the world of trade and banking, these men formed a singularly cosmopolitan group: alongside the Castillians one found Portuguese, Italians of various provenances, Wallon, Dutch, English, and German experts.[9]

The fact that the formulation of Crown policy relied on representatives from the commercial and financial sector was itself an innovation. In theory, royal policy was emitted by the monarch after he had taken into consideration the views of his councillors. Advising the king was a privilege ostensibly reserved for men drawn from the highest ranks of the clergy and nobility. Olivares departed from standard practice. So as to bypass the slow and often contentious deliberations of the official councils, he established a system of informal meetings—juntas—between various experts and himself or his close allies in which opinions were gathered and policy was laid out. As the presence and importance of financiers and merchants in the world of the court in Madrid grew, so too did the frustration and outrage of the grandees who found themselves increasingly cut off from the channels of power.

Reforms beget reactions. Opposition to Olivares's grand designs for reform was not long in forming, especially in what concerned the issue of commerce. The count-duke's courting of merchant and banking interests engendered a backlash that entwined what appears to have been a classic *réaction nobilaire* and an ideological confrontation over the appropriate relationship between the political and the economic.[10] The merchant bankers, whose vision of the economy was rooted in their daily experience in the world of the market, sought to bring the institutions and policies of the empire in line with the natural workings of the economy. This "party of commercial expansion" was inclined to believe that economic activity responded to an underlying, natural logic.[11] Drawing on the language of philosophy, one could say that its members saw the economy as ontologically prior to the polity. This conceptual framework had political implications. Statesmen seeking the prosperity of the commonwealth had to work toward achieving a harmony of interests between the state and commerce; neglecting the needs of the latter for the interests of the former spelled ruin. This intellectual framework may have been as much the product of rhetoric as of ideology. But it had an important role to play because it served to justify a series of proposals that sought to shift the mercantilist equilibrium closer to the needs of trade.

Challenging the merchant bankers, their vision, and their aims was what I call the "party of political conservation." This group brought together individuals and factions from a variety of social backgrounds, including the governing members of the *Consulados* (trading guilds) of Seville, Mexico City, and Lima; royal officials; members of the Inquisition; playwrights; clergymen; and a strong contingent drawn from the nobility.[12] Their response to the crisis facing the Spanish Empire was to push for conservation rather than for reform. According to John Elliott, this was a group leery of novelty, and for all their differences in social provenance or rank, they would in the end gather together to defeat Olivares's reformist project.[13] In part, this was a question of protecting their own interests. But their position may have had a deeper source. For many Spanish observers of the dismal seventeenth-century scene the crisis had been provoked by a derogation from the values and manners of the past. This was phrased in terms of moral decay, of God's punishment, or of the internal corruption.[14] The resolution of the crisis lay in return to the higher ideals of the past, to a golden age when Spaniards were morally upright, hardworking, and God-fearing.[15]

Confronted by the question of the place and role of commerce in the empire, they began with the needs of the polity. Though its members included individuals with direct experience in the world of trade, these formed but a small minority of the whole. For the most part, their view of matters commercial was formed from their readings and education in the canon of Catholic and classical thought. They believed that the workings and structure of commerce had to be subordinated to the higher ends of Spain's Catholic and imperial mission. In their view, the empire was a bounded *corpus mysticum*, a mystical body within which wealth needed to be retained and directed toward its head. This conception of the state had a determining influence on the party of conservation's dim view of the proposals offered by the merchants and bankers working with Olivares. Allowing trade to cross the boundaries of the imperial body politic was to condemn it to decline.[16] Encouraging intracolonial commerce presaged a weakening of the center, the head and heart of the empire. Fostering private monopolies meant the subordination of Philip's vassals to economic tyranny.

In order to bring this debate over the reform of commerce to a more concrete and manageable level, this essay examines the experience of one group of key players: the Portuguese merchant bankers active both in the Atlantic trades and in the court in Madrid. The Portuguese merchant bankers were not only closely allied to Olivares's project of commercial renovation, they also bore the brunt of its demise. What may appear as a somewhat abstract difference in views over the place of trade in the political order degenerated into a serious conflict between the Portuguese and their opponents. Over the course of the 1620s and 1630s this conflict moved from public diatribes against the self-interested avarice of the Portuguese, to their systematic judicial persecution, and finally to violence. The political crisis of 1640, which saw the secession of Portugal from the Spanish Empire, left both the Portuguese merchant bankers and their patron, the Count-Duke of Olivares, dangerously exposed. Three years later Olivares's dismissal confirmed their fall from power as they passed from being privileged vassals to traitors against the king.

The following pages break down into five general sections. The first section examines the activities and place of the Portuguese community of trade within Spain's Atlantic empire. The second section looks at how the widespread communications network on which the community's trading activities were founded came to influence their conceptualization of the workings of the Atlantic economy. The third section deals with the context and manner in which the Portuguese merchant bankers active in the court at Madrid came to publicly express their views on commerce through published treatises and pamphlets. Then the essay explores the intellectual contours of the debate over commercial reform, paying close attention to how the Portuguese came to argue that commercial expansion was the key to the commonwealth's prosperity. The ending includes a short description of the reaction engendered by the Portuguese and their consequent evacuation from the Spanish Empire.

Portuguese Merchant Bankers in Spain's Atlantic Empire

In 1625 negotiations between the Count-Duke of Olivares and representatives of the Portuguese merchant-banking community came to their successful conclusion.[17] At issue was their participation in the *asientos*—annual loans advanced by private bankers in order to finance the Spanish Crown's military campaigns in Europe. Olivares's aim was to use the presence of Portuguese financiers as a means of gaining additional leverage when it came time to negotiate the *asientos* with the Genoese banking cartel.[18] Bringing in the Portuguese would also serve to quiet the voices who decried the growing control of foreigners over the empire's trade and finances. Since the 1580 integration of the Kingdom of Portugal into the Habsburg dominion, the Portuguese had been—in constitutional theory at least—the full-fledged vassals of the King of Spain.[19] Given the general obsession with keeping the flow of bullion within the body of empire, the shift from "foreign" Genoese bankers to "native" bankers was welcomed.[20]

The relationship between the Portuguese trading community and the Spanish Empire stretched much farther back than the 1620s. It tended to be a conflictive relationship, far from the harmonious bond between king and vassals suggested by some of the rhetoric that accompanied the arrival of the Portuguese bankers to the court. Since the beginning of the sixteenth century, Portuguese merchants and seamen were a regular, if undesired, feature of Spain's Atlantic empire.[21] Given the quality of the available sources, it is difficult to establish the precise magnitude of their presence. It is nevertheless clear that there was a constant traffic of interlopers carrying European commodities and African slaves into the Spanish Indies. In exchange, they smuggled silver, pearls, and other American goods to Portugal and the Low Countries.

The 1580s, however, marked a turning point after which the Portuguese developed into the Spanish Empire's most dynamic and wide-ranging group of overseas traders, eclipsing their main rivals, the Genoese.[22] As the American silver cycle began in earnest, and the unification of the Crowns made their access into the Spanish colonies easier, they were able to integrate the various markets and production centers of the expanding European world economy. Their trading circuits, organized by tightly knit networks of families, crisscrossed the Atlantic and reached around to the Asian economy via both the Cape of Good Hope and the Acapulco to Philippines routes. In its overall structure the Portuguese community of trade connected European manufacturing and agricultural centers (both Mediterranean and northern European), African slave marts and goldfields, Asian spice and textile markets, and the mines and plantations of the Americas.

The geographical extent of the community's commercial operations was impressive. It was also the key to its overall success. In a period when early modern nation-states strove to centralize and close off their economies from their rivals, the major accomplishment of the Portuguese was to create trading routes that punctured the seal of mercantilist boundaries. Their actions inscribed themselves into the prevailing logic of commercial capitalism in which price differentials—in part caused by mercantilist policies—pushed merchants to expand their operations across space and integrate previous discrete markets.[23]

In order to do so, the Portuguese established themselves not only in the entrepôts and production centers of the Atlantic economy but also in strategic transfer points. These were ports that allowed them to organize the transfer of commodities and capital between discrete national and colonial economies. The main division to be breached was the separation between the economic system of the Spanish Atlantic empire and the northern economies of France, Holland, and to a lesser extent, England. The mid-Atlantic islands, the port of Cadiz, and the outports of the Atlantic and Algarve coasts of the western and southern Iberian Peninsula each provided relay points connecting incoming textiles and manufactured goods from the north with the silver, pearls, and dyes of the Spanish colonies.[24] The ports of San Juan de Luz, San Sebastian, and Bayonne in the Basque territories of Spain and France served as another connection between north and south Atlantic markets.[25] On the other side of the Atlantic, the Portuguese established themselves in a series of ports that would develop into the main contraband stations of the seventeenth century: Jamaica, Havana, Santo Domingo, Puerto Rico, Trinidad, Margarita, Santa Marta, Cartagena de Indias,

Porto Belo, and Buenos Aires.[26] By establishing a series of direct connections between the markets of northern Europe and the Americas, these relay points created a bypass that effectively confirmed the growing displacement of the Iberian domestic economy from its central position in the Atlantic system.

The Portuguese were also active in the burgeoning intercolonial trade that grew in response to the development of the Spanish colonies' internal economies.[27] Along certain trade circuits, such as the Peru to New Spain routes or in the intra-Caribbean trades, the Portuguese formed a strong presence though not a dominant one. It was in Buenos Aires and the Philippines that their presence was most keenly felt as they organized the contraband trade between the ostensibly separated Castillian and Portuguese colonial spheres. A small and isolated settlement, the port of Buenos Aires nevertheless sat on one of the principal outlets of contraband silver from the mines of Potosi.[28] Thanks to their connections in Africa, Brazil, Europe, and increasingly, in Potosi itself, the Portuguese came to dominate this trade. Silver from Potosi was exchanged for enslaved Africans, provisions from Brazil, and reexported textiles and manufactured goods from Portugal.[29] In the Philippines, Portuguese traders drew off silver from New Spain and Peru into the wider Asian economy in exchange for textiles and spices.

The Portuguese also flourished within the legal trades of the Spanish imperial commercial system. They controlled the *averia*—the monopoly governing the provisioning of the Indies fleet and the collection of shipping duties—during the early decades of the seventeenth century, which gave them a considerable advantage over rival trading communities.[30] I am still compiling the relative weight of their trading activity in the registered traffic of the Indies fleet. My data so far indicates that the Portuguese accounted for over 25 percent of the total trade of the dozen ships' records that I have been able to process.[31] This order of magnitude is backed up by Enriqueta Vila Vilar's work on the fleet that was seized in Porto Belo in 1617. According to her figures, two Portuguese merchants, Nicholas de los Reyes and Jorge Fernandez, controlled 30 percent of the total value of the fleet.[32] These are rough estimates of the Portuguese place in the overall Carrera de Indias, guesses that need to be supplemented by a better understanding of the participation of other trading communities. Until we have these figures there is no way of precisely knowing where the Portuguese sat in the hierarchy of the trading world of the Spanish Empire.

There was, nonetheless, a sector of the legal Atlantic trades in which the *mainmise* (control) of the Portuguese was beyond doubt: the transatlantic slave trade. The growing need of the Spanish colonial economies for enslaved African labor created a unique breach in the hermetic system of the empire.[33] The sources of the slaves were territories under the direct control of the Portuguese, a monopoly which they jealously guarded even after the unification of the Crowns. If the Indies of Castile wanted the African slaves they needed, they would have to accept the presence of Portuguese merchants in their markets. From the perspective of the officials and ministers interested in keeping the Indies free of non-Castillians, the continued operation of the Portuguese slave trade proved to be something of a Trojan horse. There was the question of the final destination of the considerable amount of silver—some 96,719,040 pesos de a ocho for the period 1595 to 1640—required to pay for this human traffic.[34] Once in the hands of the Portuguese, there was no guarantee that it would continue to circulate within the body of empire. As one of their detractors charged, it was well known that the Portuguese trafficked openly with the heretics of the North and acted as the channel through which the Indies were drained of its silver.[35]

There was also the question of contraband. The slave trade was notoriously difficult to police. Unlike the ships of the imperial fleet system, slave ships sailed throughout the year save the dangerous hurricane season of the late summer and early fall.[36] They were essentially free to come and go as they pleased, thus escaping the vigilance that was an intrinsic part of the official fleet system.[37] The slave ships were also quite small, many of which were *urcas*, ships of some forty to sixty "toneladas" with a shallow draw and low deck.[38] They were faster at sea, quicker to load and unload, and easier to hide in a wider range of natural ports.[39] In short, they were the ideal ships for the kind of traffic that wished to remain out of sight of the prying eyes of Crown officials.

The magnitude of the contraband effected under the cover of the legal slave trade is difficult to assess. All the same, the seizures of Portuguese contraband vessels allow us to glean some information about its general features. In addition to unregistered African slaves, the Portuguese slavers loaded considerable amounts of textiles and supplies from the northern markets.[40] These were either transferred directly from family members or associates in France and the Low Countries, or acquired in Portugal.[41] In return for the textiles and slaves, the Portuguese acquired silver, pearls, and precious stones that were easy to smuggle out of the Indies and into the larger Atlantic economy.

The profits generated by the activities of the Portuguese trading system were put to use in the financial markets of the period. At the head of the Portuguese trading community were a dozen or so families that had made the move from the world of overseas trade to the world of private and public finances. Drawing on the investments of Portuguese merchant houses, the bankers—or *asentistas*, as they were called in Spain—became some of the most important sources of credit for the Spanish Empire. Along with those of the Genoese (and here the Portuguese were overshadowed by the Italians), Portuguese financial networks moved millions of ducados of silver per year toward the northern economies.[42] This silver drain, a hemorrhaging of the body politic according to the imagery of the time, was one of the inevitable consequences of Spain's religious and geopolitical missions in Europe. The geographical spread of empire required regular movements of silver out of the empire to fund its military efforts in the Low Countries, Germany, and Italy. Lacking an adequate financial infrastructure, the

Spanish Empire depended on private commercial and financial networks to effect the needed transfers.[43] Traditionally, American silver destined for the financing of foreign campaigns passed through the established channels of the Spanish fiscal apparatus. Silver from the colonies arrived in Seville, where it was redistributed to the private bankers in order to settle the Crown's debts. As the transatlantic fleet system slid into decline, however, the Portuguese and Genoese bankers began to gather the Crown's silver directly from the American ports, moving it across the Atlantic through their own distribution networks.[44]

Conceptualizing the Atlantic World of Trade

As was the case with other early modern trading networks, the successful integration and operation of the Portuguese trading and financial system in the Atlantic rested on the ability of its members to efficiently coordinate flows of information among themselves. It is surprising that historians of the early modern economy have not paid more attention to the practices of communication. If, as contemporary economic theory suggests, key elements of the market mechanism such as pricing, credit markets, or the integration of markets depend on the flow of information, it seems logical that interested historians should attend to the factors influencing this movement.[45] This is especially true in the commercial sector. As we have seen, every year the Portuguese trading system moved millions of pesos worth of goods and capital—through a variety of circuits—between markets dispersed throughout the Atlantic basin. The Portuguese merchant, however, was always at one remove from the actual physical distribution of these goods and capital. His work took place either behind the writing desk, where he received and sent out a constant stream of letters throughout the Portuguese trading network, or during interactions with other merchants gathered in the marketplace.[46]

This Atlantic-wide network of communications not only permitted the organized movement of goods and capital but also gave Portuguese merchants an unparalleled view of the workings of the Atlantic economy. This vantage point allowed them to monitor markets around the Atlantic basin and also made possible a systematic understanding of the whole. They came to appreciate the growing interconnection of markets and how they influenced one another. The rippling movements of price levels, of relative currency values, of capital supply and market gluts were all charted in their correspondence. Monitoring the market was a means of mastering it. It also allowed for an intimate and practical knowledge of early modern economic causality.

In their daily correspondence Portuguese merchants wasted little ink in describing the principles that undergirded economic prosperity; they acted on them. In the world of the marketplace they were practitioners rather than theoreticians. This is not to say that they did not have a clear idea of what these principles might be. My feeling is that they did and that their understanding of the mechanisms governing the market provided the intellectual foundations of their position in the larger debate on the place of commerce within the Spanish Empire. When it came time to explain these principles to a more general public, Portuguese merchants and bankers were forceful and explicit in their argumentation. Among like-minded individuals of the world of trade, however, these principles faded into a set of unstated commonplaces.

Their view of the foundations of economic prosperity can be inferred from the general thrust of their commercial strategies. One of the guiding aims of the Portuguese banking and trading houses was the development of multilateral circuits that integrated markets from different regions and economic sectors. This meant establishing connections between, around, and through the putative boundaries established by the various states of the period. Commodity and capital flows had to follow the international contours of supply and demand. This strategy rested on the understanding that the increase in active capital, whether at the level of an individual merchant house or at the more global level of the trading system as a whole, depended on the constant circulation of goods and capital. For the merchant capitalist there was no end point at which wealth came to rest.[47] Profits were generated through the successful completion of a commercial circuit.[48] For the Portuguese this usually entailed a complicated set of exchanges that ranged across the Atlantic seaboard. As soon as they were realized, these profits were reinvested in new ventures. Merchants worked hard to knit together as many circuits as possible, in order to both maximize the total volume of exchange and reduce risk by spreading out a merchant house's active capital. The trick was to remain at the center of these commercial circuits in order to effectively direct the flow of commodities and capital within them. What was true for merchant houses also held at the level of the system. Here merchant bankers used the Dutch example in order to explain the importance of the free circulation of goods and capital. The Dutch, they pointed out, had no natural wealth to speak of, yet they had managed to transform their nation into the commercial powerhouse of the period. The key to their success lay in opening the country up to as many trades as possible so as to reap the profits of their integration.[49]

Another, even more fundamental, point of contention was the merchants' understanding of the very nature of the economy. Their opponents saw economic activity as something instrumental to the general wealth of the polity. From this point of departure one could argue that the workings of the market could be guided, altered, and even blocked for the sake of the greater good howsoever defined. The Portuguese merchants, however, saw things differently. In their view the economy was part of the natural sphere. Like other natural phenomena, individuals could observe and attempt to understand its workings, but ultimately it would follow its own course. This engendered a certain fatalism vis-à-vis the fluctuating state of the market; its swings were beyond the control of man. In periods of what we might call "secular crisis" or "cyclical downturns," the letters of the Portuguese merchants became filled with constant references to "the maliciousness of the times" or to how "like the World as a whole, this Kingdom has become an evil place," or that "the World is so completely and pervasively evil, that we hardly marveled upon finding these lands so poor."[50] One could weather the "natural" downturns of the market, but one could hardly control it.

From the Market to the Court—The Public Expression of Commercial Experience

More could be written about how the Portuguese merchants of the Atlantic world of trade understood the mechanisms of the early modern market. Their daily experiences made them well versed in a series of technical issues such as the workings of inflation, how the value of precious metals changed according to region and market, or the technicalities of currency markets. I have chosen to focus on their vision of a natural economy and the importance of the entwined principles of circulation and multilateral trading circuits because it seems to me that these lay at the very heart of the debate over the Spanish Empire's reform of the commercial sphere. Their ideological adversaries argued that the workings of the economy should be subordinated to the needs and ends of the polity, and that the common wealth of the Spanish Empire depended on the centralization of trade within a hermetic system.

The often-heated debates held in Madrid over the role of the economy and the question of state reforms were part of a wider discussion occurring in the courts and printed literature across seventeenth-century Europe. These discussions played an important role in the formulation of modern political economics precisely because, for the first time, practitioners were called on to offer their opinions on what had hitherto been the purview of statesmen or theologians. The novelty of their presence lay not so much in their understanding of the economic activity, but rather in the fact that they were publicly expressing their views in an attempt to influence the course of state policy.[51] In Spain the merchants and bankers who set their views down on paper were an important part of a larger group of pamphleteers and promoters who became collectively known as *arbitristas*.[52] These writings, which ranged from far-fetched schemes to treatises on the affairs of the state, had begun to crop up in the closing decades of the sixteenth century.[53] As Spain slipped ever deeper into crisis, the genre witnessed a veritable explosion as seemingly everyone who thought he had the solution to the empire's ills submitted his advice to the ministers and courtiers of the court at Madrid.

The installation of Olivares at the informal head of Spanish government further encouraged expansion of the discussion over the affairs of state. On arriving in power, the count-duke set about creating what Elliott has termed an alternate administration that paralleled the traditional structures of the official councils.[54] This new structure of policy making was mainly based on informal meetings, or juntas, organized in the lobbies and private apartments of Olivares's most trusted courtiers. They could also be more ostentatious affairs such as the Junta de Gran Reformación (1618–25), which commissioned opinion pieces on a range of topics in a bid to resolve the crisis facing the empire.[55] The combination of the multiplication of policy-making arenas and the explosion in production and distribution of pamphlets resulted in a marked expansion in the public sphere of the Spanish polity. Discussions over the course of the state, previously a rather genteel affair among members of the highest echelons of the Spanish clergy and nobility, now included individuals from diverse backgrounds who, in the view of one observer, swamped Madrid with their petitions, projects, and treatises in hand.[56]

The Portuguese who participated in this general discussion were part of a cosmopolitan group of merchants and bankers drawn from the various centers of the Atlantic world of trade. Some were actively recruited by Olivares to offer their expertise on economic matters; others were commissioned to present the case for particular reforms of the imperial commercial system on behalf of specific groups; while the remainder saw it as their duty as loyal vassals to offer what seemed to them key pieces of the solution to the empire's crisis. In the course of my research I found dozens of *arbitrios* written by members of the Portuguese community during the early seventeenth century. As in the case of their participation in the Carrera de Indias, it is difficult to assess their relative position in the overall production of economic pamphlets and treatises at the time without knowing more about the production of their Italian, Flemish, German, English, Catalan, and Castillian counterparts.[57] Biographical information on the Portuguese *arbitristas* is hard to come by, but what exists reveals individuals who were deeply implicated in the world of overseas trade and finance. Manuel Lopez Pereira—who pushed for the creation of trading companies, the liberalization of trade, the revival of Castile's flagging manufacturing sector, and the abandonment of Spain's strategy of land-based warfare against the Dutch—had participated in the Atlantic sugar trade before moving into the trades of the Spanish Carrera de Indias.[58] The Portuguese man of letters Antonio de Leon Pinelo, who would argue for the decentralization of the Spanish imperial trading system, came from one of the leading Portuguese families controlling the contraband trade through Buenos Aires.[59] Duarte Gomes Solis, who would write two of the most substantial treatises on the overseas trade in the empire and its reforms, was part of the Gomes Denis e Solis family of merchants and *asentistas* whose operations spread throughout northern Europe, Iberia, Italy, Asia, and the south Atlantic.[60] He had been an active merchant for many years in India and Iberia.[61] The list continues: Juan Nuñes Saraiva and Garcia de Yllan were participant bankers in the royal *asientos;* Juan Nuñes Correa held the provisioning monopoly for the imperial fleets; Cristobal Nuñez was part of the Portuguese trading community of Seville; Francisco Vitoria de Barahona had been active in the Peruvian silver trade before turning his energies toward the exportation of New Spanish cochineal and the Acapulco–Philippines circuit; while Manuel Sueyro was part of the northern European operations of the Portuguese commercial community.[62]

There existed a harmony of interests between the Portuguese merchant bankers–cum-*arbitristas* and the Count-Duke of Olivares. Along with *arbitristas* drawn from other trading communities, the Portuguese sought to wed the Spanish Empire to the cause of trade. For his part, Olivares had made the revival of Spanish commerce one of the central points of his general project of reform. Establishing the precise motives that impelled the Portuguese merchant bankers to take up the pen is largely a matter of guesswork and inference. There was, to be sure, a degree of self-interest involved. A favorable reception of their memorandums by the members of councils, juntas, or by Olivares often translated into social prestige in the world of the Spanish court or into more concrete concessions of royal privileges. There was also an element of group interest to the extent that their proposals argued for reforms that were favorable to the general liberalization of trade or to the specific activities of a particular group of Portuguese merchants. Nevertheless, if we are to take them at their word, the Portuguese *arbitristas* were also motivated by the desire to help the fortunes of the Spanish Empire as a whole. "The need to assure the common good," wrote Duarte Gomes Solis, "has obliged me, old and blind as I am, to make my way to the court in order to warn your Majesty ... of the necessity of salvaging the Indies."[63] Francisco Vitoria de Barahona opened his *arbitrio* along similar lines: "My great experience has allowed me to reflect on the means of increasing, without harm, the common[wealth]. Having firmly grasped them, and with great zeal of serving Your Majesty, I left my house and family ... and boarded ship for these Kingdoms."[64] There is, I believe, good reason to believe them. Thanks to their predominance in the Atlantic world of trade, these individuals would have continued to prosper without ever having to publish their views for a larger public. Their publication and distribution of *arbitrios* clearly suggest that they wanted their ideas to have an impact. They may have wanted to convince other groups within Spanish society of the importance of their views out of self-interested cynicism, but it seems more likely that they personally believed that the reforms they proposed would be in the interests of the greater good.

At this point their proposals took on a political dimension. So long as their writings remained clearly motivated by personal or group interests, they could be dismissed out of hand by their detractors. However, when their writings on commerce touched on the nature of the commonwealth, they managed to touch a deeper nerve, forcing their opponents to publicly reassert the established vision of the polity. Thus the debate over the place of commerce in the Spanish Empire began in earnest, as each side worked to see its vision prevail and its consequent policies carried through. It was a war of words, waged in the printed pamphlets, plays, manuscripted memos, placards, and conversations that circulated throughout the Spanish court. These words proved to have had force and consequence. To the great misfortune of the Portuguese, the discourses of their opponents came to sanction more immediate acts of prosecution and eventually violence as the party of conservation turned its energies toward the evacuation of the Portuguese trading community from the Spanish imperial sphere.

Debating the Nature of the Commonwealth

The debate over commercial reform was a dispersed affair that lasted throughout Olivares's tenure in power. It took a number of forms: written, performative, and oral. It addressed specific cases such as the proposed establishment of a mercantile nobility, just as it could delve into more fundamental and general problems such as the true nature of a republic's wealth. Examination of two general issues can lend some coherence to this disparate group of reflections and arguments. The first is the nature of the commonwealth; how individuals saw the appropriate social and political order established a framework of assumptions and ideals that constantly resurfaced, both explicitly and implicitly, in the texts pertaining to commerce. Then, in order to show how the debate played itself out, a specific case study is presented: the structural reform of the commercial system of the Spanish Empire.

Drawing from the wells of classical and Christian thought, the political imagination of seventeenth-century Spain saw the well-ordered commonwealth as an integrated whole whose fortunes rested on the harmonious interaction of its constituent parts. In order to illustrate this idea the political theorists of the period recurred to the metaphor of the *corpus mysticum*, or mystical body.[65] The image of the body conveyed the multitude of functions that existed within the polity as well as the need for their actions to be coordinated for the sake of the whole. The metaphor of the mystical body and the ideas it conveyed formed the principles that assured the success of the commonwealth. They also revealed the causes of social and political misfortune: excess and self-interest. These forms of behavior had to be sanctioned because they worked against harmony of the whole and were capable of unleashing the forces of disorder that were always latent in the body politic.[66] The belief that guided and concerted action had to be privileged over self-interest and excess was not limited to the scholars and intellectuals of the period. It formed part of the common understandings of the bases of social order at all levels of society and on both sides of the debate over the commonwealth. "I see now," fulminated the Portuguese *asentista* Andres Rodrigues Estremoz when he heard that his brother had used the house's funds for his own personal ventures, "that excess and ambition have absolute rule over you. [I remind you] that it is better to starve than to lapse into these the gravest of sins.

As for the money you have obtained in this way, it is not even worthy of the Devil."[67] An anonymous critic of the Portuguese wrote, "If we are cut off from such fruits of the Indies which are rightfully ours, it is because the wealth of the Indies has called up excesses of greed and desire amongst the Portuguese, who have entered, settled and over time come to control the best our Indies have to offer."[68]

It seems that when excess and self-interest were at play, wealth was never far from the picture. Nevertheless, another point of consensus over the nature of the commonwealth was the fact that its prosperity depended on material riches—silver in particular. Again, the metaphor of the body was called on, this time to explain the central importance of silver to the body politic. In its prefactory matter regarding the structures of trade, the compilation of the laws of the Indies stated that "the abundance and wealth of silver and gold is the principle nerve of the Kingdoms [of empire]."[69] The idea that silver was the sustaining blood of the empire appears in the economic writings of the period, including a 1642 treatise on currency: "money is the blood and vital spirit of the body of the Republic."[70] The Portuguese *arbitristas* would use similar images in their pamphlets to underscore the political importance of silver and trade. In his treatise on commercial reform Manuel Lopez Pereira wrote that "the principal artery that sustains the general wealth of your trades is in sum, Lord, the circulation of silver."[71]

The above conceptions of the principles governing the well-ordered polity and the true measure of its wealth formed a terrain of common understanding among those who participated in the debate over commercial reform. Whether theologian, official, or merchant banker, they argued from shared assumptions regarding the social order and the need for silver. Their paths would diverge sharply when they took up the entwined questions of what the ends of the commonwealth were and how, consequently, wealth should move through the polity.

In the eyes of the party of political conservation, the fortunes of the commonwealth not only depended on its internal harmony but also were safeguarded by the external actions of God.[72] The converse was true as well. The fact that the Spanish Empire had sunk into a state of crisis was attributable to God's ire.[73] The weight of God's judgment on the fate of the commonwealth meant that its actions were beholden to the imperatives of the faith—a sharp riposte to those who would argue that state policy had to conform to the natural workings of the market. The political implications of Catholic theology would thus provide the ideological legitimation for Spanish mercantilism. Given that the monarch was the instrument of God's designs on earth, the commonwealth had to be organized hierarchically in order for the king to coordinate its members toward the fulfillment of the divine will.[74] What held for the organization of power and control also held for the circulation of riches within the commonwealth: not only did wealth need to be contained within the body politic, it also had to flow toward the head of empire.

If the fate of the empire hung, in part, on the judgment of God, it could also be undermined from within. For members of the party of conservation material greed and self-interest were the chief threats to the commonwealth. "Whatever evils the Devil could not himself execute, money persuaded men to do," wrote Dr. don Aingo de Ezpeleta; he continued, "with money hatred becomes intractable and everlasting, treason is carried out, sin is introduced and fomented."[75] The moral condemnation of material wealth formed an entire genre of didactic literature in sixteenth- and seventeenth-century Spain.[76] Most echoed the reflexive attack of de Ezpeleta, but some succeeded in explaining why riches could form a corruptive presence within the commonwealth. Following in a long tradition of classical and Judeo-Christian thought, Spanish theorists such as Tomas de Mercado pointed out that material wealth was one of the most powerful lures that could distract men from the higher aims of the polity or the faith.[77] "Money itself," he wrote, "has no end, nor does the desire to acquire it."[78] The infinite nature of money established the conditions for a dangerous obsession among those whose lifework was to move and increase it. This idea hearkens back to Aristotle, who pointed out that the pursuit of wealth for its own sake logically led to excess because it was not bound by the pursuit of higher ends.[79] For Mercado, the unrelenting quest for profits encouraged individuals to consider only their own personal interests; it created a sense of personal possessiveness that was a powerful solvent against the communal bonds that held families and commonwealths together.[80] It also took away from the general welfare of the state: "thus we see how as personal fortunes advance and grow, the fortunes of the polity and the council diminish."[81]

"Self-interest is the enemy of the commonwealth," wrote one observer in the mid-seventeenth century.[82] But the machinations of self-interest could assume many forms. They could lead to monopolies—"economic tyranny," according to Mercado—in which the self-interested actions of a handful of merchants detracted from the welfare of the empire as a whole.[83] Such a situation occurred in 1637 when members of the Sevillian merchant class refused to load their goods onto the Indies fleets because they did not expect the profits that would have made the venture worthwhile. Without the shippers the Crown could not financially assure the sailing of the fleets. Without the fleets the economic lifeline to the king's vassals in the Americas would be cut off and, perhaps more worrisome, American silver would not return to meet the forthcoming demands of the royal fisc. The response from the party of conservation was unambiguous: loyal merchants should accept the reduction in their personal profits for the sake of the common good.[84] Charges of economic tyranny would be leveled against the Portuguese merchant banker Francisco Vitoria de Barahona following his proposal to establish a monopoly over New Spain's cochineal trade.[85]

The accusation of self-interest also served to delegitimate the Portuguese merchant bankers' proposals. On August 6, 1621, the counselor Mendo de Mota warned Philip IV about the growing influx of Portuguese merchants arriving to offer their commercial advice at the court. The language he used is telling: "Each of them is here on account of his own interests. Not one of them is concerned with the welfare of the King nor of the Republic. I assure you—and let anyone truthfully say that I am wrong!—that among all the people who arrive at all hours to speak with Your Majesty with their proposals, there is not one who deals with the pure and sincere desire for the Public Remedy."[86]

The party of trade had a decidedly different interpretation of the ends and structure of the commonwealth. If party opponents believed that power and resources in the commonwealth had to flow toward the center in order to best achieve the higher ends of empire, the party of trade argued that the commonwealth should be organized in such a way as to benefit its constituent parts. Neither the place nor the authority of the king was called into question. Instead, they sought to emphasize the monarch's responsibility toward his vassals in order to encourage him to enact policies more favorable to the decentralized circulation of wealth.

In his *arbitrio* on the place of merchants in Iberian society, the Portuguese *asentista* Garcia de Yllan argued that trade formed the soul of the monarchy; it had fueled Spanish imperial expansion, had assured the empire's dominion over the two Indies, and had pushed the empire "to the very summits of wealth."[87] Since the reign of Philip II, however, the state of commerce within the Spanish Empire had slipped inexorably into decline. The problem was not so much a lack of resources—few states could boast of the natural endowments God had seen fit to grant to Spain.[88] The Portuguese argued that Spain's crisis was rooted in the demise of its trades. One had only to consider the example of the empire's chief nemesis, the Dutch Republic. Throughout their tracts the Portuguese *arbitristas* made regular references to the Dutch counterexample in order to explain how commercial prosperity sustained political strength and military expansion. "The wealth and grandeur of Holland and her provinces," wrote Manuel López Pereira, "as I have mentioned, consists in commerce and shipping, the fundamental causes of wealth."[89] In another tract the Portuguese *arbitrista* continued in the same vein: "The chief strength of the Monarchy consists in the common trade of its inhabitants since it is through commerce that their capital grows and the Royal rents increase. . . . We have the bitter experience of the Rebels [which demonstrates that] though their lands were extremely limited and poor they have become powerful conquerors by means of their frequent exchanges and dealings with all the parts known to them."[90]

As shown above, the daily activities of the Portuguese merchants and bankers had convinced them that the roots of commercial prosperity lay in the free-ranging circulation of goods and commodities. The number of commercial circuits at work and the total volume of trade were the two variables that assured the general increase in capital. Forcing trade to run through a limited number of circumscribed channels toward the center of the empire might provide short-term advantages to the Crown, but it spelled long-term ruin for the commonwealth as a whole. The king, the Portuguese argued, was responsible for the economic welfare of his subjects since they formed the substance of the empire's wealth. "Reason of State," wrote Garcia de Yllan, "obliges Your Majesty to honor, esteem and sustain Your vassals. Encouraged by Your Majesty's favor and honor, they will enter into commerce and thus enrich themselves."[91] As will be seen below, the belief that freer trade increased the general prosperity of the empire and the principle of the monarch's responsibility were brought together by the Portuguese to argue for the decentralization of the empire's trading structures.

In order to convince their audience of the validity of their views on the economy and its relationship to the polity, the Portuguese adopted the rhetoric of experience and empiricism. In an interesting contrast to their opponents, the Portuguese began their *arbitrios* and pamphlets with a short description of their personal experience in the world of trade. The only worthwhile counsel, argued Manuel Ribeiro Teixeira de Morais, is that which is based on truth. "Only now," he continued, "that I have traveled, seen and navigated, noted and measured, do I feel qualified and capable of relating what is truly important to the Royal Service of Your Majesty."[92] The rhetoric of empirical observation was also an effective rebuttal to the charges of self-interest; the Portuguese argued that they were merely relating what they had observed. This device was also used to call into question the opinions of their opponents. In his tract on the importance of free trade for the economic survival of Buenos Aires, Antonio de Leon Pinelo inveighed against those royal officials who, out of passion, inflated their claims in order to convince the king. This was due not only to excesses of zeal but also to the fact that so many individuals at court allowed themselves to make spurious conjectures on the affairs of the Indies without ever having left Madrid.[93]

Their opponents could argue on grounds of religious imperative or moral principle that it was important to subordinate the workings of trade to the needs of empire, but their daily experience proved otherwise. The economy was a complicated natural entity that worked according to its own rhythms. Successful state policy consisted not in controlling the economy—this was akin to building castles in the sand—but in understanding it in order to reap the benefits of its workings. In their writings the Portuguese pointed to the state's flagrant incapacity to control the general dynamic of the economy. Cut trade off at one point and it would merely contour the blockage.[94] If the Crown wished to retain a greater share of silver from the Americas, Duarte Gomes Solis argued, it should not waste time and resources shoring up the surveillance of its boundaries. The solution was to act on the variables responsible for its movement: its purity and the value it fetched on different European markets. In order to keep more silver in the body of empire, the Crown had merely to reduce the purity of its coinage. Following such measures the Crown could lift all restrictions on the movement of silver and it would still remain in the Spanish dominion because it would have lost its desirability in the eyes of foreigners.[95]

The structures of Spanish mercantilism were built up over the course of the sixteenth century under the reigns of Charles V and Philip II. The framework of this juridical and institutional edifice followed the classical principles of mercantilism. The colonial sphere was marked off as the exclusive domain of the Spanish dominion. The movement of trade and bullion was funneled through the official fleet system. Key sectors of the economy—indigenous labor, production and supply of mercury, the minting of silver, the distribution of commodities such as salt and spices—were transferred to the exclusive domain of the Crown through the instauration of royal monopolies.[96] The development of such forms of state intervention into the economic sphere of the colonies proceeded relatively smoothly during the expansion of the Spanish Empire. Commercial competition from other colonial powers was minimal. The colonial societies of the Americas were just beginning to establish themselves and were still dependent on the resources and power of the metropolis. Overall the general conjuncture of the sixteenth century made it easy to establish and successfully run a centralized trading system that channeled the maximum amount of wealth toward the heart of the empire.

In the early seventeenth century, however, it was clear that the classical structures of the Spanish imperial mercantilist system no longer conformed to the new contours of the Atlantic economy. The domestic economy of Spain was in sharp decline, reducing its ability to provide the colonial markets with the goods they desired.[97] Its role as the principal supplier of imported goods to the colonies was increasingly taken over by the economies of northern France, the Low Countries, and eventually England. Simultaneously the colonial economies of New Spain, Peru, and Brazil had embarked on a trend of self-sustaining growth.[98] As a result of these developments the mercantilist system, which sought to bind the economic activity of the colonies to the needs of the metropolis, broke down in two key areas. The first, as was seen above, was the rapid development of contraband between the markets of the Indies and those of northern Europe. The second was the establishment of intercolonial trade, which burgeoned as colonists found that they could provision themselves and give vent to their wares more effectively in the other colonies of the empire.

Faced with these new circumstances, the statesmen and experts in seventeenth-century Spain proposed two possible solutions. The first, advocated by the party of political conservation, was to shore up the structures of the mercantilist system inherited from the sixteenth century. The second, supported by the party of commercial expansion, was to reconfigure the system so that it conformed with the new realities of the Atlantic economy. The Portuguese, it is no great surprise, placed themselves squarely at the forefront of the efforts to reform the commercial system of the Spanish Empire.

"For the conservation and the commonwealth of Spain, there is nothing more important than the conservation of the Indies ... they must remain dependent [on Spain] because they are the bank and safeguard of Spain."[99] Thus began Pedro de Avendaño Villela's written plea to stiffen the regulations of the Casa de Contratación (the Seville-based institution charged with the operation of Spain's mercantilist system). In his pamphlet Avendaño Villela would go on to warn the king of the new breaches that were "bleeding our Indies dry."[100] In addition to barely veiled accusations against the Portuguese trading community, he pointed to the growing trade between New Spain and China that diverted silver from Seville, the rising contraband of silver moved through Buenos Aires, and the expanding commerce between Brazil and Peru. The main thrust of his proposed solution to this state of affairs was to further centralize the trading system of the Spanish Atlantic. Existing regulations had to be enforced—this was a given—but also had to be joined by a greater concentration of trade movement. The Acapulco to Manila trade had to be cut off completely. Spain's connection to the Asian economy would be maintained though rerouted through a new circuit that would pass around the Cape of Good Hope and terminate in Seville. Likewise, all trade with Brazil would be shifted from Lisbon to Seville. Although Avendaño Villela wrote his tract during the reign of Philip III, the thrust of his argument was taken up and amplified under the succeeding monarch. In 1624, as the magnitude of the Portuguese contraband system between the Indies and northern Europe became increasingly evident, the Consejo de Estado (Council of State) seriously considered a proposal to shut down all but a select handful of the trading ports along the Iberian coast. In its assessment, the Consejo de Estado stated that it was in principle favorable to the idea but that its commitments to the *asentistas* had tied its hands.[101]

On the other side of the Atlantic, attention focused on the problematic case of Buenos Aires. Once again the Portuguese were singled out as the principal cause of the problem. The amount of silver that the Portuguese smuggled out of Peru via the Rio de la Plata was alarming. More worrisome, however, was the manner in which this contraband route was steadily choking the official fleet system, Spain's main connection to her American colonies. The Portuguese flooded the colonial market with relatively inexpensive goods from northern Europe. As a result, when the fleets arrived from Seville, they were unable to sell their goods unless they drastically lowered their prices. According to Alonso de Ciança, this had the expected effect of driving a good part of the Sevillian merchant class into bankruptcy.[102] Again the solution was to reduce all trade to the port to a bare minimum—a handful of resupply vessels closely surveilled by the officials of the Casa de Contratación. Other writers went a step further and called for the implantation of the Inquisition in order to eradicate the Portuguese presence. "The Holy Office," stated Manuel de Frias, "gathers intelligence from all the parts and nooks that they [the Portuguese] use for their entries and exits. [It should] mobilize all its means to capture them so that these infected people will be withdrawn."[103]

The Portuguese, however, were quick in replying to these charges. Antonio de Leon Pinelo, whose father had been deeply involved in the contraband trade in the region, published a pamphlet calling for the liberalization of trade in Buenos Aires. "The obligation of he who governs," he began, "is to treat sustaining and ruling as one and the same.... As Xenophonte said, 'The Good Prince differs in nothing from the good father.'"[104] De Leon Pinelo then argued that allowing open trade in Buenos Aires should not be seen as excessive since this would allow the vassals who lived there the means to sustain themselves. The imperative of sustenance had been used before in the case of the Canary Islands, whose residents were allowed to trade openly, as was just, in order to give vent to their products. He then moved toward the more radical points of his argument. Not only should Buenos Aires increase its traffic with Seville, he wrote, it should also be allowed free and regular access to Angola, Brazil, and Portugal. Though this directly contravened the regulations and logic of the empire mercantilist structure—not only did it sanction intercolonial trade, it would also effectively remove Seville from its position as the sole port of trade for the colony—he argued that this privilege was necessary since these were the natural markets of the South American port.[105]

The right of vassals to assure their sustenance through the liberalization of trade was an argument used in other regions of the empire. Confronted by the growing restrictions on trade enacted under the aegis of the deepening economic war with Holland, merchants and local officials in Portugal petitioned Madrid to reopen trade along the Lusitanian coast. "The Kingdom [of Portugal] has fallen into misery for lack of commerce," relayed the Consejo de Portugal (Council of Portugal) to Philip IV; the council continued, "Your vassals wonder whether the usefulness of closing off trade with the enemies is worth the damage caused by the extinguishment of commerce."[106] The Kingdom of Navarra, situated along the principal contraband route between Spain and France, was more forthright in reclaiming its rights to the prosperity engendered by trade. Navarra's representative in Madrid claimed that the Crown had violated the kingdom's *fueros* (locally accorded privileges) by cutting its trade with Lisbon, from which Navarra obtained the commodities of Asia, and its trade with Holland, from whence came the textiles from the north. "Great is the damage wrought to Your vassals," he argued, "because their principal sustenance depends on free trade and commerce."[107] Madrid, however, was resolute in its decision to cut the kingdom off from foreign trade. Two weeks later the council replied that if Navarra thought that, relative to the treatment accorded to Aragon, they were being unjustly singled out, the Crown would remedy the situation—by prohibiting trade to Aragon as well.[108]

In other spheres the Portuguese met with better success in their bid to reform the structures of Spanish mercantilism. In Madrid the Portuguese had been among the key proponents of the establishment of VOC- and EIC-style trading companies.[109] Manuel López Pereira had pushed for the creation of a trading company that would integrate the Spanish Low Countries into the Atlantic sphere of trade.[110] Backed by Olivares, the Almirantazgo de los Paises Septentrionales, as the company came to be called, was formed by royal order in 1624.[111] The company represented a new direction in Madrid's commercial policy. Not only would the regular linkage between the Spanish Low Countries and the Iberian trades reconfigure the structure of the commercial system, it also sanctioned the participation of Flemish merchants and investors in what had legally been an exclusively Castillian sphere.[112]

The Fatal Flaw—Greed, Apostasy, and Treason

It is clear that the commercial activities and proposals of the Portuguese did little to endear them to the party of political conservation. Since the beginning of the seventeenth century tracts circulated in Madrid condemning growing Portuguese dominance in the trades—both legal and illegal—of the Spanish Atlantic.[113] These attacks gathered additional force when, at the request of Olivares, they arrived in the court. What had previously been a group of interlopers and contrabandists had now become influential players in the world of the court. Not only did the Portuguese engage in the sensitive business of royal financing but they also stood out in their attempts to influence the direction of commercial policy through their writings.

The Portuguese trading community, however, contained a fatal flaw: many members were the descendants of Jews expelled from Spain in 1492. Whether or not they continued to uphold the beliefs and practices of their forefathers is beyond the scope of this essay: the question must be dealt with on a case-by-case basis, and clear supporting evidence is often missing or misleading. Their detractors had little time for such subtleties. In a concatenated series of prosecutions the various tribunals of the Spanish Empire each focused attention and resources on the prosecution of what were then known as the *Portugueses de la nación*. The wave of prosecutions crested in Portugal in 1618 before moving across the Atlantic to Brazil in 1619–20. Then came the tribunals of the Castilian half of the empire: Madrid (1623–45), Lima (1630–35), Cartagena de Indias (1634–40), Mexico City (1639–46), and finally Seville (1655–60). In many of these cases the prosecution of the Portuguese monopolized the efforts of the tribunals to such an extent that the prosecution of other offenses—for example, witchcraft, bigamy, heretical propositions—dropped off drastically and even disappeared.[114] Another noteworthy aspect of these prosecutions was their relatively short duration. Except for the revealing exception of Madrid, the inquisitors accomplished their business in four or five years.[115] This was a remarkable clip for an institution that, on average, took well over a year to try a given case.

While this surge in the Inquisition's persecutions of the Portuguese was inextricably entwined with the rise in anti-Semitism within the empire, it is important to note that these persecutions had political and social dimensions that extended beyond issues of religious orthodoxy and intolerance. What was remarkable was the degree to which the various tribunals focused their attentions on the merchants and bankers within what was a considerably larger community of Portuguese—both Old and New Christian—migrants implanted within the Spanish Empire. The Portuguese who arrived in the colonies came from all walks of life and engaged in a wide range of professions; they included, for example, mariners, artisans, and small farmers in addition to the more notorious merchants.[116] The Portuguese drawn from the lower echelons of the social ladder almost totally escaped the unwelcome attention of the Inquisition. In Cartagena, for example, the occurence of Judaizing charges by occupation for the period 1610–60 breaks down as follows: merchants, forty-six cases; surgeons, *encomenderos*, officials, and artisans, two cases each; members of the clergy, one case.[117] The same preponderance of merchants can be found for Seville in the 1640s.[118] If the Inquisition was primarily concerned with maintaining Catholic orthodoxy in the empire, one might expect the social distribution of the accused to correspond to the social makeup of the Portuguese community in the Americas.

Moreover, the Inquisition worked closely with other Crown institutions to unravel the Atlantic community of Portuguese traders. This demonstrates that the Portuguese community had proved to be a worrisome presence in the empire for reasons other than religious orthodoxy. The extent of Portuguese activities in the Spanish Empire had first become visible in the growing number of reports on Portuguese contraband filed within the Casa de Contratación's bureaucratic channels. These reports provided the impetus for judicial prosecutions on the charges of interloping and fraud. The rhythm of these prosecutions closely followed that of the Holy Office. The number of contraband or fraud cases involving Portuguese for the period 1601–40 breaks down as follows: 1601–10, ten cases; 1611–20, eleven cases; 1621–30, twenty-one cases; 1631–40, sixty-three cases.[119] In general, the Casa de Contratación punished the Portuguese in manners comparable to those of the Holy Office. Their estates were seized; they were imprisoned, publicly flogged, and then exiled or sent to the galleys.[120] Beginning in the 1620s civil authorities in Madrid began prosecuting the Portuguese who were settling in the political heart of the empire. Officers of the court (*alcaldes de la corte*) and of the city council (*alcaldes mayores*) as well as officials of the councils of exchequer all began investigations and legal proceedings against the Portuguese merchant bankers and their families. The charges ranged from the violation of sumptuary laws (for example, the wearing of swords, the use of horse-drawn carriages) to fraud.[121]

These instances of institutional persecution dovetailed with a rise in anti-Portuguese pamphleteering that not only stoked the fire of anti-Portuguese sentiment but also laid out, in explicit terms, the threat that Portuguese merchant bankers and political economists had come to pose for the imperial body politic.

The evidence generated by the empire's various judicial bodies provided ammunition to critics of the Portuguese and, by association, the count-duke himself. For their critics, the threat posed by the Portuguese had long been known but only in its generalities. Now it had become personal because direct connections had been established between the Portuguese merchant in Lima tried for Judaizing and the Portuguese banker who enjoyed the favor of Olivares, and between the financier in Madrid and his cousin in Amsterdam who openly adhered to the beliefs and practices of Judaism. For the first time in decades of anti-Portuguese pamphleteering, critics integrated into their texts the specter of an unholy alliance between the Portuguese "Jews" and the Dutch. "The financier (*asentista*) of Spain," wrote José Pellicer de Osau, "is the companion of the *Bibentebre* of Amsterdam, and together they work towards our ruin. Nor is it possible to distinguish in this plot the [Portuguese] resident in Seville from the [Portuguese] resident in Amsterdam."[122]

Pellicer's pamphlet is also noteworthy for the manner in which it braided together the different threads of anti-Portuguese discourse brought forth over the previous thirty-odd years. After laying out the international coordinates of the Portuguese trading community and their deep implication in the contraband trades, Pellicer pointed out the political threats posed by this group, which "controls the navigation and commerce of the four parts of the globe."[123] In his view, the Portuguese brought together a sinister blend of economic exploitation, apostasy, and rebellion against their sovereign lord: "these leeches ... bleed Your vassals dry" because their "lifelong hatred for [the Catholic] religion and natural spirit of rebellion has led them to conjure against Your lordship."[124] More shocking was the impertinence they exhibited in demanding honors and admission into the noble orders of the realm, a pretension that violated "all Divine and Human laws."[125] Pellicer then proceeded to point out the remedies available to the monarch. He must at all costs prevent members of the nobility from marrying with the Portuguese because this would allow "further impurities to seep insidiously into Spain." Failing such containment measures, the king should cast the Portuguese out of the realm.[126] The economic fortunes of Spain, Pellicer argued, did not rely on these perfidious bankers; it relied on the preservation of its religious mission. God had granted the gold and silver mines of the Indies to the Catholic monarchs as a reward for their expulsion of the Jews in 1492.[127] With this God-given wealth Spain was autarchical; it had no need to trade with foreigners, heretics, and apostates. Cutting foreign trades would not only undercut the Portuguese but would also shield Spain from further contamination from outside.[128]

Pellicer was joined by the famous playwright Francisco de Quevedo, who in 1638 presented *La fortuna de todos,* a barely veiled critique of Olivares's government. The play uses Olivares's close association with the Portuguese merchant bankers of Madrid to tar the chief minister with charges of greed, personal ambition, and treason. The key scene occurs on the Island of Monopantos, where the local prince, Pragas Chincollos (a readily decipherable anagram of "Gaspar Conchillos," a mixture of Olivares's first name and that of his famously *converso* great-uncle), is shown scheming with a cabal of Jews over the overthrow of the Spanish monarchy and the seizure of its wealth.[129]

At first blush, it would appear that the campaign against the Portuguese was paradoxical, if not outright self-defeating. Here were different judicial bodies, each ostensibly under the authority of the King of Spain, prosecuting the very individuals who had been brought to Madrid by the Count-Duke of Olivares in order to boost the financial capacities of the empire. In more general terms, the Portuguese had also contributed considerable commercial expertise and dynamism to the Spanish Atlantic system. All the same, not everyone within the Spanish political elite felt that the material advantages offered by the Portuguese outweighed the political costs of their presence. For a growing number of increasingly vocal opponents of the Olivares regime, the penetration of the Portuguese into the court, and into the empire more generally, represented a grievous derogation of the fundamental values of the Spanish monarchy. Thanks to Olivares's courting of the Portuguese, lucre, ambition, and apostasy had been allowed to gain ground over moral rectitude, disinterested loyalty, and religious devotion. Eradicating the Portuguese, it was conceded, may have compromised Spain's short-term commercial and fiscal interests, but it conformed to the higher imperatives of the monarchy. This view was succinctly captured by Francisco de Quevedo, who wrote after the fall of Olivares and his Portuguese allies, "now Your Majesty can truly wage war against the enemies of Spain, perhaps without any money in Your banks, but certainly with the hearts of Your true subjects."[130]

The prosecutions, which intensified in the 1630s and peaked in the years following the rebellion of Portugal, had the expected result of dismantling the entire system. While one can debate the Jewishness of the Portuguese or their political hostility to the Spanish crown (more difficult, I believe), there is little doubt as to the tightly knit and interdependent nature of the community's structure. The seizure of key merchants in one part of the Atlantic set off shock waves that rippled throughout the community as a whole. During the course of each trial, the movement of a particular merchant's goods and credit was frozen. This provoked shortfalls for corresponding merchants. The seizure of Portuguese merchants based in Lima, for example, became a problem of immediate concern for merchants in Cartagena de Indias and for monopolists in Lisbon because it radically cut the inflow of Peruvian silver required to run the African slave *asiento*.[131] Nor were the great financiers of Madrid exempt from the consequences of events occurring on the other side of the Atlantic. The capital required for the huge loans tendered by the bankers to the Spanish Crown relied on steady contributions from merchants active in the overseas trade.[132] As the colonial houses were directly or indirectly disrupted by judicial proceedings of various kinds, the financiers in Madrid were increasingly incapable of marshaling the capital needed for the *asientos*.¹³³ Given their position at the peak of the Portuguese commercial system, the liquidity of the Portuguese financiers in Madrid stood as an important measure of the commercial and financial health of the community as a whole. Beginning in 1639–40 Portuguese loans to the Spanish Crown dropped precipitously.¹³⁴ Indeed, by 1650 the Portuguese, who had previously organized and run many of the most important monopolies of the Spanish Crown, administered numerable rent farms, and loaned millions of pesos to the monarchy, had all but disappeared from the Spanish Empire. The evacuation of the Portuguese from the imperial sphere, orchestrated not only by the Inquisition but also by a variety of civil courts, had come to its successful conclusion.

The defeat of the Portuguese and of Olivares represented an incalculable symbolic victory for those who had opposed not only these individuals but also the ideas they sought to advance. By attacking the Portuguese, the party of conservation was able to clearly enunciate its vision of the nature and purpose of the empire and then, through the spectacles afforded by the autos-da-fé and other forms of public punishment, legitimate this vision before the populace as a whole. With the fall of the count-duke and his allies, those who had militated for the preservation of the traditional values of autarchy, internal purity, and hierarchy had won the struggle over the political and ideological direction of the Spanish Empire. They did not, for all that, manage to find the way out of Spain's crisis.

Conclusion

The impact that the evacuation of the Portuguese presence had on the Spanish Empire's political economy should be gauged with care. It would be difficult to argue that continued Portuguese presence would have stopped or even halted the economic decline of Spain. Over the course of the seventeenth century the Portuguese community of trade was but one of the actors in a complicated interplay of forces that included ideological confrontations, conflict between different classes, changing patterns of economic production and distribution, and underlying demographic cycles that had a profound impact on this agrarian society.

Nevertheless, to the extent that the early modern Spanish state could influence its economic fate, the political conflicts within its governing elites over the direction of economic policy bear closer investigation. In this regard, the story of the Portuguese commercial community in the Spanish polity is one of a possibility foreclosed. Drawing on the experience and understandings they gained from their activities in the Atlantic economy, the Portuguese merchant bankers had provided a novel voice in the debate over commercial reform in the empire. Their case is interesting not only because of what they said, or because of the social and ideological bases of their arguments, but also because of the reactions they engendered. The outcome of this social and ideological conflict clearly favored their opponents. The moment of reform for the Spanish Empire had come to a close.

Notes

Drafts of this article were presented at two meetings: Harvard's International Seminar on the History of the Atlantic World; and "The Emergence of the Atlantic Economy" conference held at the College of Charleston on October 14–16, 1999. I would like to thank Bernard Bailyn and the organizers of the Charleston conference, Rosemary Brana-Shute, Max Edelson, and Randy J. Sparks for the opportunity to present this piece and for the engaged commentary offered by fellow participants. Particular thanks goes to the following readers for their comments and suggestions: Carlos Álvarez-Nogal, Peter Coclanis, Malick Ghachem, Lyman Johnson, John J. McCusker, Marcy Norton, and Stuart B. Schwartz. Financial support for the archival research on which this chapter is based was provided by the Social Sciences and Humanities Research Council of Canada.

1. The phrase *el bien comun* was an inextricable part of the political vernacular of seventeenth-century Spain. Its translation presents some problems because of its double meaning. In Spanish, *bien* refers equally to good and to wealth, thus producing two translations of the phrase *el bien comun:* either the commonwealth or the common good.

2. The inescapable reference for the history of Olivares's administration, his projects, and their reception is John H. Elliott, *The Count-Duke of Olivares: The Statesman in an Age of Decline* (New Haven: Yale University Press, 1986).

3. Elliott, *Count-Duke of Olivares,* 162.

4. I. A. A. Thompson, *War and Society in Habsburg Spain* (Aldershot: Variorum, 1992); Carlos Álvarez Nogal, *El crédito de la monarquía hispánica en el reinado de Felipe IV* (Madrid[?]: Junta de Castilla y Léon—Consejeria de Educación y Cultura, 1997), 14, 20.

5. Álvarez Nogal, *Crédito de la monarquía hispánica,* 15, 355.

6. Garcia de Yllan, *Memorial en nombre de los hombres de negocios residentes en esta corte* (circa 1630s), Biblioteca Nacional de Madrid (hereafter BN-Madrid), Varios Especiales, 60–18, fol. 1r.

7. [Duarte Gomez Solis], *Memorial sobre ligar laplata,* circa 1620s, British Library (hereafter BL), Egerton Manuscripts (hereafter Eg. MSS), 1133, fol. 302r.

8. *Mendo de Mota to Junta de Comercio,* Archivo General de Simancas (hereafter AGS) Estado-2847, March 5, 1623.

9. On this cosmopolitan group of economic advisers, see Jonathan I. Israel, "Manuel López Pereira of Amsterdam, Antwerp and Madrid: Jew, New Christian and Advisor to the Conde-Duque of Olivares," in his *Empires and Entrepots: The Dutch, the Spanish Monarchy and the Jews, 1585–1713* (London: Hambledon Press, 1990), 247.

10. On the revival of the traditional aristocracy during the crisis of the seventeenth century, see I. A. A. Thompson, "Neo-Noble Nobility: Concepts of *Hidalguta* in Early Modern Castile," *European History Quarterly* 15 (1985): 379–406.

11. There existed no real "party" in the modern sense of a formal political organization. The term is used here to describe the informal conjunction of social actors and political projects that worked toward the same goal: in this case the liberalization and expansion of trade within the Spanish Empire.

12. Aside from reading their writings, I have not delved nearly deeply enough into the social backgrounds of the various individuals and groups that formed the opposition to Olivares's regime. Interested readers should turn to Elliott, *Count-Duke of Olivares;* and Jean Vilar, "Formes et tendences de l'opposition sous Olivares: Lisón y Viedma, defensor de la patria," *Mélanges de la Casa de Velasquez* 7 (1971).

13. Elliott, *Count-Duke of Olivares,* 324, 680–81.

14. John H. Elliott, "Self-Perception and Decline in Early Seventeenth-Century Spain," in his *Spain and Its World, 1500–1700* (New Haven: Yale University Press, 1989), 247.

15. Elliott, "Self-Perception and Decline," 251.

16. "I see our Spain as a human body, previously robust and filled with blood, now much debilitated," wrote Pedro Hurtado de Alcocer in his treatise on the commercial ills of Spain in 1621, *Memorial sobre los remedios de la salida de la plata y el comercio, el trafico con China y obrajes de paños* (1621), repr. in *Colección de documentos ineditos para la historia de España y de sus Indias: Tomo V la junta de reformacion, 1618–1625,* ed. Angel Gonzalez Palencia (Valladolid: Archivo Histonco Espanol, 1932), 169. For a general discussion of the organicist metaphor of the state, see José Antonio Maravall, *Téoria del estado en España en el siglo XVII,* 2nd ed. (Madrid: Centro de Estudios Constitucionales, 1997), 113–15.

17. The story of the Portuguese bankers in the court of Philip IV is given thorough treatment in James C. Boyajian, *Portuguese Bankers at the Court of Spain (1626–1650)* (New Brunswick, N.J.: Rutgers University Press, 1983).

18. For the relationship between the Spanish fisc and the Portuguese and Genoese bankers, see Carlos Álvarez Nogal, *Los banqueros de Felipe IV y los metales preciosos americanos (1621–1665)* (Madrid: Banco de España-Estudios de Historia Económica, 1997); Álvarez Nogal, *Crédito en la monarquía hispánica;* Antonio Dominguez Ortiz, *Politica y hacienda de Felipe IV* (Madrid: Editorial de Derecho Financiero, 1960); Felipe Ruiz Martin, *Las finanzas de la Monarquía Hispánica en tiempos de Felipe IV (1621–1665)* (Madrid: Real Academia de Historia, 1990).

19. Lorenco de Mendoca in his treatise *Suplicacion . . . en defensa de los Portugueses* (1630), BL, 8042.c.31, fols. 4v, 16v.

20. See Anonymous, *Discurso del buen gobierno de la hacienda contra los asentistas y fucares* (circa 1590s), BN-Madrid, Manuscritos, Ff. 9; Gerardo Basso, *Abitrio sobre el desmpeño del Reyno . . . y evitar los asientos con los Ginovesses* (1622), BN-Madrid, Manuscritos, 6731, fols. 94r–102v.

21. As early as 1513, Portuguese ships were being seized for interloping in the Caribbean; see *Accounts of the Treasury of Puerto Rico, August 15th., 1513,* Archivo General de Indias-Seville (hereafter AGI)-Contaduria, legajo 1071, no. 1, ramo 2; *Prohibition of Portuguese Ships in the Darien, 1513,* AGI-Indiferente, legajo 419, book 4, fols. 113r–113v.

22. Ruth Pike, *Enterprise and Adventure: The Genoese in Seville and the Opening of the New World* (Ithaca: Cornell University Press, 1966).

23. Immanuel Wallerstein, *The Modern World-System II: Mercantilism and the Consolidation of the European World-Economy, 1600–1750* (New York: Academic Press, 1980), 28.

24. As part of my dissertation work, I am currently working to establish a more coherent and structural view of how these transfer points were established and worked. The following references should be seen for what they are, anecdotes that give us traces of the larger structure. For the Portuguese trade in the Canaries, see *Philip II to Licenciado Nava,*

Canary Islands: Madrid, October 13th, 1571, printed in *Cedulario de Canarias: Tomo I: 1566–1597,* ed. Francisco Morales Padron (Seville: Cabildo Insular de Gran Canaria-Escuela de Estudios Hispanoamericanos, 1970), 153. For Cadiz, see Pedro Hurtado de Alcocer, *Discursos sobre la moneda y govierno de España,* n.d., n.p., BN-Madrid, MS, 1092, fol. 3r; *Proceedings against Gaspar Lorenzo, Hernando Guerra y Alonso Ramos for Docking in Cadiz without License, 1614 to 1616,* AGI-Contratación, 161. For the contraband along the coasts, see *Report of Domingo de Vegil, November 2nd, 1603 to January 3rd, 1604,* AGS-Consejo de Estado, legajo 435; Tomas Garcia Figueras, "Los factores portugueses en Andalucia en el siglo XVI," *Archivo Hispalense* 8:23 (1947): 423–24.

25. For these ports, see *Real Cedula to Licenciado Pedro Portocarrero, of the Royal Audience of Galicia, 1571,* AGI-Indiferente, legajo 426, libro 25, fols. 104v–105r; *Licenciado don Luis de Paredes to the Consejo de Estado, May 10th, 1620,* AGS—Consejo de Estado, legajo 2645, expediente 22 (25); *Consejo de Portugal to the Junta del Comercio, n.d.* (circa 1623–24), AGS-Estado, legajo 2847, loose.

26. Alonso de Cianҫa, *Discurso breve . . . en que se muestra . . . la causa que ha sido enflaquecido el comercio de las flotas de Nueva España y Tierra Firme . . .* (circa 1620s), BL, 1324.i.10 (11), fol. 3v.

27. Ruggiero Romano, *Conjunctures opposées: La 'crise du XVIIe siècle' en Europe et en Amerique Iberique* (Geneva: Librarie Droz, 1993); Carlos Sempat Assadourian, *El sistema de la economia colonial: El mercado interior: Regiones y espacio economico* (Mexico City: Editorial Nueva Imagen, 1983); Steven J. Stern, "Feudalism, Capitalism, and the World-System in the Perspective of Latin America and the Caribbean," *American Historical Review* 93, no. 4 (1988): 829–72.

28. Michel Morineau, *Incroyables gazettes et fabuleux métaux: Les retours des trésors américains d'après les gazettes hollandaises (XVI–XVIIe siècles)* (Cambridge: Cambridge University Press/Paris: Maison des sciences de l'homme, 1985).

29. Alice P. Canabrava, *O comercio portugues no Rio da Prata (1580–1640)* (Sao Paulo, 1944); Lewis Hanke, "The Portuguese in Spanish America with Special Reference to the Villa Imperial de Potosi," *Revista de Historia de America* (Mexico), no. 51 (1961): 1–48.

30. Guillermo Cespedes del Castillo, *La averia en el comercio de Indias* (Seville: Escuela de Estudios Hispano-Americanos, 1945), 82.

31. *Shipping Registers from Seville to Tierra Firme, 1631, 1639 and 1640,* AGI-Contratación, legajos 1178, 1182, 1184. A dozen ships is far from a representative sample when one considers that a single fleet during the first half of the seventeenth century was made up of between twenty and thirty ships.

32. Enriqueta Vila Vilar, "Las ferias de Portobelo: Apariencia y realidad del comercio con Indias," *Anuario de Estudios Americanos* 39 (1982): 323.

33. This issue is treated in James F. King, "The Evolution of the Free Slave Trade Principle in Spanish Colonial Administration," *Hispanic American Historical Review* 33 (1942): 33–64.

34. This is, of course, an estimate based on the exhaustive study of the Portuguese trade by Enriqueta Vila Vilar. This total was derived by multiplying her estimate for the total number of slaves imported by the Portuguese (268,664) by the average price offered on the American markets (360 pesos de a ocho). See her *Hispano-America y el comercio de esclavos: Los asientos portugueses* (Seville: Escuela de Estudios hispanoamericanos, Consejo Superior de Investigaciones Cientificas, 1977), 209, 221–26.

35. Anonymous, *Memorial dirigido a SM por un vasallo y ministro suyo noticioso de las Indias Occidentales contra los portugueses que tratan en ellas* (1640), BN-Madrid, Manuscritos, 3064, fols. 1r, 3v.

36. The rhythms of the slavers' departures can be discerned from their registers made out by the Casa de Contratación; see AGI-Contratación, legajos 2875–96.

37. Or, in the eyes of their detractors, "wreak destruction upon the commerce of our Indies throughout the course of the year"; see Alonso de Cianca, *Discurso breve,* fol. 6r.

38. AGI-Contratación, legajos 2875–96.

39. Information on the importance of small ships for the contraband trades was provided by Sergio Rodriguez Lorenzo of the University of Seville.

40. See the 1631 seizure in Buenos Aires of a single ship's cargo, valued by Crown officials at 55,000 pesos de a ocho, in *Deliberations of the Consejo de Indias Regarding the Embargo of the Goods of Diego de la Vega, June 14th, 1631,* AGI-Indiferente, legajo 757, no fol.

41. Again the case of Diego de la Vega is instructive. Many of his father's kin had settled in Amsterdam, and he maintained close commercial contacts with them and their children. See *Testimonio de Carlos Corzo de Leca y Nicolas de Ocampo Saavedra frente a la Inquisición de Lima, October 6th, 1606,* AGS-Inquisición de Lima, book 760 (10), printed in Antonio de Leon de Pinelo, *Discurso sobre la importancia, forma y disposición de la Recopilación de Leyes de las Indias Occidentales* (1623), ed. José Toribio Medina, prologue by Aniceto Almeyda (Santiago de Chile: Fondo Historico y Bibliografico José Toribio Medina, 1956), 89.

42. The yearly figures are given in Boyajian, *Portuguese Bankers,* app. B; they varied from a high of 7,327,000 ducados (1629) to a low of 1,173,000 ducados (1635). Carlos Álvarez Nogal's work allows us to see the relative importance of the different groups of bankers working the Spanish *asientos*. For the reign of Philip IV, 1621–65, the Genoese received 5,631,639,677 maravedís (15,017,706 ducados), the Portuguese received 2,562,980,264 maravedis (6,834,614 ducados), and the Germans received 1,390,212,059 maravedis (3,707,232 ducados); see Álvarez Nogal, *Banqueros de Felipe IV,* 55, 91, 110. There exists a strong discrepancy between Boyajian's and Álvarez Nogal's figures. Álvarez Nogal argues that he is calculating the silver actually received by the bankers rather than the sum of the loans decided on at the time of their negotiation, which forms the data used by Boyajian.

43. Nicolás Broens, *Monarquía y capital mercantil: Felipe IV y las redes comerciales portuguesas (1627–1635)* (Madrid: Ediciones de la Universidad Autónoma de Madrid, 1989), 13.

44. Álvarez Nogal, *Credito de la monarquía hispánica,* 352.

45. Work in this direction is beginning to appear. See Philip T. Hoffman, Gilles Postel-Vinay, and Jean-Laurent Rosenthal, "Information and Economic History: How the Credit Market in Old Regime Paris Forces Us to Rethink the Transition to Capitalism," *American Historical Review* 104, no. 1 (February 1999): 69–94; Giorgio Doria, "Conoscenza del mercato e sistema informativo; il know-how dei mercanti finanzieri genovei, nei secoli xvi e xvii," in *La republica internazionale del denaro tra xv e xvii secolo,* ed. A. de Maddalena and H. Kellenbenz (Bologna, 1986). The other manner in which economic historians have treated the impact of information flows has been through the study of transaction costs; see Douglass C. North and Robert P. Thomas, "An Economic

Theory of the Growth of the Western World," *Economic History Review,* 2nd ser., 23, no.1 (April 1970): 5–7, 12–13.

46. In May 1634, for example, Diego Lopez Fonseca would write an average of ten letters per day from Lima. More centrally located merchants such as Rodrigues d'Evora and Vega of Lisbon wrote with even greater frequency; see Gentil da Silva, *Stratégie des affaires à Lisbonne: Lettres marchandes des Rodrigues d'Evora et Veiga* (Paris: Armand Colin, 1956).

47. Immanuel Wallerstein, *Historical Capitalism with Capitalist Civilization* (London: Verso, 1996), 14–15.

48. Fernand Braudel, *The Wheels of Commerce,* vol. 2 of *Civilization and Capitalism, 15th–18th Century,* trans. Siân Reynolds (New York: Harper & Row, 1981–84), 138–48.

49. Anonymous, *Breve discurso en q se apuntan algunas caussas que ayuden a desminur las fuercas de Espana* (n.d.), BL, Eg. MSS, 339, fol. 308v.

50. See Gentil da Silva, *Stratégie des affaires à Lisbonne,* 10, 12–13; *Diogo Lopes da Fonseca and Antonio da Cunha (Lima) to Juan Alvarez and Antonio Garcia de Leon, April 25th, 1634,* Archivo General de la Nacíon (AGN)-Lima-Inquisición-Contencioso, legajo 22, fol. 186r; *Idem to Miguel Coronel, April 25th, 1634,* ibid., fol. 186v.

51. On the significance of the public arguments of these merchants, see Joseph A. Schumpeter, *History of Economic Analysis,* ed. (from MS) Elizabeth Boody Schumpeter (New York: Oxford University Press, 1954), 159–61.

52. Jean Vilar, *Literatura y economia: La figura satirica del arbitrista en el Siglo de Oro* (Madrid: Revista de Occidente, 1973).

53. For examples of sixteenth-century Portuguese *arbitristas,* see Guillermo Lohmann Villena, "Enrique Garces, Desubrido del Mercurio en el Peru, Poeta y Arbitrista," *Studia* (Lisbon) 27–28 (August–December 1969): 7–62; and the case of Duarte Lopez described in Vila Vilar, *Hispano-America.*

54. Elliott, *Count-Duke of Olivares,* 296–97.

55. Gonzalez Palencia, *Colección de documentos.*

56. Lic. don Antonio Liñan y Verdugo, *Guia y Avisos de forasteros, adonde les ensena a huir de los peligros que ay en lla vida de Corte* (1635), BL, 12490.b.18, fol. 12r.

57. Some avenues of research have been opened on these individuals. On the Italian Alberto Struzzi, see Miguel Angel Echevarría Bacigalupe, *Alberto Struzzi: Un precursor barroco del capitalismo liberal* (Louvain: Louvain University Press, 1995); on the Flemish Francisco de Retama, see José Alcalá-Zamora y Quiepo de Liano, *España, Flandes y el Mar del Norte* (Barcelona: Planeta, 1975), 480–90. Two bibliographical guides to the *arbitrios* and economic literature produced during this period provide a good starting point for future investigations: Evaristo Correa Calderon, *Registro de arbitristas, economistas y reformadores españoles (1500–1936): Catalogo de impresos y manuscritos* (Madrid: Fundación Universitaria Española, 1981); and Manuel Colmeiro, *Biblioteca de los economistas españoles de los siglos XVI, XVII y XVIII* (Madrid: Real Academia de Ciencias Morales y Politicas, 1979).

58. Israel, "Manuel López Pereira," 252–53.

59. Biographical information on Antonio de Leon Pinelo can be found in his *Discurso.*

60. Boyajian, *Portuguese Bankers,* app. A, 4.

61. For biographical details on Gomes Solis, see José Calvet de Magalhaes, "Duarte Gomes Solis," *Studia,* no. 19 (December 1966); and Mose Amzalak's edition of Gomes Solis's *Discurso sobre los comercios de las dos Indias (1622)* (Lisbon, 1943).

62. For Juan Nuñez Saraiva, see Julio Caro Baroja, *Los judios en la España moderna y contemporanea,* vol. 2 (Madrid: Ediciones Anon, 1962), 55–56; and *Trial of Juan Nuñez Saraiva,* Archivo Historico Nacional (AHN)-Inquisición-Toledo, legajo 17 1(2), expediente 4, pieza 4, fol. 234r, for mention of his submission of an *arbitrio* in the service of Philip IV. For Garcia de Yllan, see Caro Baroja, *Judios en la España moderna,* 56; and Boyajian, *Portuguese Bankers,* app. D, 209. For Juan Nuñez Correa, see *arbitrios* in the Museo Naval of Madrid, Colección Navarette, vol. 24, fols. 17ff., 88ff., 98ff., 116ff., as well as considerable documentation—trials, contracts, and accounts—housed in the Archivo General de Indias relating to the operation of the *averia* (provisioning) monopoly. For Cristobal Nuñez, see *Trial over Embargo, 1641,* AGI-Contratación, legajo 179, expediente 14. For the Peruvian activities of Francisco Vitoria de Barahona, see *Trial of Francisco Vitoria Barahona for Judaizing, 1634,* AHN-Inquisición-Lima, legajo 1648, expediente 9; for his implication in the cochineal and Asian trades of New Spain, see *Consultas of the Consejo de Indias, Feb 7th, 1635, May 26th, 1635, June 4th, 1636,* AGI-Indiferente, legajo 758, no fol. For Manuel Sueyro, see Elliott, *Count-Duke of Olivares,* 217; and Miguel Angel Echevarría Bacigalupe, *La diplomacia secreta en Flandes, 1598–1643* (Bilbao: Universidad del País Vasco, 1984).

63. Gomes Solis, *Discurso sobre los comercios,* 6–7, 11.

64. Francisco Vitoria de Barahona, *Breve discurso . . . para que se le libre el privilegio de los quarto por ciento . . . en la dos naos que todos los anos se despachan del puerto de Acapulco* (1639), BL, 1324.i.10 (2), fol. 1r.

65. Maravall, *Teoria del estado,* 115–17.

66. José Antonio Maravall, *La Cultura del Barrocco: Análisis de una estructura histórica,* 2nd ed., rev. (Barcelona: Editorial Ariel, 1996).

67. Letter from Andres Rodrigues Estemoz (Lisbon) to Juan Rodrigues Mesa (Cartagena de Indias), June 23, 1635, AHN-Inquisición-Cartagena de Indias, legajo 4816, expediente 1, fols. 12v–13r.

68. Anon., *Memorial dirigido,* fol. 1r.

69. *Recopilacion de las Leyes de Indias,* ley 1, titulo 11, libro 8; facsimile ed. (Madrid: Centro de Estudios Politicos y Constitucionales, 1998).

70. Dr. don Aingo de Ezpeleta, *Resoluciones practicas morales y doctrinales, de dudas ocasionadas de la baxa de moneda de vellon en los Reynos de Castilla y Leon* (1642), BL, 1139.1.1, fol. 226r.

71. Manuel Lopez Pereira, *Memorial sobre comercio* (circa 1620s), AHN-Consejos, libro 1428, fol. 263r.

72. Anonymous, *Breve discurso en q. se apuntan algunas caussas que ayuden a desminur las fuercas de Espana* (early 17th century), BL, Eg. MSS 339, fol. 310r.

73. Junta de Prelados i Hombres Doctos, *Discurso breve y compendioso para examinar las causas de que Dios estubiese tan enojado con la Monarchia de Espana que se halla oprimida con tantos trabajos* (1647), BL, additional MSS, 28452, fols. 302r–302v; Fray Juan de Solana, *Discursos . . . en siete tratados se refieren los muchos trabajos y plagas que padecen estos reynos de Espana . . .* (early 17th century), BN-Madrid, MS, 2471, fols. 89r–193r. See also Julio Caro Baroja, *Las formas complejas de la vida religiosa (siglos XV y XVII)* (Madrid: Akal, 1978), chap. 13.

74. Maravall, *Teoría del estado,* 194–95.

75. Aingo de Ezpeleta, *Resoluciones practicas,* fol. 231r.

76. See Abelardo del Vigo, *Cambistas, mercaderes y banqueros en el siglo de oro español* (Madrid: Biblioteca de Autores Cristianos, 1997).

77. Thomas de Mercado, *Summa de tratos y contratos de mercaderes y tratantes* (1569), Biblioteca del Archivo Historico de la Universidad de Sevilla, fols. 7r, 8v, 9 r–v.

78. Ibid., fol. 12r.

79. Aristotle, *The Politics,* trans. T. A. Sinclair, with intro. and pref. by T. J. Saunders (London: Penguin Books, 1992), book 1, chap. 9, 84–85.

80. Mercado, *Summa de tratos y contratos,* fol. 3v.

81. Ibid., fol. 4r.

82. Anon., *Breve discurso en q. se apuntan algunas caussas,* fol. 302v.

83. Mercado, *Summa de tratos y contratos,* fol. 31v.

84. Anonymous, *La pretension del comercio de Sevilla de que no vayan este anos de 637 flotas a Nueva Espana y Tierra Firme* (circa 1637–38), BL, 1324.i.5 (9), fol. 3r.

85. *Consulta del Consejo de Indias, May 30th., 1633,* AGI-Indiferente, legajo 757, no fol.

86. *Mendo de Mota to Philip IV, August 6th, 1621,* BL, Eg. MSS, 1131, fol. 17r.

87. Yllan, *Memorial en nombre,* preface.

88. Jose Pellicer y Osau, *El comercio impedido* (1640), BN-Madrid, Varios Especiales, 35–86, fol. 2v.

89. Manuel López Pereira, *Memorial en prosigicion de lo propuesto que es cosa notoria . . . el poder que los Olandeses y Engleses tienen en la Yndia Oriental,* AGS-Estado, legajo 2847, included in the *consulta* (report) of March 13, 1624, no fol.

90. Manuel López Pereira, *Memorial . . . dize que la maior fuerça de los reinos consiste en el comun comercio de sus habitadores,* AGS-Estado, legajo 2847, no fol.

91. Yllan, *Memorial en nombre,* fol. 3v.

92. Manuel Ribeiro Teixeira de Morais, *Memorial sobre varias cosas pertenecientes al buen gobierno de las Indias* (1624), BL, additional MSS, 13977, fol. 295r.

93. Antonio de Leon Pinelo, *La ciudad de la Trinidad (Buenos Aires) suplica a VM se sirva de conceder permission para navegar por aquel puerto los frutos su su cosecha a Sevilla, Brasil y Angola* (circa 1623), fols. 7r–7v. The pamphlet is reproduced in Raul A. Molina, "La defensa del comercio del Rio de la Plata por el Licenciado D: Antonio de Leon Pinelo," *Historia-Revista Trimestral de Historia Argentina, Americana y Espanola* 26 (1962): 37–112.

94. Lopez Pereira, *Memorial sobre comercio,* fol. 263r.

95. [Duarte Gomez Solis], *Memorial sobre ligar la plata,* fols. 301r–316v.

96. Luis Navarro Garcia, "Mercantilismo y sociedad estamental en la Recopilación de Indias," *Estudios de Historia Social y Economica de America,* no. 1 (1985): 21–53.

97. Carla Rahn Phillips, "Time and Duration: A Model for the Economy of Early Modern Spain," *American Historical Review* 92, no. 3 (June 1987): 531–62.

98. See n. 29, above.

99. Pedro de Avendaño Villela, *Memorial sobre el comercio y administracíon de las Indias* (1608), BL, 1324.i.10 (1), fols. 2v–3r.

100. Ibid., fol. 3r.

101. *Consulta del Consejo del Estado, December 23rd., 1624,* AGS-Estado, Legajo 2645, no fol.

102. This argument is made in Alonso de Ciança, *Discurso breve,* fols. 2r–3v.

103. Manuel de Frias (Buenos Aires) to Philip IV, February 3, 1619, AGI-Charcas, legajo 46; reproduced in Roberto Levillier, ed., *Correspondencia de la Ciudad de Buenos*

Aires: Documentos del Archivo de Indias, Tomo 2: 1615–1635 (Madrid: Colección de Publicaciones Historicas de la Biblioteca del Congreso Argentino, 1918), 154. Manuel de Frias also wrote a printed pamphlet decrying the Portuguese presence in Buenos Aires and the magnitude of the contraband that passed through its port; see Manuel de Frias, *Memorial sobre las causas que justifican la permission de los frutos de la tierra* (circa 1620), BL, additional MSS, 13992, fols. 484r–487v.

104. De Leon Pinelo, *iudad de la Trinidad,* fol. 3r.

105. Ibid., fols. 3r–5v.

106. *Council of Portugal to Phillip IV, May 16th., 1626,* BL, Eg. MSS, 324, fol. 57r.

107. *Consulta del Consejo del Estado, July 6th., 1625,* AGS-Estado, legajo 2645, no fol.

108. *Consulta del Consejo del Estado, July 30th., 1625,* AGS-Estado, legajo 2645, no fol.

109. In addition to the tracts by Manuel López Pereira, see also Duarte Gomes Solis, *Alegación en favor de la compania de la India Oriental Comercios Ultramarinos que de Nuevo se Instituyo en el Reyno de Portugal* (1622), ed. Moses Bensabat Amzalak (Lisbon, 1955).

110. López Pereira, *Memorial en prosigicion de lo propuesto.*

111. Elliott, *Count-Duke of Olivares,* 161. On the history of the Almirantazgo, see Antonio Dominguez Ortiz, "El almirantazgo de los paises septentrionales y la politica económica de Felipe IV," *Hispania* 7, no. 27 (1947): 272–90.

112. See also López Pereira's proposal to use northern capital to form a Flemish company that would deal directly with Asia: Manuel Lopez Pereira, *Memorial sobre que se haga compania en Flandes para contratar en la India Oriental* (1624), AGS-Estado, legajo 2847, part of *consulta* of March 13, 1624, no fol.

113. De Avendaño Villela, *Memorial sobre el comercio y administración de las Indias;* Hurtado de Alcocer, *Memorial;* Alonso de Ciança, *Discurso breve.*

114. This was the case for the tribunals of Lima, Cartagena de Indias, and Mexico City, the three principal urban nodes of Spain's Atlantic system. For Lima, see René Millar Corbacho, *Inquisición y sociedad en el virreinato peruano: Estudios sobre el Tribunal de la Inquisición de Lima* (Lima and Santiago de Chile, 1998). For Cartagena de Indias, see Anna Maria Splendiani, José Enriquez Sánchez Bohórquez, and Emma Cecilia Luque de Salazar, *Cinquenta años de Inquisición en el Tribunal de Cartagena de Indias, 1610–1660,* 4 vols. (Santa Fé de Bogota, 1997), 1:153–72. For New Spain, see Solange Alberro, *Inquisition et société au Méxique, 1571–1700* (Mexico City: Centre des études méxicaines et centreamericaines, 1988).

115. The prosecutions in Madrid were far more punctual and were drawn out over a longer period of time because of the protective influence of the Count-Duke of Olivares, who tried, within the limitations of his power, to shield the Portuguese from the Inquisition.

116. Enriqueta Vila Vilar, "Extranjeros en Cartagena (1593–1630)," *Jahrbuch fur Geschichte von Staat, Wirtschaft und Gesellschaft Lateinamerikas* 16 (1979) 147–84.

117. Splendiani et al., *Cinquenta años de Inquisición,* 4:121ff.

118. *Relación de causas de fé, 1644–1648,* AHN-Inquisición-Sevilla, legajo 2075 (2), fols. 1r–49v.

119. The cases can found in the following legajos: AGI-Contratación, legajos 80B, 93B, 95A, 142B, 144, 147, 148, 150, 161, 170, 175, 177, 643, 644, 797, 1774, 5711, 5713, 5718, 5720, 5732, 5737, 5738; AGI-Contaduria, legajo 403; AGI-Escribania, legajos 4, 17A, 20B, 135B, 180C, 334A, 880A, 880B, 1022A, 1079A.

120. For examples of the public punishments meted out for illegal trade, see *Proceedings against Lopez y Juan Royon,* May 5, 1566, AGI-Patronato, legajo 291, rollo 144; *Philip II to Licenciado Nava, juez oficial de la ysla de canaria: Madrid,* October 13, 1571, in Francisco Morales Padron, *Cedulario de Canarias,* 153; *Don Juan de Borja to the Consejo de Hacienda,* December 30, 1572, AGS-Consejo y Junta de Hacienda, 122 (16), 2r. These punishments were proscribed by the laws governing the Indies; see José Maria Ots Capdequi, "Los portugueses y el concepto juridico de extranjeria en los territorios hispano-americanos durante el periodo colonial," in his *Historia del derecho español en America y del derecho indiano* ([Madrid]: Aguilar, 1969), 213–63.

121. Unfortunately these cases appear as anecdotes in the secondary literature since the archives containing these trials have not yet received systematic attention. See Broens, *Monarquía y capital mercantil;* Dominguez Ortiz, *Politica y hacienda;* Caro Baroja, *Judios en la España moderna.*

122. Pellicer y Osau, *Comercio impedido.*

123. Ibid., fols. 3v, 14v.

124. Ibid., fols. 5r, 6v.

125. Ibid., fols. 6v, 17r.

126. Ibid.

127. Ibid., fol. 1r.

128. Ibid., fols. 4v, 9v.

129. Francisco de Quevedo, *La hora de todos y la fortuna con seso,* ed. Jean Bourg, Pierre Dupont, and Pierre Geneste (Madrid: Catedra, 1987). John Elliott explains the political implications of the play in "Quevedo and the Count-Duke of Olivares," in his *Spain and Its World,* 189–209.

130. Francisco de Quevedo, *Memorial contra de Conde-Duque Olivares dado al Rey don Felipe Quatro,* repr. in Antonio Valladares de Sotomayor, ed., *Semanario eruditio, que comprehende varias obras inedtias . . . de nuestros mejores autores antiguos y modernos,* vol. 15 (Madrid, 1788), 215.

131. See, for instance, Andres de Extremoz (Lisbon) to Juan Rodriguez Mesa (Cartagena de Indias), June 23, 1635, AHN-Inquisición-Cartagena de Indias, 4816, exp. 1, fol. 12r.

132. Boyajian, *Portuguese Bankers,* app. D.

133. *Deliberations of the Consejo de Hacienda, Sept 12th, 1639,* AGS-Consejo y Junta de Hacienda, legajo 795, no fol.

134. Boyajian, *Portuguese Bankers,* app. A.

Atlantic Trade and American Identities
The Correlations of Supranational Commerce, Political Opposition, and Colonial Regionalism

Claudia Schnurmann

An overwhelming function of historical studies on transatlantic interactions during the colonial period gives the impression of several, perfectly separated national Atlantic systems. When turning to Atlantic trade as a form of long-distance interaction, the emphasis is mainly on national imperial frameworks consisting of mother-country-colonies relations. Truly inspiring work has been done on the English, Dutch, Portuguese, French, and Spanish Atlantic, effectively nationalizing an ocean.[1] However, many studies concerned with the human attitude toward a natural environment unconsciously follow the orders, hopes, and wishful thinking of seventeenth-century monarchs and states, giving vivid proof of the deeply rooted belief in national histories, idealized during the nineteenth and most of the twentieth centuries.

Early modern people and societies, though, may have functioned in more than one way, following different ideals and interests and not caring for the approval of European authorities, contemporary spin doctors, or today's historians. Besides the legal Atlantic systems cherished and ordered by metropolitan laws, such as the several English acts of trade and navigation and the Dutch West India Company's charter of 1621, there flourished other Atlantic worlds whose bearers showed hardly any concern for metropolitan well-being, princes' financial needs, or national correctness. In following their own interests, they could fall back on a broad range of possibilities. Their way of creating alternative Atlantic systems either went unnoticed, embarrassed authorities who expected obedience, or annoyed rivals in the commercial battlegrounds of the respective nations. Alluding to the respective point of view, those nonconformists were branded as smugglers, pirates, interlopers, or colonists; Dutch merchants—coming by the English, at least—suffered the whole range of curses from jealous, England-based rivals.[2]

The following pages reconstruct selected elements of these much neglected and seldom fully appreciated forms of informal supranational Atlantic trade. The denial and low esteem of these forms, however, provide the necessary material for the reconstruction. By concentrating on relations among the English, the Dutch, and inhabitants of Dutch and English colonies in America during the seventeenth century, I want to find out something about the neglect of national categories by using, paradoxically, national categories as a tool. First, some dominant and characteristic types of Atlantic trade in these times are sketched. Next is a discussion of their impact and correlation to colonial mentalities, emotional identities, and transatlantic relations between Dutch and English colonies, on the one hand, and between each and their respective mother country on the other.[3]

Cash Crops and the Sense of Political Self-Will—Barbados, Virginia, and the Dutch Influence, 1620–1670s

Since their humble beginnings, the up-and-coming sugar island Barbados and the tobacco colony Virginia were closely connected through the influence of Dutch people living in the Netherlands, in New Netherland (Nieuw Nederland), and in these colonies. Dutch traders regularly visited both colonies and even moved there, supplying colonists with necessary or less-than-necessary goods in exchange for sugar and tobacco. On Barbados lived Sephardic Jews with family ties to Amsterdam as well as several Dutch Christians, who formed the "Dutch nation resident." They were all allowed to worship as they chose as long as they "comport[ed] themselves accordingly & act[ed] nothing to the disturbance of the public peace of this Island."[4] In Virginia hardly any religious conflicts between Dutch and English seem to have appeared; Dutch traders settled easily in Virginia, preferring the Eastern Shore districts of Accomack County and Northampton County. They bought land, applied for naturalization, and kept contacts with relatives, friends, and business partners in New Netherland and the old country, while easily taking to the new surroundings and being accepted. Perhaps the common faith helped to create a sense of belonging in these remote parts of the New World, as colonists everywhere in America called their new home.

Several legal cases that kept Virginian council courts busy did not endanger Dutch-English coexistence or express sincere mutual differences. They were just the result of the early modern delight in going to court that was normal in England and the Netherlands. Historians profit from this disposition because the Northampton County court records show the active participation of Dutch merchants, shippers, and settlers in the Virginian tobacco trade.[5]

Typical examples are supplied by those traders and newcomers to the Chesapeake Bay area who moved down from New Netherland. The typical New Netherlander was not of Dutch origin; only a few were born in the provinces forming the Dutch Republic. Many inhabitants of the Hudson colony came from the Spanish Netherlands, Scandinavia, or from poorer, underdeveloped territories of the Holy Roman Empire, which functioned traditionally as an important reservoir for migrants to the economically attractive Netherlands, the economic wonderland of the Dutch Golden Age.⁶ George Hack and his in-law Augustine Hermann exemplify this type. Hack was born in the Rhenish stronghold of Catholicism, Cologne, around 1620. He enrolled in the faculty of medicine at the local university, then went to Amsterdam and afterward to New Amsterdam, where he married his cousin Anna Varlett before moving to Virginia for good. Anna Varlett's siblings found partners too. In 1651 Jannetje Varlett married Augustine Hermann. Nicholas Varlett married Anna Stuyvesant, sister of the ill-famed Dutch governor Peter Stuyvesant.⁷ Of special importance became Hack's connection to Augustine Hermann. Born in Prague around 1605, Hermann was an Amsterdam refugee from imperial power in 1618, perhaps serving the Swedish Protestant hero, Gustav Adolph, in the Thirty Years' War. Hermann migrated in 1629 to North America, where he settled down in New Amsterdam as an agent of the Amsterdam merchants family Gabrie-Gabry in the 1640s. After 1660 Hermann moved to Maryland, where he ended his life as lord of Bohemia Manor. At one point in the 1640s–50s Hermann combined transatlantic trade with a vibrant intercolonial business, commuting between New Netherland, New England, and Virginia. In 1650 Peter Stuyvesant wrote to the Amsterdam chamber of the West India Company: "Augustin Hoeremans, commende uyt de Virginies liep met zynnen last voorby na d'Engelschen, en quam met het leedich schip waer aen de Manhattaes" (Augustine Hermann, who came from Virginia, passed New Netherland, and sailed with his freight and returned to Manhattan with an empty ship).⁸

Beginning in September 1652 Hack in Virginia and Hermann in New Netherland were well-adjusted colleagues. They were joined by a third man, "the leading planter, merchant, justice, military commander, squire, and patron of Accomack County, so obviously the central figure of authority," Edmund Scarborough.⁹ Their business actions soon put them in need of the regional law courts; their troubles are our luck because they show the daily routine of intercolonial, supranational transactions:

> Mr J[oh]n Custis declareth & deposeth upon oath That in the yeare 1652 about the last of August, Capt[ain] J[oh]n Dollinge [agent to Edmund Scarburgh] came to his house relatinge unto him that concerninge the Tobac[c]o w[hi]ch Mr Edmund Scarburgh hath tendred & paid unto D[o]c[t]or George Hacke, for the account of Mr Augustyne Hermann, to bee sent & dispatched to the Monhatan with . . . Hacks vessell, hee had ordre by virtue of letter of attachment from one Mr Charles Gabry & the Gouvernour Stephsant [that is, Pieter Stuyvesant] from the Monhatan arrived to Mr Scarburgh to stopp & detayne the s[ai]d Tobac[c]o in the behalfe of the s[ai]d Gabry here in the Country untill further order from him, and that hee was goeinge to execute the business w[hi]ch hee thereupon did effect. . . . the s[ai]d Tobac[c]o did lye here & rooted in the Countrye.¹⁰

Although transatlantic and intercolonial trade between Virginians and the Dutch side was not without flaws—a reality the witness had only too clearly experienced—the trade offered Virginia planters alternative markets for their one and only valuable product: tobacco. (The same could be said for Barbados sugar producers, who also relied heavily on Dutch demand for raw sugar, Dutch supplies of manufactured goods from Europe, and Dutch credits.) Instead of following English obligations, Virginians, as well as Barbadians, preferred Dutch cooperation to business with their fellow countrymen. Because tobacco dominated Virginia as sugar dominated Barbados, it was planter elites who molded the colonies' politics by opposing England and English imperial policy, choosing regional interests over national good. The pro-Dutch attitude went hand in glove with anti-English behavior, and accordingly the leading colonial planters provoked English countermeasures, in a slowly escalating process. King James I and his son, Charles I, had been content with ineffective expressions of royal displeasure (the press and the law). Whereas James I had used his writing skills, his hot temperament, and his dislike of tobacco consumption to compose philippics against tobacco and drinking,[11] his son kept cool by turning to legal measures, trying in 1637 to bring the inhabitants of the Old Dominion to reason. His efforts had no success; rather, they merely intensified Virginians' reliance on Dutch partners in 1638.[12]

During the 1640s Virginia used England's internal turmoils to steer its own political-economic course. In 1643 Virginia ex pressis verbis (in express terms) invited the Dutch to its shores, declaring trade "free and lawful for any merchants, factors or others of the Dutch nation" who were allowed "to import wares and merchandises and to trade or traffic for the commodities of the colony in any ship or ships of their own or belonging to the Netherlands."[13] An act of 1646 demonstrates the daily Dutch presence in Virginia: "Whereas dayly experience doth informe that the merchants and others, as well Dutch as English [take notice of the order], trade within the collony doe practice much deceit by diversity of weights and measures, which are comonly used by them, Be it therefore inacted, That noe merchant or trader whatsoever either English or Dutch shall sell, buy, or otherwise make use of in tradeing, any other weights and measures then are used and made according to the statute of parliament in such cases provided."[14] By 1647 the Virginia government felt so secure of Dutch support that it destroyed the last bit of national solidarity by attacking English interests. Virginians feared English merchants "on purpose to affright & expell the Dutch, and make way for themselves to Monopolize not onely our labours and fortunes, but even our p[er]sons."[15]

The royalistic mood in Virginia and Barbados, combined with their open favoring of Dutch traders in the early 1650s, however, annoyed republican post-civil-war England as much as Virginian obstinacy had embarrassed the Stuart kings. The English Commonwealth under Oliver Cromwell put much more effort into trying to bring the self-willed colonists back to the imperial line. An embargo in 1650 imposed against Virginia, Barbados, Antigua, and the Bermudas should have done the trick, but it did not work. The next step to discipline the colonists and to attack Dutch commercial dominance was in October 1651, with the passing of the act of trade and navigation. Dutch traders in Holland and Virginian tobacco planters had already joined forces against English attempts to destroy free trade. While Dutch traders protested against English confiscation of their ships sailing to and from Virginia, proudly showing their role in the Virginian economy, Virginia's governor William Berkeley forsook his customary reserve and expressed in March 1651 his idea of Virginian priorities: "we can onely feare the Londoners, who would faine bring us to the same poverty, wherein the Dutch found and relieved us; would take away the liberty of our consciences, and tongues, and our right of giving and selling our goods to whom we please"[16]

Laws, however, were not enough to organize trade, at least according to the English ideal of imperialism and anti-Dutch rivalry. Before Cromwell started his war against the Dutch Republic in 1652—a war he had not been able to win through peace talks and unity plans in 1649–51[17]—he threatened his own colonies with military power. His trial run started in the fall of 1651, shortly after passage of the act of trade and navigation, when he sent a fleet to America to bring first Barbados and then Virginia in line with the Commonwealth before it conquered New Netherland—closing with military force what he saw as the nasty gap in British North America. By forcing the two strongholds of royalist opposition and Dutch trade to accept the articles of surrender in 1651 and 1652, Cromwell implicitly had to accept the colonies' claims of being political unities to be treated as objects in their own rights. The close correlations between political demand and commercial realities are evident in both colonies. In Barbadian and Virginian waters, Cromwell's fleet surprised several Dutch ships, whose masters and crews enjoyed intensive trade with the locals, not only bringing and taking goods but also providing the always curious colonists with gossip and important news from Europe.[18] In the English point of view, each Dutch ship in English colonial waters was unmistakable proof of colonial disobedience as well as of Dutch trade power. Members of the English fleet and the High Court of Admiralty in London watched helplessly as colonists continued doing business with Dutch partners, disobeying laws and the articles of surrender after 1651 and 1652.[19] The commercial self-will was connected with political actions that ridiculed English perceptions of an empire. While the first Dutch-English war was fought in Europe without really solving problems with Dutch successes in trade, economy, and naval power, Virginians and New Netherlanders agreed on a trade treaty[20] and Barbadians intensified their emotional independence from England. Already in 1651 they had produced statements that could have come from Virginians as well:

Shall we ... be subject to the will and command of those that stayed at home? Shall we be bound to the government and lordship of a Parliament in which we have no representatives, or persons chosen by us, for there to propound and consent to what might be needful to us ... ? In truth, this would be a slavery far exceeding all that the English nation hath yet suffered. Whereas all the old planters well know how much they have been beholding to the Dutch for their subsistence, and how difficult it would have been (without their assistance) ever to have settled this place [Barbados] and even to this day [1651] are sensible what necessary comforts they bring us and how much cheaper they sell their commodities to us than our own nation; but this comfort must be taken from us by them whose will must be our law. But we do declare that we will never be so ungrateful to the Dutch for former helps as to deny them or any other nation the freedom of our ports and protection of our laws whereby they may still (if they please) embrace a free trade and commerce with us.[21]

Like other inhabitants of European colonies in America, the population of Barbados had managed to develop a series of identities and emotional belongings: they could regard themselves as part of the English nation, as Americans (a term changing its meaning from Indians to Europeans living in America), or as "we," the Barbadians, making a sense of belonging to their new home. In 1653 the atmosphere was even more strained. John Bayes reported to the committee for foreign affairs about new Barbadian claims and mental positions: "Colonial Office is a high faction caning on by some persons in the Island of Barbados, who are nowe very prevalent, to lessen the power and authority of the governor, and to make that Island, (which have cost you soe much paines and treasure in its reducement to the obedience of this common wealth) A ffree State (as they call it) to choose their owne Governor establish their owne lawes, and to have a freedom of trade, with any nation, whether in amity with England or not this in my hearing hath often bin pleaded."[22]

Taking these dispositions into account, the English imperial policy toward American colonies and Dutch trade and participation could not work. New Netherland went on organizing embassies to the tobacco colonies: to Maryland in 1659, led by Augustine Hermann; and to Virginia in 1660, led by Nicholas Varlett (a relative of both Augustine Hermann and George Hack). It was evident that both Chesapeake Bay governments formulated foreign policy without London's permission, favoring New Netherland and thereby improving their own positions,[23] which made New Netherland, as the only official Dutch bridgehead in North America, the target of English aggression.

It is remarkable that each action carried out against New Netherland was masterminded in England whereas the neighboring English colonies kept quiet most of the time, even when expansive (expansionist) interests took over, as they did in Connecticut and Delaware because of Long Island and the Jerseys. Cromwell failed in 1654, stopped by the peace treaty of Westminster and New England's hesitation to be divided between pro- and anti-Dutch factions.[24] Charles II, having given New Netherland to his brother James, Duke of York, in March 1664 without actually possessing the land, was more successful. In August 1664 the English fleet appeared in front of New Amsterdam and forced the population to surrender, which was easily done because the cosmopolitan inhabitants were less interested in their nationality and loyalty toward faraway Dutch authorities than in their personal survival and future safety.

The transformation from New Netherland to New York, in 1664 and again in 1674, however, did not fulfill English dreams of elbowing the Dutch out of the Atlantic trade or destroying Dutch direct and indirect support of colonial opposition. The commercial appearance changed, but the threads of the networks stretching out to Virginia, Barbados, the Hudson River colony, and the Netherlands continued to exist through the ensuing decades.

The Dutch Connection—New York–Holland, 1674–1704

The English takeover of the Dutch colony[25] sanctioned by European diplomacy and the peace talks in 1674 changed the legal framework and position of its population but not the emotional nor economic orientations of its people toward Holland. Tolerated or even supported by most of their English governors, Dutch New Yorker merchants who had come to America when New Netherland still belonged to the WIC went on doing business as usual with friends, relatives, and long-standing associates in the Netherlands.

There was legal trade: obeying English claims, asking for English licenses, and calling in English ports before sailing from New York, Maryland, or Virginia to Amsterdam or Rotterdam and returning to New York.[26] There was another kind of trade, on the surface out of English legal purview but playing with tricks and the holes in the English legal system, that tried to bind the colonies to the mother country's demands and interests.

The legal type was rather unspectacular and fills pages in documents of the Colonial Office and more than one thousand port books kept in the Public Record Office in Kew, Surrey. However, trade that seems to obey English laws can look remarkably different in light of other realities filed in Dutch archives, especially in the hundreds of notarial records in the Gemeentearchief Amsterdam. The former New Netherlanders—now New Yorkers—played with both political constellations and the West India Company's wishful attitude to ignore the loss of New Netherland. Even after 1674, when the Dutch Republic sacrificed New Netherland for the English-Dutch peace agreement of Westminster, the West India Company regarded the lost colony as part of its domain and New Yorkers as subjects to its monopoly, calling trade to New York trade "naar

Nieuw Nederland" and asking for duties from traders who wanted to do business with New York.

Surprisingly, many merchants in Holland and visiting merchants from New York obeyed. In November 1674 Cornelis Jacobs Moy, a distinguished New York trader living in Amsterdam who was an old hand in this business and a long-standing partner of former New Netherlanders such as the German-born Jacob Leisler, asked the WIC for a permit to send a ship to New Netherland.[27] On February 8, 1675, the Dutch master David Jochemsz asked for the same favor;[28] four days later the master of the New York–based Mayflower, William Richardson, and one of the owners of Rensselaerswijk, Jan Baptist van Rensselaer, asked the WIC's Amsterdam chamber for permission "de Mayflower met de ingeladene goederen naar Nieuw Nederlant te mogen versenden" (to send the Mayflower with her goods to New Netherland). The chamber accepted, under the condition that "de recognitien en gerechtighedden als ingevolge van den octroye" (the taxes and customs according to the charter of the West India Company) would be paid.[29] Although, in the end, the Mayflower did not make it to New York because her freighters changed their minds, Amsterdam notary Adrian van Santen produced an inventory of her freight, typical for Dutch New Yorkers and Holland–New York trade: textiles (linen, wools, mixed cloth) from Holland, Silesia, Westphalia, and the Rhineland; household goods (candles, knives, scissors, kettles, glasses, pots, mirrors, pipes); iron staves; steel; gun powder; and food (cheese, raisins).[30] But North Americans did not only ask for goods, thereby satisfying the colony's urgent demand for essentials and helping in the long run England, too; with direct and indirect tolerance by the WIC, New York's Dutch connection undermined the English mercantilistic system.

One way to undermine it was to find holes in the legal network; the other was to get around English claims and monopolistic attitudes. The first method concerns the tricks and mimicry that were performed. By apparently bowing to the acts of trade and navigation and obediently calling in English ports, English-named ships appeared to English customers, comptrollers, and searchers as being plantation-built, worked by English crews, and owned by inhabitants of English colonies, and as though their freights belonged to colonists. In fact, many of these declarations were for English ears and eyes only: two sets of bookkeeping, faked papers, or simple lies would do the trick. Ships were carried from Holland to North America in kits and built there, only so as to be able to declare them plantation-built. Ship freights were declared to be the property of colonists. While in London, a crew member declared that the freighters and owners of the New York–based *Hopewell* were identical and that therefore the *Hopewell* met English law: "some of which goods were soe laden on freight and the rest on the account and risk of Adolphus Phillipps, and Phillips French merchants of the place [New York] . . . and that they the said Adolphus Phillipps and Philip

French and one Jacob Courtland [member of an established Dutch family in New York] were the reputed owners of the s[ai]d ship."[31]

In Amsterdam, however, free from fear of punishment, the real freight owners turned up and demonstrated how they had tricked the London High Court of Admiralty: "Compareerde voor my Joan Hoekebak. [notary] . . . d'heeren Hero Moy, Livinius van Schaick, Anthony Kops, Willem Bancker, Pieter van Dyck, Jeremias Coessaart, Johannes Lepper, Steven Melony, Bernardus Holthuysen, Reinier & Jan Duythuysen alle woonende binnen dese stadt Amsterdam . . . ende alle geinteresseerdens in de ladinge van de Barcantyn genaemt de Hopewell gevoert by schipper Thomas Wright" (the notary Joan Hoekeback declared that Hero Moy, Livinius van Schaick, Anthony Kops, Willem Bancker, Pieter van Dyck, Jeremias Coessaart, Johannes Lepper, Steven Melony, Bernardus Holthuysen, Reinier and Jan Duythuysen, all living in this town Amsterdam, came to his office and are shareholders of the freight of the *Hopewell*, whose master is Captain Thomas Wright).[32] Similar cunning was performed by New York merchant Barent Reinders, son-in-law of Jacob Leisler, who had been executed in 1691 not for his role in New York's Glorious Revolution but for his difficulties with the colony's elite. This "Glorious Revolution" was an attempt to end the Dominion of New England that was triggered by England's Glorious Revolution in 1688, first in Massachusetts, then in New York, and finally in Maryland. While in Holland in 1700 Reinders bought the *Nieuw Jork Pinck* and employed a New Yorker experienced in the Amsterdam–New York route as her master[33] on her way from Texel "gedestineert naar Nieu Jork." In Amsterdam, Reinders explained his method of tricking English laws:

> Barent Reinders coopman van New Jork . . . te kennen gevende . . .dat hy het selve schip [de *Nieuw Jork Pinck*] op synen naam alleen, soo in Westindien all eenige andere plaatsen buytens lands wel sal mogen laten navigeren naar eigen geliefte, ende ook het transpoort aan hem allen was gedaan, dat ook gemelde Capt[ain] en scheepsvolk niet anders wiste ofte behoorden te weeten, dan dat het selve hem . . . alleen was toe behoorende ofte wel neffens hem aan verdere Engelse onderdanen; dog sulx alles synde alleeen om de vryheden van Engeland en die der Engelse plantagien te konnen genieten soo verclaarde hy . . . dat syne suster . . . Alida Reinders wedue wyler Jan van der Grift coopvrouwe alhier, in het selve schip en instructie van den beginne af aan is geintresseert geweest, ende nog is voor fi 2912 1/2 . . . mitsgaders syn broeder Jan Reinders mede coopman alhier voor fi 1456 1/4 . . . ende nog Michiel Haulsey voor de somme van fl 937 10.[34]
>
> [Barent Reinders, New York merchant, declares that he will give leave to the ship *New York Pink* to set sails for the West Indies and other places as is his pleasure; he further declares that he owns the freight of the said

ship and that the captain as well as the crew know perfectly well that ship and freight belong to him; to be able to enjoy English liberties and those of English plantations, he declares that his sister Alida Reinders, widow of Jan van Grift and merchant-woman in New York, from the beginning had her share in the ship and still owns shares worth 2912 guilders ½; also his brother Jan Reinders, New York merchant like himself, owns shares to the value of 1456 guilders ¼ and Michiel Haulsey who holds shares worth 937 guilders 10.]

In September 1700 the *New York Pink* arrived in New York, bringing Dutch pipes and "coopmanschappen uyt Amsterdam" (goods from Amsterdam) to Jacob van Cortlandt.[35] The *New York Pink* continued commuting between New York and Amsterdam until July 1704, freighted by Barent Reinders, among others,[36] and Jacob van Cortlandt, who supplied the former New Yorker, Amsterdam resident, and factor of Bostonian colleagues Livinius von Schaick.[37] These few cases prove a general trend: the Dutch element in Atlantic trade was not destroyed by English laws. Dutchmen in the Netherlands and New York merchants with Dutch backgrounds used their possibilities and created lucrative niches in the Atlantic trade after 1674 and well into the eighteenth century.

The second method was more difficult to detect, but it was nevertheless vehemently fought by the English Royal African Company, whose members, under the guidance of James, Duke of York, feared for their monopoly. New Yorkers used their former acquaintance with the WIC to get a share of the lucrative slave trade. As some of his New Yorker colleagues had done before, Gabriel Minvielle, a well-to-do French New Yorker who had come to New Netherland in 1669–70, had been married in New (Nieuw) Orange, New York—to a Dutch woman— and there blended perfectly into the Dutch Reformed Church as well as into the English local administration of New York after 1674.[38] In 1676 Minvielle sent a letter to the WIC's Amsterdam chamber. Notwithstanding his status as a subject of the English Crown, he asked the WIC for permission to trade between New York and the Dutch colony Curaçao. This may not have pleased London; Minvielle, however, went one step further, indirectly provoking the royal brothers, one of whom was deeply involved with the English slave trade. Minvielle likely acted with the consent of his colleague, brother in faith, and fellow citizen Jacob Leisler. In exchange for furs destined to Europe and groceries (flour, bread, pork, beef, peas, for instance) for the population of this "barren piece of ground" sent from New York, he wanted to buy Africans who had been brought by WIC slave traders from Africa to the Caribbean entrepôt.[39] To improve his chances, he asked especially for those slaves who could not be sold to Spanish America because of age, physical appearance, or mental condition.[40] After six months— the WIC always took time to consider projects—the WIC informed the director of Curaçao about upcoming events: "Wy sein te gemoet, dat met der Tyt wel een goeden handel soude konnen gedreven werden met de Ingesetenen van Nieu Jorck, die sich wel genegen thonen omme van daer schepen te senden naer Curacao, met allerhande soorten van waren en coopmanschappen, bysonder pelteryen, gelyck dan oock daer toe paspoort verleent hebben aen eenen Gabriel Minv[i]elle mitsgaders aen eenen Jacob Lycela [Leisler], te noeten omme mits betalende de geregtigheden ende recognitien vande comp[anie] aent selve Eylant te komen, ende aldaer slaven inte handelen" (We expect that with time a good trade should develop with the inhabitants of New York, who are well disposed to send ships from there to Curaçao, with all sorts of wares and merchandise, particularly peltries, for that purpose we have given a passport to one Gabriel Minvelle, together with one Jacob Lycela [Leisler], to note with the condition to heed to the laws and charges of the parties, to come to the same island and to trade there in slaves).[41] Although as yet no sources have been found to prove that the transactions took place or where the Africans should have been brought, this action demonstrates, on the one hand, the survival of the Dutch connection and, on the other hand, that the importance of regional supranational interests was stronger than national solidarity and obedience toward the metropolitan Royal African Company in London.

The Protestant Supranational—Boston-Holland, Boston-Surinam, 1670s–1702

As it did for New Yorkers, trade played an important role in the way Bostonians saw both themselves and their relationship with England. From the start, the question of commercial liberty became a matter of dispute nearly as important to Boston citizens as religious and political issues that weighed heavily on imperial contacts. Trade with Netherlanders in America and the Netherlands was not only profitable and necessary to Bostonians but also took place on a religious common ground that replaced emotional and kinship ties. Networks that connected Protestant merchants of various national backgrounds and denominations developed. Mutual sympathies fostered by faith and a sense of commercial profit had a long standing. They had already had an impact on intercolonial coexistence insofar as Massachusetts supported New Netherland, or at least kept neutrality, whereas Connecticut tried to expand at New Netherland's expense in the 1650s and 1660s.[42] In 1673, during the third Anglo-Dutch War of 1672–74, citizens of Massachusetts verbally rebelled against King Charles II, denying their support to retake New Netherland. Boston's mercantilist-orientated political elite declared Massachusetts "a free state" and "not att all to be interested or concerned in the differences or wars which His Majesty may have with other Nations." Much more interested in their individual, local, and regional welfare, their intercolonial trade, and their strong sense of self-rule, they came up with a statement that bordered on treason: "they had rather the Government and possession of New Yorke should remaine in the hands of the Dutch, then to come under the Government of such a person as Colonel [Francis] Lovelace, who might prove a worse neighbour."⁴³

Bostonian political autonomy found its mercantile expression in trade actions. In 1673 while in Boston an obedient subject to Charles II and captain of the Royal Navy was shocked by Massachusetts's obvious flouting of English law: "the Trade of New England is very great. . . . it is become a Magazine both of all American and European Commodities . . . ships daily arrived from Spain, Ffrance, Holland and Canareys . . . without coming to England."⁴⁴ Bostonians' reactions to English efforts to submit the colony to metropolitan interests resembled those of Virginians and Barbadians; like those royalist colonies, the colony of elects fought the royal will that was personified by the king's agent Edward Randolph. The clash of ideas was evident in a report that Randolph sent to Henry Coventry in 1676: "he [John Leverett, governor of Massachusetts] declares to me that the laws made by our king and parliament obligeth them [Massachusetts] in nothing but what consists with the Interest of New England."⁴⁵ The message was unmistakable: the people of Massachusetts had developed their own regional identity to go with their own regional interests. An important ingredient of this "Interest of New England" was Dutch trade. This correlation was evident and accordingly attacked by Randolph. He bombarded the lords of the committee on trade and plantations with reports of Bostonians' mercantile sins, in disgust calling Boston "the Metropolis of the American Plantations, . . . residence for fforainers and English factors that have fforaine commissions for trade."⁴⁶ In 1684 Randolph tried to destroy Boston's backbone of opposition by sailing to Amsterdam to talk people out of their interests in the Amsterdam–Boston trade.⁴⁷ His expedition was unsuccessful. In New England, however, he managed to smash the claim by Massachusetts to being a free state. The colony lost its charter in 1684 and two years later became part of the Dominion of New England, under the management of the pro-French and Catholic James II. The Stuart king tried to bring the colonies into line, ruled by a central government that was more manageable and less obstinate to metropolitan interests.

The wind of change blew far. Not only did Bostonians curse and attack Randolph even more than before,⁴⁸ but also Dutch Surinam suffered extremely under the stricter nationalization of trade. Since becoming a Dutch colony in 1667 Surinam had developed strong connections with North America, buying food, horses, and goods in exchange for sugar, molasses, and lemon juice. Fearing for their sugar, the Dutch owners of Surinam, the Sociëteit van Suriname, were not at all happy about these contacts and thus enforced in their charter of 1683 the prohibition of the export of sugar to places other than the Netherlands. Because Bostonians were forced to stay away after 1686, Surinam was devastated. In January 1688 Surinam's governor gave an explication for the sudden setback, the shortage of working animals and food, and rising prices: "en dese duerte is verooraecht om dat hier geen Engelsche scheepen syn gecomen, waer door de [Dutch] scheepers nu wederom den baes speelen" (and this rise in prices is caused by the fact that no English ships arrived, which enabled the Dutch captains to control the business).[49] His complaints went unheard because the Holland-based Sociëteit van Suriname profited from Surinam's loss: instead of disappearing in North American channels and enriching merchants and producers in New York, Massachusetts, Rhode Island, and Connecticut, nearly all raw sugar produced in Surinam during the existence of the Dominion of New England, 1686–89, was exported to the Netherlands.[50]

One of the reasons for the Glorious Revolution in Massachusetts was the strongly felt commercial setback caused by the acts of trade and navigation. It is hardly a coincidence that the declaration of April 28, 1689, explaining Boston's version of the Glorious Revolution, was given by "the Gentlemen, Merchants, and Inhabitants of Boston."[51] It was expected that William III, Dutch stadtholder and English king, would not only form a Dutch-English military alliance against France but also would replace the acts of trade and navigation with a commercial alliance. Hoping for ideal times of unlimited Atlantic trade, New Englanders gave up whatever reserve they had left and jumped head over heels for Dutch trade. A horrified Edward Randolph, in jail, wrote reports to William Blathwayt and the lords of the committee on trade and plantations about the Bostonians' criminal energy.[52] Being a prominent part of the imperial English power structure, Blathwayt served as secretary of the committee on trade and plantation from 1679 to 1696.

Summary

The perspective on Atlantic trade presented here follows discussions regarding the concept of "Atlantic history" recently debated in conferences, summer schools, and seminars.[53] One of the concept's pathfinders, Bernard Bailyn, director of the International Seminar on the History of the Atlantic World, proves the newly discovered importance of walking in the shoes of Fernand Braudel, the French historian who took the Mediterranean Sea as center stage. However, whereas Braudel judges the Mediterranean as an ocean surrounded by people of one culture, the recent concept of Atlantic history regards the ocean as a medium connecting peoples of several cultures and shaping a whole series of newly styled relations, identities, and systems. Trade and merchants, slaves and masters played important roles in expressing, establishing, and keeping up relationships and contacts within and without the national Atlantic trade systems. The trade that obeyed national claims strengthened the line connecting mother country and colonies; the illegal trade—that disobeying national laws—strengthened the colonists' position and weakened European control.

One important ingredient to the developing sense of colonial self-consciousness was the supranational trade that opposed metropolitan ideas of national trade and national benefit. The disposition to get engaged in supranational trade across the Atlantic—from North America to the Netherlands, from North America to the Dutch Caribbean, or between Holland and the Chesapeake Bay colonies—was often accompanied by remarkably strong statements, measures, and behavior of regional identities.[54] More research is needed to find out what came first: did regional identity and interest make the colonists more susceptible to opposition and Dutch trade, or did contact with alternative markets foster the colonial sense of opposition and regional belonging? Whatever the answer, it is obvious that nationalism was of less or no importance to colonial merchants and was an idea promoted by European authorities trying hard to stay in command. Therefore, studies of Atlantic economic systems should not be reduced to national categories but instead should cross and combine borders of all kinds—human-made or natural—to reconstruct the several legal and illegal, formal and informal systems, networks, and contacts that stretched across the Atlantic and made the Atlantic Ocean and its bordering societies part of an early modern global system.

Notes

1. Ian K. Steele, *The English Atlantic, 1675–1740: An Explanation of Communication and Community* (New York: Oxford University Press, 1986); Charles R. Boxer, *The Dutch Seaborne Empire, 1600–1800* (London: Hutchinson, 1965); Charles R. Boxer, *The Portuguese Seaborne Empire, 1415–1825* (New York: Knopf, 1969); Frederic Mauro, *Portugal et l'Atlantique au XVIIIe siècle, 1570–1670* (Paris: S.E.V.P.E.N., 1960); Pierre Chaunu and Huguette Chaunu, *Seville et l'Atlantique, 1504–1650,* 12 vols. (Paris: A. Colin, 1955–60).

2. Simon Schama shows some examples of the "hollandophobia" of the seventeenth century—nasty English dealings with the Dutch neighbors. Newly created idioms, Owen Felltham's *Brief Character* (1652), or Andrew Marvell's *The Character of Holland* (circa 1652) were typical for this rude fashion, which tells a lot about English mentalities, jealousies, and shortcomings. See Simon Schama, *Überflu und schöner Schein: Zur Kultur der Niederlande im Goldenen Zeitalter* (Munich: Kindler, 1988), 286–88, 694; Eric Partridge, ed., *The Penguin Dictionary of Historical Slang* (London: Penguin, 1972), 289ff.

3. See Claudia Schnurmann, *Atlantische Welten: Engländer und Niederländer im amerikanisch-atlantischen Raum, 1648–1713,* Wirtschafts- und Sozialhistorische Studien, ed. Stuart Jenks, Michael North, and Rolf Walter, vol. 9 (Cologne, Weimar, and Vienna: Böhlau, 1998). Here, I try to condense some of the findings presented at large in my second thesis, the so-called "Habilitation," given in papers to audiences on both sides of the pond. For discussing my remarks, I want to thank participants of the "International Seminar on the History of the Atlantic World, 1500–1800," Harvard University, Cambridge, Mass., August 1999, under the guidance of Bernard Bailyn; "History of the Atlantic System, 1580–1830," summer school program under the guidance of Horst Pietschmann, Department of History, Hamburg University, Hamburg, Germany, August–September 1999; and the conference "The Emergence of the Atlantic Economy," College of Charleston, Charleston, S.C., October 14–16, 1999, organized by Jack P. Greene, Rosemary Brana-Shute, Randy J. Sparks, and S. Max Edelson.

4. Barbados Public Library, Bridgetown/Barbados Council Minutes, reel 1, vol.1, fol. 67, November 8, 1654.

5. See Schnurmann, *Atlantische Welten,* passim; April Lee Hatfield, "Mariners, Merchants, and Colonists in Seventeenth-Century English America," working paper no. 99–13, "International Seminar on the History of the Atlantic World, 1500–1800," Cambridge, Mass., 1999; Susie M. Ames, ed., *County Court Records of Accomack-Northampton, Virginia, 1640–45,* Virginia Historical Society Documents, vol. 10 (Charlottesville: University Press of Virginia, 1973); Susie M. Ames, *Studies of the Virginia Eastern Shore in the Seventeenth Century* (1940; repr., New York: Russell and Russell, 1973).

6. See Herman Diederiks, "Amsterdam 1600–1800: Demographische Entwicklung und Migration," in *Niederlande und Nordwestdeutschland. Studien zur Regional- und Stadtgeschichte Nordwestkontinentaleuropas im Mittelalter und in der Neuzeit: Festschrift für Franz Petri,* ed. Wilfried Ehbrecht and Heinz Schilling (Cologne and Vienna: Böhlau, 1983), 328–46.

7. See Berthold Fernow, *The Records of New Amsterdam from 1653 to 1674,* 7 vols. (New York: Knickerbocker Press, 1897), 1:326, 3:29; Gemeentearchief Amsterdam Index Simon Hart Notarieel Archief 1094 Joost van der Ven, fol. 461, 11.8.1650; Winthrop-Stuyvesant Correspondence 1647–64, 9.6.1663, New York Public Library; Arnold J. F. van Laer, ed., *Correspondence of Jeremias van Rensselaer, 1651–1674* (Albany: State University of New York, 1932), 109.

8. Algemeen Rijksarchief The Hague/NI 1.05.01.01 17 fol. 26f 12.9.1650, "lecta" November 3, 1650.

9. Joseph Douglas Deal, "Race and Class in Colonial Virginia: Indians, Englishmen, and Africans on the Eastern Shore during the Seventeenth Century" (Ph.D. diss., University of Rochester, 1981), 149; Timothy H. Breen and Stephen Innes, *Myne Owne Ground: Race and Freedom on Virginia's Eastern Shore, 1640–1676* (New York: Oxford University Press, 1980), 49ff.

10. Northampton County, Deeds and Wills, Nos. 7–8, 1655–68, 5./15.3.1654/55, "recorded 20 Septembre [old style] 1655 p[er] Edm[und] Mathew," Colonial Williamsburg Foundation Library, Williamsburg, Va.

11. See Claudia Schnurmann, *Europa trifft Amerika: Atlantische Wirtschaft in der Frühen Neuzeit 1492–1783* (Frankfurt am Main: Fischer Taschenbuch Verlag, 1998), 215.

12. See Donald G. Shomette and Robert D. Haslach, *Raid on America: The Dutch Naval Campaigne of 1672–1674* (Columbia: University of South Carolina Press, 1988), 11ff.; Francis G. Davenport, ed., *European Treaties Bearing on the History of the United States and Its Dependencies,* vol. 2 (1917–37; repr., Gloucester, Mass.: P. Smith, 1967), 53; W. Noel Sainsbury, ed., *Calendar of State Papers, Colonial Series 1574–1660: America & West Indies,* vol. 8 (London: Longman, 1860), 250ff.

13. See the quotation by George Louis Beer, *The Origins of the British Colonial System, 1578–1660* (New York: Macmillan, 1908), 356. See also Robert Brenner, *Merchants and Revolution: Commercial Crisis, Political Conflict, and London's Overseas Traders: 1550–1653* (Princeton, N.J.: Princeton University Press, 1993), 586.

14. William Waller Hening, ed., *The Statutes at Large, Being a Collection of All the Laws of Virginia, from the First Session of the Legislature in the Year 1619,* vol. 1 (Richmond, Va.: Samuel Pleasants, 1809), 331.

15. Henry Read McIlwaine, ed., *Journals of the House of Burgesses of Virginia, 1619–1658/59* (Richmond, Va.: Colonial Press/E. Waddey, Co., 1915), 74.

16. See Schnurmann, *Atlantische Welten,* 313; Algemeen Rijksarchief The Hague/NI 1.01.04 5763/II fol. 41f., no. 1841, petition of the Dutch merchants trading to Virginia. Quotation from Henry Read McIlwaine, ed., *Journals of the House of Burgesses of Virginia, 1619–1658/59* (Richmond, 1915), 76.

17. On the English plan of union, see Simon Groenveld, "The English Civil Wars as a Cause of the First Anglo-Dutch War, 1640–1652," *Historical Journal* 30 (1987): 541–66, 554; *Secrete resolutien van de Edele Groot Mogende Heeren Staten van Holland en Westfriesland...*, vol. 2 (Utrecht, 1717), 479; Leon V. Aizema, *Herstelde Leeuw of Discourse over 't gepassieerde in de Vereenighde Nederlanden, In't Jaer 1650, ende 1651* (The Hague, 1652); Hans-Christoph Junge, *Flottenpolitik und Revolution: Die Entstehung der englischen Seemacht während der Herrschaft Cromwells,* Veröffentlichungen des Deutschen Historischen Instituts in London, vol. 6 (Stuttgart, 1980), 146.

18. "At our comming [the English fleet under George Ayscue] in sight wee saw some 12 sayle of Dutch riding... whose worke it was to make your people glad with lyes, and to strengthen their hands in wickednesse by telling them of the great prosperity of the Scots King [Charles II]" (Public Record Office Kew/Surrey CO 1/11 fol. 121 18./28.2.1651/52).

19. See the testimonies of Dutch masters in the High Court of Admiralty about their methods to deal with Virginia and circumventing English laws in Schnurmann, *Atlantische Welten,* 314f.; Public Record Office Kew/Surrey HCA 13/65 20.130.8. 1651 and HCA 13/66 16./26.9. 1652.

20. Schnurmann, *Atlantische Welten,* 95; John R. Pagan, "Dutch Maritime and Commercial Activity in Mid-Seventeenth-Century Virginia," *Virginia Magazine of History and Biography* 90 (1982): 485–501, 497f.

21. Quotations follow Brenner, *Merchants and Revolution,* 594; Gary A. Puckrein, *Little England: Plantation Society and Anglo-Barbadian Politics, 1627–1700* (New York and London: New York University Press, 1984), 118; and V. T. Harlow, *A History of Barbados, 1625–1685* (Oxford: Clarendon Press, 1926), 65. This was still the case in 1687 when English officials described the situation on the Lesser Antilles: "As they [the Dutch] come from Holland. They generally touch at all our Islands under y pretence of watering where dureing their stay which is generally 7 or 8 days the Planters come on board & there agree not only for what they have onboard (they keeping particular Invoyeces ready which are carryed from hand to hand on purpose) but watching their oppertunities they get the same on shoare to y manifest breach of his Maties laws & to y great Loss & Damage to y merchant who cannot afford their Goods so cheap (haveing payd His Matytie Duties) as y Planter this way supplys himself and the sd Flemmings haveing so disposed of their Lading go to Statia where they stay till y English Planter hath honestly sent him his sugae. ... These Dutch so haveing loaden themselves with y Produce of his Matie Islands goe with y same directly to Holland never having paid his Maties any Customs" (Public Record Office Kew/Surrey CO 1/62 fol. 224–25 report, 19./29.7.1687).

22. "John Bayes to the Committee for foreigne affaires," 4.2.1652/14.2.1653, Public Record Office Kew/Surrey CO 1/12 fol. 7r–8.

23. See Schnurmann, *Atlantische Welten,* 95, 100–105; Pagan, "Dutch Maritime and Commercial Activity," 497f.; Oliver A. Rink, *Holland on the Hudson: An Economic and*

Social History of Dutch New York (Ithaca and New York: Cornell University Press, 1986), 255; Edmund S. Morgan, *American Slavery-American Freedom: The Ordeal of Colonial Virginia* (New York: Norton, 1975), 148; Clayton Colman Hall, ed., *Narratives of Early Maryland, 1633–1684* (New York: Charles Scribner's Sons, 1910), 311–33.

24. Schnurmann, *Atlantische Welten,* 108ff.; Rink, *Holland on the Hudson,* 246–49; Ronald D. Cohen, "The Hartford Treaty of 1650: Anglo-Dutch Cooperation in the Seventeenth Century," *New York Historical Society Quarterly* 53 (1969): 311–32.

25. See John J. McCusker and Russel R. Menard, *The Economy of British America, 1607–1789* (Chapel Hill: University of North Carolina Press, 1985), 191.

26. See, for example, the contents of the port books of Dover kept in the Public Record Office Kew/Surrey E 190/663/6 1675–76, E 190/664/14 1677–78, E 190/665/4 1678–79, E 190/665/11 1679–80.

27. Algemeen Rijksarchief The Hague/Nl 1.05.01.02 330 fol. 14r-30.11.1674 (kept at the state archives of the Hague).

28. Algemeen Rijksarchief The Hague/Nl 1.05.01.02 330 fol. 618.2.1675.

29. Algemeen Rijksarchief The Hague/Nl 1.05.01.02 330 fol. 6412.2.1675.

30. Gemeentearchief Amsterdam Filmno. 3929 Notarieel Archief 3778 Adrian van Santen fols. 711–1719.7.1675 (kept at the municipal archive of Amsterdam).

31. Public Record Office Kew/Surrey HCA 13/82 fol. 312f 26.5./5.6.1701; see also Jacob van Cortlandt to Thomas Bond, BV Van Cortlandt, Jacobus 1700, Letterbook, fol. 30 26.6./7. 1700, New-York Historical Society.

32. Gemeentearchief Amsterdam Notarieel Archief 5878 Jan Hoekebak 15.11.1700.

33. Jacob van Cortlandt to John Blackall, BV Van Cortlandt, Jacobus, 1700, Letterbook Jacobus van Cortlandt, fol. 13, 18./28.7.1698, New York Historical Society; Gemeentearchief Amsterdam Notarieel Archief 5876 Jan Hoekebak, 6.5.1700; British Library Sloane MSS, 3984 fol. 205, 7./17.2. 1688, British Library.

34. Gemeentearchief Amsterdam Notarieel Archief 5876 Jan Hoekebak, 14.5.1700.

35. Van Cortlandt, Jacobus, Ledger 1700–14, fol. 1, [September] 1700, New York Public Library.

36. Gemeentearchief Amsterdam Notarieel Archief 5893 Jan Hoekebak, 19.7.1704.

37. See Jacobus van Cortlandt's "Shipments from the Port of New York, 1699–1702," *New-York Historical Society Quarterly Bulletin* 20 (1936): 113–21. For information on Livinius Schaick see Cathy Matson, "Commerce after the Conquest: I: Dutch Traders and Goods in New York City, 1664–1764," *De Halve Maen* 59 (March 1987): 8–12; Gemeentearchief Amsterdam Notarieel Archief 5884 Jan Hoekebak, 6.4.1702; Gemeentearchief Amsterdam Notarieel Archief 5887 Jan Hoekebak, 2.1.1793; Jonathan Belcher Journal, 1704, passim, Massachusetts Historical Society, Boston. See Schnurmann, *Atlantische Welten,* passim; Claudia Schnurmann, "Atlantic Trade and Regional Identities: The Creation of Supranational Atlantic Systems in the 17th. Century," in *Atlantic History: History of the Atlantic System, 1580–1830,* ed. Horst Pietschmann (Göttingen: Vandenhoeck and Ruprecht, 2002), 779–97.

38. Schnurmann, *Atlantische Welten,* 268–73; J. F. Bosher, "Huguenot Merchants and the Protestant International in the Seventeenth Century," *William and Mary Quarterly* 52 (1995): 77–100; Randall Balmer, *A Perfect Babel of Confusion: Dutch Religion and English Culture in the Middle Colonies* (New York: Oxford University Press, 1989), 166; Thomas J. Archdeacon, *New York City, 1664–1710: Conquest and Change* (Ithaca: Cornell University

Press, 1976), 64; Jon Butler, *The Huguenots in America: A Refugee People in the New World Society* (Cambridge: Harvard University Press, 1983); Joyce D. Goodfriend, *Before the Melting Pot: Society and Culture in Colonial New York City, 1664–1730* (Princeton, N.J.: Princeton University Press, 1992), passim; *The Burghers of New Amsterdam and the Freemen of New York, 1675–1866* (New York: Printed for the New York Historical Society, 1886), 39; Robert C. Ritchie, *The Duke's Province: A Study of New York Politics and Society, 1664–1691* (Chapel Hill: University of North Carolina Press, 1977), passim; New York State Archives A 1894, vol. 36, pt. 2, fol. 135 11./21.11.1690.

39. Public Record Office Kew/Surrey CO 153/2 fols. 139–62, [1673].

40. Algemeen Rijksarchief The Hague/Nl 1.05.01.02 331 fol. 181r, 2.6.1676.

41. Algemeen Rijksarchief The Hague/Nl 1.05.01.02 467 fol. 13r, 11.7.1676.

42. See Rink, *Holland on the Hudson,* 250–55; Pieter Stuyvesant to John Winthrop and John Endecott, Nieuw Amsterdam, Misc. MSS, box 1, no. 1, 6.3.1653, New York Historical Society.

43. Public Record Office Kew/Surrey CO 5/903 fol. 54/50–61/53r, 1673; Ronald D. Cohen, "The New England Colonies and the Dutch Recapture of New York, 1673–1674," *New York Historical Society Quarterly* 56 (1972): 54–78.

44. Report by Captain Wyborne [1673/74], Public Record Office Kew/Surrey CO 5/903 fols. 54–61.

45. Public Record Office Kew/Surrey CO 1/37 fol. 18f 17./27.6.1676.

46. Egerton MSS 3340, Leeds Papers, fol. 162f, 17./27.6.1676, British Library.

47. *William Blathwayt Papers,* vols. 1, 12, 16, Colonial Williamsburg Foundation Library, Williamsburg, Va.; Middleton Papers, vol. 21, fol. 1r, 7./17.10.1684, Add. MS 31823, British Library, London.

48. Schnurmann, *Atlantische Welten,* 362; HM 1716, 1686, Henry Huntington Library, San Marino, Calif.; Public Record Office Kew/Surrey CO 1/66 fol. 392ff. [1686/87].

49. Algemeen Rijksarchief The Hague/NL 1.05.03 217 fols. 175–216.

50. See Schnurmann, *Atlantische Welten,* 304f.; Johannes Menne Postma, "The Fruits of Slave Labor: Tropical Commodities from Surinam to Holland, 1683–1794" (unpublished MS, 1994); Cornelis Ch. Goslinga, *The Dutch in the Caribbean and in the Guianas, 1680–1791* (Assen and Dover, N.H.: Van Gorcum, 1985), 277.

51. W. H. Whitmore, ed., *The Andros Tracts,* vol. 5 (Boston: Prince Society, 1868–74), 11.

52. Edward Randolph to William Blathwayt, Boston, Common Goal, 22.7./1.8.1689, Public Record Office Kew/Surrey CO 5/855: "The Ketch Mary of Boston 40 ton John Updyke Mastr: by whom I send this, hath Loaded here the enumerated Comodityes without having first given Bond as y Law does require I cannot Seize her here unless my officer should be knock't o'th head There is noo Law noe Courts No Justice no Governmt all crying out against the Acts of Trade and now Vessells arrive from Holland and Newfoundland loaden wth wine Oyle and Brandy I cannot Trust the Goal wth any of my Lrs for I am lyable to be Searched every hour and that would add to my charge of Treason against their Governmt as my acting here by Comission and deputacon without their Consent is already adjudged and I am voted not Baylable. Edward Randolph"; Surrey CO 5/905 fol. 123ff.: "An account of severall ships and vessels trading irregularly . . . since the I 8th. day of April 1689."

53. Literature on the concept of Atlantic history recently gets a lot of attention. Special issues devoted to this topic include the *Journal of American History* (December 1999); and

"Forum: The New British History in Atlantic Perspective," *American Historical Review* 104, no. 2 (1999): 426–500. See also Bailyn, "Idea of Atlantic History"; Horst Pietschmann, ed., *Geschichte des atlantischen Systems, 1580–1830: Ein historischer Versuch zur Erklërung der 'Globalisierung' jenseits nationalgeschichtlicher Perspektiven* (Hamburg: Joachim Jungius-Gesellschaft der Wissenschaften, 1998).

54. On the issues of American and colonial identities and their genesis, causes, and important elements such as the distance from Europe, the experience of crossing an imaginary border by crossing the Atlantic, see, for example, Jack P. Greene, "Changing Identity in the British Caribbean: Barbados as a Case Study," in *Colonial Identity in the Atlantic World, 1500–1800,* ed. Nicholas Canny and Anthony Pagden (Princeton, N.J.: Princeton University Press, 1987), 213–66; Jack P. Greene, *Imperatives, Behaviors, and Identities: Essays in Early American Cultural History* (Charlottesville: University Press of Virginia, 1992); John Canup, *Out of the Wilderness: The Emergence of an American Identity in Colonial New England* (Middletown, Conn.: Wesleyan University Press, 1990); Michael Zuckerman, "The Fabrication of Identity in Early America," *William and Mary Quarterly* 34 (1977): 183–214; Michael Zuckerman, "Identity in British America: Unease in Eden," in *Colonial Identity in the Atlantic World, 1500–1800,* ed. Nicholas Canny and Anthony Pagden (Princeton, N.J.: Princeton University Press, 1987), 115–57; Jill Lepore, *The Name of War: King Philip's War and the Origins of American Identity* (New York: Knopf, 1998); Bernard Bailyn, *The Peopling of British North America: An Introduction* (New York: Knopf, 1986); Colin G. Calloway, *New Worlds for All: Indians, Europeans, and the Remaking of Early America* (Baltimore: Johns Hopkins University Press, 1997).

Dutch and New Netherland Merchants in the Seventeenth-Century English Chesapeake

April Lee Hatfield

Historians of Early America have long recognized the importance of Dutch trade with the seventeenth-century Chesapeake. Colonists acknowledged their reliance on Dutch ships, protesting the Navigation Acts on the grounds that the exclusion of the Dutch would ruin them economically. Although John Pagan and others have emphasized the close relationships between Chesapeake tobacco producers and Dutch merchants, these merchants heretofore have been considered, by virtue of their nationality, outsiders in the Chesapeake.[1] This is true even for regions such as the Southside counties (south of the James River) and the Eastern Shore, where immigrants from the Netherlands and from Dutch New Netherland settled disproportionately.[2]

Many Dutch merchants' involvement in Virginia and Maryland was deeper and more complicated than the historiography suggests. Several Dutch merchant families and many more individual mariners migrated from the Netherlands or New Netherland to the Chesapeake, settling permanently and becoming English denizens or naturalized citizens. These Dutch colonists fit into seventeenth-century Virginia and Maryland easily, sometimes marrying English colonists and sometimes acquiring positions of local importance. They were often virtually indistinguishable from English colonists in colonial and county court records, their Dutch background only infrequently apparent. The difficulty of identifying Dutch settlers in these records suggests that English colonists accepted Dutch merchants' settlement in the Chesapeake and perhaps that Dutch immigrants adapted to English society more consciously than did other non-English immigrants to the Chesapeake. The extent of Dutch colonists' involvement in local, colonial, intercolonial, and transatlantic networks strengthens this perception.

Economic Importance

Dutch traders were important to Virginians and Marylanders from the outset of Chesapeake colonization. Dutch prominence in seventeenth-century Atlantic shipping, Dutch markets for tobacco, and Dutch sources for dry goods made Dutch traders crucial to Chesapeake planters.[3] The Dutch-Chesapeake connection extended to include New Netherland after its settlement.[4] Within the Chesapeake colonies there were regional patterns to Dutch involvement. Transatlantic Dutch merchants traded tobacco from all parts of the Chesapeake to Europe, but intercolonial trade between Virginia and New Netherland (and via Dutch traders to other mainland and Caribbean colonies) was most important to the Maryland and Virginia Eastern Shore and to Virginia's Southside counties, and the Dutch may have carried a larger percentage of the tobacco from these regions than from other parts of the Chesapeake. New Amsterdam was also a popular entrepôt for English traders, not only because it afforded cloth and other goods not easily available elsewhere but also because traders there could sometimes avoid English duties on trade goods bound for Europe.[5]

The importance of Dutch traders to Chesapeake planters increased dramatically during the 1640s when the English civil war seriously disrupted English shipping. While Dutch merchant David Peterson de Vries reported only four Dutch ships (out of thirty-four total) loading tobacco in 1643, in 1648 the number of Dutch ships had risen to twelve (of thirty-one reported).[6] John Pagan has noted that the Amsterdam and Rotterdam Notarial Archives report only four ships bound from the Netherlands to Virginia between 1637 and 1642 but as many as thirty-three between 1643 and 1649.[7] During the 1640s Virginians actively sought out Dutch trade as well. The director of the Dutch West India Company wrote in 1646 that Virginians traveled to Curaçao to trade with the Dutch there.[8] The Virginia Assembly explicitly protected Dutch trade in 1643, reflecting its realization that diverse markets and shippers would be crucial during the upheavals then beginning.[9]

Trade Restrictions and Defense of Free Trade

During the second half of the seventeenth century, the English Navigation Acts and the Anglo-Dutch wars complicated Virginia's trade with the Netherlands and with New Amsterdam but did not stop it.[10] The importance of Dutch commerce for Chesapeake planters led them to defend that commerce as part of their right to "free trade" when Parliament began to implement trade restrictions. When, in the 1640s, London merchants began lobbying for regulations limiting Dutch trade, Virginians grew concerned, and in 1647 the Virginia Assembly declared that Dutch trade was necessary for the colony's survival.[11] When Parliament passed a 1650 law (precursor to the 1651 Navigation Act) prohibiting trade between foreigners and English colonies, Virginia governor William Berkeley protested the exclusion of the Dutch in particular, on the grounds that Virginia had been "rescued" by the Dutch during the war. The Virginia Assembly responded to the same law by reasserting its belief in Virginians' right to free trade. Their experiences of reduced English shipping during the war had taught them that dependence on English traders alone was dangerous.[12]

Virginians' opposition to the 1651 Navigation Act encouraged the colony to continue resisting the Interregnum government, resulting in England's use of a military fleet to force the colony's submission in 1652. The act, which required trade from English colonies to travel on English or English colonial ships and go directly to England, contributed as well to the first Anglo-Dutch War of 1652–54. During the war several Dutch ships were captured in Virginia, suggesting that the war hindered Dutch-Virginia trade but not totally: ships were there to be captured. Once the war ended, higher volumes of trade resumed.[13]

During the first Anglo-Dutch War, New Netherland governor Peter Stuyvesant, by order of the West India Company, tried to negotiate a commercial alliance with Virginia so that the two colonies could continue to trade despite war between their home countries. In spring 1653 he sent envoys to Virginia to negotiate an alliance, and a few months later he sent minister Samuel Drisius to propose "a provisional continuation of the commerce and intercourse between the two places" if Virginia governor Richard Bennett had not received instructions to the contrary. Drisius, a Puritan minister living in New Netherland, not only negotiated but also preached while on this trip to Virginia, illustrating the intertwining of religious and commercial and political connections linking the Chesapeake, New England, and New Netherland.[14]

The "Articles of amitie and commerce" between the two colonies were not signed until 1660, after William Berkeley had resumed Virginia's governorship. Charles II's new Navigation Act followed shortly thereafter, requiring that all ship masters and three-quarters of crew members sailing into England's colonies be English, and that the Chesapeake's tobacco go directly to England. The 1663 act stipulated that all European goods going into the colonies be from England. These Restoration Navigation Acts were better enforced and more effective than the Interregnum Navigation Acts had been.[15] Nonetheless, individual traders found ways to skirt them, and merchants of Dutch descent who had settled in the Chesapeake colonies remained there and maintained their positions in Dutch-English trade networks. After the English conquered New Netherland in 1664 many Dutch merchants there remained as New Yorkers and continued to trade as before, able to do so legally because Manhattan burghers were allowed "free denizen" status by English authorities.[16] Illegal trade continued as well, though it is impossible to measure its extent. Ships whose Chesapeake voyages were recorded only because they had problems with the Navigation Acts make it clear that even ships trading between the Chesapeake and another English port often had non-English crews and captains.[17] In 1674, for example, ship masters Isaac Foxcroft of the ship *Carolus Secundus*, John Harlow of the *Charitas*, and Jeroln Jerolnson of the *Liefde* received special permission from Charles II to sail to Virginia with their "own outlandish seamen" and to trade as freely as if they were natural-born subjects of England. Foxcroft and Harlow, described as strangers, apparently Anglicized their names, as was common among Dutch merchants trading among the English.[18] Foxcroft went further in making a show of his commitment to the English by naming his ship after Charles II.[19]

Access to markets, goods, and the safety provided by a variety of shippers are explanation enough for Chesapeake colonists' willingness to disobey various trade restrictions and even to explicitly protest such restrictions as violating their rights. The importance of Dutch traders in supplying slaves to labor-hungry Chesapeake planters may explain further why Virginia planters in particular showed little hesitation in breaking the Navigation Acts. Dutch dominance of the slave trade coincided with Chesapeake reliance on Dutch traders and with almost constant labor shortages in the Chesapeake. As is well known, the first Africans whose arrival in the Chesapeake was recorded came aboard a Dutch ship. Dutch traders or colonists were disproportionately involved in the few recorded arrivals of Africans in the seventeenth-century Chesapeake, especially on the Eastern Shore. In January 1650 two Dutchmen, Derrick Arrisson and Cornelius Clinton, presented a bond to the Northampton County Court stating their intention to bring in a "shipp with Negros into Chirryston Creeke" and to give local planters Nicholas Waddelow and Stephen Horsey first chance to buy them.[20] The largest number of slaves to arrive at once on the Eastern Shore during the seventeenth century was a shipment of forty-one Africans who were brought from Benin to New Amsterdam in August 1655. Eastern Shore intercolonial merchant Edmund Scarborough took them to Virginia seven months later.[21] Additionally, other New Netherlanders, such as members of the Varlett-Hack-Boot-Hermann family (discussed below), brought slaves from New Netherland to the Chesapeake.

Chesapeake colonists' favor toward Dutch traders recognized the access Dutch merchants and ships provided to African labor sources. When Virginia and New Netherland signed their 1660 commerce and peace agreement, Virginia charged higher tobacco export duties for Dutch shippers than for English, *unless* the Dutch had brought slaves into the colony.[22] Access to slave trade through New Netherland or the Dutch Caribbean, or simply through their contacts with Dutch merchants, may have provided advantages to Dutch merchant immigrants in the Chesapeake that would help explain their easy acceptance in the region, where English colonists would have valued anyone's ability to procure labor.

It seems likely, as well, that in addition to economic importance in general and access to African labor in particular, a sense of shared religious identity and history (especially among Puritan Virginians) made the transnational (and transethnic) connections between English Chesapeake colonists and Dutch merchants and immigrants easier, especially when such connections were illegal. Though William Berkeley, Virginia's loudest defender of the right to free trade, was also Anglican, many of those English Virginians with close Dutch connections were not only Protestant but Puritan.[23]

Merchant-Settler Interactions

The dispersed nature of settlement and trade in the seventeenth-century Chesapeake meant that a large percentage of colonists interacted with Dutch merchants and mariners and recognized their economic importance to the region. David Ormrod and Dwyrydd Jones have described England's mercantile community at the end of the seventeenth century as "thoroughly cosmopolitanized," as reflected by "willing co-operation" with foreign merchants, actions they see as resulting from the convergence of British and Dutch economic and political interests.[24] In Virginia, Maryland, and New Netherland colonists and officials displayed such willingness to see beyond ethnicity where trade was concerned during the mid-seventeenth century. Dutch merchants in the Chesapeake enjoyed easy communication and socialization with Virginia planters and officials.

Dutch merchant De Vries's experiences illustrate the kind of socializing that accompanied seventeenth-century Chesapeake trade and facilitated a familiarity that made Dutch merchants and mariners far from foreign to English Chesapeake colonists. When De Vries spent the winter of 1642–43 in Virginia, Gov. William Berkeley asked him for his company as he was "in need of society." De Vries spent several four- to five-day visits with Berkeley over the winter and was grateful "for the friendship which had been shown me by him throughout the winter." De Vries, another Dutch trader, and the ship's crew spent the winter going "daily from one plantation to the other, until the ships were ready, and had their cargoes of tobacco," as Chesapeake trading required, interacting with colonists as they did business.[25]

Friendships formed during such stays were cultivated for both their economic and social value and could be long lasting. On his way out of the Chesapeake in spring 1643 De Vries spent the night with wealthy planter and councillor Samuel Matthews at Blunt Point, near Newport News. Matthews had become a "good friend" to De Vries during the Dutch merchant's earlier visits to the region in 1633 and 1635. De Vries's social relations were not limited to elites. On his way back from Matthews's house to his ship, De Vries ran into a resident ship carpenter who welcomed him, "and was glad that he had me in his house, as I had, some years ago, on board of my ship, well treated him, and he hoped to treat me well now."[26] His host killed a turkey and some chickens to prepare a good meal and took De Vries back to his ship in the morning. These and other encounters with people he had met before in his trading, and his references to interactions on shipboard and on land, suggest intense interaction between residents and mariners, and make no reference to any difficulties of language or ethnicity.

Many colonists in Virginia and Maryland forged long-term contacts and partnerships with Dutch traders in the Netherlands or in New Netherland. More significantly, those Chesapeake colonists with Dutch connections were disproportionately instrumental in forging and maintaining Virginia's coastal trade with other *English* colonies in North America and the Caribbean.[27] Additionally, the largest presence of Dutch immigrants was on the Eastern Shore and in Southside counties, where intercolonial trade was most important, and almost all the intercolonial traders in these regions have some recorded Dutch connection or experience. Two of the wealthiest Eastern Shore merchants, Stephen Charleton and Edmund Scarborough, traded extensively to both New Netherland and New England.[28] Lemuel Mason, one of the justices for the Lower Norfolk County Court, was the attorney of Rotterdam merchant William Scapes. Cornelius Lloyd, who had migrated to Lower Norfolk from New England, traded with Scapes.[29] In May 1654 John Parker of Lynnhaven Parish in Lower Norfolk wrote a will before embarking on a voyage to "the Duch Plantacon."[30] Six months later in the same county, merchant William Vincent "of the Countrey of Virginia" willed four hundred pounds to his brother living in Amsterdam in Holland.[31] Maintaining a relationship with family in Amsterdam could be as valuable for a Chesapeake merchant as was family in England. At least two of the Lower Norfolk men who appraised Vincent's estate (Francis Emperor and William Jermyn) were intercolonial traders with Dutch connections. The inventory listed accounts in New England, including the hire of a bark there, and payment for carpenter's work and expense on the bark in Manhattan.[32] These court cases make it clear that language was rarely an issue between English and Dutch colonists, mariners, and traders. County courts recorded the frequent presence of Dutch merchants and sailors without reference to any need for translators or difficulty in communication.

Dutch Immigrants in Virginia

When the merchant De Vries wrote about his experiences in the Chesapeake, he noted the need for Dutch (or any other) merchants to have factors in Virginia.[33] Whether or not they were following his advice, many Dutch merchants trading to the Chesapeake did either move there or encourage family members or trading partners to resettle.[34] Migration and social links between Holland, New Netherland, and the Chesapeake followed the patterns established by merchants' economic networks. As a result, most Dutch immigrants moved to Virginia's Southside counties or the Chesapeake's Eastern Shore, and the most intricate intercolonial social networks between the Chesapeake colonies and New Netherland centered, as did the economic links, on the Eastern Shore. The Eastern Shore court records contain multiple denizenships for settlers explicitly described as Dutch or with obviously Dutch names.[35] In addition to the denizenships, other Dutch names appear in Eastern Shore records.[36] Some prominent

Dutch settlers in the Chesapeake, such as Minor Doodes and his wife Mary Geret, settled elsewhere (in his case in Middlesex County), but those on the Eastern Shore or in the Southside counties were more likely to maintain Dutch connections.[37] Some naturalizations, such as those for Eastern Shore merchant John Custis and Middlesex resident Nicholas Cock, were for people of English descent who had been born in the Netherlands.[38] Other immigrants identified as Dutch in Chesapeake records were in fact Huguenots (the Varlett family) or belongd to other European Protestant denominations; they had taken advantage of Dutch tolerance and commerce to establish Atlantic trade networks based in the Netherlands or New Netherland.

Dutch presence on the Eastern Shore and in Southside counties may have been related to the reliance of both Chesapeake regions on intercolonial trade products.[39] Most Dutch migrants to the Chesapeake came via New Netherland and were part of trading networks that included the Caribbean. These regions of the Chesapeake were also those with the strongest Puritan presence. That a Calvinist presence was greater in the Chesapeake regions supplying food and naval stores (as well as tobacco) may have made these regions more attractive to Dutch migrants and may have provided them with greater opportunities to establish themselves successfully than elsewhere in England's Chesapeake colonies.

Even those Dutch immigrants coming directly from Holland arrived with an eye on intercolonial as well as transatlantic trade.[40] In 1650, for example, Lower Norfolk County merchant William Moseley, "late of Rotterdam in holland," sold emerald, diamond, gold, ruby, and sapphire jewelry worth 612 guilders to Francis Yeardley for nine head neat cattle: two draught oxen, two steers, and five cows. In July, before the sale of the jewelry, Moseley's wife Susan wrote to Francis Yeardley, agreeing to the terms of the sale and explaining that the decision to sell was because of *her* "greate wante of Cattle"; she assured Yeardley that she had gone from Rotterdam to The Hague to confirm the value of the jewelry with goldsmiths there.[41] The Moseleys sold the jewelry soon after they arrived in Lower Norfolk, when cattle were much more important than jewelry to their economic establishment and ability to develop a niche in an intercolonial trade network. Another Dutch merchant in Lower Norfolk, Simon Overzee, who owned the ship *Virginia Merchant* (which traded to New England and the Caribbean), facilitated other connections between English Virginians and Dutch merchants.[42]

The most clearly documented example of New Netherland–Eastern Shore family ties is that of the Varlett-Hack-Boot-Hermann family. Casper Varlett and his wife Judith Tentenier Varlett moved from the Netherlands to the Dutch Fort Good Hope (site of Hartford, Connecticut) in the 1630s and from there to Fresh Water on Manhattan. Casper Varlett (or Varleth or Varleet) was a merchant with ties to the Dutch West India Company. The Varletts' only son, Nicholas, married

Anna Stuyvesant Bayard, the sister of New Netherland governor Peter Stuyvesant and widow of Samuel Bayard. Nicholas Varlett, also a merchant, traded to Curaçao and imported tobacco to New Amsterdam from Virginia. He was an officer for the Dutch West India Company and held several public offices in New Netherland. In 1660 and 1661 he went to Virginia as one of the representatives of New Netherland to help negotiate the commerce treaty between the two colonies.[43]

Two of Casper and Judith Varlett's five daughters (the sisters of Nicholas) moved to the Chesapeake.[44] The first was Anna, who had been born in Amsterdam before the Varletts moved to America. She and her husband, German-born surgeon George (Joris) Hack, moved to Virginia by 1651 and traded tobacco, other goods, white indentured servants, and black servants or slaves between the Chesapeake and New Amsterdam. George Hack patented almost three thousand acres in the Eastern Shore of Virginia and Maryland, and he and Anna lived in both colonies.[45] George Hack's 1658 Virginia denizenship represents his commitment to the region.[46] Anna Varlett traveled to New Amsterdam several times between 1651 and 1661, apparently by herself, in order to take care of their business there and undoubtedly also to visit her family.[47] Because George Hack was repeatedly referred to as a surgeon, and not a merchant, and because Anna did all of the recorded commercial traveling to New Amsterdam and came from a merchant family, the impulse to trade in the family came probably more from her than from her husband. In a New Netherland lawsuit she claimed a shipment of tobacco sent to her from Virginia by her husband as her private property. In September and October 1652, while she was in New Amsterdam, there was a lawsuit there concerning slaves and property that "Mrs Varleth" had purchased and that Capt. Geurt Tyssen had taken away during the night. Mrs. Varleth in that suit could have been Anna, her mother, one of her sisters, or her sister-in-law, but it seems likely, given her known trade from New Netherland to Virginia, that the cargo involved her and was either hers or destined to be shipped by her.[48] Anna Varlett's activities in New Netherland not only exhibit the commercial activity common to women in Dutch merchant families but also demonstrate a capacity to participate in legal activity to promote or defend her economic interests.[49]

In the Chesapeake, George Hack and Anna Varlett raised goods specifically for the intercolonial market, in addition to tobacco, which they sent to New Netherland for reexport.[50] They also traded Dutch goods for tobacco.[51] They owned at least one boat to carry their own trade and that of their neighbors. In 1654 Hack deeded two-thirds of his bark the *Fortune,* "now riding before my house," to Richard Prill and William Sherman.[52] Once they were in the Chesapeake, George and Anna's continued trade contacts with New Netherland helped them facilitate the migration of other Dutch settlers from New Netherland to Virginia and Maryland. Additionally, they received head rights for Africans who may have come from New Netherland. In April 1659 George Hack was granted a certificate for 1,350 acres for twenty-seven head rights, including people of English, Dutch, and African descent.⁵³

Augustine Hermann, Anna Varlett's trading partner and one of the Hacks' Virginia head rights, had moved from Prague to New Amsterdam in 1643. In December 1650 or 1651 Hermann married Anna's sister Jannetje Varlett in the Dutch Reformed Church of New Amsterdam. They moved to the Eastern Shore at the end of the decade. Hermann traded extensively in Virginia before he moved to the Chesapeake, and he was well known on the Eastern Shore. His economic relationship with Anna Varlett preceded the family relationship, which subsequently helped Anna Varlett and Augustine Hermann maintain their trade ties. The two families worked together, and both served as merchants to other colonists on the Eastern Shore, trading tobacco in their ships to New Netherland for Dutch cloth and for slaves while Augustine Hermann and Jannetje Varlett were still in New Netherland.⁵⁴ In summer 1652 Eastern Shore merchant Edmund Scarborough paid George Hack tobacco due to Augustine Hermann's account but that was sent to Manhattan in Hack's vessel.⁵⁵ The relations Hermann formed through his trade on the Eastern Shore also aided Chesapeake colonists in their own attempts to participate more directly in trade to New Netherland. On August 4, 1656, Capt. John Stringer of Accomack, gentleman, was in New Netherland, where he bought the bark *Beginning* from its owners, New Netherland merchants Augustine Hermann and James Cade. Hermann would have known Stringer from his travels to the Eastern Shore or perhaps from earlier trips Stringer had made to New Netherland. Hermann's position as merchant required that he travel incessantly, which colonists and court members understood. The summer after he had sold Stringer the *Beginning*, Hermann went to the Northampton County Court to complain that Stringer had not paid the tobacco he owed him; he claimed that he could not stay long enough to pursue a lawsuit, "his occasions not permittinge his longe staye in the Countrye." So the clerk registered the protest and promised Hermann that Stringer would see it.⁵⁶

One lawsuit in particular demonstrates the depth of Hermann's involvement in the Eastern Shore economy and his importance (and that of other Dutch merchants) to the region. Additionally, this case illuminates the often invisible network of personal communications necessary to conduct trade in the Chesapeake (without ports) and why it involved the whole society in maritime trade communities. Dutch merchants living in the Chesapeake, such as Hermann, connected English colonists to New Netherland and Dutch markets to which they may not otherwise have had access.

In late April 1657 Augustine Hermann went to the widow Grace Vaughan's house, and the two agreed that Hermann would transport her tobacco to New Netherland with his own if she would deliver it to John Custis's house, where

Hermann planned to consolidate his cargo; Hermann made similar arrangements with other Eastern Shore residents to carry their tobacco.[57] Custis (one of the colonists of English descent who was naturalized in Virginia because he had been born in the Netherlands) was then to carry the tobacco to John Green's house in Kings Creek, where Hermann would pick it up.[58] Hermann had tried to get the store at Jon (Jan?) Micheels(on?)'s house (rather than John Green's), and though Micheels refused to let him use the store, Hermann received permission "from the Dutch man that was the owner of the store . . . to put the tobacco there . . . , in spite of Micheels."[59] Robert Burrell, a mariner who had recently arrived in Northampton County, worked on Custis's sloop and laded tobacco onto it at "assorted places." The tobacco he collected included fifteen hogsheads he gathered from Grace Vaughan at her plantation. Because the mariner Burrell had to go to the individual plantations to load the tobacco, he met the owners of each plantation. Once he had loaded the sloop, he returned to Custis, who was then to deliver it for Hermann to Green's store.[60]

The case illustrates the importance of Dutch and New Netherlanders on the Eastern Shore and the ways in which coastal trade connected settlers to people with colonial experiences in New Netherland and other colonies. Not only was Hermann consolidating and carrying the tobacco, but a Dutch-born man held it. Hermann's New Netherland crew members would have spent as much time as Hermann did on the Eastern Shore. Robert Burrell's experiences loading the tobacco at settlers' plantations reveal the ways in which mariners from these ships interacted with colonists. Perhaps with Burrell and certainly with Hermann the case also illustrates that migration could follow trade or maritime contacts. Hermann was well entrenched in the Chesapeake economy well before he and Jannetje Varlett moved there from New Amsterdam.

The Hermanns, like the Hacks, purchased land in both Virginia and Maryland and ultimately moved to the Chesapeake from New Netherland. In 1655 Hermann moved servants and goods to Northampton County, Virginia, to establish a plantation there, stating that "the favor and approbation of the worthy court" had encouraged him to settle in Northampton. In 1662 he received a grant of four thousand acres in Cecil County, Maryland, for a plantation he named Bohemia Manor.[61] He held on to Bohemia Manor and spent time in both Chesapeake colonies, as well as in New Netherland.

That Augustine Hermann and Jannetje Varlett moved to the Chesapeake at least in part because they had family, George Hack and Anna Varlett, there is apparent. The two families not only maintained a commercial partnership but also patented land near one another in both Maryland and Virginia. Only three days after Hermann received the Cecil County Bohemia Manor grant, George Hack received a grant of eight hundred acres on the Sassafras River in the same county.

During spring 1665 George Hack died, and by November 1665 Jannetje Varlett Hermann had died as well.[62] Anna Varlett and Augustine Hermann applied for denizenship in Maryland at the same time in 1666.[63] They both, however, continued to spend time in both colonies, and though Anna had applied for Maryland denizenship, she apparently moved back to Virginia later that year and continued trading.[64] On May 6, 1665, on her plantation at Pungoteague in Northampton County, Virginia, Anna Varlett engaged James Fookes to build her a sloop that could carry thirty-five hogsheads of tobacco, indicating her intent to continue trading.[65] Anna Varlett and Augustine Hermann remained business partners. Hermann visited her plantation in spring 1666 and planned to use the new sloop at his Maryland plantation the following October, by which time Fookes had promised it would be finished. In spring 1667, however, the boat had not yet been built, and the partners, now including merchant Nicholas Boot, whom Anna had married, took Fookes to court in Accomack County.[66]

Merchant Nicholas Boot had also moved from New Amsterdam to Virginia. He had had contacts on the Eastern Shore and had traded between the two colonies before marrying Anna Varlett. In the 1650s Eastern Shore merchant John Custis served as Nicholas Boot's attorney on the Eastern Shore.[67] Because Boot had traded between New Netherland and the Eastern Shore for at least a decade, he surely knew Varlett, Hack, and Hermann. By 1660 Boot had moved to Gloucester County, Virginia, west of the Chesapeake Bay, and in the fall of that year the Virginia Assembly granted his petition for denizenship, on the condition that he and his family constantly reside in Virginia for two years and afterwards continue to make Virginia their primary place of residence.[68] The assembly's loosening of residency requirements after the first two years may reflect members' recognition that his occupation as merchant required mobility and that that mobility served the colony as a whole. After Boot married Anna Varlett, Varlett and Augustine Hermann remained business partners. Boot died in spring 1668, about a year after marrying Anna, and for at least ten years after Boot died, Anna continued to trade between Maryland and her plantation at Pungoteague in Accomack. She probably died in early 1685.[69]

Anna Varlett continued to form and strengthen contacts with fellow New Netherlanders and Dutch colonists in Virginia. In January 1670 she reaffirmed a power of attorney she had given in November 1668 to Cornelius Vanhoofe, specifically to sell Boot's land in Gloucester County.[70] Soon thereafter Anna agreed to sell half of a sloop to Vanhoofe.[71] When he did not pay, she sued him. Unsatisfied with the judgment of the county court, she requested an appeal to the general court, which intervened in her favor.[72] Despite her preference for a Dutch attorney (a preference that this experience may have weakened), Varlett's willingness to appeal to the general court reflects her comfort with the workings of Virginia's colonial government. Not only did she trade independently, she also used the English colonial courts to protect her interests just as male merchants commonly did, and just as she had done in Dutch New Netherland. Her success in the appeal to the Virginia General Court indicates the ability of Dutch merchants to act effectively in the public sphere in various colonies.

Anna Varlett also continued to increase her landholdings through head rights. In some of these she was responsible for continuing the migration from New Netherland to the Eastern Shore. In January 1672 she was granted a certificate for 1,250 acres due for head rights, including a Sarah Varlett.[73] In September 1674 she received a certificate for 450 acres for nine head rights, including William and Kath Varlett.[74]

The trade and migrations of the Varlett-Hack-Boot-Hermann family indicate the relationship between intercolonial economic and social ties. Intercolonial trade preceded the migrations that created an intercolonial family. Marriages and migrations strengthened the trade relationships and created webs that were not solely social or economic but both. As well, the family's experiences and the presence of other Dutch and New Netherlanders on the Eastern Shore illustrate that the intercolonial world of Virginia was not limited to other English colonies but very much included the Dutch New Netherland.

In particular, the lives of merchants Anna Varlett and Augustine Hermann illustrate the ease with which Dutch-connected merchants operated in Virginia and Maryland. (Though Hermann was Czech rather than Dutch, he came to Virginia from New Netherland and is identified in the Chesapeake primarily by those ties.) Both Varlett and Hermann were immigrants from New Netherland whose financial success in Chesapeake–New Netherland trade and ability to use Virginia's county and colonial courts to their advantage suggest that they held recognizably important positions in the colony. Violet Barbour has argued that Dutch women in early modern Europe more commonly engaged in long-distance trade than did other European women, and Dennis Maika and Martha Shattuck note that in New Netherland women were merchants and considered their husbands' business partners.[75] That Anna Varlett was active as a merchant even after moving to Maryland and Virginia suggests that Dutch women's participation in such trade extended across the Atlantic not only to New Netherland but also to parts of English America. Susan Moseley's descriptions of her decision (discussed above) to sell her jewelry for cattle shortly after arriving in the Chesapeake from Rotterdam provide further evidence that Dutch trading practices affected those women and men with Dutch heritage, even after they moved to English colonies where they were surrounded by English settlers whose expectations of women's commercial roles were probably quite different. The lack of any objection or even remarks in English Chesapeake records may suggest that women traders were familiar to English colonists for whom Dutch trade was important economically.[76] At least one Dutch woman in the Chesapeake continued to follow Dutch rather than English naming practices, using her name

Barbarah DeBarette rather than her husband's (Garrett Vanswaringen); more notably, the Maryland court recorded her name following Dutch practices, even as she was being naturalized in 1669.[77]

Ann Taft (or Toft), a spinster living in the Pungoteague region of the Eastern Shore (where Anna Varlett had her plantation), did business and made personal and economic contacts from New England to Jamaica, providing further evidence that in this region with significant Dutch presence gender conventions may have been different than elsewhere in English colonial America. On June 19, 1666, Taft appointed Connecticut governor John Winthrop Jr. her attorney to recover her half of the goods in the ketch *Virginia Merchant* (belonging to Dutch merchant Simon Overzee), to be returned to the Port of Pungoteague according to an agreement made on January 16, 1665.[78] In 1669 Ann Taft was still shipping goods in the *Virginia Merchant* (by then known also as the *Providence*). This time she was trading between the Eastern Shore and Nevis, in the Caribbean, and when difficulties arose the Northampton County Court sent an envoy to Nevis to gather information. When the envoy was instructed to seek the help of Nevis lieutenant governor Col. James Russell, Ann Taft, apparently acquainted with Russell, assured the Northampton court that Russell could be trusted to see to a thorough examination of the concerns of the *Providence*.[79]

Ann Taft also owned a four-thousand-acre plantation in Jamaica's St. Elizabeth's Parish. In 1672 she conveyed the land "along with all negroes, &c." to the executors of Eastern Shore intercolonial merchant Edmund Scarborough (the merchant who had brought forty-one Africans from Manhattan to the Eastern Shore), apparently to repay debts she owed his estate.[80] Taft did business that involved her in at least three other colonies and required that she make personal contacts throughout the Atlantic world. Her residence in a county with Dutch settlers, her repeated use of a ship owned by Dutch immigrant Simon Overzee, and her trade with Scarborough and others familiar with New Netherland may have eased her entry into a commercial world not commonly the domain of English colonial women.

Dutch and New Netherland merchants and settlers provided important economic contacts for many English colonists in the seventeenth-century Chesapeake. Financial concerns weakened ethnic prejudices and significantly reduced any Chesapeake commitment to English metropolitan mercantile visions. Such easy incorporation of Dutch merchant activity and settlement in the Chesapeake did not occur without Dutch cooperation. The apparently conscious effort some Dutch merchants made to fit in—by Anglicizing their names, Anglicizing their boats' names, speaking English, and seeking out coreligionists—contributed to their easy acceptance in Virginia and Maryland, which may have provided leeway for Dutch women to maintain independent economic activity. A. G. Roeber has noted a lack of Dutch attachment to any separate ethnic identity in New Netherland/New York, a pattern that seems to have held in the Chesapeake and been part of a commercial strategy aided by shared religious identity.[81] Seventeenth-century Virginians' frequent dependence on Dutch merchants and seamen for sufficient access to European goods and markets and African slaves, particularly during the English civil war, affected English colonists' perspectives on international rivalries and on national and individual goals of colonization in ways that facilitated significant Dutch involvement in local Chesapeake society.

Notes

1. John R. Pagan, "Dutch Maritime and Commercial Activity in Mid-Seventeenth-Century Virginia," *Virginia Magazine of History and Biography* 90 (1982): 485–501; Jan Kupp, "Dutch Notarial Acts Relating to the Tobacco Trade of Virginia, 1608–1653," *William and Mary Quarterly,* 3rd ser., 30 (1973): 653–55; Claudia Schnurmann, "Atlantic Trade and American Identities," this volume; Susie M. Ames, *Studies of the Virginia Eastern Shore in the Seventeenth Century* (Richmond, Va.: Dietz Press, 1940), 8–9, 45–67; Philip Alexander Bruce, *Economic History of Virginia in the Seventeenth Century,* 2 vols. (New York: G. P. Putnam's Sons, 1896).

2. Douglas Deal has also noted that the Eastern Shore "had more than its share of wealthy Dutch residents, who expanded the already existing commercial network that linked several prominent merchant-planters on the Shore with Dutch traders and ship captains on both sides of the Atlantic; but that network dissolved abruptly after the first of the Anglo-Dutch wars"; see J. Douglas Deal, *Race and Class in Colonial Virginia: Indians, Englishmen, and Africans on the Eastern Shore during the Seventeenth Century* (New York: Garland, 1993).

3. See Charles R. Boxer, *The Dutch Seaborne Empire, 1600–1800* (1965; repr., London: Penguin Books, 1990), for a discussion of the central place of the Dutch in seventeenth-century Atlantic shipping.

4. Most familiar is the 1619 Dutch ship that brought "twenty and odd" Africans into the James River. Because of its location, New Amsterdam was a common stopping point between New England and Virginia, and so Virginians' Dutch and New England trades overlapped. For example, Eastern Shore merchant Stephen Charleton and ship captain John Stone owned the pinnace *Virgine* together and used it to trade corn from Virginia to New England. On at least one occasion Stone stopped in New Netherland en route to New England to get water. See David Peterson [Pietersz] De Vries, *Voyages from Holland to America,* AD 1632–1644, trans. Henry C. Murphy (New York, 1853), 63–64; Susie M. Ames, ed., *County Court Records of Accomack-Northampton, Virginia, 1632–1640* (Washington, D.C.: American Historical Association, 1954), xxxvii, 22–23.

5. In 1631 Gov. John Harvey granted a commission to William Claiborne to trade with the Dutch. During the Protectorate, Capt. William Whittington and Eastern Shore merchant William Kendall made a contract with Jacob L. van Sloot to ship tobacco to Manhattan. See Ames, *Studies of the Virginia Eastern Shore* (1940), 47, citing Northampton Wills & Deeds, 1657–66, 33.

6. Pagan, "Dutch Maritime and Commercial Activity," 491, cites De Vries, *Voyages from Holland,* 112, 183; "A Perfect Description of Virginia" (1649), in Peter Force, ed., *Tracts and Other Papers Relating Principally to the Origin, Settlement, and Progress of the Colonies in North America,* vol. 2, ed. Peter Force (Washington, D.C.: P. Force, 1838), 14.

However, Ames states that in 1648 twelve of thirty-one ships trading to Virginia were Dutch, citing George Beer, *The Origins of the British Colonial System* (1908; repr., Gloucester, Mass.: P. Smith, 1959), 356.

7. Pagan, "Dutch Maritime and Commercial Activity," 491.

8. See Bruce, *Economic History of Virginia*, 2:324, citing Berthold Fernow, ed., *Documents Relating to the Colonial History of the State of New York*, 15 volumes (Albany, N.Y.: Weed, Parsons, and Co., 1856–87), 14:77. Barbadians made similar efforts to ensure access to Dutch traders during the 1640s, not just to provide shipping during the Civil War but also because the Dutch controlled access to the enslaved Africans that Barbadian planters used increasingly beginning in that decade as they began to make the transition from tobacco to sugar production.

9. The law read that "[i]t shall be free and lawfull for any merchant, factors or others of the Dutch nation to import wares and merchandizes and to trade or traffique for the commodities of the collony in any shipp or shipps of their owne or belonging to the Netherlands"; see William Waller Hening, ed., *The Statutes at Large; Being a Collection of All the Laws of Virginia, from the First Session of the Legislature, in the Year 1619*, vol. 4 (Charlottesville: University Press of Virginia, 1969), 258.

10. In 1655 Edmund Scarborough purchased slaves in Manhattan and had to petition the Dutch Council for permission to return to Virginia. The council decided that it was "the opinion of every one having been asked, to grant the request," provided that Scarborough give five thousand pounds bail that he and his mariners would not enter the Delaware Bay. Mr. Thomas Willett paid security for Scarborough. Willett, a merchant and shipowner who traded between New England and New Netherland, lived in New Plymouth and New Amsterdam. When he went to New Amsterdam in 1644, William Bradford sent a letter of recommendation to New Netherland governor Peter Stuyvesant, referring to Willett as his special friend who desired to continue trade with the Dutch. See Ames, *Studies of the Virginia Eastern Shore* (1940), 49, citing Fernow, *Documents*, 12:94.

11. H. R. McIlwaine, ed., *Journals of the House of Burgesses of Virginia 1619–1658* (Richmond: Virginia State Library, 1915), 74; discussed by Pagan, "Dutch Maritime and Commercial Activity," 493 n.

12. Ibid., 76.

13. Pagan did find complaints from Virginians that the acts disrupted shipping, but he notes that illegal trade continued during the 1650s; see Pagan, "Dutch Maritime and Commercial Activity," 496–97. Barbados, for which Dutch trade was as, if not more, important, also resisted submitting to the Interregnum government and was forced into submission by the same fleet that went to Virginia.

14. Ames, *Studies of the Virginia Eastern Shore* (1940), 48–49. A prominence in intercolonial trade of individuals who had both Puritan and Dutch ties may have originated in the communities of English Puritan exiles in the Netherlands. As well, the strong positions of New England and New Netherland in intercolonial trade may have given Puritan and Dutch Virginians an advantage in intercolonial trade.

15. Pagan, "Dutch Maritime and Commercial Activity," 498–99; Ames, *Studies of the Virginia Eastern Shore* (1940), 49–50.

16. Dennis J. Maika, "Jacob Leisler's Chesapeake Trade," *de Halve Maen* 67 (1994): 11. According to Maika, "Trade between Manhattan and the Chesapeake continued uninterrupted after the English imperial government's intrusion into New York in 1664," though

Cathy Matson argues that by that time the 1660 Navigation Act had already altered tobacco trade routes so that less Chesapeake tobacco went through New Netherland en route to Europe (Cathy Matson, *Merchants and Empire: Trading in Colonial New York* [Baltimore: Johns Hopkins University Press, 1998], 18).

17. On April 25, 1655, Richard Hincksman petitioned Oliver Cromwell that his ship *Rose of London* be allowed to proceed to Barbados with stranger mariners because he was unable to hire enough English seamen for the voyage; see W. Noel Sainsbury, ed., *Calendar of State Papers, Colonial Series 1574–1660: America & West Indies,* vol. 8 (London: Longman, 1860), 423, no. 42.

18. Clerks may have been responsible for the Anglicization, but Foxcroft's name is spelled consistently by multiple English clerks, suggesting that he was in part responsible. On February 12, 1674, Charles II wrote a "Declaration in favor of the subjects of the United Provinces" to all admirals and governors of foreign plantations that Isaac Foxcroft, master of the ship *Carolus Secundus,* had come into the kingdom on encouragement from the king. Charles wrote to the colonial officials that he had granted Foxcroft permission to sail with English goods for Virginia "with his own outlandish seamen" and to trade as freely as a natural-born subject. See W. Noel Sainsbury, ed., *Calendar of State Papers, Colonial Series, 1669–1674* (London: Eyre and Spottiswoode, 1889), 553, nos. 1219–20.

19. For another discussion of Dutch renaming of ships to avoid the Navigation Acts, see Claudia Schnurmann, "Atlantic Trade," 8.

20. J. Douglas Deal has expressed doubt that these pieces of evidence suggest particular Dutch influence on Eastern Shore slavery; see Deal, *Race and Class in Colonial Virginia,* 165, citing Northampton Deeds 1651–54, fol. 204. He is arguing against Breen and Innes, *Myne Owne Ground.* But given the dearth of evidence about the arrival of any slaves, these two pieces of evidence linking Eastern Shore slave trade to Dutch sources are significant.

21. Deal, *Race and Class in Colonial Virginia,* 165, citing Nell M. Nugent, *Cavaliers and Pioneers: Abstracts of the Virginia Lnad Patents and Grants, 1623–1800,* 4 vols. (Richmond, Va., 1934–1979), 1:328; Land Patent Book 4, 35, Library of Virginia; and Elizabeth Donnan, *Documents Illustrative of the Slave Trade to the Americas,* vol. 3, *New England and the Middle Countries* (New York: Octagon, 1965), 414, 449.

22. Hening, *Statutes at Large,* 536–40; Pagan, "Dutch Maritime and Commercial Activity," 497. See also James A. Rawley, *The Transatlantic Slave Trade: A History* (New York: W. W. Norton, 1981), 86.

23. For a discussion of the importance of shared Puritanism to seventeenth-century Atlantic commerce, see David Ormrod, "The Atlantic Economy and the 'Protestant Capitalist International,' 1651–1775," *Historical Research* 66 (1993): 197–208; Bosher, "Huguenot Merchants," 77–102. For the concentration of Puritans on the Virginia and Maryland Eastern Shores, see Babette M. Levy, "Early Puritanism in the Southern and Island Colonies," *American Antiquarian Society Proceedings* 70 (1960): 133, 139–149; James Horn, *Adapting to a New World: English Society in the Seventeenth-Century Chesapeake* (Chapel Hill: University of North Carolina Press, 1994), 56.

24. Ormrod, "Atlantic Economy," 204–5, cites D. W. Jones, *War and Economy in the Age of William III and Marlborough* (Oxford and New York: B. Blackwell, 1988), 256.

25. De Vries, *Voyages from Holland,* 183–84.

26. Ibid., 187–89.

27. On April 12, 1651, Rotterdam merchant Edward Booker discharged Thomas Allen of Lynnhaven from all debts incurred up to that point. This may have been the same Thomas Allen who transported his kinswoman from Barbados to Virginia, trading beef for sugar. See Norfolk County, Wills and Deeds C, 1651–56, 65, December 15, 1653.

28. Charleton was a member of the first vestry in 1635 and became a councillor in 1640. He was elected to the House of Burgesses in 1645 and 1653. He traded with New England from the early 1630s and later with New Netherland as well. By the time he died in 1654 he had patented a total of 3,950 acres on the Eastern Shore. See Ames, *County Court Records of Accomack-Northampton, 1640–45,* xiii. Edmund Scarborough traded with New Netherland peacefully until 1651, the date of the first Navigation Act directed against the Dutch carrying trade. John Fisher testified that he, employed by Edmund Scarborough, had made five voyages to the Delaware Bay and Susquehanna River to trade and that until the last voyage nothing had been demanded by Dutch or Swedes for customs. John Dollinge, one of Scarborough's factors, testified that on the fifth voyage, in the Delaware Bay, New Netherland governor Peter Stuyvesant demanded by violence one hundred pounds, "pretending it to be due for customs for this present voyage and the former voyages." Then, Andreas Hudson, acting governor in Stuyvesant's absence, asked Dollinge only four months before the last voyage to advise his principal (Scarborough?) to confine his trade there and to certify him that he should have no trouble or hindrance. The skipper and the pilot of Scarborough's *Sea Horse* also described a "piracy" committed by the Dutch West India Company: on the company's orders, the *Sea Horse* and its crew were carried to Fort Nassau, where their English colors were pulled down and Dutch colors put on their vessel. See Ames, *Studies of the Virginia Eastern Shore* (1940), 47.

29. On December 15, 1654, the court, after Mason showed that Lloyd had been indebted to Scapes for nineteen hundred pounds of tobacco, ordered administratrix Elizabeth Lloyd to pay (Norfolk County, Wills and Deeds C, 1651–56, 116a).

30. On May 7, 1654, John Parker gave all his chattel (after his debts were paid) to Thomas Workman, the son of Thomas Workeman of the little creek of Lynnhaven; the elder Workeman was to be his executor (recorded November 25, 1654, Norfolk County, Wills and Deeds C, 1651–56, 107).

31. The brother's name seems to be John Depotter (Norfolk County, Wills and Deeds C, 1651–56, 127–127a); the will was dated November 2, 1654, and recorded on February 15, 1655. Vincent also willed to his wife Elizabeth Vincent (who lived in England) one hundred pounds if she were alive.

32. On January 29, 1654, Gov. Richard Bennett at Nansemond ordered Mr. Francis Emperor and Mr. William Jermyn to appraise Vincent's estate. The long and complicated inventory included £15 for the bark's hire and payment of £3 14s. 6p. for carpenter's work and expense on the bark in Manhattan. The appraisal included holland cloth, tobacco, tobacco paid for boat hires, and wage payments to several men, including one with the Dutch name Cornelius Corneluson, as well as payments to Vincent for several trips to Nansemond with his boat. See Norfolk County, Wills and Deeds C, 1651–56, 129–31a, February 7, 1654, Elizabeth River.

33. De Vries, *Voyages from Holland,* 112–13.

34. Dutch denizenships and naturalizations in the seventeenth-century Chesapeake far outnumber those of any other European nation. Of 133 seventeenth-century Maryland naturalizations and denizenships that identify nationality or place of origin, just over one-half

(69) are from the Netherlands or New Netherland. The other 64 include immigrants of Swedish, French, Portuguese, German, Scottish, Spanish, and Danish origin. See Jeffrey A. Wyand and Florence L. Wyand, *Colonial Maryland Naturalizations* (Baltimore: Genealogical Publishing Co., 1986), 1–9.

35. For example, on November 23, 1669, Laurance Vanslot came to the Accomack County Court with a denizenship certificate from the Virginia Assembly; Vanslot "freely & willingly" took the oath of allegiance and supremacy, and became a denizen (Accomack County, Virginia, Order Book, October 16, 1666–January 26, 1670, Virginia Historical Society, MS 3Ac275a, typescript by Susie May Ames, 1942–46, 375. A denizen was a foreigner who received citizenship but could not hold public office or inherit real property. See Ames, *Studies of the Virginia Eastern Shore* (1940), 47–48 n.

36. As a result of this Dutch presence, the Anglo-Dutch War of 1652 caused problems for Dutch settlers and English officials on the Eastern Shore. Dutch settlers complained of "a ruinous violence, suddenly to be acted upon them," though it is not clear whether they meant physical or economic violence. The county commissioners asked the Virginia Assembly for help. The assembly, by an order of July 1653, sent several councillors to accompany the governor and the secretary across the bay "for the settlement of the peace of that county." See Ames, *Studies of the Virginia Eastern Shore* (1940), 8–9, citing Northampton County Deeds and Wills, 1651–54, fol. 162; Hening, *Statutes at Large*, 384.

37. Doodes was involved in Norfolk and Lancaster counties as well. For Doodes, see "Minor Family," *William and Mary Quarterly*, 1st ser., 8 (1899–1900): 196–98; and Charles M. Blackford, "Four Successive John Minors," *Virginia Magazine of History and Biography* 10 (1903): 97. Others I have not yet tracked down. In 1666 denizenships were granted for Andrew Herbert (who moved from Manhattan) and William Martin (from Delaware Bay), who moved with their families to Virginia; and for John de Young, a Dutchman (and "of the reformed Religion"), who married an Englishwoman, and Cornelius Noel (also of the "reformed Religion"), both of whom had lived in Virginia as freedmen and as servants. See "Randolph Manuscript," *Virginia Magazine of History and Biography* 17 (1909): 243–45. The Rappahannock County record of Noel's 1686 (April 27) naturalization explicitly stated that he was "borne in Holland." See "Historical and Genealogical Notes," *William and Mary Quarterly*, 1st ser., 27 (1918–19): 136.

38. For Custis, see "Proceedings of the House of Burgesses," *Virginia Magazine of History and Biography* 8 (1901): 391. For Cock, see Mrs. P. W. Hiden, "Smiths of Middlesex County, Virginia," *William and Mary Quarterly*, 2nd ser., 10 (1930): 215.

39. Ties between the two regions after the late 1640s, when some Puritans from Lower Norfolk (many of them merchants) migrated to the Eastern Shores of Virginia and Maryland to escape persecution, were strong. The remaining Puritans in the two regions (some of whom became Quakers) maintained communication with one another. Francis Yeardley was one of the most prominent of these migrants. He continued to travel between the two regions after he moved from Lower Norfolk to the Eastern Shore.

40. Some Chesapeake immigrants identifying themselves as coming from Holland were English who, for religious or commercial reasons, had moved to the Netherlands. Because Dutch immigrants to Virginia and Maryland Anglicized their names, it is not always possible to tell whether someone moving from Holland was of Dutch or of English descent. In either case, their presence strengthened Chesapeake-Dutch ties and weakened any sense of ethnic difference.

41. Norfolk County, Wills and Deeds C, 1651–56, 24–25a, recorded November 10, 1652, emphasis mine.

42. Overzee witnessed documents between Rotterdarn and Chesapeake merchants. See, for example, the 1651 debt release between William Harris and Francis Yeardley, Norfolk County, Wills and Deeds C, 1651–56, 8, 24. On April 15, 1652, Peter Barrister, gunner of the ship *Virginia Merchant,* belonging to Mr. Simon Overzee, brought "tydings that the Sd Shipp beinge cast away, in the River of Piscataway in Newe England, the Gunnes whereof were landed on the Sd Shoare wch Gunnes were diminished by One Capt: Samson Land [Lane?], ye takinge fower of them wth him to the Barbadoes" (Norfolk County, Wills and Deeds C, 1651–56, 9a).

43. Edwin R. Purple, "Contributions to the History of the Ancient Families of New York, Varleth-Varlet-Varleet-Verlet-Verleth," *New York Genealogical and Biographical Record* 9 (1878): 53–62, 113–25; 10 (1879): 35–38. For this and other citations on the Varlett family, I am indebted to Daphne Gentry for unpublished research notes on the life of Anna Varlett Hack Boot, compiled for the Library of Virginia.

44. Purple, "Contributions," 53–62. The three daughters who did not move to Virginia were Maria; Catherine, who married François de Bruyn of New Amsterdam; and Judith, who married Nicholas Bayard (the son of Samuel Bayard and Anna Stuyvesant Bayard Varlett). The one who married Bayard was accused of witchcraft in 1666 but lived until after 1707.

45. They lived on Pungoteague Creek on Virginia's Eastern Shore. George and Anna probably married during the 1640s. The first mention of George Hack on the Eastern Shore was on December 28, 1651. The couple may have traded with Anna's brother or father or sisters and may have moved in order for Nicholas to have a Virginia family for his tobacco importing. Nicholas may have been the source of the slaves they imported. Dr. George Hack patented one thousand acres Northampton on October 12, 1652, four hundred acres in Northampton County on July 1, 1653, and one thousand acres in Northampton County on September 23, 1661. See Nugent, *Cavaliers and Pioneers* (1623–66), 1:265, 285, 412. He was also granted four hundred acres at Anna Catherine Neck in Maryland in 1659. See Ralph Whitelaw, *Virginia's Eastern Shore: A History of the Northampton and Accomack Counties,* 2 vols. (Richmond: Virginia Historical Society, 1951), 685–86.

46. Hening, *Statutes at Large,* 499. The following month the assembly confirmed the grant. See H. R. McIlwaine, ed., *Journals of the House of Burgesses of Virginia, 1619–1658/59* (Richmond, Va.: Colonial Press / E. Waddey, Co., 1915), 112. On October 11, 1660, Hack petitioned the assembly to have his denizenship confirmed, which it did provided he and his family lived in Virginia for two years (McIlwaine, ed., *Journals of the House of Burgesses of Virginia, 1659/60–93,* 10). The following January 14 Hack petitioned that the March 1658 denizenship be renewed, which it was provided he took the oaths of allegiance and supremacy (ibid., 11). "Whereas George Hacke had formerly a commission of denizacon granted him in the year 1658 and hath petitioned in behalf of himself, his brother [Seraphin, later killed by Indians] and children that the same might be renewed to him and conferred on them, the Grand Assembly" confirmed providing they took oaths (McIlwaine, ed., *Journals of the House of Burgesses of Virginia, 1619–58/59,* 131).

47. The last New Amsterdam record with her name was in January 1661; see Purple, "Contributions," 54.

48. While in New Amsterdam in 1651 and again the following fall, she and the merchant Augustine Hermann were codefendants in several lawsuits, some instigated by her brother's brother-in-law, Gov. Peter Stuyvesant; see Purple, "Contributions," 54. George Hack was also plaintiff in New Netherland lawsuits.

49. For a discussion of women's merchant activities in New Netherland, see Dennis Maika, "Commerce and Community: Manhattan Merchants in the Seventeenth Century" (Ph.D. diss., New York University, 1995), 206.

50. In 1655 George Hack rented one hundred acres to a man whose payment included a day's work to help Hack in "reaping English grain" (Ames, *Studies of the Virginia Eastern Shore* [1940], 40, citing Northampton County, Wills and Deeds 9, 1657–66, 27).

51. In spring 1654 Hack and the Dutchman Evert Jacob(son) sued one another in the Northampton County Court regarding Holland cloth that Hack had traded Jacobson for tobacco. See Northampton County Court Order Book, March 28, 1654–June 28, 1661, typescript by Susie May Ames, Virginia Historical Society MS 3N8125a, folder 1, 15. There are four folders: (1) Northampton Co., Va. Court Order Book for March 28, 1654–January 28, 1654/55; (2) Order Book for March 28, 1655–June 5, 1657; (3) Order Book for January 29–October 28, 1657/58; and (4) Order Book for October 28, 1658–June 28, 1661. Each one is paginated separately. The April 28, 1654, jury found for Jacobson in all cases. The following month Dr. George Hack sued Evert Jacob concerning a hogshead of tobacco received for Holland; the court ordered that Hack pay Jacob all charges in the suit (ibid., 16). On April 28, 1654, Jacob(son) sued George Hack, declaring that on an action of debt for 438 pounds of tobacco, which the jury ordered Hack to pay (ibid., 6a). Holland cloth appears frequently in Eastern Shore lawsuits and inventories. Hack shipped tobacco with John Vines, master of the bark *William and Jan* of Northampton, to New Netherland merchant Cornelius Steenwick. Steenwick received the hogsheads in good condition and had paid twelve guilders apiece for them. His testimony was partly in English and partly in German. Ames does not give the date but says this occurred during the Protectorate. See Ames, *Studies of the Virginia Eastern Shore* (1940), 47–48, citing Northampton County, Wills and Deeds 9, 1657–66, 27.

52. Whitelaw, *Virginia's Eastern Shore*, 1:685–86.

53. The head rights included George Nicholas Hack; Sepherin Hack; An(n) Kathrine Hack; Domingo, a Negro; George, a Negro; Kathrine, a Negro; Ann, a Negro; Hendrick Volkerts; Rònick Gerrits; Bermon Nephrinninge; Giltielmus Varlee (Varlett?); Augustine Hermons; Barnard Ramsò; Augustine Rieters; Adrian Ramsò; Claus Gisbert; Brigitta Williams; and Cornelis Hendrickson (Northampton County Court Order Book, 1654–61, folder 4, 32–34, April 5, 1659).

54. Purple, "Contributions," 54–57.

55. Charles Gabry and Peter Stuyvesant sent letters of attachment from Manhattan for the tobacco that Scarborough paid Hack for Hermann. They sent the letters by way of the ship captain John Dolling, who took them to the house of John Custis. Dolling told Scarborough to detain the tobacco "in the [warehouse?] of the sd Gabry here in the Country" until further order from Gabry. Scarborough waited to hear from him, but no order came, and "the tobacco lay in Virginia until it rotted." See Northampton County Court Order Book, 1654–61, folder 1, 39, March 5, 1655, recorded September 20.

56. Hermann's public complaint may have been enough to ensure Stringer's payment. As Stringer was a trader to New Netherland, his reputation with Hermann was important.

On May 28, 1657, two months after the tobacco was due, Hermann, "of Amsterdam in the New Netherlands Merchant," took the bond, with Stringer's signature, to the Northampton County clerk. Living Denwood of Northampton, gentleman, testified on Hermann's behalf. By May all acceptable tobacco from the previous year's crop was gone, so Hermann was unlikely to collect that year. The clerk wrote that the amount due (seven thousand pounds of Virginia tobacco) was "a considerable Summe & quantitye of Tobacos," which Stringer was to deliver between Nuswattocks and Kings Creek in Accomack by the end of the following March. The amount was for half of the *Beginning*. This record refers to Hermann as Harmanson. See Northampton County Court Order Books, 1654–61, folder 2, 108–9.

57. In early May, Custis went to Grace Vaughan's house and demanded twenty hogsheads of tobacco. Grace Vaughan told John Custis that there were only five or six of Augustine Hermann's hogsheads at her house. Custis replied that Augustine had informed him of twenty hogsheads of tobacco that she would send with him to the Dutch. She said that she intended to send some tobacco to the Dutch plantation but that it was not ready yet and she was not certain how much there would be. Custis asked when it would be ready and complained that the only reason he had bothered with Augustine's tobacco was because he had been led to believe that the total quantity would be larger. See Northampton County Court Order Books, 1654–61, folder 3, 13–15.

58. For Custis's naturalization see discussion above and n. 38. Hermann had asked Living Denwood to deliver notes to Custis listing all the people from whom he would collect tobacco and instructing him to take all the tobacco so collected in his boat to one place. See Northampton County Court Order Books, 1654–61, folder 3, 11–12.

59. Northampton County Court Order Books, 1654–61, folder 3, 13–15.

60. Burrell gave Augustine Hermann's canoe to Vaughan as receipt (Northampton County Court Order Books, 1654–61, folder 3, 35–36). John Reyne testified that in late May he packed tobacco for Mrs. Vaughan and had intended to go to the Dutch plantation with it; he went with Thomas Teakle and John Waltam to John Custis's house, where the tobacco was being stored (ibid., 10–11).

61. Ames, *Studies of the Virginia Eastern Shore* (1940), 66.

62. Jannetje may have been dead by the time of Hack's death. By the following November she was; on November 8, 1665, Augustine Hermann wrote his first will, which said that he wished to be buried next to his wife. Hack's will, written and proved in Accomack County, provided for Anna "while she stays here and for her transportation up the Bay," indicating that she may have planned to move permanently to Maryland to be with the Hermanns after her husband died. See Accomack County Deeds and Wills, 1664–71, 11. George Hack's inventory included twenty-two books in high German and Dutch, fifty-four in Latin, and twenty in English. The will, written March 5, 1665, and proved April 17, 1665, stipulated that half of his estate was to go to Anna and that the three children were to divide the other half. In September 1665 a Northampton County, Virginia, patent for one thousand acres previously granted to George Hack went to Anna and her sons, George Nicholas Hack and Peter Hack. See Nugent, *Cavaliers and Pioneers* (1623–66), 1:525.

63. Their petition read, in part: "Augustine Herman of Prague in the Kingdom of Bohemia Ephraim Georgius and Casparus Sons to the said Augustine Anna Margarita Judith and Francina his daughters Anna Hak George and Peter her sonnes That whereas

the said ... Augustine Herman was borne at Prague in Bohemia & that ... his Sonns & Daughters were born at New York ... And that Anna Hack borne at Amsterdam in Holland George & Peter her sonnes borne at Accomacke in Virginia have long there inhabited and now removed into this province ... That your Lop humble peticoners and every of them shall from henceforth be adjudged reputed & taken as Nrall borne people of the province of Maryland" (*Proceedings and Acts of the General Assembly of Maryland, April 1666–June 1676*, vol. 2 of *Archives of Maryland* [Baltimore: Maryland Historical Society, 1884], 144–45). This is confusing, however, because there is also a Maryland denizenship for Hermann "late of Manhatans Merchant" recorded on January 14, 1660 (*Proceedings of the Council of Maryland, 1636–1667*, vol. 3 of *Archives of Maryland* [Baltimore, 1885], 398).

64. On April 16, 1666, Anna Hack petitioned to be discharged from the judgment against her husband for transporting eleven head of cattle. The order had been passed shortly before her husband's death, and Anna told the court that she was not able to pay, that Hack's partner Maccary had moved up the bay, and that the petitioner and her poor children were likely to be utterly ruined and were every day expecting an execution on the small estate left for her and her children's maintenance—"to be onliterated and in full service against principal John Maccary." See [Accomack County] Deeds and Wills, 1663–66, 119–20. In 1666 Anna had three tithables; see [Accomack County] Deeds and Wills, 1664–71. It seems likely, given her continued trade to New Netherland and her decision to have a new boat built, that her description of herself as poor may have reflected her attempt to avoid the fine rather than an actual inability to pay it.

65. Anna Hack was to find plank and a barrel of tar, and Fookes was to find nails and spikes and to make a mast and boom fitting for the sloop. Fookes at first engaged himself to be finished by December 25, 1665. On March 18, 1667, the court appointed the jury to hear the case "betweene mr Nicholas Boot plt and mr James Fookes deft" (Accomack County Order Book, 1666–70, 50). The court records of 1667 included the original articles of agreement; the jury found that Fookes did not perform his contract but that no damage had been proven (ibid., 89–90, July 16, 1667; Ames, *Studies of the Virginia Eastern Shore* [1940], 142–43).

66. Hermann complained to the court that Fookes's failure had cost him the expense of traveling down to Accomack himself about his concerns, which otherwise would have been brought up to him (Accomack County Order Book, 1666–70, 90, May 27, 1667). Hermann referred to her as "Mrs. Anne then the widow of Dr George Hack now wife of Mr Nicholas Boot." The case illustrates the cooperation between mariners and the way in which their dependence on one another for materials created the need for communication. On July 16, 1667, William Chase testified that the previous February, Anna (Hack) Boot sent him to Mr. Martindale's ship to get some rigging for his sloop and bolt ropes for the sails. On July 4, 1667, Thomas Saywell testified that the previous September, Anna had bought a sail from the ship *Daniell of Dublin* (on which he was then a crewman) and had it delivered. Within a few days of her purchase, the ship was loaded and had departed. Saywell (or the clerk) referred to her as "the widow of Goorge VanHack" (ibid., 91).

67. In April 1657 John Custis collected 1,453 pounds of tobacco from Eastern Shore merchant William Kendall for the use of Nicholas Boot and sent to Manhattan by his order an additional 1,320 pounds, which paid Kendall's accounts in full (Northampton County Court Order Books, 1654–61, folder 3, 9, January 29, 1658; see also ibid., folder 4, 55a, November 28, 1659).

68. Boot had settled in Gloucester County during the 1650s. On September 16, 1660, Robert Jones, aged thirty-six, testified that he was present in the chamber of Col. Samuel Matthews, deceased, when Mr. Boate brought some papers for him to sign (McIlwaine, *Journals of the House of Burgesses,* 1659/60–93, 10).

69. Boot's will was written January 9, 1668, proved April 8, 1668, and recorded April 18 ([Accomack County] Deeds and Wills, 1664–71, 68). Nicholas was sometimes referred to as Claus. Boot and also appears as Boodt, Bout, Boat, or Bootsen. Anna Varlett's name appears last in a commercial transaction in 1677. On July 8, 1685, her two sons qualified as administrators of her estate, and on December 22, 1685, they referred to her in a deed as "Ann our mother lately deceased." See *Archives of Maryland,* 2:144–45.

70. On January 10, 1670, Anna Varlett (Boot), as widow of Nicholas Boot, acknowledged that on November 17, 1668, she had made Cornelius Vanhoofe her attorney and confirmed that he was to act as her attorney in the Gloucester County Court to sell 150 acres on Pepper Creek to William Plummer (Accomack County Orders and Wills, 1671–73, 20).

71. On January 25, 1671, Lydia Prichard testified that she had heard Anna say that she would have no partner with her in the sloop ownership and that she was "a widdow woman and had nobody to do her business for her" and so concluded to sell half of the sloop to Cornelius Vanhoofe for fifty-five hundred pounds of tobacco. Vanhoofe agreed and gave her a bill for tobacco to be paid, deducting what she owed him for his former service in her employment. Anna Varlett (Boot) replied that if she could trust him with her sloop she could as well trust him with the remainder of the tobacco and so made the bill of sale. See [Accomack County] Orders and Wills, 1671–73, 58.

72. On September 18, 1672, the court appointed two referees to audit the differences in accounts between Cornelius Vanhoofe and Anna Boot; see [Accomack County] Orders and Wills, 1671–73, 134. On November 19, 1672, the General Court ordered the Accomack County Court to rehear the case; see H. R. McIlwaine, ed., *Minutes of the Council and General Court of Colonial Virginia, 1622–1632, 1670–1676* (Richmond, Va., 1924), 320.

73. January 16, 1672 ([Accomack County] Orders and Wills, 1671–73, 48).

74. September 11, 1674 ([Accomack County] Wills, etc., 1673–76, 180). The following month (on October 8) Anna Boot patented 1,350 acres in Accomack, 900 being part of 1,000 granted her under the name of Ann Hack widow, 450 for nine persons including William Varlett and Kath Varlett. See Nugent, *Cavaliers and Pioneers* (1666–95), 2:158. Her business activities apparently involved more than transporting the products of her plantations for imports from New Netherland. In 1668 in Accomack she commissioned John Richards to make her nine tables, ten forms, twelve cupboards, six spinning wheels, and four chests. He was to finish the work within twelve months, but on August 19, 1673, she sued him because he still owed her the work. See [Accomack County] Orders and Wills, 1671–73, 224.

75. Violet Barbour, "Capitalism in Amsterdam in the Seventeenth Century," *The Johns Hopkins University Studies in Historical and Political Science* 67 (1949): 140; Maika, "Commerce and Community," 206; Martha Dickinson Shattuck, "A Civil Society: Court and Community in Beverwyck, New Netherland, 1652–1664" (Ph.D. diss., Boston University, 1993), 164.

76. English records in Virginia refer to Dutch women by their unmarried (or previously married) names more often than is the case for English women, though this may have been because of their activity as merchants rather than because of their nationality.

77. The naturalization record lists entries for Garrett Vanswaringen "born in Reensterdwan, Holland"; Barbarah DeBarette "born in Valenchene, in the Low Countries when under Spanish rule"; Elizabeth Vanswaringen "born in New Amstel, daughter of Garrett and Barbarah"; and Zacharias Vanswaringen "born in New Amstel, son of Garrett and Barbarah" (Wyand and Wyand, *Colonial Maryland Naturalizations,* 5).

78. Endorsed June 28, 1666, "Mrs Ann Taft To the Honoble John Wintropp Esqre Govmor of the Southern parts of New England" (Winthrop Papers, Massachusetts Historical Society, Boston, microfilm reel 8).

79. Ann Taft indicated to the Northampton court members that she knew Governor Russell and that he was trustworthy and qualified to carry out their requests (Accomack County Order Book, 1666–70, 94–95, 261–62).

80. The executors had instructed Vassall to send the slaves back (to Virginia?) and declared that they intended to desert the plantation. The Jamaica Council ordered that Scarborough's executors, within the following twelve months, make clear that they really intended to settle the land "and comply with the bonds for bringing on their number of hands." If not, the land was to return to the king to be disposed of as the governor pleased. See St. Jago, Minutes of the Council of Jamaica, 1672, in Sainsbury, *Calendar of State Papers, Colonial Series, 1669–1674,* 382, no. 881.

81. A. G. Roeber, "'The Origin of Whatever Is Not English among Us': The Dutch-Speaking and the German-Speaking Peoples of Colonial British America," in *Strangers within the Realm: Cultural Margins of the First British Empire,* ed. Bernard Bailyn and P. D. Morgan (Chapel Hill: University of North Carolina Press, 1991), 220–83. Such a conclusion would confirm the work of David Ormrod and J. F. Bosher about the importance of Calvinist Protestantism to Atlantic trade, which is particularly noticeable in Virginia, a colony whose officials were attempting to define it as Anglican even at times during the Interregnum. See Ormrod, "Atlantic Economy"; Bosher, "Huguenot Merchants."

Official Duplicity

The Illicit Slave Trade of Martinique, 1713–1763

Kenneth J. Banks

In late November 1736 the captain of the French coast guard vessel *St. Jacques,* one Dupont, spied an English ship off the French sugar island of Martinique. Dupont ordered his crew to give chase. The *St. Jacques* boarded the English ship easily, for it was heavily laden with slaves, riding low in the water, and expecting no harassment from a French vessel. The English ship was a slaver, the *Scipio*[1] out of London, crammed with at least 240 slaves locked below decks. To the astonishment of the English captain, Alexander McPherson, and his sailors, Dupont placed a prize crew on board, and the two vessels sailed in tandem to Martinique's main port of St. Pierre. McPherson was brought before the French Admiralty court on charges of smuggling. He protested vigorously, arguing that his ship had strayed into French waters by mistake, driven by strong winds and currents near what he thought was the neutral island of Dominica. Despite some support for the English captain from local French mariners called to testify on sailing conditions, the court found McPherson guilty, fined him personally one thousand livres, and ordered his ship confiscated and its miserable human cargo sold. Already many of the African prisoners on board were ill, so a local merchant hastily arranged an auction, although not before the three chief officials of Martinique took two slaves each, as was their due by custom in smuggling cases.[2] The remaining slaves were snapped up within two hours on labor-starved Martinique. Among those presumably benefiting from the sale were the governor-general of the French Windward Islands (or Îles du Vent) and the governor of Martinique, both of whom owned extensive plantations. McPherson and his English crew were allowed passage to Antigua, where the seizure immediately became a cause célèbre championed by the colony's governor, who claimed that the French were merely retaliating for his seizure of two French vessels, also accused of smuggling, the previous year. The case dragged on for another four years before reaching the highest diplomatic circles at Versailles and the Court of St. James.[3]

The affair of the *Scipio* highlights one small corner of the enormously important, highly complex, and yet scantily studied problem of illicit trade in the early modern Atlantic world economy. Many studies touch on illicit trade, and even proclaim its importance, but few have analyzed the problem in any depth. As the seizure of the *Scipio* suggests, smuggling proved to be a far more complex matter encompassing imperial designs, local commercial and planting interests, and official participation. The boundaries of what constituted contraband were not agreed on by the European nations competing in the Caribbean: one nation's smuggler was another nation's legitimate merchant. Most striking, and the least commented on, is the strangely acquiescent role of colonial officials regarding illicit trade in general and slave smuggling in particular.

Historians have been highly ambiguous in their treatment of official complicity in smuggling. One of the first such historians, and arguably still the finest, Richard Pares, cites example after example of both English and French colonial authorities' explicit roles in illicit trade. Yet he mitigates his charges by insisting that government efforts to suppress contraband trade were genuine, and that official involvement depended on the personality of the officer. Although shocked by smuggling, Pares argues, officials authorized it since they were unable to stop it. He contends that "even if the officers had always been honest, they had very little power" to enforce penalties against smuggling.[4] Since the appearance of Jean Tarrade's work on the *Exclusif mitigé* in 1972, historians have gradually accepted a more complex interplay of royal designs, metropolitan mercantile interests, planters' demands, and *philosophe* theories of commerce in the formulation of royal ordinances aimed at suppressing illicit trade.[5] Tarrade nevertheless echoes the ambiguity between official suppression and unofficial support by faithfully reporting government edicts to suppress smuggling while sketching the outlines of a voluminous illegal trade encouraged by officials. For example, Tarrade observes that the Comte d'Estaing, the newly appointed governor of St. Domingue in 1765 (and later the admiral who ensured American independence at Yorktown), believed that "hindering interlope commerce [the eighteenth-century French term for smuggling] is a pretension which my personal experience has demonstrated to be useless." Yet only a few pages earlier (see p. 335, n. 6), Tarrade states that in the same period d'Estaing concluded a notorious contract with a New England merchant to carry Acadians to St. Domingue and shiploads of prohibited New England products in the process.[6] Later historians perpetuate the same confusing assessment, being content, as Liliane Crété is, to sympathetically note that "[g]overnors and Intendants were torn between their duty and their good sense" in stamping out illicit trade.[7] Did colonial officials simply accept the ubiquity of illicit trade and muddy their own hands when it was to their personal profit? Or did officials systematically engage in smuggling and consciously support a culture of contraband? The issue is important for it colors our perception of the Caribbean's role in the economy of the early modern Atlantic world. Did the Caribbean function merely as a ground for self-enrichment and exploitation, or was it a testing ground for new concepts and networks of free trade?

Because of the nature of smuggling as an extralegal activity, its volume and means are extremely hard to investigate or even estimate. There are three major obstacles to studying smuggling. The first is the attempt to grasp the enormity of the trade. In the eighteenth century colonial officials could only report on activity within their jurisdictions. It was up to the Ministry of the Marine, which directed France's overseas colonies, to make the linkages, and the staff of three to five who handled the massive volume of all colonial correspondence were either unable or perhaps unwilling (given the workload) to compile any overview. At this stage of early bureaucratization and national records management, it also may not have occurred to them to do so. The second problem is recognizing the multiple forms of smuggling based on commodities, methods, people, and the regions involved. Poorer French farmers, supplementing their incomes from cassava farms on the officially neutral island of St. Lucia with smuggling ventures, had different needs and resources than did an English slave ship sailing directly from West Africa. Each type of contraband imposed unique demands and problems. Even within the realm of slave smuggling, two kinds of smuggling existed: a large international traffic involving the English, Dutch, Portuguese, and Spanish; and an apparently smaller, but no less worrisome, domestic one involving French ship captains. Each had different political ramifications and led to very different spectrums of attempted solutions by the state. The third problem is related to sources. Most historians have relied exclusively on official complaints about smuggling to document the problem. As the seizure of the *Scipio* suggests, officials were hardly a disinterested group.

These three challenges can best be met by examining one aspect of contraband on a single island. As the most important French possession in the New World in the seventeenth and first half of the eighteenth centuries, Martinique offers rich documentation and the added advantage of geographical compactness. Second, by concentrating on slave smuggling, we are better able to see its relation to other forms of contraband. It can be suggested that slave smuggling in fact provided the foundation on which all other contraband depended and shows clearly how the state intervened to handle both international and domestic smuggling. Expanding the source base to include official reports on diplomatic matters and on colonial social relations, interested corporative bodies, and unofficial reports and letters by merchants provides insight into the intricacies and transatlantic dimensions of illicit trade. The mercantile correspondence of Nantes merchants in the departmental archives of the Loire-Atlantique are particularly valuable. Nantes, the preeminent slave-trading port in France, stood to lose the most from slave smuggling, and its merchants were at greater pains to point out irregularities to the Ministry of the Marine, which directed France's overseas colonies.[8] This essay is an overview of slave smuggling on the French island of Martinique with a focus on the role of colonial officials. While the evidence is far from conclusive, it would appear that from at least the War of the

Spanish Succession (1702–13), French colonial leaders did not merely tolerate smuggling but used their positions to foster an elaborate contraband economy within the context of prevailing patron/client relationships.[9] The three top officials, the governor-general and the intendant of the Windward Islands and the governor of the Island of Martinique, each had his own small staff, in addition to controlling the appointments of men, usually junior officers, to several lesser posts. These posts not only paid set amounts but also were stepping-stones to higher positions. While the upper-echelon officials were usually French, the lower were often drawn from the upper ranks of planter society (the *grand blancs*). Patron/client relations, then, had a transatlantic dimension, and it is possible to view the relations of lower- and upper-echelon officials as a form of exchange in which metropolitan protection and legitimization were traded for colonial contacts and support.

Illicit trade with the English, Spanish, and Dutch began with the first occupation of Martinique and Guadeloupe as pirate bases in 1635.[10] By most accounts, a Dutch refugee from Brazil, Daniel Trexel, established the first French sugar plantation on Guadeloupe in 1639, using experienced slave workers he had brought with him. Not surprisingly, he relied on the extensive trade contacts of his fellow Dutch to market his crop in northern Europe. Martinique and Guadeloupe were first under the jurisdiction of the Company of the Islands of America and then were sold in the late 1640s to their respective governors. Since there were no royal restrictions yet imposed, the colony's officials considered the trade with Holland perfectly legal, although perhaps a taint on French honor and a hindrance to regional groups of French-speaking merchants (Normans, Bretons, Poitevans), who were in competition with each other. The selling of slaves to develop Martinique's plantations progressed as a side venture to the much larger landing of slaves illegally in the Spanish Caribbean.[11] In 1664 Jean-Baptiste Colbert (the de facto secretary of state for the Marine) united the French Windward Islands under royal rule and initiated policies designed to destroy Dutch control of trade in the Caribbean. Colbert sought to harm Dutch trade in three ways: ejecting them by force, encouraging French shipping by lowering duties, and founding the Compagnie des Indes to aggressively import slaves from West Africa. These policies ultimately proved successful, although the third was distinctly the least successful. By 1680 the two hundred or so Dutch ships that had engaged in trade to the Îles du Vent had been largely replaced, although not totally eliminated, by a roughly equal number of French ships. Nevertheless, colonial governors continued to allow Dutch traders to import slaves: at least twelve thousand arrived in the Îles du Vent between 1664 and 1665.[12] In effect, Colbert's regulations policies outlawed what had been considered legitimate trade before 1664.

The illicit slave trade served as the impetus for illicit trade as a whole for one key reason: the successor companies to the Compagnie de Indes established after

1674 could never adequately supply the French sugar islands with enough plantation field slaves.[13] The formal addition of St. Domingue by the Treaty of Ryswick in 1697 immediately increased demands on an already inefficient system. The acquisition of the *asiento,* or license to land slaves in Spain's American colonies, by France in 1701 placed further strains on supply.[14] To acquire slaves for their own possessions, the French resorted to raiding the ships and towns of the Spanish Main, at least until 1697. During wartime they added English and Dutch targets as well. A spectacularly successful French naval raid against Spanish Cartagena by Governor Du Casse of St. Domingue in 1696 provided him and several fellow officers with enough specie to buy slaves from Curaçao and Jamaica. In another case, a French "naval" operation led by the Canadian Pierre Le Moyne, Sieur d'Iberville, carried off nearly eighteen hundred slaves from the English island of Montserrat in 1706 and held the planters there to ransom for an additional fourteen hundred. French pirates continued this tradition for a few years after 1713, although they sold their cargoes of slaves at French Grenada or neutral St. Lucia. At roughly the same time French metropolitan and colonial merchants forged contacts with foreign entrepôts. In 1700 the intendant of the Îles du Vent pronounced himself shocked to discover that even French ships were bypassing Martinique for the higher returns and ready specie at Danish St. Thomas and English St. Kitts.[15] Another problem appeared after 1713. With the rise of St. Domingue and the founding of New Orleans in Louisiana, French slavers shifted from supplying the Windward Islands to these newer, growing areas. As early as 1721 Martinique's officials noted with alarm the redirection of slaves to St. Domingue. French merchants believed that it was easier to collect long-term planter's debts, that they received higher prices for slaves, and that they had more opportunities to resell their human cargoes to the Spanish eastern side of the island.[16] From 1700 until the Seven Years' War, colonial officials continually bombarded the secretary of state for the Marine with complaints over the lack of slaves.[17] From the perspective of French planters and officials on the Windward Islands, the supply of African slaves to power the sugar mills existed at least as early as 1700 and merely accelerated during the phenomenal economic growth during the "Long Peace" of 1713–44. The number of slave laborers determined the amount of sugar, coffee, indigo, and other tropical products and also the amount of food and building materials needed to keep the plantations producing.

It is difficult to make any estimate of the size and profitability of smuggling as a whole, let alone that of contraband slaves. Some scattered official estimates for Guadeloupe after 1763 place that island's contraband trade in the range of 30–40 percent by value of all colonial produce shipped.[18] However, we can gain some idea of at least the potential size of the smuggling trade, as well as the potential profits, by comparing the perceived needs for slaves with the actual numbers imported. In the early part of the eighteenth century, when Martinique was the premier colonial produce-exporting island among French possessions, officials determined that some 11,651 African slaves landed on the island during the eight years between 1714 and 1721, augmenting the existing labor force of about 25,000. The high numbers reflect the desire by planters to replenish the labor force after the War of the Spanish Succession. In his correspondence the intendant considered these arrivals, about 6.6 percent of the existing slave population per year, to be barely adequate.[19] By 1736 one official complained that French slave ships never provided even one-quarter of the required replacements at a time when legal French imports averaged between 1,000 and 2,000 in the late 1730s. This meant a shortfall of 4,000, given the perceived need of about 6,000 slaves per year; that is, the French slave trade provided only 33 percent of the slaves needed. Three years later officials judged the shortage of slave labor to be acute, based on erratic arrivals of between 1,300 and 3,400 slaves per year.[20] In 1755 Intendant Hurson recommended that 25,000–30,000 slaves were needed each year in the entire French Windward Islands for an enslaved population of about 90,000–100,000. In the five-year period 1751–55 about 2,700 slaves on average were landed by French slavers in the French Windward Islands, or about 11 percent of perceived needs. Immediately after the Seven Years' War, Governor-General Fénelon recommended 40,000 slaves per year as a minimum to replace a total enslaved population of about 130,000. In 1763 French slave ships brought 1,238 slaves, about 3 percent of perceived needs, and these numbers barely rose in the next five years. Even at the height of the massive slave importation into occupied Guadeloupe (1758–63) and Martinique (1762–63) during the Seven Years' War, English slave ships managed to land just under 25,000 African slaves for the entire duration of the occupation, or about 20 percent of needs based on the lower prewar estimates.[21] At the same time, the French Windward Islands experienced a dramatic growth in exports and its enslaved population. During the 1700–1755 period sugar production increased 221 percent, coffee increased by nearly 700 percent (1730–55, after its introduction from 1727), and the slave population on Martinique alone rose from 14,600 to nearly 67,000.[22] Given the normally harsh conditions, which led to high death rates, and low birth rates associated with sugar plantation slavery, both the increase in the enslaved populations and the rise in export production could not be possible with the known slave imports to Martinique during this period.[23] It is probable that officials engaged in the common ancien régime practice of grandly overestimating the numbers needed in order to increase the number of people actually received and as a way of anticipating future growth in colonial produce exports. Even if we allow that officials in their estimates asked for triple the number of slaves actually needed, it is clear that after 1721 slave imports into Martinique provided only a fraction of the slave manpower required: 75 percent in 1736, 27 percent in 1755, and barely 10 percent in 1763. As a rough and conservative estimate based on these revisions of official perceptions, it is clear that from the late 1730s at least

1,000 extra slaves per year were desired by Martinique's planters, and this demand grew to perhaps 7,000 per year on the eve of the Seven Years' War. We can even pinpoint the mid-1720s as the last era when French slavers, however irregularly, supplied the French Windward Islands with a sufficient number of African laborers.

Given this incessant demand for more and more slaves, smugglers could expect enormous profits. Even in the "legal" sale of slaves, sick or young slaves fetched up to nine hundred livres (normally the price of a male field hand in the prime of life, or *pièce d'Indes*), and prime field hands up to seventeen hundred or eighteen hundred livres when arrivals were scarce. These sums are at least twice the amount normally paid, or at least those paid after currency stabilization after 1726.[24] Profits in the "legitimate" slave trade remain a point of debate for French slavers, but profits were probably higher than most other types of trades, at least before the beginning of the Seven Years' War in 1756. Official reports found by Tarrade for St. Domingue demonstrated that profits from slaving voyages decreased from 302 percent in 1753 to about 99 percent in the late 1780s.[25] The lower figure is still far above the normal return of 5–10 percent expected from most trade voyages. As the capture of the *Scipio* shows, there were other costs involved, including the privileges claimed by colonial leaders and the costs of advertising and mounting an auction. Smugglers evaded paying these costs, as well as the duties. Clearly, the potential profits for smugglers were enormous. Slaves were somehow reaching Martinique at precisely the same time that complaints over the scarcity of labor were loudest.

All forms of smuggling in and out of Martinique shared basic characteristics. Even the Marine understood the basic operations. These descriptions filtered into Versailles from irate chambers of commerce officials in the port towns, who in turn relied on the complaints and reports of French merchants and ship captains. Colonial governors and intendants proclaimed the severity of the problem but provided few details, perhaps because it may have appeared suspicious that an official could know so much. One such independent report by a naval captain found its way to the Nantes Chamber of Commerce. Lieutenant de Rossel, the first naval captain sent by the Marine to suppress smugglers in 1729, described the problem in some detail.[26] Smugglers landed goods and slaves, he reported, in the many sandy coves scooped out of Martinique's coast. In two of the smaller outports, Cul-de-Sac Marin and Vauclin, small sloops anchored offshore by prearranged agreement at night and could unload their cargoes using small skiffs or locally made boats (*canots*) within three hours. He implied that at least some minor royal officers protected the smugglers, noting that they seldom caught anyone in the few raids they undertook. But these were not the only venues. He believed that most of the exchange occurred in the "Neutral Islands" of Dominica and St. Lucia, which sandwiched Martinique between them in the arc of the Lesser Antilles. By 1700 French squatters and debt refugees had carved out their own simple farms and even some small plantations on the sufferance of the few remaining Carib islanders. Some English settlers had joined them, but neither European nation had enforced any jurisdiction over the islands by 1730. De Rossel reported that between fifteen and twenty English ships from Barbados or Antigua could be found at any one time at "the Carénage" in St. Lucia (today the capital city of Castries) trading with small schooners and even large canoes from Martinique. All negotiations were conducted on board, and barter appeared to be the rule.[27] Smugglers exchanged the mundane but essential items that kept the sugar plantations in operation: flour, meats, butter, wood planks, mules, iron tools, textiles, and above all, African slaves from Barbados.

Lieutenant de Rossel recognized, however, that the true heart of illegal operations remained the bustling port of St. Pierre, Martinique's commercial heart and largest town. St. Pierre nestled on a wide bay on the northwestern side of Martinique, where an open roadstead with steady winds allowed ships to anchor at all times of night or day. Wharves and sheds crowded a long, gentle arc of beach, making it difficult to isolate illegal activities and easy to clear off if soldiers or the militia attempted a raid. Moreover, ship captains found it easy to hide newly arrived slaves by blending them in with the large enslaved population of the port. In terms of sailing logistics, St. Pierre lay astride an important northwest-southeast axis of shipping routes that arched north to Guadeloupe and St. Eustatius. In this way the port served as an entrepôt of smuggled goods and slaves for Guadeloupe and the smaller French settlements northward.[28] This axis of trade could be extended north as far as the English mainland colonies of New York and Rhode Island. Southward the same route reached Trinidad and the Guyanas of the South American mainland. French ship logs of the eighteenth century stressed the ease of sailing up and down this axis. Of equal importance, Martinique enjoyed a reputation among ship captains as the second easiest island to find (second to Barbados) for ships from Europe or West Africa on the transatlantic run.[29] Returning to western Europe proved just as easy, which helps explain why Martinique's merchants maintained some illicit connections with Bermuda and the Portuguese Cape Verde Islands off North Africa.[30]

Sloops and brigantines from Martinique also roamed south to the Venezuelan coast, which opened two thorny problems: trading with the Spanish Main (legal in French eyes, illegal in Spanish) and trading to Dutch Curaçao (illegal in French eyes, legal in Dutch). However, the exchange of mainly French manufactured luxuries and wine for tobacco, cacao, leather goods, and mules for the island's sugar mills sputtered.[31] With these natural advantages, St. Pierre grew into a haven for pirates, corsairs, and smugglers during the 1680s. There is no dearth of reports by exasperated officials on the predilection for dealing in smuggled goods and slaves in St. Pierre. In 1714 a new intendant, Vaucresson, reported that his rigid measures to prevent smuggling had merely forced daytime landing into becoming a night-time activity, an observation echoed by a royal tax collector a quarter-century later and by Governor-General Bompar yet again in 1754.[32] While contraband could be traded anywhere, it appears that smugglers preferred St. Pierre, or secondarily the sheltered outports on the southern side of Martinique.

The assignment of responsibility to those engaging in illicit trade tells us more about metropolitan/colonial relations than anything else. Contemporary French accounts seem equally divided in blaming greedy merchants and competitive planters, the latter driven to outshine each other by imported clothes, jewelry, and furnishings.[33] Famed philosophe Thibault de Chanvalon noted the "ostentation" of the planters yet claimed that they were morally incapable of deceit. Planters blamed merchants and in particular the commercial brokers of St. Pierre, while French merchants blamed planters and the avaricious English.[34] However, most metropolitan officials took it for granted that all white colonists, whether ennobled planters or unemployed artisans, engaged in smuggling. A kind of communal conspiracy among white colonists seemed to be at the core of the problem. Intendant Blondel, writing in 1725, noted that "if a denouncer should be discovered amongst them [the colonists] he would find it hard going."[35] Surveying the situation in 1765, one anonymous official wrote: "Smuggling is here an epidemic disease, which infects all members of society, the small and the great, rich and poor, men of substance and their subordinates, gentlemen and rogues: all here engage in, tolerate, and protect this hideous commerce."[36] In his 1730 report Lieutenant de Rossel sided with local planters, who lumped colonial and metropolitan merchants together as the true culprits; de Rossel noted wryly that the French merchants who cried the loudest over the abuses of contraband were those most heavily engaged in it.[37] Even some members of the clergy were not above suspicion. The most infamous case concerned Father Antoine Lavallette, the manager or business agent (*procureur*) for the Jesuit mission in St. Pierre and later its superior. His spectacular bankruptcy, based on a sudden concurrence of losses during war, triggered the metropolitan reaction against the Jesuits and the subsequent investigation that ended with their banishment from France in 1762.[38] As early as 1756 Lavallette shipped sugar and coffee to a Dutch broker named Teminck in St. Eustatius, using the St. Pierre merchant partnership of Rachon and Cartier as a front to hide his activities. From St. Eustatius his cargoes traveled either to Amsterdam or to Cadiz, to be reexported (either the colonial produce itself or bills of exchange for them) to his agents Lioncy and Gouffre in Marseille.

Historians have accepted that the dominant players in all aspects of economic life in the French Windward Islands, including smuggling, were the "shady" commercial brokers of St. Pierre, collectively known as the *commissionaires*. These were colonially based (but not necessarily colonial-born) merchants who bought and sold merchandise on their own account, not as agents of French merchants or firms.[39] However, these charges must be used with caution. The original references to the *commissionaires* sprang from complaints in the mid-1720s by the Nantes Chamber of Commerce, most of whose membership were involved in the French slave trade and who remained an outspoken and bitter voice against both English slave smuggling and colonial debt repayments. These charges were reechoed notably by royal officials, who, as we saw in the *Scipio* affair, were themselves beneficiaries of slave shipments. It is striking that even in the official correspondence few *commissionaires* are singled out by name, although governors and intendants readily identified French ship captains who caused trouble. We remain largely ignorant of who the *commissionaires* were, who they married, how many existed, how much capital they controlled, or even how they arranged their financial operations.[40] It is also striking that these "shadowy" merchants, so vilified in the official sources, represented the only wealthy and literate residents in the islands who were not directly dependent on the patronage and favors dispensed by the governors and intendants. Many of the officials either were from the colonies or, as in the case of intendants, strongly identified with and represented planter interests to Versailles. Lieutenant de Rossel depicts the *commissionaires* in a distinctly positive light, as merchants who helped planters dispose of their sugar crops and supplied their needs on relatively good terms.[41] His views probably reflect a metropolitan bias, one not shared by metropolitan governors. Thus, while it is certainly reasonable to accept the charges against the *commissionaires,* it is equally plausible that these St. Pierre merchants were convenient scapegoats.

Historians routinely ignore one powerful group as major players in smuggling: colonial officials. Their complicity in smuggling is surprisingly well documented. The most common informing came from other officials, often new leaders eager to distinguish themselves from their predecessors or rivals, or distance themselves from the conduct of underlings. Some examples will suffice. In 1713 Intendant Vaucresson charged the late Governor-General Phélypeaux with slave smuggling. He noted that immediately after the proclamation of peace ending the War of Spanish Succession, an English merchant captain from Antigua anchored at the capital of Fort Royal and unabashedly demanded to "resume the old understanding," including the landing of slaves.[42] In 1744 a merchant at Cul-de-Sac Marin on Martinique's southern tip offered the king's lieutenant of the area a bribe of one hundred gold louis to his wife after being caught with 120 slaves from Barbados. Apparently known for her local philanthropy, the merchant suggested that the money be "distribute[d] to the poor." While one might commend this officer for his honesty, in the world of patron-client relations it had a price. The officer, Lt. Martin de Poinsable, recounted the incident to demonstrate his commitment to the king's service (*zèle*) and distance himself from the actions of his fellow officers, thereby pursuing his own advancement in the ranks. In the same letter he denied charges circulating among Canadian ship captains that officials regularly allowed English ships to dock in the port.[43]

Governor-General Caylus, himself a noted smuggler (see below), fingered his subordinates several times during his short stint as governor-general in 1745–50.[44] Nearly ten years later Governor Bompar and Intendant Hurson felt it necessary to report disciplinary actions against the king's major at the small port of Marin for allowing slaves to be landed.[45] The disciplinary action consisted of a written reprimand.

These examples are in addition to the lively "flag-of-truce trade" (*bateaux parlementaires*), as described by Pares, between French and English islands during wartime. Officially, these ships returned French prisoners of war to French soil, but they also served as convenient excuses for smuggling. Pares cites several examples of English governors in New York, Rhode Island, Pennsylvania, and Jamaica selling the rights to carry these prisoners to the highest bidder; French officials turned a blind eye to contraband.[46] The pervasiveness of slave smuggling might even provide the pretext to press for officially sanctioned slave imports. On at least one occasion Governor Champigny and the new intendant, César-Marie de Lacroix, asked permission to issue two-year licenses to Martinique ships that would trade for slaves in West Africa, as means of attacking the contraband sale in slaves. Given that Governor-General Champigny and his brother were both major plantation owners (on Guadeloupe and the neighboring island of Marie-Galante, respectively) and that both governors and intendants traditionally enjoyed a set number of slaves from each cargo landed, the requests should not be surprising. In addition, control over permissions would undoubtedly go to merchants who were patronized (or "protected") by the governor and the intendant. The minister of the Marine, Maurepas, flatly refused the request.[47]

Few officials engaged so enthusiastically in illicit trade as did Charles de Thubières, Marquis de Caylus, governor-general of the French Windward Islands during most of the War of Austrian Succession (1744–48). Historians have long suspected Caylus of engaging in an assortment of sordid activities.[48] However, we now know that he maintained a long and prosperous business relationship with the Roux family of Marseille while governor-general of the French Windward Islands. In one particularly revealing letter he requested that Roux handle some delicate business affairs, converting the profits from his illegal trading ventures through the neutral Dutch islands of St. Eustatius and Curaçao (using Teminck, the same agent Lavellette used), where the letters of exchange and produce would be shipped on Dutch ships to Amsterdam. If the letters and cargoes escaped capture by English privateers, Caylus directed, they were to be exchanged for other letters drawn on merchants in Marseille, where he had many debts to settle. "I ask you," he added, "to observe in all these transactions an inviolable discretion, since you know as well as I the consequences." He noted that the lack of convoys had forced the French Islands to rely on Dutch ships. He ended this extraordinary document by offering to be "useful" to Roux in some unspecified way in the future.[49] In many respects, Caylus managed his operations in a way typical of other sugar island merchants, who risked their money and their commercial reputations by engaging in illicit trade with neutrals or even direct trade with the English colonies. At the same time, he constructed the conditions under which contraband might thrive, since the de facto authorization to allow trade with the Dutch came from his desk. That Caylus was personally corrupt is clear. Of more interest is his offer to be "useful," which displayed more than politesse. Caylus was a client of the Marquise de la Villière, the mother-in-law of Maurepas and thus an influential player in the early court of Louis XV, and therefore no stranger to patronage. He signaled to Roux his desire to engage in reciprocity of action, a cornerstone of patron-client relationships. In passing we might note that from the letters it is hard to determine whether Caylus or Roux is the patron. This exchange reflects the merging of his social and economic roles as both sword nobility and merchant, at a time when trade and discussions over money still sent shivers down the spines of the French nobles.[50] While Caylus demonstrates one extreme of official corruption, the question remains whether he constructed these contacts on his own or adapted to a system already in place.

That smuggling for officials had already become semi-institutionalized is suggested in a rare, scathing report written in the personal hand of the Sieur de Neuville, director of the King's Domaine, the semiofficial state agency that in ancien-régime France oversaw tax collection. In 1739 Neuville advised newly arrived intendant Lacroix of the extent of the smuggling problem, only to be dismissed as overreacting.[51] Neuville decided to bypass Lacroix to reach the Marine and forwarded his letter privately on a merchant ship, and not with the official correspondence scanned regularly by clerks under the governor and the intendant. Among other charges, Neuville made several serious claims: that the royal ships sent to catch smugglers in effect ran a "protection" racket; that at least one English ship landed slaves with the knowing consent of the royal commander of St. Pierre; and that a royal clerk who wrote out the depositions on an English ship seized for smuggling in 1739 had to go into hiding for fear of his life from superior officers. Neuville cited as an instance of irregularity a letter he had intercepted that was written by the secretary of the king's lieutenant of St. Pierre, who happened to be the half brother of a suspected smuggler, one Gachet. The letter conclusively documented the landing of 101 slaves at a cove near the port by an English ship from St. Eustatius.[52] The confluence of these examples during the tenure of Governor-General Champigny may have marked a low point in Martinique corruption. But the continuity of official involvement throughout the first half of the eighteenth century is the most striking aspect. In short, while it was probably true that all members of Martinique's white society collaborated with smugglers at least some of the time, it is certainly true that only colonial officials, and their clients, were in a position to profit from those collaborations all the time.

To counter slave smuggling and limit contacts with foreign merchants in the Windward Islands, the state pursued two contradictory policies regulating trade and contact. First, the Marine gradually loosened the number of restrictions on shipping. From 1713 to the de facto acceptance of free trade by neutral merchants in 1756, there was a subtle, yet unmistakable trend toward freer trade to the West Indies. Efforts to reinvigorate the French slave trade after 1713 began with the issuing of the Letters Patent of 1716, which opened the French slave trade to free competition, cut duties on the produce exchanged for slaves from 5 percent to 2.5 percent (in effect lowering the tax on most of the sugar imported into the kingdom by half), and provided for the issuing of certificates to guarantee the trading privileges of ships from designated ports. These new regulations did not have the desired effect of rapidly increasing the slave trade. After a period of some confusion on both sides of the Atlantic, a definitive statement on state policies appeared in the form of the letters patent of October 1727, which remained the basic document governing colonial commerce until the end of the Seven Years' War.[53] These regulations awarded a monopoly of French commerce and commercial communications to a prescribed number of metropolitan ports. At the time the Marine proclaimed these new regulations as an introduction to freer trade since they increased the number of participating French ports (to fifteen). They also removed limitations on ports of origin for metropolitan products, including some Spanish ports in the circuit of French shipping, and for the first time allowed direct trade on some goods between Ireland and the French Caribbean islands.[54] The majority of the regulations, however, were clearly constructed to snuff out contraband. For the first time they identified French and foreign smugglers as enemies of French commerce, effectively as enemies of the state, and stipulated rules for their capture and punishment. Stiff penalties were assigned to smugglers, including the sentence of perpetual life as galley slaves if caught. Further unknotting of restrictions followed the 1727 regulations. New orders allowed salt beef to be imported directly from Ireland beginning in 1728 (the major product desired by white colonists), allowed direct trade with Cadiz in 1737 and with the Portuguese Cape Verde Islands in 1740, and permitted importation of butter and cheese from Denmark (which effectively legalized trade with Danish St. Thomas) in 1741.[55] These regulations were designed, according to official explanations, to supplement French trade, not as a replacement for it.

While the Letters Patent of 1727 tightened the grip of the state on colonial trade, it also opened important loopholes in what would otherwise appear to be draconian measures. Foreign ships suffering storm damage or in need of water were allowed to dock in thirteen major French Antilles ports, including St. Pierre, for a limited period of time. While cash was preferred for the funding of repairs or to obtain supplies, foreign captains were allowed to land part of their cargoes as payment, so long as they obtained permission from local authorities.[56] Foreign merchants, especially English captains from Barbados and Antigua, swiftly took advantage of the loophole. Claimed instances of storms suddenly increased markedly in the Lesser Antilles, and English ships that had been "hurricaned" began appearing regularly at St. Pierre.[57] Colonial officials carefully submitted the appropriate paperwork, but they could not disguise their complicity from metropolitan merchants, who protested vehemently to Maurepas.[58] Colonial leaders also took advantage of emergencies to issue trade licenses that contravened the regulations. In the most blatant case, Governor-General Champigny and Intendant Lacroix legitimized the entry of New England vessels between 1738 and 1740, when two (real) hurricanes struck Guadeloupe in successive years and a fire burned about half of St. Pierre. Although this led to a flurry of protests and culminated in Neuville's letter mentioned above, the minister of the Marine, Maurepas, merely scolded the two for "incautious action" and did not rescind their orders.[59] In the 1750s Governor-General Bompar and Intendant Hurson vehemently defended their decision to allow French ships to dock at Dutch Curaçao in case of pursuit by the Spanish Guarda Costa (coast guard), contrary to Marine orders. Although they based their claim on the well-known ruthlessness of Spanish customs officials, we should also note that Curaçao thrived as a major illicit transit port to the Spanish Main. Of course, the permissions to dock there (all French ships carried such permissions if sailing toward the Spanish Main) could only be obtained directly from the governor-general and the intendant.[60] In this respect, loopholes or exemptions increased the control over commerce that the top leadership in the Îles du Vent could exercise. Judging by the high volume of complaints against which these leaders defended their policies, they increased smuggling activity, whether they actually profited from it or not.

Less than a year after issuing the regulations, it had become clear that without patrols, the Letters Patent of 1727 were useless. The outgoing intendant of Martinique, Blondel, broached the idea to Maurepas of creating the colony's own *guarda costa* of four ships, with two to be kept sailing continuously around Guadeloupe and Martinique and with crews paid from prize money.[61] The Domaine would fund the patrols. By 1729 the Domaine armed two small ships, probably sloops (*pataches*), one based in Martinique and the other on Guadeloupe. They sailed irregular patrols of three to four weeks around these islands or, more rarely, Dominica and St. Lucia. Although no complete records of their activities have survived, the official correspondence provides us with an idea of the scope of their operations. Table 13 shows the year, location, and number of seizures made by these coast guard boats from their first year of effective operation until the period, by 1742, when colonial officials reoriented their tasks from catching smugglers to preparing for war. Most seizures were of boats, although on two occasions slaves who had already been landed on Martinique were seized. Clearly the bulk of activity occurred around the coasts of Martinique and Guadeloupe. It is perhaps not surprising that seizures were rare around the two known

Table 13: Contraband cargoes/ships seized 1729–1741, French Windward Islands

Year	Martinique	Guadeloupe	St. Lucia	Other	TOTAL
1729	2	0	0	0	2
1730	1	0	0	0	1
1731	1	5+	1	0	7+
1732	2	3	0	2*	7
1733	3	3	1	0	7
1734	1+	0	0	0	1+
1735	0	4+	2+	0	6+
1736	1	2	2	1**	6
1737	2	3+	1	0	6+
1738	0	0	0	1**	1
1739	4	2+	0	0	6+
1740	1***	0	0	0	1
1741	1	0	0	0	1
TOTAL	19+	22+	7+	4	52+

*Both off St. Martin.
**Seized off Dominica.
***Seized thirty-eight slaves after landing near Ft. Royal.

and prominent smuggling harbors on the islands of Dominica and St. Lucia. The table also suggests that there seems to have been a "quota" of seizures at about seven vessels per year. About three-quarters of the ships captured were English vessels. Given the enormity of the trade (an estimated two hundred vessels were based in Martinique alone in the 1750s),[62] it seems probable that the French coast guard was barely effective. If these ships did not catch many smugglers, why were the patrols maintained?

A closer examination of the funding and use of these ships suggests that they were useful for tasks other than patrols. For example, in the year beginning December 1737, the sloop *St. Louis* patrolled Martinique for one month, returned, then ventured to Dominica for one month (confiscating a single vessel on the latter cruise), carried the new governor of French Guyana to Cayenne from March to June, was refitted on its return, cruised Martinique again for about two weeks in late August, left in early October for a month to help officials salvage royal property damaged during the hurricane that had ravaged Guadeloupe, and undertook a final cruise of the sea lanes between Martinique and Guadeloupe for about three weeks starting in late November. The other sloop was so damaged that it had to be replaced by a chartered ship for a short cruise in June (which returned empty-handed). The two vessels combined patrolled the waters for only four and a half months.⁶³ Given the cost of the ship (a "bargain" sloop cost twenty-nine thousand livres, roughly a third of the Domaine's yearly operating expenses), the victualing, the officer (appointed by the governor-general) and crew salaries (between sixteen and twenty for each ship), and maintenance, in light of the meager results it is difficult not to see the patrols as a type of government-subsidized employment, whose positions were controlled by colonial leaders through the Domaine. The director at this time, Neuville, indicated as much in his private letter to Maurepas.⁶⁴ Of course, officials consistently cited the patrols in their letters to Versailles as indicative of both their determined efforts to catch smugglers and the nature of the Sisyphean task involved. Although demonstrably ineffective, the new French officials who assumed control of the sugar islands after 1763 argued for the reintroduction of patrols. Perhaps benefiting from past experience, the Marine opted instead to send naval frigates directly from France.⁶⁵

At the same time that the state attempted to eliminate contraband by force, it also implemented procedures to control contraband by more efficient record-keeping. This second type of control applied not to foreign commerce but rather to a second form, the domestic smuggling by French slave-ship captains. To institute the new procedures the Marine simply increased the number of clerks and customs officials, a move that had the benefit of increasing the number of entry-level patronage positions under the control of governors and intendants in both France and the colonies. The problem of tracking slaves provides a good example of half-hearted implementation by authorities and easy evasion by merchants. In the regulations of 1716 the Marine firmly subordinated slave trading to French commercial interests and metropolitan needs. Application of the regulations rested on instituting simple declarations of merchandise, or certificates, that verified lawful exchanges of cargoes. As mentioned above, merchandise obtained from the sale of slaves was taxed at half the rate of other exchanges. Complaints were few until 1731, when the director of the tax-collecting agency in Nantes began rejecting the certificates because they were not properly signed by the intendants of either St. Domingue or Martinique. In addition, and rather incredibly, the regulations did not require the recording of the numbers of slaves landed, only the amount of merchandise traded for them.⁶⁶ This meant that captains could underdeclare their cargoes and sell the remaining cargo without paying duties, by exaggerating the cost of produce received in exchange. French tax officials charged that lower officials in both colonies had been forging the intendant's signature and issuing the certificates for a fee.⁶⁷ Since captains or supercargoes paid only half the customs duties, they could pocket the difference themselves.

By 1734 the Marine issued a new ordinance that outlined an improved certificate system.⁶⁸ At least two copies were ordered to be made for each document carried by a slave ship, with one to be deposited with the tax office in the French port of origin, one to be retained by the captain, and the original to be left with the Domaine's colonial office. Officials constructed the process so that any given ship's cargo could be tracked by authorities on either side of the Atlantic by comparing copies from one office with those deposited in the other. The cargo was in effect under bond until the certificates could be matched. The system was simple although highly labor-intensive, given that a ship's merchandise invoices alone often covered fifteen to twenty full manuscript pages. The system appeared to function smoothly until a scandal erupted on Martinique in 1741. The Marine discovered that clerks in Intendant de Lacroix's office at St. Pierre had again resorted to issuing false trade certificates for St. Domingue.[69] In another practice slave ship captains would sell part of their human cargo clandestinely in St. Pierre, load more slaves at St. Thomas or St. Eustatius up to the number just sold, and arrive at St. Domingue with the numbers complete and their papers in legal order.[70] Recognizing these abuses, tax officials in France issued new regulations and new forms in 1742. These new rules explicitly demanded that colonial officials adhere to making copies of each transaction, specified that exchanges were to be recorded in two columns so that the sale of slaves (presumably whether individually or by lot) corresponded with an exact amount and value of produce exchanged either immediately or to follow in the future, that the Domaine's clerks were to keep all bills, and that the records must show a final balance between the exchange of slaves and produce. Most important, only the clerks, not the captains, could write on the certificates and risked a five-hundred-livre fine for each contravention. Only when a ship arrived back in port with all the papers in order could the outfitters claim, in person, the duty reduction.[71] The slave traders of Nantes protested this new form immediately, calling the quest for more detailed information "ridiculous" and adding indignantly, "It is with this measure that the *fermier* [the tax-collecting agency in France] has begun to infringe upon the integrity of his Majesty."[72] Shortly thereafter the Nantes Chamber of Commerce recommended replacing the old handwritten forms with cheaper and standardized printed ones, and these new forms continued in use to at least 1758.[73] However, with the uncertainties of war in 1744–48 and the scramble to resupply the Îles du Vent after 1749, the use of these certificates appears to have been haphazard.

As France and England prepared for war in late 1755 and early 1756, another battle erupted in France over the control of contraband. Despite widespread opposition from merchants in the French ports, the new minister for the Marine, Moras, proposed that neutral ships from Holland and Denmark be allowed free entry into France's colonial possessions. French chambers protested that this freedom would only act as a "subtle poison [which] will creep into the hearts of our fellow citizens, only to bring discouragement, consternation and despair";[74] the Chambers won.[75] They demanded, and were accorded, the right to issue the passports, which some did issue, if sparingly. From a longer perspective, it was clear that the smugglers were winning the larger war. The business of smuggling had grown to become too important, with a tradition of support, or at least self-interested neglect, from colonial leaders. The point here is not to indict specific players, but to suggest that the very nature of the colonial economy demanded far greater commercial elasticity, particularly in the procurement of plantation slaves, than regulations could allow.

It appears from this brief inquiry that colonial officials may have used their offices as patronage positions, dispensing freedom to trade in slaves when and with whom they found it expedient to do so. What should be addressed in future research is whether patron-client relationships were a useful, or perhaps the only, way to develop and maintain rewarding and secure smuggling operations. We must also ask who these smuggled slaves were and how they fared after their importation into the French Windwards. How many were African, and how many Creole? What proportions were men, women, and children? Did they speak some English, Dutch, or another language, and if so, how did this condition their integration into a French Creole cultural milieu? Did they constitute a more rebellious group than slaves imported directly into the French colonies, as several French officials hinted?[76] It is perhaps the greatest irony, and the greatest shame, that we can learn more about illegal smuggling operations than about the African men and women on the *Scipio,* who were the objects of so much deceit.

With the end of war in 1763, and the subsequent reorganization of a new, but geographically compact French American empire centered on St. Domingue, the new minister of the Marine, Choiseul, on the urging of his Martinique-born *premier commis,* authorized the creation of several free ports in the French Caribbean, including the Môle St. Nicholas on St. Domingue and the Carénage on St. Lucia. Not surprisingly, these ports were well established as smugglers' dens before 1756. Yet the lack of slave labor continued to haunt the development of the French Windward Islands, even as the massive importations into St. Domingue created the foundation for an independent, black, and ultimately free Haiti.

Notes

1. French documents record the ship as *Le Scipion,* but it was actually the *Scipio.* See David Eltis, Stephen D. Behrendt, David Richardson, and Herbert S. Klein, eds., *The Transatlantic Slave Trade: A Database on CD-ROM* (Cambridge: Cambridge University Press, 1999), voyage 76573.

2. The governor-general of the French Windward Islands, the governor of Martinique, and the intendant claimed two each. This law, a kind of feudal privilege on labor, seems to have been established in the islands well before 1700.

3. Drawn from *Archives Nationales: Archives des Colonie, Centre d'Archives d'outre-mers* (hereafter *AC*), ser. C8A (Martinique), 47, fols. 250–67v., d'Orgeville to Maurepas, December 25, 1736.

4. Richard Pares, *War and Trade in the West Indies, 1739–1763* (Oxford: Clarendon Press, 1936), 344, 356, quotation from 397.

5. Jean Tarrade, *Le Commerce colonial de la France à la fin de l'Ancien régime: L'evolution de regime de l'exclusif de 1763 à 1790*, 2 vols. (Paris: Presses Universitaires de France, 1972), 1:55–85.

6. Ibid., 1:101–3; 104–5; quotation from 1:104–5.

7. Liliane Crété, *La traite des nègres sous l'Ancien Régime* (Paris: Perrin, 1998), quotation from 228; Charles Frostin, *Les révoltes blanches à Saint-Domingue aux XVIIe et XVIIIe siècles* (Paris: L'Ecole, 1975), 147–48; Robert Louis Stein, *The French Slave Trade in the Eighteenth Century: An Old Regime Business* (Madison: University of Wisconsin Press, 1979), 26–27.

8. Responsibility for the navy, coastal defense, and overseas colonies was joined and given to a secretary of state for the Marine, a position held first by Colbert from 1674. In 1736 Louis XV created the Ministry of the Marine, theoretically independent of the minister holding the position. For sake of clarity, I will refer to the "Ministry of the Marine" throughout.

9. On the now extensive literature on patronage, good introductions are Sharon Kettering, "P in Early Modern France," *French Historical Studies* 17 (1992): 839–62; and the classic work by William Beik, *Absolutism and Society in Seventeenth-Century France: State Power and Provincial Aristocracy in Languedoc* (Cambridge: Cambridge University Press, 1985). In an entirely different chronological and geographical context but also with valuable insights into patronage, see Kathryn Meyer and Terry Parssinen, *Webs of Smoke: Smugglers, Warlords, Spies, and the History of the International Drug Trade* (Lanham, Md.: Rowman and Littlefield, 1998), which concentrates on early twentieth-century China.

10. Louis-Philippe May, *Histoire économique de la Martinique (1635–1763)* (1930; repr., Fort-de-France: Société de Distribution et de Culture, 1972), 209–13; Jean Meyer et al., *Histoire de la France Coloniale* (Paris: Armand Colin, 1991), 70–71.

11. Wim Klooster, *Illicit Riches: Dutch Trade in the Caribbean, 1648–1795* (Leiden: KITLV Press, 1998), chap. 5.

12. Ibid., 109.

13. Frostin, *Révoltes blanches,* 146–47; Crété, *Traite des nègres,* 230–31; Stein, *French Slave Trade,* 26, 46–47.

14. Awarded at the outset of the War of Spanish Succession, indeed one of the areas of contestation, the contract called for a minimum of thirty-eight thousand slaves to be shipped to the Spanish American colonies over ten years during war, or forty-eight thousand over the same period during peace (Crété, *Traite des nègres,* 23).

15. AC, C8A 12, fols. 77–78v., Robert to Pontchartrain, January 8, 1700.

16. Crété, *Traite des nègres,* 226; see also, as an example, AC, C8A 60, fol. 240, Bompar & Hurson to Rouillé, May 9, 1754.

17. These are too numerous to list completely. For examples, see ibid., 27, fols. 129–33v., Fequières & Bénard to Marine Council, November 9, 1720; ibid., 47, fols. 306v–7, Givry to Maurepas, May 25, 1736; ibid., 65 fols. 102–4, Memorandum concerning the Negroes, [signed Ponthieu & Fénélon], March 30, 1763.

18. Tarrade, *Commerce colonial,* 1:109–12.

19. *AC,* C8A 29, fol. 264, Account of the Negroes which have been imported into Martinique since the First of January 1714, [signed Intendant Mesnier], August 22, 1721. These figures must be treated with extreme caution; according to one hasty 1719 census, Martinique had 35,472 slaves; on this point, see Christian Schnakenbourg, "Statistiques pour l'histoire de l'économie de plantation en Guadeloupe et Martinique, 1635–1835," *Bulletin de la Société d'histoire de la Guadeloupe* 31 (1977): 10 n. 7. What I believe is significant here is the perceived need by officials, which in turn reflects the perceived needs of major planters, who in turn were the largest purchasers of slaves.

20. *AC,* C8A 47, fol. 306v. Givry [Controller] to Maurepas, May 25, 1736; ibid., 50, fol. 28v., Champigny & de Lacroix to Maurepas, March 21, 1739; ibid., fol. 79–81v., Champigny & de Lacroix to Maurepas, July 10, 1739.

21. Ibid., 60, fol. 275–75v., Bompar & Hurson to Rouillé, November 29, 1754; ibid., 65, fol. 104, Memorandum concerning the Negroes [signed Ponthieu & Fénélon], March 30, 1763. All numbers of arrivals are drawn from Eltis et al., *Trans-Atlantic Slave Trade.*

22. Schnakenbourg, "Statistiques pour l'histoire de plantation," tables I-3, II-4, and III-7. Combining the totals for Guadeloupe and Martinique gives a number close to the totals cited by officials for 1755 and 1763. The tremendous growth of coffee production on Martinique may help to account in part for the population increase since coffee is usually associated with lower death rates.

23. On conditions on West Indian plantations, see, for example, Michael Craton, "Hobbesian or Panglossian? The Two Extremes of Slave Conditions in the British Caribbean, 1783–1834," *William and Mary Quarterly,* 3rd ser., 35 (April 1978); Richard S. Dunn, *Sugar and Slaves: The Rise of the Planter Class in the English West Indies, 1624–1713* (Chapel Hill: University of North Carolina Press, 1972); Gabriel Debien, *Les esclaves aux Antilles françaises (XVIIe–XVIIIe siècles)* (Basse-Terre, Guadeloupe: Société d'histoire de la Guadeloupe et Société d'histoire de la Martinique, 1974); Barry W. Higman, *Slave Populations of the British Caribbean, 1807–1834* (Baltimore: Johns Hopkins University Press, 1984). The figures after 1736, it should be underscored, are far greater than the 5 percent death rate of slaves cited by Tarrade for the 1763–89 period; see Tarrade, *Commerce colonial,* 1:50.

24. *AC,* C8A 29, fol. 111, Judgment Rendered . . . by Us, [signed Bénard], March 30, 1721; ibid., 60, fols. 226–28, Bompar & Hurson to Rouillé, March 6, 1754.

25. Ibid., 140–41 n. 66.

26. *Archives départementales de Loire-Atlantique* (Nantes, hereafter *ADLA*), C-735, fol. 6, Memorandum of Sieur de Rossel, December 1730. I have not yet been able to determine de Rossel's full name and background.

27. On the role of the Neutral Islands, see the invaluable section in Pares, *War and Trade,* 195–216.

28. Anne Pérotin-Dumon, "Commerce et travail dans les villes coloniales des Lumières: Basse-Terre et Point-à-Pitre, Guadeloupe," *Revue française d'histoire d'Outremer* 75 (1988): 278:36–38.

29. May, *Histoire économique,* 211–12; Kenneth J. Banks, "'Lente et assez fâcheuse traversée': Navigation and the Transatlantic French Empire, 1713–1763," in *Proceedings of the Twentieth Meeting of the French Colonial Historical Society,* ed. A .J. B. Johnston (Cleveland: FCHS, 1994), 80–95.

30. *Archives départementales de Gironde* (Bordeaux, hereafter *ADG*), 7B-1828, Pierre Pellet to Jean Pellet, May 31, 1727.

31. *AC,* C8A 39, fols. 367–68v., Memorandum on . . . the Windward Islands, [signed Blondel], December 6, 1728; ibid., F3 256, fol. 672, Maurepas to Lacroix, October 20, 1738; May, *Histoire économique,* 147–53.

32. *AC,* C8A 20, fols. 48–51, Vaucresson to Pontchartrain, April 11, 1714; ibid., 50, fols. 412–20v, Neuville [director of King's Domaine in St. Pierre] to Maurepas, November 17, 1739; ibid., 60, fols. 225–28, Bompar & Hurson to Rouillé, March 6, 1754.

33. *ADLA,* C-735, Letters of Monsieur X, Merchant in Martinique to Monsieur Y, Merchant in Marseille, August 1727. A cover letter to this piece explains that the printers at Chez Verger in Nantes were to edit and publish it; I have not been able to determine if this was done. While the letter may have in fact come from a merchant in Marseille, it is at least as likely that this was a literary device.

34. *AC,* C8A 39, fols. 473v.–76, Response from Martinique to the memorandum from Nantes dated October 7, 1727, April 1728, [unsigned, but marginalia indicates memorandum written on behalf of planters of the island]. I have not yet located the original Nantes memorandum; for the French view see, for example, *Archives de la Chambre de Commerce et l'industrie de Marseille* (hereafter *CCM*), Series H, box 20, Messieurs the Directors of the Chamber of Commerce of Guyenne to [those of] Marseille, April 4, 1726, 3.

35. Ibid., 34, fol. 133v., Blondel to Maurepas, January 14, 1725. Tarrade believes that the harsh penalties proclaimed in the 1727 regulations created a bond of conspiracy since no white colonial wanted to see a relative, friend, or neighbor punished by reduction to slavery on the galleys (Tarrade, *Commerce colonial,* 1:108). I have not found any record in the official correspondence that colonial courts ever meted out any punishment other than fines.

36. Anonymous military official writing in 1765, cited in Tarrade, *Commerce colonial,* 1:109 n. 83.

37. *ADLA,* Memorandum of Sieur de Rossel, December 1730, fols. 3–4v.

38. Camille de Rochemonteix, *Le Père Antoine Lavalette à la Martinique* (Paris: Alphonse Picard & fils, 1907), 136–37, 149–50, 165–66.

39. Modern historians have followed the lead of Louis-Philippe May and Richard Pares, who in turn followed earlier writers of the island such as Pierre Desalles and Sydney Daney. See Pares, *War and Trade,* 187–89, 290; May, *Histoire économique,* 217–18; Clarence Gould, "Trade between the Windward Islands and the Continental Colonies of the French Empire," *Mississippi Valley Historical Review* 25 (1939): 473–90; Tarrade, *Commerce colonial,* 1:31, 100–101; Dale Miquelon, *Dugard of Rouen: French Trade to Canada and the West Indies, 1729–1770* (Montreal: McGill-Queen's University Press, 1978), 92.

40. The destruction of St. Pierre's notarial records in the tragic eruption of Mount Pelée in 1902 destroyed bankruptcy proceedings, notarial records, and birth registrations used by historians and sociologists to reconstruct merchant networks in other ports.

41. *ADLA,* Memorandum of Sieur de Rossel, December 1730, fols. 1v., 3v.–4v.

42. *AC,* C8A 19, fols. 440v.–41, Vaucresson to Pontchartrain, November 2, 1713.

43. Ibid., C8A 56, fols. 133v.–136v., Poinsable to Maurepas, January 8, 1744, quotation from fol. 133v.

44. Pares, *War and Trade,* 353–55.

45. *AC,* C8A 60, fol. 225, Bompar & Hurson to Rouillé, March 6, 1754.

46. Pares, *War and Trade,* 356–57, 446–55.

47. AC, C8A 50, fols. 28–30v., Champigny & de Lacroix to Maurepas, March 21, 1739.

48. Sydney Daney, *Histoire de la Martinique depuis colonisation jusqu'en 1815,* vol. 2 (1846; repr., Fort-de-France: Société d'histoire de la Martinique, 1963), 119–26; James Pritchard, "The Naval Career of a Colonial Governor: Charles de Thubières, Marquis de Caylus, 1698–1750," in *Proceedings of the Sixteenth Meeting of the French Colonial Historical Society* (Lanham, Md.: University Press of America, 1990), 12–23.

49. *CCM,* box 9, no. 690, Caylus to Roux, August 16, 1747.

50. See, for example, William Doyle, *The Oxford History of the French Revolution* (Oxford: Oxford University Press, 1989), 26–30; Guy Chaussinand-Nogaret, *The French Nobility in the Eighteenth Century: From Feudalism to Enlightenment,* trans. William Doyle (Cambridge: Cambridge University Press, 1989), 86–113.

51. *AC,* C8A 49, fols. 297–308v., de Lacroix to Maurepas, August 8, 1738.

52. Ibid., C8A 50, fols. 412–20v., Neuville to Maurepas, November 17, 1739.

53. *ADLA,* C-741/5, January 25, 1716, Arrêt of Council of State . . . ; *AC,* A 25, fols. 51–56, Letters Patent of the King, April 1717; ibid., C-735, Letters Patent of October 1727.

54. Ibid., fols. 83v.–90, Letters Patent of the King, October 1727.

55. Ibid., fols. 143–43v., *Arrêt* of December 19, 1728; ibid., fols. 240–40v., *Arrêt* of September 30, 1737; ibid., fols. 258, *Arrêt* of December 27, 1740; ibid., fol. 258v., *Arrêt* of February 7, 1741.

56. Ibid., articles 11–16.

57. See, for example, *AC,* C8A 42, fols. 210–12v., d'Orgeville to Maurepas, June 8, 1731, quotation from fol. 211v.

58. Ibid., 41, fols. 73–78, Champigny & d'Orgeville to Maurepas, October 19, 1730.

59. Ibid., 49, fols. 18–28, Champigny & d'Orgeville to Maurepas, March 24, 1738; ibid., fols. 210–14, d'Orgeville to Maurepas, February 2, 1738; ibid., fols. 387–89v., Longueville to Maurepas, December 16, 1738; ibid., 50, fols. 141–54v., Champigny & Lacroix to Maurepas, November 21, 1739.

60. Ibid., 60, fols. 53–56, Memorandum on the Coasting Trade of the Windward Islands [signed Bompar & Hurson], December 24, 1753.

61. Ibid., 39, fols. 367–68v., Memorandum on the Intendant's position in the Windward Islands of America [signed Blondel], December 6, 1728.

62. Ibid., 59, fol. 158, Bompar & Hurson to Rouillé, November 14, 1751.

63. Ibid., 49, fol. 208–8v., d'Orgeville to Maurepas, January 10, 1738; ibid., fols. 216–17v., d'Orgeville to Maurepas, February 12, 1738; ibid., fol. 261–61v., d'Orgeville to Maurepas, May 23, 1738; ibid., fols. 269–70, de Lacroix to Maurepas, June 6, 1738; ibid., fol. 317–17v., de Lacroix to Maurepas, September 15, 1738; ibid., fol. 322–22v., de Lacroix to Maurepas, October 13, 1738; ibid., fol. 332–32v., de Lacroix to Maurepas, November 2, 1738; ibid., fols. 355–57, de Lacroix to Maurepas, December 10, 1738; ibid., 50, fols. 219–23, de Lacroix to Maurepas, January 28, 1739.

64. Ibid., 50, fols. 419v.–20, Neuville to Maurepas, November 17, 1739.

65. Tarrade, *Commerce colonial,* 1:105–6.

66. *ADLA,* C-741/28, In regard to the certificates for Merchandise derived from the sale of Blacks . . . , February 17, 1731; ibid., C-741/11, Ordinance of the King Roy regulating the style of certificates for the trade of Negroes in the French islands of America, July 6, 1734.

67. Ibid., C-741/62, Copy of observations . . . made by the Controller-General in regard to representations made by the Council of Nantes, September 27, 1733.

68. Ibid., C-741/11, Ordinance of the King . . . , July 6, 1734.

69. *Beinecke Collection of the Lesser Antilles,* Hamilton College, N.Y., NCH 1/76, fols. 18–19, Memorandum of Monsieur Lacroix, February 25, 1741.

70. *AC,* C8A 50, fols. 134–36v., Champigny & de Lacroix to Maurepas, November 6, 1739.

71. *ADLA* C-741/89, Ordinance of the King concerning the exemption accorded to merchandise derived from the Trade in Negroes . . . , March 31, 1742.

72. Ibid., C-741/92, Observations of the Guinea Merchants of Nantes . . . , March 8, 1742.

73. Ibid., C-741/90, Copy of a Letter Written by the Judges and Consuls of Nantes . . . , March 4, 1744.

74. *Chambre de Commerce de La Rochelle,* 24/8534, piece 8, Bordeaux Chamber of Commerce to the Count Garde des Sceaux, March 23, 1756.

75. Pares, *War and Trade,* 359–75, esp. 366.

76. For example, see AC, F3 259, fol. 287, Machault to Beauharnais, March 10, 1758.

The Spanish Empire and Cuban Tobacco during the Seventeenth and Eighteenth Centuries

Laura Náter

Due to its international prestige, Cuban tobacco was the Spanish Crown's option to compete in the European market. The strategy had two axes: (1) Seville, as elaboration, distribution, and export center; and (2) Cuba, as the main raw material supplier for Seville's factory. Since the 1680s Spain experimented with different ways to implement the strategy; this achievement was finally obtained in 1760 with the creation of the Havana *factoría*. But the success of the *factoría* lasted less than two decades. Its extreme dependence on Mexican silver prompted its early decline and eventual collapse.

From the beginning of the conquest of the Americas, the Spanish Crown's priority was to control mining in Peru and New Spain and bring an efficient and quick return of the wealth to the Iberian Peninsula. This led to the articulation of a restrictive commercial system in which the colonies became a source of precious metals and a closed market for Seville's commercial monopoly.

The other European powers of the time, which were determined not to be excluded from trade in the Americas, had recourse, at first, to piracy and looting. Ships attacked vessels carrying precious metals to Europe and to the Spanish settlements in the Caribbean. In both cases the objective was to take possession of the wealth monopolized by Spain. But in the first decades of the seventeenth century, Spain's competitors incorporated a new strategy. The Dutch, and later the English and French, established permanent settlements on islands that had not been efficiently populated by the Spaniards. Without abandoning piracy, they then concentrated on forging illegal commercial relationships with the Spanish colonies. This generated a growing and important smuggling network in the whole region, which shifted some Spanish wealth toward other European countries and thus undermined the Spanish power that continued to be based on commercial exclusivism.[1]

The situation got more complicated for Spain when the new colonies experienced what is known as the "sugar revolution" in the mid-seventeenth century. The non-Hispanic Caribbean islands became colossal sugar producers, offering impressive earnings to their respective metropoles at the same time that intense commercial traffic was generated in the Atlantic world. The so-called triangular trade, based on the three axes that sustained it (the Caribbean, Africa, and Europe), provided slaves to the nascent sugar plantations that needed abundant manpower, supplied the European sugar market, and distributed European-manufactured articles.[2]

The Caribbean became one of the most dynamic regions for international trade. Consequently, from the mid-seventeenth century to the end of the eighteenth, it was the stage on which many of Europe's rivalries in both commercial competition as well as warlike confrontation played out. Spain, in spite of preserving its more important colonies in the Caribbean and controlling the mining production of Peru and New Spain, was outmatched. Its commercial system of fleets and galleons was in decline. From 1669 to 1700 the fleet weighed anchor on only fourteen occasions, and the galleons involved never numbered more than eight.[3] This meant that Spanish colonies, particularly the poorest ones, did not have the necessary goods for the subsistence of their populations, nor a sure way to sell their products. Smuggling was almost their only alternative—and quite an attractive one—since Spain's enemies showed great interest in it and because it generated trade with the Hispanic islands.

Although Spain had not shown much interest in stimulating colonial industries, its agricultural concerns, especially cacao and tobacco, in this area increased. Paradoxically, the Spanish Crown did not, at first, decide to stimulate these crops officially. In the case of tobacco, for example, it preferred to combat smuggling by prohibiting cultivation for years in Santo Domingo, Cuba, Margarita, Puerto Rico, Cumaná, and Nueva Andalucia.[4] Instead of trying to control the trade, the Spanish authorities tried to eliminate production that their enemies could market. This could be interpreted as recognition of their weak standing in the commercial arena. The smuggling of tobacco nevertheless continued to increase, not only in the Americas but even on the Iberian Peninsula.[5]

The Spanish, however, faced a problem even more serious than smuggling. The only product in which they played a dominant international role was precious metals. These had to be used to pay state debts as well as for imports that, given the relative backwardness of Spanish industry, were quite considerable. Peninsular production was not enough to supply Spain's own necessities and those of her colonies. Due to these factors, the Spanish economy suffered a continuous leakage of gold and silver that could not be recovered because it did not have sufficient products to sell in international markets.

Beginning in the last two decades of the seventeenth century, tobacco became the option of the Spanish Crown in its attempt to overcome the described difficulties—though still in a weak and incipient way. When Spain's rival powers settled in the Caribbean, the region acquired great relevance in the context of Atlantic trade, and the Hispanic metropolis had to confront the problem of being at a serious disadvantage in mercantile competition. A great quantity of the empire's wealth escaped through smuggling. At the same time, it was the beginning of large-scale cultivation of tropical products, particularly sugar. Spain, in an effort to measure up to its rivals, turned to Cuban tobacco, which enjoyed a high price because of its prestige in Europe. The strategy consisted of the following: first, Seville would be converted into the center of elaboration, distribution, and export of tobacco products; second, but no less important, Cuba would become the main raw material supplier for the huge Seville factory.

Spanish regulation of tobacco began as an answer to the new commercial dynamics that had been developing in the Caribbean since the middle of the seventeenth century. But Spain had to wait almost a century longer to see its policies toward tobacco become really effective. This was achieved with the establishment of the monopoly in Cuba in 1760. However, the bases were initially established, with the first decree to regulate the tobacco business enacted in 1684. The logic of the political economy of tobacco did not change much from then on. In subsequent decades and through the eighteenth century, all efforts were directed to finding mechanisms that allowed effective instrumentation. When the Bourbons arrived on the Spanish throne, they did not discard this policy. On the contrary, they incorporated it as an important piece of their general policies of imperial renovation. The new dynasty maintained intact the logic of articulation of the tobacco complex, with Cuba as tobacco leaf production center and Seville as elaboration, distribution, and export center.

Tobacco vs. Sugar

During the seventeenth century the two tropical products in highest demand in Europe were tobacco and sugar. All the powers that settled in America experimented with one or the other. But the only place both industries flourished simultaneously on a large scale was in Brazil. In the Caribbean islands, which had more limited territory and smaller geographical variety, only one of these two crops succeeded, usually stimulated by the respective metropole.

Early British and French settlers in the Caribbean devoted themselves to cultivating tobacco in small plots. In fact, Fernando Ortiz has argued that tobacco was the main inspiration behind the early colonization of Spain's rivals.[6] England experimented in the 1630s with a nominal tobacco monopoly, and the French colonies were, in their first years, essentially tobacco producers.[7] But from the second half of the century on, big sugar-cane plantations displaced tobacco cultivation in the non-Hispanic Caribbean, except in Haiti, where the change took place later.

Since the early seventeenth century, tobacco played a prominent role among European countries battling to control Atlantic trade and to eliminate, as much as possible, enemy competition. In 1614, for example, the King of England established taxes on foreign tobacco to favor the tobacco grown by his colonies. In return, Felipe III of Spain lifted the prohibition on cultivating tobacco in his Caribbean territories and imposed capital punishment on smugglers. He was hoping to force the English to go to Seville and to pay dearly for the best tobacco of the time.[8]

Not long after the new colonies—especially in the Caribbean and on the North American continent, mainly Virginia—began to produce tobacco, a crisis of overproduction took place, causing a drop in prices. Nevertheless, tobacco-pricing scales also depended on the quality of the tobacco and on the care put into preparation and packing. The tobacco of the non-Hispanic Caribbean never achieved the levels of quality acceptable to the European market. At the end of the seventeenth century, an observer declared that tobacco arrived in Europe "dry, odorless, rusty, stuck together, worm-eaten, sandy and almost entirely rotten."[9] (He was referring to chewing tobacco—not tobacco for smoking or snuff—which was the dominant preference in Europe during the seventeenth and eighteenth centuries and, therefore, the most in demand.)

The decline in prices and the leaf's bad quality partly explain the change in crop focus in the middle of the seventeenth century.[10] But there were other explanations for the decline of tobacco and the rise of sugar. Dutch participation in the process was particularly important.

Foreign trade constituted the main reason for the prosperity of Amsterdam, which supplied all of Europe with tropical products. The earnings of the colonial trade, as much American as oriental, went directly to Dutch merchants' pockets. This led to the development of manufacturing centers to process the raw material, so that Amsterdam had factories to refine sugar and to produce powdered tobacco. The Dutch, furthermore, had settled in Brazil in 1624 and were the largest sugar producers until that moment. Their merchants, moreover, were prepared to offer the colonists of any nationality capital and technical knowledge, to extend them long credits for acquiring slaves and factories, and then to buy the resulting crops. With each new colony in the Caribbean, Dutch sailing increased and Spain received a hard blow. It is not surprising then, that the Dutch encouraged and aided the nascent colonies of France and England.[11] These two metropoles would eventually see the Dutch as rivals, but during the first half of the seventeenth century they were more concerned with creating a common front against Spain. For these reasons, the non-Hispanic colonies in the Caribbean had the necessary capital to undertake the big sugar enterprises that transformed them into colossal producers and the most profitable possessions of their metropoles. In turn, the colonies discarded the production of poor quality tobacco, the price of which was already in decline.

Although Spain had harvested cane in its Caribbean colonies since the beginning of colonization, Spain bet on tobacco. Before the end of the sixteenth century, the stagnation of the sugar industry in the Spanish Antilles was already evident. The noted specialist in sugar history, Sidney Mintz, has pointed out some factors that help explain that stagnation: (1) the scattering of the settlers toward Mexico after the conquest of Tenochtitlan (1519–21); (2) the Spanish obsession with precious metals; (3) the excessive authoritarian controls imposed by Spain on all productive private enterprise in the New World; (4) the chronic lack of capital for investments; and, (5) the so-called dishonor of the work attributed to the Spanish settlers.[12] The rigidity and inefficiency of the fleet and galleons system were also, without a doubt, decisive in the premature stagnation.

The Spanish Crown encouraged the emergence of early sugar industries in its Caribbean colonies to provide the islands with some form of subsistence. Nevertheless, the monarchy had no intention of making sugar a great source of revenue; it believed that the mines of Mexico and Peru would be enough. But when Spain's European rivals began to establish colonies in America and even snatched away important territories of the Greater Antilles (Jamaica and half of Hispaniola), other considerations began to appear.

The European rivals began acquiring as many possessions as they could. For the Spaniards, to lose the Caribbean meant to lose the bases of trade and defense. Furthermore, precious metals were leaking out of Spain's economy through international trade and smuggling. At the same time, the Dutch, followed by the English and French, were demonstrating that tropical products trade could provide spectacular earnings. The weakness of the Spanish economy became obvious. But, as Jan de Vries affirms, Spain was not ignorant of what was happening; an entire school of economic reformers wrote mountains of treatises defending new measures, including proposals to revive industry by prohibiting raw material exports and manufactured imports.[13] On the other hand, the a new and vital importance had been injected in the Caribbean region, transforming it into a center of international trade, and Spain could not close its eyes to that development.

To recover land in the Caribbean and in the Atlantic trade through revitalizing the sugar industry required a lot of capital to be invested in technology and manpower. Spain did not have it. The non-Hispanic colonies were able to develop sugar industries, thanks to the support of the vigorous Dutch trade. Also, their sugar had brought prices with which it was difficult to compete. In a 1701 document, the Consulado of Seville's merchants stated that Cuban sugar had been completely displaced from the peninsular market due to the impossibility of counteracting the prices. While Cuban sugar was sold in Spain for more than four pesos per *arroba*, Portuguese sugar hardly cost two.[14] Cubans had expressed the same complaint in a 1690 town council meeting, in which they alleged that their sugar was not in demand because that of Brazil, Jamaica, Haiti, Barbados, and other places in the Americas had invaded the peninsular market.[15]

Cuban Tobacco—A Trademark

Spain, however, had a trademark product: Cuban tobacco.[16] Tobacco consumers had already realized that Cuban tobacco was superior to any other. Its only serious competitor was Virginian tobacco, but even that was not able to match it in quality. According to a contemporary observer, Cuban tobacco was considered throughout the seventeenth century to be superior to that of Virginia, which is why English smokers paid the surcharge willingly.[17] The fame of the Cuban leaf had eclipsed that of its rivals to such a level that in foreign markets its price doubled and even tripled the price fixed for tobacco sourced elsewhere.[18]

Cuban tobacco's characteristic delicious taste and scent, as well as its excellent combustibility, spread its fame quickly. Foreign competition thus did not affect Cuban tobacco to the same degree that it affected tobacco from other places. The Cuban leaf enjoyed a constant and consistent demand that guaranteed its high price. Ramón de la Sagra, an early nineteenth-century expert in agriculture and economy, remarked on the privileged situation of Cuban tobacco, the crop par excellence of the island. He believed that Cuban tobacco had to fear neither foreign competition nor a possible limit to its production caused by reduced consumption.[19] At the beginning of the nineteenth century, when the convenience of abolishing Cuba's tobacco monopoly was discussed, Spanish authorities recognized that the prestige of Cuban tobacco had influenced the Crown's policies.[20] Keeping in mind some of Jean-Baptiste Colbert's declarations, tobacco was the logical option for Spain. The French minister, who worked persistently to consolidate the economy of his country, said, "if I had the tobaccos and wools of Spain, then France would be happy."[21]

In summary, the non-Hispanic Caribbean islands made an early attempt to promote tobacco, but they did not achieve a level of quality acceptable for the European market. However, they had sufficient capital to develop the sugar industry. The Spaniards, on the contrary, did not have capital to invest in sugar. Moreover, given that their rivals had achieved a high level of productivity and that foreign prices were so low, they found it difficult to compete. However, Spain had Cuban tobacco, which enjoyed prestige and acceptance among the Europeans. England and France competed in the battleground of the sugar market, alternating in preeminence. Spain opted to take advantage of the privileges of Cuban tobacco, cleverly avoiding competition in sugar, a field it would have entered at a serious disadvantage.

Strategy Outline

To obtain the most benefit from international trade competition through promoting Cuban tobacco, Spain had to take some measures. First, Spain had to preserve its privileged situation in the market. For example, the merchants' practice of mixing Cuban tobacco with cheaper leaves to obtain bigger earnings injured its prestige among consumers. The same result occurred when tobacco was adulterated with other substances, including sometimes earth, to increase its weight and consequently affect the sales price. Second, Spain had to control distribution in the European market so that it could guarantee the administration of earnings. In both cases smuggling was harmful.

The Crown's ministers were aware of the difficulties, as well as of the importance that tobacco was acquiring in the international market. A 1682 document from the Consejo de Indias demonstrated this concern. According to Guillermo Céspedes del Castillo, the document says that at the end of the sixteenth century, the first transatlantic route that would be able to supply all of Europe with tobacco would be developed, with Havana as the export center and Seville as the distribution center. The document asserted that if free navigation were allowed and if cultivation would be supported by financial stimulus and protection, that route would be very successful. But this last depended on, among other things, the reform of traditional policies of commercial exclusivism. Tobacco traffic was, therefore, precarious.[22]

It was necessary to find a solution that harmonized new interests with old policies. The new strategy concentrated on the metropolis, particularly Seville, from where the state tried to manage the nascent business and to combat fraud and smuggling. That strategy was inaugurated in 1684 with an *Instrucción* (decree) that regulated the tobacco business. But the strategy also required developing the infrastructure to allow its implementation.

From the beginning of the seventeenth century, increased demand had stimulated the creation of Spanish factories in which cigarettes and powder were made with tobacco arriving from the Americas. The factory that became the most important, as much for volume of production as for the fame of its tobaccos, was Seville's, which had begun work in 1620 as a private enterprise. The considerable earnings it had produced ever since it was opened suggested to the state the wisdom of acquiring it and establishing a royal monopoly.[23]

In 1636 the tobacco monopoly was established in Castile and Aragon. The Seville factory was designated as the only production center for the different tobacco products, that is, for making cigarettes and snuff.[24] These measures can be interpreted as a reaction to the initial peak of the tobacco business. But, more than anything, they reflect the growing financial burdens caused by the war crisis of 1618. New taxes became necessary to cover payment of the monarchy's considerable debts and to meet the urgent need to obtain more revenues. Since tobacco use had already taken root and spread into wide sectors of society, the state trusted its revenue possibilities.[25] From that moment on, the government periodically leased the administration of the tobacco monopoly (Renta del Tabaco) in exchange for increasingly large amounts of money. The leasings included the Seville factory, the cigar stores and other sales offices on the peninsula. This system continued until the decade of 1680–90.[26]

In 1684 the state suspended the leasings and turned the monopoly's administration over to Seville's factory, which proceeded to depend directly on the royal treasury and became the center and head of the tobacco monopoly. Production exclusivity was granted to Seville's factory, and the closing of all others was ordered. This was a mechanism to reduce fraud, necessary because the products of the other factories were of poor quality. Imitation of Seville's production, on the other hand, was not a concern for authorities since its quality had no competition.[27]

José Manuel Rodríguez Gordillo, a specialist in the history of tobacco in Spain, has analyzed the *Instrucción* of May 3, 1684, that established the monopoly. He concludes that the text has a remarkably mercantilist spirit, and he supports this conclusion by noting the firm control that the Crown tried to establish in all activities of the tobacco business; the thoroughness in the supervision of, for example, prices and qualities; and an initial project of a colonial pact.[28]

The *Instrucción* of 1684 stressed mainly the Crown's intention to protect Caribbean tobacco production in general and Cuban production in particular. The first article established that the Seville factory could use tobaccos only from Havana, Trinidad de la Havana, Trinidad de la Guayra, Puerto Rico, and Santo Domingo. The second article prohibited the sale of any tobacco originating from any other lands. In both articles exception was made for the "Brazil leaf," which was usually dedicated to chewing and thus did not compete directly with Cuban tobacco, which was consumed as cigarettes or snuff.[29] That the source of the tobacco was settled in the first two articles shows that the metropolitan regulations were intimately related with the circumstances of production and commercialization in the colonies. That bond was the axis around which the new tobacco policies were organized.

To be able to fulfill the expectations of the first two articles, the fifth article ordered the governors of the Caribbean colonies to encourage tobacco cultivation. Cultivation on the peninsula was specifically forbidden. The rest of the colonies could harvest tobacco, but the production could only be dedicated to local consumption, in light of the commercial restrictions of the time.[30]

Snuff—the type of tobacco most heavily consumed at the time—was made in the Seville factory. This was the only tobacco powder that could be sold in the Indies. That made in Havana had to be remitted to the metropolis, where it was reprocessed and distributed together with the peninsular type. On the fringe of the *Instrucción,* but in the same context, the Crown tried to prohibit the making of snuff in Cuba. It was not successful, however, due to great opposition on the island. Even so, the attempt reveals the metropolitan intentions of concentrating the production of leaves in the Caribbean and of controlling the elaboration and commercialization from Seville.

The *Instrucción* reveals Spain's determination to protect Caribbean tobacco and its commercialization, but Spain also contemplated other objectives. The Crown was interested in guaranteeing fiscal revenues by controlling the factories and tobacco consumption on the peninsula. By this point Cuba had already become the main producer of tobacco leaves for the European market, and the metropolis also wanted to assure earnings for American tobacco sales. At the same time, this could be a mechanism to avoid the leakage of capital to other nations through the trade of a product in such high demand. Also, the *Instrucción* tried to guarantee an appropriate supply of tobacco to Spain in an effort to prevent a shortage that could harm the monopoly. When tobacco became scarce in Spain, it was necessary not only to acquire it from foreign colonies but also to face the consequences of smuggling, both of which were detrimental to the interests of the royal treasury.

These considerations, together with the now notorious prosperity of the tobacco industry in Havana, made the royal treasury's directors think about the convenience of establishing a second monopoly—in Cuba. While the local authorities were eventually able to do so, they recommended acquiring the largest possible quantity of the tobacco harvested on the island, which should be sent to Seville's factory. In that way the Crown could improve its control over the sales and distribution in England, Holland, France, and other European nations. This practice was not very successful at first, but it was ratified in 1698, producing better results. After that, tobacco purchases carried out by the royal treasury in Cuba continued uninterrupted, although by different forms, until the beginning of the nineteenth century.[31]

The seventeenth-century Spanish Imperial State did not have the appropriate forces to sustain the initiatives taken in Cuba and on the peninsula. Cuban governors, for example, made efforts to combat smuggling. But they continually complained that the chronic shortage of resources frustrated their intentions. It was not until the Bourbons arrived on the Spanish throne that the purposes of establishing a tobacco monopoly on the island were formulated with greater force and effectiveness.

Bourbons and Tobacco

When the Bourbons ascended to the throne, they demonstrated that they knew tobacco policies and their importance. To this awareness was added the influence of important thinkers, whose economic and political thought weighed decisively in the reorganization processes of the absolutist state. They began to emphasize the importance of the royal authority's material base and the belief that the state should assume primary and active responsibility for the prosperity of its citizens. Any reforms taken should point to the progress of the monarchy as much as of the people, changing the economic structure as well as the state organization. For economic commentators of the time, the population's prosperity—as much in numeric terms as in quality of life—would bring an increase in consumption that, in turn, would stimulate productive and commercial activities. In the long run, it would mean a bigger fiscal reward, but this could occur only if tributary loads did not become excessive.

These ideas did not appear in a clearly favorable rational context. The Bourbons inherited a country desolated by the War of Spanish Succession, with an inadequate army and a weak economic structure. Therefore, it was urgent to apply an economic policy that would return Spain to a first-order power among the European nations. For this purpose, new and lucrative sources of public revenues were needed, but the initiatives could not be so heavy as to hinder the possibilities of economic development on the peninsula.

Control over the tobacco industry emerged as one of the most attractive alternatives. First, the population's basic necessities were not harmed because tobacco consumption was not obligatory or indispensable for survival, thus fulfilling the Crown's goal of offering as much prosperity to the people as to itself. Also, tobacco consumption continued to rise and had proven to be an invaluable source of revenue for the royal treasury as long as it maintained efficient administration.

With the arrival of the Bourbons, establishing a tobacco monopoly was manifested in a constant and systematic coherence with the Crown's objectives of achieving a substantial increase in royal treasury revenues. The economic ideology of the time, into which the tobacco monopoly already fit well, was reinforced by the fact that at the beginning of the eighteenth century tobacco revenues were of considerable importance to the monarchy. In 1702 tobacco contributed 14.3 percent of the net revenues collected by the Crown of Castile. By 1713 this figure had risen to 24.9 percent, more than any other individual revenue.[32]

The ideological influences and the proven fiscal benefits of the tobacco monopoly placed it in an important position in the treatises on political economy written during the first half of the eighteenth century. The theories about the advantages and possibilities of tobacco monopoly were best absorbed by Gerónimo de Ustáriz in his *Teórica y práctica de comercio y marina,* written in 1724 and published in 1742. According to Ustáriz, the tobacco monopoly was the most flourishing revenue in the royal treasury. Only the well-administered monopolies in Havana and Spain could sustain a larger army and navy than other European kings maintained with all their patrimony.[33]

The tobacco monopoly became an ever more advisable fiscal resource with the growing conviction that it could increase earnings. For this reason, according to Ustáriz, it was necessary to improve the administration of the tobacco monopoly, to renovate and receive the maximum profit from the Seville factory, and mainly to guarantee product supply for both Spanish consumption and export to the rest of Europe. Ustáriz thought that Cuba should receive special attention because it was called on to supply the demand of the peninsular market and of the metropolitan trade with the European continent. The Crown, on the other hand, would assure the annual purchases of tobacco. Ustáriz also recommended sending royal officers to Havana to work with local producers and offer them assistance in matters concerning purchase, preparation, and transport.[34] Last, a tax with the characteristics of the tobacco monopoly would reduce tributary loads on other items that directly affected basic needs of the population. This would increase consumption, which in turn would translate into incentives for the economy in general.[35]

The logic applied by Ustáriz was not different from that of the *Instrucción* of 1684. Cuba was the production center par excellence and Seville was the center of elaboration, distribution, and export. Ustáriz insisted, as did the ministers of the previous century, on Cuban tobacco being a gourmet product, able to sustain Spanish trade with the rest of Europe. The difference was that with a more rational public administration, the Bourbons were trying more persistently to solve problems using concrete alternatives to enable the effective execution of their policies. As John Lynch says, the decades prior to and after 1700 continued the uninterrupted course of Spanish history.[36]

From Theory to Practice—Spain's Tobacco Monopoly

To put this whole theory into practice, the Spanish state concentrated on two fronts: Cuba and Seville. In terms of royal regulations, each place almost always received distinct treatment, that is, measures dictated for one were not necessarily applied to the other. But the two were never seen as detached because the success of the Spanish tobacco policy rested on how well each complemented the other in order for tobacco to most benefit the Crown. It is necessary to repeat that Cuba operated as a leaf-production center and Seville as elaboration, distribution, and export center. The differences in treatments received by these two places were results of their roles. For Cuba, royal measures were designed to guarantee the purchase of tobacco in large quantities to satisfy the needs of Seville's factory. On the peninsula, the objective was to increase and improve industrial production and product marketing.

For the Spanish Crown, it was more complicated to find appropriate measures to make Cuba a functional enclave within the tobacco complex. The opposition of the colonial elite was determined, as were European rivals in the Caribbean. On the peninsula, the methods used to put the Crown's policies into practice were articulated and implemented earlier and served as a model for those to be used in Cuba and, later, in the rest of the colonies.

The direct administration of the tobacco monopoly by the royal treasury, ordered in the *Instrucción* of 1684, had a short life—hardly one year. After this trial period the Crown returned to the practice of leasing. But the Seville factory remained the exclusive elaboration center in the peninsula, which was an achievement of the 1684 decree. As soon as the Bourbons arrived on the throne, they returned the factory's administration to the royal treasury, restarting a process that would not again be reversed. At the same time, in order to bolster the tobacco business, they produced regulations against fraud and took measures to guarantee tobacco purchases in Havana. The Seville factory's role as the axis of the monopoly was reinforced. The War of Succession, however, made it difficult to implement the steps in a rapid and effective way.[37]

Finally, in 1731, the Crown established the "universal administration" for the tobacco monopoly in Spain. From that moment on, the monarchy exercised effective control over all aspects of the peninsular tobacco world. In 1740 the "Universal Rules for the Best Government of the Tobacco Monopoly" reinforced this situation. These "Universal Rules" imposed the legal regulation that governed the monopoly until the nineteenth century. They took over all the acquired experience on the administration and tobacco sales; they advised and ordered the most convenient and effective methods to obtain good results; and they tried to prevent the most common frauds. The document, which was reprinted in 1767 and 1788, served as a model for other monopolies established successively in all the colonies during the eighteenth century.[38]

The Bourbons also looked at the Seville factory's infrastructure, the object of continuous expansion. Up to 1758, at least, the objective of those material reforms was to enlarge the factory's industrial facilities and to improve technology, that is, to make the monopoly adapt production to growing demand.[39]

In 1740 the tobacco monopoly in Spain was officially established, with its axis in Seville's factory. From then on, exports and supply to the local market depended exclusively on Seville. But the factory, in turn, depended on the raw material supplied by the colonies, especially Cuba. The Crown did not cease its efforts to find the most appropriate measures to guarantee purchases in Cuba as the only way to assure adequate supply for the factory.

Cuba—The Second Axis

In 1717 the king promulgated a royal decree to buy all the tobacco harvested in Cuba on behalf of the royal treasury.[40] The document states that the two fundamental concerns of the Crown regarding tobacco were to ensure both an adequate supply for the peninsula and foreign trade competition. During the previous century the monopoly had grown considerably in the metropolis, due to an increase in tobacco consumption and to administrative improvements. By 1720, however, this situation began to change. The supply was not elastic enough to meet the increasing demand.[41] Smuggling, in turn, increased as much on the peninsula as in Cuba, creating a continual shortage of tobacco leaves in Seville.

This combination of factors impacted the state's other great concern: losing advantages in foreign trade. On the one hand, Spain's enemies could win control of a part of the tobacco trade through direct purchases in Cuba, either by illegal means or by taking advantage of obtained concessions (such as the English received with the Treaty of Utrecht).[42] On the other hand, tobacco exports from Spain to the rest of Europe could be demolished or diminished because of inadequate supply.

Governed by mercantilism, European metropolises favored a system based on manufacturing articles for exportation and importing raw materials from their colonies, which would result in accumulation of the precious metals on which each nation's wealth depended. To that end, it was also necessary to exclude enemies from the markets.[43] In conjunction with these principles, Spanish authorities were devoted during the entire century to rehearsing alternatives that allowed the nation to overcome the problems identified in the tobacco trade. With Cuba as the main producer in the Spanish Empire, it became indispensable to control the insular situation from the planting phase until those of commercialization. But the task was not simple, largely because of conflicting interests in the colony.

Historically, tobacco had been the main export of Cuba. This had led to the emergence of an elite of harvesters and merchants who sustained their power on participation in the industry. Until the end of the seventeenth century they had enjoyed relative freedom in the business, and they were not willing to give that freedom up easily. But this elite was not homogeneous, and thus its clash with the state was exacerbated by inner conflicts.

The *vegueros* (tobacco growers on small properties) depended on merchants to export their crops. In addition, they depended on the landlords or the church that leased them the lands. The merchants managed the prices to their convenience and granted loans to the *vegueros* over the value of their harvest. The clergy received the tithe in tobacco and so were also partly interested in the business.[44]

The most influential merchants tried to take advantage of the metropolitan policies to use as much against their local colleagues as against their Cadiz ones. The *vegueros* fought to defend their interests against the merchants. The Crown's officers on the island—sometimes Cubans, sometimes Spaniards—formed another power group and made alliances with the different sectors in search of personal benefits. The English, supported by the Treaty of Utrecht, also took their place in these conflicts.

The history of the successive Crown measures regarding Cuban tobacco shows its interventionism, mediated by conflicts as much local as international. The imperial state looked for the most effective measures to prevent losing control of the Caribbean trade and, at the same time, to guarantee the peninsula's supply on which the monopoly's success depended. But vested interests tempered these attempts and forced multiple redefinitions. The most important landmarks in the process culminated with the establishment of the Havana *factoría* in 1760.

By 1684 the Seville factory depended directly on the royal treasury and administered the tobacco monopoly that included the peninsula's sales as well as extra- and intraimperial exports. All the tobacco from India arriving in Spain had to enter through the factory. But due to royal contracts, merchants who bought the leaves in the Americas sold the king what suited them or what they could not hide. The merchants kept most of the tobacco for personal benefit through secret sales. Consequently, the factory faced a continuous shortage, which diminished treasury revenues.

In search of a solution, the Crown began in 1698 to purchase tobacco in Cuba on behalf of the king. This was also a mechanism to direct a part of the Cuban tobacco business's substantial earnings toward the state. In April 1698 Carlos II ordered the purchase of Cuban tobaccos on behalf of the treasury. This form of purchase continued for some years. Although there was not, at the time, a tobacco *situado* with fixed quantity and predetermined to these effects, the purchases in Cuba were financed from the beginning with New Spain's silver.[45]

These purchases were still not enough to guarantee appropriate supply to the metropolis. So in 1717 the Crown established a general monopoly in Cuba. The monopoly would take charge of the purchases and of conditioning the tobacco remission to Seville, certain Spanish American colonies, and the Canary Islands. The 1717 measures restricted the freedom that Cuban harvesters had previously enjoyed and forced them to sell their products to the treasury at officially fixed prices But repeated *veguero* seditions made it fail in a short time. In 1720 the authorities had no recourse but to decree a return to freedom in the tobacco business.[46] A *factoría* continued to administer official purchases, but only as one more buyer. The old problem had yet to be resolved: how to achieve control of the tobacco business.

In those years most Cuban production went to satisfy the demand of English buyers established on the island. The Cubans preferred to reserve their first-quality tobacco to this trade, from which they obtained better prices. The Spanish Crown, needful of large supplies, had no alternative other than to accept the poorer quality leaves. The Crown's biggest concern, at this time, was to ensure that Spain did not lack tobacco to satisfy peninsular demand and to please European demand with the Seville factory's products.

In search of an advantageous alternative for the treasury, the Crown suppressed direct purchases in 1736. It was expected that conceding privileges and exclusivity to an experienced merchant would increase the effectiveness of the Crown's partial control of Cuban tobacco commercialization and improve the supply efficiency. A contract was granted to Joseph Antonio Tallapiedra, a merchant from Cadiz. In 1739 the contract was transferred to another merchant, the Marqúes de Casa Madrid, with the same conditions. A year later the contract was transferred again, this time to the Havana Company, formed by Cubans with a capital of 20 million reales. None of these alternatives produced the expected results.[47]

Cuban Monopoly

In 1760, one year after Carlos III's arrival on the Spanish throne, the Havana *factoría* was established.[48] Its main mission was to buy the entire tobacco harvest in Cuba. The Crown believed that this was a way to combat smuggling and to guarantee that Seville would always be well supplied. With this establishment, a new monopoly was inaugurated in Cuba.[49] After almost a century of diverse attempts that did not produce the expected results, the metropolis opted for the production and commercialization ruling, under the administration of the treasury. The Havana *factoría* began work formally on March 1, 1760. In August 1762 the English captured Cuba, and the monopoly was interrupted.

The Treaty of Paris, signed on February 10, 1763, ended the Seven Years' War and returned Cuba to Spain. The *factoría* was reactivated immediately. From then on, the monopoly experienced a period of growth and consolidation that lasted until 1773. The consistent growth created an optimistic atmosphere, and Spanish authorities believed that they had finally achieved success. They were convinced that the *factoría* guaranteed optimal business operations at an imperial level. Indeed, between 1766 and 1773 the *factoría* was successful in fulfilling its objectives. The *factoría*'s records identify four well-defined stages: the 1766–73 stage was characterized by consistent growth; 1774–82 saw decline; 1783–88 were years of recovery; and the years 1789–1812 saw the beginning of definitive decline.

The indicator that best reveals the *factoría*'s effectiveness is the remittances to Spain, since the fundamental objective of its establishment was to guarantee supply to Seville's factory. During the first and second stages, that is, until 1782, the curves of entries and remittances to Spain are similar (see figure 9.1). But contrary to the entries, remittances could not recover. As I will explain later, the war against Great Britain (1779–83) delivered a decisive blow to Cuban tobacco exports to Spain. Nevertheless, it calls attention to the high volume of remittances in 1783, which reflects the accumulation during the previous years in which the war interrupted transportation. In 1779, the year Spain entered the war, remittances decreased greatly and the gap that separated them from the entries widened significantly. Neither in 1780 nor in 1782 were there any remittances to Spain, so the storage of several years in the Havana warehouses is what appears in the records for 1783. This is corroborated by the fact that the entire 1783 remission was snuff (see figure 9.2). When tobacco leaves did not exit promptly, local officials opted to increase powder production to diminish the risk of loss and to facilitate storage. After 1783 the totals of remittances to Spain and, mainly, their proportion compared to the entries, never again reached the levels of the previous periods. In other words, 1766–73 constitutes the only period in which the Havana *factoría* fulfilled without setbacks its fundamental objective of guaranteeing supply to the Seville factory.

Examining the records of the *factoría*, one finds that local sales and sales to other Spanish American colonies seem insignificant compared to remittances to the peninsula. But that does not decrease the importance of these items. The tobacco *situados* that arrived from Mexico were used, mainly, to pay farmers for purchases, to acquire slaves, to liquidate debts, or to finance pending investments in infrastructure. The general management expenses of the *factoría* and the salaries of its employees, however, depended in good measure on the earnings from sales on the island and other Spanish American colonies.

Returning to 1766–73, the amount of tobacco in the *factoría* became so large that by 1768 it was necessary to construct new warehouses. Shipments to Cadiz and Seville increased in such a way that every merchant and warship left on the island was used for those purposes. In a few years the peninsula's reserves were so excessive that there were more than twenty million spare pounds of tobacco in the Seville factory.

But all this success hung on a fragile thread. The *factoría* had a high priority objective to guarantee the purchases of all the tobacco harvested on the island by sending it to the Seville factory. For such purposes the Crown had committed to buy the entire Cuban crop. The purchases were paid with fixed contributions, known as tobacco *situados,* that New Spain should remit. These consisted of an annual consignment of four hundred thousand pesos until 1767, when it increased to five hundred thousand. When international events or other circumstances hindered the flow of these *situados,* the *factoría* began to collapse.

Tobacco Situados

Since their inauguration at the beginning of the eighteenth century, the purchase of tobacco in Cuba on behalf of the royal treasury was financed with New Spain's silver. In 1718 the consignment ascended to three hundred thousand pesos. In the contracts of Tallapiedra, Casa Madrid, and the Havana Company (1735, 1738, and 1740, respectively) it was specified that New Spain would annually give two hundred thousand pesos for purchasing tobacco. In 1744 the consignment increased to four hundred thousand.[50]

In 1760 this practice was reiterated and became the base on which the entire imperial system of tobacco was built. To ensure supply to the Seville factory, it was necessary to guarantee the purchases in Cuba. And to verify these purchases, New Spain's silver was indispensable. As a result, the whole engagement depended on the tobacco *situados.* Between 1766 and 1773 tobacco *situados* always arrived complete, but frequently with considerable delays. The irregularity caused dysfunctions in the *factoría* and concerned the local and metropolitan authorities. The *factoría*'s vulnerability became evident.

At least once a year New Spain's viceroy received an exhortation from Madrid to make an effort to remit the tobacco *situados* on time. But *situados* always arrived with delay, sometimes accumulating for several years (mainly in wartime). The continual lack of capital carried serious consequences for the *factoría.* In 1769, for example, the Havana governor notified New Spain's viceroy that the next crop could fail because it had not been possible to pay the *vegueros* for the previous one.[51] This warning served little use, and the consignment did not arrive until August 1770.[52] Meanwhile the *factoría* directors had no alternative but to appeal for loans from local merchants to finance expenses and pick up the tobacco. This situation was repeated year after year.

The loans became good business for the local elite. The *factoría* directors were aware that in light of the *situado*'s irregularity, the operation of the establishment depended on these loans and therefore tried to make them attractive to the merchants. In 1768 they ordered that payments for the borrowed quantities be made in silver pesos as a way to guarantee that similar loans would be available in future emergencies.⁵³ The American-minted peso fuerte (silver peso) was equal to four piezas of two reales each, while the peninsular-minted one was equal to five piezas. Therefore, it was quite lucrative to introduce Spanish pesos into the colonies and take out the American ones.⁵⁴ Havana merchants lent to the *factoría* in peninsular-minted pesos to collect in silver pesos. In this way the moneylenders monopolized control of the better money remitted from New Spain, which allowed them to secure investments in international commerce and other economic activities.

The tobacco monopoly officers also took advantage of these circumstances, developing sophisticated forms of speculation through which they obtained important economic benefits. Among these forms was the common practice of taking a loan out of the *situado* money and eventually restoring it with weaker currency. The direct access of the high-ranking officers to the flow of money that passed through the island facilitated and supported their full involvement in colonial economic life and created strong bonds between them and the local elite. This did not escape the eyes of critics, who pointed to the situation as one of the problems besetting the monopoly.⁵⁵

Through the merchants' loans to the factory and the officers' scheming, the Mexican silver stimulated the local economy and strengthened the Havana elite. The consequences for trade and the sugar industry (and the interest groups linked to these activities) were positive. However, for the tobacco monopoly it had adverse repercussions. While particular individuals benefited from control of the American-minted silver, the weak currency was going to the royal treasury. For monopoly operation this was not a great problem because the objective of the tobacco *situados* was to pay farmers at the local level for the tobacco purchases. But for imperial interests it meant more leakage of silver. On the other hand, insofar as the Cubans had capital to invest in tobacco—most of the time in mills and illicit factories—smuggling increased and the practice of sending lower-grade tobacco to the *factoría* was accentuated. The most significant effect, however, was that these injections of capital stimulated the development of the Cuban sugar economy, to the detriment of the treasury's interests and thus harming imperial priorities.

While the cultivation of sugar acquired importance, the *vegueros* did not depend exclusively on tobacco. When they faced problems that threatened their subsistence (such as the recurrent lack of payments), they had alternatives, including work as sugar wage-laborers or as producers of basic goods. Such problems led contemporaries to observe that the most noxious effect of the irregular arrival of the *situados* was the injuries caused for the *vegueros*, injuries that, in turn, redounded adversely royal interests. In its simpler and more evident manifestation, lack of liquidity meant that the crop could not be paid to the *vegueros*, who worked for months, and sometimes more than a year, without receiving a cent. Lacking incentives and money to finance new sowing, the *vegueros* abandoned tobacco for other crops. As a result, the *factoría* risked that the necessary production levels to supply the Seville factory would not be reached, despite this being the *factoría*'s main objective. On the other hand, sometimes the *vegueros* preferred to sell their tobacco to smugglers, going either directly to foreigners or through local merchants, to guarantee payment. Multiple documents allude to these problems. Good examples are the repeated exhortations of the ministers in the Indies to New Spain's viceroys: the ministers begged for punctual remission of the *situados* because the lack of funds carried disastrous repercussions for imperial interests.[56]

The *vegueros* suffered worse from the lack of payments. The *factoría* gave them receipts for the quantity of money corresponding to the payment owed for the given crop, but the silver took a long time to arrive. The *vegueros*' needs were urgent, and they were forced to endorse the documents to particular merchants, who kept as much as 25 percent. Another difficulty was added to this situation. If a container were damaged or wet (a quite frequent accident), the tobacco lost its value and neither the royal treasury nor the merchants received it.[57]

The receipt benefited the detail merchants at the expense of the *vegueros*, who opted to switch to other crops. Such a situation was a constant threat to the royal treasury. These problems, however, did not diminish the enthusiasm on both sides of the ocean for the continuous growth of the *factoría* purchases and tobacco remittances to Spain. The Anglo-American War, however, changed the scenario because of its multiple consequences on Cuba in general and on the tobacco business in particular.

The Anglo-American War and the Decline of the Havana Factory

The war's effects were felt even before Spain entered it. In 1774 the thirteen colonies closed their ports to the products of British Caribbean colonies, and a year later they prohibited exports to them.[58] The Spanish and French possessions found in this good commercial opportunities. Through metropolitan concessions or through smuggling, they could fill the vacuum left both in the North American side and in their Antillean neighbors. Immediately the figures of tobacco entries in the Havana *factoría* fell, as did the figures for remittances to Spain. In 1779 Spain declared its participation against Great Britain in the war. In 1781 and 1782 the *factoría* reached its lowest-ever levels of tobacco entries and remittances to the metropolis.

One of the most direct effects on the monopoly was the dramatic decrease in the tobacco *situados* arriving from New Spain. Even with irregular and almost always late arrival, the quantities consigned for purchase of tobacco had been arriving in full since 1768. In the three years prior to Spain's entry into the war (1776–78), the *factoría* received 1.8 million pesos from the *situados*. During the five years it was in the conflict (1779–83), however, this decreased to 970,713 pesos, or half the amount received in the previous three-year period.[59]

At the same time there was an enormous increase in the usage of Mexican *situados* to cover the growing war expenses. Between 1779 and 1783, according to Carlos Marichal and Matilde Souto Mantecón, these expenditures exceeded the capacity of New Spain's tax structure to provide funds, and the viceroy was thus obliged to call for a series of forced and voluntary loans from all sectors of the Mexican population.[60] Given such pressure, as well as wartime priorities, it is not strange that funds for tobacco purchases were scarce. All remittances went to maintaining the Spanish military forces in the Caribbean, which were concentrated in Havana.

Until the 1779–83 period, and for some years after the Anglo-American war, the consignments received from New Spain constituted more than 75 percent of the total entries in the Havana *factoría*. Without its main source of revenues, the *factoría* could barely operate. Also crucial to the success of the monopoly had been the support of the Havana elite who saw the *factoría* as a mechanism that guaranteed the flow of capital to the island, from which they, of course, had benefited. During the war, however, the *factoría* lost this attractiveness. The silver arrived in greater quantity than ever before, but it was assigned to other purposes, namely the war. Local merchants, in continuous search of silver, looked toward those who were receiving the flow of money. The *vegueros,* on the other hand, were informed that the *factoría* could not pay them for their harvest. For that reason they preferred to sell their harvest to the smugglers or to change crops entirely. On occasion they even opted to retain the tobacco, refusing to surrender it to the *factoría* without the assurance of remuneration.

The war's consequences for the Cuban tobacco monopoly, however, were much greater. With the onset of their War for Independence, the thirteen colonies' tobacco production diminished notably. The British market that had been supplied, fundamentally, out of that production now faced a shortage, so merchants had to appeal to other places. This further encouraged the smuggling of Cuban tobacco, mainly via Jamaica. The product arrived in London in greater and greater quantities, and English consumers began to demonstrate a preference for it. Once the thirteen colonies achieved independence and regularized their commercial relationships with the old metropolis, North Americans had to import leaves from the island to mix with their own crops in order to create a product that would sell in the coveted English market.[61] The war, then, gave place to the growth of smuggling not only during wartime but also in the long term.

On the other hand, during the Anglo-American war a great number of Spanish military troops arrived in Cuba (the operation center), increasing the demand for food. The provisions trade, either locally produced or imported, became an attractive source of earnings.[62] This further prompted some *vegueros* to abandon tobacco. After all, the *factoría* continued to be the only official buyer of leaves.

But neither the new local production nor New Spain's supplies were enough to satisfy the demand for provisions, in spite of the pressures exercised on the viceroyalty. Consequently, Spain authorized the Cubans to trade with neutrals, and the nascent United States became the main supplier of flour, shortening, and meats. At the same time the interruption of the commercial relationships between the rebel colonies and the British Caribbean opened the North American market to Cuban sugar. This created commercial links that the return to peace could not undo.

The strengthened Cuban relationship with North America had other adverse effects for the monopoly. On the one hand, invigorated sugar production required the expansion of the land area dedicated to sugar cane cultivation, gradually displacing tobacco from many of its traditional lands. On the other hand, the increase in the sugar labor force and the tendency toward monoculture opened an internal food market that allowed the *vegueros* who had abandoned tobacco not to have to return to it after the war's end.

In short, the Havana *factoría* came out quite battered by the Anglo-American war. At the same time, the expenditures to cover war expenses had left New Spain's treasury exhausted and indebted. Between 1768 and 1778 the consignments for tobacco purchases in Cuba had arrived complete despite delays. But from the end of the war in 1784 until 1811, the entire sum (or greater) consigned for the tobacco *situados* was received only in nine years. The problem was already alarming in 1788 and 1789 when the *factoría* did not receive a single coin from New Spain.

The monopoly authorities, both in the colony and in the metropolis, reactivated pressures on New Spain in an attempt to regularize tobacco *situados* and avoid the total ruin of the establishment. They obtained good results: between 1790 and 1793 the amount of Mexican silver reaching the *factoría* surpassed the five hundred thousand consigned pesos. But a new war (the French Convention, 1793–95) spoiled the efforts to guarantee the incoming *situados*.

Collapse of the Havana—Factoría

The war with France interrupted once more the silver remittances for tobacco purchases. After the good results of 1790–93, the *situado* incomes again fell, and did not recover. Aside from exceptional remittances in 1801 and 1809, the figures never reached their full consignment of five hundred thousand pesos again.

To the chronic lack of money and its already routine consequences was added another problem. The 1791 Haitian Revolution put an end to the French colony's sugar production, which supplied 50 percent of the world market at that time. Cuba greatly benefited from the void, and by 1792 it occupied third place among sugar producers of the world, behind only Brazil and Jamaica.[63]

Looking at Cuban history of those years through the prism of tobacco, it is evident that the establishment of the Havana *factoría* was decisive in providing a certain indispensable basis for the sugar expansion at the end of the century. The *factoría* favored the population's concentration of riparian settlements. In addition, the *factoría* businesses opened new communication roads, as much internal as with international trade. On the other hand, the *situados*—both for tobacco and for other purposes—injected important capital into the island, without which it would have been difficult to develop an industry with high investment requirements. Furthermore, the *factoría* supported the growth of small and medium free harvesters and contributed to the importation of African slaves. In this way the monopoly instigated the consolidation of a large labor force (both free and slave). In the wake of the difficulties with tobacco, this labor force could be easily transferred to the sugar plantations.[64]

The sugar industry required good roads for communication, abundant manpower, and capital to invest in technology. Without intending to, the *factoría* had facilitated these three requirements. When the Haitian Revolution opened the doors to the European market, the Cuban elite had the capacity to expand sugar production and thus to benefit from the international situation.

Starting from the sugar expansion caused by the Haitian Revolution, the Cuban economy experienced a dramatic change, one directed by the sugar aristocracy. According to Manuel Moreno Fraginals, the *vegueros* were the first to feel the impact. The increase in sugar production created a growing need for new lands that had to meet four basic requirements: proximity to forests for a supply of firewood; access to livestock to move *trapiches* (sugar mills) and to draw carts; plains for sowing the cane; and access to ports. The tobacco plots were fertile and naturally irrigated. They were also sufficiently discounted to proceed immediately to the cultivation of cane. The forest had been conserved. These lands had already been located within a network of roads that united them to the ports. And they were settled in the only populated areas, which guaranteed the availability of wage laborers for sugar plantations. Therefore, tobacco plots were the preferred lands for sugar investments.[65]

The decisive element in the collapse of the *factoría* was the chronic lack of funds it had suffered since the onset of the Anglo-American war. So long as the tobacco *situados* arrived complete, the *factoría* worked productively. But when the *situados* failed to appear, the *factoría* entered a decline from which it was not able to recover. The peak of the *factoría*'s success helped to endow the island with the necessary basis to respond vigorously to economic changes. Paradoxically, the economic revitalization created by the *factoría* was the agent of its demise. The material basis created by the *factoría* provided Cubans at different social levels with alternatives. Cubans found themselves in a position to undertake different initiatives to diminish or eliminate the dependence tobacco that had dominated the island's economy since the mid-seventeenth century.

The *factoría* experienced a different fate. The monopoly had been designed to operate with the support of New Spain's silver. Without this flow of funds it could not fulfill its main objective of buying tobacco for the Seville factory and could hardly sustain its own administration. The *factoría* was part of a system designed to maximize profits in the metropolis. All the money that entered the *factoría* came out immediately, often committed ahead of time. When New Spain's remittances diminished and eventually disappeared, the monopoly lost its engine. When it could not fulfill its objective of sending raw material to Seville, the Cuban monopoly also lost its reason for being.

The *factoría* was officially abolished in 1817. In practice it had died in 1810, if not earlier. Its foundation in 1760 represented the culmination of imperial tobacco policies that had been articulated since the late seventeenth century. The *factoría* was also the most successful attempt to put those policies into practice. But its operation and eventual disappearance were, at the same time, proof of its vulnerability, especially to the dependence on Mexican silver. That vulnerability, in turn, mirrored that of the empire in general, which was administered under the same premise that governed the monopoly: Mexican silver could solve all problems.

Notes

1. See Arturo Morales Carrión, *Puerto Rico and the Non Hispanic Caribbean: A Study on the Decline of Spanish Exclusivism* (San Juan: University of Puerto Rico, 1974).

2. See Franklin W. Knight, *The Caribbean: The Genesis of a Fragmented Nationalism* (New York: Oxford University Press, 1990); Eric Williams, *Capitalismo y esclavitud* (Buenos Aires: Ediciones Siglo Veinte, 1973).

3. John R. Fisher, *Relaciones económicas entre España y América hasta la independencia* (Madrid: Editorial Mapfre, 1992), 98.

4. José Pérez Vidal, *España en la historia del tabaco* (Madrid: Consejo Superior de Investigaciones Científicas, 1959), 184.

5. For Cuba, see José Rivero Muñiz, *Tabaco, su historia en Cuba,* 2 vols. (Havana: Instituto de Historia, 1964–65), 1:17–25. For Spain, see Pérez Vidal, *España,* 347–63.

6. Fernando Ortíz, *Contrapunteo cubano del tabaco y el az Úcar* (Caracas: Biblioteca Ayacucho, 1987), 395.

7. Jacob M. Price, *France and the Chesapeake: A History of the French Tobacco Monopoly, 1674–1791, and of Its Relationship to the British and American Tobacco Trades,* 2 vols. (Ann Arbor: University of Michigan Press, 1973), 1:4–17.

8. Ortíz, *Contrapunteo,* 395.

9. Price, *France and the Chesapeake,* 1:95.

10. J. H. Parry and Philip Sherlock, *Historia de las Antillas* (Buenos Aires: Ediciones Kapeluz, 1976), 72.

11. Ibid., 58–65.

12. Sidney W. Mintz, *Dulzura y poder: El lugar del azúcar en la historia moderna* (Mexico City: Siglo Veintiuno Editores, 1996), 66.

13. Jan de Vries, *La economía de Europa en un periodo de crisis, 1600–1750* (Madrid: Ed. Cátedra, 1992), 40.

14. Lutgardo García Fuentes, *El comercio español con América, 1650–1700* (Seville: Diputación de Sevilla/Escuela de Estudios Americanos, 1980), 344–45. *Arroba* is a Spanish weight unit equal to twenty-five pounds.

15. Rivero Muñiz, *Tabaco,* 1:65.

16. Fernando Ortíz has an entire chapter about the prestige of Cuban tobacco, which he considers the best in the world; see Ortíz, *Contrapunteo,* 431–38.

17. H. E. Friedlaender, *Historia económica de Cuba* (Havana: Jesús Montero Editor, 1944), 35.

18. José Rivero Muñiz, *Las tres sediciones de los vegueros en el siglo XVIII* (Havana: Academia de la Historia de Cuba, 1951), 9

19. Ramón de la Sagra, *Historia económico-política y estadística de lla isla de Cuba* (Havana: Imprenta de las viudas de Arazoza y Soler, 1831), 118.

20. "Informe sobre la abolición de la Factoría de tabacos de la Habana, 24 de abril de 1816," Archivo General de Indias (hereafter AGI), Audiencia de Santo Domingo (hereafter ASD), legajo 2001.

21. "Estudio para la formación de Instrucciones para el arreglo de la Renta del Tabaco en Perú, 1773," Archivo General de la Nación, México (hereafter AGNM), Fondo Renta del Tabaco, vol. 3.

22. Guillermo Céspedes del Castillo, *El tabaco en Nueva España* (Madrid: Real Academia de Historia, 1992), 41–42.

23. Pérez Vidal, *España,* 184, 227.

24. José Manuel Rodríguez Gordillo, "La real fábrica de tabacos" (photocopy courtesy of the author), 155.

25. José Manuel Rodríguez Gordillo, "El fraude en el estanco del tabaco (siglos XVII–XVIII)" (photocopy courtesy of the author), 63.

26. José Manuel Rodríguez Gordillo, "Sobre la industria sevillana del tabaco a fines del siglo XVII," in *Cuadernos de Historia,* 7 (1977): 536.

27. Pérez Vidal, *España,* 75, 228–29.

28. Rodríguez Gordillo, "Sobre la industria sevillana," 538.

29. There is a partial transcription of the articles in ibid., 540.

30. In practice, tobacco production in Santo Domingo and Puerto Rico and even in Venezuela never grew as much as in Cuba, and the Crown's support never was significant.

31. Rivero Muñiz, *Tabaco,* 1:58–73.

32. Miguel Artola, *La hacienda del antiguo régimen* (Madrid: Alianza Editorial/Banco de España, 1982), 222.

33. Gerónimo de Ustáriz, *Teórica y práctica de comercio y marina* (Madrid: Ediciones Aguilar, 1968), 370.

34. Ibid., 366–69.

35. Ibid., 368.

36. John Lynch, *El siglo XVIII: Historia de España, XII* (Barcelona: Editorial Critica, 1991), 5.

37. José Manuel Rodríguez Gordillo, "El tabaco: Del uso medicinal a la industrialización," in *La agricultura viajera* (Barcelona: Lenwerg, 1990), 64.

38. Ibid., 64; Pérez Vidal, *España,* 337.

39. Rodríguez Gordillo, "Real fábrica."

40. "Real Cédula de 11 de abril de 1717," AGNM, Fondo Reales Cédulas Originales (hereafter RCO), vol. 38, exp. 15, fols. 40–41.

41. Agustin González Enciso, "Organización y valores de la Renta del Tabaco en la primera mitad del siglo XVIII," in *Actas del I Symposium Internacional: Estado y fiscalidad en el Antiguo Régimen,* ed. Carmen M. Cremades Griñán (Murcia: Caja de Ahorros de Murcia, 1989), 263–64.

42. The Treaty of Utrecht (1713) finished the Succession War (1700–1713), by which Great Britain obtained exclusive permission to supply Spain's colonies with African slaves, which propitiated smuggling. In Cuba's case, slaves were frequently paid with tobacco leaves.

43. See Pedro Pérez Herrero, *América Latina y el colonialismo europeo (siglos XVI–XVIII)* (Madrid: Editorial Sintesis, 1992).

44. See Rivero Muñiz, *Tres sediciones,* 24–25; Julio Le Riverend, *Historia económica de Cuba* (Havana: Editorial de Ciencias Sociales, 1985), 126–27.

45. In the Spanish Empire the term *situado* was used specifically to refer to the remittances or transfer of royal funds from one caja of the royal treasury to another to cover expenses of strategic importance. See Carlos Marichal and Matilde Souto Mantecón, "Silver and Situados: New Spain and the Financing of the Spanish Empire in the Caribbean in the Eighteenth Century," *Hispanic American Historical Review* 74, no. 4 (November 1994): 588.

46. See Rivero Muñiz, *Tres sediciones.*

47. "Real Cédula de 15 de agosto de 1736," AGNM, RCO, vol. 56, exp. 50, fols. 120–22; "Real Cédula de 13 de agosto de 1739," AGNM, RCO, vol. 59, exp. 94, fols. 294–96. For more details, see Laura Náter, "Integración imperial: El sistema de monopolios de tabaco en el Imperio Español: Cuba y la América española del siglo XVIII" (Ph.D. diss., El Colegio de México, 2000).

48. As *factoría,* it was understood to be a tobacco monopoly administrative district. See Susan Dens-Smith, *Bureaucrats, Planters, and Workers: The Making of the Tobacco Monopoly in Bourbon Mexico* (Austin: University of Texas Press, 1992), 324.

49. "Ynstrucción que se forma de orden de Su Majestad para el establecimiento de la Factoria del Tavaco en la Havana . . . ," AGI, ASD, leg. 2002.

50. "Real Cédula de 15 de agosto de 1736," AGNM, RCO, vol. 56, exp. 50, fols. 120–22; "Real Cédula de 13 de agosto de 1739," AGNM, RCO, vol. 59, exp. 94, fols. 294–96; "Real Cédula de 2 de agosto de 1744," AGNM, RCO, vol. 64, exp. 77, fols. 264–66.

51. "Carta de Antonio María de Bucareli, gobernador de La Habana, al Marqués de Croix, virrey de Nueva España, 7 de noviembre de 1768," AGNM, Fondo Correspondencia de Diversas Autoridades, vol. 12, exp. 2, fols. 4–5.

52. Rivero Muñiz, *Tabaco,* 2:8–13.

53. Ibid., 4, 17.

54. Le Riverend, *Historia,* 124. For the monetary problems in the Spanish Empire and its impact on the colonial and international commerce, see Pierre Vilar, *Oro y moneda en la historia (1450–1920)* (Barcelona: Ediciones Ariel, 1969), 348–61; Antonio Miguel Bernal, *La financiación de la Carrera de Indias (1492–1824): Dinero y crédito en el comercio colonial español con América* (Seville: Fundación El Monte, 1992), 315–32.

55. "Manifiesto sobre las siembras, beneficio y compra de los tavacos en la Havana y demás territorios de aquella Isla . . . 17 de diciembre de 1782," AGI, ASD, leg. 2017.

56. "Julián de Arriaga al Marqués de Croix, 21 de mayo de 1767," AGNM, RCO, vol. 90, exp. 136, fols. 232–33; "Julián de Arriaga al Marqués de Croix, 18 de julio de 1769," AGNM, RCO, vol. 94, exp. 170, fols. 297–97; "El Marqués de Sonora a Bernardo de Gálvez, 28 de noviembre de 1785," AGNM, RCO, vol. 132, exp. 179, fols. 309–309vto.

57. "Cultura del tabaco en la Isla de Cuba," AGI, ASD, leg. 2002.

58. Johanna Von Grafenstein, *Nueva España en el Circuncaribe, 1779–1808: Revolución, competencia imperial y vínculos intercoloniales* (Mexico City: UNAM, 1997), 127.

59. "Estado que manifiesta los caudales ingresados en la Tesorería de la Factoría de la Habana por consignaciones . . . desde el año de 1761 hasta último de diciembre de 1812," AGI, ASD, leg. 2023.

60. Marichal and Souto Mantecón, "Silver and Situados," 606.

61. Rivero Muñiz, *Tabaco*, 2:61–62.

62. Von Grafenstein, *Nueva España*, 132.

63. Manuel Moreno Fraginals, *El ingenio: Complejo económico social cubano del azúcar*, vol. 1 (Havana: Editorial de Ciencias Sociales, 1978), 40.

64. It is important to point out the role of the *factoría* as provider of slaves. This was the principal recourse to please the *vegueros*. The *factoría* bought slaves and delivered them to the *vegueros*, who paid with tobacco at the moment of carry the harvest to the monopoly sites. Nevertheless, there were no guarantees that the slaves would not be sold at a later time.

65. Moreno Fraginals, *Ingenio*, 52–55.

The Drudgery of the Slave Trade
Labor at Cape Coast Castle, 1750–1790

Ty M. Reese

In 1776, when accusations of mismanagement caused Parliament to ask the Company of Merchants Trading to Africa for an account of its expenses, the report created by the Council of Cape Coast Castle demonstrated the company's reliance on the local African elite and both free and unfree laborers. In the period from 1770 to 1776 the company paid out £7,426 9s. 8d. in "Black Men's Pay," £20,622 8s. 4.5d. for "Castle Slaves," and £6,741 17s. 6.7d. for "Free Canoemen and Labourers hired"; the company spent £10,628 5s. 2.3d. on "Presents and Dashees," while "White Men's Salaries" accounted for the largest expenditure at £59,243 4s. 2d.[1] The company's expenditures on hiring free and unfree African, English, and mulatto labor, along with continually working to maintain a favorable and profitable relationship with the local elite, demonstrate the agency and importance of Africans and laborers in the coastal slave trade. An examination of the company's relationship with and dependence on these people illustrates the opportunities created by the slave trade for Africans and how a coastal trading infrastructure was created and maintained.

The success of England's late eighteenth-century slave trade stemmed from a combination of factors. One of the more important involved the ability of English slavers to procure slaves along the West African coast. In 1750 Parliament created the Company of Merchants Trading to Africa not to trade in slaves but to maintain the coastal trading infrastructure.[2] The company, created on the basis of protected free trade, inherited the decrepit structures of the Royal African Company and was to receive a yearly parliamentary grant. The major problem the company faced from 1750 to 1790 involved obtaining enough laborers to build, rebuild, and maintain the company's coastal forts, castles, outposts, warehouses, and numerous other structures. Laborers, including wage, slave, and pawns, were an important element in the success of the slave trade while demonstrating, through the commodities they received in pay, the material extent of the Atlantic economy.

The company's administrative center in West Africa was at Cape Coast Castle on the Gold Coast. While Cape Coast Castle was not a major slave trading center, its administrative activities were vital to England's slave trade. An examination of the various ways in which the company procured and utilized laborers at Cape Coast Castle is important for several reasons. First, by focusing on these coastal laborers a relatively unexplored aspect of the slave trade becomes clearer and increases our understanding of the coastal trading environment. The coastal slave trade involved more people than just the buyers and sellers of slaves. Second, the toil of laborers at Cape Coast Castle, and all along the coast, allowed the slave trade to occur. An examination of these laborers demonstrates the various systems used to procure and utilize them. The free and unfree laborers used by the company illustrate that Africans beyond those who controlled the slave trade benefited from the trade. Third, these laborers were part of the Atlantic economy. Their everyday toil allowed the Atlantic economy to continue to grow while, because they were paid in commodities rather than specie, they were both producers and consumers within this economy.

The Slave-Trade-Created Elite

On the Gold Coast the English presence extended and intensified the social divisions found within African society. At all ten of their coastal posts, the company maintained its relationship with the local African elite, the *caboceers* and *penyins*, through a system of presents, *dashees*, employment and customary rights and dues.[3] This elite allowed the company to remain on the coast. On October 10, 1781, the Council of Cape Coast Castle recorded: "That it is necessary from our present weakness to keep black men of power in our pay, that through their influence, we may live in peace and amity with the natives who would otherwise molest us, knowing we have not a sufficient force to protect ourselves."[4] This statement justified the large sum of money spent on presents and *dashees* in Africa. Most of these presents and *dashees* went to the local *caboceers*, leaders of a tribe or village, and *penyins*, the elders of the various states, tribes or villages. To create an alliance with the Fante, the English focused their diplomatic energies on them but not to the exclusion of others.

The nature of the Fante state allowed local leaders great autonomy, while along the coast there remained numerous independent towns, peoples, and states. The local elites dealt and interacted with the company's representatives in a variety of ways. When a slave ship arrived, the captain customarily went ashore and inquired into the supply and price of slaves. The captains found it advantageous to invite the local *caboceer* and *penyins* aboard his ship, where he presented them with *dashees*.[5] In many areas the local elites were slave intermediaries as their political authority gave them control over the slave paths and the exchange of slaves. In 1753 a pawn, the son of "one of the chief priests of Fante," wanted to see England. Governor Melvil explained to the London African Committee that a small monetary expenditure might bring the company great benefits; the powerful position of the pawn's father was an important factor in this event.[6]

The African elites most benefited from their control of the slave trade. They became a new type of slave merchant who weekly went to the interior market to procure slaves and then delivered them directly to the fort or the "road" where the slavers were. If there was no "vent" for the slaves, they were returned to the market.[7] Only the local elite had the money, authority, and knowledge to participate so directly in the slave trade. The African slave merchants actively dictated the nature of the coastal slave trade.

The most important African at Cape Coast was Cudjoe Caboceer, who until his death in May 1776 played a vital role in creating and maintaining the company's relationship with the Fante. After his arrival Governor Melvil expressed his concern to Cudjoe of the town's rampant lawlessness. He inquired how many men could enforce the town's laws and Cudjoe estimated one hundred. When Melvil expressed his concern over the expense of one hundred white soldiers, Cudjoe suggested obtaining Gambia men and women to uphold the law. Cudjoe probably believed that foreign peoples could more easily enforce the laws as they remained distant from local squabbles. While the company engaged Cudjoe in many trivial affairs, his most important role involved maintaining the profitable relationship between the company and the Fante and with the various other coastal peoples. In September 1752, when Melvil attempted to negotiate a political treaty with the Fante, the various *caboceers* demanded one thousand bendies each to sign the treaty.[8] In reaction, Melvil presented them with brandy and sent Cudjoe to negotiate with each separately. Cudjoe's role in the treaty's creation was indispensable, and whenever the Fante demanded something new, Cudjoe negotiated for the company's benefit.[9]

Cudjoe found ways, other than direct employment, to profit from the company's precarious position. In 1767 when the company desperately needed labor, Cudjoe presented a group of laborers for hire. Early on, the laborers worked hard, but they quickly became lazy and disruptive. Since it involved too much time and money to oversee them, the company fired them. Cudjoe agreed to this and, when it was time to pay wages, collected them all. The company quickly realized that Cudjoe had tricked them into hiring his personal slaves as wage labor.[10] In May 1776, when Cudjoe died, the company remembered him as their strongest African supporter and immediately concerned itself over his successor.[11] This quickly subsided when Cudjoe's brother, Caboceer Bothy, succeeded him. Caboceer Bothy, along with Cudjoe's son, Caboceer Aggerie—captain of the town's black soldiers—would both prove "useful and loyal" to the company.[12] Aggerie was called into action in April 1780, when the *caboceers, penyins,* and townspeople arrived in the castle's hall and demanded presents and *dashees* for the assumption of a new governor. To rectify this dilemma the company hired Aggerie at £50 coast money, plus presents, to appease the locals.[13] The company's ability to maintain a strong relationship with the *caboceers* of Cape Coast guaranteed its continued survival.

The transfer of commodities from the company to the African elite signified their importance. In February 1750 Cudjoe, in his position as company linguist, received £70 coast money per annum, castle bomboy James Hinch £50, messenger extraordinary George Bunissee £48, warehouse keeper and servant Essinee £27, and six black soldiers £18 each. In that month the Cape Coast *penyins* received, once a week, their customary flask of rum. On February 8 the *penyins* received another flask as a *dashee,* while on the 16th Cudjoe received an anchor of brandy. Indirect payments such as customary ground rent and water custom supplemented the direct payments to the African elite. In March and April 1751 the company paid £24 in ground rent and water custom.[14] August 1766 saw pay of three and one-half gallons of rum, worth £1 13s. 4d., delivered to various "Black Men," while for September–October they received £32 10s. in commodities. The company paid the £32 10s. in iron bars, rum, Halfsays and Tassaties (varieties of textiles), and brandy.[15] In 1776 the council submitted a report to Parliament explaining expenses for 1770–76. In that time the company paid out over £7,426 in "Black Men" salaries while spending over £10,628 on "Presents and Dashees."[16] The goods paid to this elite involved a sizable portion of the company's budget, given that it received yearly parliamentary grants of between £10,000 and £15,000. In 1764 Gov. William Mutter requested the following gifts be sent for the local elite: three black hats with silver lace, another three with gold lace, and six "hickory canes with silver heads"; Mutter added that "neither the cloths, the hats, nor the lace, should be fine, but gaudy and ostentatious."[17] The company's dependency on the African elite did not create respect. The company maintained its relationship with the elite for assorted reasons, the most important being its reliance on African labor. This relationship with the local elite allowed company officials access to local laborers, thus giving the slave trade's direct participants control over its indirect participants. The company's dependency on the African elite satisfied its long-term goals, but its daily survival relied on its ability to procure laborers.

Coastal Wage Labor

Canoemen

The dispersion of the company's West African possessions over hundreds of miles of coast required the company to utilize coastal laborers. At Cape Coast Castle the most important group of indirect participants were the wage laborers whose toil maintained the coastal trading infrastructure. The geography of the Gold Coast, especially the lack of a natural harbor, coupled with the company's expansive coastal presence made employing local canoemen a vital element in the coastal slave and commodity trade.[18] The arrival of supply ships at Cape Coast Castle, usually late with spoiled or unwanted goods, made it the governor's responsibility to supply the outposts. The problem was that the coastal surf was constantly rough and dangerous. Although past the breakers and out to sea it became calm, the tantamount problem remained of moving the commodities from ship to shore and the slaves from shore to ship. This was where the canoemen came in. Paul Isert's journal of his voyage to Guinea describes the coastal waters as very shallow. This forced most ships to drop their anchors one and one-half miles off the coast. Isert reported that most European attempts to reach shore in a small boat resulted in its being capsized. Only the coastal fishermen possessed the skill, bravery, and dexterity to successfully get their canoes through these breakers, and yet even they were not always successful.[19] On May 12, 1762, while the supply ship *Phoenix* was being unloaded, the rough surf destroyed four or five large canoes. This loss caused Gov. Charles Bell to declare May the worst time to unload ships. On June 16, 1762, in another correspondence to the London African Committee, Bell commented that the rough seas slowed the *Phoenix*'s unloading, but he happily reported no destroyed canoes.[20]

The multitude of tasks for canoemen increased their value to both the company and the slavers plying the coast. As shown, one use involved unloading the supply ships. Canoemen also loaded ships with supplies and carried slaves out to the slavers, but this occurred outside company control. In June 1755 Governor Melvil rejoiced when the canoemen unloaded the annual supply ship in three days.[21] Soon thereafter Melvil reported that the free canoemen carrying water to ships lying on the road received excellent compensation.[22] Another use for the canoemen developed in 1764 when the company required timber to continue its repairs at Cape Coast Castle. Gov. William Mutter reported that to obtain timber company slaves traveled ten to twelve miles inland, where they felled the trees and sawed them into planks. Since by customary right the local peoples supplied the forts with wood, the company hired free laborers to load the canoes and then canoemen to bring the timber to the fort. The company additionally employed canoemen to carry supplies along the coast to the various outposts and to deliver messages, correspondence, and presents along the coast and inland rivers. The numerous ways that the company utilized canoemen's labor made them an important element in the slave trade and coastal economy.

The company's need for the canoemen created economic opportunities for them, and the canoemen used their skills to profit from the European presence sanctioned by their rulers. In 1754 the refusal of the Annamaboe canoemen to work for what the company offered forced Governor Melvil to send Cape Coast canoemen to Annamaboe to unload a supply ship.[23] This wage dispute was common as the company attempted to pay the canoemen as little as possible yet continually complained of the expense of hiring so many. When Melvil first arrived, he complained of the high cost of the canoemen. This complaint was reiterated in 1778 and 1780, but at those times by the London African Committee. In May 1780 the committee was unhappy to learn that the chiefs of their forts gave the canoemen *dashees* before they left. The committee demanded the end of this practice for all but three-hand intelligence canoes (those manned by three canoemen).[24]

While the wages they received were low, especially for the physical labor that they performed, the canoemen profited from their labor in other ways. They developed a customary right to appropriate any commodity that spilled in their canoe. This custom developed naturally as supervision of the canoemen only occurred when they were loading or unloading their canoes. When the company hired bomboys to supervise the "launching, drawing and landing of canoes," they discovered that the African bomboys habitually looked the other way when offenses occurred.[25]

Another way in which canoemen benefited from the English slave trade was through employment as sailors. The slave trade's brutality was not enacted just on slaves as sailors, too, experienced high death rates, especially when a ship laid off the coast for months. This made many a slaver captain desperate for men to make the westward voyage across the Atlantic. The canoemen's familiarity with the Atlantic and African coasts, along with their bravery and sense of adventure, made them perfect recruits, even though many did not possess the knowledge or skills to sail a rigged ship. Private traders hired these African sailors to operate their own ships that patrolled the coast searching for the cheapest slaves. In 1766 one of these coastal sailors, wanted for murder, attempted to escape on a Liverpool slaver ready to sail for the Americas.[26] Because Africans were hired as sailors a small percentage of Africans who crossed the Atlantic to the Americas did so not as human chattel but as free men.

The records of Cape Coast Castle for February 1751 illustrate the diverse uses for canoemen. Under the category of "presents and *dashees,*" canoemen received a present whenever they fitted out a new canoe. Presents were also given to the various messengers coming and going by canoe. The category of "free canoemen and laborers hired" further demonstrated the canoemen's importance. On February 2 canoemen received one flask of rum and one fathom of tobacco as subsistence, while the canoemen who transported the Danish governor and his wife to Cape Coast Castle received three flasks of rum. On February 3 canoemen with an express for Succondee received a gallon of rum and a fathom of tobacco. Rum and tobacco were the most common forms of payment, but other forms were used as well. Two canoemen going to Winnebah received a keg of tallow and one sheet, while a nine-hand canoe going to Winnebah received textiles that included one Perpet and four sheets. The other form of payment involved seven canoemen voyaging to Commenda, who received one long cloth, tallow, and tobacco for their labor. The at-ready canoemen on the beach received a weekly wage of alcohol whether or not they worked. Canoemen also received pay when they helped to rectify the almost continuous series of coastal palavers. To pay off those participating in palavers involving the company, goods needed to be sent, and so the company hired canoemen to carry these goods.[27] The diversity and amount of commodities paid out to the canoemen in one month demonstrate their ability to profit from and their importance to the company. The canoemen's worth was based on their physical labor of propelling their canoes up and down rivers, along the coast, and through the breakers, as well as in their ability to move commodities, supplies, slaves, messages, people, and presents.

African Wage Labor

Along with the canoemen, another important element contributing to the company's success and stability in West Africa was the skilled and unskilled wage labor employed to maintain the coastal trading infrastructure. The company's dependence on free African labor was based on necessity and on developing racial attitudes. In 1753 Governor Melvil wrote that "the white laborers are almost all sick, I never expected much good from 'em for this is not country for Europeans to work in the sun, even though they are sober men"; that same year Mr. Apperley, chief engineer and commander of the fort at Annamaboe, reported: "These white men which I have at present that are not artificers (which is four) are useless for me as no white man can work at labourer work in this country. The white bricklayers can work but five hours a day and the blacks seven hours in the day. The sun being so extremely hot here; as I find the black bricklayers are the people I am to depend on for building the fort, out of the 23 men slaves Captain Bruce brought [from] Gambia, I've made twelve bricklayers, three carpenters and three smiths."[28] The company hired African laborers because it lacked European laborers and also believed that in the African environment Africans worked more, harder, and for less money. Of course, if slavery comprised the dominant labor force of the Americas, it would seem logical that the company, so near the source of slaves, would use slaves exclusively. The company used slaves and pawns, and yet a reflection by Governor Mutter illustrates the dilemma under which the governors of Cape Coast Castle worked: "As to company slaves, it would undoubtedly be necessary to have a supply of them, but till they could be procured [mainly paid for], free labourers might be hired, and they would come full as cheap as company slaves, but then they must not be relied on entirely, for if they once saw you could not proceed without their assistance, extravagant wages and insolent behavior, would in spite of the greatest indulgences, knock all our schemes in the head."[29] The company did not want free labor to realize its importance within the growing coastal economy.

The majority of the company's hired wage labor repaired and improved, and in a few cases built, its warehouses, castles, and forts. When the company assumed the responsibility of insuring England's West African interest, the forts and castles transferred from the Royal African Company were in a decrepit state. The period from 1750 into the late 1770s was one of constant rebuilding and improving. Governor Melvil arrived to find Cape Coast Castle in a state of disrepair intensified by the lack of laborers and building materials required to repair it. Apperley, ordered to construct a fort at Annamaboe, mainly because of a French threat to do so, experienced the same problems. The constant want of bricklayers and carpenters made highly skilled laborers in demand. Apperley complained that the hospitalization of seven African bricklayers and one African carpenter brought his work to a halt.[30] The continuous rebuilding and rot because of the two rainy seasons necessitated constant repairs and an endless supply of building materials. In 1775 Gov. David Mill worried about his lack of bricklayers after he lost six of them to worms; he was impatient to get the castle's arches repaired before the rainy season began.[31]

The company's diary of employment for 1777 illustrates the use of free coastal labor. On July 10 the company employed eleven bricklayers, seven carpenters, four sawyers, five smiths, three armorers, four coopers, nine artificer boys, seventeen laborers, thirty-two labouresses, and six stone blowers. Throughout 1777 and 1778 the number of workers employed remained constant, with the majority being bricklayers, laborers, and labouresses. It is interesting to see so many women employed as unskilled labor. In West Africa physical labor was not the exclusive domain of men; therefore women actively participated in the slave trade.[32] The use of free labor depended on several variables: the company's need for labor, its ability to pay, and the status of its slave force.

Mulattos

Another source of free labor was the growing mulatto population. The company hired mulattos into various positions, but the most common task was soldiering. In 1774 Governor Mill reported the enlistment of twelve mulatto soldiers into the garrison, as they were "fittest for this climate"; Mill believed that this policy helped the company through Cape Coast Castle being better garrisoned while ending the cost of crimping and indenting soldiers in London.[33] In December the African Committee argued that the garrison consisted of too many mulattos and, although they were good soldiers, wanted the number reduced to one-fourth the current level.[34] This did not end their employment in the garrison for in February 1776 Jon Moll, a mulatto, signed a three-year indenture as a soldier.[35] In early 1774 Cape Coast Castle employed fifty-three soldiers in its garrison, including six mulatto band members and seventeen mulatto soldiers; the mulatto soldiers received the same pay of twenty-seven pounds coast money per annum as the white soldiers.[36] Many mulattos possessed other skills, just as the white soldiers did; thus, some were hired for other positions. William Norman, a mulatto carpenter, received employment early in 1772 at the rate of thirty-six pounds coast money per annum.[37] A few mulattos received European educations and consequentially found employment as artificers, factors, and writers. This brought them greater pay and authority.

English Wage Labor

The other source of wage labor came from England. With this labor the company experienced two problems: acquiring men willing to journey to West Africa for little pay; and finding quality men. Once the workers arrived in West Africa the problems continued, especially as disease and the harsh local environment decimated these European workers. The responsibility of obtaining and transporting laborers was that of the London African Committee. This committee consisted of nine men, three each from London, Bristol, and Liverpool, annually elected to their positions. The trouble the committee encountered centered on securing men willing to do physical labor in West Africa.

In early February 1764 the committee commissioned Erasmus Carver to crimp two masons and two house carpenters. They wanted "sober, good working men" and hoped that Carver could find them "six able bodied soldiers, from 20 to 30 years old." Carver enticed the masons and house carpenters by offering forty to fifty pounds coast money per annum and promised the soldiers twenty-five pounds coast money per annum. To supply themselves before embarking for Cape Coast Castle, the soldiers received uniforms and two guineas while the masons and house carpenters received four pounds for the voyage. The company paid the passage of all its men, and provided each with a hammock, bedding, beds, food, and drink during the voyage. Any man willing, or forced, to take these terms signed a three-year indenture.[38] Obtaining soldiers/laborers for the company entitled Carver to a bounty.[39]

The printed indenture signed by the men, either freely or through the auspices of a crimp, was standard for the time. Those indentured agreed to serve the company faithfully at any of its posts in Africa for a specific number of years to be agreed on. This service officially began on arrival in West Africa. In return for their service the company agreed to pay their passage to Africa and subsistence on the ship both before and after it sailed, with the indentured worker stating both the amount and schedule of pay. This pay for each would be in "goods and merchandise at a fair and market price according to the custom of the said coast for his maintenance and support."[40] This allowed the company to pay the men at coastal values and in commodities, not specie. When his indenture expired, a man could renew it for another three years. If he did, he received a bounty. In March 1778 Thomas Fryer and William Howard renewed for two years and received a bounty of £4 10s. coast money each.[41] While some men renewed their indentures, many others petitioned to be sent home.

When the indentured laborers/soldiers arrived, they encountered a harsh and strange environment in which they often toiled to exhaustion or death. Generally the governor, chiefs, and officers viewed their European laborers as worthless. Soon after his arrival Governor Melvil reported that the European soldiers were worthless, and Melvil argued that the company would be better off using Gambia slaves as soldiers. Melvil was also unimpressed with the white sailors he found along the coast, stating, "There are sometimes a dozen worthless sailors living in this town, getting drunk and abusing the Negroes, these fellows think themselves above all law"; Melvil viewed these sailors as the "most abandoned men in the world" as after they were paid in alcohol they went wild in a lawless town.[42] This negative opinion held sway whether they worked hard or not. Under Melvil's reign Slater, an artificer, was a good worker, but his constant drinking offset this attribute.[43] Apperley reported that "white men as artificers and laborers are quite useless to me here therefore look upon their wages as money thrown away."[44] An incident occurred under Gov. Charles Bell when the supply ship *Phoenix* arrived in May 1762. The *Phoenix* contained nineteen soldiers, but on the voyage from London one had died. Referring to this death, Bell wrote: "which I suppose is no great loss to your service, for in my life I have never saw such Cretans [sic], I think I should be wanting in my duty if I did not assure you that your sending such people here, is just so much of the public money thrown away, as one half of them will never be able to do a house duty."[45] The low opinion the company's officials had of their European laborers did not disguise the fact that these laborers were vital to their position and success in West Africa.

The laborers sorely needed were those skilled in the building trades. The wet climate wreaked havoc on the company's structures, especially those made of mud and bricks. With this in mind, early on the company decided that everything should be rebuilt using stones and a lime-based mortar. This ambitious reconstruction plan demanded skilled bricklayers, carpenters, and various artificers. In some cases the bricklayers and other skilled workers sent over were incompetent in the trades they claimed to belong to; in other cases when a good worker arrived the environment quickly took him away. In March 1753 Apperley complained that four out of five of his bricklayers "know nothing of the bricklayers' work."[46] Skilled workers were important not only for their work but in that they could teach their skills to others. Those soldiers/laborers who practiced no trade could be taught one along with some of the company's African workers. In January 1753 James Skinner apprenticed one of the company's boy slaves to a black carpenter. He reported to the African Committee that if they sent him a white carpenter he could teach both of them and consequentially all three would be great attributes for the company.[47]

The nature of their labor and the precariousness of their life expectancy drove many men to drink. The fact that they were partly paid in rum or brandy amplified this problem. In June 1766 Governor Hippisley encountered a problem when, with food supplies running low, he discovered that several soldiers continually sold their daily rations for alcohol. This problem of drunkenness was intensified when, in July, Cape Coast experienced its worst rainy season in memory.[48] With little to do because of the rain, the men turned to alcohol. For soldiers' work, especially labor, the committee felt that drinking was not enough reason to expel a man. For clerical positions this was not the case. In February 1771 the writer Thomas Smith was discharged when the governor discovered that he was daily in a "state of stupefication occasioned by drunkenness ever since his arrival."⁴⁹ The constant drinking created other problems. In May 1765 a group of men gathered in Mr. Williamson's room to drink punch. At this party the antagonism between the accountant John Crichton and the surveyor John Smith erupted into violence. Crichton entered the room with a three-inch-thick stick hidden under his coat. He walked up to Smith and struck him two "bloody and murderous blows to the head." Crichton was quickly grabbed and detained and soon after was dismissed from service, although Smith survived the blows.⁵⁰

The problem of finding hardworking men to indenture themselves to three years' service on Africa's West Coast intensified in the late 1770s because of the manpower drain caused by the war against England's North American colonies. In early 1781 an English expeditionary force led by Captain Mackenzie arrived at Cape Coast Castle with orders to attack and take the Dutch forts. The problem was that the majority of these soldiers were convicts released to fight the Dutch in Africa. Governor Weuves reported to the African Committee that these men had become "the terror of all your servants as well as [the] natives." They plundered everything and everyone they could.⁵¹ The following month the problems with Captain Mackenzie's soldiers persisted, causing Governor Weuves to plead to the company: "We surmise [the] government will be disposed again to send out some of the convicts—in such case for God's sake send us good locks, for we have already experienced that those we have here are not proof of the villainy of these wretches . . . indeed unless a power is sent out to try these most notorious of them to hang, they must be kept always in irons, for how in the name of God can it be thought the lives of eight or ten officers are safe among such a crew of felons."⁵² The problem with the convicts continued through the year, and at one point several deserters were locally captured by Africans. This allowed Captain Mackenzie to make an example out of one of them. He placed the man in front of a nine-pound cannon and "sent him . . . to the next world to answer for his conduct in this."⁵³ By early 1783 Governor Miles worried that the government would continue using West Africa as a dumping ground for felons.⁵⁴ Governor Miles's concerns escalated when instructions from the African Committee stated that more convicts were on their way.⁵⁵

Although the problems encountered in using European laborers on the Gold Coast were numerous, the company could not function without these workers. This dependence was reflected especially in pay. In 1750, under the category of "Officers," Gov. John Roberts received 300 pounds per annum, the factor John Meers 80 pounds per annum, and the writer Nathaniel Parker 60 pounds per annum, while John Goldfrey, inspector of fortifications, received 100 pounds a year. Concurrently the highest-paid individual, under the category of "Artificers and Soldiers," was John Hippisley, who held the positions of surgeon, secretary, and French translator and received 200 pounds per annum. The next were John Soveiger, paneyor of the garden, and sergeant Hugh Invin, both at 50, pounds followed by corporal Peter Falcongreen at 36 pounds and drummer John Little and thirteen soldiers at 27 pounds each.[56] For September–October 1766 the total whitemen's salaries for the entire coast was 6,660 pounds; this was paid out not in species but in commodities.[57]

As the officers controlled the commodities used as wages, those at the bottom probably received the least valuable of the tradeable commodities. The payment of salaries in overinflated coast money caused continual discontent. In June 1781 there was a concerted effort by the men to receive their wages at European rather than coastal prices. This effort, of course, failed.[58] Those Europeans who entered the company's service at the lowest levels did the hardest work for the least amount of opportunity.

Coastal Unfree Labor

The company found that, while useful, wage labor, be it African or European, was not their only option. The company's job was to insure both the infrastructure and the supply of slaves for the slave trade. The commodity of which they insured a constant supply could be used as a labor source. This made slaves direct and indirect participants in the slave trade as they served as both commodities and as laborers who maintained the trade's infrastructure. The only hindrance to using slave labor was the company's parliamentary prohibition of selling slaves. The act that created the company allowed it to buy slaves for use in its possessions along the coast; thus, because of their proximity to the source of slaves, slave labor became an important element in the company's daily operations and upkeep. Pawns were the other source of unfree labor available to the company, but the possession and use of pawns created complications. For this reason the company avoided any circumstance that might bring more pawns. Slaves and pawns competed with African and European wage labor in doing the company's work, and yet the company never found one source of laborers superior to the others.

Slaves

Important issues within studies of slavery and African history during the slave-trade period involve the history of African slavery and the difference between African and Western slavery. Suzanne Miers and Igor Kopytoff examined African slavery and how Western slavery prohibited one from understanding African slavery within its cultural context.[59] An important question is what happened to African slavery and European slavery when they existed side by side? At Cape Coast Castle the company used its slaves differently from local practices and from American plantation practices. While their slaves were viewed as commodities, the company paid them wages and they were given the same privileges as the wage laborers. It can be guessed that, in West Africa, contact between the two types of slavery caused each to change—at least locally. More study is needed to determine the consequences of this contact.

The company had many options in purchasing slaves, and yet they quickly learned important lessons that helped them to efficiently employ slave labor. The first lesson involved acquiring slaves from far away for local use. If the company purchased slaves from a local seller, there was always the possibility that the slave might be local. This increased the chance of the slave running away or trouble with family or friends.[60] For the period under study the company's officials attempted to buy all of its slaves for factory use from Gambia. Because Gambian slaves had little in common with the locals, the chance of escape was minimal. Also, company officials believed that Gambian slaves were better laborers than local slaves. In December 1771 the African Committee informed Gov. David Mill that the next supply ship contained extra goods—many being printed textiles—sent to buy twenty-five healthy and young male slaves from Whydah. While the committee preferred that the slaves be from Gambia, their last report stated that the Gambia slave paths were closed.[61] In December 1773 Governor Mill reported to the committee that he had purchased ten more slaves, "fine young men" who would learn a trade and prove profitable to the company.[62]

The slaves engaged in a multitude of tasks, but the most time-consuming and important ones involved the repair and strengthening of the castle. Constant maintenance prevented the castle's deterioration, and concurrently the company believed that if the castle appeared formidable to the Africans then this facade of power would keep them docile. During the summer of 1765 the company's slaves busily rebuilt one of Cape Coast Castle's walls. By autumn 1765 the company engaged its slaves in "paving the spur" to prevent a new tank from being destroyed by the rain; their next job involved repairing the south wall, but deterioration of the magazine's roof interrupted this work.[63] During January 1767 the slaves rebuilt the south bastion and were slowed only by the lack of materials.[64] For their excellent job in building and repairing the castle Governor Petrie the following year commended the slaves, especially the three slave carpenters who excelled beyond the company's two white carpenters. This improvement was especially important as it appeared that the Asante and Fante would soon go to war.[65] More castle repairs were done during late 1770, when Governor Mill reported that if the company slaves were not paid he would have to hire thirty to forty laborers to carry stones. At this time Governor Mill experienced trouble in hiring free laborers and therefore desired to purchase twenty or thirty young Gambian slaves.[66] Slave labor was vital to the maintenance of the slave trade's infrastructure and helped to insure the continuation of English profits in the trade.

Slave labor was not restricted to repairing and maintaining the castle and other buildings. In January 1753 Governor Melvil used company slaves to unload a supply ship rather than hire free canoemen. While the slaves did a good job, Melvil reported that "other ships can not be expected to be unloaded with such expedition, as it would destroy all of our slaves."[67] The use of slaves to unload the supply ship was an unusual occurrence since the local canoemen were much more qualified for the job; yet it demonstrated the company's willingness to use slaves over wage labor whenever possible. The same year, in an effort to keep his bricklayers employed just laying bricks, Apperley requested that he be allowed to use slaves to blow stones; the company, whenever possible, attempted to use its unskilled slaves to do menial physical labor because of the scarcity of skilled laborers.[68] Gov. Thomas Mutter, in a correspondence to the African Committee, explained the company's policy toward free and slave labor; according to Mutter, the hiring of free labor only occurred when the company did not possess enough slaves to do the job.[69] Of course, the company's endemic underfunding continually prohibited it from possessing enough slaves.

Later the same year Governor Mutter proposed a plan to allow the company to depend almost exclusively on slave labor. As they worked to repair Cape Coast Castle and other decrepit outposts, Mutter attempted to procure thirty to forty Gambian slaves. These slaves could be instructed in the bricklayer, smith, and carpenter trades and, if no artisans could teach them, could be sent to England "to learn these trades."[70] This plan was never put into action, and yet the idea of teaching its slaves skills remained attractive to the company.

Another way the company utilized its slaves was as soldiers. The problem with this was that arming one's slaves went against the European notion of slavery. In September 1778 Governor Miles reported the increasing number of French men-of-war and American privateers causing trouble along the West African coast. The fear of a coastal war among European states intensified because, while the rebuilding of Cape Coast Castle made it stronger, the castle's garrison consisted of eighteen men; at that time only ten were fit for duty and all were mulattos. Governor Miles considered using slaves but quickly realized that the consequences would be more detrimental than beneficial.[71] By June 1780, when the possibility of war included the Dutch, slaves were reconsidered as possible soldiers. The Council of Cape Coast Castle decided that some of the more trustworthy castle slaves could fire artillery and, hopefully, some of the local European free traders would take up arms and help.[72] The council probably figured it was harder to turn an artillery piece than a rifle on one's master.

The company's reliance on slaves can be seen in a March 1756 list of slaves at Cape Coast Castle. Assigned there were thirty-seven male slaves and seven female slaves. Out of the male slaves nine were bricklayers, with one being old, another a boy, and three listed as sick. Four male slaves possessed the skill of carpenter, with one being old and two being boys. There was one brick maker, one sick goldsmith, one blacksmith, one canoeman, one copper's boy, and nineteen laborers. Of these, six were sick and six were boys. Each of the female slaves was listed as "labouress," with two of them sick.[73]

In February 1751 the company paid its slaves £13. A bricklayer named Coffee was advanced on his pay one fathom of tobacco, while an elderly female "doctress" received four fathoms of tobacco for curing a slave's illness. The same month Winnebah Tom received one gallon of rum while Quamino, warehouse porter, received two gallons. These payments can be compared to the other company expenses for the same month: over £8 on "presents and dashees," £32 on "free canoemen and labourers hired," £111 on "palavers," and over £22 on "stores furnished in Africa."[74]

The buying and maintaining of slaves became important parts of the company's yearly budget. In April 1751 the castle slaves received over £12 in a combination of the following items: long cloths, Blue Basts, and Niconne textiles, along with brandy, rum, cowries, and tobacco.[75] The cost of maintaining its slaves continued to rise throughout the company's reign. From May to June 1757 the company spent over £437 to purchase and maintain its slaves, and this amount remained constant for the rest of the year.[76] For January to mid-August 1770 the company spent £412 on its slaves; this was used to purchase 571 gallons of rum for £285 10s. and 506 fathoms of tobacco for £126 10s. This amount was less than that paid to its white servants (£725) but more than black men's pay (£24), fort repairs (£377), free canoemen and laborers hired (£114), presents and *dashees* (£94), and ground rent and water custom (£4).[77]

Pawns

The other form of unfree labor available to the company involved the use of pawns. The coastal meaning of "pawns" remains rather ambiguous even after a thorough examination of the company's records. A pawn, while considered a form of debt peonage, was not a slave, in the European definition of the term, because some amount of personal freedom remained. Toyin Falola and Paul Lovejoy have worked to place pawnship in its proper historical perspective as it correspondingly developed with slavery. They illustrate how pawnship is related to questions of "indebtedness, labor control, gender and capital flows in societies that were only perfectly connected to world markets." Pawnship emerged out of coastal poverty and was related to the attempt of families to survive at a subsistence level. When a family could not afford the commodities it desperately needed, a pawn, usually female, was contracted to the merchant. The pawn's labor, now controlled by the merchant, would cover the interest on the debt and continue to provide subsistence for the family. This meant that the debt remained to be paid, which, in turn, made it hard to pay off the pawnship contract. Falola and Lovejoy stress that the pawn was not property but only a source of labor and that there existed legal channels to prevent abuse. This was important in that most pawns were held locally and thus their families and friends could easily observe their treatment.[78] The locality of pawnship created difficulties for the company as pawns could not be transferred to other forts for labor.

For the company, pawnship constituted the least attractive source of labor. While accounts of accepting and using pawns exist throughout the company's records, they were minor compared to the other sources of labor. One atypical situation occurred in March 1753 when one of the company's pawns, destined to "be one of the chief priests of the Fante," expressed a desire to see England. The record states that the pawn was obtained "for the observance of the law," with Governor Melvil arguing that it would be worthwhile for the company to spend money to educate him in England. An English education would make the pawn a useful servant of the company and, concurrently, would help to further strengthen English/Fante relations. Governor Melvil concluded his report by stating: "And may enable us the better to keep up our connections with the inland Fante; besides his father is a man of great personal authority expects that his son shall be taught; and in my opinion he ought to be gratified, as he is one of the principle [sic] actors in procuring the law: I know there are objectives to teaching the Negroes to read and write, but I believe they would not hold good in the present case."[79] A little education could go a long way in firming the company's position on the coast, and yet the majority of pawns did not receive this type of treatment from the company. In August 1774 the company resolved a palaver between Accroans and the people of Mumford and Lagoe by paying the palaver to the Accroans. The company at that time possessed enough slaves and so decided that it would take pawns from Mumford and Lagoe for the debt of paying the palaver. The council employed the pawns as laborers and paid each "four ackies in trade goods per month for their subsistence." The council stated that its motivation for becoming involved was to keep the paths open.[80] In January 1775 Gov. David Mill reported that the company had just received pawns who would be used as laborers but that a few would be taught trades. The following year Mill concluded that the only way the company could get its money back in its pawnship contracts was to sell the pawns.[81] This created its own problems.

Conclusion

An examination of the laborers of Cape Coast Castle illustrates their roles in the slave trade and the Atlantic economy. The elite, both African and English, who participated in the slave trade depended on coastal laborers to maintain the coastal trading infrastructure and to keep the slave paths open. The procurement and utilization of labor at Cape Coast Castle was a vital determinant in the economic success of England's slave trade. A mixture of wage and unfree systems ensured that the laborers worked while crimping, indentures, purchasing, or the enticement of commodities obtained laborers. The labor systems of Cape Coast Castle depended on the company's ability to maintain a mutually beneficial relationship with the local elite who allowed the company to remain on the coast. Cape Coast Castle's laborers were racialized, marginalized, exploited, and gendered; yet these differences did not allow one group of laborers to receive better treatment than the others. The position of the European laborers was probably the worst as they labored in a foreign environment for overvalued commodities; many turned to alcohol, thus intensifying their problems. An important issue is that labor at Cape Coast Castle, the administrative center of England's slave trade, was not entirely slave labor; wage labor proved more effective than slave even though the company had access to the best and cheapest slaves. Cape Coast Castle also provides an excellent example of the interaction and contributions of direct and indirect participants in the slave trade and the consequences of European activity on the Gold Coast.

Notes

1. Public Records Office (hereafter PRO), Kew Gardens, U.K., Treasury Office Records, African Companies, T70/155, *Report of Council of Cape Coast Castle, 1770–76*.

2. A copy of the parliamentary act creating the Company of Merchants Trading to Africa is in Elizabeth Donnan, *Documents Illustrative of the Slave Trade to the Americas*, vol. 2, *The Eighteenth Century* (New York: Octagon Books, 1969), 474–85.

3. PRO T70/1035, Day Book, January to March 1774, lists the following English stations: Cape Coast Castle, Appalonia Fort, Dixcove Fort, Luccandee Fort, Commenda Fort, Annamaboe Fort, Tantumquerry Fort, Minnebak Fort, James Fort at Accra, and William's Fort at Whydah. An examination of these forts is in A. W. Lawrence, *Trade Castles and Forts of West Africa* (Stanford, Calif.: Stanford University Press, 1964); and his *Fortified Trade Posts: The English in West Africa 1645–1822* (London: Jonathan Cape, 1969).

4. PRO T70/152, Cape Coast Castle Council Minutes 1770–81, October 10, 1781, fol. 52. This theme of keeping the local elite happy can be found in Margaret Priestly, *West African Trade and Coast Society: A Family Study* (London: Oxford University Press, 1969). The council consisted of the governor and the next two highest-ranking officers available at the time. These were usually officers from Cape Coast Castle or the chiefs of the forts closest to Cape Coast Castle. The English records distinguish between presents, which they offered the Africans, and *dashees,* which the Africans demanded.

5. Alexander Falconbridge, *An Account of the Slave Trade on the Coast of Africa* (1788; repr., New York: AMS Press, 1973), 7. It is interesting to note that Falconbridge reported how the slave trade disrupted relations among the various African people.

6. PRO T70/30, Inward Letter Book, Africa to England 1750–62, Gov. Thomas Melvil to African Committee, March 10, 1753, 8.

7. Ibid., March 17, 1755, 86–87.

8. A bendie's value was eight pounds.

9. PRO T70/29, Inward Letter Book, Africa to England 1751–53, Gov. Thomas Melvil to African Committee, September 23, 1752, 50. Throughout the records for 1752 the importance of Cudjoe can be seen.

10. PRO T70/31, Inward Letter Book, Africa to England 1762–73, Gov. Gilbert Petrie to African Committee, June 31, 1767, 237.

11. PRO T70/32, Inward Letter Book: Africa to England 1773–81, Gov. David Mill to African Committee, May 7, 1776, 33.

12. PRO T70/32, Gov. John Roberts to African Committee, July 14, 1780, 110–11.

13. PRO T70/152, Council Minutes, April 27, 1780, fol. 28; ibid., May 17, 1780, fol. 35.

14. PRO T70/425, Cape Coast Castle Account Journal #1 for February 1750/1.

15. PRO T70/459, Cape Coast Castle Account Journal #31 for August to October 1766, 15, 47.

16. PRO T70/155, Report of Cape Coast Castle Council 1770–76.

17. PRO T70/31, Gov. Thomas Mutter to African Committee, February 27, 1764, 76–77.

18. Kwame Yeboa Daaku, *Trade & Politics on the Gold Coast 1600–1720: A Study of the African Reaction to European Trade* (Oxford: Clarendon Press, 1970), 33, illustrates the coastal economic dependency on the canoemen. Other works concerning the importance of canoemen to West Africa include Robert Smith, "The Canoe in West African History," *Journal of African History* 11, no. 4 (1970): 515–33; Peter C. W. Gutkind, "The Canoemen of Southern Ghana," in *The Workers of African Trade,* ed. Catherine Coquery-Vidrovitah and Paul E. Lovejoy (London: Sage Publications, 1985).

19. Paul Erdmann Isert, *Letters on West Africa and the Slave Trade: Journey to Guinea and the Caribbean Islands in Columbia,* trans. and ed. Selena Axelrod Winsnes (1758; repr., Oxford: Oxford University Press, 1992), 27–28.

20. PRO T70/31, Gov. Charles Bell to African Committee, May 12, 1762, 1; ibid., June 21, 1762, 2.

21. PRO T70/30, Gov. Thomas Melvil to African Committee, June 9, 1755, 82.

22. Ibid., March 17, 1755, 85.

23. Ibid., July 1, 1754, 63.

24. PRO T70/29, Gov. Thomas Melvil to African Committee, July 11, 1751, 4; PRO T70/69, African Committee to Cape Coast Castle, December 30, 1778, 266; T70/152, May 16, 1780, fol. 34.

25. PRO T70/152, June 16, 1780, fol. 44.

26. PRO T70/31, Gov. John Hippisley to African Committee, June 14, 1766, 189.

27. PRO T70/425, *Cape Coast Castle Journal for February 1751.* This is the most thorough journal in that it lists the actual wages paid instead of just combining them under their heading. John Atkins, *A Voyage to Guinea, Brazil and the West Indies* (1735; facs. repr., London: Frank Cass, 1970), explains that a palaver is a local dispute and that, if proven by the palaver, the plaintiffs have the right to *panyar* (take something to settle the dispute).

28. PRO T70/30, Gov. Thomas Melvil to African Committee, March 14, 1753, 11; ibid., April 22, 1753, 27.

29. PRO T70/31, Gov. William Mutter to African Committee, January 10, 1764, 50.

30. PRO T70/30, Gov. Thomas Melvil to African Committee, March 10, 1753, 6–7.

31. PRO T70/32, Gov. David Mill to African Committee, April 15, 1775, 24.

32. PRO T70/1469, Diary of Employment, 1777–78.

33. PRO T70/32, Gov. David Mill to African Committee, July 29, 1774, 15.

34. PRO T70/69, African Committee to Cape Coast Castle, December 5, 1774, 230.

35. PRO T70/152, February 20, 1776.

36. PRO T70/1325, Garrison Ledger for January to June 1774; PRO T70/1335, Garrison Ledger for January to June 1779.

37. PRO T70/152, February 1, 1772, fol. 5.

38. PRO T70/69, African Committee to Mr. Erasmus Carver, February 2, 1764, 1.

39. Ibid., February 15, 1764, 2.

40. PRO T70/143, Minutes of the African Committee Meetings 1750–55, draft of an indenture to be printed, October 11, 1752, fol. 91.

The Drudgery of the Slave Trade   295

41. PRO T70/152, March 1, 1778, fol. 16; ibid., May 20, 1778, fol. 16.

42. PRO T70/29, Gov. Thomas Melvil to African Committee, December 26, 1751, 17–18; ibid., January 8, 1752, 21. A contemporary account that fully explains the devastating effects of the slave trade on sailors is Falconbridge, *Account of the Slave Trade*.

43. PRO T70/30, Gov. Thomas Melvil to African Committee, April 24, 1753, 29.

44. Ibid., Mr. Apperley to African Committee, September 8, 1753, 34.

45. PRO T70/31, Gov. Charles Bell to African Committee, May 12, 1762, 1.

46. PRO T70/30, Mr. Apperley to African Committee, March 10, 1753, 5.

47. Ibid., James Skinner of James Fort to African Committee, January 23, 1753, 47.

48. PRO T70/31, Gov. John Hippisley to African Committee, June 14, 1766, 190; ibid., July 13, 1766, 193.

49. PRO T70/152, February 28, 1771, fol.3.

50. PRO T70/31, Act of Council, May 10, 1765, 143.

51. PRO T70/33, Gov. Bernard Weuves to African Committee, April 29, 1782, 35.

52. Ibid., Gov. Richard Miles to African Committee, June 22, 1782, 42.

53. Ibid., August 6, 1782, 45.

54. Ibid., February 1, 1783, 55.

55. PRO T70/153, Cape Coast Castle Council Minutes 1781–99, January 16, 1783, 29.

56. PRO T70/425, Pay Bill for Officers of This Castle and Pay Bill for Artificers and Soldiers. The well-paid John Hippisley continued to move upward in rank and pay, and by 1766 he was governor of Cape Coast Castle.

57. PRO T70/459, Cape Coast Castle Journal #31, 1766, *Whitemen's Salaries* for September–October 1766, 42–46.

58. PRO T70/145, Minutes of London African Committee 1780–86, June 20, 1781, 61.

59. Suzanne Miers and Igor Kopytoff, "'Slavery' as an Institute of Marginality," in *Slavery in Africa: Historical and Anthropological Perspectives,* ed. Suzanne Miers and Igor Kopytoff (Madison: University of Wisconsin Press, 1977).

60. PRO T70/32, Gov. David Mill to African Committee, December 4, 1773.

61. PRO T70/69, African Committee to Cape Coast Castle, December 4, 1771, 200.

62. PRO T70/32, Gov. David Mill to African Committee, December 4, 1773.

63. PRO T70/31, Gov. Mutter to African Committee, July 20, 1765, 136; ibid., October 25, 1765, 149–50.

64. Ibid., Gov. Gilbert Petrie to African Committee, January 31, 1767, 235–36.

65. Ibid., March 31, 1768, 290–91.

66. Ibid., Gov. David Mill to African Committee, November 19, 1770, 393.

67. PRO T70/29, Gov. Thomas Melvil to African Committee, January 7, 1753, 53.

68. PRO T70/30, Mr. Apperley, at Annamaboe, to African Committee, September 8, 1753, 34.

69. PRO T70/31, Gov. Thomas Mutter to African Committee, January 10, 1764, 50.

70. Ibid., May 10, 1764, 83.

71. PRO T70/32, Gov. Richard Miles and Council to African Committee, September 25, 1778, 82–83.

72. PRO T70/152, June 9, 1780, fol. 42.

73. PRO T70/30, Gov. Charles Bell to African Committee, March 1756, 144.

74. PRO T70/425, Castle Slaves Delivered to Sundry Accounts, February 1751, fols. 1–13.

75. Ibid., April 1751, fol. 22.

76. PRO T70/437, Cape Coast Castle Journal #12 from January to June 1757, Castle Slaves Delivered to Sundry Accounts, May–June 1757.

77. PRO T70/466, Cape Coast Castle Journal #38 from January 1 to August 10, 1770, 1–27.

78. Toyin Falola and Paul Lovejoy, eds., *Pawnship in Africa: Debt Bondage in Historical Perspective,* African Modernization and Development Series (Boulder, Colo.: Westview Press, 1994), 1–6.

79. PRO T70/30, Gov. Melvil to African Committee, March 10, 1753, 8.

80. PRO T70/152, August 1, 1774, fol. 10.

81. PRO T70/32, Gov. David Mill to African Committee, January 5, 1775, 21; ibid., May 7, 1776, 34.

Indians and the Economy of Eighteenth-Century Carolina

Peter C. Mancall, Joshua L. Rosenbloom, and Thomas Weiss

On April 15, 1729, seventeen ships were docked at the Fort Royal harbor in South Carolina. They ranged in size from small vessels with only one hand on board to larger transatlantic ships—one of which had seventy hands and another sixty. But perhaps the most impressive thing about these ships was the fact that only six were local. The other eleven vessels had made their way to Fort Royal from around the Atlantic basin—from Philadelphia and New York, Rhode Island, Barbados, London, Amsterdam, Bermuda, and Kingston.[1] Without detailed inventories of those ships' cargoes it is impossible to know exactly why they had docked at Fort Royal, but the fact that they jostled for space in the port in the late 1720s tells an important story: those who owned or commanded those ships had guided them to South Carolina's coast to take advantage of what was becoming one of the most profitable colonies in English America. In later years hundreds of ships annually cleared the colony's ports, hauling the region's produce to far-flung markets.[2]

Historians have long known that the basis for wealth in South Carolina was rice. The development of the rice trade, so beautifully described in works by Peter Wood, Peter Coclanis, and Philip Morgan, fit into the economic dreams of British strategists in the eighteenth century. Reliance on the labor of African slaves made sense to the English, who had earlier extracted labor from Africans in the West Indies and the Chesapeake region. Once planters figured out how they could produce rice on their plantations and manage to survive the dangers of the lowlands environment, which they accomplished by spending much of their time in the marginally healthier climes of Charleston, they knew that the way to wealth was to produce rice for the European market.[3] Over time, indigo also became a profitable staple, but rice remained the dominant export of South Carolina.[4]

South Carolina's economy eventually hinged on rice production and the savage labor regimes it entailed, but that commerce was not the most important economic activity for the native peoples of the region. For those Indians, which included those who lived within the territorial boundaries of Carolina (such as the Catawbas) as well as those who lived beyond the colony but who traded extensively with colonists in Carolina, the English colonization of the southern low country meant incorporation into the Atlantic economy. Indians might have participated in long-distance trade less frequently than colonial rice merchants, but their production of deerskins constituted a valuable component of the colony's exports.[5] And though it would be odd indeed to analyze eighteenth-century South Carolina history as a case study in Native American entrepreneurship, it is time to correct the opposite historical assumption that Native Americans there, as in other colonies, were mere dupes of profit-minded European traders. The Indians of the Lower South suffered horrendous population loss during the colonial period, but the survivors figured out ways to improve their lives through creating trade networks that ultimately bound them to other producers and suppliers of goods in the Atlantic basin.

Quantitative estimates are provided to show Indians' economic activity in the southern low country during the eighteenth century. Because Native Americans in this period did not keep the kinds of accounting records left by colonists, and because Indians' economic activities are not always clear in surviving documents, the results presented here are less complete than are similar results produced by analyses of the colonial economy. Nonetheless, since it is our goal to reconstruct the workings of the colonial economy as a whole and to provide more reliable time series by using conjectural estimating techniques to include the economic activity of all early Americans (including Indians),[6] what follows will in the end constitute one part of a reassessment of the entire economy of the Lower South of the mainland British American colonies.

Early Trade and Demographic Decline

Long before the English arrived in Carolina, the Native Americans of that region, like Indians elsewhere, had participated in trade. Archaeological evidence confirms the existence of trade across North America in the centuries before European contact; in the Southeast commerce between groups of Indians had allowed residents of particular regions to enjoy products they could not obtain locally.[7] When Europeans arrived they learned the proper protocols for trading with Indians.[8] In the area that became the Southeast of the English American mainland colonies in the seventeenth century, the first Europeans to engage in extensive trade were the French, who established a post at Fort Caroline in 1562. For the brief duration of that settlement's existence—the Spanish took over intercultural commerce in the Southeast when they established their outposts at St. Augustine (in 1565) and Santa Elena (in 1566)—Europeans and Indians engaged in trade. The French offered manufactured goods such as knives, scissors, axes, and beads; in exchange the Indians provided deerskins, the hides of bison, and pearls. From that point forward trade proceeded in the region. By the time the English arrived to establish Carolina, Timucuas, Guales, and Apalachees, among others, had a long tradition of engaging in commerce with Europeans.[9]

For Native Americans the ongoing contact with Europeans also meant sustained exposure to Old World pathogens that devastated Indian communities. Scholars continue to debate the scale of the demographic catastrophe that Europeans unwittingly precipitated in the Americas, a debate made especially difficult by the lack of reliable population figures for virtually all Native American groups.[10] In the region that became the Southeast of the English mainland colonies, the catastrophe struck with differing force. The Carolina Algonquians, who inhabited Roanoke, disappeared, and many smaller groups bound themselves together and took on new collective identities in a process of ethnogenesis that led to the growth of nations such as the Catawbas and the Choctaws.[11]

It is impossible to understand the relationship between southeastern Indians and the Atlantic economy of the eighteenth century without first stressing that by 1700 or so the population of Native Americans in this region was approximately 50 percent of what it had been before Europeans first arrived in the sixteenth century. Just as important, the economy of the region also reflected the demographic success of the two peoples who invaded the Southeast: European colonists who came willingly and African slaves who had no choice about their destination. In these population figures lie the first clue to understanding Indians' participation in the Atlantic economy (see tables 14, 15, and 16).

As even a brief glance at these numbers reveals, no one could argue that Native Americans in the Southeast benefited without question from the arrival of Europeans. As table 16 reveals, in 1680 Native Americans constituted 95 percent of the population of the Southeast. Yet less than fifty years later Indians' share of the regional population was less than 50 percent, and by 1770 Indians accounted for only one out of every ten individuals in the area; at the end of the century only 4 percent of the population of the Southeast was of Native American ancestry. That table describes the demise of the broadest group of Indians in the Lower South, but the picture is almost the same if we look at more narrowly defined groups (in tables 14 and 15). In all cases the Indian population declined, on average, at a rate of 0.4 or 0.5 percent each year and fell to a minuscule part of the population of the Lower South by 1800.

But demographic catastrophe constitutes only the first component of any understanding of Native Americans' place in the Southeast's economic history. After all, the future still lay ahead for survivors of smallpox and influenza epidemics. Indians remembered their fallen relatives and friends in elaborate rituals, but those who remained in the region did not abandon all hope and collapse into life-ending misery and depression. Instead, as had been the case with other peoples facing catastrophic circumstances, the survivors had to figure out how to best cope with what had become for them a new world.

Table 14: The population of the Lower South at selected dates, 1680 to 1800
(narrow definition of Indian population)

	Number of persons (in 1,000s)				Percentage shares		
Date	White	Black	Indian	Total	White	Black	Indian
1680	6.0	0.6	39.9	46.5	13%	1%	86%
1685	7.6	1.0	35.0	43.6	17%	2%	80%
1690	9.7	1.8	30.7	42.2	23%	4%	73%
1700	13.6	2.9	23.7	40.2	34%	7%	59%
1710	19.3	6.7	19.5	45.5	43%	15%	43%
1715	21.9	9.9	18.1	49.9	44%	20%	36%
1720	24.8	14.9	16.7	56.4	44%	26%	30%
1730	34.0	26.0	15.0	75.0	45%	35%	20%
1740	62.8	50.2	15.0	128.0	49%	39%	12%
1745	71.8	54.3	15.0	141.1	51%	38%	11%
1750	82.4	60.8	14.9	158.1	52%	38%	9%
1750	119.6	90.1	15.0	224.7	53%	40%	7%
1770	190.2	155.6	14.9	360.7	53%	43%	4%
1774	227.9	175.1	15.0	418.0	55%	42%	4%
1780	305.9	210.3	15.2	531.4	58%	40%	3%
1783	358.0	218.7	15.3	592.0	60%	37%	3%
1790	521.9	240.6	15.6	778.1	67%	31%	2%
1793	574.9	268.5	15.8	859.2	67%	31%	2%
1800	739.0	352.4	16.1	1107.5	67%	32%	1%

Sources: U.S. Bureau of the Census, *Historical Statistics of the United States, Colonial Times to 1970,* ser. Z (Washington, D.C.: Government Printing Office, 1975), 1–19; U.S. Census Bureau, *Second Census: Return of the Whole Number of Persons* (Washington, D.C., 1800). The 1790 figures are from the U.S. Census as shown in Rossiter (Washington, D.C., 1909);

Table 14 (continued)
the figures were taken from an electronic file provided by Michael Haines. See Peter Coclanis, *The Shadow of a Dream: Economic Life and Death in the South Carolina Low Country, 1670–1920* (New York: Oxford University Press, 1989), 64; Peter Wood, "The Changing Population of the Colonial South: An Overview by Race and Region, 1685–1790," in *Powhatan's Mantle,* ed. Peter Wood, Gregory A. Waselkov, and Thomas Hatley (Lincoln: University of Nebraska Press, 1989), tab. 1, 39.

Our population series consist of separate estimates for the free, black, and Native American populations. The free and black population figures cover the colonies and states of Georgia, North Carolina and South Carolina, and Tennessee, the latter because we wanted the region to be that in which resided the Native Americans who interacted with the colonists. John McCusker and Russell Menard in *The Economy of British America, 1607–1789* (Chapel Hill: University of North Carolina Press, 1985), 172, made slight revisions to the figures for 1710, 1720, and 1740 but did not report the white and black populations separately for each colony. Their figures, as well as those shown in *Historical Statistics,* differ slightly from the figures reported by Wood for some of these years. The black population for the colonial years includes both slaves and free blacks. The black population in 1790 and 1800 refers to the slave population; the small number of free blacks is included with the white (free) population. The Native American figures include those persons in North and South Carolina who, according to Peter Wood, resided east of the mountains and the Creeks who resided in Georgia and parts of Alabama.

The figures from *Historical Statistics* were reported at decadal benchmark dates, 1680, 1690, and so on, while Wood's estimates for Native Americans were reported at fifteen-year intervals from 1685 to 1790. In order to have comparable coverage of dates for the various series we calculated figures for years between the benchmark dates that were not reported in each of the sources. We derived these figures for each population component in each state or territory by interpolating at a constant the rate of change between the nearest benchmark dates. Thus, for example, the rate of change for the Creek Indians between 1700 and 1710 was assumed to equal that implied by Wood's figures for 1700 and 1715. The Indian population for 1800 was obtained by extrapolating the 1790 figure based on the rates of growth of the Indian population in each state and territory between 1775 and 1790.

Table 15: The population of the Lower South at selected dates, 1680 to 1800 (intermediate definition of Indian population)

Date	Number of persons (in 1,000s)				Percentage shares		
	White	Black	Indian	Total	White	Black	Indian
1680	6.0	0.6	80.3	86.9	7%	1%	92%
1685	7.6	1.0	67.0	75.6	10%	1%	89%
1690	9.7	1.8	56.1	67.6	14%	3%	83%
1700	13.6	2.9	39.7	56.2	24%	5%	71%
1710	19.3	6.7	32.1	58.1	33%	11%	55%
1715	21.9	9.9	29.3	61.1	36%	16%	48%
1720	24.8	14.9	27.6	67.3	37%	22%	41%
1730	34.0	26.0	25.5	85.5	40%	30%	30%
1740	62.8	50.2	24.4	137.4	46%	37%	18%
1745	71.8	54.3	24.0	150.1	48%	36%	16%
1750	82.4	60.8	23.3	166.5	49%	37%	14%
1760	119.6	90.1	22.2	231.9	52%	39%	10%
1770	190.2	155.6	23.0	368.8	52%	42%	6%
1774	227.9	175.1	23.4	426.4	53%	41%	5%
1780	305.9	210.3	23.2	539.4	57%	39%	4%
1783	358.0	218.7	23.1	599.8	60%	36%	4%
1790	521.9	240.6	23.1	785.6	66%	31%	3%
1793	574.9	268.5	23.1	866.5	66%	31%	3%
1800	739.0	352.4	23.0	1114.4	66%	32%	2%

In table 15 the Native American figures include those contained in table 14 plus the Cherokees, who resided for the most part west of the mountains in the Carolinas but who were engaged in trade with the colonists.

Table 16: The population of the Lower South at selected dates, 1680 to 1800
(broad definition of Indian population)

	Number of persons (in 1,000s)				Percentage shares		
Date	White	Black	Indian	Total	White	Black	Indian
1680	6.0	0.6	118.9	125.5	5%	0%	95%
1685	7.6	1.0	102.0	110.6	7%	1%	92%
1690	9.7	1.8	87.8	99.3	10%	2%	88%
1700	13.6	2.9	65.7	82.2	17%	3%	80%
1710	19.3	6.7	54.5	80.5	24%	8%	68%
1715	21.9	9.9	50.1	81.9	27%	12%	61%
1720	24.8	14.9	46.0	85.7	29%	17%	54%
1730	34.0	26.0	39.8	99.8	34%	26%	40%
1740	62.8	50.2	38.9	151.9	41%	33%	26%
1745	71.8	54.3	38.5	164.6	44%	33%	23%
1750	82.4	60.8	37.9	181.1	45%	34%	21%
1760	119.6	90.1	37.1	246.8	48%	37%	15%
1770	190.2	155.6	38.8	384.6	49%	40%	10%
1774	227.9	175.1	39.6	442.6	51%	40%	9%
1780	305.9	210.3	40.0	556.2	55%	33%	7%
1783	358.0	218.7	40.2	616.9	58%	35%	7%
1790	521.9	240.6	40.9	803.4	65%	30%	5%
1793	574.9	268.5	41.2	884.6	65%	30%	5%
1800	739.0	352.4	41.9	1133.3	65%	31%	4%

See tables 14 and 15. Table 16 includes those Indians included in table 15 plus the Choctaws and Chickasaws. Wood, "Changing Population," 66–72, puts these Indians in Mississippi and Alabama. The budget accounts for South Carolina discussed in the text indicate that the colony had dealings with these tribes, so we have produced this variant of the population to show the relative importance of these Indians.

Sources: These estimates are derived from A. S. Salley, ed., *Journals of the Common House of Assembly of South Carolina* (Columbia: Historical Commission of South Carolina, 1909–49); J. H. Easterby et al., eds., *The Journal of the Commons House of Assembly,* 14 vols. (Columbia: Historical Commission of South Carolina, 1951–83). For additional details about these figures, see Peter C. Mancall, Joshua Rosenbloom, and Thomas Weiss, "The Public Finances of the Colonies of the Lower South," paper presented at the NBER Summer Institute on the Development of the American Economy, July 1999, tab. 2A.

By the beginning of the eighteenth century, Indians in the Southeast embraced the opportunities afforded by access to the then-booming economy of the Atlantic basin. And by making that choice they became actors in the economic ascendance of Carolina during the eighteenth century.

Colonists' Payments to Native Americans

How important were Native Americans to the economy of South Carolina during the eighteenth century? It is virtually impossible to measure the entire value of Indians' labor in the colonial era. What value can be placed on Native Americans' prior clearing of fields that were later claimed and planted by colonists?[12] What is the precise value of Native Americans' provisions of food to colonists during the early years of the colonial era, or the value of a bilingual cultural broker who acted as a go-between to minimize potential conflicts between colonists and their Indian neighbors? How can one put a precise value on the fact that some southeastern Indians captured runaway slaves and returned them to their colonial owners? Estimating the price of the slave and compensating the native slave catcher would be parts of the equation, of course, but so would the less calculable value of teaching other slaves that running away often led to even worse treatment once they were returned by Indians.

One measure of Indians' economic worth to the colonists can be judged from the amount of money spent on Indians by colonial officials (see figure 2). From 1701 to 1716 expenses on Indians averaged 211 pounds in Carolina currency per year, or approximately 4 percent of the entire public expenses during that period. Thereafter the relative importance of public expenses for Indians generally increased—to 7 percent in 1736, 9 percent in 1739, 15 percent in 1745, 19 percent in 1746, and a high of 28 percent in 1756, the year the Seven Years' War began in North America.[13] Though figures did not always progress upward, the trend is nonetheless clear: over time, at least until 1756, colonial administrators in South Carolina spent both more money and a higher proportion of their funds to provide goods, such as entertainment expenses at treaty sessions and presents, to Indians. Although these transactions might not fit most scholars' definitions of economic transactions—it could be argued that the expenses had nothing to do with Indians' economic contributions to the colony but instead were made to retain the allegiance of Indians during turbulent times—such logic underestimates the crucial role that Indians played in the colony; without the expenses to satisfy Indian neighbors, colonial administrators would understandably have worried about the fate of the rice and indigo economies during times of war.[14]

To get a clearer idea of Indians' economies and the relationship between those economies and the economies of the Atlantic world it is necessary to go beyond these summary observations based on the total expenses of colonial administrations. Fortunately, the annual budgets of South Carolina provide some details

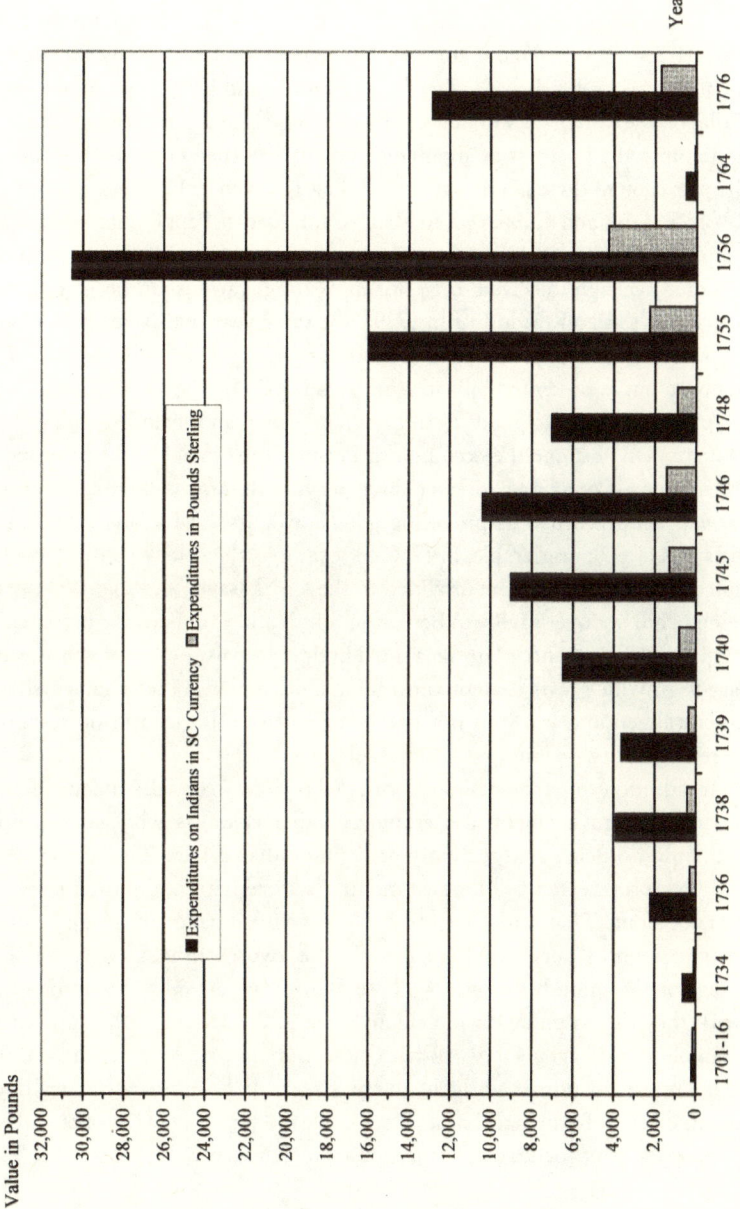

Figure 2: Expenditures on Indians by the colony of South Carolina at selected dates

about nearly 400 economic transactions that involved Native Americans in and near the colony in the thirteen years for which we have examined the extant documents.[15] Though these transactions constitute a minority of the notations in the annual budgets, they accounted for a sizable minority—nearly a fourth of the 1,757 transactions we have recorded so far.

Carolina officials spent public money on Native Americans in a variety of ways. Some expenses went directly to colonists who provided goods for Indians. As early as 1724 the colony authorized a payment of £60 to pay for presents—including a laced red coat, a laced hat, a saddle and bridle, and a gun—for the Tallapoos headman Tickhonobee.[16] By the end of the 1730s various colonists had gotten into the business of supplying Indians and then charging the colony for the provision of these goods. James Crockatt received £241.3 for providing goods to Chickasaws and Cherokees in 1736,[17] Capt. Daniel Pepper received £252.3 for supplying various goods to Choctaws in Savannah in 1738,[18] and Samuel and George Eveleigh received £284 for providing various unspecified goods to Chickasaws at New Windsor in 1739,[19] the same year that Alexander Wood got £615.5 for goods he provided to a group of Creeks.[20] Over the next forty years many colonists presented bills for similar services. By the late 1740s the number of colonists providing goods to Indians had grown and included women as well as men; in 1748 alone the accountants keeping the official books recorded forty transactions—an average of over three per month—for individuals reimbursed for expenses recorded as providing goods or "gifts" to Indians.[21] The value of gifts was often considerable; in 1756, for example, the colony paid Jerome Courtonne £870 for presents he provided to the Chickasaws, and that same year the colony paid out over £1,400 to Benjamin Smith and Company for presents.[22] The frequency of such entries in the annual budget reveals the fact that it was necessary to provide goods to maintain Indian allies and also that such a system was decentralized and put into practice by colonists authorized to do so and who were not otherwise employed by the colony.

In addition to payments to colonists who were essentially independent contractors, the government also employed other colonists who worked directly with public officials charged with managing Indian affairs. Thus in 1738 Nathanial Jackson received £40 for two months' service with Maj. Hugh Butler.[23] He was not alone. That same year the budget included payments to Philip Jackson for two months' service, Hugh Morphy for two months' service, and Robert Lang for two months' service.[24] Those salaries were paid to these men for the work they did to maintain the colony's peaceful relations with the Cherokees. The colony paid agents to work with other Indians too. Accountants authorized payments to an unnamed agent to the Creeks (who received £4 per day), an unnamed clerk to the Creeks (at £2 per day), and four men who assisted them (at £20 per month); for services rendered from January 1, 1736, to April 5, 1736, these six men received a total of £786.²⁵ In addition to such routine service, colonial bureaucrats also authorized payments to colonists who had less regular but nonetheless vital contacts with Indians directly or who did work for the colony that related to Native Americans. To take one particularly expensive example, Col. Joseph Fox and two of his assistants received £402 in 1738 for a mission to the Cherokees to "fetch" a Dr. Priber.²⁶

The annual budgets often contain only vague references to the types of goods Indians received; too often, it seems, whoever kept the accounts was satisfied to write only that money was needed to reimburse individuals for providing "sundry goods" or "presents" to Indians. One particularly detailed account from the Georgia agent Benjamin Martyn suggests the range of goods that Native Americans in the Southeast wanted by the mid-eighteenth century. According to Martyn's list of goods needed for presents in Georgia in 1750, which he sent to the Board of Trade at the end of 1754, the colony required:

20 pieces striped Duffils, the stripes bright
28 half pieces blew Strouds (deep Colours)
14 half pieces red Do.
10 pieces blew plains corded and Wormed for Women
200 Yards of embroider'd Serge the patterns large
2500 lb. F. Gunpowder
150 Wilson's trading Guns
40 Fowling pieces
12 Saddles with Cruppers and Bridles
8 Do a better Sort with Housings
2 Gross Stone Rings
12 Doz. Horn Combs
6 Doz. Ivory Do.
4 Gross black and spotted Clasp knives
12 Doz. Razors
12 Doz. Pair Scyssors
12 Doz. looking Glasses
12 Nests of red gilt trunks
19 Doz. Check Shirts
18 Doz. White Garlisc Do
15 pieces of Calicoe 18 yards in Each.
50 cwt. trading Bells
34 second hand scarlet, red, and blew coats
6 Do. A better sort, and 6 Wastcoats for head Men
34 tinsel laced Hats
6 tinsel laced Hats a better Sort for Head Men
6 Gross Body Cadis in pieces 12 yards each

6 Gross figured and Star Gartering
30 lb. Vermilion
14 Gros long Pipes
60 Gross Hunters Do
100 lb. Shag cut tobacco
40 lb. Bright brass wire sorted
6 Gross Hawks Bells smallest size
12 Dozen Oval-eyed Hatchets
250 lb. brass Kettles sorted
10 Nests tin Kettles 15 in Each
4 Doz. quart tin Pots
4 Doz. ' Pint Do
4,000 black flints for trading Guns
1,000 Do for fowling Pieces.[27]

Despite the vagueness of many records, some of those record keepers did historians a favor and enumerated the specific goods and services provided by colonists to native groups in the region. In 1734, for example, the colonist Nicholas Lynch received £7 for "physick and bleeding" some ill Indians.[28] From that point until the end of the colonial period other colonists too received payments for tending to sick natives. In 1734 John Martini received £4 for physic and bleeding a Cherokee,[29] and in 1739 Dr. Thomas Dale received £24.3 for treating a group of Catawbas.[30] Also in 1739 Thomas Brown got £17 for feeding five Catawbas, two of whom were sick; he provided them with rum, sugar, and food.[31] The colony recorded no payments for medical services during the 1740s and only sporadic payments thereafter: in 1756, for example, Dr. Oliphant and Dr. Garden received £26 for treating an unspecified group of Indians; and in 1764 George Miligan received £15 for his work to set the fracture of a Catawba.[32] Despite these provisions of medical care, the native population of the region continued to succumb to infectious diseases. Epidemics remained the "greatest Enemie" of the Catawbas and other Indians throughout the colonial period.[33]

Yet if Native Americans did not often seek medical attention from colonists, preferring instead to seek cures from Indian healers, other details in the accounts reveal the diverse types of economic exchanges that brought Indians and colonists together. Surviving documents identify the precise goods or services that Indians wanted from their new neighbors. For example, in 1734 John Milner received £193.1 for "mending indian guns," an extraordinary expense incurred to maintain a product that natives did not possess before the arrival of colonists;[34] the existence of this payment also reflects the fact that in between times of warfare colonists working for the government helped the Indians to stay armed. Five years later the colony paid Capt. Thomas Cooper £38.3 for providing 450 pounds of bullets for Chickasaws, the same year that the colony reimbursed

Samuel and George Eveleigh (who had been involved in the provisioning trade) £245.9 for providing "guns, bullets & sundries" to Catawbas, Chickasaws, and Creeks.[35] In 1740 the colony paid Nicholas Chinnery £500 for powder and bullets that he had provided to the Chickasaws; that same year it issued a payment of £373.5 to James Maxwell, Esq., for "ammunition and presents" for the Cherokees.[36] Even when the murmuring of war spread through the hinterland, the colony continued, on occasion, to provide weapons to some Indians, as it did in 1756 when it reimbursed the trading house of Otniel Beale & Co. for providing guns to unspecified natives or when, that same year, it paid Jerome Courtonne for hauling twenty-nine "horse loads of Guns & Ammo" to the Chickasaws, or when, also that year, it paid out £256 to John Scott and another £70 to John Dodd for their work "mending indian guns."[37] As late as 1764 colonial officials were still willing to pay for the upkeep of Indians' weapons, as demonstrated when they paid Dodd (again) almost £19 for gunsmith work he had done for some natives.[38] Other expenses were equally unpredictable. The colony paid Samuel West the modest sum of £8 for "stabling" the horses of Indians in 1740 and that year paid approximately the same amount to John Barton for pasturage for a group of Wateree Indians' horses.[39] In other words, colonists provided maintenance for Indians' animals—animals that arrived in the region when Europeans arrived. In 1738 the colony authorized a payment of £400 for surveyors who had been hired to mark out 21,774 acres of land near New Windsor; but unlike other surveyors, who typically worked for colonists eager to establish their families' farms or plantations, these surveyors had been at work marking lands to be used by Chickasaws.[40]

Perhaps the most important details in the accounts relate to the European and colonial goods that Native Americans desired. These entries, combined with accounts kept by merchants and traders, allow us to measure with some precision the types of goods that Indians wanted in the eighteenth century; combined with exports of deerskins, such data also make it possible to quantify a valuable component of the Carolina economy. At times those who provisioned Indians reported that they provided natives with rum or sugar, though most entries included no specifics. It is thus impossible to know, at least through these official accounts, if disruptions in Indians' economies had forced some communities to seek basic foods, such as corn (maize), on a regular basis; impossible to know if the expansion of colonial settlements onto lands long owned by specific Indian communities meant loss of access to orchards filled with apples or peaches,[41] or to streams that ran thick with anadromous fish on their way to spawn in the autumn; impossible to know if the decline in the deer population, precipitated mostly by European demand for deerskins though possibly increased through the expansion of colonial farms,[42] meant decline in sufficient protein. Still, the few references to the provision of specific foods in the official accounts suggest the extent of the loss of reliable foods. In 1755, for example, the colony paid £500 for corn for the Catawbas; that same year accountants reimbursed colonists who had provided beef to Indians on at least five occasions.[43] Gov. James Glen realized that such expenses were necessary for "our Friends the Catawbas," who were suffering from depleted food supplies due to a drought and had lost many members in epidemics and wars. He also recognized that the expansion of colonial settlements had limited the chances for the Catawbas' economic prosperity. "A bad Crop was not so great a Calamity to them in former Times," he informed the assembly, "[f]or then they had a wide Range to hunt in; and Venison, Bear, and Buffalo, in some sort, supplied the want of Grain, and other Provisions; but the near Neighborhood of the English, they say, drives away their Game; and deprives them of the means of subsisting on such Emergencies."[44] But if providing food to the Catawbas was a reflection of these natives' diminished ability to provide for their own dietary needs during times of dearth, what could it have meant in 1755 when the colony paid James Withers for six cords of wood for the Creeks?[45] Had some Creek communities lost access to sufficient wood for their fires? Could deforestation, which commonly followed the expansion of colonial settlements, have been so extensive in some areas that the woods were no longer there for some native communities? Or could the reason instead be that the community had lost so many members that it lacked the labor to provide for its own survival?

On some occasions the accountants recorded reimbursements for goods that suggested quite clearly the seemingly nonessential goods that Indians wanted. The official accounts are, regrettably, less complete than the accounts of trading houses; there is no parallel in the colony's accounts for the detailed inventories to be found, for example, in the ledgers of the Philadelphia-based trading firm Baynton, Wharton, and Morgan, which did its business throughout the colonial hinterland.[46] But the official records nonetheless reveal how Indian communities had changed as a result of colonial expansion. The advent of the horse trade led, invariably, to demand for such things as saddles, and in 1748 Benjamin Addison received £8 for providing saddles to Indians.[47] Perhaps sensing that this was a growing business, Addison kept at it; in 1755 he and Thomas Nightengale each received over £90 for the saddles they had provided to unspecified natives.[48] In 1739 the colony reimbursed Jonathan Scott for providing three and one-half yards of "scarlet whitneys"[49] to the Catawbas; that same year William Mathewes provided a "Scarlet coat trimmed with Silver" to "one of the Indian Chiefs," for which the colony paid him £37.1.[50] Indians who did business with the colony seem to have had a particular desire for scarlet material. In 1739 the colony reimbursed "Messrs. Oswald & Stewart" the sum of £31.5 for providing four and one-half yards of scarlet cloth to a group of Creeks.[51] The next year Benjamin Stead received payment for a gift of "scarlet Whitney & laced hats" that he had provided to Indians in August 1739.[52] As in other colonies, manufactured cloth remained popular with Indian consumers. Hannah Proctor took advantage of that demand when she made "gowns etc. for Indian women" in 1746, for which she received £14.8.[53] Alexander Smith's estate was reimbursed almost £50 that same year in exchange for "making cloathes for Indians."[54] In 1755, apparently responding to a different type of demand for cloth, Margaret Boone received £16 for "making 2 flags for indians."[55]

Rum, guns, physic, scarlet witneys, cords of wood, sugar, beef, saddles, lace hats, pasturage for horses—these are the things, along with thousands of pounds of unspecified goods, that filled the ledgers of South Carolina's accounts. We would like to know more about the full extent of such exchange: why colonial officials at a given time authorized certain payments; why some colonists and not others became involved in the provisioning business; what effect these transactions had on the prices of commodities and the availability of deerskins; and whether such transactions helped to maintain peace between English colonists and their myriad native neighbors. We lack the resources to compile each of these stories, and indeed some would be impossible to produce, but efforts to understand better these transactions seems well worthwhile. Instead of complete records, we have too often encountered tantalizing glimpses of the nature of this economy. For example, a 1756 entry in the official accounts reveals that nerves must often have been frayed, especially in times of turmoil. That year the colony paid the firm of John McQueen and Company over £1,100 in reimbursement, at least in part, for a reward that he had given to the Cherokees in return for scalps.[56] Everything, it seems, had a price that could be calculated.

Economic Agency among Native Americans

Public expenses directed toward Indians reflected colonial government officials' concerns about Indians and their proper place in a region where they were an ever-decreasing minority. But even as their numbers shrank, Native Americans remained in the region, and some of them, such as the Catawbas, figured out how to survive even when their communities were surrounded by colonists and their fields. Surviving documents, including correspondence between colonial officials (in the region and back and forth to London) as well as references in inventory estates and material remains unearthed in archaeological digs, reveal in more clarity the myriad relationships that Indians created with envoys of the Atlantic economy.

Colonists and Indians alike realized the central importance of trade. In 1716 the Indian Trade Commission began to establish precise values for goods used in the deerskin trade. In that initial calculus certain items were to have fixed costs: 20 deerskins for a pistol; 16 deerskins for a white blanket; 3 to 5 deerskins for a hoe, depending on its width; 14 deerskins for a petticoat; a single deerskin for a knife or 12 flints or 30 bullets or a pair of scissors.[57] As early as 1717 colonists and Cherokees had come to an agreement about the price of goods.[58] A 1733 treaty called by the colonists the "Ratification of Articles of Friendship and Commerce with the Lower Creeks in Georgia" laid out in precise terms specific protocols for trade, in particular, and elements of Indian-colonist relations more generally. Thus the treaty required the Lower Creeks to return any runaway slaves, to maintain peaceful alliances with the English, and to protect colonial traders. Colonists, for their part, were to regulate the behavior of traders who worked among Indians. Of crucial importance was the establishment of acceptable prices for trade goods. This treaty was more than just a convenient way of determining the value of goods. By agreeing to its terms, colonial negotiators and Lower Creeks established the ground rules for trade to continue indefinitely. As long as Creeks arrived with deerskins, colonists would be there to sell them goods—blankets, guns, knives, axes, hoes, brass kettles, mirrors, hats, buttons. This agreement, and the many exchanges that followed and conformed closely to these prices, demonstrated that Native Americans in the region had come to rely on certain goods produced elsewhere and knew what to expect when they met with colonial traders.[59] By 1762 the list of goods in such agreements had become extensive. That year the directors of the Indian trade issued two separate lists that together provided the prices in deerskins for 132 specific goods.[60]

Establishing prices for the deerskin trade proved important because of the value of that trade to both Native Americans and colonists. From 1698 to 1715 colonists exported between 53,000 and 54,000 deerskins each year. By the mid-1710s the Yamasees, at least, were having such trouble finding deer that they feared they would be captured and sold into slavery if they were unable to pay their debts to traders; this anxiety, one historian has reported, was the real motivation for their participation in the conflict that now bears their name.[61] While the volume of the business dropped sharply during the Yamasee War—surviving figures for 1716 reveal that colonists shipped only 4,702 deerskins that year—the postwar recovery was a success; by the early 1720s exporters shipped approximately 60,000 skins. The volume of the trade continued to grow. In 1748 colonists exported 160,000 deerskins. In the early 1750s one Savannah merchant noted the shipment of approximately 140,000 pounds of deerskins in one year sent by deerskin traders from Augusta, a total reflecting the shipment of perhaps 70,000 deerskins in a single year. By the end of that decade Charleston exporters shipped approximately 177,000 deerskins each year, and after 1763 deerskin exports emanated from East and West Florida as well. In 1764 John Stuart, the southern superintendent for Indian affairs, claimed that annual exports approached 800,000 pounds of deerskins (the hides of approximately 400,000 individual deer).[62] After the American Revolution the number declined, but even in 1799 the firm of Panton, Leslie and Company still reported its annual exports at 124,000 deerskins per year.⁶³ Still, despite such harvests, local Native Americans had complained since the mid-1760s that the supply of deer was diminishing, especially in areas that had come under the control of colonists.⁶⁴ It is worth noting that despite the attention scholars have paid to the deerskin trade, even at its height this commerce had a relatively low impact on Native American economies, at least as judged by the value of the deerskin trade in relation to the entire economic performance of the Southeast's native peoples. Based on the available evidence, it seems unlikely that the value of the trade in skins amounted to more than 5 percent of the value of total production per person among the Indians of the Southeast.⁶⁵

Whatever its actual value, working in the deerskin trade made sense to many Native Americans. According to one historian of the Southeast, Indians' participation in the trade was a straightforward response to the expansion of the Atlantic market; by hunting skins for European colonists Native Americans demonstrated how the "modern-world system," to use the phrase of the historian Immanuel Wallerstein, penetrated new territories along the periphery of the zone of European expansion.⁶⁶ But it was not the deerskin trade alone that brought Indians to work for colonists. In certain places Native Americans also worked for wages, performing specific tasks for payment. In one example a Charleston clock maker in 1727 paid £20 to "an Indjon for Cutting Clock Wheels."⁶⁷ In another example, in 1756 colonial officials in South Carolina reimbursed two traders for expenses they incurred for the colony, including four yards of stroud (worth £9) that they gave to a runner to "go after" the gun merchant and his people, who were then "about 100 Miles in the Woods"; they also received £3 15s. to pay them back for corn they provided to Indians who "were left behind to take care of the Headmen's Horses" when the gun merchant and his entourage traveled to Charleston.⁶⁸ Such labor was in addition to payments made to Indians who responded to colonists' needs in pressing circumstances, such as capturing runaway slaves or killing slaves who had taken up arms during the Stono Rebellion of 1739.⁶⁹

In addition to such direct participation in the colonial economy, Native Americans in the Southeast modified their economic practices to accommodate other changes caused by the expansion of the Atlantic economy. Some Indians became involved in the slave trade, capturing runaway African Americans or even keeping slaves themselves, though the practice of slavery seemed so dangerous that the Creeks, presumably among others, chose not to become involved.⁷⁰ Colonial expansion and the alienation of Indian lands, whether by force or through treaty, led to a redefinition of the landscape. In many low-lying areas colonists created plantations to produce rice, and they peopled those plantations with African American slaves (many of whom were born in the West Indies); they also reshaped the lowlands to make them more suitable for rice production.⁷¹

But rice planters were not the only individuals to create the newly colonized landscape of the region. Farmers eager to plant crops also took up land, and over the course of the eighteenth century many of those farmers fenced more and more of their fields. Fences in Carolina, as in New England (where their effects have been described by the environmental historian William Cronon[72]), served a variety of purposes. Wherever they appeared fences demarcated property boundaries, usually between colonists. Fences also protected crops from roaming animals or, conversely, contained animals from roaming far, a decided shift from the earliest years of Carolina when planters had allowed their livestock to range freely.[73] Fences were necessary in an economy based at least in part on the cultivation of food crops or the maintenance of livestock. Before colonists had arrived, Indians in Carolina had not fenced their fields. Though they grew crops to sustain themselves, there was no need to protect their fields from roaming livestock since the most destructive animals—hogs and cattle—had not yet arrived; local pests, such as squirrels, might have been a nuisance, but there is no indication of any persistent threats to Indians' food supplies before colonists arrived. However, once colonists had quite literally planted themselves on the landscape, the logic changed. Fences impeded movement for Indians hunting deer; fences served as a stark reminder about the alienation of lands; fences around colonists' fields protected colonists' corn and grains but did little to protect Indians' fields if colonists still allowed their livestock to range freely. In other words, fences became markers of the expansion of the Atlantic economy, an economy based (in this region at least) on the spread of a market-defined value of real estate and the construction of physical barriers to insure the success of the emerging economy.

If Native Americans had rejected the Atlantic economy, they would also have rejected the notion of fencing fields. But this is not what happened. By the end of the eighteenth century, according to officials of the newly created United States government, the Creeks (among others) were well on their way to fencing their fields.[74] Such fencing was necessary in order to protect their crops and also to maintain the livestock that Indians had purchased from Europeans.

Into the Nineteenth Century

In 1801 the federal Indian agent Benjamin Hawkins offered his views on life among Native Americans in the Southeast. In his "Sketch of the present state of the objects under the charge of the principal agent for Indian affairs South of the Ohio," he paid particular attention to the transformations of Creek society. The Creeks were, he wrote, avid raisers of cattle. "This is more relished by the Creeks than any part of the plan devised for their civilization," he wrote. "They are now eagerly acquiring cattle, by every means in their power." They had also embraced European-style agriculture. "[A]ll of them fence their fields," he asserted, noting that they had a continuing demand for plows. "There is a nursery of peach trees in the Lower Creeks, and one has been lately established among the Upper Creeks: and the Indians begin to accept of, and to plant them; nearly five thousand have been raised and distributed since the arrival of the agent." The Creeks were also cultivating flax and cotton and engaging in a wide variety of agricultural tasks. "The early white and brown wheat is ripe by the middle of May," he noted. "Apple trees, grape vines, rasberies, and the roots, herbs, and vegetables, usually cultivated in good gardens, have lately been introduced; and they all thrive well." In other areas, too, the Creeks had adopted economic practices first introduced by European colonists. "The present spring, the agent has delivered to Indian women, one hundred pair cotton cards, and eighty spinning wheels," Hawkins noted. "There are eight looms in the nation, four of them wrought by Indian or half breed women, and the remainder by white women. There is a woman employed as an assistant, to teach the Indian women to spin and weave, and the agent has appointed, as a temporary assistant, a young Englishman, from a manufactory in Stockport, in England, who can make looms and spinning wheels, and every thing appertaining to them, and he understands weaving." A nascent hickory nut oil business and the continued need for blacksmiths to live among them revealed yet other signs that the Creeks had begun to live like their non-Indian neighbors.[75]

The fact that Creeks had adopted elements of an economic system that had originated across the Atlantic Ocean did not mean that these Native Americans or others had ceased to live as they had. Their cultural identity remained intact, of course, as was evident to any observer and, later, to the federal government, which in the 1830s had authorized a policy of "removal" that one historian has recently likened to "ethnic cleansing."[76] But lost in President Andrew Jackson's self-serving cant about Indian savagery was the sense that the native peoples of the Southeast had, over the course of the eighteenth century, become deeply entwined in an economic system that spanned the Atlantic basin.[77] Indians captured runaway slaves, some of whom had been born in Africa. They sold their deerskins to colonial traders who then shipped them to the West Indies or to Europe. They carved local woods into parts for clocks so that colonists could maintain their sense of time. They wore a variety of European clothing and rode on saddles made by colonists on horses whose ancestors had come from Europe. When the federal government decided that it should pay a man from England to supervise the production of cloth on looms, the government was acknowledging the deep changes in Indians' economies that had been wrought from participation in a transatlantic system.

Historians might see the transformation in the Indians' economies as signs of what might be termed the "penetration" or "intrusion" of the European market into Indian country. But that perspective denies to Creeks, Choctaws, Cherokees,

Catawbas, and other native peoples of the Southeast the agency that they possessed. Indians were not naive victims in a scheme to thin the land of them and their pesky deer; they embraced the deerskin trade because such commerce proved a viable way of improving their lives in an age of demographic catastrophe and enormous loss of land.[78] As William Bartram wrote when he encountered the Lower Creeks during his tour of the southern backcountry in the mid-1770s, these natives enjoyed "a superabundance of the necessaries and conveniences of life, with the security of person and property, the two great concerns of mankind. The hides of deer, bears, tigers and wolves, together with honey, wax and other productions of the country, purchase their cloathing, equipage and domestic utensils from the whites"; as a result, Bartram concluded, they "seem to be free from want or desires."[79] Bartram's report might have been overly optimistic, but he did realize that Native Americans participated in the fur trade in the Southeast because they recognized the economic gains of this commerce.

Colonists knew that they would succeed best if they could work with local Indians and not against them. The fact of price agreements dating to the early eighteenth century suggests how much colonial officials wanted the new system to work. After all, by establishing such agreements officials explicitly denied to colonial traders the right to sell goods for whatever they could get for them. The need to manage the trade persisted through the colonial period. When John Stuart, superintendent of Indian affairs for the southern colonies, offered his assessment of Indian-colonist relations after the conclusion of the Seven Years' War, he justified the annual expenditure of eleven thousand pounds to maintain "peace with good Order Among the Nations that surround us.[80] As he and other colonial officials realized, long-term needs were more pressing than the short-term profits for any particular trader and well worth even substantial public expenses. Fortunately for the southeastern Indians, demographic catastrophe had convinced many Native Americans that working in the deerskin trade or other pursuits with colonists was the way to security in an unstable and dangerous world.

Notes

The research reported here is part of the NBER program on the Development of the American Economy. Any opinions expressed are those of the authors and not those of the National Bureau of Economic Research.

This research is funded in part by the National Science Foundation (SBR9808516) and by the General Research Fund of the University of Kansas. The paper has benefited from the comments of Peter Coclanis and Robert Olwell and the participants of the Charleston conference on "The Emergence of the Atlantic Economy." We also thank Jasonne Grabher O'Brien and Maril Hazlett for all the assistance they have provided.

1. "Reasons humbly offer'd for fortifying Port Royal harbour in So. Carolina & for erecting an Hospital and store houses there," n.d., Add. Mss. 22680, fol. 12, British Library.

2. On the number of ships leaving Charleston from 1717 to 1766, see Peter Coclanis, *The Shadow of a Dream* (New York: Oxford University Press, 1988), 100.

3. Peter H. Wood, *Black Majority: Negroes in Colonial South Carolina from 1670 through the Stono Rebellion* (New York: Knopf, 1974); Coclanis, *Shadow of a Dream;* Philip D. Morgan, *Slave Counterpoint: Black Culture in the Eighteenth-Century Chesapeake and Lowcountry* (Chapel Hill: University of North Carolina Press, 1998). The profitability of rice made at least some South Carolinians wealthy. As the historian Kenneth Morgan has put it: "By 1774, South Carolina had the highest per capita wealth among the white population of the mainland colonies, and much of it came from rice"; see Kenneth Morgan, "The Organization of the Colonial American Rice Trade," *William and Mary Quarterly,* 3rd ser., 52 (1995): 433–52, quotation from 433–34.

4. From 1768 to 1772 rice accounted for over 55 percent of the exports from South Carolina and indigo, which developed only in the 1740s, accounted for approximately 20 percent. See Marc Egnal, *New World Economies: The Growth of the Thirteen Colonies and Early Canada* (New York: Oxford University Press, 1998), 101.

5. Deerskins were the most profitable export until the rise of the rice trade and remained the second most valuable export until the later rise of indigo; from 1768 to 1772 deerskins still comprised approximately 5 percent of South Carolina's exports. See Egnal, *New World Economies,* 110–11, 101. For the relative value of the deerskin trade at midcentury, see Coclanis, *Shadow of a Dream,* 80–81.

6. See Peter C. Mancall and Thomas Weiss, "Was Economic Growth Likely in Colonial America?" *Journal of Economic History* 59 (1999): 17–40.

7. For precontact trade in the Southeast, see Patricia Galloway, *Choctaw Genesis, 1500–1700* (Lincoln, Neb., 1995), 27–74, passim; Kathryn E. Holland Braund, *Deerskins & Duffels: The Creek Indian Trade with Anglo-America, 1685–1815* (Lincoln: University of Nebraska Press, 1993), 27; James H. Merrell, *The Indians' New World: Catawbas and Their Neighbors from European Contact through the Era of Removal* (Chapel Hill: University of North Carolina Press, 1989), 29. For precontact trade elsewhere, see, among recent sources, Neal Salisbury, "The Indians' Old World: Native Americans and the Coming of Europeans," *William and Mary Quarterly,* 3rd ser., 53 (1996): 435–58; Laurier Turgeon, "French Fishers, Fur Traders, and Amerindians during the Sixteenth Century: History and Archaeology," *William and Mary Quarterly,* 3rd ser., 55 (1998): 585–610.

8. On how such processes took place, see James Axtell, "At the Water's Edge: Trading in the Sixteenth Century," in his *After Columbus: Essays in the Ethnohistory of Colonial North America* (New York: Oxford University Press, 1988), 145–81; James Axtell, "The First Consumer Revolution," in his *Beyond 1492: Encounters in Colonial North America* (New York: Oxford University Press, 1992), 125–51.

9. Gregory A. Waselkov, "Seventeenth-Century Trade in the Colonial Southeast," *Southeastern Archaeology* 8 (1989): 117–33.

10. For a review of the numbers and the debates over population, see John A. Daniels, "The Indian Population of North America in 1492," *William and Mary Quarterly,* 3rd ser., 49 (1992): 298–320; Douglas H. Ubelaker, "North American Indian Population Size: Changing Perspectives," in *Disease and Demography in the Americas,* ed. John W. Verano and Douglas H. Ubelaker (Washington, D.C.: Smithsonian Institution Press, 1992), 169–76; Russell Thornton, *American Indian Holocaust and Survival: A Population History Since 1492* (Norman: University of Oklahoma Press, 1987), esp. 42–90.

11. On the Carolina Algonquians, see Karen Ordahl Kupperman, *Roanoke: The Abandoned Colony* (Totowa, N.J.: Rowman and Allanheld, 1984). On the Choctaws, see Galloway, *Choctaw Genesis*. On the Catawbas, see Merrell, *Indians' New World*, esp. 8–48.

12. It is impossible to put a precise figure on the value of land clearing; yet it would be unwise to ignore the value of such work. As Robert Gallman recognized for the antebellum period, "[f]arm improvements made with farm materials accounted for nearly half of real gross domestic investment (less changes in inventories) in the decade 1834–43"; see Robert E. Gallman, "Gross National Product in the United States, 1834–1909," in *Output Employment and Productivity in the United States after 1800,* ed. Dorothy S. Brady, Studies in Income and Wealth, vol. 30 (New York, 1966), 3–76, quotation from 24. Based on Gallman's method of estimation we have estimated that it cost approximately £2.5 sterling to clear an acre of land in the late colonial period.

13. These estimates are derived from A. S. Salley, ed., *Journals of the Common House of Assembly of South Carolina* (Columbia: Historical Commission of South Carolina, 1909–49); J. H. Easterby et al., eds., *The Journal of the Commons House of Assembly,* 14 vols. (Columbia: Historical Commission of South Carolina, 1951–83) (hereafter *Col. Recs. South Car.*). For an examination of these figures in the context of public spending in the eighteenth-century South, see Peter C. Mancall, Joshua Rosenbloom, and Thomas Weiss, "The Public Finances of the Colonies of the Lower South," paper presented at the NBER Summer Institute on the Development of the American Economy, Cambridge, Mass., July 1999, table 2A.

14. For a discussion of this issue in the context of the Canadian fur trade, see Ann M. Carlos and Frank D. Lewis, "Trade, Consumption, and the Native Economy: Lessons from York Factory, Hudson Bay," *Journal of Economic History* 61 (2001): 1037–64.

15. To date we have analyzed the records for 1724, 1734, 1736, 1738, 1739, 1740, 1745, 1746, 1748, 1755, 1756, 1764, and 1776.

16. A. S. Salley, ed., *Journals of the Common House of Assembly of South Carolina* 20. Here and elsewhere in this paper we have converted figures originally denominated in pounds, shillings, and pence into pounds with decimals. Thus, for example, twenty pounds, six shillings would be rendered as £20.3 here.

17. *Col. Recs. South Car.,* 1:324.

18. Ibid., 2:111.

19. Ibid., 2:318.

20. Ibid., 2:323.

21. Ibid., 9:378–90.

22. Ibid., 14:452.

23. Ibid., 2:108.

24. Ibid.

25. Ibid., 1:325.

26. Ibid., 2:111.

27. "Memorial of Benjamin Martyn, agent for Georgia, to the Board of Trade, Jan. 28, 1755," in Kenneth Coleman and Milton Ready, eds., *Original Papers of Governor John Reynolds 1754–1756* (vol. 27 of *Colonial Records of Georgia*) (Athens: University of Georgia Press, 1977), 30–31. For similar lists for South Carolina, see Goods Supplied to Indians by Colonel Byrd, April, 1758, and Return of Provisions received by Lieutenant

Coytmore, April 14, 1759, in W. L. McDowell, ed., *Documents Relating to Indian Affairs 1754–1765* (Columbia: South Carolina Archives Department, 1970), 456–57, 482–83.

28. A. S. Salley, ed., *Journals of the Common House of Assembly of South Carolina*, 169.

29. Ibid., 170.

30. *Col. Recs. South Car.*, 2:318.

31. Ibid., 2:321.

32. Ibid., 14:454; A. S. Salley, ed., *Journals of the Common House of Assembly of South Carolina*, 170.

33. Merrell, *Indians' New World*, 136–37, 193–96.

34. A. S. Salley, ed., *Journals of the Common House of Assembly of South Carolina*, 169.

35. *Col. Recs. South Car.*, 2:318.

36. Ibid., 2:539, 542.

37. Ibid., 14:452.

38. Salley, *Journal . . . , January 8, 1765 to August 9, 1765*, 169.

39. *Col. Recs. South Car.*, 2:540.

40. Ibid., 2:109.

41. Peach trees were not indigenous to the Southeast, but by the eighteenth century they had become common; see Alfred Crosby, *Ecological Imperialism: The Biological Expansion of Europe, 900–1900* (New York: Cambridge University Press, 1986), 156–57.

42. As William Cronon has argued in his study of colonial New England, Native Americans' practice of burning forests in the generations before Europeans arrived could have meant the expansion of deer populations since deer were often attracted to the so-called "edge" habitats on the margins of woods; it is also possible that the population of deer in the eighteenth century benefited from the decline in their traditional predators, especially wolves. On the "edge" effect, see William Cronon, *Changes in the Land: Indians, Colonists, and the Ecology of New England* (New York: Hill and Wang, 1983), 51. But despite the possibility that the population of deer increased in some places, abundant evidence points to depopulation linked directly to the deerskin trade and, less directly, to the loss of habitat in regions settled by colonists. See Timothy Silver, *A New Face on the Countryside: Indians, Colonists, and Slaves in South Atlantic Forests, 1500–1800* (New York: Cambridge University Press, 1990), 91–94; Braund, *Deerskins & Duffels*, 71–72.

43. *Col. Recs. South Car.*, 14:275.

44. Terry W. Lipscomb, ed., *Journal of the Commons House of the Assembly, Nov. 20, 1755 to July 6, 1757* (volume 14 of *The Colonial Records of South Carolina*) (Columbia: Historical Commission of South Carolina, 1989), 7.

45. *Col. Recs. South Car.*, 14:165.

46. See the papers of Baynton, Wharton and Morgan, Pennsylvania Historic and Museum Commission, Harrisburg, Pennsylvania, and scattered papers from the same firm in the Historical Society of Pennsylvania, Philadelphia.

47. *Col. Recs. South Car.*, 9:226.

48. Ibid., 14:275.

49. A witney was a heavy and loose woolen that was made into blankets at the Oxfordshire town of Witney.

50. *Col. Recs. South Car.*, 2:317, 318.

51. Ibid., 2:320.

52. Ibid., 2:541.
53. Ibid., 7:365.
54. Ibid.
55. Ibid., 14:276.
56. Ibid., 14:452.

57. William L. McDowell, ed., *Journals of the Commissioners of the Indian Trade, September 20, 1710 to August 29, 1718,* Colonial Records of South Carolina, ser. 2 (Columbia: Historical Commission of South Carolina, 1955–70), entry for July 6, 1716; Philip Brown, "Early Indian Trade in the Development of South Carolina: Politics, Economics, and Social Mobility during the Proprietary Period, 1670–1719," *South Carolina Historical Magazine* 76 (1975): 123.

58. Mary U. Rothrock, "Carolina Traders among the Overhill Cherokees, 1690–1760," *East Tennessee Historical Society Publications* 1 (1929): 14.

59. See Leslie F. Church, *Oglethorpe: A Study of Philanthropy in England and Georgia* (London: Epworth Press, 1932), 114–15.

60. "Table of Goods and Prices for the Indian Trade, July 19, 1762," and "Table of Goods and Prices for the Indian Trade, November 20, 1762," in McDowell, *Documents Relating to Indian Affairs, 1754–1765,* 566–69, 576–79.

61. Richard L. Haan, "The 'Trade Do's Not Flourish as Formerly': The Ecological Origins of the Yamasee War of 1715," *Ethnohistory* 28 (1981): 341–58.

62. It is worth noting that Stuart's estimate appears implausibly high as it is approximately three times the volume of deerskin exports recorded in any of the preceding twenty-five or so years.

63. Braund, *Deerskins & Duffels,* 97–98; W. O. Moore Jr., "The Largest Exporters of Deerskins from Charles Town, 1735–1775," *South Carolina Historical Magazine* 74 (1973): 144–50; "Observations of Superintendent John Stuart and Governor James Grant of East Florida on the Proposed Plan of 1764 for the Future Management of Indian Affairs," *American Historical Review* 20 (1915): 818. See also Verner Crane, *The Southern Frontier 1670–1732* (Durham, N.C.: Duke University Press, 1928), 111.

64. Braund, *Deerskins & Duffels,* 71–72. It is worth noting that estimates on the volume of deerskin exports based on the records of the public treasurer in South Carolina yield different results; according to Edward Murphy, who recently provided estimates for the period 1736 to 1767, there were no clear trends over time (except, possibly, for the period after 1763, when exports decreased—from 328,480 pounds of skins in 1763 to 148,960 pounds in 1767). According to his estimates, there were 200,720 pounds of deerskins exported in 1736, but the volume fluctuated, reaching a high in the mid- to late 1740s (when there were 314,400 pounds shipped in 1743, 376,160 pounds in 1745, 323,920 pounds in 1746, and 368,080 pounds in 1748). But for 1763, the year that Stuart provided the estimate used here, Murphy calculated exports of 328,480 pounds of skins, far less than the superintendent believed. See Edward Murphy, "The Eighteenth-Century Southeastern American Indian Economy: Subsistence Versus Trade and Growth," in *The Other Side of the Frontier: Economic Explorations into Native American History,* ed. Linda Barrington (Boulder, Colo.: Westview Press, 1999), 152.

65. Between 1736 and 1767 the value of deerskins exported averaged about two-thirds of a pound sterling per Indian using the narrowest definition of the native population of

the Southeast (see table 14). Using the broader definition (see table 16), the average value of exports per Indian was only one-fourth of a pound sterling. Only a fraction of these export earnings accrued to Indians, however. Based on evidence in Brown, "Early Indian Trade," 118–28; and Murphy, "Eighteenth-Century Southeastern American Indian Economy," 153–55, the proportion of the final price of deerskin exports that the Indians received appears to have been around 40 percent in the early 1700s. Evidence on how this fraction changed over time is scanty, but it appears that it may have risen to a peak near the middle of the century and then fallen back. Thus the likely income from skins (no more than one-quarter of a pound sterling) per Indian appears quite small in comparison to our estimate of Native American income per head of around eight pounds sterling. See Peter C. Mancall, Joshua L. Rosenbloom, and Thomas Weiss, "Conjectural Estimates of Economic Growth in the Lower South, 1720 to 1800," in *History Matters: Essays on Economic Growth, Technology, and Demographic Change,* eds. Timothy W. Guinnane, William A. Sundstrom, and Warren Whatley (Stanford: Stanford University Press, 2004), 389–424.

66. Immanuel Wallerstein, *The Modern World System* (New York: Modern Academic Press, 1974). Charles M. Hudson, "Why the Southeastern Indians Slaughtered Game," in *Indians, Animals, and the Fur Trade: A Critique of Keepers of the Game,* ed. Shepard Krech III (Athens: University of Georgia Press, 1981), 155–76.

67. Wood, *Black Majority,* 197.

68. Lach. McGillivray to Glen and the Council, February 17, 1756, in McDowell, *Documents Relating to Indian Affairs, 1754 to 1765,* 104.

69. Braund, *Deerskins & Duffels,* 74; *Col. Recs. South Car.,* 2:65.

70. Theda Perdue, *Slavery and the Evolution of Cherokee Society* (Knoxville: University of Tennessee Press, 1979); Claudio Saunt, "'The English has now a Mind to make Slaves of them all': Creeks, Seminoles, and the Problem of Slavery," *American Indian Quarterly* 22 (1998): 157–80.

71. Mart A. Stewart, *"What Nature Suffers to Grow": Life, Labor, and Landscape on the Georgia Coast, 1680–1920* (Athens: University of Georgia Press, 1996), 89–94.

72. Cronon, *Changes in the Land,* 108–26.

73. Wood, *Black Majority,* 28–31.

74. See Benjamin Hawkins, "A Sketch of the present state of the objects under the charge of the principal agent for Indian affairs South of the Ohio," in *American State Papers* (Washington, D.C.: Gales and Seaton, 1832–61), 7:647.

75. Ibid., 647–48.

76. John Mack Faragher, "'More Motley than Mackinaw': From Ethnic Mixing to Ethnic Cleansing on the Frontier of the Lower Missouri, 1783–1833," in *Contact Points: American Frontiers from the Mohawk Valley to the Mississippi, 1750–1830,* ed. Andrew R. L. Clayton and Fredrika J. Teute (Chapel Hill: University of North Carolina Press, 1998), 304–26.

77. See David M. Wishart, "Could the Cherokee Have Survived in the Southeast?" in *The Other Side of the Frontier: Economic Explorations into Native American History,* ed. Linda Barrington (Boulder, Colo.: Westview Press, 1999), 165–89.

78. On this point, see James Axtell, *The Indians' New South: Cultural Change in the Colonial Southeast* (Baton Rouge: Louisiana State University Press, 1997), 48–63; J. Russell

Snapp, *John Stuart and the Struggle for Empire on the Southern Frontier* (Baton Rouge: Louisiana State University Press, 1996), 11–14.

79. William Bartram, *Travels through North & South Carolina, Georgia, East & West Florida, the Cherokee Country the Extensive Territories of the Muscogulges, or Creek Confederacy, and the Country of the Chactaws; Containing an Account of the Soil and Natural Products of Those Regions, Together with Observations on the Manners of the Indians,* ed. Mark Van Doren (1791; repr., New York: Dover, 1955), 182. This excerpt is also included in Gregory A. Waselkov and Kathryn E. Holland Braund, eds., *William Bartram on the Southeastern Indians* (Lincoln: University of Nebraska Press, 1995), 57.

80. "Observations of Superintendent John Stuart," 824.

Planters' Exchange Patterns in the Colonial Chesapeake
Toward Defining a Regional Domestic Economy

Laura Croghan Kamoie

In 1985 John McCusker and Russell Menard called the domestic economy a neglected topic in Chesapeake history. Scholars of economic history have focused overwhelmingly on the export sector and in many cases expressed interest in the activities of local markets only to the extent that they seemed to be short-term responses to fluctuations in the export sector.[1] Works since McCusker and Menard's have made important strides toward analyzing the significance and defining the parameters of the colonial domestic economy on its own terms. This scholarship has most frequently taken a microhistory approach, focusing on the county or region.[2] In every case scholars of local markets and domestic economies underscored the fact that the export sector of the colonial economy was most responsible for long-term regional growth. However, they also noted that export earnings accounted for about one-third of the total colonial output.[3] Some scholars, such as P. M. G. Harris, therefore caution that we have perhaps overemphasized the tobacco trade in attempting to understand the contours of the Chesapeake colonial economy. Harris and others have argued that, from the 1730s on, those engaged in business relied increasingly less on income from tobacco and increasingly more on income derived from new alternative sources.[4] In the colonial Chesapeake, planters developed exchange relationships to create and access these alternative economic activities and understood the importance of diversification for their own individual wealth as well as for the success and growth of the regional domestic economy.

Throughout the eighteenth century planters exhibited a diversified approach to plantation management that encompassed commercial agriculture and an array of merchant, industrial, and other business services. This diversification, combined with an entrepreneurial inclination among the elite of the planter class, formed the basis of the Chesapeake's regional economy. Planters diversified their holdings into mixed agriculture, agricultural processing, iron making, shipbuilding, capital investments, and craft-service activities, among others. While planters exported the majority of their products in iron and agriculture, for example, to British merchants, an important minority of those products remained in the colonies and passed as trade goods in the domestic economy. As McCusker describes it, "while such activities [the organization and growth of the domestic market] were as yet of minimal quantitative significance, they represented a notable qualitative shift."[5]

In addition, planters founded a variety of plantation craft industries that made goods and offered services for local customers. These shops frequently became neighborhood centers where planters bartered, bought, and sold goods and services. In attempting to enumerate all the relevant economic activities that would need to be taken into account for defining a national economy, Robert Gallman includes the value of nonmarketed goods (such as clearing and breaking new farmland), food and clothing production for home consumption, and household craft production.[6] In the South such household craft production took place on plantations most frequently at the hands of slave laborers. During the colonial era traditionally "urban" economic activities in the South were sustained in rural communities and on plantations. Most farmers and planters combined their farming activities with other trades and industries. "Urban" goods and services were available in the South but in the countryside.[7] Charles Farmer notes that in Southside Virginia, almost every sizable plantation included at least one major service activity. Where adjacent plantations offered other desirable services, residential clustering (what he designates as the open-country neighborhood pattern) frequently occurred. In many cases these plantation clusters were in close proximity to the local courthouse, tavern, and ferry.[8] Thus, craft-service activities influenced the regional domestic economy and the settlement patterns related to that economy.

Planters also contributed to the development of a regional domestic economy by encouraging other business-minded men in their efforts to diversify. Many planters invested capital in a variety of new enterprises, either indirectly through loans or more directly by participating in partnerships. Planters joined together to form land speculation companies; provided capital for the founding of country stores, ordinaries, and taverns; and invited one another to become partners in new mining and other industrial ventures. At a minimum, many planters functioned as formal financial institutions later would—extending credit, advancing cash, and paying creditors. As Myra L. Rich long ago recognized, few people were only the debtors or creditors. Many aspects of the Chesapeake's domestic economy were supported by exchange relationships based on debt and credit. Most of Virginia's debts were contracted and held among the colonists. In the absence of banking, paper money, and commercial laws, then, credit served as a medium of exchange on which Virginians relied for their business endeavors.[9] Planters most frequently developed such exchange relationships with family members, immediate neighbors, and the local elite families of a region.

Table 17: Tithables of the Northern Neck of Virginia, 1722–1783

County	1722	1729	1745	1755	1782/3
King George	915	1,275	1,744	1,788	2,490
Lancaster	1,147	1,390	1,538	1,610	4,108
Northumberland	1,521	1,572	2,176	2,414	7,734
Richmond	1,020	1,839	1,837	1,997	6,832
Westmoreland	1,763	1,998	2,471	2,532	7,722 (1790)
TOTAL TITHABLES	6,366	8,074	9,766	10,341	28,886

The Chesapeake encompasses a variety of distinct geographical landscapes (for example, the Eastern Shore, the James River, the Northern Neck of Virginia, southern Maryland, the Southside), each characterized by its own natural resources, access to water routes, soil types, and settlement patterns. Therefore, for the purposes of discussing the particulars of the relationship between planters' exchange patterns and the regional domestic economy, this chapter will focus on the Northern Neck region of Virginia (see map 12.1). Virginia's Northern Neck comprises the peninsula between the Potomac and Rappahannock rivers and includes five counties: King George, Westmoreland, Richmond, Northumberland, and Lancaster. In 1722, 6,366 tithables inhabited the Northern Neck counties. That number grew to 10,341 by 1755 (see table 17). By the 1780s the tithable population of the Northern Neck had tripled, to approximately 30,000.[10]

The earliest settlers moved into this region during the 1640s and immediately broke the land for tobacco. By the 1730s, however, planters growing Oronoco tobacco in this area had added wheat and corn to their market-crop mixes. Indeed, planters in the Northern Neck, as well as on the Eastern Shore and in western Virginia, dedicated more of their lands to grain cultivation and steadily withdrew their reliance on the tobacco staple by about midcentury.[11] The introduction of wheat and other grains spurred several significant developments in prerevolutionary Virginia. Corn and wheat were staples with considerable spread effects or linkages. In other words, grains required many more people and services to process, package, and transport them than did tobacco. The result was a more diversified economy that could better withstand the shock of economic contraction. In many years the local market provided an important source of income for planters and even proved the difference between profit and loss.[12] The move toward grains and away from tobacco required planters to find alternate profitable ways to use their slaves' time. While tobacco required year-round attention, wheat and other grains did not. Therefore, as planters shifted greater amounts of their acreage into grains, they required less field work from their slaves. This availability of slave-labor time further fueled planter entrepreneurship and agricultural diversification. Planters had to keep all hands busy at all times in order to maintain their profitability. Many slaves began to specialize in a variety of plantation craft industries, while others learned new skills in more complex industries such as iron making, shipbuilding, and textiling. While some planters began hiring out or selling their "excess" slave population, most planters readily created new enterprises or found new tasks to which they assigned their slaves.[13] Agricultural diversification in the Northern Neck and throughout the Chesapeake therefore spurred the growth and development of regional domestic economies.

The geographical unit of the region is useful for studying exchange relationships and domestic economies. A focus on the regional level allows us to study the interaction between production for the export market and production for the local market—both important activities within a regional economy—on individual plantations and within neighborhoods. Numerous scholars of colonial New England and the colonial Chesapeake have emphasized the importance of the community for illuminating patterns of association and interaction, patterns central to understanding the workings of a regional domestic economy.[14] In the Chesapeake the county especially provided the geographical space around which institutions formed and people socialized and interacted. People in counties and surrounding regions were linked by kin groups, residential proximity, local politics, and religious and other institutions. It was these relationships that most determined exchange patterns within the domestic economy. Colonial Virginians were more likely to seek credit, goods, and services from those closest to them, both in terms of familial relationships and distance. The wealthiest members of the planter class used their political clout, available capital, ability to get credit, and external contacts to dominate local business activities and even the broader regional domestic economy.

In the 1770s John Tayloe II (1721–79) owned over twenty thousand acres of land in the Northern Neck. Tayloe was one of the wealthiest planters in Virginia during the eighteenth century. His exchange relationships within Richmond County and the Northern Neck can help shed light on the nature, scope, and significance of planters' exchange patterns relative to the domestic economy. Tayloe's estate stretched for miles along both sides of the Rappahannock River. His home plantation, Mt. Airy, was supported by six separate but interdependent farms in Richmond, Essex, and King George counties: Old House, Forkland, Marske, Menokin, Gwinfield, and Hopyard. He also had other plantations in nearby Stafford County and across the Potomac River in southern Maryland. Between 1750 and 1770 Tayloe sold to British merchants about fifty to one hundred hogsheads of tobacco per year from the Rappahannock plantations.[15] At the same time Tayloe began turning increasing amounts of his acreage over to wheat and corn.

Since Tayloe's agricultural records are incomplete, it is difficult to ascertain precisely when he began planting significant crops of wheat, corn, and other grains. The existence of grist mills on the estate of John Tayloe I (1687–1747) proves that at least some level of grain growing and processing regularly took place as early as the 1720s.[16] Grains comprised part of Tayloe's crop mix at least by 1755, when he recorded in an account book that he sold four hundred bushels of oats and numerous smaller quantities of corn to surrounding neighbors. In 1762 Tayloe reported to his neighbor Landon Carter that "the corn looked very bad the Tobo. was all cut . . . & the wheat was then sowing."[17] Two years later Carter recorded in his diary that Tayloe, like most other planters in 1764, was complaining about the damage that rain had caused to the size and quality of his wheat crop.[18] Certainly by the 1760s and 1770s wheat was a regular and important part of Tayloe's annual agricultural routine. For example, in 1767 Tayloe purchased the Landsdown estate from the Carters, which included a mill he intended to use "for wheat." In 1771 Tayloe ordered Thomas Lawson, his manager at the Neabsco Ironworks, to build a "new merchant mill" in expectation of future "good crop[s] of wheat."[19] These marked, at a minimum, the fourth and fifth grist mills Tayloe built or added to his holdings.[20] Between 1770 and 1775 Tayloe produced an average of over nine hundred bushels each of wheat and corn per year.[21]

Tayloe furthered his commitment to agricultural diversification by including craft industries and services on his Mt. Airy plantations. Besides the grist mills, Tayloe employed his slaves in a blacksmithing shop, in a carpentry shop, at shoemaking, and at spinning, weaving, and fulling cloth. Beyond the Northern Neck, Tayloe had an additional one hundred–plus slaves laboring at two iron plantations in Prince William County. There, besides their duties directly related to iron making, slaves were employed at shipbuilding, blacksmithing, and forging. Tayloe's iron concerns allowed him to play important roles in the domestic economies of both the Northern Neck and Northern Virginia. Tayloe made these craft and industrial services available to his neighbors and others for a cost.

Tayloe's account books are replete with evidence about his exchange patterns. While these account books mostly record his export activities for tobacco and iron with more than a dozen British merchants, they also record transactions conducted within the local market. Tayloe filled the role of the country store for many of his neighbors. He sold not only goods imported from London but also products made and grown on his plantations. For example, between 1755 and 1756 Tayloe recorded a series of transactions with Richmond County locals Thomas Maddox, Thomas Shirredin, and William Black for items including dress wigs, rum, brown sugar, chalk, molasses, corn, oats, clover seed, and wheat.

At other times between the 1750s and late 1770s Tayloe sold his neighbors tools, shoe thread, bar iron from his Neabsco and Occoquan ironworks, cloth, flax, and salted beef. Invariably his customers came from among his neighbors (such as William Brockenbrough, Jesse Garland, and William Garland) and family members (brothers-in-law Richard Corbin and Mann Page Jr. and Ralph Wormeley). Nor were these exchange relationships one-sided. On several occasions Tayloe recorded making purchases from some of these same people. In 1777 Tayloe bought homemade cider from Brockenbrough for himself and his sick slaves. Another time he purchased six hogsheads of oyster shells from William Alderson of Richmond County. John Goldsby supplied Tayloe with "fish and Crabbs" throughout the summer of 1779.[22]

Tayloe also performed financial functions for his family and neighbors. On numerous occasions Tayloe recorded lending money ranging from a few to several hundred pounds. Marmaduke Beckwith of Richmond County spent over ten years paying off a 1,500 pounds debt he owed Tayloe. Corbin frequently borrowed 5 or 10 pounds here and there. On several occasions Tayloe lent similarly small sums to Brockenbrough. As was common, Tayloe was also a debtor. For example, a 1764 notation indicated that Tayloe had run up a 517-pound tab with Fredericksburg merchant William Allason. Tayloe also made third-party payments on behalf of some of his customers. In 1751 Tayloe paid for some locally made shingles for Corbin. In 1768 Tayloe paid ironmaster John Jordan's 80-pound debt for bar iron to Baltimore Company partner Charles Carroll. Tayloe settled Walker Tomlin's account with another ironmaster, John Hunter, in 1777.[23] These transactions are representative of numerous others found throughout Tayloe's accounts.

Fortunately, portions of Tayloe's records allow for more than just an anecdotal approach to his exchange patterns. Between 1775 and 1781 Tayloe kept detailed accounts of all the transactions made at his blacksmithing shop. Blacksmithing had been a regular part of the business activities at Mt. Airy under Tayloe's father, whose 1747 estate inventory included an entry for "Black Smiths Carpenters & Joyners Tools" valued at ten pounds.[24] Mt. Airy apparently evolved into the community blacksmithing center at least by the 1770s, as small and great planters from surrounding lands in Richmond County regularly patronized Tayloe's shop. The Mt. Airy blacksmiths worked year-round but tended to be busiest between February and June.[25] Tayloe's blacksmiths were talented craftsmen who performed basic tool making or repairing services as well as more intricate work on looms, chariots, guns, and cotton gins. Typically, the slave blacksmiths spent their days making and repairing plows and other agricultural tools, as well as shoeing horses. In the eight years (1773, 1775–81) for which there are records, the Tayloe blacksmiths made or repaired 236 plows and shod 83 horses. They worked constantly to make or repair tools such as hoes, axes, saws, shovels, files, chisels, wedges, spades, pitchforks, scythes, wheat fans, and irons.

Less frequently they made weapons such as tomahawks and bayonets, mended or made cast hollowware items, or performed mill work.

Eighty-six individuals patronized Mt. Airy's blacksmith shop during the period 1773 to 1781. Tayloe's customers included small planter families such as the Garlands and Beales as well as gentry families such as the Lees, Carters, and Pages. Not surprisingly, Tayloe's immediate neighbors were among his regular customers at the Mt. Airy smith shop. William Brockenbrough was Tayloe's most frequent customer, patronizing the Mt. Airy smith shop eighty-six times in two years, 1776 and 1777, and spending £26 13s. 6d. Virginia currency. Brockenbrough lived west of Tayloe's estate bordering the original Old House lands (figure 12.1). John Belfield, whose lands sat across the Rappahannock Creek from Mt. Airy, required smithing services fourteen times in the three-year period from 1776 to 1778, which cost him only £3 19s. 2d. The Beale family of contiguous Chestnut Hall sought Tayloe's blacksmithing services thirty times between 1775 and 1779, spending a total of £44 10s. 1d. Moore Fauntleroy and Landon Carter, who bordered Tayloe on the west and south, were among his most frequent customers, visiting the smith shop forty-seven and twenty-seven times, respectively. Fauntleroy spent £37 15s. 1d. in three years while Carter spent only £10 11s. 6d. during the same period. Richard Neale, the Garland family, and Lindsey Opie concluded the list of Tayloe's adjacent neighbors. Neale purchased £5 6s. worth of services in thirty visits over three years, while Opie spent £7 16s. 6d. in eleven visits between 1776 and 1779. The Garland family, which included Tayloe's trusted manager Griffin Garland, collectively patronized the Mt. Airy smith shop eighty-eight times in four years, spending £88 12s. 11d.

Most blacksmithing services cost less than £1 Virginia currency. Tayloe made the most money at the smith shop in 1778 when he provided £126 17s. 9d. worth of services. During that year the average transaction value equaled about 18s. Considering that his costs consisted mainly of slave-labor time, most of Tayloe's annual income at the smith shop was likely profit, although the precise amount is difficult to determine. Tayloe's blacksmiths charged about 2s. to shoe a horse or between 2s. and £1 to mend a plow, depending on the amount of iron required to complete the repairs. Some tasks were more intricate, time-consuming, and costly. Mill work; making intricate pieces such as buckles, locks, or nuts and screws; and repairing and assembling carriages or carts tended to be jobs for which the blacksmiths charged over £1. Thus, the Mt. Airy blacksmith shop brought in a regular but generally small annual income.

George Washington's blacksmithing shop operated similarly and attracted its customers from the same local radius. Washington's shop operated at Mount Vernon in Fairfax County between 1755 and 1799, offering the same services as Tayloe's shop. Like the Mt. Airy blacksmiths, Washington's blacksmiths served a steady clientele, 134 individuals, mostly neighbors—some of whom patronized the shop for twelve to twenty-five years. Over 75 percent of Washington's customers lived within five miles of Mount Vernon. Only a handful of men came from as far as ten miles away. Planters were generally unwilling to travel great distances to obtain basic services, and therefore Tayloe's and Washington's shops served as community service centers. Six miles south of Mount Vernon, George Mason operated a smithy shop at Gunston Hall. Thus, Washington's shop lured the customers closest to it while Mason's served its own radius of customers in the next neighborhood.[26]

The customer base of a mill belonging to John Tayloe III (1771–1828) proves the firmness of the exchange relationships depicted by the blacksmithing shop. In 1810 the younger Tayloe completed construction on a new grist mill not far from Mt. Airy.[27] Tayloe operated his mill as a merchant mill, meaning that his neighbors could grind their grains at the Tayloe mill for a toll, usually between one-sixth and one-eighth of the grain ground. His customers were mostly neighbors and residents of the Northern Neck.[28] Indeed, while Tayloe frequently ground his own corn and wheat at the new mill, his neighbors accounted for 50 percent of the mill's business and output. Wealthy and middling families alike patronized Tayloe's mill. The Carters, Fauntleroys, and Belfields were as frequently customers as were small-farm or tenant families such as the Garlands, Lawsons, Sissons, and Giburnes. Altogether, Tayloe's neighbors brought their grains for grinding on 463 occasions throughout 1810. Many customers patronized the mill on a weekly basis. For example, Capt. John Belfield and Vincent Shackelford were two of Tayloe's most frequent customers, using the mill forty-six and forty-one times, respectively, in 1810 alone. Peter Northern and Tayloe's manager Griffin Garland brought their grains to the mill thirty times each. Others visited less frequently, such as Captain Kelsick, Robert Wormeley Carter, and John Sisson, who appear in the records eleven, sixteen, and twelve times, respectively. The families patronizing the third Tayloe's mill in 1810 were for the most part the same families patronizing his father's blacksmithing shop during the 1770s. The Tayloes gained a reputation throughout Richmond County and even into the broader Northern Neck region for providing necessary services using skilled slave artisans. The Tayloe plantations were therefore able to dominate the "urban services" provided in their neighborhood and thus shaped the locus of activity in the regional domestic economy.

The establishment of such strong exchange relationships among Virginia's planters laid a foundation that allowed them to rely on one another for other business opportunities. An examination of the one hundred wealthiest Virginians of the revolutionary era indicates that the majority of planters exercised a diversified entrepreneurial approach to their business activities and valued exchange relationships for helping them to further this approach. In 1954 Jackson Turner Main produced a list of the one hundred wealthiest Virginia planters of the revolutionary era based on their holdings in land and slaves (see table 18).[29] Not surprisingly, most of Virginia's first families and political leaders appeared on the list, including the Carters, Harrisons, Fitzhughs, Lees, Pages, and Randolphs. Patrick Henry, Thomas Jefferson, and George Washington also held places on the list. John Tayloe II was the wealthiest Virginia planters.

Extensive manuscript evidence is available for sixty-five of the one hundred. Out of that number 89 percent, or fifty-eight out of sixty-five, owned, operated, or invested in some form of business in addition to the cultivation of tobacco.[30] These sixty-five planters all demonstrated the entrepreneurial behavior that served as the foundation of diversification and thus of the development of regional domestic economies. To describe planters as entrepreneurial is to say they made business decisions prudently, willingly endured reasonable risks, and demonstrated business intelligence in gathering information before making financial decisions. In the language of the day, these planters were "adventurers and undertakers," men of action and innovation who invested, diversified, and speculated in such a way as to maintain their—and Virginia's—long-term economic growth.[31]

A brief analysis of several planters' activities will help to illuminate how their entrepreneurial behavior furthered the diversification and development of regional domestic economies. Roger Atkinson (1725–84) was a merchant-planter in Richmond and Petersburg. While Atkinson owned forty thousand acres and one hundred slaves in a half-dozen counties, his merchant activities were his top priority and main source of income. Atkinson established general stores in the cities of Richmond and Petersburg and had trading connections with almost a dozen English mercantile firms. He supported the development of smaller towns in Virginia, such as Pocahontas and Appomattox, and founded flour mills to support the processing of wheat and other grains. Atkinson believed strongly in agricultural diversification and was convinced that Virginia's economic future rested on planters' ability and desire to diversify from tobacco. He invested in smaller enterprises, including several wine-making schemes, and speculated in land in the neighboring colony of North Carolina.[32] Atkinson's career highlights the possibility that, while most often entrepreneurship involved planters branching out into business, it also could include businessmen branching out into planting.

Edmund Pendleton (1721–1803) farmed on a smaller scale; he owned 7,283 acres located mostly in Caroline County as well as fifty-one slaves. Pendleton thus ranked among the third quarter of the one hundred in terms of wealth, making it likely that the success of his various investments and speculations was all the more important to his financial security. Pendleton, also a lawyer, speculated in land and ginseng, and he opened an ordinary. His land speculation proved the most troublesome, as land in which he invested became tangled in boundary disputes between Virginia and North Carolina. He petitioned on behalf of internal improvements and supported the creation of new towns in the interior. In addition, he operated at least one mill, New Gate, to process the grains he cultivated.[33]

Table 18: The One Hundred

Richard Adams	Archibald Cary	Nathaniel	Edmund
William	W. Miles Cary	Harrison	Randolph
Alexander	William	James Henry	Peyton Randolph
William Allen	Churchill	Patrick Henry	Thomas
John Ambler	Allen Cocke	Adam Hunter	Randolph
John Armistead	Chastain Cocke	Thomas	Thomas M.
Roger Atkinson	John Cocke	Jefferson	Randolph
Henry Banks	John H. Cocke	Joseph Jones	William
Burwell Bassett	Francis Corbin	Peter Jones	Randolph
John Baylor	Gawin Corbin	Robert Lawson	Thomas Roane
Edmund	Richard Corbin	Henry Lee	William Ronald
Berkeley	John P. Custis	Richard Lee	David Ross
Robert Beverley	Nicholas Davis	William Lee	Edmund Ruffin
Theoderick	Francis Eppes	Warner Lewis	Henry Skipwith
Bland	Francis Eppes	William	Peyton Skipwith
William Blunt	George Fairfax	Lightfoot	James Southall
Carter Braxton	Moore	George Mason	Alexander
William Brent	Fauntleroy	Stevens Mason	Spotswood
Cuthbert Bullitt	Henry Fitzhugh	Joseph Mayo	John Tabb
Lewis Burwell	Thomas	Daniel McCarty	Richard
Nathaniel	Fitzhugh	Thomas Nelson	Taliaferro
Burwell	William	Thomas Nelson	John Tayloe
Joseph Cabell	Fitzhugh	Wilson Nicholas	John Taylor
William Cabell	William	John Page	Alexander Trent
Charles Carter	Fitzhugh	Mann Page	George
Edward Carter	Muscoe Garnett	John Paradise	Turberville
George Carter	Philip Grymes	David	John
John Carter	Benjamin	Patterson	Turberville
Landon Carter	Harrison	Edmund	George
Robert Carter	Carter B.	Pendleton	Washington
Robert W. Carter	Harrison	John Perrin	Ralph Wormeley

Archibald Cary (1721–87) of Ampthill in Chesterfield County owned over seventeen thousand acres and 240 slaves. While agriculture served as Cary's main source of income, he also dedicated himself to developing industry. Cary greatly expanded several enterprises he had inherited from his father, established a furnace and foundry on Falling Creek in Chesterfield, and founded flour mills in Warwick. He also supported the development of the limonite iron ore mining industry in Buckingham County. In addition, Cary established and operated a ropery in the city of Richmond. As did his contemporaries, Cary invested in a company encouraging the development of the wine, olive oil, and silk industries in Virginia.[34]

David Ross (1740–c. 1817), one of Virginia's leading ironmasters, owned over one hundred thousand acres and almost 450 slaves. Ross's business activities were numerous: he was a merchant, a shipowner, and a director of the James River Company; he operated several mills on his estate and owned coal mines. He speculated extensively in land as far south as Georgia and Mississippi. While Ross profited from all of these activities, those earnings did not compare to those from his various ironworks. David Ross is best known for his association with the Oxford Ironworks in Campbell County, which manufactured sixteen hundred tons of pig iron annually. However, Ross also invested in Calloway's Furnace in Campbell County, Stonewall Furnace in Appomattox, and David Ross Forge and Furnace in Tennessee. For Ross, agricultural activities served to support his other business activities, especially iron making.[35]

Robert Carter (1728–1804) of Nomini Hall in Westmoreland County was one of the most committed and successful planter-businessmen. Carter owned over sixty thousand acres and almost 450 slaves in at least nine Virginia counties. He owned, operated, and sometimes rented out numerous grist, saw, and merchant mills. He owned several schooners, a productive salt mine, and a one-quarter interest in the Frying Pan copper mines.[36] On his plantations Carter established blacksmithing shops and a "Manufactory of Woolen, Cotton & Linen Clothes." Carter profited greatly from his sales of textiles during the Revolutionary War and explained to his Baltimore business associates that if he should have more money to invest, "it should be employed in a Linen and Woolen Manufactory."[37] Like Ross, Carter was also an ironmaster. Carter owned a one-fifth interest in the Baltimore Iron Works, a prominent and successful Maryland company that operated between the 1730s and the 1770s.[38] His share in the company's works and mines was valued at approximately ten thousand pounds and netted him a minimum annual income of five hundred pounds.[39] Most significantly, Carter derived more income from rents than from any of his other enterprises, agriculture included. He rented lands to several hundred tenants and netted thirty-five thousand pounds of tobacco annually worth over two thousand pounds Virginia currency.[40]

As these men demonstrate, planters invested in the full spectrum of business opportunities necessary for developing local markets and economies. Some of their investments, such as tobacco and iron, were directed toward the export market, while others, such as stores, ordinaries, and mills, characterized the different ways planters interacted with the local market. Capital collaboration, either through loans or partnerships, was an important way the elite of Virginia facilitated the diversification that allowed for the development of regional markets. The elite planters were connected by more than just their wealth; they were also connected by their political power and dominance in their respective neighborhoods. Planters' political positions at the county and colony levels allowed them to make the connections, influence the legislation, and seize the financial opportunities that enabled their entrepreneurial approach to their economic activities.

John Tayloe's connections with members of "The One Hundred" on numerous occasions enabled him to pursue business opportunities through partnerships that alone he could not have attempted. In 1751 Tayloe joined thirteen other planter-businessmen in forming the Ohio Company, a land speculation company that had been granted "about Five Hundred Thousand Acres on the Branches of the Ohio and other Branches of the River MISSISSIPPI within the Colony and Dominion of Virginia."[41] Besides Tayloe, other members of "The One Hundred" in the Ohio Company included Robert Carter, Gawin Corbin, Richard Lee, and George Mason. Tayloe's participation in the Ohio Company was related closely to his investment in the Patton Association, another land speculation partnership that received a similarly vast land grant in the same region in 1749. Both companies hoped to secure the inland Indian provisioning and fur trade.[42] Using his sales of iron from his ironworks, Tayloe advanced the company funds as necessary for surveying, construction, purchases, and other expenses.[43] Tayloe's ability to reap the rewards of large-scale speculation depended on the participation of other elite planters in such partnership ventures.

On occasion Tayloe invested in proposed enterprises by other, smaller planters. During the 1760s Tayloe attempted to purchase four thousand acres in Princess Anne County on behalf of himself, John Wadman, and others. John Wadman proposed "to make oil of Tarr, and fish oil . . . [and] mak[e] some experiments in salt and other things which may be useful to this Colony." Unfortunately, Tayloe's and Wadman's attempts to establish fishing, salt, and tar-oil industries on Cape Henry intruded on local residents' ideas that lands that had long supported a common fishing hole should not be patented for private use.[44] While it is difficult to tell whether or not Tayloe and Wadman persevered in their plans, Tayloe's investment behavior demonstrates the type of capital collaboration characterizing the exchange relationships that facilitated the diversification and therefore development of the regional domestic economy.

During the 1770s Tayloe once again teamed up with other elite planters to pursue new business opportunities through partnerships. Instead of joining together to facilitate land speculation, however, in both of these instances planters partnered to promote merchant endeavors or the founding of new agricultural industries. In 1771 Tayloe spearheaded an effort to establish "a Patriotic Store." He reasoned that the current import trade was "extremely prejudicial to the industrious planters, by unavoidably involving them greatly in debt, through the excessive price at which goods have for many years been sold." To rectify "this evil," Tayloe and a group of other prominent Northern Neck planters, including Landon Carter and Richard Henry Lee, proposed to create a store that they would operate in a way more advantageous to Virginians. The store's directors intended to sell goods at far lower rates than those prevailing in Virginia at the time, limit its profit margin to 10 percent, limit quantities sold to any one individual or family, and sell goods only for ready money or tobacco. Tayloe figured that this endeavor required at least six thousand pounds sterling in start-up capital and would require approximately five years to return a profit to investors. The outcome of Tayloe's proposal is unrecorded, but Tayloe felt strongly that it was a "most useful undertaking" and knew that its success depended on the participation of other elite planters.[45]

In 1774 Tayloe joined an industry-promoting partnership "for the Purpose of raising and making Wine, Oil, agruminous Plants [herbs], and Silk." Working with the well-known Italian businessman Philip Mazzei, who was to act as a factor for the new company, the partnership intended to import "sufficient quantities of eggs of silk worms from Italy and Sicily"; thousands of "vines which bear the best grapes" from Italy, France, Spain, and Portugal; and four thousand "olive trees from Provence, Lucca and Nice where the best olive oil is made." Mazzei's duties included personally inspecting the products at each of these locations before shipping them to Virginia as well as hiring fifty farmers experienced in making silk, wine, and olive oil who were willing to relocate to the colony. The partners sold subscriptions for partnership into the company at fifty pounds sterling each in order to fund the purchasing of the vines, trees, and eggs as well as the four thousand backcountry Virginia acres thought necessary for the venture. Fifteen of Virginia's wealthiest planters subscribed to this partnership, including Tayloe, Peyton Randolph, George Mason, George Washington, John Page, Thomas Jefferson, Benjamin Harrison, Thomas Nelson, Theodorick Bland, Archibald Cary, W. Miles Cary, Allen Cocke, Mann Page, John Tabb, and Charles Carter.[46] As all of these examples make clear, planters regularly encouraged other business-minded men in their efforts to diversify by investing capital in a variety of new enterprises, through either loans or partnerships.

It was not just in these large speculative companies that planters supported one another in developing the regional economy. Within and across regions planters joined forces to offer merchant services and make iron. During the revolutionary era Henry Banks and David Ross, both on the list of one hundred, operated their own mercantile companies using partnerships. Banks was a named partner in the Richmond firm of Banks, Hunter & Co., while Ross participated in at least three mercantile firms during his career: Ross & Forde, David Ross & Co., and Ross & Currie.[47] Edmund Pendleton chose not to operate his own ordinary but instead invested in one managed by his local business associate Thomas Wild.[48] Because ironworks required large investments of capital, they too were ripe fields for capital collaboration. Robert Carter owned a one-fifth interest in the Baltimore Iron Works, a prominent and successful Maryland company that operated between the 1730s and the 1770s.[49] Although no similar study of Maryland's wealthiest planters has been conducted, the Baltimore Company partners, Daniel Dulany, Dr. Charles Carroll, Benjamin Tasker, Charles Carroll of Annapolis, and Daniel Carroll, would certainly top such a list for Maryland. In addition, highlighting the significance of familial relationships in the exchange patterns that dominated regional domestic economies, Carter secured his shares by marrying into the Tasker family.[50]

Ironmaster David Ross owned and managed the Oxford Ironworks in Campbell County and also invested in and operated several other works. For example, he partnered in 1779 with J. Calloway to start Calloway's Furnace, also in Campbell.[51] Archibald Cary headed up the partnership that also included William Cabell, Edward Carter, and Alexander Trent and that managed the Albemarle Ironworks in Albemarle County. Charles and Robert Carter each owned a quarter interest in the Frying Pan Copper Mine in Fairfax and Loudoun counties.[52] John Tayloe was able to expand his iron-making endeavors by enlisting the financial support of Presly Thornton, a wealthy planter from Northumberland County in the Northern Neck. After experiencing the financial benefits of his Neabsco Ironworks, Tayloe in 1755 joined with Thornton to acquire the nearby Occoquan Company. Tayloe served as the hands-on manager, while Thornton acted as more of a silent partner, supplying managerial advice and capital when needed. The partnership outlasted both men and was only dissolved in the 1790s when Thornton's son expressed his disinterest in the old works.[53]

Iron making was a profitable business that could double a planter's annual income and provide important hedges against depressions in the tobacco market. Tayloe's iron making can serve as a representative example. The per-ton prices Tayloe received for his iron fluctuated from one transaction to the next each year and seemed to coincide with depressions in Virginia's tobacco economy.[54] While iron and tobacco prices generally were depressed simultaneously, the combined income Tayloe received in depressed years was far more than he would have received for tobacco alone.[55] When Tayloe's tobacco brought only £4 16s. 10d. per hogshead for 153 hogsheads he sold in 1763, he received £6 14s. 6d. per ton for

214 tons of pig iron. His total income from both commodities that year reached just over £1,957 sterling. Had Tayloe been dependent on tobacco alone, he would have made just £712 (see table 19). Certainly iron making was more lucrative than most of Tayloe's activities oriented toward the local market, such as the blacksmithing and milling activities discussed above. Iron is, however, representative of the ways in which planters used diversification to lessen their dependence on the tobacco market. While goods produced for the export market generally comprised the major part of a planter's income, goods produced for the local market helped secure the hedge between the tobacco economy and their financial security.

Chesapeake planters created a regional domestic economy during the eighteenth century based on their entrepreneurial, diversified approach to plantation management that encompassed commercial agriculture and an array of merchant, industrial, and other business services. An important minority of export-oriented products, such as tobacco, iron, and other crops, remained in the colonies and passed as trade goods in the domestic economy. In addition, planters founded a variety of plantation craft industries that made goods and offered services for local customers. These shops frequently became neighborhood centers where planters bartered, bought, and sold goods and services. Through such activities planters created and expanded on a variety of exchange relationships that provided the foundations for other business activities within the domestic economy. The regional economy of the colonial Chesapeake can therefore be defined as a variety of exchanges between planters, including debt and credit, buying and selling, bartering and trading, and capital collaboration. Kinship ties and residential proximity figured prominently into the nature of planters' exchange relationships. It is interesting to note, for example, that John Tayloe II was related to four other members of "The One Hundred": Robert Beverley, Landon Carter, Mann Page III, and Ralph Wormeley. In addition, the Tayloe family was connected through more distant kin ties to the Corbins, Lees, and Washingtons, as well as with equally wealthy and prominent planter families in Maryland. Tayloe could thus dominate the domestic economy of his neighborhood through the urban-type craft services he offered; he could also operate businesses at the colony level by partnering with elite planters from other neighborhoods and counties. He is representative of the other members of "The One Hundred" in these respects.

Any understanding of the nature of regional domestic economies in the colonial Chesapeake has to start with an understanding of (1) the role of diversification in sparking regional growth and development, and (2) the exchange relationships that facilitated that diversification. These, of course, are only starting points for analyzing and defining the regional domestic economy. Anecdotal and quantitative evidence show how planters' exchange relationships facilitated diversification and supported economic interaction at the neighborhood level.

Table 19: John Tayloe II tobacco and iron production, 1751–1774*

† = portion of annual amount was lost at sea
a = no value recorded for portion of exports, or value listed without tonnage figures

Year	Hogsheads of Tobacco	£ Sterling Received	Tons of Pig Iron	£ Sterling Received
1751	45	£27	—	—
1752	53	£303	—	—
1753	59	£246	—	—
1754	97	£430	109	£657
1755	101.5	£781	40.5	£256
1756	75.5	£626	416.5	£2549
1757	50†	£478	124	£706
1758	194†	£865	281†	£1049
1759	89†	£654	450†	£2343
1760	125	£986	258†	£1112
1761	127†	£932	110.5	£566
1762	129	£635a	289	£1617
1763	153†	£712	214†	£1245
1764	119	£696	60	£338
1765	60	£517	24†	£97
1766	75	£540	129†	£667
1767	42	£320	67†	£603a
1768	36	£292	35†	£179a
1769	64†	£606	93†	£550
1770	23	£204	54	£325
1771	28	£198	0	0
1772	47†	£115	120†	£365
1773	19	£94	76†	£167
1774	12†	0	40†	£20

*John Tayloe II Account Book, 1749–68; John Tayloe II Ledger, 1747–87; Accounts, Bonds, Orders, 1756–1762; John Tayloe II Account Book, 1770–76; Thomas Lawson's Occoquan Accounts, 1757–85, file 171.

Diversification fueled the development of individual wealth among the elite planters and the development of regional domestic economies. The challenge, of course, with the microhistory approach used here is the relevance of the individual, neighborhood, and county experiences to the overall regional or colonial domestic economy. More studies like the one done here, and especially like the analyses of southern Maryland, the Chesapeake tobacco regions, and Southside Virginia completed by Lorena Walsh, Lois Green Carr, Russell Menard, and Charles Farmer, will be required before any synthesis at the regional and colony-wide level materializes.

Notes

1. John J. McCusker and Russell R. Menard, *The Economy of British America, 1607–1789* (Chapel Hill: University of North Carolina Press, 1985), 127.

2. Lorena S. Walsh, "Summing the Parts: Implications for Estimating Chesapeake Output and Income Subregionally," *William and Mary Quarterly,* 3rd ser., 56 (January 1999): 53–94; Lois G. Carr and Russell Menard, "Wealth and Welfare in Early Maryland: Evidence from St. Mary's County," *William and Mary Quarterly* 3rd ser., 56 (January 1999): 95–120; Frank D. Lewis and M. C. Urquhart, "Growth and the Standard of Living in a Pioneer Economy: Upper Canada, 1826–1851," *William and Mary Quarterly* 3rd ser., 56 (January 1999): 151–81; P. M. G. Harris, "Economic Growth and Demographic Perspective: The Example of the Chesapeake, 1607–1775," in Lois Green Carr, *The Chesapeake and Beyond—A Celebration* (Crownsville: Maryland Historical and Cultural Publications, 1992), 55–92; Charles J. Farmer, *In the Absence of Towns: Settlement and Country Trade in Southside Virginia, 1730–1800* (Lanham, Md.: Rowman and Littlefield, 1993); Frances C. Robb, "Industry in the Potomac River Valley, 1760–1860" (Ph.D. diss., West Virginia University, 1991); Richard B. Sheridan, "The Domestic Economy," in *Colonial British America: Essays in the New History of the Early Modern Era,* ed. Jack P. Greene and J. R. Poles (Baltimore: Johns Hopkins University Press, 1984), 43–85. Robert E. Gallman analyzes the difficulties of speaking about a national domestic economy for the colonial period in "Can We Build National Accounts for the Colonial Period of American History?" *William and Mary Quarterly,* 3rd ser., 56, no. 1 (January 1999): 23–30.

3. See, for example, Walsh, "Summing the Parts," 57; John J. McCusker, "Measuring Colonial Gross Domestic Product: An Introduction," *William and Mary Quarterly,* 3rd ser., 56, no. 1 (January 1999): 4; Charles Tiebout, "Exports and Regional Economic Growth," *Journal of Political Economy* 64 (1956): 167.

4. Harris, "Economic Growth and Demographic Perspective," 61, 65, 70, 73; Carr and Menard, "Wealth and Welfare in Early Maryland," 102; Walsh, "Summing the Parts," 57–58, 66; Laura Croghan Kamoie, "Three Generations of Planter-Businessmen: The Tayloes, Slave Labor, and Entrepreneurialism in Virginia, 1720–1830" (Ph.D. diss., College of William and Mary, 1999), 22 n. 3, passim.

5. McCusker and Menard, *Economy of British America* (1985), 295.

6. Gallman, "Can We Build National Accounts," 23.

7. Carville Earle and Ronald Hoffman, "Urban Development in the Eighteenth-Century South," *Perspectives in American History* 10 (1976): 13; Farmer, *In the Absence of*

Towns, 9, 89, 90; David Goldfield, "Communities and Regions: The Diverse Cultures of Virginia," *Virginia Magazine of History and Biography* 95, no. 4 (1987): 436.

8. Farmer, *In the Absence of Towns,* 54, 136.

9. Myra L. Rich, "Speculations on the Significance of Debt: Virginia, 1781–1789," *Virginia Magazine of History and Biography* 76, no. 3 (1968): 302, 205; Farmer, *In the Absence of Towns,* 159, 180.

10. Evarts B. Greene and Virginia D. Harrington, *American Population before the Federal Census of 1790* (New York: Columbia University Press, 1932), 143–55. Tithables included all white males, black males, and females above sixteen years of age. Tithables are generally thought to represent about one-third of the overall population.

11. Lorena S. Walsh, "Plantation Management in the Chesapeake, 1620–1820," *Journal of Economic History* 49 (1989): 394, 396; Richard L. Bushman, "Markets and Composite Farms in Early America," *William and Mary Quarterly,* 3rd ser., 55, no.3 (July 1998): 358, 369; Harold B. Gill Jr., *Cereal Grains in Colonial Virginia,* Research Report Series (Williamsburg, Va.: Colonial Williamsburg Foundation, 1974), 9; William H. Siener, "Economic Development in Revolutionary Virginia: Fredericksburg, 1750–1810" (Ph.D. diss., College of William and Mary, 1982), 14–15; Peter V. Bergstrom, "Markets and Merchants: Economic Diversification in Colonial Virginia, 1700–1775" (Ph.D. diss., University of New Hampshire, 1980), 139; Allan Kulikoff, *Tobacco and Slaves: The Development of Southern Cultures in the Chesapeake, 1680–1800* (Chapel Hill: University of North Carolina Press, 1986), 120; Earle and Hoffman, "Urban Development," 28–31; Gregory A. Stiverson, *"Gentlemen of Industry, Skill, and Application": Plantation Management in Eighteenth Century Virginia,* Research Report Series (Williamsburg, Va.: Colonial Williamsburg Foundation, 1975), 99–116; Thomas M. Preisser, "Alexandria and the Evolution of the Northern Virginia Economy, 1749–1776," *Virginia Magazine of History and Biography* 89 (1981): 289; David Klingaman, "The Significance of Grain in the Development of the Tobacco Colonies," *Journal of Economic History* 29 (1969): 271–77; Walsh, "Summing the Parts," 57–58; Kamoie, "Three Generations of Planter-Businessmen," 117, passim.

12. McCusker and Menard, *Economy of British America* (1985), 23–25, 323, 325; Thomas Berry, "The Rise of Flour Milling in Richmond," *Virginia Magazine of History and Biography* 18 (1970): 390; Siener, "Economic Development in Revolutionary Virginia," 22, 24–25; Louis Morton, *Robert Carter of Nomini Hall: A Virginia Planter of the Eighteenth Century* (Charlottesville, Va.: Dominion Books, a division of the University Press of Virginia, 1965), 178.

13. Ralph V. Anderson and Robert Gallman, "Slaves as Fixed Capital: Slave Labor and Southern Economic Development," *Journal of American History* 44 (June 1977): 29; Christine Daniels, "Gresham's Laws: Labor Management on an Early-Eighteenth-Century Chesapeake Plantation," *Journal of Southern History* 62 (May 1996): 217–18; Gerald W. Mullin, *Flight and Rebellion: Slave Resistance in Eighteenth-Century Virginia* (New York: Oxford University Press, 1972), 125; Walsh, "Plantation Management in the Chesapeake," 394, 396; McCusker and Menard, *Economy of British America* (1985), 127; Lucia Stanton, *Slavery at Monticello* (Charlottesville: University Press of Virginia, 1993), 24.

14. See Goldfield, "Communities and Regions," for a good historiographical discussion of the significance of communities and regions. For the Chesapeake, Goldfield rightly emphasizes the community studies of Darrett and Anita Rutman, Rhys Isaac, Allan Kulikoff, and Richard Beeman.

15. John Tayloe II Account Book, 1749–68, Tayloe Family Papers, Virginia Historical Society, Richmond, reel 2:frames 179–214. A large part of the Tayloe Family Papers at the Virginia Historical Society (hereafter VHS) have been microfilmed as part of the *Records of Ante-Bellum Southern Plantations,* Series M, part 1: "The Tayloe Family." These papers will hereafter be expressed as TFP, reel:frame, to distinguish them from Tayloe family collections that are not part of the microfilm collection located at the VHS and other repositories. See also John Tayloe II Ledger, 1747–87, Library of Virginia, Richmond (hereafter LVA; this is a copy of the 1749–68 account book but with some additional entries made by Tayloe's executors); Accounts, Bonds, Orders, 1756–62, TFP, 56:392–427; John Tayloe II Account Book, 1770–76, Tayloe Family Papers, VHS.

16. Beverley Fleet, comp., ed., *Virginia Colonial Abstracts,* vol. 17 (Richmond, Va.: Genealogical Publishing Co., 1934), 125.

17. John Tayloe, Mt. Airy, to Colo. Landon Carter, October 16, 1762, Carter Family Papers, VHS. See, for example, John Tayloe Ledger, 1747–87, 2; Miscellaneous Accounts, 1755–1882, TFP, 6:681.

18. Jack P. Greene, ed., *The Diary of Colonel Landon Carter of Sabine Hall, 1752–1778,* vol. 1 (1965; repr., Richmond: Virginia Historical Society, 1987), 275.

19. John Tayloe, Mt. Airy, to Robert Wormeley Carter, March 20, 1767, Carter Family Papers, VHS; Thomas Lawson, Neabsco, to John Tayloe, December 2, 1771, file 171, Fredericksburg Court Records, Fredericksburg, Va.

20. Berry, "Rise of Flour Milling," 387–88, argues that the expansion of wheat acreage correlated to increased numbers of milling facilities.

21. Stephen Loyde and John Tayloe Account Book, 1708–78, TFP, 2:1–173.

22. John Tayloe II Account Book, 1749–68; John Tayloe II Ledger, 1747–87; Accounts, Bonds, Orders, 1756–62; John Tayloe II Account Book, 1770–76.

23. Ibid.

24. John Tayloe I Estate Inventory, November 2, 1747, Richmond County Will Book 5, 547–553.

25. This discussion of and all tables about Tayloe's blacksmithing activities at Mt. Airy come from his accounts in the John Tayloe Account Book, 1776–86.

26. Dennis J. Pogue, "Blacksmithing at George Washington's Mount Vernon," *Northern Neck of Virginia Historical Magazine* 46, no. 1 (December 1996): 5379–81.

27. Richmond County Deed Book 19: 32. The Richmond County Court in 1810 ordered Tayloe to compensate three of his neighbors for the six acres they collectively lost to flooding caused by Tayloe's mill dam.

28. This discussion of Tayloe's mill activities comes from the John Tayloe Account Book, Tayloe Family Papers, Mss1T2118G11, VHS.

29. Jackson Turner Main, "The One Hundred," *William and Mary Quarterly,* 3rd ser., 11 (1954): 354–84.

30. Main based his list of "The One Hundred" on tax and census records from the 1770s and 1780s. Therefore, he necessarily identified the basis of planter wealth as being those things recorded by tax lists (land) and census records (slaves). These sources record little about planters' other business activities besides agriculture. However, other types of primary sources provide a more detailed glimpse into planters' business activities; wills and estate inventories are especially important. When wills and inventories were not readily identifiable for a particular member of the list, family manuscript collections that

included correspondence and account books offered depth. On occasion secondary sources were also consulted.

31. For example, a 1727 statute providing for the founding of ironworks was entitled "An Act for Encouraging Adventurers in Iron-Works"; see William Waller Hening, ed., *The Statutes at Large; Being a Collection of All the Laws of Virginia, from the First Session of the Legislature, in the Year 1619,* vol. 4 (1820; repr., Charlottesville: University Press of Virginia, 1969), 228. Similarly, Robert Carter declined an invitation from John Tayloe I "to be a joynt Undertaker with your new Society untill I am better acquainted with [your] progress"; see Robert Carter to Colo. John Tayloe, January 29, 1728/9, Robert Carter Letterbook, 1728–30, VHS.

32. William B. Bynum, "Roger Atkinson: Merchant-Planter in Revolutionary Virginia" (M.A. thesis, University of Virginia, 1981), 1, 4, 10, 17, 25.

33. David John Mays, ed., *The Letters and Papers of Edmund Pendleton, 1734–1803* (Charlottesville: University Press of Virginia, 1967), 7, 78, 91, 361, 589.

34. Robert K. Brock, *Archibald Cary of Ampthill, Wheelhorse of the Revolution* (Richmond, Va.: Garrett and Massie, 1937), 12; "Proposals for forming a Company or Partnership for the Purpose of raising and making Wine, Oil, agruminous Plants, and Silk," Mss1Ad198a2070s, and "Outlines of a Plan for introducing into the Colonies . . . the different Products of Europe," Mss1Ad198a206, Adams Family Papers, VHS.

35. Charles B. Dew, "David Ross and the Oxford Iron Works: A Study of Industrial Slavery in the Early Nineteenth-Century South," *William and Mary Quarterly,* 3rd ser., 31 (April 1974): 189–224.

36. Morton, *Robert Carter,* 19, 149–50, 179–81, 183, 184, 198–99.

37. Ibid., 96, 175–77.

38. Keach Johnson, "Genesis of the Baltimore Company," *Journal of Southern History* 19 (May 1953): 157–79.

39. Morton, *Robert Carter,* 39, 166; 1787 deed, Carter Family Papers, Mss1C2468a2057, VHS.

40. Morton, *Robert Carter,* 72–78.

41. Ohio Company Articles of Agreement, May 23, 1751, Business Papers, LVA. The articles are reproduced in Alfred P. James, *The Ohio Company: Its Inner History* (Pittsburgh: University of Pittsburgh Press, 1959), 205–11.

42. Pamela C. Copeland, *Five George Masons: Patriots and Planters of Virginia and Maryland,* vol. 1 (Charlottesville: University Press of Virginia, 1975), 124–28; James, *Ohio Company,* passim.

43. John Tayloe II Account Book, 1749–68, TFP, 2:182; John Tayloe to James Russell, March 25, 1774, Virginia Colonial Records Project (VCRP), SR01022, 1, originals in London Class Russell Papers, bundle 17, Coutts & Co., Bankers, London.

44. John Wadman Petition, 1771, VHS. The disagreement over water rights in Princess Anne County in this situation was similar to the types of disagreements that occurred in revolutionary Rhode Island. See Gary Kulik, "Dams, Fish, and Farmers: Defense of Public Rights in Eighteenth-Century Rhode Island," in *The Countryside in the Age of Capitalist Transformation: Essays in the Social History of Rural America,* ed. Steven Hahn and Jonathan Prude (Chapel Hill: University of North Carolina Press, 1985), 25–50.

45. "Proposals for a Patriotic Store," *Virginia Gazette,* January 31, 1771. See T. H. Breen, *Tobacco Culture: The Mentality of the Great Tidewater Planters on the Eve of Revolution* (Princeton, N.J.: Princeton University Press, 1985), 161, 191–95, for a description of the Association movement of which this patriotic store was likely a part.

46. "Proposals for forming a Company," November 1, 1774, and "Outlines of a Plan."

47. John Ambler Papers, UVA, MS 1140, box 2; Emory Evans, *Thomas Nelson of Yorktown: Revolutionary Virginian* (Williamsburg, Va.: Colonial Williamsburg Foundation, distributed by University Press of Virginia, 1972), n.p.; Dew, "David Ross," 206 n. 63.

48. William Kelso, *Kingsmill Plantations, 1619–1800: Archaeology of Country Life in Colonial Virginia* (Orlando, Fla.: Academic Press, 1984), 98, 100; Ledger, 1758–63, Acc. 20472, LVA; Mays, *Letters and Papers of Edmund Pendleton,* 7, 78.

49. See Johnson, "Genesis of the Baltimore Company," 157–79.

50. Morton, *Robert Carter,* 39, 166; 1787 deed, Carter Family Papers.

51. Dew, "David Ross," 192–94; William Peden, ed., *Notes on the State of Virginia by Thomas Jefferson* (New York: W. W. Norton, 1982), 27–28.

52. William Reynolds, "An Account of the Albemarle Iron Works," *Magazine of Albemarle County History* 50 (1992): 46, 48, 52; Charles Carter Will, May 10, 1803, Mss2C24534a1, VHS; Morton, *Robert Carter,* 19.

53. John Ballendine to John Tayloe, May 13, 1756, TFP, 54:1034–35; Tayloe and Thornton Land Lists, TFP, 5:153; Prince William County Deed Book P, 201–10, Prince William County Courthouse, Manassas, Va. See also David Curtis Skaggs, "John Semple and the Development of the Potomac River Valley," *Virginia Magazine of History and Biography* 92, no. 3 (1984): 288; Presly and Susan Thornton to John Tayloe, Deed, January 1, 1798, TFP, 5:592.

54. Kulikoff, *Tobacco and Slaves,* 119; McCusker and Menard, *Economy of British America* (1985), 62–63, 121; Ronald Hoffman, *A Spirit of Dissension: Economics, Politics, and the Revolution in Maryland* (Baltimore: Johns Hopkins University Press, 1973), 18.

55. See McCusker and Menard, *Economy of British America* (1985), 119, 126–27, for a discussion of motivations for and the impact of diversification on the tobacco economy.

The Characters of Commodities
The Reputations of South Carolina Rice and Indigo in the Atlantic World

S. Max Edelson

In a brief passage scrawled in the back of his letter-book, Carolina planter Richard Hutson cast an admiring eye toward Spanish America and the noted reputations of its celebrated commodities: "Cochineal is a production almost peculiar to New Spain. Quinquine, or Jesuit's Bark, the most salutary simple, perhaps, and of most restorative virtue . . . is found only in Peru, to which it affords a lucrative branch of commerce. The Indigo of Guatimala is superior in quality to that of any Province in America. Cocoa, though not peculiar to the Spanish Colonies, attains to its highest state of Perfection there. The Tobacco of Cuba, is of more exquisite flavour than any brought from the New World."[1]

Low-country planters produced and exchanged plantation produce to generate returns on capital, but they also invested commodities with a range of meanings beyond a purely rational calculus. The acquired reputations of commodities, especially those regarded as place-defining "staples," attested to their producers' skills and served as emblems for American regions abroad. When the merchant Henry Laurens declared in 1756, "We hate a bad Commodity of any sort," he underscored the importance of commodity quality and reputation as components in the construction of a collective provincial identity.[2] South Carolina's eighteenth-century staples, rice and indigo, testified to the accumulation of adaptive expertise that made planting fortunes possible in volatile environments. As exports, these plantation goods carried with them images of the Lower South abroad and seemed to transmit the very character of low-country society. Early modern participants in Atlantic exchange used terms that straddled social and economic spheres of endeavor when they described the reputations that commodities and individuals bore.[3] They struggled to project a commendable outward veneer and fought to ward off the stigma that a flawed appearance lent to assessments of the qualities of staples as well as people. The impulse to construct hierarchies of quality stemmed in part from a desire to impose a categorical order on an Atlantic world in which vast distances disrupted direct scrutiny and the reliable ascription of value. Letters of introduction eased an individual's transition from an established social position on one side of the Atlantic to an analogous stature on the other. The regional reputations that commodities acquired functioned similarly to surround American goods with an associative framework that allowed European buyers to prejudge their purchases.

Low-country rice served admirably in this quest for transatlantic recognition. Its early eighteenth-century rise to prominence in European markets seemed to rest as much on the unparalleled whiteness, flavor, and shape of the Carolina grain as it did on the capacities of planters to supply it to markets efficiently. South Carolina indigo, however, exported in significant quantities from the 1740s, gained a notoriety for adulteration, impurity, and inconsistency that permanently suppressed its price in London markets in relation to imports from French and Spanish colonies. This chapter examines the material causes and cultural consequences of the divergent reputations of South Carolina's staples. Rice's good character endorsed the planters' quest to broadcast images of a refined and advancing colony to the metropolis. Indigo's bad character abroad, however, seemed to confirm their worst fears: that South Carolina might instead succumb to the crudeness and savagery that marked colonial settlements as inherently inferior versions of European societies. The contrasting statures of rice and indigo supported two contrasting visions of the Atlantic economy. Planters saw their skillful adaptation of rice agriculture to the novel environments of the Lower South rewarded with metropolitan praise and the high returns of an even-handed, even benevolent, market. Unwilling to accept the censure of being associated with inferior, low-priced indigo, some accused self-interested brokers and traders of maligning the dyestuff's reputation unfairly. The characters that these commodities bore brought South Carolina planters into a prosperous but culturally complex engagement with the broader Atlantic world.

Concerns for the ways in which reputations circulated to secure or impair group economic fortunes flourished long before transplanted English settlers negotiated the standing of their commodities in the Atlantic world. Late medieval town authorities regulated local exchange by monitoring false weights and short measures in the marketplace to ensure "their town's reputation for peaceful and honest trading."[4] As the early modern English household became enmeshed in local creditor and debtor relationships "householders sought to construct and preserve their reputations for religious virtue, belief and honesty in order to bolster the credit of their households so that they could be trusted." As the extension of credit moved from a relatively confined circuit of personal and neighborhood interaction and toward larger spheres of contracted debt and interdependence by the early seventeenth century, reputations communicated reliability across "chains of friends and business associates, and became the basis of deciding who could then be added to structural chains of obligation." As economic prospects came to depend on household reputation, a tainted reputation, even one unfairly assigned through slander or mistaken information, threatened the household with the specter of exclusion from networks of lending and a potentially rapid descent downward in social and economic status.[5] As a central idea in contemporary works of drama and political economy that cataloged this transformation of social experience, "honor" came to be associated with "a bottomless line of credit, a claim or protection against the contingencies of the social marketplace where reputations fluctuated like so much stock."[6]

The key factor that stimulated the widespread circulation of household reputations in England was the increased distance between borrower and lender; this factor operated on a more expansive scale in the setting of transatlantic exchange, where reputations traversed an ocean and where subject and audience were separated in time as well as by space.[7] The new terms of maintaining and manipulating transatlantic character were revealed most dramatically in the political arena, where rivals tarnished the reputations of opponents with such abandon that their battles created a "climate of conspiracy, slander, and general foul play" that "pervaded the public life of the Anglo-American world."[8]

South Carolina planters, from the first decades of the eighteenth century, benefited from an increasingly active credit market that financed the development of the plantation countryside. Low-country debtors responded to this development by devoting new energy to establishing and maintaining reputations as capable and careful planters.[9] When South Carolina planters began exporting commodities for European consumption, they entered a transatlantic forum for the articulation and elaboration of reputations. Such reputations adhered to the province as a whole, rather than to discrete households, and were embodied by actual commodities, as opposed to the less tangible exports of rumor, calumny, and invective by which political actors found their statures diminished abroad. Commodity reputations flourished in the early modern Atlantic economy, in part, because they performed an economic function for European merchants. The time and space that separated importers from areas of production made it impossible for them to gauge with any certainty the quality of produce until long after they had issued orders to factors and chartered ships to colonial ports.[10] Imposing regional reputations on imported commodities gave merchants a crude but serviceable means of predicting the quality and thus the expected market price that unseen commodities might command. Just as tarnished personal reputations could linger with damaging effect in the political and social realms, even if unfounded, such reputations bore an uncertain relationship to the "true" value of commodities over time.[11]

Lower South planters anchored a sense of their cultural stature to the standing of their commodities abroad. Rice's reputation as the early modern world's finest testified to the planters' experience and skill. Every European encomium that held their chief staple up for special praise seemed also to imbue the low country as a whole with some measure of legitimacy, as a refined rather than a crude society in which discernment, not degeneracy, prevailed.[12] From its beginnings as a significant transatlantic commodity, South Carolinians celebrated their staple as "Rice of the best kind," "the best rice that is brought to England from any part of the world," and, without any apparent sense of hyperbole, "the best yett known in the world."[13] As the eighteenth century progressed, rice retained this status. When the planter Ralph Izard toured southern France on the eve of the Revolutionary War, he noted with pride that "large quantities of rice from Carolina" earned the preference of Marseilles buyers at the expense of other varieties. William Gerhard De Brahm, royal surveyor for the southern colonies during the 1760s, considered low-country rice to be a production "brought . . . to the highest perfection, and as such known in all the European and American markets."[14] Throughout the century rice planters experimented with several varieties of *Oryza sativa*, seeking out grains that appeared larger, whiter, and brighter. After 1750 two types, known as "white" and "gold," became the most commonly produced.[15] Charleston merchants employed few distinctions in categorizing rice quality. Most planters were able to produce rice of a standard size, shape, and color with small quantities in each harvest downgraded as "Ordinary" or "Second & third rate" or marked out for distinction and price premiums as "uncommonly fine."[16] When bad frosts, droughts, or flooding damaged rice grains, leaving them small or easily broken after processing, such impaired crops were sometimes sold locally in the "rough" for provisions or vended in less discriminating American markets.[17]

The deterioration of otherwise good rice, "being a Perishable Commodity Especially in a Hott Climate," dominated concerns for commodity quality and influenced marketing strategies.[18] Toward the close of the shipping season in late spring, "Old Beat Out Rice" disintegrated into dust and flour and became prey to the "Weavil" and the "worm." Rats made "great destruction" among parcels stored in Charleston warehouses for late export, and some observers suspected that "the heat of the Ships hold" accelerated its deterioration.[19] After slaves pounded rice to remove its outer husk, they "polished" it by removing the brown inner cuticle in large wooden mortars. Grinding away the germ inhibited the discoloration and spoilage that affected the grain as it aged and gave Carolina rice its trademark whiteness. But overpolishing led to noticeably "burnt" rice, a flaw that perhaps gave it a brownish cast but left rice otherwise "very little the worse for being so" and increased the percentage of damaged and broken grains that contributed to dull-colored, "dusty," and "flowery" parcels.[20] In the second half of the eighteenth century, mechanized pounding and polishing technologies made controlling rice appearance as it proceeded through processing more certain, but in the decades that preceded these innovations, environmental volatility and the inconsistencies of hand-processing affected rice quality to a greater degree.[21] In every crop exported, some rice that bore the marks of damage and age accompanied the whole.

European buyers assessed rice quality by its appearance and opened random parcels to sample a larger shipment. Charleston merchants inspected the rice they purchased with an eye toward these evaluation practices and sought to avoid shipping rice that appeared discolored or "of a dull aspect."[22] The planters' influence in the local market, however, often forced export merchants to assume the risks of shipping subpar rice in order to gain the opportunity to buy the bulk of any given producer's crop. When John Guerard exported an entire rice cargo, one that might well have exceeded one hundred or two hundred barrels, the preponderance was "all Choice good Excepting that small Parcel" of eleven barrels, "which we could not avoid Shipping." He feared that one of these might "be the first Open'd which if not Liked might be a Discredit to the rest as it might be thought the whole Cargo is the Same Sort." Instructing the ship's captain to send ashore "a Cask or two of it at a Time," he hoped "it will not be Perceived." Of utmost importance in this 1754 transaction was that his English associate, to whom the cargo was consigned, would take heed of the same careful notations of these distinctions, as did Guerard himself, "to prevent any Pretence or Plea on Score of the Quality."[23]

When Dutch brokers condemned two of Henry Laurens's rice cargoes as unsalable, only to purchase the shipment at a fraction of their market value at auction, he accused them of plotting to defraud him. He suspected that "the hurry of expeditious Cowes-Factors" impaired perceptions of his rice's quality when they "for the sake of dispatch tumble the several parcels of one Cargo into one promiscuous heap from whence the Barrels were filled again." Laurens endorsed the rice he shipped with the stamp of his own expertise. When assembling outbound cargoes in Charleston, he asserted, "I always judge of myself & depend upon no other eyes than my Own." British factors, by severing the link between merchant and commodity, undercut the premiums that Laurens believed should accrue from a cultivated discernment of quality and depressed his trading income by averaging his crop selections with those by export merchants who were "not over nice in the Choice of Rice." He then insisted in London that "my Rice be Shipped distinctly from other parcels & take its chance according to its own merit," and he demanded in Lisbon that his rice should "not Suffer in the Sale by being connected to such as [are] inferior."[24] Because planters typically sold their rice in Charleston, perceptions of rice quality abroad were problems that fell to the merchants' lot. These experiences, however, suggest the terms of an emerging colonial critique of the metropolis. Predatory rice buyers made spurious claims about quality that damaged the reputations and finances of Charleston export merchants. British associates often failed to protect their colonial counterparts from disadvantageous intrigue. When small parcels of inferior rice tainted the sale of entire cargoes, the Charleston merchants could only remonstrate from a distance and bemoan the lack of knowledge demonstrated by those on whom they depended for commodity returns. British merchants who handled large quantities of grain treated it as a true commodity in which individual parcels were interchangeable and could thus be combined and repackaged for reexport. Maintaining associations between discrete barrels of rice and their actual producers and exporters proved a cumbersome liability to high-volume trade, and doing away with such distinctions foreshadowed nineteenth-century developments in the storing and shipping of large quantities of grain for world markets.[25] The export merchants' insistence on maintaining a relationship with the physical parcels of rice they purchased, however, demonstrated the degree to which the qualities of goods were seen to embody and reflect the qualities of the individuals who produced and vouched for them.

After the South Carolina Agricultural Society requested that Thomas Jefferson, as minister to France, help promote the importation of Carolina rice into that country in 1787, the society's elite planter members expressed their thanks for a canister of Italian seed rice of the kind favored by French consumers. They remained confident that their ability to grow and process high-quality rice would render changing over to the Lombardy variety unnecessary to gain leverage in this new market. "When I was in Italy," wrote Ralph Izard to Jefferson, "I visited some of the best rice plantations in that country, and was surprised to find how inferior their management of the grain was to ours. . . . You may observe how much whiter our rice is than theirs." But the French complained that Carolina rice dissolved when "dress'd au gras" and contained too many broken grains, a byproduct of the polishing process. Contemplating the losses involved in separating out whole from partial grains, William Drayton argued that "it is only the Eye, that would be gratified by this Separation; for the broken Grains are equaly well tasted." He recommended that the French boil rice in the Carolina fashion to appreciate its virtues.[26] Comparatively inexpensive and uncommonly white Carolina rice had earned the Lower South a dominant share of the northern European market by the 1730s. Some fifty years later planters defended the qualities that had made their rice famous for goodness and resisted proposals that might change its appearance, even when faced with market incentives to do so. Although planters and merchants demonstrated that they could engage in the Atlantic economy with a calculating, rational concern for accumulation, their concerns for rice quality were embedded as much in a quest for a viable colonial identity as they were with maximizing returns on investments.

At the turn of the eighteenth century, Carolina immigrant Elizabeth Hyrne asked that her "mother and the children come over as well cloethed as you can, for if they should not apear very handsome at there first arrivall" in the colony, "it may doe us a prejudis."[27] In strikingly analogous language, one of indigo's leading advocates warned in 1746 that if the blue dye "comes to the market bad at first, it will not be easy ever to regain its Character." The first shipments of South Carolina indigo to arrive in England, however, lacked "the bright metallick substance, or copper colour, which . . . is the distinguishing characteristik of good indigo" and instead crumbled on inspection "into small, roundish, and square pieces about the brightness of horse beans, with grey, mouldy, or dull edges." Soon after, the commodity seemed "to Labour under so bad a Character" as was likely "greatly [to] prejudice what may come . . . hereafter."[28]

The first unseemly indigo perused by London brokers was followed by other maligned shipments, and South Carolina indigo acquired a reputation as adulterated, impure, and inferior that would outlast the industry itself.[29] This persistent judgment against the planters' second staple forced a search for explanations and a reconsideration of the status of their peripheral plantation economy. Self-abasing admissions that indigo planters lacked diligence in the intricate processing phase of dye production suggest that indifference to quality was responsible for the commodity's failings in European markets.[30] A crisis of confidence urged planters to throw up their hands in the face of a natural world they managed to channel so efficiently toward improvements in the rice industry but could not make answer to the commercial imperatives of making good indigo. Although blaming the environment deflected the self-doubt of admitting that experience could not be turned into expertise, casting aspersions on the land confirmed the worst indictments of the Lower South as a wasteland immune to improved culture.[31] When some producers learned to make high-quality indigo and their dye nevertheless sold at low prices in England, they began probing the means by which commodity reputations were acquired. In defense of their capabilities, planters leveled a critique at a marketing system that privileged indigo buyers at the expense of colonial producers and came to view the market itself as a partial arbiter of quality and a vehicle for the corrupt exercise of interest.

In the first years after the dye's introduction in South Carolina in the mid-1740s, indigo's promoters took comfort in the expectation that, with time, its quality would improve.[32] A decade later the commodity had become an important export complement to rice, but observers viewed persistent quality problems with less optimism. "There is something Extreamly unacountable in the working of Indigo amongst us. We shall make it very fine today & tomorrow without any visible alteration in the weather with the Same weed, the Same water, Steeping, & beating the most Experienced of Our makers shall not be able to make Either the Same quantity or quality." As planters increased their exports of the dye, they wondered why "their assiduous pursuit of a business which is extreamly troublesom & intricate" could not help supplant the commodity's bad reputation with a good one. The low-country environment, which appeared open to the cultivation of a wide range of exotic produce in the first decades of settlement, seemed to conspire against the reliable manufacture of good indigo. South Carolina "planters almost to a man make it as good as they can, but there is something at times either in the air or water that is not discover'd which confounds those of the best experience."[33] Heavy rains, untimely frosts, and intermittent droughts took a frequent toll on growing indigo in the fields, and temperature fluctuations affected the processing phase in which the compounds in the plant's leaves were extracted and precipitated into usable dye.[34] Planters with little experience in British East Florida and Tobago produced indigo that quickly established a reputation as "very fine," won prizes from the Royal Society of Arts, and commanded extraordinary market premiums in London—all of which confirmed suspicions that tropical and near-tropical climes were most conducive to good quality.[35] Those Lower South planters known and celebrated for the quality of their indigo invariably produced a few casks of "indifferent" or even "extreamly bad" dye, a pattern that also suggests that environmental causes, rather than a slovenly indifference to quality, sustained the commodity's negative image.[36]

Although derided by London buyers, South Carolina and Georgia indigo was consumed in progressively larger quantities over the course of the eighteenth century. Two dyers testified before a parliamentary committee debating the merits of granting a bounty on British indigo imports in 1748. After relying for years on distinctively colored and formed cakes of French dye, each noticed that the British American product "did not appear to the eye equal to the French" and indeed seemed "at the first Sight, to be unfit for any Use." Actual trials of the cheapest Carolina indigo revealed that it provided 75 percent of the dyeing strength of its French competitor, and yet it sold for less than a third of the price. The elaboration of quality categories based on regional reputations accounted for this disparity between use value and market value. When dyers articulated a set of criteria for evaluating indigo, the South Carolina variety passed muster because it "opened kind, worked free, and gave as good a colour as the French." The "Carolina Indico stains as well and as deep" as either the French or Spanish in tests, and although the best "Flora" "looks finer . . . the Colour of the Carolina is as durable, and will answer all the Uses of Flora in Callico Printing."[37]

British indigo brokers, by contrast, judged the dye in terms of its appearance before use and its point of origin. Color distinctions among progressively more expensive "copper," "blue," and "purple" or "flora" indigo reflected long experience importing dye from Spanish Guatemala and French St. Domingue. South Carolina indigo appeared "muddy and very dark blue" or "of a very light or pale blue colour," unfamiliar hues that made importers suspect that the product was adulterated.[38] Aesthetic notions of quality influenced indigo's market value because the most advanced tests of the dye's potency—burning as sample to see what matter was left behind, or measuring its ability to dissolve in water—offered uncertain gauges of the underlying chemical composition. "Purity" was associated with light weight, sweet odor, regular consistency, smooth texture, and most important, luminous color.

Buyers placed great emphasis on shape and proportions of the finished indigo cakes, favoring the traditional French and Spanish sizes that had become trademarks of high quality. South Carolina colonial agent James Crokatt urged planters to "make all the indigo as near as possible to [the French] size of stone" or to conform to the Spanish standard, "in small pieces about the size of a nutmeg ... this shape passes here as Spanish indigo, the finest Guatimalo is made up in that manner." The British East India Company attempted to enhance the reputation of its indigo by similarly improving its presentation. "At present there is a prejudice against it for its shape and appearance," wrote an official in the company's London office to its Bengal agent in 1785, "which we conceive might easily be remedied by making it in square cakes and cleaning the cube of sand and dirt." Well into the nineteenth century evenly proportioned indigo obtained the highest prices, for "if the corners are much broken, or the Indigo cracked, it has the look of being imperfectly prepared, or *old* and ill used; a purchaser will, in such case, reject it, unless tempted by a low price: for, it is supposed, by every merchant, that there must be some good reason for others, refusing to buy."[39]

Indigo's bad reputation in British markets comprised a direct impeachment of planter skill. Planters and their skilled subordinates, slave and free, determined when to harvest indigo, they eyed the colors in the steeping vat to mark the exact point at which precipitation should begin, and they presided over the curing of the finished cakes. As much as planters felt slighted by the quality premiums offered to imperial competitors to the continuing discredit of their own product, two economic imperatives operated to impede the achievement of producing indigo good enough to force a reappraisal of its troubled reputation.

Planters sought immediate returns from the produce of their plantations. They sculpted their cubes of indigo to meet the standards for appearance that British buyers imposed but shipped them damp. As they dried, the regularly shaped cakes cracked, losing weight and symmetry. Planters rushed their dye to market to claim the best prices, and few waited the two months often required for thorough curing.[40] After gaining experience in producing indigo, planters also discovered an inverse relationship between quality and quantity. The finer varieties that mimicked the best French or Spanish "yeilded so little to a vatt, that it was more Proffitable to make Copper Indigo," sold at a reduced price.[41] Compared to the finest varieties of indigo, standard copper indigo could be produced in twice the quantity in one-third the time and using a quarter of the labor. The "Guatimala Flora," it was assumed, was "made there by Indians who set no value upon their time. Were we to manage it in the same way it would not pay a quarter part the hire of our Slaves."[42] Especially when Carolina indigo's bad reputation rendered price premiums for the highest quality uncertain in the London market, planters followed a familiar economic calculus of gearing production toward the best returns per slave laborer. Collectively, these behaviors made indigo's reputation a self-fulfilling prophecy. For the most part, planters relinquished a favorable stature in metropolitan markets to avoid devoting land and labor to more uncertain ventures.

This compromise with the biases of London's indigo buyers and the exigencies of plantation finances did not sit well with active agricultural improvers and export merchants, who increasingly identified the London mercantile community's interest in low prices for colonial indigo as the chief rationale for demeaning its quality. Charleston indigo merchants began questioning the fairness of indigo's reputation with the arrival in 1756 of Moses Lindo, a Jewish merchant with extensive West Indian connections. As an experienced London indigo broker, Lindo offered his expertise to planters on commission and promised to endorse the best Carolina indigo with his respected stamp of approval, given as the colony's official "Surveyor and Inspector General of Indigo" from his appointment to this office in 1762 until his death in 1774.[43] Lindo, aware of the importance of the commodity's shipping container as an indicator of its quality, affixed a special seal to each parcel he inspected. Guaranteeing that the indigo he approved would be free from adulteration or mixture, he attracted the business of the most careful planters and the orders of the larger London trading houses. Competing indigo exporters soon accused him of attempting to engross the trade and "Quash little folks." They saw him buy up parcels previously deemed inferior at higher prices and suspected that he wished to "throw a blemish upon all Indigo that is not sanctify'd by his Seal."[44]

Lindo's apparent successes at obtaining higher London prices for previously maligned Carolina indigo, however, forced merchants to reconsider the fairness of a reputation that could be so artfully manipulated. Robert Raper reported that "several Quantities of Indico last year & this has been sent from hence to London via Jamaica & there Cleared as French & sold as such in London." When French prize indigo was sold in Charleston at a substantial premium to locally manufactured dye, despite appearing to be "a good deal inferior," some grew to suspect that a cabal of conspiring merchants derided Lower South indigo in order to buy it at bargain prices.[45]

As a planter determined to produce indigo of the highest quality on his Mepkin Plantation and after long experience as an export merchant, Henry Laurens believed that he knew "good Indigo as well as any body." Yet he had "seen such a difference in sentiments upon that Article, often depending upon caprice, the fashion, or the demand for it, that I never think myself sure of having Indigo which we call best on this side pass for the same thing on yours." Indigo was a "valuable article & gives temptation & scope for too much Artifice," he claimed. "Men of great seeming Riches who carry their heads very high & will serve their own Interest first as tend to puzzle & embarrass the most judicious fair Trader" suppressed prices when the commodity was "down and out of repute."[46] Far from reflecting the real value of Lower South indigo, "Tricks & cunning" were at play when "a glutted & declining Market create[d] a thousand blemishes in any commodity." Laurens blamed the inattention of his English associates in not guarding "against the artifices of those people who appear for the purchasers on your side, else whence that clamour that is heard about the size & shape & that preference given to a piece of Indigo 2 Inches square to the same piece broke into

6 parts."⁴⁷ His suspicions of a brokers' conspiracy to maintain the bad reputation of Carolina indigo seemed to be confirmed during a trip to England in 1772. Laurens presented a sample of his own production to "some of the Wise Men call[e]d Brokers and Dyers" without revealing its regional origins. "They admired it much for East Florida Indigo. One . . . was very sorry we could not make such Indigo in Carolina. This proves the Strength of their Prejudices more than the Clearness of their Judgment."⁴⁸ Confident that his indigo was "intrinsically better than it appears," Laurens abandoned what he viewed as a corrupt English market for the more impartial French in 1786.⁴⁹

The early modern transition to an economy pervaded by long-distance exchange altered the characters of commodities. Once stable entities easily valued in terms of their "weight, purity, and sovereign statement," goods became fluid entities when evaluated from within the matrix imposed by market exchange, their value open to "Calculations, anticipations, expectations, possibilities of use or non-use, alternations of plenty and scarcity—a sinuous course of things real, felt, imagined and calculated." South Carolina planters stood on the cusp of this transformation as they responded to the ways in which rice and indigo were valued in the Atlantic economy. Planters' economic behaviors reflected a recognizably modern notion of commercial exchange, one that sought the most efficient means of generating income from investments in slaves and land. Rice was a valuable crop that supported an increasingly refined planter material culture, but as a substitute grain for the northern European poor it lacked the exotic cachet that inhered in products such as silk, olives, and wine, which South Carolina and Georgia were never able to produce profitably. Indigo, with its long commercial history as a precious dyestuff, promised to perform the role of a status-granting commodity, but Lower South producers found themselves supplying a raw material for a nascent textile industry serving the emulative aspirations of an expanding, and decidedly middling, consumer group.⁵⁰ When opportunities to sacrifice quantity for quality presented themselves, planters opted, more often than not, to pin their fortunes to the economies of scale they could generate rather than competing for the prestige that French rice consumers and London silk dyers conferred by paying premiums for the best commodities. Planters manipulated supply and demand information to obtain the highest price for their produce, and they pursued such tactics without a hint of compunction for distorting the "real" value of their commodities.⁵¹

Yet at the same time, merchants and planters celebrated rice's reputation for high quality in ways that transcended concerns for market position. Despite the growing market for their indigo in Britain, they acknowledged that their second staple's character as an inferior product was an evil that necessitated reform and innovation. Challenges to rice and indigo quality, however, evoked charges of complicity against metropolitan commodity handlers in the defaming of Lower South commodities. Some went so far as to envision the Atlantic economy as a system in which corrupt agents at the center profited at the expense of producers on the periphery. Reports of bad commodities abroad punctured a faith in planter expertise and portrayed plantation societies as backward and unrefined. The planters' ability to supply the British textile industry and feed Europe's hungry posed a challenge for settlers who saw plantation production as a means of promoting cultural improvement. The range of responses evoked by the divergent reputations of the Lower South's staples suggests that planters were economically, but not ideologically, prepared to undercut claims to refinement in exchange for reliable returns on plantation investments.

Notes

1. Richard Hutson Letterbook, South Carolina Historical Society, Charleston (hereafter SCHS).

2. Henry Laurens to Devonsheir, Reeve, and Lloyd, August 26, 1756, in *The Papers of Henry Laurens,* ed. Philip M. Hamer et al., 16 vols. (Columbia: University of South Carolina Press, 1968–2003), 2:299 (hereafter *PHL*).

3. On South Carolinians' perceptions of "credit" as these applied to Georgia, see Henry Laurens to James Read, October 15, 1762, ibid., 3:137–38.

4. Dorothy Davis, *A History of Shopping* (London, 1966), 6–9.

5. Craig Muldrew, *The Economy of Obligation: The Culture of Credit and Social Relations in Early Modern England* (Basingstroke: Macmillan, 1998), chap. 6, 148–72, 148–49, 152–54. On the role of reputation in structuring long-distance exchange in London, see Natasha Glaisyer, "Merchants at the Royal Exchange, 1660–1720," in *The Royal Exchange,* London Topographical Society, publication no. 152, ed. Ann Saunders (London: London Topographical Society, 1997), 201–2.

6. Jean Christophe Agnew, *Worlds Apart: The Market and the Theater in Anglo-American Thought, 1550–1750* (Cambridge: Cambridge University Press, 1986), 181–83.

7. On the constraints imposed by Atlantic navigation on communication and commerce, see Ian K. Steele, *The English Atlantic, 1675–1740: An Explanation of Communication and Community* (New York: Oxford University Press, 1986), passim.

8. Patricia U. Bonomi, *The Lord Cornbury Scandal: The Politics of Reputation in British America* (Chapel Hill: University of North Carolina Press, 1998), 2, passim. See also Alec B. Haskell, "'To declare in this publick Manner,' Reputation Defenses in the *Virginia Gazette,* 1736–1770," paper presented to the Seminar in American History, Johns Hopkins University, Baltimore, April 15, 1998. On the ideological imperatives that encouraged colonists to scrutinize the distance between political reputation and true intention, appearance and interest, see Bernard Bailyn, *The Origins of American Politics* (New York: Knopf, 1967), 139–44.

9. Russell R. Menard, "Financing the Lowcountry Export Boom: Capital and Growth in Early South Carolina," *William and Mary Quarterly* 51 (1994); Michael Woods, "The Culture of Credit in Colonial Charleston," *South Carolina Historical Magazine* 99 (1998): 358–80. On the emergence of collective standards by which planting expertise was evaluated, see S. Max Edelson, "Planting the Lowcountry: Agricultural Enterprise and Economic Experience in the Lower South, 1695–1785" (Ph.D. diss., Johns Hopkins University, 1998), 474–99.

10. On the effects of Atlantic navigation and commerce on planter marketing strategies and experiences in colonial Charleston, see Edelson, "Planting the Lowcountry," 400–433.

11. Planters employed regional categories in a similar fashion when they articulated preferences for slave labors by region and ethnicity. Such preferences seem to have included both calculated assessments of valuable and region-specific attributes, and crude stereotypes of ethnic personalities and sensibilities. See Daniel C. Littlefield, *Rice and Slaves: Ethnicity and the Slave Trade in Colonial South Carolina* (Baton Rouge: Louisiana State University Press, 1981), 8–21; Ira Berlin, "Time, Space, and the Evolution of Afro-American Society on British Mainland North America," *American Historical Review* 85 (1980): 58–59.

12. On the symbolic role of tobacco, see T. H. Breen, *Tobacco Culture: The Mentality of the Great Tidewater Planters on the Eve of Revolution* (Princeton, N.J.: Princeton University Press, 1985), 58–73.

13. Records in the British Public Records Office Relating to South Carolina, South Carolina Department of Archives and History, Columbia (hereafter BPRO), July 19, 1715, 6:99; John Norris, "An Interview with James Freeman, 1712," in *The Colonial South Carolina Scene: Contemporary Views, 1697–1774,* ed. H. Roy Merrens (Columbia: University of South Carolina Press, 1977), 43; BPRO, circa 1706, 5:152–53. See also sources cited in Lewis C. Gray, *History of Agriculture in the Southern United States to 1860,* 2 vols. (1933; repr., Gloucester, Mass.: P. Smith, 1958), 1:283.

14. Anne I. Deas, ed., *Correspondence of Mr. Ralph Izard of South Carolina from the Year 1777 to 1804* (New York: Charles S. Francis and Company, 1844), 11; William Gerhard De Brahm, "Philosophico-Historico Hydrogeography of South Carolina, Georgia, and East Florida," in *Documents Connected with the History of South Carolina,* comp. P. C. J. Weston (London, 1856), 199.

15. R. F. W. Allston, *Essay on Sea Coast Crops* (Charleston, S.C.: A. E. Miller, 1854), 28; Duncan Clinch Heyward, *Seed from Madagascar* (Chapel Hill: University of North Carolina Press, 1937), 4–8; David L. Coon, *The Development of Market Agriculture in South Carolina* (1972; repr., New York: Garland, 1989), 169; Henrietta McBurney, *Mark Catesby's Natural History of America: The Watercolors from the Royal Library* (London: Merrell Holberton, 1997), 99–100; John Drayton, *A View of South-Carolina, as Respects Her Natural and Civil Concerns* (Charleston, S.C.: W. P. Young, 1802), 115; Norris, "Interview with James Freeman," 43; Gray, *History of Agriculture,* 1:283. On the production and export of "Ancony Rice," see *South-Carolina Gazette,* January 24, 1736.

16. See Henry Laurens to Henry Byrne, January 14, 1764, *PHL,* 4:130–31; Henry Laurens to Thomas Mears, December 22, 1763, ibid., 4:98. See also Robert Pringle to James Goodchild, March 31, 1741, in Walter B. Edgar, ed., *The Letterbook of Robert Pringle,* 2 vols. (Columbia: University of South Carolina Press, 1972), 1:306; Robert Pringle to William Cookson and William Welfitt, September 25, 1742, ibid., 1:421; Henry Laurens to John Nutt, February 26, 1757, *PHL,* 2:469–70; Henry Laurens to John Knight, January 31, 1756, ibid., 2:85; Robert Raper to Thomas Boone, May 13, 1768, Robert Raper Letterbook (photoduplicate of original in West Sussex Record Office), South Carolina Historical Society, Charleston; Felix Warley to John Tarleton, December 7, 1771, Letters 1772–80, Henry Laurens Papers, SCHS. These small variations in quality were not apparently sufficient to encourage planters to frequently consign rice for sale in Europe

in order to obtain the best prices that metropolitan markets might offer on account of high quality.

17. On the effects of environment on rice quality, see John Guerard to Messrs. Patride and Sons, January 9, 175[3], John Guerard Letterbook, SCHS; John Guerard to Messrs. Warr Lesueur and Trollope, December 17, 1753, ibid.; Henry Laurens to Stephenson, Holford, and Company, December 29, 1756, *PHL,* 2:385; Robert Raper to John Colleton, March 19, 1760, Raper Letterbook, SCHS; Robert Raper to John Beswick, January 2, 1764, ibid.; Elias Ball to Elias Ball, February 10, 1790, Elias Ball XIV Family Papers, folder 7, SCHS. On rice quality variations due to soil quality, soil exhaustion, and "degeneracy" due to infestations of "red rice," see McBurney, *Mark Catesby's Natural History of America,* 99–100; Allston, *Essay on Sea Coast Crops,* 28. On the alternative marketing of low quality rice, see Henry Laurens to Devonsheir, Reeve, and Lloyd, May 18, 1756, *PHL,* 2:193; John Lewis Gervais to Henry Laurens, October 21, 1778, John Lewis Gervais and Henry Laurens Correspondence, SCHS.

18. Robert Pringle to Michael Lovell, October 24, 1743, in Edgar, *Letterbook of Robert Pringle,* 2:592. See also Henry Laurens to Smith and Baillies, February 9, 1764, *PHL,* 4:167; [James Glen], *A Description of South Carolina* (London, 1761), facs. rpt. in Chapman J. Milling, ed., *Colonial South Carolina: Two Contemporary Descriptions* (Columbia: University of South Carolina Press, 1951), 99. See also Robert Pringle to William Cookson and William Welfitt, September 25, 1742, in Edgar, *Letterbook of Robert Pringle,* 1:423; Robert Pringle to Thomas Johnson and Samuel Carter, March 14, 1743, ibid., 2:528; Henry Laurens to John Knight, August 17, 1763, *PHL,* 3:529.

19. On climate, pests, and quality, see Robert Pringle to Thomas Burrill, June 1, 1740, in Edgar, *Letterbook of Robert Pringle,* 1:218; Robert Pringle to Andrew Pringle, September 10, 1740, ibid., 1:245; Robert Pringle to Thomas Hutchinson and Co, July 12, 1742, ibid., 1:391; Samuel and William Vernon to Austin and Laurens, December 8, 1756, *PHL,* 2:367; Henry Laurens to Smith and Baillies, ibid., 4:4. On rats and storage, see Josiah Smith Jr. to Francis Philips, January 10, 1772, Josiah Smith Jr. Letterbook, SHC; Henry Laurens to James Parode, February 21, 1749, *PHL,* 1:213; Henry Laurens to Mayne, Burn, and Mayne, April 30, 1763, ibid., 3:431. On shipboard deterioration, see Robert Pringle to John Keith, November 4, 1743, in Edgar, *Letterbook of Robert Pringle,* 2:597; Henry Laurens to Devonsheir, Reeve, and Lloyd, July 31, 1755, *PHL,* 1:304.

20. Felix Warley to John Tench, August 16, 1771, Letters 1772–80, Laurens Papers, SCHS. See also Judith Carney, "Rice Milling, Gender, and Slave Labour in Colonial South Carolina," *Past and Present,* no. 153 (1976): 116–18.

21. See Drayton, *View of South-Carolina,* 121–22; Gray, *History of Agriculture,* 2:729–30.

22. Henry Laurens to Thomas Easton and Company, March 3, 1756, *PHL,* 2:122; Henry Laurens to Sarah Nickleson, August 1, 1755, ibid., 1:309; Henry Laurens to Richard Oswald and Company, January 21, 1757, ibid., 2:425; Henry Laurens to Myler and Hall, October 2, 1756, ibid., 2:326.

23. John Guerard to Capt. William Best, January 12, 1754, Guerard Letterbook, SCHS; John Guerard to William Jolliff, January 17, 1754, ibid.

24. Henry Laurens to Grubb and Watson, March 30, 1763, *PHL,* 3:394; Henry Laurens to John Nutt, February 15, 1763, ibid., 3:259; Henry Laurens to Charles Crokatt, June 11, 1764, ibid., 4:306–7; Henry Laurens to Dennistoune, Munro, and Company,

April 14, 1764, ibid., 4:245–46. See also Henry Laurens to George McKenzie and Company, January 18, 1764, March 29, 1763, ibid., 4:130–32, 3:387; Henry Laurens to Cowles and Harford, January 20, 1764, ibid., 4:136–37.

25. William Cronon's discussion of grain storage and shipping in nineteenth-century Chicago has identified a similar tension between the commercial advantages of handling high volumes of commodities by severing "the link between ownership rights and physical grain" and the complaints of farmers who "had been complaining for years that prices paid in Chicago markets did not adequately reflect differences in quality among different shipments of grain"; see William Cronon, *Nature's Metropolis: Chicago and the Great West* (New York: W. W. Norton, 1991), 114–19.

26. Ralph Izard to Thomas Jefferson, April 4, 1787, "The Letters of Ralph Izard," *South Carolina Historical Magazine* 2 (1901): 201–2; William Drayton to Thomas Jefferson, November 25, 1787, William Drayton Papers, SCL.

27. [Elizabeth Hyrne] to [Burrell Massigberd], [c. 1701 or 1702], "Hyrne Family Letters, 1701–10," in *The Colonial South Carolina Scene: Contemporary Views, 1697–1774,* ed. H. Roy Merrens (Columbia: University of South Carolina Press, 1977), 19, 21.

28. James Crokatt, "Further Observations Intended for Improving the Culture and Curing of Indigo, etc., in South Carolina," in *The Colonial South Carolina Scene: Contemporary Views, 1697–1774,* ed. H. Roy Merrens (Columbia: University of South Carolina Press, 1977), 152–53; Crokatt quoted in Coon, *Development of Market Agriculture,* 228; *Journals of the House of Commons,* 90 vols. to date (London, 1803–), 25:634; Henry Laurens to George Austin, December 27, 1748, *PHL,* 1:200.

29. Claude Louis Berthollet, French chemist and author of *Eléments de l'art de la teinture* (Paris: F. Didot, 1791), a work recognized as the first empirically rigorous study of the chemistry of dyeing, affirmed this reputation when he classed indigo into three categories: "indigo flore," "coppery indigo," and "much less pure kinds, as that *from* Carolina." See also Barbara W. Keyser, "Between Science and Craft: The Case of Berthollet and Dyeing," *Annals of Science* 47 (1990): 244–46; Claude L. Berthollet and A. B. Berthollet, *Elements of the Art of Dyeing,* trans. and ed. A. Ure, 2nd ed., 2 vols. (London: T. Tegg, 1824), 2:36. John J. Winberry first discussed the causes and consequences of indigo's reputation at length in "Reputation of Carolina Indigo," *South Carolina Historical Magazine* 80 (1979): 242–50.

30. This view has been endorsed by Winberry, "Reputation of Carolina Indigo," 247; Joyce E. Chaplin, *An Anxious Pursuit: Agricultural Innovation and Modernity in the Lower South, 1730–1815* (Chapel Hill: University of North Carolina Press, 1993), 201–5; Gray, *History of Agriculture,* 1:294.

31. One critic charged that "lands in our Southern colonies are extreamly poor and sandy, and have a barren driness in them, which renders them very unfit to produce such a crop [indigo]"; see [John Mitchell], *The Present State of Great Britain and North America with Regard to Agriculture, Population, Trade and Manufactures* (London: T. Becket, 1767), 149–50.

32. See Robert Pringle to Andrew Pringle, March 1, 1745, in Edgar, *Letterbook of Robert Pringle,* 2:830; Henry Laurens to William Stone, May 14, 1748, *PHL,* 1:138–39.

33. Henry Laurens to Richard Pattison, September 16, 1756, *PHL,* 2:320; Henry Laurens to Augustus and John Boyd and Company, September 23, 1755, ibid., 1:340.

34. See Josiah Smith Jr. to George Appleby, March 30, 1784, Josiah Smith Jr. Letterbook, Southern Historical Collection, University of North Carolina, Chapel Hill; Robert Raper to John Colleton, September 23, 1759, Raper Letterbook, SCHS; Henry Laurens to John Knight, February 26, 1756, *PHL,* 2:109; Henry Laurens to Augustus and John Boyd and Company, November 15, 1756, ibid., 2:351–52.

35. William Gerhard De Brahm, *Report of the General Survey in the Southern District of North America,* ed. Louis De Vorsey Jr. (Columbia: University of South Carolina Press, 1971), 214; Josiah Smith Jr. to George Austin, February 25, 1772, Smith Letterbook, Southern Historical Society; David Macpherson, *Annals of Commerce, Manufactures, Fisheries and Navigation,* vol. 3 (1805; repr., New York: Johnson Reprint Corp., 1972), 514. Henry Laurens's indigo failed to obtain the society's prize, and his own appraisal of East Florida indigo was largely negative, despite the fact that the "Florida Indigo was vaunted off in our Charles Town News Papers"; see Henry Laurens to Gabriel Manigault, March 20, 1772, *PHL,* 8:228. After an initially favorable reception by London brokers, East Florida indigo's reputation appears to have declined, despite the colony's climatic advantages. See David Hancock, *Citizens of the World: London Merchants and the Integration of British Atlantic Community, 1735–1785* (Cambridge and New York: Cambridge University Press, 1995), 160, 163.

36. Crokatt, "Further Observations," 150; Robert Raper to John Colleton, December 17, 1760, Raper Letterbook, SCHS; Henry Laurens to James Cowles, December 8, 1755, *PHL,* 2:29; Henry Laurens to Richard Shubrick, January 17, 1756, ibid., 2:72; Henry Laurens to John Knight, February 26, 1756, ibid., 2:109; Henry Laurens to Rawlinson and Davison, April 9, 1756, ibid., 2:150; Henry Laurens to Devonsheir, Reeve, and Lloyd, May 18, 1756, ibid., 2:192; Henry Laurens to James Cowles, August 28, 1756, ibid., 2:305; Henry Laurens to Rawlinson and Davison, January 11, 1757, ibid., 2:407–8. The London price for Carolina indigo in 1748 varied from 18d. to 5s. per pound; see *Journals of the House of Commons,* 25:635.

37. *Journals of the House of Commons,* 25:635.

38. For indigo color criteria, see Alexander Hewit, "An Historical Account of the Rise and Progress of the Colonies of South Carolina and Georgia," in *Historical Collections of South Carolina,* ed. B. R. Carroll (1779; London, 1836), 1:360; Crokatt, "Further Observations," 148.

39. Crokatt, "Further Observations," 149, quoted in Dena S. Katzenberg, intro., and commentary, *Blue Traditions: Indigo Dyed Textiles and Related Cobalt Glazed Ceramics from the 17th through the 19th Century* (Baltimore: Baltimore Museum of Art, 1973), 19; A. Campbell Dunlop, "On the Cultivation and Preparation for Market of the Bengal Indigo," *Southern Agriculturalist* 2 (1829): 208.

40. S. Max Edelson, "Colour and Enterprise: South Carolina Indigo and the Atlantic Economy" (M.Litt. thesis, University of Oxford, 1994), 172–74. Planters watched their naval stores industry collapse as they failed to meet more rigorous quality standards necessary to produce the "green tar" that was specified in metropolitan bounties granted during the 1730s. The technique required that pines be barked for at least one and up to three years before being processed into tar. See *SCG,* February 12, 1737; Converse D. Clowse, *Economic Beginnings in Colonial South Carolina, 1670–1730* (Columbia: University of South Carolina Press, 1971), 208.

41. Henry Laurens to Richard Pattison, January 11, 1757, *PHL,* 2:411; Henry Laurens to Richard Pattison, September 16, 1756, ibid., 2:319; Henry Laurens to John Knight, January 27, 1757, ibid., 2:439; Peter Manigault to Benjamin Stead, December 13, 1767, Peter Manigault Letterbook, SCHS. See also William Elliott, "Reflections on the State of Our Agriculture, Especially on the Advantage of Cultivating Indigo, &c," *Southern Agriculturalist* 1 (1828): 65. Planters did strive for high quality indigo, however, to compensate for harvest shortfalls. See Henry Laurens to Devonsheir, Reeve, and Lloyd, August 26, 1756, *PHL,* 2:299; Henry Laurens to Rawlinson and Davison, August 26, 1756, ibid., 2:301; Peter Manigault to Ralph Izard, August 19, 1765, Manigault Letterbook, SCHS. Sources that indicate a general knowledge of this relationship between quality and quantity include J. F. D. Smyth, *A Tour of the United States of America,* vol. 2 (Dublin: Price Moncrieff [etc.], 1784), 36–37; Hewit, "Historical Account," 389; Berthollet, *Art of Dyeing,* 2:33; *SCG,* October 29, 1744; Crokatt, "Further Observations," 150.

42. Henry Laurens to William Cowles and Company, October 31, 1769, *PHL,* 7:184; Henry Laurens to Richard Pattison, September 24, 1755, ibid., 1:341–42.

43. Leila Sellers, *Charleston Business on the Eve of the American Revolution* (Chapel Hill: University of North Carolina Press, 1934), 165–66; Coon, *Development of Market Agriculture,* 252–53. See *PHL,* 2:344 n. and 8:408–9 n. Hugh Swinton filled this office in 1774; see Miscellaneous Records, RR, 62, South Carolina Department of Archives and History, Columbia.

44. Sellers, *Charleston Business,* 166; Henry Laurens to Cowles and Harford, October 12, 1762, *PHL* 3:131; Henry Laurens to Rawlinson and Davison, October 25, 1756, ibid., 2:344; Henry Laurens to Joseph Brown, January 27, 1763, ibid., 3:222–23.

45. Henry Laurens to John Knight, October 23, 1769, ibid., 7:171. Laurens was among Lindo's most vocal critics, but he paid for the inspector's services; see *SCG,* July 23, 1772. In November 1768 Laurens paid Lindo £82 12s. "for inspect[ing] Indigo"; see Henry Laurens Account Book, Robert Scott Small Library, Special Collections, College of Charleston, Charleston, S.C. On French prize indigo, see Henry Laurens to Samuel Munckley, John Adlam, and Francis Rogers Jr., March 11, 1757, *PHL,* 2:489. On Carolina indigo sold as French, see Robert Raper to Messrs. James and Charles Crokatt and Company, December 7, 1759, Raper Letterbook; "The State of Indigo Manufacturing in South Carolina," *Gentleman's Magazine* 31(1761): 440.

46. Henry Laurens to William Cowles, November 17, 1768, *PHL,* 6:170; Henry Laurens to Cowles and Harford, December 22, 1763, ibid., 4:102; Henry Laurens to Gabriel Manigault, March 8, 1773, ibid., 8:601; Henry Laurens to Ross and Mill, May 21, 1768, ibid., 5:686.

47. Henry Laurens to Ross and Mill, October 8, 1767, ibid., 5:336–37.

48. Henry Laurens to Gabriel Manigault, April 1, 1772, ibid., 8:228. See also ibid., 2:502, 4:434, 4:459–60.

49. Henry Laurens to Bridgen and Waller, January 7, 1786, ibid., 16:626–27; Henry Laurens to Babut and Fils and la Bouchere, February 25, 1786, ibid., 16:635–37.

50. Joyce Appleby quoted by J. G. A. Pocock, "To Market, To Market: Economic Thought in Early Modern England," *Journal of Interdisciplinary History* 10 (1979–80): 305. On textiles consumption, see Beverly Lemire, *Fashion's Favourite: The Cotton Trade and the Consumer in Britain, 1660–1800* (Oxford: Oxford University Press, 1991).

51. Edelson, "Planting the Lowcountry," 406–33.

Contributors

Kenneth J. Banks is assistant professor in the Department of History, University of North Carolina–Asheville.

Peter A. Coclanis is Albert R. Newsome Professor in the Department of History, University of North Carolina–Chapel Hill.

Robert S. DuPlessis is Isaac H. Clothier Professor of History and International Relations at Swarthmore College.

S. Max Edelson is assistant professor with the Department of History at the University of Illinois, Urbana-Champaign.

David Hancock is associate professor in the Department of History, University of Michigan, Ann Arbor.

April Lee Hatfield is assistant professor in the Department of History, Texas A&M University.

Laura Croghan Kamoie is assistant professor in the Department of History at American University.

Peter C. Mancall is professor in the Department of History, University of Southern California.

R. C. Nash is senior lecturer with the Department of History, University of Manchester, England.

Laura Náter is assistant professor in the Department of History, University of Puerto Rico.

Ty M. Reese is assistant professor in the Department of History, University of North Dakota.

Joshua L. Rosenbloom is professor in the Department of Economics, University of Kansas.

Claudia Schnurmann is assistant professor in the Department of History, Georg-August-Universität, Göttingen, Germany.

Daviken Studnicki-Gizbert is Stagière Postdoctoral Fellow with the Département d'histoire, Université de Montréal.

Jan de Vries is the Sidney Hellman Ehrman Professor of History and Economics at the University of California, Berkeley.

Thomas Weiss is professor in the Department of Economics, University of Kansas.

Index

Acapulco-Philippines trade route (Spain), 156, 163, 170
Accomack County (Va.), 187, 188, 213, 215
Accroans, 292
Adams, John, 13
Adams, Richard, 332
Addison, Benjamin, 310
Adolph, Gustav, 188
Albany (N.Y.), 55
Albemarle County, 336
Albemarle Ironworks, 336
Alderson, William, 328
Alexander, William, 332
Algonquians, 299
Allason, William, 328
Allen, William, 55, 332
Almirantazgo de los Paises Septentrionales, 172
Amazon River, 4
Ambler, John, 332
American Revolution, xv, xvii, 38, 40–43, 55, 58, 59, 96, 100, 110, 115–19, 124, 127, 131, 230, 269–72, 313, 333, 347
Amory, John, 38
Amory, Jonathan, 38
Ampthill (Va.), 333
Amsterdam, 3–9, 12, 16, 17, 101, 106, 133, 174, 188, 192–95, 197, 206, 210, 237, 255, 297. See also *Beurs*
Anderson, B. L., 114
Anderson, James, 36
Andrews, Charles M., xi
Anglo-Dutch Wars, 8, 190, 196, 206, 207, 222. See also Westminster, Peace of
Angola, 171
Annamaboe, 281, 283
Annapolis, 119, 336

Antigua, 34, 190, 229, 236, 238, 241
Antilles, Dutch, 9
Antilles, French, 9, 241
Antilles, Greater, 256
Antilles, Spanish, 255
Antwerp, 133
Apalachees, 298
Apperley, Mr., 283–84, 286, 290
Appomattox, 331
Aristotle, 166
Armistead, John, 332
Armit, John, 37
Arrison, Derrick, 208
Asante, 289
Atkinson, Roger, 331, 332
Augusta (Ga.), 313
Australia, 1
Austrian Succession, War of, 239
Azores, 39, 43

Bahia, 4
Bailyn, Bernard, xi, 198
Baltimore, 34, 119, 130–32, 333
Baltimore Company, 328, 336
Baltimore Ironworks, 333, 336
Bancker, Willem, 194
Bank of North America (Philadelphia), 130–32
Banks, Henry, 332, 336
Banks, Hunter & Co., 336
Banks, Kenneth J., xvi
Barahona, Francisco Vitoria de, 163, 166
Barbados, 7, 8, 23n15, 34, 107, 122, 187, 189–92, 197, 241, 256, 297; slave trade in, 98–99, 102, 219n8, 236, 238. See also sugar
Barbour, Violet, 216

Barette, Barbara De, 217
Barton, John, 309
Bartram, William, 316
Bassett, Burwell, 332
Batavia, 2, 3
Bayard, Anna Stuyvesant. *See* Stuyvesant, Anna
Bayard, Samuel, 212
Bayes, John, 191
Baylor, John, 332
Baynton, Wharton and Morgan, 310
Baynton & Wharton, 37
Bayonne, 156
Beale family, 329
Beckford, Peter, 123
Beckwith, Marmaduke, 328
Beekman, James, 115
Belfield, Capt. John, 329, 330
Belfield family, 330
Bell, Gov. Charles, 281, 286
Bengal, 352
Benin, 208
Bennett, Richard, 207
Berbice, 15
Berkeley, Edmund, 332
Berkeley, William, 190, 206, 208, 209
Bermuda, 34, 190, 236, 297
Beurs (Amsterdam), 4, 6
Beverly, Robert, 332, 337
Biddle, Clement, 40
Birket, James, 54
Black, William, 327
Blackwell Hall, 126
Bland, Theodorick, 332, 335
Blathwayt, William, 198
Blondel, Intendant, 237, 242
Blunt, William, 332
Blunt Point (Va.), 209
Bohemia Manor, 188, 214. *See also* Hermann, Augustine
Bompar, Governor-General, 237, 239, 242
Boone, Margaret, 311
Boot, Nicholas, 215, 227
Boston, 34, 38, 40, 43, 49–51, 100–101, 103, 109, 120, 122, 196–98
Brahm, Gerhard De, 347

Braudel, Fernand, xi, 198
Braventon, William, 38
Braxton, Carter, 332
Brazil, 4, 6–7, 13, 17, 22–23, 26, 121, 157, 169, 170–72, 232, 254–56, 271
Breen, Timothy, xiv, 72, 81, 83
Brent, William, 332
Bristol, 36, 97, 102, 104, 110–13, 115, 126, 128, 285
British East India Company, 352
Brockenbrough, William, 328, 329
Brown, House of, 130, 132
Brown, Thomas, 308
Bruce, Capt., 283
Bruchey, Stuart Weems, 131
Buck, Norman Sidney, 115–16, 118
Buckingham County (Va.), 333
Bucks County (Pa.), 37
Buenos Aires, 157, 162, 168, 170, 171
Bulley, Robert, 37
bullion. *See* gold
Bullitt, Cuthbert, 332
Bunisee, George, 280
Burd & Swift, 37
Burges, Gedley Clare, 36
Burrell, Robert, 214
Burwell, Lewis, 332
Burwell, Nathaniel, 332
Bushman, Richard, 83
Butler, Maj. Hugh, 306
Byrd, William, 54

Cabell, Joseph, 332
Cabell, William, 332, 336
Caboceer, Aggerie, 279
Caboceer, Bothy, 279
Caboceer, Cudjoe, 279–80
Cade, James, 213
Cadiz, 156, 237, 241, 264–66
calicoes. *See* textile trade
Calloway, J., 336
Calloway's Furnace, 333, 336
Camden (S.C.), 79
Campbell, John, 34
Campbell, Malcolm, 35
Campbell, Patrick, 55

Campbell County (Va.), 333, 336
Canary Islands, 43, 95, 171, 265
Cape Coast Castle (Gold Coast), xvii, 277–93
Cape Henry (Va.), 334
Cape Horn, 1
Cape of Good Hope, 3, 14, 156, 170
Cape Verde Islands, 236, 241
Carénage. *See* Castries
Carlisle (Pa.), 37
Carlos II (Spain), 264
Carlos III (Spain), 265
Carlos V (Spain), 169
Caroline County (Va.), 331
Carr, Lois Green, 339
Carrera de Indias, 157, 162
Carroll, Charles, 328, 336
Carroll, Daniel, 336
Cartagena des Indias, 156, 172, 173, 175, 233
Carter, Charles, 332, 335, 336
Carter, Edward, 332, 336
Carter, George, 332
Carter, John, 332
Carter, Landon, 327, 329, 332, 335, 337
Carter, Robert, 55, 56, 332, 333–36
Carter, Robert Wormeley, 330, 332
Carter family, 329–31
Carver, Erasmus, 285
Cary, Archibald, 332, 333, 335, 336
Cary, W. Miles, 332, 335
Casa de Contratación (Seville), 170, 173
Casa Madrid, Marqúes de, 265, 267
Casse, Gov. Du, 233
Castillo, Guillermo Céspedes del, 258
Castries (St. Lucia), 236, 246
Catawbas, 297, 299, 308–10, 311, 316
Catholicism, xi, xv, 1, 82, 154, 165, 174, 188, 197. *See also* Inquisition
Cayenne, 243
Caylus, Marquis de, 239–40
Cecil County (Md.), 214
Champigny, Governor-General, 239, 240, 242
Chanvalon, Thibault de, 237

Chapman, Stanley D., 116, 117
Charles I (England), 189
Charles II (England), 192, 196–97, 207–8
Charleston (S.C.), xiii–xv, 297, 313; indigo trade in, 353; rice trade in, 104, 109, 124, 347–48; slave trade in, 102, 124; sugar trade in, 114; textile trade in, 72–78, 80, 81; wine trade in, 34, 40, 56, 57;
Charleton, Stephen, 210, 221
Chastellux, Marquis de, 59
Cherokees, 306–8, 311–12, 315
Chesapeake region, xvi, xvii–xviii, 34, 100–106, 108, 111, 127, 187, 191, 199, 205–18, 297, 323–39; Dutch settlers in, 205–18; slavery in, 208, 212–13; tobacco production and trade in, 8, 17, 98, 122–24, 205–15. *See also* Maryland, Virginia
Chester County (Pa.), 37
Chesterfield County (Va.), 333
Chickasaws, 306–10
China, 119, 170
Chinnery, Nicholas, 309
Choctaws, 299, 306, 315
Choiseul, Minister, 246
Christiana Bridge (Pa.), 38
Churchill, William, 332
Ciança, Alonso de, 170
Clemens, Paul E., 112, 114, 115
Clinton, Cornelius, 208
Clunow, James, 37
cochineal, 344
Cocke, Allen, 332, 335
Cocke, Chastain, 332
Cocke, John, 332
Cocke, John H., 332
Coclanis, Peter, 297
cocoa, 253, 344
Coessart, Jeremias, 194
coffee, 10, 12, 39, 95, 110, 233, 234, 237
Colbert, Jean-Baptiste, 232, 257
Cologne, 188
Commenda (Gold Coast), 282
Company of Merchant Adventurers, 98, 112

Company of Merchants Trading to Africa, 277, 279–93
Company of the Islands of America, 232
Cone, John, 35
Connecticut, 7, 34, 192, 198, 217
Consejo de Indias, 258
contraband. *See* illicit trade
Cook, Nicholas, 211
Cooper, Basil, 35
Cooper, Capt. Thomas, 308
commission system, 97–133
commissionaires, 237–38
Compagnie des Indes Occidentales, 8, 232
Corbin, Francis, 332
Corbin, Gawin, 332, 334
Corbin, Richard, 328, 332
Corbin family, 337
Cork (county), 36
Correa, Juan Nuñes, 162
Cortlandt, Jacob van, 194, 195
cosmopolitanism, 58–59, 98, 209
cotton. *See* textile trade
Courtland, Jacob. *See* Cortlandt, Jacob van
Courtonne, Jerome, 91n29, 306, 309
Coventry, Henry, 197
Creeks, 306–10, 313–16. *See also* Lower Creeks, Upper Creeks
Crété, Liliane, 230
Crichton, John, 287
Crockatt, James, 306, 351
Croft, John, 58
Cromwell, Oliver, 189, 190, 192
Cronon, William, 314, 319n42, 358
Cuba, xvi–xvii, 8, 252–73, 344
Cul-de-Sac Marin (Martinique), 235, 238, 239
Cumaná, 253
Cunningham, Waddell, 36
Curaçao, 7, 13, 15, 28n63, 195–96, 206, 212, 236, 239, 242; Jews in, 26n42; slave trade in, 6, 10, 233
Custis, John, 188, 211, 213–15, 225, 332

David Ross & Company, 336
David Ross Forge and Furnace, 333
Davies, K. G., 98, 122
Davis, Nicholas, 332
Davis, Ralph, 125, 126
deerskin trade. *See* fur trade
Delaware, 7, 192
Denmark, 241, 245. *See also* St. Thomas
d'Estaing, Comte de, 230
Detroit, 78, 92n34
Deutz, Willem Gideon, 12
Dodd, John, 309
Dodd, Dr. Thomas, 308
Doerflinger, Thomas, 106, 131
Dolling, John, 188, 221, 224
Dominica, 229, 235, 242–43
Donaldson, Andrew, 36
Donk, Adriaen van der, 7
Doodes, Minor, 211
Drayton, William, 349
Drisius, Samuel, 207
Dublin, 36
Dulany, Daniel, 336
Dunaway, Wilma, xi
DuPlessis, Robert S., xiv–xv
Dutch East India Company (EIC), 1, 20, 171
Dutch West India Company (WIC), 1, 3–18, 21, 186, 188, 192–93, 195, 206, 207, 211–12
Dutch-Asian trade, xiii, 1–3, 5, 18–20
Duythusen, Jan, 194
Duythusen, Reiner, 194
Dyck, Pieter van, 194

Eastern Shore (Va.), 206–17, 218n2, 325
Edelson, Max S., xviii
EIC. *See* Dutch East India Company
Elliott, John H., 154, 161
Elmina, 7, 9, 13
Emperor, Francis, 210
Engels, Friedrich, xi
England, 6–15, 18, 20, 95–133, 156, 169, 186–99, 229, 231–37, 240, 245, 252, 254–57, 260, 263–66, 269, 270, 277–93, 298, 326–27; colonies of—*see* Barbados, Bermuda, Gold Coast, Jamaica; indigo trade in, 350–54; rice trade in, 95, 102,

109–11, 119, 124, 345–51, 354–55; slave trade and, xvii, 7, 95–99, 102–8, 111–15, 121–26, 129, 133, 208, 277–93, 297; and sugar trade, 95–99, 103, 107–10, 113–14, 117, 122–24, 127; textile trade in, xiv, 96, 110–13, 116–20, 126–28, 132–33, 206, 354–55; tobacco trade in, 31, 95, 97, 100–104, 107–15, 119, 122–24, 127, 132–33, 254; wine trade in, 31–35, 39, 43, 54, 57, 59
Enkhuizen, 4
Eppes, Francis, 332
Essex County (Va.), 326
Estremoz, Andres Rodrigues, 164
Eveleigh, George, 306, 309
Eveleigh, Samuel, 306, 309
Everard, Thomas, 59
Evertsen, Adm. Cornelis, 8
Ezpeleta, Dr. Don Aingo de, 166

Fairfax, George, 332
Fairfax County (Va.), 329, 336
Falcongreen, Peter, 287
Falola, Toyin, 291
Fante, 278–79, 289, 292
Farmer, Charles, 324, 339
Fauntleroy, Moore, 329, 332
Fauntleroy family, 330
Felipe II (Spain), 254
Fénélon, Governor-General, 234
Fernandez, Jorge, 157
First Bank of the United States, 130
First National Bank of Massachusetts, 130
Fithian, Philip Vickers, 55–56
Fitzhugh, Henry, 332
Fitzhugh, Thomas, 332
Fitzhugh, William, 332
Fitzhugh family, 331
Florida, 351, 354
Fookes, James, 215, 226
Fort Augusta (Pa.), 37, 78
Fort Caroline (S.C.), 298
Fort Good Hope (Hartford), 211
Fort Royal (Antigua), 238
Fort Royal (S.C.), 297

Fox, Col. Joseph, 307
Foxcroft, Isaac, 207–8
Fraginals, Manuel Moreno, 272
France, xvi, 6–12, 20, 156, 169, 197, 198, 229–46, 252, 255–56, 269, 271, 290, 298; colonies of—*see* Antilles, French, Guadeloupe, Guyana, French, Martinique, New France; indigo trade and, 351–54; rice trade and, 345, 347, 349; slave trade and, 7, 158, 229–46; sugar trade and, 257; tobacco trade and, 104, 236, 254, 260; wine trade and, 31, 42, 43, 335
Franklin, Ben, 32; his *Poor Richard's Almanack,* 58
Fredericksburg, 328
French, Philip, 193–94
French and Indian War, 42
French Revolution, xv, 96, 116
Fryer, Thomas, 285
Frying Pan Copper Mines, 333, 336
Funchal, 39, 60
fur trade, 3–6, 17, 23n18, 75, 78, 195, 298, 309–13, 315–17, 334

Gabry, Charles, 188
Gallman, Robert, 324
Gambia, 279, 283, 285, 289–90
Garden, Dr., 308
Garland, Griffin, 329, 330
Garland, Jesse, 328
Garland, William, 328
Garland family, 329, 300
Garnett, Muscoe, 332
Georgia, xvii, 307, 312, 333, 351, 354
Geret, Mary, 210
Germany, 98, 104, 158
Gibbes, John, 57
Giborne family, 330
Gibson, John, 37
Gilroy, Paul, xi
Glasgow, 104, 105, 111, 124, 125, 133
Glen, Gov. James, 310
Glorious Revolution, 194
Glorious Revolution (America), 194, 198
Gloucester County (Va.), 215

gold, xiii, 2, 4, 6, 118, 155, 156, 165, 169, 174, 211, 253
Gold Coast, 277–78, 280, 287. *See also* Cape Coast Castle
Goldfrey, John, 287
Goldsby, John, 328
Gordillo, José Manuel Rodríguez, 259
Gordon, Thomas, 35, 36. *See also* Newton & Gordon
Green, John, 214
Green Bay, 78
Grenada, 117, 233
Grift, Jan van, 195
Grimes, Philip, 332
Grisley, Samuel, 38
Guadeloupe, 232, 233, 236, 239, 242–43
Guales, 298
Guatemala, 344, 351–52
Guerard, John, 348
Guiana, Dutch, 9
Guinea, 281
Gunston Hall (Va.), 330
Guyana, 8, 10, 12, 13, 18, 28
Guyana, French, 9, 243

Hack, George, 188, 191, 208, 212–15, 223, 225
Hackshaw, Robert, 145
Hague, The, 211
Haiti, 246, 254, 256
Haitian Revolution, xvii, 271, 272
Halifax, 34
Hamilton, Hance, 37
Hampshire County (Mass.), 43, 48, 50–51
Hancock, David, xiv, 98, 105
Hancock, John, 38
Hancock, Thomas, 38, 58
Harlow, John, 207
Harris, John, 38
Harris, John, Jr., 37
Harris, P. M. G., 323
Harrison, Benjamin, 332, 335
Harrison, Carter B., 332
Harrison, Nathaniel, 332
Harrison family, 331
Harris's Ferry (Pa.), 37, 38

Hatfield, April Lee, xvi
Haulsey, Michael, 195
Havana, 156, 253, 258–73
Havana Company, 265, 267
Hawkins, Benjamin, 314
Hayes, Carlton J. H., xi
Heligoland, 117
Henry, James, 332
Henry, Patrick, 331, 332
Hermann, Augustine, 188, 191, 208, 213–16, 224–26
Heyn, Adm. Piet, 4
Hill, Henry, 37–38
Hill, Dr. Richard, 35, 37
Hill, Richard, Jr., 37
Hinch, James, 280
Hippisley, John, 286, 287
Hoekeback, Joan, 194
Holland. *See* Netherlands
Hoorn, 4, 5
Horsey, Stephen, 208
Hothuysen, Bernardus, 194
Howard, William, 285
Hudson, Pat, 118
Hudson River, 5, 7, 16, 194
Hunter, Adam, 332
Hunter, John, 328
Hurson, Intendant, 234, 239, 242
Hutson, Richard, 344
Hyrne, Elizabeth, 349

Îles du Vent. *See* Windward Islands
illicit trade, xiii, xv, xvi, 7, 20, 28n63, 158, 169, 171, 173–74, 192–99, 207, 229–46, 252–55, 263. *See also* slave trade
Illinois, 75
India, 34, 42, 119, 162, 264
Indian Trade Commission, 311
Indians. *See* Native Americans
indigo trade, xviii, 297, 317n4, 317n5, 344–45, 358n29; in Charleston, 353; in England, 95, 102, 109–10, 350–54; and France, 351–54; and Jamaica, 353; and Native Americans, 352; and the Netherlands, 10; quality of, 345, 349–54; slavery and, 233, 352; in South

Carolina, xviii, 297, 344–45, 348–54; and Spain, 344, 351–52
Industrial Revolution, xv, 96
Inikori, J. E., 114
Inquisition, 170, 172–73, 176
Invin, Hugh, 287
Ireland, 95, 97, 241
iron, 126, 331–38
Iroquois, xi
Isert, Paul, 281
Israel, Jonathan, 8
Italy, 39, 158, 162, 335
ivory, 4, 6
Izard, Ralph, 347, 349

Jackson, Andrew, 315
Jackson, Nathaniel, 307
Jackson, Philip, 306
Jamaica, 98–99, 107, 122–24, 146n90, 156, 217, 239, 256, 271; indigo trade and, 353; slave trade in, 102, 233; and sugar trade, 271; tobacco trade and, 270; wine trade in, 34, 35, 43, 49–53. *See also* sugar
James, Duke of York, 192, 195
James I (England), 189
James Buchanan & Co., 127
James River, 55, 205, 325
James River Company, 333
Japan, 7, 13
Java, 3
Jefferson, Thomas, 331, 332, 335, 349
Jermyn, William, 210
Jerolnson, Jeroln, 207
Jerseys, 192
Jews, xvi, 4, 6, 14–16, 22n13, 26n42, 98, 172–75, 187, 353
Jochemsz, David, 193
John McQueen and Company, 311
Johnson, Joshua, 115
Johnston, Alexander, 35, 36
Jones, Dwyrydd, 209
Jones, Joseph, 332
Jones, Peter, 332
Jones, Robert, 36
Jordan, John, 328
Junta de Gran Reformacion, 162

Kamoie, Laura Croghan, xvii–xviii
Kelsick, Capt., 330
Kershaw, Ely, 79
King George County (Va.), 325, 326
King's Domaine, 240, 242, 244–45
Kingston (Jamaica), 297
Knox, Dr. Robert, 35
Kops, Anthony, 194
Kopytoff, Igor, 288

Lacroix, César-Marie de, 239, 240, 242, 245
Lagoe, 292
Lamar, Hill, Bisset & Co., 37
Lancashire, 117, 125, 128
Lancaster City (Va.), 325
Lancaster Town (Pa.), 37–39
Lang, Robert, 306
Laurens, Henry, 93, 344, 348, 353–54
Lavalette, Father Antoine, 237
Lawson, Robert, 332
Lawson, Thomas, 327
Lawson family, 330
Leacock, John, 35
Leacock & Sons, 56
Lee, Henry, 332
Lee, Richard, 332, 334, 335
Lee, William, 55, 332
Lee family, 329, 332, 337
Leeds, 116, 118, 133
Leeward Islands, 15, 98–99, 107
Leisler, Jacob, 193–96
Lemire, Beverly, 80
Lenox, Robert, 36
Lepper, Johannes, 194
Leverett, John, 197
Lewis, Warner, 332
Lightfoot, William, 332
Lille, 9
Lillie, Samuel, 145
Lima, 154, 172, 174, 175
Lindo, Moses, 353
Linebaugh, Peter, xi
linen. *See* textile trade
Lisbon, 38, 60, 170, 171, 175
Little, John, 287

Liverpool, 36, 102, 104, 105, 111, 114–20, 124, 126, 128–33, 282, 285
Lloyd, Cornelius, 210
Logan, William, 37
Lombardy rice, 349
London, 8, 33, 35–40, 54, 57–60, 81, 82, 96–133, 190, 191, 194, 195, 206, 229, 270, 284–86, 297, 312, 327, 345, 348, 352–53
London African Committee, 278, 281, 284–87, 289, 290
Long Island, 192
Loudon County, 336
Louis XIV (France), 9
Louis XV (France), 240
Louisiana, 74–77, 80, 81, 233. *See also* New Orleans
Lovejoy, Paul, 291
Lovelace, Francis, 197
Lower Creeks, 312, 315, 316. *See also* Creeks
Lower Norfolk County (Va.), 210, 211
Luanda, 7
Lucca, 335
Lutherans, 15
Lynch, John, 262
Lynch, Nicholas, 308
Lynnhaven Parish (Va.), 210

Mackenzie, Capt., 287
Maddox, Joshua, 37
Maddox, Thomas, 327
Madeira (island), 33–36, 38, 40, 59, 95
Madeira (wine), xiv, 30–61, 95, 97; consumption of, 41–54; cultural implications of, 54–61; distribution of, 34–41; production of, 32–34. *See also* wine trade
Madrid, 152, 154, 155, 161, 162, 168, 171–76, 267
Maika, Dennis, 216
Main, Jackson Turner, 330
Mancall, Peter C., xvii
Manchester (U.K.), 119
Mantecón, Matilde Souto, 270
Margarita, 156, 253
Marichal, Carlos, 270

Marie-Galante I, 239
Marin. *See* Cul-de-Sac Marin
Marseille, 237, 239
Martini, John, 308
Martinique, xvi, 7, 8, 229–46
Martyn, Benjamin, 307
Marx, Karl, xi
Maryland, 102, 192, 194, 212–17, 327; Dutch settlers in, 188, 205–6, 209, 210, 212–17; slave trade and, 212–13; tobacco trade and, 115, 191, 205; wine trade and, 34, 35, 37. *See also* Baltimore, Chesapeake region
Mason, George, 330, 332, 334, 335
Mason, Lemuel, 210
Mason, Stevens, 332
Massachusetts, 34, 38, 52, 100, 194, 196–98
Massie, Joseph, 105
Mathewes, William, 310
Matson, Cathy, 101
Matthews, Samuel, 209
Maurepas, Minister, 239, 240, 242, 244
Maurits, Count Johan, 13
Maxwell, James, 309
Mayo, Joseph, 332
Mazzei, Philip, 335
McBride, Duncan, 58
McCall, Samuel, 37
McCarty, Daniel, 332
McCusker, John, 323–24
McPherson, Capt. Alexander, 229
Mediterranean Sea, 198
Medway, 8
Meers, John, 287
Melvil, Governor, 278–79, 281, 283, 285–86, 289, 292
Menard, Russell, 323, 339
Mepkin Plantation. *See* Laurens, Henry
Mercado, Tomas de, 166
Meredith, Reese, 37
Merwick, Donna, 14
Mexico, 252, 255, 256, 270, 271, 273
Mexico City, 154, 172
Micheels, Jon, 214
Michilimackinac, 78
Midlands, 115, 126

Miers, Suzanne, 288
Miles, Gov. Richard, 287, 290
Miles, Samuel, 37
Miligan, George, 308
Mill, Gov. David, 284, 289, 292
Milner, John, 309
Ministry of the Marine (France), 231, 233, 235, 239–41, 244, 247
Mintz, Sidney, 255
Minvielle, Gabriel, 195–96
Mississippi, 333
Mississippi River, 334
Mitchell, John, 40
Môle St. Nicholas (St. Domingue), 246
Moll, Jon, 284
Montreal, xv, 55, 72–79, 81, 82
Montserrat, 233
Moore, Samuel Preston, 37
moradores (Portuguese planters), 4, 6, 23n13
Morais, Manuel Ribeiro Teixeira de, 168
morannen (runaway slaves), 11, 17–18
Moras, Minister, 245
Morgan, Philip, 297
Morphy, Hugh, 306
Moseley, Susan, 211, 216
Moseley, William, 211
Mota, Mendo de, 152, 166
Mount Airy, 326–30
Mount Vernon, 329–30
Moy, Cornelis Jacobs, 193
Moy, Hero, 193
Moyne, Pierre Le, 233
mulattoes, 4, 277, 284
Mumford, 292
Murdoch, Thomas, 34, 69n42
Mutter, Gov. William, 280, 281, 283, 290

Nantes, 231, 235, 238, 244, 245
Napoleon, 117
Napoleonic Wars, xv
Nash, R. C., xv, 101
Náter, Laura, xvi
Native Americans, xvi, 1, 95, 297–316, 334; and indigo trade, 352; population of, 89n15, 92n31, 93n37, 299–304; and slave trade, 304, 312, 314, 316; in South Carolina, xvii, 82, 297–316; and sugar trade, 310; and textile trade, 72–75, 77–82, 91n29, 315, 316; and tobacco trade, 308. *See also* fur trade
Navigation Acts (England), xvii, 8, 32, 41, 87, 113, 119, 139, 190, 193, 198, 205–8
Neabsco Ironworks, 327, 328, 336
Neale, Richard, 329
Neave, Meredith, 37
Nelson, Thomas, 332, 335
Netherlands, xvi, 1–21, 98, 125, 156, 160, 167, 171, 186–99, 205–18, 256, 287, 290; colonies of—*see* Antigua; Antilles, Dutch; Curaçao; Guiana, Dutch; Guyana; and illicit trade, 31, 231–33, 236, 239–40, 245, 252; and rice trade, 104, 348; and slave trade, 6–12, 17–18, 22n12, 195–96, 208, 212–13, 217–18, 218n4, 219n10; and sugar trade, 4–10, 187, 189, 197, 255; and textile trade, 193, 206, 213; and tobacco trade, 17, 23n18, 189–91, 205–15, 260; and wine trade, 34. *See also* Dutch East India Company, Dutch West India Company, Dutch-Asian trade, New Netherland
Neuville, Sieur de, 240, 242, 244
Nevis, 217
New Amsterdam, 8, 14, 17, 188, 192, 206, 208, 212–15
New France, 9, 81, 87–88n8, 345
New Hampshire, 54
New Holland, 5–6
New Netherland, 4, 6–10, 13–18, 187–96, 205–18. *See also* patroonships
New Netherland Company, 3
New Orange (N.Y.), 195
New Orleans, xv, 72–79, 81, 83, 233
New Spain, 169, 170, 252, 253, 267–73, 344
New Windsor (S.C.), 306, 309
New York, 98, 192–98, 236, 239; and wine trade, 33–36, 43, 49–53
New York (city), xiii, 33–36, 40–51, 101, 103, 109, 115, 119–22, 130, 192–96, 207, 210, 211, 213, 217, 297
Newfoundland, 34, 95, 100, 104, 111

Newport News (R.I.), 209
Newton, Francis, 35, 36
Newton, Thomas, 35, 36
Newton & Gordon, 35, 36, 56, 57
Newton & Spence, 36
Nice, 335
Nicholas, Wilson, 332
Nightengale, Thomas, 310
Nixon, Richard M., xi
Nomini Hall. *See* Carter, Robert
Norman, William, 284
North Carolina, 331
Northampton County (Va.), 187, 208, 213–15, 217
Northern, Peter, 330
Northern Neck (Va.), xviii, 325–39
Northumberland County (Va.), 325, 326
Nova Scotia, 34
Nueve Andalucia, 253
Nuñez, Cristobal, 162

O'Callaghan, E. B., 16
Occoquan (Va.), 328, 336
Ohio Company, 334
Ohio River, 315
Oliphant, Dr., 308
Olivares, Count-Duke, xv, xvi, 152–55, 161–64, 172, 174–76
Oliver, Robert, 131, 132, 144n74
One Hundred, the, 332, 334, 337
Oostindie, Gert, 18
Opie, Lindsey, 329
Orinoco River, 4
Ormrod, David, 125, 209
Ortiz, Fernando, 254
Osau, José Pellicer de, 174
Otniel, Beal & Co., 309
Overzee, Simon, 211, 217
Oxford Ironworks, 333

Pagan, John, 205, 206
Page, John, 332, 335
Page, Mann, Jr., 328, 332, 335
Page, Mann, III, 337
Page family, 329, 331
Panton, Leslie and Company, 312

Paradise, John, 332
Pares, Richard, 123, 124, 126, 127, 230, 239
Paris, 81
Paris, Treaty of, 266. *See also* Seven Years' War
Parker, John, 210
Parker, Nathaniel, 287
Parratt, Samual, 37
patroonships, xiii, 15–17
Patterson, David, 332
Patton Association, 334
Pemberton, Israel, 37
Pemberton, James, 37
Pendleton, Edmund, 331, 332, 336
Pennsylvania, 35, 74, 78–79, 81, 98, 101, 239
Pepper, Capt. Daniel, 306
Pereira, Manuel Lopez, 162, 165, 167, 171
Perrin, John, 332
Perry, Micajah, 122
Peru, 157, 169, 170, 252, 253, 256, 344
Petersburg (Va.), 331
Petrie, Gov. Gilbert, 289
Phélypeaux, Governor-General, 238
Philadelphia, 101, 103, 106, 109, 120, 131, 150n119, 297, 311; textile trade in, xv, 72–75, 78; wine trade in, 33–40, 42, 55. *See also* Bank of North America
Philip II (Spain), 152, 154, 167, 169
Philip III (Spain), 170
Philip IV (Spain), 152, 167, 171
Philippines, 157. *See also* Acapulco-Philippines trade route
Phillips, Adolphus, 193
Pinelo, Antonio de Leon, 162, 168, 171
Pintard, John Marsden, 59
Plunderleath, James, 35
Pochahontas (Va.), 331
Poinsable, Lt. Martin de, 238
Poland, 17
Pope, John, 56
Porto Belo, 157
Portugal, xv, 4, 13, 31, 40, 43, 59, 121, 154–77; colonies of—*see* Brazil; and illicit trade, 31; and slave trade, 7, 156–58, 175; and textile trade, 156–58;

and wine trade, 6, 34, 54, 335. *See also moradores*
Potomac River, 325, 326
Potosi, 157
Poyas, James, 80
Prague, 188, 213
Priber, Dr., 307
Price, Jacob M., 112, 114, 115, 126, 127, 132
Prill, Richard, 212
Prince William County (Va.), 327
Princess Anne County (Va.), 334, 342
Pringle, Robert, 94n52
Proctor, Hannah, 311
Provence, 335
Provost, John, 36
Puerto Rico, 8, 156, 253, 249, 274
Pungoteague (Va.), 215, 217
Punta de Araya (Venezuela), 2–4. *See also* salt

Quakers, 37
Quebec, 34
Quevedo, Francisco, 174–75

Rainy Lake, 78
Randolph, Edmund, 332
Randolph, Edward, 197, 198
Randolph, Peyton, 332, 335
Randolph, Thomas, 332
Randolph, Thomas M., 332
Randolph, William, 332
Randolph family, 331
Raper, Robert, 353
Rappahannock River, 325, 326
Reading (Pa.), 38
Recife, 4, 26n42
Redwood, William, 37
Reese, Ty M., xvii
Reformed Church, Dutch, 1, 14–15, 23n17, 195, 213
Reinders, Alida, 195
Reinders, Barent, 194–95
Reinders, Jan, 195
Rensselaer, Jan Baptist van, 193
Rensselaer, Kiliaen van, 16

Reyes, Nicholas de los, 157
Rhineland, 193
Rhode Island, 34, 198, 236, 239, 297, 342
rice trade, 314, 317n3, 317n5, 344–49, 354–55; in Charleston, 104, 109, 124, 347–48; in England, 95, 102, 109–11, 119, 124, 345–51, 354–55; in France, 345, 347, 349; and the Netherlands, 104, 348; quality of, 345–49, 354–55; and slavery, 347; in South Carolina, xviii, 104, 109, 124, 297, 344–49, 354–55; and Spain, 345
Rich, Myra L., 324
Richardson, David, 114
Richardson, William, 193
Richmond, 331, 333, 336
Richmond County (Va.), xviii, 325–28, 330
Rio de la Plata (Peru), 170
Roane, Thomas, 332
Roanoke, 299
Roberts, Gov. John, 287
Robertson, Andrew, 35
Roche, Daniel, 80
Roeber, A. G., 217
Ronald, William, 332
Rosenbloom, Joshua L., xvii
Ross, David, 332, 333, 336
Ross & Currie, 336
Ross & Forde, 336
Rossel, Lieutenant de, 235–38
Rotterdam, 192, 206, 210, 211, 216
Roux family, 239–40
Royal African Company, 8, 97–99, 104, 121, 123, 195–96, 277, 283. *See also* Company of Merchants Trading to Africa
Royal Society of Arts, 351
Ruffin, Edmund, 332
Russel, Col. James, 217
Ruyter, Adm. Michael de, 8
Ryswick, Treaty of, 233

Sa Jorge da Mina (Gold Coast), 4
Sagra, Ramón de la, 257
St. Augustine, 298
St. Domingue, 230, 233, 235, 244–46, 351

St. Elizabeth's Parish (Jamaica), 217
St. Eustatius, 8, 10, 28–29n63, 236, 237, 239, 240, 245
St. James, Court of, 229
St. Kitts, 34, 233
St. Lucia, 230, 233, 235, 236, 242, 246
St. Pierre (Martinique), 229, 236–38, 240–43, 245
St. Thomas, 233, 241, 245
Salem (Mass.), 34
salt trade, 6, 169, 334. See also Punta de Araya
San Juan de Luz, 156
San Sebastian, 156
Santa Elena, 298
Santa Marta, 156
Santen, Adrian Van, 193
Santo Domingo, 156, 253, 259, 274
Sargent, John II, 58
Sarly, Anthony, 35
Sarvia, Juan Nuñes, 162
Sassafras River, 214
Savannah, 306, 313
Scapes, William, 210
Scarborough, Edmund, 188, 208, 210, 213, 217, 219, 221, 228
Schafferstown (Pa.), 38
Schaick, Livinius van, 194, 195
Schnurmann, Claudia, xvi
Scotland, 36
Scott, John, 309, 311
Searle, John, 36
Seven Years' War, 37, 125, 233–35, 241, 266, 304, 316. See also Paris, Treaty of
Seville, xvii, 154, 159, 166, 170–74, 252–73
Shackleford, Vincent, 330
Shattuck, Martha, 216
Sheridan, Richard B., 122
Sherman, William, 212
Shippen, Edward, 37
Shippensburg (Pa.), 37, 38
Shirredin, Thomas, 327
Shoemaker & Pennington, 37
Sibbald, John, 37
silk. See textile trade

Silver, 4, 156–59, 163–69, 170, 174, 175, 252, 253, 265, 267–68, 270
Sisson family, 330
Skinner, James, 286
Skipwith, Henry, 332
Skipwith, Peyton, 332
slave labor, in Chesapeake, 208, 212–13
slave trade, xi, xii, 4–12, 102–8, 111–15, 121–26, 229–46, 276n64, 277–93, 314; in Barbados, 98–99, 102, 219n8, 236, 238; and Brazil, 4; in Charleston, 102, 124; in England, xvii, 7, 95–99, 102–8, 111–15, 121–26, 129, 133, 208, 277–93, 297; and France, 7, 158, 229–46; and indigo trade, 233, 352; in Jamaica, 102, 233; in Maryland, 212–13; and Martinique, xvi, 229–46; Native Americans and, 304, 312, 314, 316; and the Netherlands, 6–12, 17–18, 22n12, 195–96, 208, 212–13, 217–18, 218n4, 219n10; and Portugal, 7, 156–58, 175; in South Carolina, 81–82, 102–3, 124, 297, 299, 304, 312, 324, 326, 347; and Spain 4, 7, 253, 272; and textile trade, 75, 77, 79–83; and tobacco trade, 208, 291, 326, 331–33; in Virginia, 108, 208, 217–18, 326–33. See also illicit trade, morannen, Royal African Company
Smith, Adam, 60, 127
Smith, Alexander, 311
Smith, Benjamin, 306
Smith, George, 37
Smith, John (Quaker), 37
Smith, John (surveyor), 287
Smith, Thomas, 286
Sociëteit von Suriname, 17, 197–98
Solis, Duarte Gomes, 162, 163, 168
South Carolina, 75–82, 114, 297–316, 344–55; indigo trade in, xviii, 297, 344–45, 348–54; Native Americans in, xvii, 82, 297–316; rice trade in, xviii, 104, 109, 124, 297, 344–49, 354–55; slave trade in, 81–82, 102–3, 124, 297, 299, 304, 312, 324, 326, 347; and textile trade, 75–82; and wine trade, 33, 34, 43, 49–53. See also Charleston

South Carolina Agricultural Society, 349
South Sea Company, 10
Southall, James, 332
Soveiger, John, 287
Spain, xv–xvi, 1–3, 6–10, 15, 121, 152–77, 197, 233, 241–42, 252–73; colonies of—see Antilles, Spanish, New Spain, Peru; and illicit trade, 231, 232, 236; and indigo trade, 344, 351–52; and rice trade, 345; and slave trade, 4, 7, 253, 272; and sugar trade, 162, 252–57; and tobacco trade, xvi–xvii, 252–73; and wine trade, 31, 41, 43, 335
Spanish Succession, War of, 10, 231–32, 234, 238, 260, 262. *See also* Utrecht, Treaty of
Spence, George, 36. *See also* Newton & Spence
Spotswood, Alexander, 332
Stead, Benjamin, 310
Stedman, Alexander, 37
Stedman, Charles, 37
Stedman, John Gabriel, 17–18
Stonewall Furnace, 287
Stono Rebellion, 313
Storke, Samuel, 122
Stringer, Capt. John, 213, 224–25
Stuart, John, 312, 316
Studnicki-Gizbert, Daviken, xv
Stuyvesant, Anna, 188, 212
Stuyvesant, Peter, 188, 207, 212, 221
Succondee (Gold Coast), 282
Sueyro, Manuel, 163
Suffolk County (Mass.). *See* Boston
Sugar Act (1764), 54
sugar trade: and Barbados, 7, 189; and Brazil, 4–5, 271; and Cuba, 252–57, 268, 271, 272; and England, 95–99, 103, 107–10, 113–14, 117, 122–24, 127; and France, 257; and Martinique, 232–34, 236; and Native Americans, 310; and the Netherlands, 4–10, 187, 189, 197, 255; and Jamaica, 271; and Spain, 162, 252–57
Surinam, 9–18, 26n42, 27n51, 28n63, 196–98

Tabb, John, 332, 335
Taft, Ann, 217
Taliaferro, Richard, 332
Tallapiedra, Joseph Antonio, 265, 267
Tallapoos, 306
Tarrade, Jean, 230, 235
Tasker family, 336
Tayloe, John, 327
Tayloe, John, II, xvii, 326–31, 332, 334–38
Tayloe, John, III, 330
Taylor, John, 332
Tenochitlan, 255
Texel, 194
textile trade, xiv–xv, 72–85; calicoes, xv, 77–82, 110; in Charleston, 72–78, 80, 81; cotton, xv, 75–83, 96, 110, 116, 118, 156, 315, 333; and England, xiv, 96, 110–13, 116–20, 126–28, 132–33, 206, 354–55; linens, 73–83, 110, 126, 193, 333; Native Americans and, 72–75, 77–82, 91n29, 315–16; and the Netherlands, 193, 206, 213; in Philadelphia, xv, 72–75, 78; and Portugal, 156–58; silks, 73, 76, 78, 81, 83, 333, 335; and slavery, 75, 77, 79–83; in South Carolina, 75–82; woolens, 73–82, 110–12, 116–18, 120, 126, 133, 193, 333
Thirty Years' War, 188
Thornton, Presly, 336
Thubières, Charles de. *See* Caylus, Marquis de
Tickhonobee, 306
Timucuas, 298
tobacco trade, 7, 187–91, 205–15, 252–73, 331–39; in Chesapeake, 8, 17, 98, 122–24, 205–15; and Cuba, xvii, 252–73, 344; in England, 31, 95, 97, 100–104, 107–15, 119, 122–24, 127, 132–33, 254; in France, 104, 236, 254, 260; in Jamaica, 270; in Maryland, 115, 191, 205; Native Americans and, 308; and the Netherlands, 17, 23n18, 189–91, 205–15, 260; and slavery, 208, 291, 326, 331–33; and Spain, xvi–xvii, 252–73; and Virginia, 108, 187–91, 205–15, 255–27, 325–27, 331–39

Tobago, 8, 15, 351
Toft, Ann. *See* Taft, Ann
Tom, Winnebah, 291
Tomlin, Walker, 328
Trent, Alexander, 332, 336
Trexel, Daniel, 232
Trieste, 117
Trinidad, 156, 236
Trinidad de la Guayra, 259
Trinidad de la Havana, 259
Turberville, George, 332
Turberville, John, 332
Tyseen, Capt. Geurt, 212

United East India Company (VOC), 3, 5–6, 13, 20–21, 171
Upper Creeks, 315. *See also* Creeks, Lower Creeks
Ustáriz, Gerónimo de, 261–62
Utrecht, Treaty of, 10, 263, 264. *See also* Spanish Succession, War of

Vanhoofe, Cornelius, 215, 227
Vanswaringen, Garrett, 217
Varlett, Anna, 188, 212–17, 223, 226–27
Varlett, Caspar, 211–12
Varlett, Jannetje, 188, 213–15, 225
Varlett, Judith Tentenier, 211–12
Varlett, Kath, 216
Varlett, Nicholas, 188, 191, 211–12
Varlett, Sarah, 216
Varlett, William, 216
Varlett family, 208, 211
Vauclin (Martinique), 235
Vaucresson, Intendant, 236, 238
Vaughan, Grace, 213–14, 225
Venezuela, 2, 8, 274
Versailles, 229, 235, 238, 244
Vilar, Enriqueta Vila, 157
Villela, Pedro de Avendaño, 170
Villière, Marquise de la, 240
Vincent, William, 210
Virginia, xviii, 187–92, 205–18, 324–39; Dutch settlers in, 187–92, 205–18; and slave trade, 108, 208, 217–18, 326–33; and tobacco trade, 108, 187–91, 205–15, 255–27, 325–27, 331–39; and wine trade, 33, 34, 54, 55, 59
Virginia Company, 121
VOC. *See* United East India Company
Vondel, Joost van, 17
Vries, David Peterson de, 206, 209
Vries, Jan de, xiii–xiv, 256

Waddelow, Nicholas, 208
Wadman, John, 334
Wales, 43
Wallace, James, 37
Wallerstein, Immanuel, xi, 313
Walsh, Lorena, 339
Warwick (Va.), 333
Washington, George, 54, 55, 59, 329–31, 332, 335
Washington, William, 56
Washington family, 337
Waterees, 309
Waterford, 36
Waterhouse, David, 109, 122, 145
Weiss, Thomas, xvii
West, Samuel, 309
Westminster, Peace of, 192
Westmoreland County (Va.), 325, 333
Westphalia, 193
Weuves, Gov. Bernard, 287
Whydah (Gold Coast), 289
WIC. *See* Dutch West India Company
Wild, Thomas, 336
Wild Coast, 4, 9, 17
William III (William of Orange), 198
Williamsburg (Va.), 55
Windward Islands, xvi. *See also* Martinique
Wine Islands, 40, 43. *See also* Madeira
wine trade: in Charleston, 34, 40, 56, 57; in England, 31–35, 39, 43, 54, 57, 59; in France, 31, 42, 43, 335; in Jamaica, 34, 35, 43, 49–53; in Maryland, 34, 35, 37; and the Netherlands, 34; in New York, 33–36, 43, 49–53; in Philadelphia, 33–40, 42, 55; in Portugal, 6, 34, 54, 335;

in South Carolina, 33, 34, 43, 49–53;
and Spain, 31, 41, 43, 335; and Virginia,
33, 34, 54, 55, 59. *See also* Madeira
Winnebah (Gold Coast), 282
Winthrop, John, Jr., 217
Withers, James, 310
Wood, Alexander, 306
Wood, Peter, 297
Wormeley, Ralph, 328, 332, 337
Wright, John, 54, 58
Wright, Capt. Thomas, 194

Yamasee War, 312
Yamasees, 312
Yeardley, Francis, 211
Yllan, Garcia de, 162, 167, 168
York (Pa.), 37, 38
Yorkshire, 111, 116–18, 125–29
Yorktown, 230

Zahedieh, Nuala, 122
Zeeland, 4, 5, 7, 11, 17

www.ingramcontent.com/pod-product-compliance
Lightning Source LLC
Chambersburg PA
CBHW030602230426
43661CB00053B/1809